RAILWAY ANCESTORS

RAILWAY ANCESTORS

A GUIDE TO THE STAFF RECORDS
OF THE RAILWAY COMPANIES OF
ENGLAND AND WALES 1822–1947

DAVID T. HAWKINGS

WITH A FOREWORD BY LORD TEVIOT

This book is dedicated
to my friend Keith W Gilbert,
whose remarkable knowledge of
early railways was my inspiration.

First published 1995
This edition published 2008

The History Press Ltd
The Mill, Brimscombe Port
Stroud, Gloucestershire, GL5 2QG
www.thehistorypress.co.uk

© David T. Hawkings, 1995, 2008

The right of David T. Hawkings to be identified as the Author
of this work has been asserted in accordance with the
Copyrights, Designs and Patents Act 1988.

British Library Cataloguing in Publication Data.
A catalogue record for this book is available from the British Library.

ISBN 978 0 7509 5058 9

Typesetting and origination by The History Press Ltd
Printed in Great Britain

CONTENTS

Appendices

FOREWORD
BY LORD TEVIOT

It was a joy to the ears when David Hawkings told me that he proposed writing a book on railway staff records. I remember saying 'Do you really know what you are taking on?' All forms of genealogical research can become frustrating at one time or another when one cannot find what one is looking for. Hitherto railway sources came top of the list. No one has been brave enough to tackle the immense problems most searchers had in trying to find railwaymen in the records.

Before 1923 there were many railway companies of varying sizes. Companies had grown out of other companies; staff records were therefore a nightmare. This work is extremely horough and very detailed in setting out what staff records are available in The National Archives and elsewhere. You will, with any luck, be able to pick up this book and find the exact reference you want without spending much wasted time referring to lists and documents which are irrelevant.

There has always been something romantic about railways. Journeys were speeded up considerably; the country rapidly became much smaller. Entirely new forms of employment came into being and many employees remained their whole working lives on the railways. Generations followed and the work carried certain status, hence jobs were much coveted. Readers will be able to gain much pleasure in tracing their railway forebears from the good offices of this excellent book.

Teviot

PREFACE TO THE FIRST EDITION

At an early stage in my genealogical researches I was anxious to learn all I could about the more obscure historical sources which could fill in the details of the lives of family members. In the summer of 1972, over a cup of tea in the members' room at the Society of Genealogists, I mentioned to the late Miss Florence Toop that I was perplexed by an entry in the 1861 population census returns. Thomas Hawkings, a brother of my great grandfather, had been recorded as a 'St. Porter'. Did this, I wondered, mean a *street porter* or a *station porter*? Thomas Hawkings lived close to Bedminster station (in a suburb of Bristol) on the then Bristol and Exeter Railway and only a mile from Temple Meads station on the Great Western Railway. 'Have you searched the railway archives?' asked Miss Toop. I had no knowledge of such records and little did I know at the time that this suggestion was to set me on a long exploratory trail. British Rail Records Centre at Porchester Road, Paddington, held all the then known surviving historic records of the railway companies of England, Wales and Scotland. It was a great disappointment to find that there were apparently no surviving staff records for the Bristol and Exeter Railway. For the Great Western Railway, however, I was astonished to discover dozens upon dozens of large registers recording staff from its early days. I could find no trace of Thomas Hawkings but much to my surprise (and to that of the rest of my family) I discovered that, in 1900, my grandfather Thomas William Hawkings had been employed at Bristol Temple Meads as an engine cleaner, at the age of 17 years, for which he had been paid 1s 10d a day. Clearly this was not the job for him; after only one week he resigned. There could be no doubt about his identity; like every other employee, his date of birth was written next to his name in the staff register.

Many years later I began to explore the surviving records of the Bristol and Exeter Railway Company. A search through some of the minutes of the Board of Directors' meetings revealed that the appointments of porters, policemen and clerks were recorded. Apparently each member of staff was actually interviewed by the Board, the names of these employees being easy to trace as each volume of minutes is indexed. (Individuals are not listed as separate entries in the index but may be located under 'appointments'.) Thomas Hawkings has not been found in these records and therefore it is concluded that he was a street porter and not a station porter. Furthermore, the Board's minutes of this company for 27 October 1852[1] record, '. . . reduce the Standard for Porters from 5' 8" to 5' 7" but continue that of Policemen 5' 9"'. It is believed that Thomas Hawkings was probably under 5 ft 7 in tall and therefore too short to be a railway porter.

Exploration through many of the miscellaneous classes of railway records has revealed numerous previously unknown records of staff. After many years of research a detailed guide has been produced which it is hoped will assist family historians with railway connections to make full use of the railway archives. The RAIL group alone contains over 80,000 pieces (books, boxes, folders, etc.) occupying about 2½ miles of shelving in The National Archives at Kew. Railway staff records have also been discovered in some country record offices and elsewhere. This book brings together details of all known staff records for English and Welsh railway companies. It also includes those Scottish railways which crossed the border into England. It is very probable that further material will come to light; this will be added to any future edition.

David T. Hawkings
August 1995

1. TNA, RAIL 75/19

PREFACE TO THE SECOND EDITION

The first edition of this book met with much enthusiasm from both family historians and railway enthusiasts. I was indeed delighted to receive an Award of Excellence for it in 1997 from the Literati Club.

Some readers took the trouble to write to me with details of minor corrections and additions. I am most grateful to the following for their comments and suggestions: Michael Back, Peter Bancroft, Desmond Brailsford, Bill Duffin, Cliff Edwards, Ken Farenden and Glynn Waite. Once again I must thank Keith Gilbert for so kindly answering my many queries and checking my corrections.

Three more railway companies have been added to Appendix 1. These are The Fareham and Netley Railway Co., The Settle and Carlisle Railway Co., and The Southwold Railway Co. This now brings the total number of railways which ran in England and Wales, to 991. Some further railway staff records have been located and have been added to Appendix 3.

Further exploration at The National Archives through MT6 files has revealed much detail about the early inspection of railways where a letter was found from George Stevenson to the Board of Trade suggesting procedures to ensure the safety of railways. (see Chapter 3). A letter was also found from Charles Dickens and is reproduced on page 182.

The search goes on.

David T. Hawkings
September 2008

ACKNOWLEDGEMENTS

My thanks go to the following for their help and support during my many years of research for this book:

At the Public Record Office, Mrs M. Barton, Miss G. Beech, Mrs A. Cameron, Mr C.D. Chalmers, Mr N. Coney, Mrs A. Crawford, Mr A. MacDonald, Mr F. McCall, Mr J. Murray and Mr M. Rogers; the archivists of all county and other record offices in England and Wales for answering my enquiries; Mr J. Worthy of Brunel University Library for help with the Clinker Collection; Dr Alison Rosie and Mr I. Hill of the Scottish Record Office; Mr C.P. Atkins of the National Railway Museum Library; Mr R. Linsley and Mr R. Wood, Record Officers of British Rail; Mr R. Taylor, London Transport Archivist; the staff at the Guildhall Library, London; the staff at the British Library, Bloomsbury and the Newspaper Library at Colindale; Mr T.M.B. Silcock, Secretary of the Railway Librarians Association; Mr N.J. Bridger, Mr D. Bromwich, Mr I. Coleby, Mr K.W. Gilbert, Mr A. Miller and Mr D. Pennington for detailed information.

A very special thank you must go to Mrs Susan Overton and her husband, Brian, for so kindly typing and preparing for the publishers the appendices to this book. I would also like to express my gratitude to the editorial and production staff at Alan Sutton Publishing, in particular Clare Bishop, Mary Critchley and Tracey Moore, for all their hard work and their patience.

Transcripts, photographs and facsimiles of records from British Rail archives are reproduced by permission of the British Rail Record Officer. Photographs held by the National Railway Museum, York, are reproduced by permission of the Librarian. The drawing of the London, Birmingham, Liverpool and Manchester Railway is reproduced by permission of the Trustees of the British Museum. The drawings of views showing the Bristol and Exeter Railway and Great Western Railway are reproduced by permission of the Somerset Archaeological and Natural History Society. Transcripts of Ministry of Transport (MT) documents and the references given in Appendix 3 and 4 are reproduced by permission of The National Archives. Transcripts of Somerset Quarter Sessions records are reproduced by permission of the Somerset County Archivist. Document references to Scottish records, given in Appendices 3 and 4, are reproduced by permission of the Scottish Record Office. Transcripts of documents from London Transport Archives, held at the London Metropolitan Archives, are reproduced by permission of the London Transport Archivist.

LIST OF ABBREVIATIONS

Amalg.	Amalgamation
Ang RO	Anglesey Area Record Office
App	Appendix
Beds RO	Bedfordshire Record Office, Bedford
Brist Ref Lib	Bristol Reference Library
Brist RO	Bristol Record Office
Brun/Cl	Clinker Collection, Brunel University, Uxbridge
Ches RO	Cheshire Record Office, Chester
Corn RO	Cornwall Record Office, Truro
Cum RO	Cumbria Record Office, Carlisle
Dev RO	Devon Record Office, Exeter
G Man RO	Greater Manchester County Record Office, Manchester
GWR	Great Western Railway
Leic RO	Leicestershire Record Office, Leicester
LMA	London Metropolitan Archives
LMS	London, Midland and Scottish Railway
LNER	London and North Eastern Railway
NRM	National Railway Museum
PRO	Public Record Office, Kew, Surrey
RCHS	Railway and Canal Historical Society
RCTS	Railway Correspondence and Travel Society
Scot RO	Scottish Record Office, Edinburgh
SoG	The Society of Genealogists, London
SOM RO	Somerset Record Office, Taunton
SR	Southern Railway
Staf RO	Staffordshire Record Office, Stafford
Suf RO	Suffolk Record Office, Ipswich
Swin Mus	Swindon Railway Museum
TNA	The National Archives, Kew, Surrey
TWAS	Tyne and Wear Archives Service, Newcastle upon Tyne
Wilts RO	Wiltshire Record Office, Chippenham

INTRODUCTION

In 1972 the Public Record Office took over the historical records relating to English and Welsh railway companies held at the British Rail Records Centre, and in 1976 transferred them to their Office at Kew. Those records relating to Scottish railways were sent to the Scottish Record Office, Edinburgh. Since then further records for more recent dates have also been transferred from British Rail to the Public Record Office at Kew (now renamed The National Archives).

No detailed and illustrated guide existed for railway records at that time, like so many other archive sources. I therefore began to compile a handbook which outlined all known railway staff records. It was to be a brief guide of limited use and Mr Anthony Camp, Director of the Society of Genealogists, suggested to me that it would be useful to include a list of all historic railway companies. This was excellent advice but neither of us realized the size of such a list or the work that would be involved in compiling it.

After extensive research an alphabetical list has been compiled of railways which existed in England and Wales up to Nationalization in 1947. This list comprises some 991 railways and is given in Appendix 1. It includes some tramways which were initially horse-drawn and were converted to steam or acted as 'feeders' to steam railways. As this book concentrates on those records held by The National Archives at Kew, Scottish railway records are not included, except for those railways which crossed the border into England. Some railway companies changed their name before opening a line. These companies are included in Appendix 1 with their name changes.

It was already known that staff records survived for 94 pre-1923 English and Welsh railway companies, and much additional material has been found for many of these. Records referring to named staff have been found for another 44 companies, plus the LMS, LNER and SR, which gives a total of 141 companies with some staff records, i.e. 14 per cent of the total number of railways listed in Appendix 1. Taken in isolation, however, this statistic is misleading as some companies' records have details of only a few staff and most do not cover the full life of particular railways. Furthermore, 110 of the companies listed in Appendix 1 were renamed. Another 25 were taken over by, or amalgamated with others before opening. It is not always certain whether some of these companies, though under the control of successors, ran under their original names. It is probable that an absorbed company would continue to be known by its original name, locally if not officially. It is known, for example, that the Chester and Holyhead Railway, which was vested in the London and North Western Railway Company in 1859, continued under its own name until 1879. It might reasonably be assumed that the staff of an absorbed company were paid for by the parent company and may never have been listed under their original company's name. The actual number of running companies therefore reduces by 135, to 856. This then means that the percentage of companies with some surviving staff records increases to 17 per cent of the total number listed. Records of staff taken over by another company are sometimes found in the parent company's records thus increasing this percentage still further. An indication is given in column 6 of Appendix 1 as to whether or not records of staff have been found for each particular company. The researcher must then refer to Appendix 3 where staff records are listed in detail.

The earliest staff record found is a petition,[1] dated 17 March 1801, from George Harris requesting an increase in wages. He was, however, an employee of the Monmouthshire Canal Company, which later combined with the Blaenavon Tramroad and was reincorporated as the Monmouthshire Railway and Canal Company on 31 July 1845. The earliest located staff records for a railway company are paybills dating from 1822 for the construction of the Stockton and Darlington Railway. Records also survive for the traffic staff of this railway dating from its opening in 1826.

Appendix 3 includes all miscellaneous records which have been found to give details of staff by name. Petitions to the Board of Directors of some companies include lists and often signatures of employees. These have been included, but petitions which do not have names of staff or are from other bodies have been omitted.

The arrangement of the staff registers themselves varies from one company to another. Some records arrange employees numerically by their individual staff numbers and others are fully indexed by surname. Some staff are found listed in their *depot* or *station* and in some large companies records are arranged by *division*. Clerical staff are usually listed separately from uniformed staff, and skilled and unskilled workmen are often entered in different registers.

Exploration through the mass of records has revealed records of staff in unlikely places. 'Leaders Books' record the movement of goods but also name the engine drivers, and 'Books of Vouchers' often include fortnightly pay sheets usually with the names and signatures of the staff.

Sickness and accident records include not only staff but often those passengers who were injured while on a railway company's train or property. Such detailed records were necessary in case of compensation claims against the company. In some instances details of compensation payments to staff and passengers are recorded. The Board of Trade was required to investigate all serious railway accidents and enquiries recording these include detailed statements made by members of railway companies' staff.

1.   TNA, RAIL 500/43

Some staff registers record the whole career of an employee and include reprimands and commendations. These may also record the date of retirement and eventual death of the employee. Other records may be a single-line entry recording only the rank, location and pay of an employee at a particular date. Some group photographs of railway company staff have been found, though those photographed are not always named. Examples of a variety of staff records are given in Chapter 1.

Many railway companies worked jointly with others, sharing the same station or track. Some joint lines and joint stations were actually built under a joint agreement. Some joint companies were formally incorporated as such. In order to control and administer such an undertaking a joint committee was formed from representatives of each member company. Many of the minutes of the meetings of these committees refer to staff by name. Changes of staff were of particular note. Clearly the pay of these staff was of importance and had to be agreed by the joint committee. The following is recorded in the minutes of the Bristol Joint Station Committee, 18 November 1870.[2]

> Either company to have power to put on their own porters at their own expense, leaving the Joint Committee to make such an allowance for the service so performed as in their judgement relief is given to the General Station expenses!

The staff of joint companies often had their own particular uniform. In a few cases a description of uniforms for various grades of joint staff are described in the joint committee minute books (see Chapter 6). Some abstracts from joint committee minutes, giving details of staff, are also given in Chapter 6. In a few instances records of joint staff were recorded in separate registers. If a researcher is unable to locate an employee in the records of a particular company (or there are no staff records for that company) a search should be made through any likely joint committee staff records or joint committee minutes. These are listed in Appendix 4, which also gives the companies which formed each joint committee.

Minutes of the meetings of the Boards of Directors of the railway companies should not be overlooked. Many made note of the offences and subsequent reprimands or dismissals of staff, and fines imposed on employees were often recorded. Accidents were enquired into, and details of the damage to both the company's property and that of others, such as private railway carriages, were recorded. The employees of some companies, particularly those staff who were to come into contact with the travelling public (porters, policemen, booking clerks, etc.) were selected, interviewed and appointed by the Board of Directors. Some boards also interviewed and passed judgement over those staff charged with offences contravening the company's rules and regulations. Many a porter has been recorded as 'drunk on duty' and consequently dismissed. It was particularly interesting to discover that the board of the Bristol and Exeter Railway Company recorded in its minutes the appointment of porters, policemen and clerks. Even more rewarding was the discovery that these minutes are indexed. The names of individual staff are not usually given in the indices but lists of employees may be found under 'appointments'

2.   TNA, RAIL 80/4

of their respective grades, i.e. 'porters', 'policemen', 'clerks', etc. Some Board of Directors' minutes index lists of staff under 'appointments', 'wages', 'salaries' or 'establishment'. In other companies it may be necessary to look under the name of the department, e.g. 'accountant, 'chief engineer', 'locomotive', etc.

Some of the larger railway companies set up sub-committees to administer particular aspects of their business. The Great Western Railway Company, for example, had over twenty committees which are known to have discussed staffing matters, including the following:

The General Committee
The Refreshment Room Committee
The Engineering Committee
The Locomotive, Carriage and Stores Committee
The London Committee of Management
The Traffic Committee
The Committee as to Allowances on Retirement
The Clerks Appointment Committee

The minutes of the meetings of each of these committees have been found to record staff by name. There was also a 'Sub-committee on the Progress of Works and Other Committees'. This committee recorded the appointments of policemen, porters, guards, conductors, etc. Names of those appointed were recorded. Examples of abstracts from the minutes of these, and other committees are given in Chapter 5.

In order to assist researchers, lists of all railways which ran in each historic county, with dates of opening, are given in Appendix 2. This is intended as a guide only, to enable the researcher to initiate the investigation of these railways and further branch openings. No attempt has been made to record the routes along which these railways ran. Such detail would add substantially to the size of this book and is considered outside its scope. Further information can be obtained from the many published railway histories (see Bibliography).

Family historians wishing to identify the railway on which a known family member in a county may have been employed, should also consider adjacent counties. By the end of the nineteenth century some men travelled many miles on one railway to their place of employment on another railway.

The name of a railway can sometimes be misleading. The Manchester and Milford Railway Company, for example, was promoted in 1845 to build a railway from Crewe to Milford Haven via Oswestry and Newport, a distance of about 230 miles. The only part of this route built by this company ran in central Wales, from Pencader via Lampeter to Aberystwyth, a distance of 40 miles. It is important therefore to investigate the actual routes built and used by a railway company and not assume its location from the place-names in its title.

A detailed search has been carried out through all records at The National Archives which might possibly record details of staff. Those found to give staff by name (with the exception of the various committees mentioned above) have been included in

Appendix 3 with references. Staff records held by county record offices and elsewhere are also included.

Many paybills have been located but not all these give the names of railway staff. Some are merely summary accounts for various company departments. Other paybills record payments made only to tradesmen and contractors. All paybills found are given in Appendix 3 with an indication as to whether or not staff are recorded by name. Examples of some paybills are given in Chapter 2. Books of accountants' vouchers have been found to include paybills and other records of staff. Some of these are also given in Chapter 2. Examples from a selection of staff sickness registers, and records of railway accidents are given in Chapter 3. The minutes of the meetings of Boards of Directors often record staff by name and some abstracts from various board minutes are given in Chapter 4.

TNA document class RAIL 1172 is listed as 'Management and Correspondence Files'. This class contains a large number of appeals by trades unions on behalf of railway workers for pay increases, regarding and improvement in conditions of service. These documents take the form of printed or typed reports and often record verbatim the statements made by both unions and members of the Industrial Court. Such records give an insight into the pay and working conditions of various grades of railway workers in the early twentieth century. Most are dated after the 1923 Grouping. The only pre-1923 records are for employees of the Great Northern Railway in 1920. The others relate to the GWR, SR, LMS and the LNER. Some of these files may be regarded as general correspondence because they do not name railwaymen. All workers that are named in these records are included with the staff records for each particular railway in Appendix 3. It is interesting to note that there are very few claims and disputes involving the GWR. Summaries of eleven cases from these records are given in Chapter 8. No attempt has been made to include in this book historic records of the various related trades unions. (Some trade union records are deposited at Warwick University.[3])

Some railway companies produced their own journals, all of which include references to staff. Retirements and obituaries are of particular note. Some examples from these are given in Chapter 9. A list of railway magazines is given in Part Two of the Bibliography. Local newspapers are another good source of biographical information.

The Railway Clearing House was established in 1842 at Euston, London. When a passenger travelled on a journey which involved using more than one railway his fare was divided among the various railways in proportion to the mileage he had travelled on each. Such permutations were calculated and allocated by the Railway Clearing House. Some staff records survive and are given in Appendix 5.

The Great Western Railway Company, incorporated in 1835, survived in its own name at the 1923 Grouping. Appendix 3.2 lists all the railways which were absorbed by the various GWR Absorption Acts. Also given in Appendix 3.2 are all surviving GWR staff records dating from 1835 to 1947. Details of the railways which were grouped together to form the LMS, LNER, and SR, together with details of their staff records, are given in Appendix 3 (3.3, 3.4 and 3.5 respectively).

3.   Warwick University Library, Coventry, CV4 7AL

Men and women of a very large number of trades and occupations were employed by railway companies. These trades are listed in Appendix 6.

The major events in British railway history are given in Appendix 7.

Access to the Records

Railway staff registers contain some detail which is of a personal nature. Researchers wishing to consult these must sign an undertaking stating that they will only use such information for family history purposes. All such records less than 75 years old are not available to the general public.

Note

This book has taken many years to compile. Despite intense research it is possible that some early railway companies have been omitted from Appendices 1 and 2. The author will be pleased to receive details of additional railways and suggested corrections to the dates of opening of those given. Information about the location of any unrecorded staff records will also be gratefully received.

CHAPTER 1

STAFF REGISTERS AND STAFF HISTORIES

The detail contained in staff registers varies considerably from company to company but undoubtedly the records of the Great Western Railway Company are the most extensive. The registers of some companies record merely the name, grade, place of employment (station or depot), and pay of individuals. Others contain much more, such as date of birth, previous occupation, reference to service in the armed services (particularly the First World War), promotions and commendations, date of retirement, pension details and date of death.

Some registers are indexed or have separate indices and others have their staff entries arranged alphabetically by the first letter of the surname. It is therefore a simple matter to seek out a particular employee from these. A number of companies have entered their employees chronologically by the date on which they joined the company. Sometimes an employment number has been allocated. If these registers are not indexed it may be a time-consuming exercise to search through for a particular individual.

The larger companies' records are usually grouped into divisions or departments (or both), which may assist in locating an employee. Station staff are often recorded separately from others and may be found under the name of the station.

Every type of employee will be found in the larger companies' records, from labourer to lavatory attendant, typist to chief clerk, porter to engine driver, ganger, gateman, storeman, accountant, auditor, station master and superintendent. A list of all the trades of employees found in the larger railway companies is given in Appendix 6.

Some of the very varied entries from staff registers are given overleaf.

Stockton and Darlington Railway Company. A list showing the names, builders and drivers of locomotives, September 1828. (TNA, RAIL 667/654). A transcript of this document is given on the following page.

RAIL 667/654   Stockton and Darlington Railway Company
Staff List, 1828

The following is a list of names of the first engines supplied to the above railway, with the names, builders and drivers of each engine from its commencement.

	ENGINE	BUILDER	DRIVER		ENGINE	BUILDER	DRIVER
1	Locomotion	Stephenson	James Stephenson	16	Director	Stephenson	Henry Lancaster
2	Hope	do	do	17	Lord Brougham	Timothy Hackworth	Ralph Waite
3	Blackdiamond	do	Robert Murray	18	Shildon	do	John Holmes
4	Diligence	do	George Jemminson	19	Darlington	Stephenson	Michael Law
5	Royal George	Timothy Hackworth	William Gowland	20	Adelaide	do	Richard Parkinson
6	Experiment	Stephenson	Michael Law	21	Earl Grey	Hawthorne	Thomas Lancaster
7	Rocket	do	James Stephenson	22	Lord Durham	Stephenson	Gorge Jemmison [sic]
8	Victory	Timothy Hackworth	John Montry	23	Wilberforce	Hawthorne	Edward Corner
9	Globe	Stephenson	John Morgan	24	Magnet	Timothy Hackworth	John Montry
10	Planet	do	Joseph Gladden	25	Enterprise	A. Kitchen	William Gatiss
11	North Star	do	George Newcombe	26	Arrow	Timothy Hackworth	Edward Corner
12	Magestic [sic]	Timothy Hackworth	William Baxter	27	Swift	Hawthorne	do
13	Coronation	do	William Gladstone	28	Sunbeam	do	do
14	William the Fourth	do	John Morgan	29	Queen	A. Kitchen	do
15	Northumbrian	do	George Newcombe	30	Raby Castle	do	Appleby

RAIL 623/66   Shropshire Union Railway and Canal Company
Staff Book

List of Persons in the employ of General Office Chester
Manager's Office

William Jones, manager	
Entered Service	Apr. 1844
Annual Salary	£600
August '76	£750
Resigned 31/10/79	

Cashier's Office

T.W. Chalton	Junior Clerk Feb. 1873
Annual Salary	£50/annum
1 June '79	To Carrying Dept.

This volume also contains staff in the Secretary's Office, Engineer's Office, Estate Office, Accountant's Office, Audit Office, Stores, Telegraph Office and Messengers.

RAIL 410/1805   London and North Western Railway Company
Staff register [indexed by station]

Lichfield

Man's Number	526
Name	Mooney, Richard
Last Employment	Confectioner
By Whom recommended	The late Sir Robert Peel
By Whom Nominated	Not known
Date of Appointment	June 1847
Age at Time of Joining Company's Service	42
Height	5 ft 6 inches
Occupation	Gateman
Pay	17/6

RAIL 770/80   Hull and Selby Railway Company*
Clerk's Salaries

Salaries Due to Clerks in the Merchandise Department, Hull.
Month ending 31 Mar 1848

Name	Occupation	Rate per Annum	£	s	d
M.T. Ring	Chief Clerk	150	12	10	0
Richard Spence	Correspondent	100	8	6	8
G.B. Watson	Checking Acc^t	100	8	6	8

---

*   RAIL 770 is the record class for the York and North Midland Railway. The Hull and Selby Railway was leased to the York and North Midland Railway from 1 July 1845. (This is an example where the records of a particular railway are to be found with the records of its parent company.)

Name	Occupation	Rate per Annum	£	s	d
Henry Denniss	Up Porter	100	8	6	8
Thomas Duck	Collector and Truckage Acc[t]	100	8	6	8
Edwin Storry	Up Traffic Book Acc[t]	80	6	13	4
Thomas Walker	Station Traffic	80	6	13	4
George Dowkin	Declarations &c	80	6	13	4
Dennis Taylor	Booker	80	6	13	4
William Sale	Down Porter's Acc[t]	70	5	16	8
George Saint	Porter's Delivery Book &c	70	5	16	8
J.C. Richardson	Advice Notes &c	65	5	8	4
Joseph Watson	Division of Traffic	70	5	16	8
John Corbett	Down Traffic Book	60	5	0	0
Thomas Morley	Clearing House	60	5	0	0
William Jackson	Down Ledger and Book	60	5	0	0
James Booth	Up Ledger and Book	60	5	0	0
John Scrafton	Copying up Invoices	60	5	0	0
John Marshall	Ass[t] Up Traffic Book	25	2	1	8
Thomas Watson	Ass[t] Down Traffic Book	20	1	13	4
Thomas Marshall	Sundry	15	1	5	0
			£125	8	4

RAIL 264/18   Great Western Railway Company
Register of Drivers and Firemen [1841 to 1864]

Thomas CLAPHAM
Date of Birth 8 June 1840*

* Unable to obtain certificate of birth.

His parents are both dead and family bible giving the date of birth which passed into possession of his elder brother, since deseased [sic], has been lost. Copy of letter from sister with family bible giving the age of Clapham examined at Swindon 7/12/03.

Entered Service	12 Nov. 1864	at 7/-
Fireman	8 Dec. 1864	at 7/6
3 Nov. 1906	Resigned on account of old age.	
5 Nov. 1906	M.A.S.† Assurance £55 paid to Clapham in consequence of his old age.	
4 Feb. 1927	Deceased.	

Name   David OWEN
Date of Birth   13 Apr. 1837

PROMOTIONS AND RATES OF WAGES			STATIONS AND DESCRIPTION OF WORK	
Date	Rate	Position	Station	Description of Work
3 Feb. 1860		Fireman	Gobowen	
5 Feb. 1860	3/-			
6 Jan. 1861	3/3			

† Mutual Assurance Society   *Cont.*

5

PROMOTIONS AND RATES OF WAGES			STATIONS AND DESCRIPTION OF WORK	
Date	Rate	Position	Station	Description of Work
10 Nov. 1861			Salop	
19 Jan. 1862	3/6			
18 Jan. 1863	3/9			
1 Dec. 1863			Gobowen	
6 Dec. 1863	4/-			
10 Apr. 1864	4/6			
11 Apr. 1864		Engine Turner		
7 May 1865	5/-			
8 May 1865		Engineman		
6 May 1866			Salop	
4 June 1866	5/6			
17 June 1867	4/-	Fireman	Wolverhampton	
4 Nov. 1867	5/-			
29 Nov. 1868	5/6			
1 May 1870	6/-			
30 Apr. 1871	6/6			2nd Class
12 May 1872	7/-			
9 May 1875	7/6			
31 Jan. 1893		Dismissed		
9 Sept. 1896		M.A.S. cheque £100 paid to cousin		

RECORD OF FINES			
Date	Locality	Penalty	Circumstances
5 Jan. 1861		Fined 1/-	
24 Jan. 1868		Fined 10/-	Being concerned in the damage to No. 266 Engine's Tender, and refusing to give such information as to show by whom it was actually done.
26 Apr. 1869	Bushbury	Fined £2	Damaging wagons when shunting.
4 Feb. 1870		Fined 2/-	Not seeing that the road was clear before moving his engine in the shed thereby damaging her.
13 Apr. 1874	Market Drayton	Reprimanded	Not sending to Wolverhampton for assistance by a goods train which passed him at Market Drayton when he had failed and waiting for Telegraph Office to open.
2 Dec. 1876		Severely reprimanded	Allowing dirt to accumulate in the sides of the fire box of No. 61 Engine.
11 Apr. 1878	Oxley siding and Codsall	Fined 2/-	Neglecting to see that the set screws were secure before leaving the Shed causing right big end cotter of No. 67 Engine to work out when running between Oxley Siding and Codsall causing delay to his own and a passenger train.

RECORD OF FINES			
Date	Locality	Penalty	Circumstances
4 March 1881		Fined 2/-	Leaving Shed late to take out his train causing late start.
12 Jan. 1882	Harbury Station	Suspended five days and severely reprimanded	Leaving when starting signal was at danger.
4 March 1885	Round Oak	Fined 2/-	Starting away without receiving the Guard's signal or seeing that his van was following and leaving van and guard behind.
5 March 1884			Not recommended for promotion. Incapacity.
13 Feb. 1884			Declined removal from Wolverhampton.
19 July 1887	Warwick	Fined 1/- and strongly reprimanded	Neglecting to stop at Warwick with goods train in accordance with time table.
23 July 1892		Dismissed	Owen caused the leading axle of his engine to be quite spoilt through neglect, and he did not again present himself for duty until 31 Jan. 1893. Owen's general conduct has not been satisfactory for the last few years and he was therefore told on 31 Jan. 1893 that he must consider himself dismissed.

Note: Owen applied for removal to Wolverhampton in June 1867 and as there was no vacancy for an Engineman or Engine Turner he elected to go and take employment as a Fireman.

Name George WEBBER
Date of Birth 28 July 1833

PROMOTIONS AND RATES OF WAGES			STATIONS AND DESCRIPTION OF WORK	
Date	Rate	Position	Station	Description of Work
7 Jan 1858		Fireman S.D.R.*	Falmouth	
17 June 1865		Engineman S.D.R.		Branch
at time of amalgamation	7/6	Passenger Engineman		
11 Apr. 1887	3/6	Chargeman Cleaner	Truro	Chargeman of Cleaners

RECORD OF FINES			
Date	Locality	Penalty	Circumstances
15 Feb. 1881	Truro	Cautioned	Engine thrown off line at turn-table.
17 Jan. 1882	Falmouth	Fined 2/-	Leaving without water in the tank and consequently the engine failed between Truro and Perranwell.

*   South Devon Railway   *Cont.*

RECORD OF FINES			
Date	Locality	Penalty	Circumstances
31 Mar. 1886	Perranwell	Fined £1 by Cornwall Directors	Failing to notice that van and trucks were not coupled up to train until they had run about 2 miles and then stopping so suddenly as to cause the last truck to break coupling and run back into collision with the trucks left on line causing considerable damage.
5 Aug. 1886	Falmouth station yard		Webber was engaged putting tallow in the lubricators just after starting from Falmouth with the 2.50 p.m. train and on returning to the footplate his foot slipped and he fell to the ground, the step of the front carriage striking him. Back and thigh bruised and spine shaken.
8 Dec. 1886			Webber was returning from Falmouth to Truro with empty engine 'Roberts', after working down the 11.32 a.m. ex Truro, to work down the 1.38 p.m. ex Truro, and when running between $309\frac{3}{4}$ and 310 mile posts felt his engine knock something. He stopped at Penryn to examine his engine and found portions of blood and hair and other matter sufficient to conclude someone had been run over, which proved to be the case, as on arrival at Truro he was informed that ganger Collins had been ran [sic] over and killed. There was a heavy hail and snow storm at the time which prevented the engineman and fireman seeing the man and it is supposed prevented Collins seeing the approaching engine. Verdict at inquest, Accidental, partly in consequence of the weather. In consequence of this accident Webber went temporarily out of his mind and was placed in the Bodmin Lunatic Asylum on 15 Dec. 1886. He was released on 1 Mar. 1887 and re-employed as Chargeman Cleaner on 11 Apr. 1887.
17 May 1888			Mutual Assurance Society Cheque for £70 paid to George Webber on account of disablement by accident.

RAIL 640/30   South Wales Railway Company
Staff at Chief Offices, *c.* 1860

Names	Length of Service	Present Salary
	Secretary's Department	
Mr Saunders	In 18th year	£1000 per annum
Mr Seargeant	In 15th year	£ 360 "
Mr Adams	In 8th year	£ 110 "
Mr Casman	In 4th year	£ 40 "
Registration		
Mr Baynes	In 10th year	£ 400 "
Mr W.R. Barwis	In 10th year	£ 130 "
Mr Caillet	In 7th year	£ 95 "
Mr R.G. Marwood	In 11th year	£ 130 "
Mr Watson	In 4th year	£ 40 "
Draftsmen &c		
Mr Wilkey	In 5th year	£ 80 "
Mileage Office		
Mr G.W. Bond	In 10th year	£ 140 "
Mr Bowles	In 9th year	£ 90 "
Mr C. Barwis	In 4th year	£ 70 "
Mr Barker	In 3rd year	£ 70 "
Mr King	In 2nd year	£ 45 "
Mr Lyon	In 7th year	£ 70 "
Mr Mothersole	In 5th year	£ 70 "
Mr Prentis	In 8th year	£ 50 "
Mr Snow	In 6th year	£ 70 "
E. Turner	Recently joined	6/- per week

RAIL 527/1898   North Eastern Railway Company
Salaries of Officers; Darlington Section

Salaries for the Month of Sept. 1866

Name	Salary	Name	Salary
T. MacNay	£250	Thomas Lee	£18–15
E. Towns. Jr	£75	Fred. Davison	£10–00
J.E. MacNay	£62–10	G.W. Barlett	£21–5
W.T. Ord	£42–10	S. Remington	£38–10
I.K. Kirsop	£8–15	J.H. Garbutt	£25–00
Joseph Thompson	£45–00	J. Simpson	£12–10
Thomas Garbutt	£30	T. Barker	£10–00
G.C. Lee	£30	J. Bellerby	£13–15
H. Cuthbertson	£30	W. Bygate	£11–5
John Cooke	£25		

Newcastle and Carlisle Railway Company. Wages book. (TNA, RAIL 509/96)

North Eastern Railway Company, Haydon Bridge staff (undated). Back row, left to right: Irwing Wray (P.W. Inspector), Mr Harding, William Boyd (platelayer), S.M., K. Kindred (signalman), Bob Wood (clerk), Edward Smith (ganger), George Wray (platelayer). Second row: Joe Todd (signalman), G. Thom (clerk), Jim Todd (porter), Matt Mews (porter), Billy Reay (W.E.), Jos. Elliot (foreman, porter). Front row: Billy Todd (junior porter), J. Telford (clerk); W.H. (bookstall). (NRM, 219/87)

RAIL 527/1895   North Eastern Railway Company
Appointments and Salaries for Clerical Staff and Draughtsmen in Workshops

Darlington
Works Manager's Staff

Name	E. Mackay
Born	15 Aug. 1853
Date Entered Service	Jan. 1872
Salary and Date of Receipt	£120 Jan. 1908

Note: Occasionally lists of staff transferred from one railway company to another, following an amalgamation, are also found. The following are examples:

RAIL 264/310   Great Western Railway Company
Register of Enginemen and Firemen employed on Amalgamated Lines
[1867—1923]

Bristol and Exeter Railway 1 Jan. 1876
Enginemen

Name		Station	Rate	Name		Station	Rate
Lyalli	G.	Bristol	7/6	Fulford	C.	Bristol	6/1
Ansell	R.	"	"	Elson	J.	"	6/-
Harle	R.	"	"	Payne	W.	"	5/9
Millman	I.	"	"	Tucker	J.	"	5/8
Dunscombe	W.	"	"	Tomkins	P.	"	5/6

Railway. 1 Jan.ʸ 1876.

Firemen.

Name		Station	Rate	Name		Station	Rate
Bryant	J	Bristol	4	Wilkins	G.	Bristol	3/
Bennett	F.	.	.	Gregory	Walter H.	.	.
Webber (1)	J.	.	.	Humphry	F.	Barnstaple	.
Millard	G.	Yeovil	.	Wiltshire	Cb.	Bristol	.
Star	G.	Wells	.	Ponsford	Cb.	.	.
Dainton	J.	Bristol	3/9	Coggins	John	.	.
Wilkins	E.	.	.	Bryant	G.	.	.
Randall	Cb.	.	.	Johns	Cb.	Barnstaple	.
Evans	Cb.	.	.	Newton	J.	Bristol	.
Blackmore (1)	F.	.	.	Day	Albert	.	.
Hotwood	Cb.	Yeovil	.	Brown	Frederick	.	.
London	Cb.	Bristol	.	Callow	R.	.	.
Adams	F.	Chard	.	Perry	R.	Taunton	.
Randall	F.	Clevedon	.	Harvey	S.	Bristol	.
Gait	E.	Taunton	.	Denham	E.	"	.
Simmonds	H.	Bristol	.	Parsons	Cb.	Taunton	.
Casling	F.	Yeovil	.	Brown	Henry	Bristol	.
Dodge	Cb.	Barnstaple	.	Hole	F.	.	.
Snell	H.	Taunton	.	Squire	Cb.	Barnstaple	.
Hoskins	S.	.	.	Gregory	Wallace	Bristol	.
Carey	A.	Bristol	3/6	Barrett	J.	"	.
Blackmore (2)	F.	Taunton	.	Evans	A.	.	.
Jarman	J	Weston	.	Lee	E.	.	.
Webber (2)	J	Bristol	.	Poultney	F.	.	.
Crew	Cb	.	.	Brewer	S.	.	.
Tucker	F.	Barnstaple	.	Wells	S.	Yeovil	.
Pursey	F.	Taunton	.	Jarman	S.	Bristol	.
Perry	S.	Barnstaple	.	Thomas	J.	.	.
Goff	D	Bristol	.				
Evans	J		.				
Bartlett	J	.	3/				

Great Western Railway Company, 1 January 1876. A list of firemen from the Bristol and Exeter Railway after amalgamation. (TNA, RAIL 264/31)

Name		Station	Rate
Scott	J.	"	"
Gorwill	I.	"	"
Nash	W.	"	"
Robson	T.	"	"
Robson	G.	Clevedon	"
Hawkins	R.	Weston	"
Gair	S.	Yeovil	"
Rowland	J.	Chard	"
Hobbs	G.	Taunton	"
Rogers	W.	Bristol	7/-
Sanger	A.	Bristol	7/-
Hannaford	W.	Taunton	"
Jones	J.	"	"
Sims	J.	"	"
Frost	H.	Barnstaple	"
Green	J.	"	"
Braund	J.	"	"
Ridge	A.	Wells	6/4
Coggins	G.	Bristol	6/3
Underhill	J.	"	"
Williams	F.	Yeovil	"
Harding	F.	"	"
Williams	A.	Barnstaple	"
Panis	C.	"	"
Neades	J.	Bristol	6/1

Name		Station	Rate
Corbitt	J.	"	"
Millard	R.	"	"
Legge	J.	Weston	"
Newport	S.	Bristol	5/-
Coggins	J.	"	"
Lane	S.	"	"
Ricketts	G.	"	"
Dressell	J.	"	"
Ridge	T.	"	"
Rice	R.	"	"
Neades	W.	"	"
Sheppard	H.	"	"
Clutterbuck	S.	"	"
Aslat	T.	"	"
Bruford	F.	Chard	"
Coggins	A.	Clevedon	"
Pocock	G.	Yeovil	"
Jefferies	M.	"	"
Millard	W.	Weston	"
Pyne	H.	Taunton	"
Panes	J.	"	
Helps	J.	"	"
Hillman	J.	"	"
Howell	C.	"	"
Derman	J.	"	"

Bristol and Exeter Railway 1 Jan. 1876
Firemen

Name		Station	Rate
Bryant	J.	Bristol	4/-
Bennett	F.	"	"
Webber	J. (1)	"	"
Millard	G.	Yeovil	"
Steer	G.	Wells	"
Dainton	J.	Bristol	3/9
Wilkins	E.	"	"
Randall	W.	"	"
Evans	W.	"	"
Blackmore	T. (1)	"	"
Horwood	W.	Yeovil	"
London	W.	Bristol	"
Adams	T.	Chard	"
Randall	F.	Clevedon	"
Gait	E.	Taunton	"
Simmonds	H.	Bristol	"
Casling	F.	Yeovil	"
Dodge	W.	Barnstaple	"
Snell	H.	Taunton	"
Hoskins	S.	"	"

Name		Station	Rate
Wilkins	G.	Bristol	3/-
Gregory, Walter Henry		"	"
Humphry	F.	Barnstaple	"
Wiltshire	W.	Bristol	"
Ponsford	W.	"	"
Coggins	John	"	"
Bryant	G.	"	"
Johns	W.	Barnstaple	"
Newton	J.	Bristol	"
Day, Albert		Bristol	"
Brown, Frederick		"	"
Callow	R.	"	"
Perry	R.	Taunton	"
Harvey	S.	Bristol	"
Denham	E.	"	"
Parsons	W.	Taunton	"
Brown, Henry		Bristol	"
Hole	F.	"	"
Squire	W.	Barnstaple	"
Gregory, Wallace		Bristol	"

13

Great Western Railway Company, Swindon Firemen (undated). (TNA, RAIL 1014/48)

Name		Station	Rate
Carey	A.	Bristol	3/6
Blackmore	T. (2)	Taunton	"
Jarman	J.	Weston	"
Webber	J. (2)	Bristol	"
Crew	W.	"	"
Tucker	T.	Barnstaple	"
Pursey	T.	Taunton	"
Perry	S.	Barnstaple	"
Goff	D.	Bristol	"
Evans	J.	"	"

Name		Station	Rate
Barrett	J.	"	"
Evans	A.	"	"
Lee	E.	"	"
Poultney	F.	"	"
Brewer	S.	"	"
Wells	S.	Yeovil	"
Jarman	S.	Bristol	"
Thomas	J.	"	"
Bartlett	J.	"	"

RAIL 463/219   Manchester, Sheffield and Lincolnshire Railway Company Staff Ledger

[*Note inserted inside back cover*]

Mr Birt to Mr Fearn, 27 October 1886

I have had two cases before me recently where persons have been admitted into the service over 35 years of age. One case before me this morning is that of a man 65 years of age, past work, who wants an allowance from the Company, and who has only been in the service 11½ years.
I direct your particular attention to that rule which forbids any one over 35 years being engaged. The rule is not to be departed from in any case without my sanction.

RAIL 236/727 Great Northern Railway Company
Staff Register [indexed]

Mr Herbert Anderson
Clerk
6 Woodville Road
Boston
Born 9 Oct. 1887
Joined Company service 19 Apr. 1903
Entered Sack Dept.   8 May 1904   11/- per week
                         19 Apr. 1904   14/-
                          9 Oct. 1905   20/-
                          9 Oct. 1906   22/-
                          9 Oct. 1907   24/-
                          9 Oct. 1908   26/-
                          9 Oct. 1909   28/-
                          9 Oct. 1910   30/-
                          9 Oct. 1912   32/-
                          9 Oct. 1914   £90 per an.
                          9 Oct. 1916   £95 per an.
Enlisted in RNAS* as an Air Craftsman 28/1/18
Returned to Sth Depot 22/9/19
Graded Class 5, 1 Aug. 1919
To Boston Goods 14/1/24
* Royal Naval Air Service

RAIL 674/11 Stratford upon Avon and Midland Junction Railway Company
Staff Register

No. S716

R. Harrison	labourer		
Born	1851		
Joined	1887		
Station	Stratford Upon Avon		
Rate	Nov. 1911	18/6	
	Feb. 1913	19/6	
	1 Feb. 1915	20/6	per week plus 1/- bonus
	15 Feb. 1915	20/6	per week plus 2/- bonus
	18 Nov. 1915	20/6	per week plus 4/- bonus
	16 Sept. 1916	20/6	per week plus 9/- bonus
	16 Apr. 1917	20/6	per week plus 14/- bonus
	5 Nov. 1917	19/6	per week plus 21/- bonus
	1 Jan. 1920	58/-	per week including bonus
	1 Apr. 1920	59/-	per week including bonus
	5 Apr. 1920	8/6	per week, flat rate. difference between rural and industrial rate
	14 June 1920	67/6	per week including bonus
	1 July 1920	69/6	per week including bonus

Cont.

Rate	1 Oct. 1920	71/6	per week including bonus	
	1 Jan. 1921	72/6	per week including bonus	
	1 Apr. 1921	68/6	per week including bonus	Granted a flat rate of 2/3 per
	1 July 1921	64/6		week owing to withdrawal of bread subsidy

Retired from service 16 July 1921
Paid a retiring allowance of 15/- per week in recognition of his 34 years service.

RAIL 227/450   Great Eastern Railway Company
Superintendent's Department; Salaried Staff Register

Date of Entry   4/2/89
Age at Entry   16
Charles Edward Reeve BANYARD

Grade	Station	Pay	Date	
Probationary Clerk	Aldeburgh	6/-	4/2/89	
Lad Clerk	"	10/-	1/12/90	
	"	12/-	29/2/92	
	"	14/-	6/3/93	
	"	16/-	12/3/94	
	"	18/-	4/8/97	
Goods Clerk	Eye	20/-	14/11/98	
	"	22/-	11/12/99	
Goods Clerk	Leiston	23/-	15/10/00	
	"	24/-	31/12/00	
	"	25/-	31/12/01	
Second Parcels Clerk	Ipswich	28/-	4/1/04	
District Relg. Bkg. Clerk*	"	25/- + expenses	19/12/04	
District Relg. Bkg. Clerk (Station Master 14/10/13)	"	£70 + do	23/7/07	
		£75 + do	1/9/08	
	"	£80 + do	1/1/11	
		£85 + do	1/1/14	
		£90 + do	1/4/15	
Station Master	Thurston	£100 + House	1/2/16	
		£110 do	1/1/18	
		£120 do	1/7/19	
Station Master (4th Class)	"	£230 + £23 F.B.†	1/8/19 Rent £21 Bonus £5 1/4/20	
			£25 1/7/20	
		£230 + £18 F.B.	1/7/21	
		£230		

To folio 589 Operating Dept.

*   Relieving Booking Clerk
†   fixed bonus

		Branch		Station	
Name	Age	Rank	Pay	Date of entering the service	Remarks
Halcroff, Adam	26	Station Master	24/-	Jan. 1853	Under Porting Clerk, 6th Jan. 1857. Resigned Jan. 1857.
Whittingham, John	38	Carriage Cleaner	16/-	Oct. 1854	Dismissed for being drunk, 2nd July 1856.
Sweetly, William	46	Lampman	16/-	Jan. 1853	Resigned
Rodgers, John	32	Porter	15/-	March 1856	Promoted to Clerk at Silecroft 19 May 1856
Morgan, John	24	Porter	15/-	April 1856	Under Bowl Guard 1st Sept 1857
Johnston, Richard	34	Switchman	16/-	May 1850	Has a house, rent free. Promoted to Permanent Pilot 1st Dec. 1856
Brundson, Josiah	48	Signalman	12/-	Sept. 1852	Has a house, rent free
Johnston, John	41	Night Watchman	16/-	April 1849	Removed to Signalman, Eskate Junction 13 May 1856
Barnes, William	14	Messenger	6/-	Jan. 1856	Resigned 22nd Dec. 1856
Higgin, Henry		Charwoman	7/-	Dec. 1854	Has a house, rent free
Pile, Joseph	24	Porter	15/-	12 May 1856	Changed to Fire-lighter at Broughton 1st July 1856

Whitehaven and Furness Junction Railway Company. Staff book. (TNA, RAIL 744/9)

RAIL 489/21 Midland and South Western Junction Railway Company
Staff Register

Name	Cooke James		
Married or Single	-----		
Born	23 Apr.	1876	
Appointed	Jan.	1893	
Grade	Cleaner		
Promotions, Rewards and Remarks	8 Nov.	1896	Put on coalstage for leaving shed without leave
	7 July	1897	Promoted to Fireman at 3/- per day
	Jan.	1898	Suspended 2 days for not locking up tool box. Removed to Andover Junction thro' allowing engines to blow off unevenly at Stations
	4 Apr.	1898	Removed to Cheltenham
	7 July	1898	Advanced to 3/6 per day
	7 July	1899	Advanced to 4/- per day
	27 May	1901	Commended and given 5/- for seeing points wrong at Cricklade and signals off, 9.15 ex Andover Junction. Advanced to 4/6 per day
	4 Jan.	1904	Reduced to 4/- per day for passing signals at danger at Andover Junction with engineman A. Butler on 10.25 a.m. ex South'ton 18 Dec. 1903
	27 June	1904	To Chargeman and Boiler Washer at 4/6
	June	1905	To Cirencester, Spare Engineman
	21 May	1906	To Cheltenham
	23 Sept.	1907	To Swindon Driving
			Registered as an Engineman at 5/- per day
	11 Mar.	1908	Removed from Swindon to Cheltenham
	23 Sept.	1908	Advanced to 5/6 per day
	23 Sept.	1909	Advanced to 6/- per day
	23 Sept.	1910	Advanced to 6/6 per day
	30 Nov.	1910	Commended for the vigilance displayed on 24 Nov. when he stopped at Foss Cross with the 3.5 p.m. ex Cheltenham in order to inform the Stationmaster that a truss of Hay was lying across the up road near the Station
	6 Mar.	1911	Placed in charge of No. 7 Passenger Engine.
	27 May	1911	Hot connecting rod brasses on No. 7 Engine on the 4.50 a.m. ex Cheltenham
	23 Sept.	1911	Advanced to 7/- per day
	23 Sept.	1912	Advanced to 7/6 per day
	13 Feb.	1916	Appointed Foreman at Cheltenham at 58/4d per week
	28 Aug.	1916	Advanced to 63/- per week
	24 Dec.	1917	Advanced to 70/- per week
	24 Feb.	1919	Advanced to 85/- per week
	2 May	1920	To Head Office, Inspector at £350 per annum plus 20% and back pay from 1 Aug. 1919

Lancashire and Yorkshire Railway Company, female labourer cleaners at Horwich engine shed, 1917. (TNA, RAIL 343/725)

RAIL 410/1814   London and North Western Railway Company
Old Northampton Staff Register, No. 3

Irthlingboro' Station
Coaching Department

Jesse Allen		
Grade	Porter	
Date of Birth	20–9–79	
Date of Entry into Service	14–12–95	Date
Rate of Salary or Wage	£–s–d	17–2–99
	16–0	17–2–99 C. Ashby [Cold Ashby]
Date and Where Transferred from or to,	[from]	29–11–99 Wellingbro
or, Date and Cause of Leaving	[to]	

RAIL 635/306   South Eastern Railway Company
Staff Register, Goods Department

Erith Station

Number	1614
Name in Pull	H. Roberts
Rank	Porter
Date of Appointment	17 June 1895
Weekly Wage	£ 1/-/-
Yearly Salary	£52
Date of Birth	9 June 1869
Remarks	Resigned
Date of Leaving the Service	19 May 1896
Successor	Holland, G.T.

South Eastern Railway Company, Canterbury West station staff (undated). (NRM, 1497/87)

RAIL 328/16   Isle of Wight Central Railway Company
Staff Register, [1864 to 1915]

Labourers
Ticket Collectors
Painters
Messengers
Porters
Signalmen

Secretary & Traffic Manager's Office
Sandown
18 Nov. 1898
Re vacancy as No. 2 Passenger Guard owing to J. Exton's illness.

As there does not seem any probability of Exton returning to his duty it has been decided to fill up this position permanently.
Both Corbett and Lee have applied for it and as there is nothing to choose between the two men it must go by seniority and this being so the appointment is due to Lee as he has been guard on BH Rly* since 1887. Corbett being appointed to his position at Ryde when Lee was transferred to Bembridge.

Read this to Corbett and say in justice to Lee I am sorry I cannot give any other decision and ask him whether he would wish to take up the position of guard on the BH Railway.

Yours Truly
M. Wherray

Inspector Phenay
Brading

* Brading Harbour Railway

RAIL 574/13   Port Talbot Railway and Docks Company
Register of Staff

General Manager's Office
Salaried Staff

Relief Clerk	W. Stevens
Date of Entering Service	7 Feb. 1898
Date appointed to present post	16 Apr. 1914
Date 27/2/14	£5
27/2/15	£5
27/2/17	£10

Girl Clerk	Olive Milson
Date of Entering Service	26 Mar. 1917
Date appointed to present post	26 Mar. 1917
Present Wages	15/- per wk.

Unidentified group of railwaymen. LMA SC/PHL/02/625/84/1658

RAIL 583/54   Rhymney Railway Company
Register of Dates of Men Employed

Cleaners, Cardiff

Name	Age	Date When Taken On	Date of Leaving	Remarks
William Liddell	16/5	Feb. 16, 1901	Mar. 28, 1901	Last day worked
Arthur Shute	16/3	Feb. 19, 1901	June 27, 1901	
Thomas Evans	15/10	Feb. 20, 1901	Mar. 12, 1901	Last day worked
David Williams	19/10	Feb. 21, 1901	Feb. 28, 1901	
James Tranter	19	Feb. 22, 1901	May 17, 1902	
Frederick Singleton	24/6	Mar. 5, 1901	Did not start	
William Bell	17	Mar. 8, 1901	Jan. 30, 1902	Dismissed
Charles Townsend	15/1	Mar. 11, 1901	Apr. 15, 1901	
William Jones	24	Mar. 13, 1901	--------	Refer to page 38*
James Belt	15/2	Mar. 19, 1901	--------	
William R. Jones	16/4	Mar. 22, 1901	Sept. 20, 1901	Left without notice

This volume also contains: helpers, drivers, firemen, washers out, packers, coalers, fitters, turners, screwers and drillers, boys, coppersmiths, tinmen, gas fitters, smiths, strikers, boiler smiths, pattern makers, carpenters, wagon repairers, sawyers, signal fitters and examiners, wagon inspectors, greasers, masons, labourers, painters, enginemen and watchmen.

---

*   Page 38 shows that he was employed as a packer

Cambrian Railways, carriage shop men, Oswestry Works, 1909. Back row, left to right: A. Hodgson, W. Benbow, W. Rowlands, A. Edwards, I.H. James, J. Morgan, J.W. Green, E. Evans. Second row: R. Evans, W.E. Lewis, T. Davies, H. White, J. Richards, D. Jones, L. Jones, S. Lewis, C. Humphreys, W. Lewis, E. Williams. Third row: T. Davies, C. Thomas, A. Martin, F. Parry, J. Hack, C. Lloyd, W. Tudor, W. Woollam, J.F. Thomas, G. Sperrins, F. Frost, E. Hill, G. Humphreys, G. Jenkins. Front row: W.H. Parry, W.P. Evans, T. Morgan, T. Price, J. Adams, J. Martin, A.E. Matthew, H. Gough, J. Brown, B. Jones. (TNA, RAIL 92/136)

Cambrian Railways, turning shop men, Oswestry Works, 1909. Back row, left to right: S. Vaughan, E.O. Griffiths, E. Jones, E.W. James, H.G. Glasscondine (died 31/10/12), R. Ellis, D. Vaughan, W.R. Finchett, W.A. Jones, J. Rogers, W. Ward, J. Jones (one name is missing from this row). Second row: H.J. Foulkes, H. Roberts, E. Hampson. Third row: J. Hughes, T.P. Jones, R. Edwards, C. Plimmer, S. Jones, J. Owen, L. Stewart, A. Ellis, M. Jones, E. Vaughan, H. Young, A. Morris, E. Williams, R. Martin. Front row: J. Pearce, W. Swan, T. Archer, E. Jones, E. Cox, W. Gwynn, W. Kilvington, T. Holland, A. Frost, W. James, P. Vaughan, H. Cawley, W. Davies. (TNA, RAIL 92/136)

RAIL 532/58   North Staffordshire Railway Company
Staff Book, Traffic Department [arranged by station]

RUSHTON STATION

Brassington, S.	Porter	
Age on entering service [born]	6–3–97	
Date of appointment	6–7–14	
To present grade	6–7–14	
To present position	6–7–14	
Rate of pay	13/-	
Resigned Jan. 11/15		

RAIL 633/343   South Eastern and Chatham Railway Company
Register of Punishments and Awards to Enginemen

Frederick George Harris	Faversham
Born	22/3/95
Cleaner	27 May 1914
Fireman	2 Nov. 1914
Passed	30 June 1914
Appointed Driver	13 Jan. 1936
18 Mar. 1922	Cautioned. Causing derailment of Engine 468 in Loco Yard, Faversham
29 Apr. 1944	Reprimanded. Running thro' crossing gates at Queensboro' (Whiteway Crossing)

RAIL 410/1979   London and North Western Railway Company
Unappointed [dismissed] Clerical Staff Employed at Liverpool Goods Depot

Alexandra Dock
Female Clerks

Gertrude Beatrice BATES	female clerk		
Born	29 Apr. 1898		
Entered Service	2 Apr. 1917		
Salary		16/-	
Advance	29 Apr. 1917	4/-	20/-
	29 Apr. 1918	3/-	23/-
	29 Apr. 1919	2/-	25/-
Date and Cause of Erasure	3 May 1919	Put off	

RAIL 264/307   Great Western Railway Company
Register of Officers, salaried and supervisory staff taken over from amalgamated lines

This includes:
Barry Railway
Rhymney Railway
Taff Vale Railway
Cardiff and Penarth Docks
(Continued on p. 26)

Cornwall Railway

List of Staff employed in the Traffic Department at the undermentioned Stations

Name		Occupation	Date of entering Service		Salary or Wages	
Plymouth						
Scantlebury	W	Inspector	May	62	1	15
Searle	H	Pass: Guard	Oct	59	1	8
Westaway	W	" "	April	60	1	8
Kelly	R	" "	Jan	61	1	8
Hammett	R	" "	June	60	1	8
Hocking	J	" "	Feb	67	1	8
Uren	H	" "	Oct.	59	1	8
Hurd	H	" "	March	63	1	7
Johnson	J	" "	"	72	1	6
Bullock	G	Goods "	July	69	1	7
Lobb	S	" "	Dec	72	1	7
James	W	" "	"	74	1	4
Harvey	J	" "	Nov	73	1	4
Scott	T	" "	Feb	86	1	10
Freethey	J	" "	July	67	1	10
Ireland	J	" "	Oct.	73	1	4
Squire	W	" "	Nov.	73	1	5
Salk	W	" "	March	75	1	6
Bray	W	" "	Aug	78	1	4
Secretary & Accountants Offices						
Pickford	EW	Messenger	Dec	85		8
Scantlebury	W	Housekeeper				7

Cornwall Railway Company, 1889. Staff at amalgamation with the Great Western Railway Company. (TNA, RAIL 134/40)

Alexandra Docks and Railway
Port Talbot Railway and Docks Co.
Cambrian Railways
Brecon and Merthyr Railway
Neath and Brecon Railway
Burry Port and Gwendreath Valley Railway
Cardiff Railway Gasworks Section

Example:
Rhymney Railway – Salaried Draughtsmen
Geoffrey Gwyther JONES
Assistant Draughtsman

Born	19 May 1901
Entered Service	3 Jan. 1921
Left	11 Nov. 1922
To Swindon D.O.†	
Ticket No. 110.	
Date of Transfer	12 May 1922

†   Drawing Office

Cambrian Railways, iron foundry men, Oswestry Works, 1909. Back row, left to right:
W. Roberts, F. Thomas, G. Thomas, S. Jones, E. Jones, J. Nicholls. Second row: E. Phillips, J.H.
Matthews, A. Beaton, R. Lewis, C. Thomas, C.R. Bland. Front row: H. Williams, S.F. Davies,
T.J. Ruscoe, H. Williams, J.R. Griffiths, E. Jones, E. Rogers. (TNA, RAIL 92/136)

CHAPTER 2

PAYBILLS AND VOUCHER BOOKS

Paybills often give only the summary total payments to the various departments of a railway. In some cases, however, detailed lists have been found giving the names of all employees, arranged by grade and department.

Voucher Books contain the receipts collected together by accountants and sometimes include weekly or fortnightly lists of wages paid. They also give the names of the employees, whose signatures or marks are often appended. On some occasions pay has been signed for by one person on behalf of another.

Examples of some of these documents are given in this chapter.

RAIL 772/106   York, Newcastle and Berwick Railway Company
Gateshead Station

Paybill for the fortnight ending 4 January 1845
Engineering, Locomotive and Carriage Department

Name	Occupation	Time	Rate	Gross Amount £ s d
	Gatemen			
Jno. Lee	Park Lane	12	2/-	1 4 0
Will. Phillipson	"	12	2/-	1 4 0
Will. Hay	Felling	12	1/4	0 16 0
Thos. Moor	Boldon Lane	12	1/4	0 16 0
Thos. Watson	"	12	1/8	1 0 0
Rich. Robinson	Shields	12	2/6	1 10 0
Thos. Hayton	"	12	2/6	1 10 0
Will. Daglish	Green Lane	12	2/6	1 10 0
Jos. Hewitt	Stanhope Crossing	12	2/6	1 10 0
Jos. Dobson	Shields	11	2/6	1 7 6
Will. Fenton	S & D* Crossing	12	2/9	1 13 0

*   Stockton and Darlington Railway

Name	Occupation	Time	Rate	Gross Amount £ s d
E. Binns	" "	12	2/9	1 13 0
Will. Wilson	Chilton	12	2/6	1 10 0
E. Moys	Byers Green	12	2/6	1 10 0
Henry Hewitt	Rainton	12	2/6	1 10 0
Jno. Willis	New Bottle Lane	12	1/3	0 15 0
Jno. Lishman	Cleaning Quicks	15	1/6	1 2 6
Rich[d] Batey	" "	12	1/6	0 18 0
Geo. Renwick	" "	12	1/6	0 18 0

RAIL 667/1481   Stockton and Darlington Railway Company
Voucher Book

Wear Valley Railway
Labrous [sic] time for October 1849
Platelayers and (extrey) men, maintenance
Laying new siding at Eals Bec

Platelayers	Mentenence [sic] of Way Days	Laying new siding at Eals Beck Days	Albung and Longthug Siding at Dryburn	Quantity of Days	Per Day	Switch Money	£ s d
John Stout	11½		15	26½	2/6	6	4 1 1
John Ridley	12		15	27	2/8		3 12 0
Robert Hart	28			26	2/10	6	3 19 8
John Liddle	18		9	27	2/8		3 12 0
John Atkinson	22	5		27	2/10	6	4 2 6
W[m] Fryer	21	5		26	2/-		2 12 0
John Lynn	14		12	26	2/10	6	3 19 8
John Fryer	15½		10	25½	2/8		3 8 0
John Ells	27½			27½	2/10	6	4 3 11
Christopher Willson	15		12	27	2/8		3 12 0
Robert Fryer				27	5/-		6 15 0
etc.							

Note: The Wear Valley Railway Company was leased to the Stockton and Darlington Railway Company in 1847 and amalgamated with that company in 1858.

RAIL 704/17   Vale of Neath Railway Company
Paybill Book

Merthyr Road Station
Week ending 1 October 1851

Name	Occupation	Time	Amount
D. Thomas (from 10 July to 23 Sept.)	Station Master	[blank]	8 0 0
			7 0 0 15 0 0
W[m] Venables	Policeman		1 10 0
Thomas Sparks	Porter		1 17 0
Morris Griffiths	Porter		1 15 0

RAIL 253/174   Great Western Railway Company
Paybill Book

General Manager's Office for 4 weeks ending 26 January 1868

Name	A. Beasley
Occupation	Chief Clerk
Time	4 weeks
Rate	£250
Amount	19–3–7
Income Tax	9/7
Superannuation	9/7
Amount Received	18–4–5

RAIL 99/57   Carmarthen and Cardigan Railway Company
Voucher Book

General Traffic Wages
Weekly Pay List, 2 weeks ending Friday the 8th and 15th day of October 1869

Names	Sat.	Sun.	Mon.	Tu.	Wed.	Th.	Fr.	Rate	£ s d	Totals	Signatures
Carmarthen											
Wm. Lewis	2	2	2	2	2	2	2	23/-	2 6		W. Lewis
Jno England, Guard	2	2	2	2	2	2	2	22/-	2 4		J. England
Edw Mason	2	2	2	2	2	2	2	18/-	1 16		E. Mason
W. Bartlett, Switchman	2½	2	2	2	2	2	2	19/-	1 19 4		Wm Bartlett
D. Thomas	2	2	2	2	2½	2	2		1 19 4		D. Thomas
Jno Griffiths, Foreman	2	2	2	2	2	2	2	18/-	1 16		J. Griffiths
D. Lloyd, Porter	2	2	2	2	2	2	2		1 16		D. Lloyd
D. Davis	2	2	2	2	2	2	2	17/-	1 14		D. Davis
G. Howlett	2	2	2	2	2	2	2	16/-	1 12		G. Howlett
T. Price	2	2	2	2	2	2	2		1 12		Thos Price
D. Williams	2	2	2	2	2	2	2	12/-	1 4		David Williams
J.W. Jones	2	2	2	2	2	2	2	10/-	1		J.W. Jones
J. Lewis, Gateman	2	2	2	2	2	2	2	17/-	1 14		Js Lewis
W. Jones, Nightman	2	2	2	2	2	2	2	15/-	1 10		W. Jones
J. Morris	2	2	2	2	2	2	2	6/-	12		Jas Morris
										24 14 8	
Abergwilli Junction											
T. Davis, Signalman	2	2	2	2	2	2	2	21/-	2 2		T. Evans*
										2 2	
Bronwydd											
R. Shaw, BC†	2	2	2	2	2	2	2	16/-	1 12		R. Shaw
										1 12	
Conwil											
E. Evans, BC	2	2	2	2	2	2	2	19/-	1 18		E. Evans
										1 18	
Llanpumpsaint											
Thos Evans, BC	2	2	2	2	2	2	2	18/-	1 16		T. Evans*
										1 16	

*   These signatures are identical

†   Booking Clerk

Continued on p. 31

Pay Sheet 2 Weeks Ending January 22 - 1859

MEN'S NAMES.	Days.	Rate.	Amount.			Amount Due.		SIGNATURE.
John Vernon	12	3/.	1 16	5		2 1		J. Vernon
Clark Grainger	12	2/6	1 10			1 10		C. Grainger
J. Douglas	11-2	2/6	1 8 9			1 8 9		J. Douglas
Vernon & Weeks Blacksmiths Work						6	5 5 9	
William Brown	12	3/.	1 16	5		2 1		William Brown
William Batty	12	2/6	1 10			1 10		William Batty
George Witty	12	2/6	1 10			1 10		George Witty
Brown & Weeks Blacksmiths Work						6	5 7	
Thomas Ryder	12	3/.	1 16			1 16		Thomas Ryder
Walter Taylor	12	2/6	1 10	5		1 15		Walter Taylor
John North	12	2/6	1 10			1 10		John North
Ryder & Weeks Blacksmiths Work						6	5 7	
Robert Morris	12	3/.	1 16			1 16		Robert Morris
William Rowland	12	2/6	1 10	5		1 5		William Rowland
Ben Brown	12	2/6	1 10			1 10		Ben Brown
Morris & Weeks Blacksmiths Work						6	4 17	
Francis Clark	12	2/.	1 4			1 4		Fraince Clark
Joseph Curtis	12	3/4	2			2		Joseph Curtis
William Keating	12	3/.	1 16	5		1 11		Wm Keating
							4 15	
						Total	25 11 9	

January 29 1859
Received of Mr Maltman £25 11 9
in payment of wages as above

Joseph

Hull and Holderness Railway Company. Pay sheet, 22 January 1859. (TNA, RAIL 313/22)

Names	Sat.	Sun.	Mon.	Tu.	Wed.	Th.	Fr.	Rate	£ s d	Totals	Signatures
Pencader											
Jno. Lloyd, BC	2	2	2	2	2	2	2	23/-	2 6		J. Lloyd
Owen Evans, Porter	2	2	2	2	2	2	2	16/-	1 12		J.L. for O. Evans
										3 18	
Pencader Junction											
R. Mills, Signalman	2	2	2	2	2	2	2	18/-	1 16		R. Mills
										1 16	
Llandyssil											
J. Morris, Foreman	2	2	2	2	2	2	2	18/-	1 16		J. Morris
T. Davis, Porter	2	2	2	2	2	2	2	14/-	1 18		T. Davis
										3 4	
P & S Junction											
J. Williams, Signalman	2	2	2	2	2	2	2	21/-	2 2		J.M. Williams
										2 2	
										43 2 8	

RAIL 747/37   Whitland and Taff Vale Railway Company Voucher Book

[Payments made to various contractors and also includes Wages Lists]

Maintenance Permanent Way
PAY BILL for the Fortnight ending Friday the 28th day of July 1876

Name	Occupation	Days	Rate		Amount		
			s	d	£	s	d
Benjamin Jones	Ganger	12	3	4	2		
Thomas Rowlands	Repairer	8	2	10	1	2	8
James Beynon	"	11½	2	10	1	12	7
Thomas Thomas	"	11½	2	10	1	12	7
Stephen Lewis	"	4	2	10		11	4
Joseph Davies	Ganger	11	3	4	1	16	8
William John	Repairer	11	2	10	1	11	2
David Lewis	"	11	2	10	1	11	2
Titus Davies	"	5	2	10		14	2
Edward Jones	Ganger	11	3	4	1	16	8
Daniel Richards	Repairer	11½	2	10	1	12	7
Benjamin Davies	"	10	2	10	1	8	4
Thomas Harris	"	9½	2	10	1	6	11
John Gibbon	Carpenter	12	4	2	2	10	–
Daniel Rees	Smith	12	4		2	8	–
					£23	14	10
					[signed] David Roberts		

A CHALLENGE

SENT TO THE DIRECTORS OF THE EASTERN COUNTIES RAILWAY COMPANY.

The following is an exact copy of a Letter sent to the Directors of the Eastern Counties Railway Company :—

7, Chester Street, Green Street,
Bethnal Green, August 26th, 1856.

To the Chairman and Directors
    of the Eastern Counties Railway Company.

Gentlemen,

    Your Engines seem to be taking it *very easy*. I have an old **Donkey** that I will guarantee to beat some of your **Business Trains** in speed. For example, your Time Table allows 6, 7, and 8 Minutes from Cheshunt to Waltham. Now, I will back my old Donkey to do it in 4 Minutes, and thus leave me time to get my breakfast before the Train starts.

    This little Donkey is 15 years old, or I would back him to run against some of your Trains from Cheshunt to London. I know he could have beaten them 4 or 5 years ago, and I think he might do so now, but I am not willing to tax the powers of my old friend. He will do what I have stated *with ease,* and have a good bray afterwards, as if in contempt of the inferior power of **Eastern Counties Steam.** If you are willing to accept the Challenge, name the day, and have an umpire on a fast horse to see all fair, and I will be ready for you.

                 I am, Gentlemen,
                    Your humble Servant,
                     (Signed)   GEORGE HOY.

Eastern Counties Railway TNA, RAIL 186/100

CHAPTER 3

SICKNESS AND ACCIDENTS

Some railway companies have surviving sickness and accident registers of their employees. Many more records survive for train accidents. Not only did railway companies maintain their own records of accidents but the Board of Trade enquired into every serious accident and published very detailed reports. Every railway employee who witnessed, or was involved in an accident was interviewed. Such reports therefore record the statements made by railway workers and others. These reports are found in TNA document class RAIL 1053 and date from 1840 to 1975. A set of these reports is also held by the National Railway Museum Library at York.

The official printed annual reports by the Inspecting Officers of Railways contain accident reports. These are found in TNA document class MT 29 and date from 1840 to 1964.

TNA document class MT 6, *Railway Correspondence and Papers*, also includes accident reports. (MT 7 is a general index to MT 6.)

The following are some examples from the records of accidents.

MT 6/1/7   A Letter from George Stevenson to the Board of Trade suggesting various ways of improving and controlling safety on railways.

Containing observations relative to the regulations of Railways by Government.
Received 1st April.

> George Stevenson
> Tapton House
> near Chesterfield
> 31st March 1841

To the Right Hon. H. Labouchere
President of the Board of Trade
Sir,
   Since my examination before the select committee of Railways I see the difficulties you have to contend with from the opposing members to your bill in bringing forward a measure for the management and better regulation of Railways. I am quite sure that some interference on the

part of government is much wanted; perhaps I ought to be the last man to admit this (the whole system of Railway and Locomotive Engines having been brought out by my executions), but when I see so many young engineers, and such a variety of notions I am convinced that some system should be laid down to prevent wild visionary schemes being tried, at the great danger of injury or loss of life to the public. I consider it right that every talented man should be at liberty to make improvement but that the supposed improvement should be duly considered by proper judges. Then the question follows, from the opponents to the Bill who are those judges to be? I beg to lay before you my views on this point.

Suppose any Engineer has any improved plans for the better working of Railways to propose, he should submit his plan to the Engineer belonging to the Board of Trade, but before that Engineer should give his decision as to the utility of the scheme he should have full power to call together the chief Engineers of the principal Railways of the Kingdom, and after the subject has been duly discussed votes should be taken, for and against this measure. The discussion should be laid before the Board of Trade accompanied with the observations of the government Engineers and if approved of should then be placed into his hands to carry out.

I should propose for the consideration of the different Engineers, that the speed of Locomotives should not exceed forty miles per hour on the most favourable Lines, excepting on special occasions curved Lines to diminish in velocity according to the radius. I am quite aware that this cannot be carried out to any great necity [necessity], but still it would be a check upon the Drivers.

Collateral Lines require government consideration, in every strong point of view. Uniformity of signals is another desirable point.

As several persons are now turning their attention to the construction of self acting breaks [*sic*], it will soon appear that great benefit, and safety to travelling, will be found by their adoption. In the mean time no train should be allowed to travel which has not the breaksmen [*sic*], and form coaches, in each train should be provided with breaks[*sic*] to allow for contengencies [*sic*].

It is my opinion that no contrivance can be found out by which the breaks [*sic*] can be dispensed with. Six wheeled Engines and carriages, are much safer than four, any person riding one hundred yards upon an Engine or coach constructed upon this plan would discover the difference. The rim of all Railway wheels ought to be made the same width and the axle trees for all coaches of a strength approved of by the Engineers, both wheels, springs and axles should bear the government stamp to being made of the best materials, as every practicable means ought to be made use of in order to have them made of the best iron.

All disputes between Railway Companies should be decided by the Board of Trade.

It appears to me that the above suggestions might be carried out with success without interfering injuriously with Railway property. I hope that you will not consider that I am intruding by sending you these observations.

I am Sir,

Yours most ob. Servant

Geo. Stevenson

MT6/1/18   Grand Junction Railway
Return of Prosecutions by the Company
Rec^d 3rd January 1842

Return of Prosecutions instituted by the Grand Junction Railway Company against Persons other than Servants of the Company under the Bye Laws and Regulations or Act of Parliament of the Company, or under the Act III & IV Vict. C97 regulating Railways.

Date of Offence	1841 Dec[r] 20th	Dec[r] 23rd
Description of Offence	Leaving gates open after passing through	Riding in a coach to Wolverhampton having only booked and paid fare to Warrington
Name of Accused	Robt Ridyard	Benj[n] Bardsley
By Laws, Regulations or clause of acts of Parliament under which Prosecution was instituted	1 and 2 Vict clause 17th	1 and 2 Vict clause 8th
Magistrates before which the Case was tried	Wm Stubs, Thos Lyon, H. Gaskell, W. Hall, Esq[rs]	H. Hill Esq[r]
Date of Trial	Dec[r] 27th	Dec[r] 23rd
Result of Trial	Fined 10/- and costs	Fined 30/6 including costs

Mark Huish, Sec.

There then follows in the same file 42 pages detailing the type of accidents which occurred in 1853 with their causes. The first page reads:

From these returns it would appear that the total number of accidents to Trains and Engines which have been reported by Railway Companies as having occurred during the year 1853 is 103. Of these 76 have been more especially brought before the notice of your Lordships by the Reports of the Inspecting Officers, or by the correspondence which has taken place upon them. These accidents may be generally classed as:-

First   Accidents appertaining to the Rolling Stock and Road.
Secondly Accidents appertaining to the management of Railways

Rail 667/485   Stockton and Darlington Railway Company
Accident Reports

1831   10 Feb.
Thomas Johnson, fireman Etherley Engine, killed whilst braking the loaden [sic] waggons down the Incline.

MT29/1   Railway Inspectorate: Inspectors' Reports [indexed]
London and Birmingham Accident of 12 Nov. 1841*

Royal Engineers Office
21 James St.
Buckingham Gate
13th November 1840

To the Lords of the Committee of Privy Council for Trade

The Report of Lieut Colonel Sir Frederick Smith of the R Engineers, on the accident which occurred on the London and Birmingham Railway on the evening of the 12th November.

My Lords,
I have the honor [sic] to acknowledge the receipt of your Lordship's orders of this date,

* This is presumably an error and should be 1840

35

District Railway Company, Earls Court staff, *c.* 1874. The man in the top hat is Thomas Samuel Speck, the first locomotive superintendent and resident engineer. The station was situated on the east side of Earls Court Road. The wooden building was destroyed by fire in 1875.
(NRM, 2624/52)

directing me to enquire into the causes of the accident which occurred on the London and Birmingham Railway yesterday evening, and pursuant to your directions I proceeded to the Terminus at Euston Square and afterwards to the Harrow Station at which places I obtained the information that enabled me to lay before you the following report:

It appeared that two Luggage Trains leave Birmingham daily for London one at 6 a.m. and the other at ½ past 10 am.

The former, which yesterday consisted of 14 carriages, left Birmingham at the usual hour; and proceeded without interruption until it arrived at about a mile and ¾ on the London side of the Harrow Station. Here a waggon, which is represented to have been over loaded at Burton, broke both its axle-trees and was in consequence thrown off the line, dragging with it three other waggons which were immediately behind it.

The waggon with the fractured axles was the seventh from the Engine, and as its coupling chains broke the six preceding waggons were liberated, and after a short delay continued their journey to Camden Town where as well as at the Harrow and Watford Stations notice was given of the accident.

The 11 o'clock passenger train from London to Birmingham had been assisted up to Tring by Engine No. 15 driven by a man of the name of Bradburne and arriving at Harrow Station on its return to Camden Town the driver was directed to proceed to the spot where the axle-trees above alluded to had broken in order to aid the workmen who were collected on the spot in clearing the line for the trains expected up from Birmingham.

The red signal was immediately exhibited at the Harrow Station to inform approaching trains of the danger of proceeding beyond that point and a Policeman was sent to the first crossing to the Northward of Harrow to direct trains or engines destined for London to cross to the down line. In consequence of this arrangement three passenger trains did so cross, and after travelling a few miles on the down line and thus avoiding the obstruction caused by the waggons that were off the rails. They recrossed to their proper line & reached Euston Square at the hours respectively appointed for them.

Between five and six o'clock in the afternoon Engine No. 15 was sent to the Harrow Station from the spot where the up line was obstructed, the driver Bradburne being charged with a message to the Clerk of the Harrow Station, directing him to stop any trains that might arrive there till after the five and six o'clock trains from London should have passed that station.

It appears that Bradburne stopt [*sic*] at the station, quitted his engine and accompanied the Clerk out of the Station House to give direction on some other matter. It also appears that the Fireman went into the office for a few minutes and that the Porter (John May) who was outside and saw a luggage train approaching from Watford at great speed called to the Fireman to put his

Engine in gear and move from the Station. John May states that the Fireman acted according to this advice but observing that the Luggage Train was continuing on its course, notwithstanding the signals that were made to arrest it, jumped off the engine and left it to its fate.

The Luggage Train, which consisted of eighteen waggons, had left Birmingham at ½ past 10 a.m. and was drawn by Engines No. 1 and No. 82, the former being driven by a man of the name of Brown and the latter by Simpson.

John May and the Engine driver Brown state that the red light was exhibited, warning the train to stop, and that in consequence the steam was shut off from Engine No. 1 and the break [*sic*] applied to the tender. Brown states that the driver of No. 82 did not shut off his steam or apply the break. John May on the contrary is of opinion that the driver of No. 82 had shut off his steam. Be this however as it may this train proceeded at a sufficient velocity to overtake Engine No. 15 and a collision ensued in consequence of which the Engine driver of No. 82 and the Fireman of No. 1 was [*sic*] killed on the spot and the Fireman of No. 82 seriously injured.

On enquiring into the characters of the Drivers, Brown and Simpson, I was informed that they were both considered steady men, but that the latter had on a former occasion, shown a similar disregard of signals at the Harrow Station. The porter John May states that when the train passed the Harrow Station last evening it was running at the rate of at least 20 miles an hour and when it is considered that this was upon a descending plane of 1 in 330 and that the gross loads of the waggons and the goods they contained could not have been much less than 110 tons, it will he obvious that the momentum of such a train could not he easily arrested. The end waggon was provided with a break but it is doubtful whether it was used or not on this unfortunate occasion.

If however it had been used it is a great question with me whether it would have prevented this accident, as the breaks attached to the Luggage Waggons are by no means powerful and a single break can merely be considered as a feeble auxiliary to the Engines in retarding the progress of such a train as that of yesterday evening.

I considered it my duty to enquire into the ordinary extent of the Luggage Trains on this line and I found that they varied considerably, but that it was not unusual to see them amount to fifty waggons and that on one occasion a Luggage Train had consisted of upwards of 80 waggons.

Now the evil of allowing Luggage Trains to exceed the gross weight of 80 tons is, that in order to make up for the loss of speed in the ascending planes they are obliged to travel at such a velocity on the descending planes as to acquire a momentum beyond the prompt control of the engine and break. As a general principle I would state that no train whether containing passengers or goods should consist of so many carriages as to require to be drawn by more than one engine, because when two or more are employed it is impossible to regulate them so that they shall employ equal power, and be so manageable as to be equally safe for the passengers. But I am aware that in a line of such traffic as that on the London and Birmingham Railway it would be difficult if not impossible to dispense on all occasions with assistant engines.

Nevertheless it should be considered as the general rule not to extend the trains beyond the power of a single engine. I would suggest that at those seasons of the year or periods when the Luggage traffic is considerable the number of trains should be increased. At present the first Luggage Train leaves Birmingham at 6 o'clock a.m. and arrives at Woolverton at ½ past 9; it waits there till ½ past 11 o'clock to allow two passenger trains to pass it; it then proceeds on to Tring where it remains on a siding to allow another passenger train to pass and finally it arrives at Camden Town at 4 o'clock.

The next Luggage Train leaves Birmingham at ½ past 10 and proceeds in a similar manner stopping at Woolverton and Tring to allow Passenger Trains to pass.

A third Luggage Train from Rugby brings luggage from the Midland Counties and goes into sidings at Woolverton and Tring like the preceding trains.

37

It does not appear that any accident has yet happened from this system but I cannot help regarding it as one not quite free from danger, as I think that in order to avoid all risk from collisions the course of the various trains should be continuous and uninterrupted, like the revolution of an endless chain. I would submit the expediency of the heavy goods trains being worked at night after the departure from the termini of the latest Passenger Trains and that the only Luggage Trains that should travel in the day time should be such as might be so limited as to keep their time between the passenger Trains.

In my report on the Hull and Selby accidents I suggested 'that Buffer Springs should be adopted for every carriage, waggon, truck or horse box used on railways'. Had the tenders and waggons of the Luggage Train in which the loss of life occurred yesterday been provided with Buffer Springs this lamentable accident in all probability would not have happened.

In the same report I suggested the expediency of engine drivers being licensed. I beg to repeat that suggestion and to add that if it should be adopted the Railway Companies should be invited to report for your Lordships' information all important instances of neglect in these servants, in order that when it may appear they may be deprived entirely or for a limited period of their licenses.

If Simpson, the unfortunate sufferer by the accident of yesterday had been suspended for his former misconduct, it would in all likelihood have acted as a salutary warning to himself and to others. I am of opinion that an engine should under no circumstances be left on a line of Railway by its driver; and that a general order should be issued to that effect by the managers of all Railways. In the event of such a regulation being now in existence, in the London and Birmingham Railway which from the great foresight and attention which prevails in that company is extremely probable it would be proper that the driver Bradburne should be discharged.

I would recommend that the maximum speed of the Luggage Trains should be fixed and on no account departed from. This is perhaps the more important as it is well known that in almost all Railway Companies the most inexperienced drivers are those attached to the Luggage Trains, and it is to be borne in mind that this is the third accident which has happened in the space

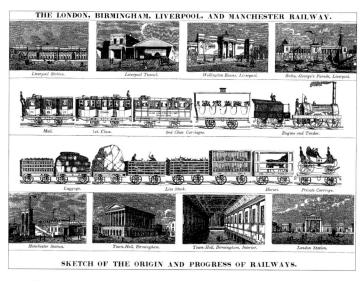

London, Birmingham, Liverpool and Manchester Railway Company, sketch of the origin and progress of railways. (British Museum, Transport f. c 242)

of three weeks to goods trains, viz on the Whitstable Line, The Great Western and lastly the accident of yesterday.

I have to add that I conceive it would be a proper check on the drivers of the Luggage Trains if the Station Clerks were to keep the same record of the time at which these trains pass their respective stations as they do in regard to the passenger trains so that the superintendents of the several lines might have a knowledge of any irregularity at intermediate stations, and take proper steps to prevent their recurrence.

In the event of the adoption of this suggestion I have offered as to running the Luggage Trains at night I would recommend as a necessary check on the sobriety of the engine drivers, firemen and guards, that at certain fixed stations the clerk should hold such communication with them as to enable him to feel satisfied that they are in the state to pursue their journey.

Both the axle-trees of the waggon which caused the accident to the first Luggage Train of yesterday broke close to the shoulder of the left wheels and the waggon took a course to the left of the rails completely confirming the observation I made in my report on the North Midland Railway accident that if the axles had broken before the carriage left the rails they would from the fracture being close to the right wheels have taken a course to the right of the rails, whereas they turned off to the left, in the direction to which the switch improperly left near the rails conducted them.

I found the fractured axle-trees of the Luggage Waggons so covered with mud when I inspected them at Harrow and the weather was so unfavourable for the purpose that I was unable to examine the quality of the Iron but I shall avail myself of an early opportunity of narrowly inspecting it. However this accident adds strength to the recommendation which I had the honor to make to your Lordships in my report of the 16th ulto on the North Midland Railway that the form and dimensions of axle-trees should be the subject of scientific investigation.

I have to observe that owing to the admirable arrangements and the promptness of action of the various officers of the London and Birmingham Company no interruption was given to the numerous passenger trains that were travelling up and down the Line between the time of the overturning of the Luggage Waggons and the final clearing of the rails, nor was injury done to any passenger.

When the Inquest takes place it is possible that additional information as to the causes of this accident may be obtained, but I feel no hesitation in pronounceing [*sic*] that it is attributable to the following causes:–

1st   The overloading of the Burton Waggon and consequent fracture of its axle-trees.

2nd   Either to the bad quality inferior workmanship or want of substance of the Iron of which its axle-trees were made and to their being of a defective form.

3rd   To this Waggon having only four wheels.

4th   To the over extent of the Luggage Train and the consequent necessity of employing two engines.

5th   To excessive driving.

6th   To the neglect of the driver Simpson.

7th   To the absence of the driver Bradburne from his engine.

8th   To the want of Buffer Springs.

> I have the honor to be
> My Lords
> Your Lordships' obedient Servant
> Frederick Smith
> Lieut. Colonel
> R¹ Engineers

Recapitulation of recommendations

To examine into the qualifications and to license the Drivers.

To improve the form and construction of axle-trees.

Engines never to be left on the Railway without their drivers.

All carriages to have six wheels and Buffer Springs.

RAIL 1053/19   Manchester, Sheffield and Lincolnshire Railway Company
Collapse of bridge over Spital Road near Gainsborough, 30 April 1850

SIR,   May 2, 1850.

The Commissioners having directed me to inquire into the circumstances connected with the fall of a cast-iron girder bridge on the Manchester, Sheffield, and Lincolnshire Railway, near Gainsborough, I have the honour now to inform you that I arrived there on Tuesday, the 30th ultimo. I was met by Mr Fowler, the chief engineer, and Mr Potter, the resident engineer; Mr Ibbotson, the engineer, under whose superintendence the bridge was constructed, was absent. I requested he might be in attendance next morning.

The accompanying sketch of the cross section of the bridge shows the disposition of the girders, and the dimensions of the several parts. The span of the bridge, which is a square one, is 35 feet over the Spital-road, close to the town of Gainsborough; the bridge is close to the points leading into the goods-siding, which renders it necessary for all goods-trains to cross the bridge before they can be shunted into the siding. It was under this operation that the bridge failed. The tender of the engine had just cleared the bridge when the failure occurred; both girders of the down-line giving way, the engine went down chimney-end foremost, leaving the trailing-wheels resting against the upper part of the western abutment. I annex a sketch taken shortly after the failure, which will assist to illustrate the state of affairs. The inner girder was broken into five or six pieces, the outer one into two; and as this latter casting appeared to be a sound one, I am led to believe that its rupture must have occurred from the strain at the time of the inner-girder yielding being thrown laterally upon it. From the fracture which the inner-girder presented, it is only astonishing that the bridge, which has now been opened for a year, has stood so long, and did not yield with the first load passing across it. In some of the fragments the bottom flange has separated from the vertical web, the fracture presenting the appearance of the pieces not having been cast at the same moment; in other instances the vertical web has separated from the bottom flange with a large laminated part of the flange adhering; the top flange and middle-web were clean and smooth, but the bottom flange showed many flaws and air-bubbles.

After examining the bridge, I thought it desirable to inquire into the history of the girder from its casting to its leaving the foundry; I therefore requested the attendance of Mr Farmer,

The scene after the accident caused by the collapse of the bridge over Spital Road, Manchester, Sheffield and Lincolnshire Railway, 30 April 1850.

at whose foundry it was cast. He informed me that he kept an ironmonger's shop; that he was unacquainted with a founder's business, and that he intrusted all to his foreman, who had worked formerly in some large foundry. I therefore sent for the foreman, and he informed me that he had been employed in the Phoenix Works at Sheffield; that the castings there were confined to machinery, and that he had never been engaged in a casting of the same magnitude as the girder. I then visited the foundry, which proved to be a very small affair, in very confined premises. It consisted of two cupolas, one capable of containing five tons of metal, the other much smaller. My inquiries terminated here for the evening. The impression on my mind, after the examination of the premises, apparatus, and means, together with the total want of experience and practice on the part of the founder in making girders, that it was next to impossible that sound castings could be turned out of such a place of the magnitude of those in question.

The next morning I was waited upon by Mr Potter, the resident engineer, and Mr Ibbotson, the engineer under Mr Potter, who superintended the construction of the bridge. Mr Ibbotson then made to me the following statement:

> The founder was unused to making such large castings, and made two or three attempts before being able to produce what he considered a proper casting; at last he produced the girder which Mr Ibbotson believes is the one which caused the failure of the bridge. The bottom flange was very imperfect, and he rejected it, pointing out the imperfections to Mr Potter. The girder lay for many weeks at the foundry: the founder then commenced casting for smaller bridges, and having become more expert in the mode of casting, they commenced again on the large girders. These girders, as well as the rejected ones, were all tested with about 16 tons on the centre – some with a dead weight, and others differently; the particulars I have yet to get from Mr Fowler. Mr Ibbotson objected to the mode of testing, the weights having been applied to the top of the girder instead of the flange. There were none of the girders perfect, but the one objected to was pre-eminently defective. Mr Lister says, the castings were rough ones, but he considered them sound. Mr Lister also says, that Mr Ibbotson *did* object to the girder, but that Mr Potter afterwards passed it, and believes that Mr Ibbotson's objection was to the imperfection in the flange. He further states, that there is one up now still more imperfect, and which, he believes, is the one Mr Ibbotson objected to. The condition on which Mr Potter passed it, was its bearing the tests. The deflections were roughly taken, and did not in any case exceed half an inch. Mr Ibbotson says, that when the first engine was about to pass over the bridge he got off, being afraid of its strength.

Mr Fowler promised to call upon me to-day, which he has not yet done. As I have not seen him since hearing Mr Ibbotson's statement, I refrain from passing any comments, and I would have

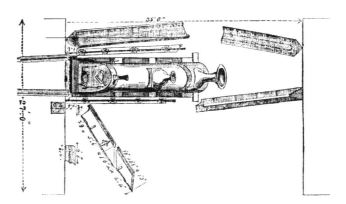

A plan of the accident, 30 April 1850.

41

delayed sending in a report till I had seen him; but as I learn that there are five other bridges on the line, the girders of which have been cast at the Gainsborough Foundry, I think it right to lose no time in drawing the attention of the Commissioners to this circumstance, and to express my decided opinion that, from the evidence of Mr Ibbotson, whose statements were not contradicted with regard to the castings, none of which he said were perfect, and the fact that the founder had neither apparatus, space, nor experience for making castings of the magnitude of those in question, that all these bridges should be immediately replaced by others on which confidence can be placed, or that they should be subjected to such tests and examinations as will leave no doubt of their stability, and that in the mean time they should all be shored up under their centres. I have already directed that three of them, one of 35 feet span and two of 25 feet span, should be supported in this manner; and I think the remaining two should be similarly treated, though one of them is but 12 feet span, and the other is an over-bridge.

As I was the Government officer who inspected and passed this bridge, I beg to state the grounds on which I did so. Taking the moving load at one ton per foot, and the permanent load at half a ton per foot, which is just the weight of the superstructure, including the girders; the breaking weight of the bridge (calculated by Mr Hodgkinson's formula, which gives value to the vertical web) is, as nearly as possible, four times the greatest practical load; and though this is a margin much below what the Iron Commission have stated might be considered safe, our then knowledge of iron structures and practice of engineers would not have justified me in reporting it as of insufficient strength; the upper flange, and the vertical web, as far as it could be seen, presented the appearance of a good casting, and the imperfections in the lower flange I did not detect.

After I have seen Mr Fowler I will again communicate to you on the subject.

I have, &c.

Capt. Simmons, R. E.,   GEO. WYNNE,
&c.   &c.   Capt. Royal Engineers.

Office of Commissioners of Railways,
SIR.   Whitehall, May 7, 1850.

I am directed by the Commissioners of Railways to forward to you the accompanying extracts from a report made to them by Captain Wynne, upon the failure of the Spital-road bridge, near Gainsborough, on the Manchester, Sheffield, and Lincolnshire Railway, and to request that you will call to the attention of the Directors the very serious matters relative to the construction of the bridge therein related, upon which they are desirous of receiving any remarks which the Directors may have to offer.

The Commissioners have also desired me to inform you that, under the circumstances stated by Captain Wynne, they hope that the Directors will see the propriety of adopting precautions for the safety of the public, not only at this bridge which has partially failed, but at the other bridges on the line erected under Mr Potter's superintendence, or the iron-work of which was cast at the Gainsborough Foundry, until such time as those bridges shall have been re-inspected and tested, which they have considered it their duty to desire Captain Wynne to do, and specially to report thereon.

I have, &c.

The Secretary of the   J.L.A. SIMMONS,
Manchester; Sheffield and Lincolnshire Railway Company.   Capt. Royal Engineers.

SIR,   *July* 3, 1850.

I have the honour to acquaint you that, in compliance with the directions of the Commissioners, that I should examine and test the cast-iron bridges of the Manchester, Sheffield, and Lincolnshire Railway, the girders of which were cast at the Gainsborough Foundry, I proceeded to Gainsborough on the 12th June for that purpose, and remained there till the 13th, when being called away on other business without having completed all the bridges, I returned there again on the 21st, and completed what I had left undone on the former occasion.

The girders of five of the under bridges were cast at Gainsborough; two of these were of 35 feet span, two of 25 feet span, and one of 11 feet 6 inches span; the two former have had entirely new girders substituted for the former ones, which were cast at a large foundry in Staffordshire, they have every appearance of sound castings, and their breaking weight is considerably greater than the old ones they have replaced.

The arrangement made for testing the girders of the two bridges of 25 feet span was by suspending weights on their centres. The apparatus for this purpose consisted of a wrought-iron saddle made to rest upon the top flange, and which reached below the bottom flange; to this was suspended, by means of chains, the body of a truck with the wheels taken off, and the weights used were short rails, having the weight marked on each; the saddle had a bearing of 17 inches on the top flange of the girder; the weight suspended averaged about 16 tons on each girder, and the distributed weight of the roadway and of each girder was about 5 tons; the breaking weight of the girder being 47 tons, and the weight suspended averaging 16 tons, would, with the distributed load, make the test something more than owne-third the breaking weight. I applied the weights as nearly as I could by three tons at a time, taking the deflections each time by means of a level and staff, from which I could read off with tolerable accuracy to the ·005 of a foot. The apparatus employed was rough in character, but the necessity of having to keep open for traffic both the railway above and the roadway underneath, precluded the adoption of more refined means.

The result of the tests to the eight girders of the two bridges I have annexed in a tabular form at the end; but it may be briefly stated, that equal additions of weights gave nearly equal deflections, which were for every three tons ·01 of a *foot*, the greatest ultimate deflection of any of the girders was ·66 of an *inch* – another deflected ·54 of an inch, and the others varied from ·36 to ·48 of an inch. On the weights being removed, each girder returned to its former level, showing that its elasticity was in no way impaired.

With the girders of the small under-bridge of 11 feet 6 inches span, I did not consider it necessary to subject each to the same test; but having loaded the roadway with 15 tons of rails, I passed a heavy engine over, and the greatest deflection I obtained was 0·18 of an inch. The calculated breaking weight of these girders is 30 tons on the centre.

The result of the above tests in my opinion establishes the soundness of the castings, as far as it can be done without inflicting permanent injury on the girders.

With regard to the girder that failed over the Spital-road, there seems some difficulty in accounting for its standing a year, and then giving way under a load which must frequently have passed over it. From the total want of adhesion amongst its parts which its fracture exhibited, it appears surprising that it should not have given under the weight of the first engine that passed over it, and the only way in which I can account for its now doing so, is by supposing that, from the unsoundness of the casting, its breaking weight was but a small fraction above the weight of the engine under which it failed, and that in the operation of shunting the engine must from some cause have jumped, and thus the momentum from impact exceeded the breaking weight.

I have, &c.

Capt. Simmons, R. E.,   GEO. WYNNE, *Capt. R.E.*
   &c.   *&c.*

RAIL 1053/55   Cornwall Railway Company
Returns of Accidents to the Board of Trade [1859]

RAILWAY ACCIDENTS
CORNWALL RAILWAY

Railway Department Board of Trade,
Whitehall, June 27, 1859.

SIR,

    I am directed by the Lords of the Committee of Privy Council for Trade to transmit to you the enclosed copy of the report made by Capt. Ross, RE.* the officer appointed by them to inquire into the circumstances which attended the accident that occurred to a passenger train on the 6th of May, near the Grove Lake viaduct on the Cornwall Railway, and to state, that my Lords trust that the remarks of the inspecting officer will receive the careful consideration of the directors.

    I have, &c.

DOUGLAS GALTON,
Captain, RE.

The Secretary of the
    Cornwall Railway Company.

Whitehall, May 31, 1859.

SIR,

    I have the honour to report for the information of the Lords of the Committee of Privy Council for Trade, that in compliance with your instructions, I have inquired into the circumstances attending a fatal accident which occurred on Friday, 6th of May, to an ordinary passenger train travelling on the Cornwall Railway from Plymouth to Truro. The train in question was timed to leave Plymouth at 7.25 p.m. It consisted of a tank engine, second-class carriage, first-class carriage, second-class carriage, and truck. It stopped at Saltash station, and is said to have left that station one minute late, and it was traversing an embankment between Saltash and St Germans, when the engine appears to have mounted the right rail, and to have got off the line. It was then approaching a timber viaduct called the 'Grove Lake viaduct.' It came into collision with the end of the framework forming the right parapet of this viaduct, and clearing away a considerable portion of the parapet, plunged off the viaduct into the creek below, a depth of nearly 30 feet, carrying with it the two leading carriages. A guard in the leading compartment of the second-class carriage was killed, the driver and fireman were suffocated or drowned, and the passengers in the two carriages, upwards, it is believed, of 14 in number, escaped – some unhurt, and some with severe cuts and bruises. The train had just passed along a curve of 63 chains, with a fall of 1 in 83, but it had been running nearly 100 yards over a part of the road that was straight and level when the accident occurred. The roadway had not been travelled over by engines until the opening of the line a few days previous to the accident. The embankment is said to have been standing about six months, and the ballasting to have been completed six weeks before the accident, both having been effected by horse-power.

    The roadway is of the description in use on the Great Western Railway, with longitudinal timbers and transoms. These had been 'lifted,' not more, I am assured, than 1½ inch, on the Tuesday morning preceding the accident. On that day the directors had for the first time passed over the whole line, and ordinary trains with passenger traffic bad been travelling upon it on Wednesday, Thursday, and Friday. Thus, when the accident occurred on Friday evening, the roadway had been worked over perhaps thirty times by an engine. There had been heavy rain on Wednesday and Thursday, but this portion of line had been examined by the inspector of permanent way, with a ganger, on Friday morning, and found to be in good order.

*   Royal Engineers

A notice announcing a
swimming match to be
held at Blackpool, South
Devon.
(TNA, RAIL 57/19)

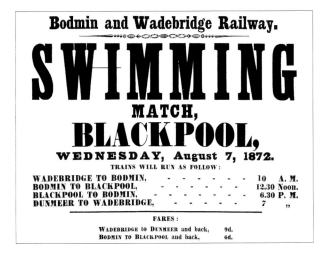

Bodmin and Wadebridge Railway.

SWIMMING

MATCH,

BLACKPOOL,

WEDNESDAY, August 7, 1872.

TRAINS WILL RUN AS FOLLOW :

WADEBRIDGE TO BODMIN,	10 A. M.
BODMIN TO BLACKPOOL,	12.30 Noon.
BLACKPOOL TO BODMIN,	6.30 P. M.
DUNMEER TO WADEBRIDGE,	7 ,,

FARES :

WADEBRIDGE to DUNMEER and back,	9d.
BODMIN TO BLACKPOOL and back,	6d.

The roadway was subjected to a close examination after the accident by the engineers of the line. They state that the roadway was fully ballasted, that the longitudinals *maintained their level*, and that the ballast seemed well packed up to them. They could find nothing whatever to account for the accident. The first mark was that of a left wheel of the engine dropping inside the *left* rail at a distance of 148 feet from the end of the viaduct. Corresponding to this mark there is a joint of the longitudinal timber of the right hand side under the *right* rail. The left longitudinal and rail were undisturbed, but the longitudinal timber in advance of the joint on the right hand side was driven out of gauge, and two lengths of rail upon it were curved outwards, with marks upon them of the right wheels having mounted and crossed them.

There was a transom close to the joint. The strap bolts upon it had not lost the nuts connecting them to the longitudinals, and the right longitudinal was set free by the strap bolt being torn from the transom.

The track of the left wheels of the engine was indicated as usual upon the transoms of the roadway, some of which were broken.

The gauge was *correct* up to the spot where the right longitudinal timber was driven out of gauge, and as the road had been travelled over by the same engine, it seems reasonable to conclude that the fault was not in the gauge.

The engine was a new bogie engine, corresponding nearly in its details to those which have been running for the last eight years on the South Devon Railway, a line which is very similar to the Cornwall Railway in its characteristics of sharp gradients and curves. This engine had travelled several trips upon the South Devon Line, and also on the Cornwall Line, and is said to have been reported by the driver, Biscombe, upon the morning of the accident to '*be doing as well as she possibly could do.*'

The driver, Biscombe, who so unhappily lost his life, was himself a man of considerable experience upon the South Devon Railway, and of steady habits.

The engine was found after the accident, on its back, wheels uppermost. The locomotive superintendent could not discover that any part of the motion machinery was either broken or lost, and the wheels were correct to gauge. The machinery was said not even to have been strained, each part being taken off with perfect ease by the fitters employed to remove the engine.

The distribution of weight is stated to have been –

		Tons	Cwts
On the bogie wheels	–	12	18
" middle "	–	13	12
" trailing "	–	12	10
Tons	–	39	0

The engine had four driving wheels 5' 6" in diameter, four bogie leading wheels 3' 6" in diameter, and cylinder 16½ diameter. The stroke was 24 inches.

The train was timed to arrive at Saltash at 7.42, and at St Germans at 7.56, the distance between them being 5¼ miles. This, allowing five minutes for stopping and getting up speed, would be at the rate of 35 miles an hour.

The surviving guard of the train and the passengers appear to have noticed nothing remarkable in the speed at the time of the accident. The incline down which the train had just come was of no great length, as shown by the annexed section A B of the line travelled over by the train from A, to the scene of the accident B, and, as the train had left Saltash nearly to its time, there seems no reason why the driver should have been travelling at a speed inconsistent with that which had been prescribed for his journey.

It is inferred that the engine was actually travelling at the rate of between 30 and 40 miles an hour, and the probability doubtless is, that such was the speed.

On the whole I see no grounds for imputing blame to the driver, nor is there anything to show that either the engine or the roadway was accountable for the accident.

I am of opinion, however, that the Cornwall Company have acted very wisely since the accident in very considerably reducing the regulated speed between Saltash and St Germans.

There are no less than ten stopping places for ordinary trains between Plymouth and Truro, and the rate by *time table* for performing the journey of 53¾ miles was from 19 to 20 miles an hour; but deducting five minutes for each stopping place, the speed to be maintained between stations by ordinary passenger trains, varied from the rate of 22½ miles an hour to that of 39 miles an hour on different sections of the line. Thus between Saltash and St Germans, as already stated, the average speed would have been 35 miles an hour.

This was no light trial to a new road unused to engines, and worked over by a tank engine of nearly 40 tons weight, especially after heavy rain, and to this combination of circumstances the accident must, I think, be attributed.

Comparing the express speeds with the express speeds in use upon the South Devon line, I find that on an average they are below the latter, but that they approximate very closely to them.

Liverpool Street Station Swimming Club, c. 1913. (TNA, RAIL 227/511)

It would, I think, have been prudent to have made a more considerable deduction from the rate of travelling which had proved safe upon the South Devon Railway, when framing time tables for the untravelled over Cornwall line.

I believe the roadway to be in good order for reasonable speeds, and it is certainly smooth to travel over.

On the subject of the letters addressed to their Lordships by a person signing himself W. Webber and H. Adams, and referred to me by your minute in connexion with this accident, it will have been gathered from my report that the writer was mistaken as to the spot where the accident happened. The scene of it was the Grove Lake viaduct, and not the Notter viaduct, as supposed by him, and the accident originated upon an embankment and not upon a viaduct.

From the inquiries I made it appears that Mr Adams is not known to the officials nor to the contractors of the railway, and I conclude that his employment has been upon the mail road from Plymouth to Truro, and that he has been imperfectly informed upon the details of the viaducts.

The tests to which Colonel Yolland submitted these timber structures by means of heavy weights imposed upon them gave excellent results; I am not aware of any more satisfactory way of ascertaining their present strength, and their stability under the continued passage of heavy trains will doubtless have the close attention of the officers of the Company.

At the eastern extremity of the Notter viaduct, questioned by Mr Adams, a timber platform is employed, as elsewhere upon the line, for maintaining the level of the viaduct at its junction with the embankment, and for compensating any settlement that may take place.

I see no reason to apprehend danger from this cause under the necessarily close vigilance with which the viaducts must be watched.

I have, &c.

GEORGE Ross,

Captain Galton, R.E.
Captain, R.E.
&c.   &c.

RAIL 527/1904   North Eastern Railway Company Staff Files

Injury to an Engineman

Carlton Street
Dairy Coates
Newington
Hull
Oct. 3rd 1881

Dear Sir,

Mr Stroughhair informs me that your reply to my letter to you of August 25 is that you would give me a short coal train down in the North. I did not ask you for a run of no description but for some employment off an engine for some time till I was able to bear my present Employment. I asked this solely on account of my Injury. Now after nearly 30 years service and the service I rendered you in your difficulty it seems as cold an insult as could well be oferd and not wat might of reasonabley been expected from a gentleman whome I had served so well. It clearley proves to me that your kind offer as been prompted by one who would be afeard of me nowing wat he ad said for this reason. I did ask Mr Stroughair some time ago about a short milage run to Gool and I consider it very hard to have to ask for work to be always on at nights especley under circumstances which was from no neglect of my own.

Continued on p. 50

Copy

D4/256. Goods Dept.
West H'pool. Feby. 27.

Sir,
Accident in Goods Yard, 25th inst.

I beg to inform you that about 8/30 p.m.
on the 25th inst whilst Pilot Engine 869
which had been left in charge of Fireman
Sheraton & R. Addison Guard, was shunting
into No. 4 Siding Goods Yard, their waggons
came in contact with other waggons in No.
10 Siding, which had been put in by them
a few minutes previously, causing one wag-
-gon to leave the rails. No damage done.
9-0 p.m. Express goods detained 10 mnts.
After Addison observed the waggons were not
clear, he gave the Fireman a Signal to stop, but
he did not do so, until the wagon was off the
line. Had Driver Royal been on his Engine,
the accident might have been prevented.
I am given to understand by our Foreman
Shunters that it has of late been become a
daily occurrence when the Locos. Foremen
and myself are not in the yard for the
Drivers to leave their Engines and especially
this man when any of the Main line Engines
are in the yard.
Will you please take up before anything
more Serious happens.
Yours truly,
J. Bland Esqr.   J. Roper.

North Eastern Railway Company. An accident to an engineman, 27 February 1882.
(TNA, RAIL 527/1903)

RAIL 1053/59
Return Relative to Railway Accidents

RETURN of the Number and Nature of the ACCIDENTS and the INJURIES to LIFE and LIMB which have been reported to the Board of Trade as having occurred on all the RAILWAYS open for Traffic in *England and Wales, Scotland,* and *Ireland,* respectively, from the 1st of January to the 31st of December 1870.

ENGLAND AND WALES

Date of Accident	NAME OF RAILWAY COMPANY	Passengers Killed or Injured from Causes beyond their own Control.		Passengers Killed or Injured from their own Misconduct or want of Caution.		Servants of Companies or of Contractors Killed or Injured from Causes beyond their own Control.		Servants of Companies or of Contractors Killed or Injured from their own Misconduct or want of Caution.		Persons Killed or Injured whilst crossing at Level Crossings		Trespassers		Miscellaneous		NATURE OF ACCIDENT
		Killed	Injured	Killed	Injured	Killed	Injured	Killed	Injured	Killed	Injured	Killed	Injured	Killed	Injured	
1870:																
6 Apr. –	Brecon and Merthyr	–	–	–	–	–	–	1	–	–	–	–	–	–	–	Shunter run over and killed in Brecon yard through his own want of caution.
23 Sept. –	- ditto - - -	–	–	–	–	–	–	1	–	–	–	–	–	–	–	Breaksman [sic] fell from a waggon near Rhiwdein and was run over and killed.
20 Jan. –	Blyth and Tyne	–	–	–	–	–	–	1	–	–	–	–	–	–	–	Goods guard fell between trucks in motion at Shields Station, and was run over and killed.
19 Sept. –	- ditto - - -	–	–	–	–	–	–	–	–	–	–	–	1	–	–	Trespasser knocked down and injured by an engine near Percy Mains.
19 Sept. –	- ditto - - -	–	–	–	–	–	–	1	–	–	–	–	–	–	–	Labourer in service of company run over and killed near Benton Station, from his own want of caution.
4 June –	Bristol and Exeter	–	–	–	–	1	–	–	–	–	–	–	–	–	–	Servant of contractor killed whilst uniting a coal train. Accident occurred from causes beyond control of deceased.
20 July –	- ditto - - -	–	–	–	–	–	–	–	–	1	–	–	–	–	–	Run over and killed at a public footpath crossing at Nailsea.

etc.

As there appears nothing can be done I ask that you will remit to me that which is due to me from my comencing to Drive at the strike up to Oct. 21st 1871 togather with 5^{pr} cent compound intrest up to the present time, togatber with £1.15.0 deficancy in my wages duering the time I was of duty through Injury and this will assist me for the time I am compeld to work when the strike took place I was the onley goods man at Hull that was capable of taking a main line goods train that stud by you, and my agreement is 7/- per day of 10 hours. It was also promised by the Directors circular and that I as one should be considered one of their oldest servants and entitled to their special consideration and as honourable Gentlemen I have no fear that they will depart their promise.

Instead of receiving 7/- per day I received 6/- per day under protest and did not rise to 7/- till Oct. 21st 1871 there was men that came in at the strike that could not be maid Enginemen of and got 7/- per day. I have always fulfild my duty and why should my wages not of been according to agreement. As to my Injury that is a question for after consideration. Your earley attention to this will no doubt stay further unplesentness.

Yours Obediantly

E^{d} Fletcher Esqr F Smith
Loco Engineer   Engineman
                                        Dairy Coates

RAIL 1053/75   London and South Western Railway Company
Returns of Accidents to the Board of Trade [1886]

Board of Trade, (Railway Department)
1, Whitehall, London, SW.,
29th June 1886.

SIR,

I have the honour to report, for the information of the Board of Trade, in compliance with the instructions contained in the Order of the 22nd instant, the result of my inquiry into the causes of an accident which occurred on the 19th instant, between Wareham and Corfe Castle stations, on the London and South Western Railway.

In this case, as the 1.20 p.m. mixed train from Wareham to Swanage (consisting of engine and tender, running tender first, eight loaded goods waggons, third-class break-carriage [sic] one third-class, two first-class, and one second-class carriages, guard's break-van, and goods break-van) was runnilng on the Swanage branch between Worgret junction and Corfe Castle stations, one of the goods waggons, probably the fourth from the engine, which was loaded with coals, left the rails, and was followed by the 11 vehicles behind it.

The engine, tender, and three leading waggons remained on the rails, and ran forward for about 100 yards before coming to a stand; the fourth waggon was upset into a field on the left side of the line; the fifth was abreast of it on its side at the foot of the low embankment on which the line is carried at this point; the sixth was lying bottom upwards on the slope of the embankment, and nearer to the engine than the fifth; the seventh was bottom upwards in a stream crossed by the line; the eighth, also bottom upwards, was behind the seventh, half in and half out of the stream; and the third-class break-carriage was on its wheels on the slope of the embankment, close to the edge of the stream, and with the leading end knocked out by the corner of the waggon in front of it. These last three vehicles were nearer to the engine than the fourth, fifth, and sixth waggons, and were over the bank on the night side of the line.

The remaining vehicles in the train were all off the rails, but upright and on the line, and the whole of the couplings behind those between the sixth and seventh waggons were unbroken.

Two passengers and the acting guard of the train are returned as being injured.

The whole of the vehicles which left the rails were damaged, the third-class break carriage and six of the waggons being badly smashed.

A full return of the damages to the rolling stock is given in the Appendix.

In the permanent-way 47 sleepers and 50 chairs were broken, and 12 rails were bent.

Description

The Swanage branch, which leaves the main line to Weymouth at Worgret junction, 1 mile 14 chains west of Wareham, is a single line, and was opened for passenger traffic in May 1885.

The permanent-way is of the standard London and South Western pattern, and is composed of 82-lb bull-headed steel rails in 24-ft and 21-ft lengths, 40-lb cast-iron chairs, each fastened to its sleeper by three hollow oak trenails with spikes, rectangular transverse redwood sleepers, 9 ft long and 10" x 5" in section, creosoted, and laid at an average distance apart of 2 ft 8 in, fish-plates 18 inches in length, and weighing 23 lbs per pair, outside compressed keys, and ballast of broken stone and gravel.

The point where the waggon left the rails is 52 chains from Worgret junction, 1 mile 66 chains from Wareham, and 4 miles 23½ chains from Corfe Castle, and at this point the line is straight and on a falling gradient of 1 in 165.

In approaching this spot from the junction, the line is upon a curve to the left for about 35 chains, and is then straight, passing over a double-span bridge over a stream, a six-span viaduct

London and South Western Railway Company telegraph staff at Southampton, 1864. Left to right: C. Farenden, T. Hewlett, T. Hill, W. Watkins, S. Reeve. (NRM, 304/87)

over the River Frome, and then a single-span bridge 34 ft wide over another stream, into which part of the train fell.

The gradient is a falling one of 1 in 80 to the first of these bridges, a distance of 34 chains, and from this point it is a falling one of 1 in 165 for about 286 yards, the line becoming level some 38 yards beyond the point where the first vehicle left the rails, continuing level for 242 yards, and then rising on a gradient of 1 in 165 for a considerable distance.

The waggon which left the rails first, a long goods waggon, No. 5,883, was built in 1877, and was last lifted in December 1884.

It was, after the accident, found to have two axles bent, the dimensions of the axles being $4^{3}/_{8}$" diameter at centre, $5^{1}/_{8}$" at back of boss, and 5" at boss.

The axles were manufactured by the Patent Shaft and Axle-tree Company, Limited.

Evidence

William Banks states: I have been 16 years in the service, and 13 months a passenger driver. I have worked on the Swanage branch since it was opened on the 20th May 1885. On the 19th instant I came on duty at Swanage at 6.30 a.m. I was doing fireman's duty till noon with another driver, and afterwards took engine 'Locke' for work on the branch. The engine is a six-wheeled engine with trailing and driving wheels coupled, and a six-wheeled tender, and is fitted with steam break and vacuum apparatus. I brought the 12 o'clock train from Swanage to Wareham, – a mixed train. I arrived at Wareham at 12.50. I felt nothing at all wrong on the line on that journey. The men were working on it near the Frome bridges. I returned then with the 1.20 p.m. from Wareham, which left at 1.24 p.m. It was also a mixed train with eight waggons, six carriages, and a goods van at rear. I was running tender in front. I took four minutes to run to the junction. I came slowly through the junction with steam off, and applied a little steam through the cutting. On getting near the foot of the bank, when I was running at no more than 15 miles an hour, I felt the engine oscillate, quite enough to cause me alarm. I looked round and saw one or more waggons were off the road. I cannot be sure which waggon was off first, but it was one behind the third from the engine. I applied the steam break and hand break to pull up, and stopped 98 sleepers beyond the bridge. I then had three waggons attached behind the engine and on the rails. I went back and found the train lying in the position shown on the plan produced. Behind the break carriage, which was over the bank, the passenger carriages were all off the rails, but on the line and upright. I examined the line behind the train. For some distance it was broken up, and it was twisted badly back as far as the mile post. This was some distance back from the point where there was the first mark on the sleepers of a wheel flange running off the rails. I examined the waggons which remained attached to the engine, and they were to all appearance in very good order. I did not see any broken draw-bar. When I came up from Swanage with the first train at 7.30 we were brought on over this part of the line with a red flag, and on the return journey with the 8.30 from Wareham with a green flag. With the 10.15 from Swanage the ganger gave us an all-right signal. I think the road gave under the engine, and that caused the oscillation. It was a fine clear day. I did not touch the regulator after running through the cutting. The men were working a little on the Swanage side of the mile post.

Walter Chisham states: I have been about 18 or 19 years in the service, and about 14 years a fireman. On the 19th June I was fireman to Banks. I have heard my driver's evidence, and it is correct.

Harry George Clark states: I have been about five years in the service, and seven months a guard. On the 19th instant I was guard of the 1.20 p.m. down mixed train from Wareham, having brought the 12 o'clock from Swanage. The 1.20 train was made up as follows: engine (running tender first), eight goods waggons, all loaded, third-class break-carriage, one third-class, two first-class, and one second-class carriages, passenger break-van and goods break-van. The waggon next the engine was a Somerset and Dorset waggon. I do not know how it was loaded. Then came two loaded timber waggons, then four loaded coal waggons, then one sheeted waggon with four barrels of cement and some slates. I was in the third-class break-van. There was an assistant guard in the rear break-van. There were 11 passengers in the train, nine in the leading break-carriage, and two in the next carriage. We started four minutes late. We came very slowly through the junction, and at a speed of about 14 or 15 miles an hour down the bank. The first I felt wrong was a slight shock, just sufficient to knock about some crockery which was in the van. Immediately afterwards there was a great crash, and I felt the van run over the bank. I was a good deal shaken, but not otherwise injured. I was thrown through the front of the van, which was broken out. I found the train lying somewhat in the position shown on the plan produced. The couplings between the break-carriage and the waggon in front were not broken, but the front of the break compartment was against the corner of the waggon and the end was knocked out. All the couplings behind the break-carriage remained unbroken, the carriages being off the rails but upright. The leading end of the carriage next behind the break-carriage was driven in, but the others were not much damaged. Only one passenger complained of injury. I examined the line behind the train, and it appeared to me in good order. It was broken up for some distance back, but behind that I could not see much amiss. I had felt nothing at all wrong with the line when running from Swanage with the 12 o'clock train.

Alfred Besant states: I am gauger in charge of a length of 2½ miles of the Swanage branch, commencing at Worgret junction. I walk it every morning, and was over it between six and seven o'clock on the morning of the 19th instant. When the accident occurred, I was working a little on the Swanage side of the mile post, No. 127. I saw the train coming, and it was running down the bank at moderate speed and apparently all right. When it had run a few yards past me I heard a crash, and thinking something was wrong I got out of the way. I did not actually see the first vehicle leave the rails. I was on the right-hand side looking towards Swanage. I was on the Wareham side of the level crossing. The train was, after the accident, in much the position shown on the plan produced. I found a sleeper marked inside the right rail with a wheel flange. The road behind that was crooked for some distance, two or three rail lengths at least, but there were no marks of a wheel flange on the sleepers or chairs. I was working with two gangs during the morning straightening that part of the line. We were working from the level crossing towards the mile post. We had completed and filled in the ballast for six or seven rail lengths behind the first marked sleeper. Behind that, and as far as the mile post or a little farther, the line was opened up. I did not think it was necessary for me to caution the driver. I had done so with the two first trains in the morning, showing a red flag to the first and a green flag to the second, but I thought it was not necessary after that. I had not been lifting the line at all that morning, only straightening, putting it in proper line. The gauge was quite correct. There were no low joints. In ordinary repairs it is left to the discretion of the ganger to say whether cautious running is necessary or not. I think that the accident was caused by a defect in the coal waggon. It was not due to speed.

Samuel Cobb states: I am a permanent-way man in Besant's gang. At the time of the accident I was working near the level crossing, filling in the ballast. We had been straightening the line, not lifting it. I was on the right side of the line. I saw the train coming, but did not notice it much until it was over the first bridge. I then noticed that one of the waggons was knocking about from one side to the other, It was the fourth or fifth from the engine, and it left the rails not far from the level crossing, near where the first sleeper is marked with a wheel flange. I went to the carriages to give assistance, and did not look much at the line, but I saw that it was crooked for some distance behind the first marked sleeper. We had cautioned the two first trains in the morning, as the middles of the sleepers were not then packed. They were all packed when this train came over, except some near the first bridge. We did not think it necessary to caution this train. We did not loosen any fish-plate bolts in order to straighten the line. No fish-plates or bolts were broken. I did not notice how much the line was crooked.

Charles Russell states: I have been nine or 10 years in the service, and seven years a signalman. On the 19th instant I came on duty in Worgret junction box at 9 a.m. for 11 hours. When the 1.20 p.m. train to Swanage passed my box it was not running at more than 10 miles an hour.

C. Hailes states: I am foreman examiner in the carriage department. On the 22nd instant I examined the vehicles which formed the 1.20 p.m. mixed train from Wareham to Swanage on the 19th instant, which ran off the line about 3/4 mile from Worgret junction, and hand in a return of the damage. I thoroughly overhauled all the vehicles, but failed to find any defect in any of them which would cause them to leave the rails.

<u>Conclusion</u>

From the foregoing evidence, the marks on the permanent-way, and the positions in which the vehicles were found after the accident, it is clear that the first vehicle to leave the rails was the fourth goods waggon behind the engine, which was loaded with coals, and was upset over the embankment on the left side of the line.

This waggon left the rails towards the left side, the first mark of any kind being an abrasion on the inside of the right rail, and the next being a mark of a wheel flange on the sleeper inside this rail about 4 ft further on, while the first mark of a wheel flange on the left side was on the next sleeper outside the left rail.

Behind the first mark the line was, according to the evidence of the permanent-way men, as well as that of the driver and fireman, considerably twisted, although there was no trace of any wheel being off the rails, and this twisting of the line extended for a distance of probably some 20 or 30 yards at least.

The driver states that the first thing which he felt wrong was a violent oscillation of the engine, which was running tender in front, and as far as can be judged this oscillation took place just about where the line was found to be twisted. At this point the line had been opened up by the permanent-way men, who had been at work straightening the line back towards the junction from the point where the train ran off the rails, but the evidence is to the effect that the ballast had been filled in at the place where the line was twisted. Behind this, however, it is admitted that the sleepers were opened up, and it is stated that the two first trains in the morning had been brought over this part of the line at caution.

The axles of the first waggon which left the rails were, after the accident, found to be bent, and the evidence of one of the permanent-way men is to the effect that this waggon was swaying about from side to side for some distance before it left the rails.

I believe the accident to have been due to the line, at the place where it was not ballasted up properly, giving way under the engine, causing it to oscillate so much as to twist the line, and that upon the waggon reaching this part of the road it swayed from side to side so much that it left the rails, the axles possibly bending before it did so.

I think that it was an error of judgement on the part of the ganger of permanent-way to have discontinued the cautioning of trains, which he had started in the morning when he first opened up the line, for it is far better to delay the traffic a little than to run the risk of accident.

The rule in the Company's book of regulations states that 'When repairing or lifting the line, or performing any operation so as to make it necessary for a train to proceed cautiously, the foreman or ganger must send a man back at least half a mile * * * * who must exhibit the caution signal.'

This rule leaves the responsibility of deciding when cautious running is necessary upon the ganger, and judging from the rare occurrence of accidents from this cause, the responsibility is judiciously placed, although in this case I think the ganger, who is stated to be a very careful man, made a mistake.

I believe, moreover; that an ordinary passenger train would probably have kept the rails in spite of the slight twisting of the line, for in such a train, properly coupled up and equipped, the oscillation set up would have been far less than in this case, where the front portion of the train was composed of a lot of loosely coupled and unequally laden goods waggons.

In some measure, therefore, I attribute this accident to the pernicious practice of running mixed trains with the good waggons in front of the passenger carriages, which practice leads to far too many accidents.

Mixed trains in any form are to be avoided, and where, owing to small traffic and poverty of a line, it is impossible to avoid running them, the waggons, unless properly constructed for running in passenger trains, should be behind the passenger carriages. On a line occupying the position of the London and South Western Company they should be unknown, and I should think that this narrow escape from a very serious accident ought to lead to their immediate disappearance from this line.

I was informed that the reason of the engine of this train being a tender engine, running tender in front, was that the tank engine regularly worked on this branch was under repair. Under such circumstances another tank engine ought to have been provided.

I have, &c.

The Assistant Secretary,	F.A. MARINDIN,
Railway Department, Board of Trade.	*Major*

————————

APPENDIX

London and South Western Railway.

Carriage Department,

W. PAINTER, ESQ.

Bishopstoke Station,

SIR,

June 28, 1886.

I traced out on Sunday where the waggons damaged in the Wareham accident were last examined, and the following are the particulars as to dates of passing examining stations, and I find four of them were examined at Wimborne and one at Dorset [*sic*].

No. 4,845 long goods waggon passed Wimborne loaded for Hamworthy per 6.30 p.m. goods from Bishopstoke on the 18th instant, and was loaded at that station for Swanage branch and sent on, on the 19th instant.

No. 4,350 long goods waggon passed Wimborne loaded for Wareham on the 14th instant, was loaded at that station and sent on to Hamworthy on the 17th instant, re-loaded on the 19th instant and sent on to the Swanage branch the same day.

No. 4,965 long goods waggon arrived at Wimborne on the 7th instant, left that station on the 9th instant loaded for Hamworthy, stood on hand at the last named station till the 19th instant, when it was loaded and sent on the Swanage branch.

No. 5,883 long goods waggon arrived at Wimborne on the 8th instant, left that station for Hamworthy the same day and remained on hand at the last named station till the 19th instant, when it was loaded and sent on the Swanage branch.

No. 6,630 long goods waggon loaded from Weymouth to Moreton passed Dorset per 12.50 p.m. up train on the 8th instant, when it was loaded and sent on to Hamworthy. It remained on

55

hand at that station till the 19th instant, when it was loaded and sent on to the Swanage branch. I have attached examiner's reports as to condition when they passed their stations.

Yours obediently,

[*Signed*]   C. HAILES

Accident on Swanage Branch Line

Wimborne, June 27th 1886.

No. 4,845 long goods waggon passed here per 6.30 a.m. down goods on the 17th instant in good condition. Train examined by 'S. Puddy.'

No. 4,350 long goods waggon passed here per 6.30 a.m. down goods on the 14th instant in good condition. Train examined by 'S. Phillimore.'

No. 4,965 long goods waggon arrived here per 10.50 a.m. down goods on the 7th instant, and left on the 9th instant in good condition. Train examined by 'W. Nessling' and 'S. Phillimore.'

No. 5,883 long goods waggon arrived per Somerset and Dorset goods due at 1.9 p.m., Blandford to Hamworthy, and left per down goods due at 2.12 p.m. the same day in good condition. Train examined by 'S. Phillimore.'

[*Signed*]   W. NESSLING

Accident on Swanage Branch

Dorset, June 25th 1886.

No. 6,630 long goods waggon – The above waggon passed this station on the 4th instant, with the 12.50 p.m. goods train, loaded from Weymouth to Moreton, and was examined by myself and found to be in good condition.

[*Signed*]   J. WILLIAMS

RETURN OF DAMAGES TO ROLLING STOCK

No. 338, first-class. – Wheels correct to gauge, one spring broken.

No. 373, first-class. – Wheels correct to gauge, foot-board damaged.

No. 119, second-class. – Wheels correct to gauge, one side spring broken, quarter and end panel damaged.

No. 319, third-class. – One axle bent about 1½ inches, buffer-casting, door, quarter, end panel, foot-boards, step-irons, and break-work broken, and one draw-bar bent.

No. 260, passenger guard's van. – Wheels correct to gauge, two axle-guards bent, headstock and foot-boards damaged.

No. 115, goods van. – Wheels correct to gauge, side door displaced.

These vehicles were put on the road and taken to Wareham:

No. 243, third-class break. – Wheels correct to gauge, both ends, two quarters, one door, and end of roof destroyed, two buffer-rods, both headstocks, break-work, foot-boards, body and soles broken, both draw-bars bent and three side springs crippled.

No. 4,845, long goods. – Wheels correct to gauge, two sole-bars, headstock, end, quarters, two axle-boxes, one draw-bar, and one axle-guard broken, and three axle-guards bent. Built 1871, last lifted 1/4/85.

No. 4,350, long goods. – Wheels correct to gauge, both sole-bars, headstock, quarters, end, and three axle-boxes broken, and four axle-guards bent. Built 1866, last lifted 20/5/85.

No. 6,630, long goods. – Wheels correct to gauge, headstock, three end boards, two end pillars, and two axle-boxes broken, four axle-guards and break-guard bent. Built 1880, last lifted 11/3/85.

No. 4,965, long goods. – Wheels correct to gauge, both sole-bars, buffers, draw-bars, two quarters, side flap, and two axle-boxes broken, and one axle-guard bent. Built 1873, last lifted, one end 3/86.

No. 5,883, long goods. – Both axles bent, two axle-boxes, one headstock, and both draw-bars broken, and two axle-guards bent, and two quarters damaged. Built 1877, last lifted, 24/12/84.

Printed copies of the above report were sent to the Company on the 31st July.

RAIL 521/15   London and North Western, Midland and North London Railway Joint Committee
Minutes of Meeting

13 Dec. 1893
Reported the following accidents as returned to the Board of Trade:
1.   6 Nov. Miss Champion, finger pinched in carriage door Kew Bridge Claim settled for £19/9/0 including legal and medical fees. Approved
2.   9 Oct. N.L. Guard Dennis, ankle sprained. Acton
3.   13 Oct. N.L. Under Guard Pratt, leg injured. South Acton
4.   13 Oct. Wallace (child) severely injured. Fell out of train. South Acton
5.   1 Dec. R. Salter, hands and face hurt. Fell whilst crossing the line. Woodstock Road level crossing
6.   3 Dec. Porter S. Martindale, shoulder blade broken, fell over bridge. South Acton

Robert Benson, a director of the London and North Western Railway Company and Chairman of the Railway Clearing House, 1873 to 1875. (TNA, RAIL 1085/79)

RAIL 1057/2248   Vale of Glamorgan Railway Company
Accidents to Staff

Dear Sir,   9/2/00
C. Gould

I visited and carefully examined the above named and find that the three outer fingers of his right hand have been completely removed, the remaining index finger very much injured, whilst the back of his hand to the wrist was severely lacerated. He will not be able to attempt any kind of work for 6 or 8 weeks and of course he will never be able to do other than light selected work with the injured hand.

George Neale
surgeon
James Bell esq.

Dear Sirs,   14 April 00
Charles Gould

I am in receipt of your letter of 12th instant inclosing copy of Mr T.J. Hughes' letter to you, and of the notice he enclosed. The following are the facts of the case: Gould was a servant of the company, a quarry labourer. On 9 February he was loading stones into a skip at Ewenny Quarry when one rolled against his right hand and crushed it severely; three fingers have since been amputated.

The accident is reported to have been due to his own want of care.

Yours faithfully,
W. Mein

To Messrs Downing and Handcock [solicitors]
Cardiff

RAIL 23/53   Barry Railway Company
Accident Register

G.260538   On Oct. 26, 1910, a lady named Miss Dorothy Clark alighted from the 8:30 p.m. train ex Cardiff at Dinas Powis Station and went down into the subway. She was found there shortly afterwards by some passengers, lying on her back, having fallen down. When questioned by the Stationmaster she stated she felt dizzy whilst in the train and must have fainted.

RAIL 236/728   Great Northern Railway Company
Staff Sickness Register

	from	to	Resumed
Mr East	16 Apr.	20 Apr.	22 Apr. 1911

A certificate states that Mr J. East of 64 High Street [town not given] was suffering from debility.

RAIL 583/61 Rhymney Railway Company
Register of Accidents

No.	Name	Occupation	Date of Accident	Date when resumed duty	Nature of Accident	Rate per Week	Weeks Paid	Half Pay	Amount Paid £	s	d	Correspondence Ref No.	Remarks
45	John Davies	Turner	Feby 3 1903	Feby 10 1903	Left hand bruised							10808	no compensation
46	Joseph Browning	Labourer	Feby 13 1903	Feby 23 1903	Two small toes of right foot bruised							10808	no compensation
47	John Smith	Driver	Feby 16 1903	April 13 1903	Injury to ribs	42/-	$5\frac{4}{6}$	Maximum 20/-	5	13	4	10812	
48	Frederick Williams	Driver	Feby 21 1903	June 29 1903	Right leg broken above the ankle	45/-	16	Maximum 20/-	16	0	0	10812	
49	Thomas Parry	Shunter	May 9 1903	May 18 1903	Thumb and second finger of left hand injured							10812	no compensation
50	John Bowen	B. Smith*	May 12 1903	May 25 1903	Left leg bruised above knee							10808	no compensation
51	George Gurney	S. Fireman†	May 18 1903	June 6 1903	Severe bruise to large toe on right foot	15/-	1	7/6		7	6	10812	
52	Aaron J. Moses	Boy	May 19 1903	May 25 1903	Severe cut on back of left hand near the first finger							10808	no compensation
53	John Jones	Cleaner	May 21 1903	May 27 1903	Thigh slightly scalded							10812	no compensation
54	James Allen	Sheet Repairer	May 26 1903	June 4 1903	Severe cut on crown of the head							10808	no compensation
55	William Eades	PS Labourer‡	May 28 1903	June 29 1903	Shock to system and back bruised	21/-	$2\frac{1}{2}$	10/6	1	6	3	10808	
50§	Ernest Searles	Machinist	July 4 1903	July 13 1903	Right arm slightly bruised							10808	no compensation
51	Frederick Cawsey	Mason	Aug 5 1903	Sept 7 1903	Blood poisoning of arm	35/-	$2\frac{1}{3}$	17/6	2	0	10	10808	
52	George Harris	Fireman	Aug 27 1903	Sept 1 1903	Part of nail of third finger torn off, lump of coal fell on it							10812	no compensation
53	John Llewellyn	Carpenter	Sept 22 1903	Oct 19 1903	Crushed fingers on left hand	34/6	$1\frac{7}{18}$	17/3	1	10	8	10808	
54	Arthur Henley	Cleaner	Nov 12 1903	Jany 11 1904	Bone in front of right leg broken about 6" above instep	10/-	$6\frac{1}{3}$	5/-	1	11	8	10812	
etc.													

* Blacksmith or boiler smith
† The meaning of the S is unclear
‡ possibly painter's labourer
§ The error in the numbering is as in the original

Note: This volume also includes Superannuation Allowance.

RAIL 684/116   Taff Vale Railway Company
Register of Accidents to Company's Servants

Ref. to Papers	Date of Accident	Place	Name	Grade & Where Employed	Nature of Injury and Cause	Ordy Rate of Wages per Week	Date certified by Co's Medical Officer fit to work	Date Resumed	No. of days away or on Acct Fund	No. of days away after 1st fortnight	Earnings Gross Annual £ s d	Average weekly s d	50% Average weekly s d	Compensation Paid £ s d
A100680	1904 Apr. 27	Aberdare Goods Yard	Thos E{d} Brimmell	Guard Cathays	Inj{d} finger (slight). Placing scotch under wheel of coach and his finger was caught between scotch and rail.	31/-	Worked on							
A100709	Apr. 28	Cathays Yard between No. 1 & 2 Carr. Rds.	Albert Horton	Brakesman Cathays	Inj{d} legs (slight). Stepping off coaches of C42 train after turning on gas he fell over a buffer shell lying between the roads.	21/-	Worked on							
A100721	Apr. 28	Ystrad lower end Goods Yard	Evan Davies	Guard Treherbert	Sprained leg. Riding on step of R & SB*. Horsebox No. 2 when handle which he was holding turned causing him to slip and fall.	31/-	Not seen	May 9	8					
A100771	Apr. 28	Roath Dock Storage	Samuel Saint	P. Guard Roath Branch	Inj{d} knees, shin & leg (slight). Getting off step of Eng. 91 his foot slipped causing him to fall on his knees.	29/-	Worked on							
A100834	May 4	High Level East Dock No. 4 Tip	Wm Jno. Loosemore	Brakesman Cathays	Inj{d} shoulder & knee. Getting off end wagon of train of 50 his foot caught in brake lever causing him to fall to ground.	23/-	June 20	June 13	33	21	53 0 8	20 5	10 2½	1 15 9
A100881	May 4	Y. Standard Colliery Siding	Wm G. Gilbert	Brakesman Ferndale	Inj{d} lip. Releasing brake on Standard wagon 535 with coupling stick lever sprang up suddenly & forced stick against his face.	22/-	Not seen	May 9	3½					
A100912	May 6	Station Terrace Maerdy	Edgar Edmund Phillips	Carr. Cleaner Maerdy Stn	Sprain. Wheeling barrow load of parcels up a hill his nose began to bleed, he having sprained himself.	18/-	Not seen	May 11	3					
A100935	May 9	Penarth Jc.	Robert Jervis	Guard Cathays	Inj{d} back. Holding pin-tumbler points & turning to signal his Driver he was struck in the back by step of Eng. 177 which was passing on adjoining road.	31/-	June 22 " 27	June 27	41	29	86 15 5	33 4	16 8	4 0 7
A101041 failed 2nd time 3rd time	May 11 July 6 July 28	Bwllfa Lower	John Cornish	Brakesman Aberdare	Inj{d} abdomen. Gravitating wagons & applying brake of Bwllfa Dare wgn. 483 by means of brake-stick, stick slipped & lever sprang up & caught him in the abdomen.	22/-	June 18	June 20 July 11† Sept 12‡	33 4	21 4	57 3 3	22 -	11 -	1 18 6 7 4
														2 5 10

* Rhondda and Swansea Bay Railway
† July 11, as groundman, Cwmbach Jc.
‡ Sept. 12, as signalman, Bwllfa No. 1

Ref. to Papers	Date of Accident	Place	Name	Grade & Where Employed	Nature of Injury and Cause	Ordy Rate of Wages per Week	Date certified by Co's Medical Officer fit to work	Date Resumed	No. of days away or on Acct Fund	No. of days away after 1st fortnight	Gross Annual Earnings (£ s d)	Average weekly (s d)	50% Average weekly (s d)	Compensation Paid (£ s d)
A101036	Apr. 13	Roath Line Jc. Down Sidings North end	Henry Jas. Atkins	Groundman Roath Line Jc.	Inj^d big toe (slight). Releasing points after train has passed into Siding & ball of lever fell on his foot.	22/-	Worked on							
A101244	Apr. 18	Penarth Jc.	Jas. Hy. Quick	Groundman & Brakesman Penarth Jc.	Died at Halse, Somerset May 10/05. Inj^d foot. Attending C15 & 17 trains, tumbler lever turned over on his foot.	23/-	Not seen	May 18	9½					
A101336	1904 May 20	N^r Llwyncelyn	Jonathan Thomas	Guard Coke Ovens	Inj^d head. While in charge of X14 train & sitting down in his van some thing struck off his cap & grazed the top of his head. Fireman G.R. Mason riding in van.	31/-	1904 Not seen	1904 June 13	19	7	*			
A101316	May 21	Pwllyrhebog Junction	E^d Richards	Guard Cathays	Inj^d back. Letting part of train (C42) down to join front portion & getting out brake of G.W.R. truck from rack he strained his back.	30/-	July 12 } July 30 }	Aug. 1	60	48	72 9 2	27 10	13 11	5 11 4
A101591	May 27	Roath Goods Yard	Geo. Taylor	Groundman Roath Dk. Storage	Inj^d (slight). Coming out from under buffers after coupling up & rising to upright position he struck small part of back against buffer.	22/-	Worked on							
A101632	June 1	Treorchy Warehouse	Fred. Coombes	Guard Treherbert	Inj^d hip & back. Assisting in loading G.W. truck 61836 & while stepping off the load he slipped & fell across the buffer.	29/-	June 20	June 20	15	3	78 12 3	30 3	15 1½	7 7
A101853	June 8	Woodfield Colliery Siding	Albert Cooksley	Guard Coke Ovens	Inj^d leg (slight). Turning pair of points weight or ball fell over on his leg.	28/-	Worked on							
A101854	June 8	East Branch No. 6 Tip	Ernest Wm Giddings	Tipper East Branch	Inj^d fingers (2). R.H. Gravitating Rhymney Co's wagon 27 to weighing machine lever sprang up and caught his hand.	24/-	Worked on July 31	Aug. 2	45	33	71 15 10	27 7	13 9½	3 15 10
A101949	June 11	Ely Mills Up Starter Down Line	Alfred Robinson	Yardman Ely Mills	Inj^d Knee (slight). While Down the line opposite the Mills he fell over a signal wire.	23/-	Worked on							
A102016	June 12 (Sunday)	Cardiff Goods Yard	Andrew John Keegan	Porter Cardiff	Strain of stomach. Lifting sheets on to a truck of theatrical scenery he felt a pain across his stomach.	21/-	Not seen	June 27	11½					
A102092	June 15	Aberdare Goods Yard	Edward Walters	Porter Aberdare	Inj^d shoulder & hand. Stooping down to place stone under wheel of L.N.W. tk the brake of which was on other side he slipped & somehow caught between buffers.	18/-	Not seen	June 26 (Sunday)	9					

etc.

* Not treated as an accident

RAIL 23/53   Barry Railway Company
Register of Accidents

On Saturday February 21st 1914, the 2.30 p.m. train ex Barry arrived at Barry Dock Station with door of one of the compartments open in the front part of the train. The Station Master at the latter Station and one of the Porters searched the line and discovered a lad lying unconscious in the four-foot way of the down passenger line with his left leg cut off below the knee. A Doctor and the County and Dock Police were summoned, and the lad was conveyed to the Accident Hospital where he afterwards died. This youth was identified as William Harris residing at 77 Princess Street, Barry.

The Driver of the 1.37 p.m. train ex Porth confirms the statement that the door was open when he passed the up train, and he added that he observed an object on the down line in front of him. After passing the spot he considered the matter and then reported the occurance on reaching Barry Station. The fastenings of this train appeared to be in perfect order and on leaving Barry Station the doors of all the compartments were properly closed.

An inquest was held before the Coroner Mr David Rees at Barry Police Court on Monday February 23rd. After hearing the evidence the Jury returned a verdict of 'Accidental Death' and no blame was attached to the Company in connection with the mishap.

RAIL 414/636   London, Brighton, and South Coast Railway Company
Staff Absences

Dates Absent		Working Days Absent	Name	Rank	Station	Cause
From	To					
1919						
Oct. 29	Nov.10	10	C. Peircy	Clerk	B'ton	Ill
20	Nov. 3	2 wks	Miss A. Bickerstaff	Clerk	"	"
27	30	3	E. Goodman	"	"	"
27	Dec.15	7 wks	H. Ridge	Timekeeper	Coulsdon	Haematemesis
"	Nov. 3	1 wk	W. Cook	Foreman	New Cross	Influenza cold
31	5	4	C.F. Dyer	Jr. Clerk	"	Injured thigh
Nov. 3	12	8	G. Want	"	Brighton	Inflamed foot
5	7	2	J.M. Cloak	Inspector	"	Quinsey [sic]
6	7	1	C.R. Ming	Jr. Clerk	New X	Illness
11	21	9	W.J. Bennett	Foreman	B'ton	Cold
11	24	2 wks	Miss Bennett	Clerk	"	"
11	14	3	S. Smith	Jr. Clerk	"	"
10	17	1 wk	Miss Chamberlain	Clerk	"	Neuristhenia [sic]
17	19	2	H. Barnden	"	"	Chill
Dec. 1	2	1	W.H. Payne	"	"	"
8	Jan. 19	5 wks	H.L. Chalcroft	Acting Inspector	"	Ill
11			J. Ellis	Foreman	"	"
9	10	1	G. Grace	"	"	"
16			F.P. Maitland	Inspector	"	"
31	Dec.31	½ day	N. Ridge	Timekeeper	Coulsdon	"
28	30	2	W. Cook	Foreman	New X	"
30	Jan. 27	4 wks	F. Reeves	Clerk	T. Wells	Injured elbow (football)

Dates Absent		Working Days Absent	Name	Rank	Station	Cause
From	To					
1920						
Jan. 12			G. Want	Clerk	B'ton	Mental overstrain
Jan. 13			H. Ridge	"	Coulsdon	Died 12/4/1920
7	11	4	W. Powell	Foreman	W. Croydon	Sciatica
22	Mar. 1	5 wks	C. Webb	Clerk	B'ton	Nervous breakdown
23	24	1	H. Chapman	Clerk	"	Ill
26	28	2	C.L. Ming	"	New X	"
28	29	1	A. Cobby		B'ton	"
27	28	1½	H. Chapman		"	"
30	Feb. 2	2	Miss Baker	"	"	Neuralgia
31	2	1	E. Bendclar	Foreman		Ill
Feb. 2	3	½	A. Worlley	Lad	"	Cold
13	Mar. 5	3 wks	W. Jenman	Foreman	"	Nervous breakdown
10	11	1	W. Cooper	Inspector	Battersea	Ill
16	19	3	W. Dalladay	Asst. Timekeeper	New X	Influenza
etc.						

London, Brighton and South Coast Railway Company, Bognor station staff, May 1912.
(NRM, 403/63)

RAIL 65/35   Brecon and Merthyr Tydfil Junction Railway Company
Register of Accidents of Company's Servants

1919

ref 901	
Date and Time	12 Nov. 9.50 a.m.
Name of Injured	J. Lloyd
Age	42
Occupation	Examiner
Place where accident occurred	Newport
Resumed	8 Dec. 1919
Weekly Compensation	20/-
Total Compensation	4/7/6
Nature of Injury	Two ribs fractured
	Left eye and left knee bruised

RAIL 23/53   Barry Railway Company
Register of Accidents

As the 6.20 p.m. passenger train from Barry to Bridgend was travelling between Gileston and Llantwit Major on the 22nd August 1919 the engine collided with a farmer's dray loaded with wheat which was crossing the line at the Level Crossing between the 7½ and 7¾ mile posts.

The Driver stated that he had a clear sight of the crossing as he was approaching and did not notice anything until he was about a train's length away when he saw the first horse's head and although he blew his whistle and applied the brakes he was unable to prevent the engine colliding with the rear end of the dray, badly damaging it and upsetting the load.

From the enquiries made it would appear that the Driver of the dray crossed the line to open the gates at the other side of the line and left his horses to come along by themselves without ascertaining whether any train was approaching.

After a delay of about 10 minutes the train proceeded on its journey.

Stanley Robinson residing at 17 Laura Street, Cadoxton, arrived at Cadoxton by train from Barry Dock at 9.45 p.m. on the 1st September 1919 and whilst running down the stone steps from No. 3 Platform he fell, sustaining a slight concussion and bruised left leg.

After being detained at Cadoxton about 20 minutes he was able to walk home.

The steps were in good condition and were well lighted.

A. Chappell, a labourer in the employment of Mr R.M. Dilwyn, Castle-upon-Alum, St Brides Major, was unloading concrete slabs from a railway wagon at Southerndown Road Station Goods Yard on the 19th September 1919 when a concrete slab fell on the fingers of his right hand practically severing one finger end.

It appears that on the arrival of the Down Vale Goods in charge of Guard G. Chick, Chappell was advised that the wagon was about to be shunted but he remained in it holding a slab and when the engine was drawing away the jerk caused the slab to fall and his fingers were caught between it and the other slabs in the vehicle.

He was conveyed by his employer to the Bridgend Hospital.

Festiniog Railway Company. The station master, Mrs Bessie Jones at Tan-y-Bwlch, c. 1930. (TNA, RAIL 1057/2846/10)

RAIL 343/901   Lancashire and Yorkshire Railway Company Accident Report

The following is part of a long report on a fatal accident at Victoria station, Manchester, on 26 February 1919. This accident caused so much concern that many photographs of the area were taken. The railway company was obliged to fit a warning horn to the overhead traveller. The photograph overleaf shows a young woman posing on top of a carriage in the position at which Alice Golding was struck by the overhead traveller.

RAILWAY DEPARTMENT
Board of Trade
47 Victoria Street
Westminster
S.W.1.
26th March, 1919

Sir,

  I have the honour to report for the information of the Board of Trade in accordance with the order of the 15th March, the result of my inquiry into the circumstances attending the fatal

Accident at Victoria station, Manchester, 1919. A young woman poses on the top of a coach showing the position at which Alice Golding was struck by the overhead traveller. (TNA, RAIL 343/901)

accident which occurred on the 26th February, to Alice Golding, at Victoria Station, Manchester on the Lancashire and Yorkshire Railway.

At 7.0 p.m. Golding who was employed as a Glober, was on the roof of one of the coaches of a train standing at No. 14 Platform, for the purpose of lighting the lamps, when she was struck by the basket of the overhead motor traveller; and was thrown into the adjoining six-foot way, with fatal results.

Victoria Station is provided with overhead electric travellers to which basket containers are slung, and into which parcels and other goods are placed to be transported to the various platforms and other points. The rails on which the travellers run are suspended from the roof and encircle a considerable area of the Station. During the day-time only one traveller is in operation, and its working is confined more or less to the eastern section of the Station. At 7.0 p.m. the second traveller is brought into use to work over the western portion of the circular route backwards and forwards. The operator sits in a saddle facing the motor. To look ahead in the outward direction he has to slew himself round in the saddle, while on the return journey he has to lean over to one side or the other of the motor and gear, with the possibility of coming in contact with the live wire at the side. Weight is of importance as the machines are necessarily of light construction, and boys, after being trained, are usually employed as operators. The traveller rails are carried over the different lines in the Station, and with the baskets raised to clear the loading gauge there may be a clearance of from 1' 10" to 2' 10" between the bottom of the basket and the roofs of coaches, according to the varying height of the stock. The motors which have a speed of 400 feet a minute, can be stopped by the brakes provided in 12½ feet. Globers when on the top of carriages for lighting up purposes, are liable to be struck by the traveller baskets where the overhead rails pass

Lancashire and Yorkshire Railway Company, Tabulating Room, *c*. 1917. (TNA, RAIL 343/725)

over platform roads nos 13, 14, 15 and 16 East and West end, and platform roads nos 2 to 10 East end Suburban Section. The travellers are not fitted with any warning arrangement, and although the staff have been verbally cautioned to keep a look out for them there were no instructions on the subject. In this case the traveller was being worked backwards by motor-driver William Abbott, a youth of 17 years of age.

He was necessarily facing the motor and consequently could only keep an indifferent look out ahead as his back was towards the direction of travel. Abbott informs me that he was only about 6 feet from the woman when he first saw her, and although he switched off the current and applied the brake, he was unable to stop in time to avoid the accident. Abbott was aware that lighting up work is regularly performed on 13, 14, 15, and 16 platform roads, and it is to be regretted that he failed to look round in sufficient time before approaching those roads to be able to stop the traveller short of anyone who might be engaged upon the roofs of stock standing thereon. He has been employed as a motor-driver for twelve months. The electric travellers were installed in 1905, and some 2,000,000 journeys have been made by them up to date. Only two personal accidents including the one under notice, have occurred during the whole of the period. To enable the operator to keep a constant look out ahead, and thereby lessen the risk of a similar accident taking place, the saddle should if possible be lowered, and the gear so arranged that he will always face in the direction of travel. It would be well also to provide horns having a distinctive sound, and brought into action automatically at the danger points where employees engaged upon the roofs of carriages are liable to be struck by the baskets. The Company should consider the advisability of improving matters in the directions indicated. Golding had been on duty six hours and a half when the accident occurred.

Carriage & Wagon Department
Newton Heath
19 March 1919

NOTICE

The special attention of all employees, whose duties require them to work on the roofs of carriages, standing in Victoria Station, Manchester, is called to the verbal warning given them when entering the Company's employ, to exercise special vigilance when working near the overhead parcel carrier track, so as to avoid being struck by the basket. In spite of this warning a serious accident has recently occurred.

Employees are warned that they must not allow anything to interfere with their personal safety but must keep a sharp look out for the carrier when working under the track.

If the carrier should come upon them suddenly injury can be avoided by immediately lying down flat on the roof of the carriage.

RAIL 1053/110 London and North Eastern Railway Company
Returns of Accidents to the Board of Trade [1924]

REPORTS BY THE ASSISTANT INSPECTING OFFICERS OF RAILWAYS ON ACCIDENTS TO RAILWAY SERVANTS AND OTHER PERSONS ON RAILWAY PREMISES.

SIR,

I have the honour to report, for the information of the Minister of Transport, in accordance with the Order of the 30th July, the result of my Inquiry into the circumstances attending the fatal accident, which occurred on the 10th July, to E. Warren, between Hythe and Wivenhoe, on the London and North Eastern Railway.

Warren, who was employed as a sub-ganger, was engaged with ganger John Frostic renewing keys on the down line between Hythe and Wivenhoe. On the morning in question there was a fog, the density of which varied considerably from time to time. The men, however, appear to have continued their work regardless of this feature, with the result that at about 7.25 a.m., when the fog was very dense, a train approached unobserved on the line on which they were working. Warren, who was in the four-foot way, was knocked down and killed instantly, while the ganger, who happened to be in a more favourable position, escaped injury. The responsibility for the accident rests with ganger Frostic, who allowed the work to continue, although Rule 273 (f) directs that men must desist from work of this sort during fog, and the Company should take suitable notice of this disregard of their rule.

Warren had been on duty less than half an hour when the accident took place.

I have, etc.,

J.L.M. MOORE.

SIR,

I have the honour to report for the information of the Minister of Transport, in accordance with the Order of the 8th August, the result of my Inquiry into the circumstances attending the accident, which occurred on the 17th July, to F. Donovan, at Bridgehouses, Sheffield, on the London and North Eastern Railway.

Donovan, who was employed as a caller-off, was assisting a foreman to transfer a large case from a road vehicle to an open goods wagon by means of a 2-ton hydraulic crane.

This wagon happened to be standing between two covered wagons, and as the jib of the crane was slewed round, the case caught against the corner of one of these wagons. Donovan immediately stepped forward to release it, but in doing so he thoughtlessly placed himself in such a position that when the case swung clear it forced him against the corner of the adjoining wagon, and he sustained injury to his ribs.

The accident appears to have been due to over-anxiety on the part of Donovan to expedite the work, which caused him temporarily to forget to take thought for his own safety.

At the time of the occurrence Donovan had been on duty 5 hours.

I have, etc.,

J.L.M. MOORE.

RAIL 1053/110   Great Western Railway Company
Returns of Accidents to the Board of Trade [1924]

REPORTS BY THE SUB-INSPECTING OFFICERS OF RAILWAYS ON ACCIDENTS TO RAILWAY SERVANTS AND OTHER PERSONS ON RAILWAY PREMISES.

GREAT WESTERN RAILWAY

Date, time and place of Accident – 2nd July, 1924, 5.10 p.m., Stormstown Sidings, Abercynon. *Name, grade and age of Person* – Richard Harris, goods guard, 56. *Booked working hours and time on duty* – 8; 3 ¾ hours. *Nature of Injury* – Fatal.

Shunting operations were being conducted by Harris and goods guard T.A. Godfrey. Sixteen wagons were being propelled by an engine off No. 3 Carn Parc towards No. 2 Merthyr siding. As the wagons were approaching the points for the cross-over road from Merthyr road to the back road, Godfrey, who was working the ground frame, gave a hand signal to the engineman to stop. Harris was then about to detach the seven leading wagons, and to do so he had to step on a wooden covering of the point rodding. In doing so, however, he slipped and fell towards the moving wagons. His clothing became entangled, and he was dragged towards the four-foot way, falling with his head on the rail, and a wheel of the ninth wagon from the engine passed over the crown of his head as the wagons ran out after they had buffered up to the engine as a result of the application of the engine brake.

Harris lost his balance owing to a portion of the wooden covering of the point rodding eleven inches in width nearest the rail being missing. The accident was due to this defective wooden covering.

I was informed that it is the intention of the Company to remove this ground frame, and to work these sidings by the means of hand point levers.

In the meantime, attention should be given to the making good of the defective wooden coverings, and to the ramping of the present trunking, some of which projects from two to three inches above the ground level. The defect which caused this accident had been made good at the time of my inquiry.

WM. WORTHY COOKE.

Date, time and place of Accident – 9th July, 1924, 8.30 p.m., Barry Docks. *Name, grade and age of Person* – Arthur Benjamin Hinder, coal trimmer, 65. *Booked working hours and time on duty* – 8; 6 ½ hours. *Nature of Injury* – Fatal.

Hinder had come ashore from the S.S. *Ithaki* which was coaling at No. 34 tip. He was proceeding to a coal trimmers' tool box which is situated close to the capstan house at No. 33 tip. In order to reach this box it was necessary for him to cross the running rails leading to No. 5 movable tip, which was working at the time. While crossing the empty wagon road he was knocked down by a wagon and sustained injuries which subsequently proved fatal.

It was not necessary for Hinder to cross these roads where he did, since about 40 yards ahead he would have avoided passing between the wagons and crossed the running lines on a practically level timbered crossing which leads direct to the tool box.

The accident was not witnessed, but it was clearly due to Hinder's own want of caution. The removal of the trimmers' tool boxes to positions where the men would have access to them without crossing the running rails should receive the attention of the Company.

WM. WORTHY COOKE.

Date, time and place of Accident – 2nd September, 1924, 5.30 a.m., Paddington Goods. *Name, grade and age of Person* – Henry Rodolphus Turner, goods porter, 67. *Booked working hours and time on duty* – 9; 1½ hours. *Nature of Injury* – Back, right arm and leg bruised.

At this station there are several drawbridges arranged to cross different lines for the purpose of conveying goods from one platform to another. When not required, or when necessary to move wagons along the shed lines, the bridges are withdrawn under the floor of the shed by electric hydraulic power. The operations are performed by capstanmen. On the occasion in question, just as the bridge was being withdrawn from over the Nos. 14 and 15 lines, porter Turner, who had conveyed some goods to the opposite side of the shed, was returning with his empty barrow to the No. 15 platform when, failing to notice that the bridge was being withdrawn from the No. 14 platform, he pushed his barrow over the edge of the platform. Keeping hold of the barrow Turner was pulled from the platform, and with his barrow he fell on the rails and sustained injuries as stated above. From the position in which capstanman H.R. Andrews was necessarily standing he could not see Turner approaching the bridge, but foreman A.E. Lunn, who was on the No. 15 platform, saw Turner, and called to him to 'keep clear of the bridge.' At that moment Turner is said to have been looking along the platform, and neither saw the bridge nor heard Lunn's call.

I attribute the mishap to want of care, but for future safety I recommend that before a bridge is withdrawn a red flag should be placed at the edge of the platforms affected, or that someone should stand on the platform from which the bridge is being withdrawn for warning purposes.

AMOS FORD.

RAIL 270/30   Great Western Railway Company
Register of Accidents

Date of Accident	Station	Name of Injured Person	Particulars of Accident	Result of Departmental Inquiry & Recommendation	Result of Board of Trade Inquiry & Recommendation	How dealt with
1925 7 Feb. 10.5 a.m.	Tiverton B.T.* 630	J. Dascombe Person on business *Fatal* *Verdict* Accidental Death	Assisting his employer to push a truck of coal in position on siding in the yard when a goods train came in contact with the truck and Dascombe was knocked down, the wheels passing over both legs. Died in hospital.	Rule 112 observed by G.W. Shunter Oak, but man's employer failed to obtain the shunter's permission to move the wagon. No negligence on part of Company's servants. No recommendation.	Accident arose through failure on the part of Reed and Dascombe to tell the Shunter they were going to move the wagon, and to neglect on the part of Shunter Oak to comply with Rule 112(a). Shunting Staff should be advised that all movements made into this siding should be preceded by one of the men and warning given before any movement is made.	Instructions given for Rule 112(a) to be complied with.
7 Mar. 4.15 p.m.	Btn St Briavels & Redbrook B.T. 1191	J.J. Boulton Fireman (Five passengers complained of shock)	As the 3.55 p.m. Passr train ex Monmouth was running between Redbrook and St Briavels it became derailed on the right hand side of the track.	Not possible to assign any definite cause for the accident. No recommendation.	Derailment due to a combination of circumstances, including lateral hunting between rail and flanges and pronounced oscillation, the somewhat small clearance between the axle boxes and horn ties on the engine and the fact that the engine was running bunker first. No one to blame. Company to consider whether other types of engines than those of 0-6-0 class are not better suited for working on branch lines where no speed restrictions exist, also provision of larger clearance between the axle boxes and the horn tie on these locomotives.	Company unable to agree with the conclusions arrived at by Major Hall, but in view of fact that his Report was already printed and circulated, matter allowed to drop.
24 Apr. 10.15 a.m.	Coton Hill B.T. 2117	S. Hill wagon repairer (employed by Wagon Repairs Ltd)	Hill was putting a new buffer pad on Clee Hill wagon No. 202 standing with others in a siding when some wagons were shunted against it and he was slightly pinched between the buffers. He had not obtained permission before starting to carry out the work, neither did he exhibit a red flag in accordance with the regulations.	Own want of care. No recommendation. None held.	Accident due to Hill's neglect to give effect to the regulations with which he was fully conversant. No recommendation.	
etc.						

* Board of Trade. B.T. 630 is presumably a reference to a Board of Trade document

71

RAIL 425/2   London, Midland and Scottish Railway

ACCIDENT at WINWICK JUNCTION BOX, WARRINGTON,
28. 9. 34.

Nine passengers killed or subsequently succumbed to their injuries.

Mr Joseph Malone,
73, Vincent Street,
St. Helens.

Mr Sherlock,
(address not yet known).

Miss Jennie Hutchinson,
Visita Road,
Earlestown.

Mr James Turner, (age 61)
11, Edditch Grove,
Bolton.

Mrs Mary Ann Rowe,
12, Sankey Terrace,
Earlestown.

Four passengers (2 men and 2 women) who were killed not yet identified.

---

1 Servant Killed:

Guard John Lyden, St Helens, in charge of the local train.

---

13 Passengers injured and detained in
Warrington General Infirmary.

Mr Albert Victor Layton (age 44),   Fractured left ankle and shock.
18 Trafford Avenue,
Warrington.

Mrs Carrie McHugh,   Injuries to head and shock.
96, Whelley,
Wigan.

Miss Clarice Bunting (age 24),   Severe injury to nose.
Employed at:
Savoy Hotel,
Blackpool.
Thought to reside at Sheffield.

Mr Thomas Dennett (age 27),   Facial injuries and contusions
1, Grayson's Yard,   of left foot.
Wigan Lane,
Wigan.

Mr William Fowles (age 49), 23, Argyle Street, Wigan.	Feet bruised and shock.
Mr J. Horrobin, (age 29), 41, Frog Lane, Wigan.	Abrasions of left foot, compound fracture lower end right leg and shock.
Mr Thomas Evans (age 51), 9, Rectory Road, Neath, S. Wales.	Fractured ribs.
Miss Violet Johnson (age 21), 35, Regent St., Earlestown.	Severe lacerated scalp, concussion, abrasions to left leg and shock.
Miss Ethel Laird (age 17), 11 Hotel Street, Earlestown. Condition critical.	Compound fracture of right leg, scalp and face wounds.
Miss Beryl Wilkes, 73, King Edward Street, Darlaston, Staff.	Cuts on right knee and face.
Miss Katherine Walls, (age 25) Hall Lane, Wigan. Condition critical.	Lacerated scalp, right clavicle fractured and compound fracture of right tibia.
Mr William Bentley, Raven Hotel, Wigan.	Fractured right leg and wound on right elbow.
Miss Mona H. Rodway, (age 16), 4, Park Avenue North, Wargrave, Earlestown.	Fractured right leg. Injuries to to face and shock.

---

3 Passengers detained in Newton-le-Willows
Cottage Hospital.

Mr Matthew Gibson, 18, Russell Street, Wigan.	Fractured leg.
Mr William A. Dove, 99, Homeslack Lane, Preston.	Fractured leg.
Mr Herbert Taylor, 36, Nevill Street, Earlestown.	Fractured leg.

---

4 Servants detained in Warrington General
Infirmary.

Driver George Hope,
   Chester.
      Working local train.

Fractured scapula, ribs,
clavicle and shock.

Goods Guard W. A. Higham, (age 42),
   Preston.
      Thought travelling as passenger.

Shock.

Thos. Woodward, (age 41),
   Loco. Fitter,
      Warrington.

Laceration of back, compound
fracture of right leg and shock.

Guard John Jones, (age 39),
   Wednesbury.

Scalp wound and shock.

Copy of report from Mr. C. R. Byrom, Euston, to Mr. G. L. Darbyshire, Euston, dated 29. 9. 34.

Collision at Bletchley, October 1939. (TNA, RAIL 1020/12)

74

5.20 p.m. express passenger train, Euston to Blackpool colliding with the rear of the 8.55 p.m. ordinary passenger train, Warrington to Wigan via Newton-le-Willows, Winwick Junction Signalbox, Warrington, Friday, 28th Sept., 1934.

With reference to my report of date.

The lines were opened for traffic as follows:

> Up Slow 9.55 a.m.
> Up Fast 10.50 a.m.
> Down Slow to Earlestown Branch 11.24 a.m.
> Down Slow to Main 3.50 p.m.
> Down Fast 6.0 p.m.

I am informed that only one of the twelve vehicles forming the two trains concerned was of all-steel construction, namely the third vehicle of the express, bogie van No. 3955.

The fire referred to in the first paragraph of the third sheet of my previous report occurred between the second and third compartments of the leading vehicle of the local train, and the C. & W.* staff definitely report that it was due to fusing of an electric wire.

As already reported the Inquest was opened for the purpose of taking evidence of identification at the Police Court, Warrington, at 2.30 p.m. today, when the Company were legally represented, and the Coroner has decided to resume the Inquest at the Police Court, Warrington, at 12. 0 noon on Tuesday next, the 2nd proximo.

With regard to the list of killed or fatally injured, I learn that Mr Sherlock's full particulars are as follows:

> John Reid Sherlock,
> 5, Robson Street,
> Warrington.

Of the four passengers who were unidentified it has since transpired that one was a man and three were women, not two men and two women as previously stated, and they have been identified as follows:

> Ralph Draper,
> 12, Atherton Street,
> Newtown,
> Wigan.

> Hilda Dunning,
> 45, Haydock Street,
> Earlestown.

> Catherine Beatrice Aston,
> The Cottage,
> Wood Green,
> Wednesbury.

> Harriet Ann Anderton,
> 15, Wigan Lane,
> Wigan.

* Carriage and wagon

Further enquiries shew that the local passenger train had been offered forward by the signalman at Winwick Junction Box to the Box in advance in the Earlestown direction and accepted under Regulation 3 at 9.2 p.m. and consequently there was no reason whatever why the train should not have been allowed to proceed.

I may add that it is shewn that the signalman gave the 'Train out of section' signal for the local train to the box in rear at 9.5 p.m. when he was offered and accepted the 'Is line clear' signal for the express train, received the 'Train entering section' signal at 9.7 p.m. and the train was offered forward from Winwick Junction Box on the main line and accepted by the Box in advance at 9.5 p.m.

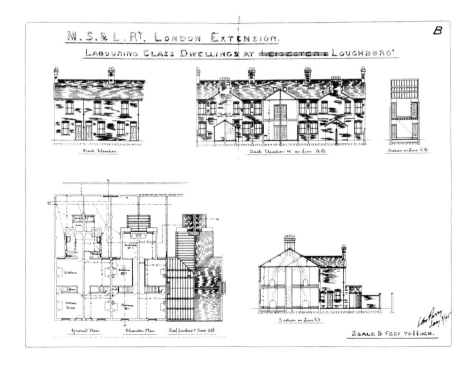

Manchester, Sheffield and Lincolnshire Railway, labourers' houses. TNA, RAIL 226/179

CHAPTER 4

BOARDS OF DIRECTORS' MEETINGS

The Board of Directors of each railway company met regularly to control and administer the company's affairs. The minutes of many companies' meetings record only the most important issues. It is assumed that the less important administrative matters were delegated to other committees or individuals. It is surprising, however, to find that some directors were concerned with much of the detailed administration. The Bristol and Exeter Railway Board actually interviewed all applicants for porters and policemen and recorded the names of successful applicants in the minutes of their meetings. All manner of events affecting staff may be found in these minutes, in particular accidents were discussed and compensation payments recorded. Reprimands, dismissals and commendations may also be found.

A selection of abstracts from various railway companies' Board of Directors' minutes are given here, illustrating the wide range of detail to be found relating to staffing matters and where staff are named.

RAIL 315/7   Hull and Selby Railway Company
Board of Directors' Meetings

29 May 1840
That Mr Thomas Brown be appointed the private Ledger Clerk at a salary of £120 per annum, and that he give Security to the amount of £250 one month's notice to be given if a change is made.

That Mr George Coverdale be appointed the Ledger Clerk for up and down Goods at a salary of £90 per annum, he giving security for £200.

That Mr M. Ring and Mr W. Witby be the junior Clerks in the Goods Office at a Salary of £70 per year each.

That Mr George Pearson be the second Clerk in the Booking Office at a Salary of £80 per annum, security to be given for £200.

That Mr William Wilson be the junior Clerk in the Booking Office at a Salary of £40 per year. Security to be given for £100.

That Aaron Weatherill be the House Porter, and that his wages be 18/– per week in addition to a House and Coals and that his wife be allowed 3/- per week for cleaning the Offices &c.

That John Auckland, Robert Smith, Thomas Smith, James Coates, and Francis Fugill be porters at 20/- per week each, with a Velvet Jacket yearly. The Secretary to appoint one of them to deliver and receive parcels who shall have 21/- per week, he giving Security for £50.

That Richard Twidle and John Doy be the two Foremen for Goods up and down, the wages to be 28/- per week to each, and Security for £50 to be taken from each.

That Mr Wallis Metcalf be appointed the Managing Clerk at the Selby Station with a Salary of £100 per annum and a Dwelling House, Security to be taken for £200.

That Benjamin Quest, Matthew Moment, George Todd, Richard E. Peel, John Longbone, John Smith, John Peach, Charles Patteson and Samuel Mason be the Gatekeepers on the line, the wages to be 18/- per week, and the Box to reside in. Samuel Mason to be placed at the Manor House Street Gates and to be allowed 19/- per week if he has not a Box.*

4 June 1840
Mr Pearson the Booking Clerk, being called in stated his approval of the terms of the engagement which had been made with him and he was informed he would have to go to York and Leeds to make himself familiar with the mode of booking Passengers at those places, paying his own expenses, but that his salary would commence on the day he set off for that purpose. Mr Pearson named Mr Abbey and Mr Proctor as his Surities.

The communication from Mr Holloway of York, relative to an engagement with Mr Aslett of the London and Birmingham Railway as principal booking Clerk being referred to, it was moved by Mr Liddell, seconded by Mr Gresham, and Resolved:

That Mr Holloway be informed the Directors will probably not object to give Mr Aslett a salary of £130 per annum if he is at liberty, and makes application to the Company.

RAIL 315/8   Hull and Selby Railway Company
Board of Directors' Meetings

26 December 1840
The Secretary read Mr Gray's Report of the accident near Brough on the 23 Inst. with the train coming from Leeds to Hull, owing to the breaking of the Axle of a wagon belonging to the Leeds and Selby Railway Company. The conduct of the Engine Driver, Pierce Naylor was most praiseworthy by gradually bringing the Train to a stand after the accident further mischief was prevented, the only person injured was Smith, the Guard who leaped off the Carriage on which he was riding, and his shoulder was bruised in consequence.

23 January 1841
The conduct of Pierce Naylor who was the Driver of the Engine when the accident occurred lately near Brough was considered, and being most praiseworthy it was thought that some mark of approbation should be confirmed on him. Moved by Mr Henwood, seconded by Mr Egginton and Resolved.

That a Silver Medal be presented to Pierce Naylor as a mark of approbation of his conduct when the accident took place near Brough on the 23 Dec[r].

---

* A box was a small country house

RAIL 631/1   South Devon Railway Company
Board of Directors' Meetings

31 March 1846
The Board having proceeded to the election, the following persons were appointed:

Station Clerks	Henry Bending
	John Blackborow
	Gilbert Burrington
	Richard Cross
	William Elliott
	David Ker
	J.P. Morgan
	Andrew Patey
	Edward Peck
Guards	William Bastin
	James Hobbs
	C. Maitland
	John Wensley
	Richard Williams, conditional on his obtaining the sanction of the Gt. Western Co. to his application and sufficient testimonials

Charles Skivins ⎫   were approved of as supernumerary
Thomas Padrick ⎬   Guards for eventual appointment

Policemen	George Barry	George Payne
	George Cockerell	John Skinner
	William Dart	James Stoke
	Richard Gardner	William Symes
	John Harcombe	William Veale
	Charles Newberry	H.P. Voysey
	George H. Norman	
Porters	John Browning	John Pallette
	James Collins	John Sampson
	Henry Hooper	James Vicary
	William Lavers	Robert Vilvin
	William Lear	William Wyatt
	Thomas Moorman	

RAIL 631/2   South Devon Railway Company
Board of Directors' Meetings

14 March 1848
That pursuant to the above Regulations the following be the salaries of the several Clerks referred to:

Mr Arliss	@	£60	until	1 Oct.	1848
Bastin		60		"	
Batt		80		1 Apr.	1849
Bendall		80		"	
Blackborow		70		1 Oct.	1848
Blewitt		70		"	1849
Chivers		70	until	"	1848
Cross		80		1 Apr.	1849
Cuddeford		60		1 Oct.	1848

Cont.

Digby	70	1 Apr. 1849
Drew	60	1 Oct. 1848
Elliott	90	1 Apr. 1849
Gedye	80	"
Hannaford	60	1 Oct. 1848
Hedger	80	1 Apr. 1849
Hood	70	1 Oct. 1848
James	60	"
Ker	100	1 Apr. 1849
(on opening to Laira)		
Morgan	90	"
Palmer	60	1 Oct. 1848
Parr	70	"
Patey	80	1 Apr. 1849
Peck	80	"
Rendell	70	"
Sloper	80	"
Stuart	80	"
Tuckett	80	"
Virtue	50	"

26 September 1848

Offences Policeman W[m] Irish was dismissed for being asleep in his box at the Old Quay Signal, Teignmouth on the night of the 15th September.

7 November 1848

Offences The Chief Superintendent reported W. Wyatt, porter, for intoxication on the 30th October. W. Wyatt was dismissed the service.

RAIL 772/6   York, Newcastle and Berwick Railway Company
Board of Directors' Meetings

24 May 1850
Minute No. 1568
Lesbury Station

That Mr Bowes, now employed under the Engineer, be appointed Station Master at Lesbury and that Holmes, the present Station Master there, return to Newcastle.

RAIL 772/10   York, Newcastle and Berwick Railway Company
Board of Directors' Meetings

4 November 1852
Minute No. 401

Mr Christison reported that the staff in the Booking Office at the Central Station consisted of the following clerks:

Mr Dewar at a salary of   30/- a week
Mr Halliday   20/-
Mr Ridsdale   20/-
Mr Donnison   20/-

the latter of whom was not efficient

Mr Christison was directed to take Mr Stamper, lately a clerk with Messrs Bainbridge and Co. of Newcastle, on trial for a week in the Booking Office, and to report as to his fitness.

RAIL 575/2 Portsmouth Railway Company
Board of Directors' Meetings

16 September 1853

The Secretary reported that Mr Hatch who was appointed Clerk under Minute No. 204, having declined to accept the situation, he had obtained the services of Mr John Packer formerly a Clerk in the Oxford, Worcester and Wolverhampton Office at a salary of £100 per annum.

Resolved. That this appointment be, and it is hereby approved and confirmed.

RAIL 56/6 Blyth and Tyne Railway Company
Board of Directors' Meetings

Agenda Book
Meeting of Directors,   15 October 1853

Mr Grey mentioned a person named Robert Care as a likely person for a Clerk or Gatekeeper, wages at 20/- to 25/- a week.

RAIL 640/7 South Wales Railway Company
Board of Directors' Meetings

23 December 1853

Resolved   Mr G.P. Pike was approved as Clerk at a salary of £60 per annum, security £300
              Mr Geo. Dunkin was approved as Clerk at a salary of £60, security £300
              Mr Geo. Clift was approved as Clerk at a salary of £70, security £300
              James Dobbs was approved as Guard
              William Rowland was approved as Porter

RAIL 250/9 Great Western Railway Company
Board of Directors' Meetings [indexed, with names of staff, porters, policemen, clerks, etc.]

3 July 1856

Mr Stevens reported that the undermentioned clerks in the Goods Department, who had been on probation during the same period of two months had proved themselves efficient for the Service and he recommended their appointment at the Salaries set opposite to their respective names, viz:

Mr Woolcott	at	£70 per annum
Mr Wilson	at	£70 " "
Mr Hughes	at	£60 " "
Mr Hawkins	at	£40 " "

which was sanctioned by the Board.

1 November 1855

Thomas Hamilton, switchman at Bath, was called in, charged with neglecting his points on the 22nd ulto. The fact being proved he was fined 40/- and cautioned as to his future conduct.

7. If three men can pack 20 boxes in four hours, how long will it take five men to pack 30 boxes?

10 Marks allowed.

The Candidate is here required to describe any Railway journey he has made.

10 Marks allowed.

The furthest railway journey I can remember was when I went to Bognor for a couple of days by the sea. I passed a good many railway stations on the way and I found some were bigger than others.

The country stations were not so big as the others of town stations, But it was better going through country ones because it seemed a lot fresher. There were fine views in the country but there were no good views in London.

South Eastern and Chatham Railway.

Clerks' Department.

JUNIOR CLERK'S EXAMINATION PAPER.

Date of Examination Tuesday, March 9th 1915

Name of Candidate in full ... Philip Burrell

Address ... 67 Mayall Rd. Sr Sydenham 86

Date of Birth ... January 24th 1901

Where Educated ... Haseltine Road school

Residence and Profession of Parents ... 67 Mayall Rd. Sr Sydenham

Date of leaving School and been employed since ... January 22nd 1915

General Health ... good

TIME OCCUPIED IN EXAMINATION (To be filled in by Examiner)

South Eastern and Chatham Railway Company. Part of a junior clerk's examination paper. 1915. (TNA, RAIL 414/554)

Great Western Railway Company. Kelston Bridge near Bath. (Somerset Archaeological and Natural History Society)

1 November 1855

The usual premium of £5 each was ordered to be paid to the following switchmen for one year's service without complaint or accident, viz:

James Harvey	Chippenham
John White	Cheltenham
Samuel Pope	Sapperton
William Heath	Gloucester
John Skater	Cheltenham
Henry Barnes	Gloucester
John Wilks	Gloucester
William Brown	Swindon

3 April 1856

Arthur Harris, a porter at Swindon, was reported, charged with entering the Service through the medium of fictitious testimonials to character and not appearing was dismissed.

RAIL 527/9   North Eastern Railway Company
Board of Directors' Meetings

8 August 1856

Resolved.   That the following alterations and appointments be made:

Captn O'Brien as General Manager at a salary of £500 per annum.

Mr Cleghorn to be Secretary at a salary of £400 per annum.

Mr Christison to be Passenger Superintendent for the whole of the line at a salary of £400 per annum.

Mr Eglinton of the Transfer Office to be Assistant Passenger Superintendent at a salary of £250 per annum.

Mr Wilson to be Goods Manager of the Southern District at a salary of £400 per annum.

Mr Robert Pauling to be Agent at Leeds at a salary of £200 per annum. And the salary of Mr Crier to be advanced to £200 per annum.

11 December 1857

Resolved.   That the salary of Mr Wilson, Goods Manager, Southern Division be advanced from £400 to £600 per annnm. Also that the salary of Mr Christison, General Passenger Superintendent be advanced from £400 to £500 per annum both from the 1 January next.

RAIL 250/11   Great Western Railway Company
Board of Directors' Meetings

25 June 1857

In consequence of the recent death of Mr W.C. Rea the Manager of the Swindon Works, Mr Gooch attended the Board with an application from his brother (Mr William F. Gooch) to succeed to that appointment. His testimonials were read and Mr Gooch recommended him as a most competent and proper person for the charge of the works. Being interrogated as to the fitness of the person, Mr Fraser, who had charge of the works during Mr Rea's illness, Mr Gooch replied that he had not been sufficiently educated for that appointment and could not therefore be recommended for so responsible an office. The Board decided to postpone any decision on this subject until the next Meeting. Upon enquiry respecting the Salary, it appears that Mr Rea had been raised in March 1856 to £550 per annum. Mr Gooch informed Capt. Bulkeley in reply to his enquiry that his brother would expect to receive £500 per annum if appointed to the same office.

Read letter from Mr Reginald Cocks addressed to Mr Micklethait complaining of the inefficient manner in which the business of the Company appears to be conducted at the Maidenhead Station, instancing on one occasion that he could not obtain admission into the Booking Office at the proper time and on another that several tickets were omitted to be collected in consequence of the absence of the Policeman whose duty it was to perform that Service. Mr Lucy the Station Clerk was called in and being interrogated on these complaints, stated with reference to Mr Cocks not having been admitted into the Booking Office on his arrival, that the Up Train by which he intended to travel had arrived several minutes before its proper time while the Down Train was also in the Station. He was compelled therefore in his discretion to act as he had done in closing the Booking Office for a short time while every attention had been paid by the persons on duty to Mr Cocks, who had suffered no inconvenience, inasmuch as after he had obtained his Ticket and even taken his seat in the carriage an interval of three minutes had elapsed previously to the Train starting. The Waiting Room also had been open while the Booking Office was closed. With regard to the allegation that certain Tickets had not been collected, Mr Lucy stated that the omission was entirely attributable to the fact of the porter having to perform the duty of the Policeman during his absence, who at the time was unavoidably engaged in the performance of other duties. Mr Lucy suggested an addition to the present staff at Maidenhead in order to prevent the recurrence of similar complaints which was considered but the Traffic of the Station having been referred to it was not deemed necessary at present to increase the Establishment at that Station.

John Horton a Policeman at Swan Village was reported for neglecting his signals and not appearing to answer the charge was dismissed the service.

Henning & Andrews Messrs 5
Hill Anthony S. 303
Heyford, accident at S. 21.
Half yearly General Meetings 13. 22. 24. 50. 53. 61. 66. 67. 74. 78. 90. 347. 375. 381. 385.
Hanson Mr. Clerk, 18.
Hodgson John Esq. 24. 60. 50.
Hayward I. E. Esq. 29
Hawes Mr. Thomas 30. 47.
Hill Mr. George, 32.
Holmes Mr. Clerk, 43
Hartnell Mr. H.N. 46. 130. 145. 268.
Hill Mr. Christopher 47. 171.
Hungerford & Devizes Railway 51. 328. 338. 406.
Hereford Ross & Gloucester Railway 70. 182. 151. 152. 255
Hellier, Engineman, 71
Hennet Mr. 93.
Harborough, Porter, 96.
Holland Mr. Clerk, 96. 121.
Hammond Mr. J. Clk, 98.
Head Mr. W. Clk, 98
Holloway Mr. Clk, 99
Horne Mr. James N. 105
Heron Joseph Esq. 106
Hockwell, Porter, 122
Horses, reserve of, to be purchased, 130.
Hooper Mr. Clk, 145
Hutton W., Switchman, 147.
Holt & Staverton, Memorial from, 149
Hall Mr. Clk, 157
Hippesley John Esq. 166.
Hamberger Monsr 169
Hatten, Porter, 170.
Henley Branch, 182. 195. 266. 268.
Hardisty Mr. 186.
Haskins, Porter, 208.
Hall, Guard, 209.
Holford R. S. Esq. 246. 267. 287.
Huggins, Policeman, 258. 277.
Householders Coal Company 262. 280.
Henley Fares &c 300
Holt Station, New Road to, 305.
Horton J. Policeman, 306.
Henderson, Messrs 307
Hendry Mr. Clk, 308. 351.
Hellier Mr. Clk, 309

H I K L M N O P Q R S T V W X Y Z

Great Western Railway Company. Page of index to Minutes of the Board of Directors
Meetings. (TNA, RAIL 250/11)

Mr Kelley reported that Webb a Porter at Wellington had had his arm amputated in consequence of an accident when employed in shunting the Waggons and had asked for assistance until his recovery; an allowance of 10/- per week was ordered to be allowed to him for a period of two months.

C. Baxter, a Guard on the Northern Division was reported for being absent from duty and found asleep, he was called in and informed that he cannot be retained in the Service.

Mr Kelley reported that Mr Williams the Station Clerk at Gresford had reported Evans a Porter at that Station for insubordination by writing about some Passengers Luggage which was missing, without communicating with him, and for being the worse for liquor some time previously. Evans was admonished for not informing Mr Williams about the Luggage and informed that had Mr Williams brought the charge of intoxication against him at the proper time he would have been dismissed and Mr Williams was reprimanded for not having done so.

Ogbourne a Porter at Birmingham was reported as incompetent and being called in, he was discharged. Mr Forbes brought a charge of great carelessness against Mr Stephenson, a Clerk at Warminster for having detained some loaded Trucks for 15 days and for neglecting to send a Way Bill with some Trucks loaded with wool which were consequently sent to a wrong destination. He was called in and informed that he cannot be retained longer in the Service, being incompetent for the duty he has to perform.

Mr Forbes reported that Mess[r] Wellington of Gloucester had conveyed by one of the Company's Trains two boxes of Lucifer Matches declaring them to be Biscuits, but which had been detected and he was instructed to take proceedings against Mess[r] Wellington for this breach of Law respecting the transmission of Lucifer Matches under a fraudulent declaration.

Mr Forbes mentioned that Messrs Henderson Solicitors of Bristol had sent in a claim for Costs respecting the irregularity of the delivery of some cheese and explained the circumstances when he was instructed to inform Mr Henderson that the Directors do not admit the Company to be liable.

Mr Stokes a Clerk at Slough was reported for carelessness as well as for having refused to give change to a passenger. He was called in and examined and informed that under the circumstances the Directors are of opinion he must retire from their service.

Dance a Foreman Porter and Welsh a Porter both in the Goods Department at Paddington, were called in and examined on a charge of a great neglect in not having examined a van after the arrival of the train in consequence of which the goods in it had not been removed but were forwarded to Bristol. Dance was severely reprimanded and informed that had it not been for his long Service and general attention he would have been severely punished.

Welsh whose special duty it was to examine the vans was fined 10/- and cautioned to be more careful in future.

Burden a Policeman at Oxford was reported for insubordination to Mr Burch which having been proved he was called in and dismissed.

Willlams a Luggage Stower at Oxford was called in and examined for using insolent language to Mr Quelsh. He was dismissed.

Cordey a Porter at Southam was reported for charging 4d above the usual Rates which he had misappropriated. He admitted the offence and was dismissed.

A charge against Morrell for backing a Goods Engine improperly was postponed as the Engine Driver was not in attendance to give his evidence.

Perkins a Porter at Solihull was called in and examined on a charge of neglecting orders and for insubordination, which being proved he was dismissed.

Mr Hendry a Clerk in the Goods Department at Paddington was reported for neglecting to deliver 10 of Hams which it was his duty to have done on receiving the Order. He was called in and stated in his defence that having delivered a similar number of bearing the same mark only a few days previously to receiving the Order, he concluded they must be the same. Messr Cherry the Owners of the Hams have made a claim of £20 in consequence of loss of sale which was ordered to be defrayed, and Mr Hendrey was ordered to pay £2 towards the loss and was severely reprimanded for his neglect of duty.

The following were recommended for appointment to the Permanent Establishment of the Company having undergone the usual probationary Service of two months. They were accordingly appointed as Clerks at the Salaries set opposite to their respective names.

Mr J.R. Richard	Goods, Banbury	at £80 per annum
Mr Relton Atkinson	Goods, Paddington	70
Mr H. Martin	Paddington	70
Mr G.H. Kidd	Leamington	60
Mr R. Izand	Birmingham	60
Mr E. Tillery	Paddington	50
Mr F. Moor	Paddington	50

Read letter from Capt. H.B. Hellier dated West Drayton yesterday soliciting permission for the return of his son Mr B. Hellier to the employment of the Company after having resigned his situation. The Secretary was instructed to aquaint Capt. Hellier that his request cannot be complied with, inasmuch as an existing rule precludes such an application being allowed.

Frank Ponsonby,
Chairman

RAIL 313/4   Hull and Holderness Railway Company
Board of Directors' Meetings

17 October 1857

Ordered 157   The Secretary reported that one of the Gates at Hedon had been broken by an approaching Train on the evening of the 12th inst. in consequence of the negligence of the porter. That he be fined to the amount of Half the cost of the repair.

31 October 1857

Ordered 169   That John Harmson be appointed Station Master at Burstwick at a salary of 20/- per week.

Ordered 170   That Henry Atkinson be appointed Station Master at Ottringham at a salary of 20/- per week.

Ordered 171   Minute 158 reconsidered. Ordered: That W. Smith the porter at Hedon be dismissed and that the Secretary give him the usual notice.

RAIL 250/12   Great Western Railway Company
Board of Directors' Meetings

31 December 1857

A claim made by Mr Wm Barnett for £8.10.0 as compensation for the value of an Ox, killed upon the line near Snow Hill Station at Birmingham on the night of the 19 November, was submitted. The circumstances attending this accident were investigated when it appeared to have occurred from the inattention of Mr Izard the Clerk, and Porters Young and Kerry. Mr Izard was ordered to pay 40/- and each of the Porters 20/- towards it. Mr Bill was instructed to obtain, if possible, a reduction of the amount claimed.

RAIL 463/5   Manchester, Sheffield and Lincolnshire Railway Company
Board of Directors' Meetings

Friday 26 October 1860
Minute No. 441
A petition signed by Richard Dinnis on behalf of the Engine Drivers, asking the Company to reduce their hours of labour to 10 hours per day was laid on the table.

RAIL 604/3   Severn and Wye Railway and Canal Company
Board of Directors' Meetings

18 November 1863
Read letter dated 15th November Inst. from Mr Geo. Wm Keeling, Engineer of this company, applying for an increase of salary on the ground of the extent of his duties and length of service. Resolved unanimously that Mr G.W. Keeling's salary be increased from £100 to £150 per annum, the same to commence from the 30 September last.

1 March 1865
The Secretary having submitted to this meeting the arrangements and duties in the respective departments of engineering and accounts which must now he put in force for carrying on the new branch of business appertaining to the supply of Locomotive power. It was unanimously resolved that the salary of Mr Geo. Wm Keeling, the Engineer, be increased to £250 per annum the said increase to commence from the 25 March last. Also that a further sum of £40 per annum be paid to Mr Gilbert Jas. Keeling for keeping the Locomotive Account Books to commence from the 25 March last.

14 November 1867
Read letter dated 13 November Inst. from Mr Geo. W. Keeling, Engineer, applying to this Board for an increase of salary on the ground of the heavy and important duties which have latterly devolved upon him, and the length of service.
Resolved unanimously that Mr Geo. W. Keeling's salary be increased from £250 to £300 per annum the same to commence from the 1 October last.

27 April 1871
That it be referred to the Executive Committee to consider what remuneration should be awarded to Mr Keeling for past services of an Extraordinary Character also the amount at which his future salary should be fixed; and to enquire as to the most convenient mode of providing for the increasing of Office business of the Company. The Committee do now report: That they consider it to be their duty to inform themselves upon various circumstances relating to Mr Keeling's long service with the Severn and Wye Company from the year 1847 to the present time, which, although not expressly referred to in the foregoing resolution were entitled to exercise an influence upon the results to which their investigation was directed. It will be enough to remind the Board that these measures which they regard as essential to the stability of the Company were chiefly instigated by Mr Keeling, and that their promotion has entailed upon him during the last four years an extra-ordinary amount of labour, anxiety and responsibility. —— the Committee have come to the conclusion that the sum of Five Hundred Pounds would be an appropriate award to be made to Mr Keeling in recognition of past services of an extraordinary character. —— they are of opinion that it is desirable to augment Mr Keeling's salary to £800 per annum. In making the latter recommendation they think it right to remind the Board that Mr Keeling's present salary of £600 has remained stationary for eleven [sic] years.

The present position of the Office Staff is that Mr Davies (who has long been engaged in the Engineering Department) transfers his services to the Office as Senior Clerk at the same salary as heretofore, being still available for occasional assistance in Engineering business. That Mr Smith succeeds his father (deceased) as second Clerk and that the Lord Trotter assists in Junior Clerks works. In the transitional state of the Company business it cannot be supposed that the work has settled into its ultimate form, but Mr Keeling reported this arrangement is promising to work well and states that he already finds much relief from the assistance of an extra clerk of such good capacity as Mr Davies, to whom he can depute the organisation of the new business of the Traffic Department and that the concentration of business in the New Offices is attended with great economy of time and labour.

RAIL 75/39   Bristol and Exeter Railway Company
Board of Directors' Meetings

4 April 1866
Appointment of Porters &c. It having appeared on the recent appointment or confirmation of appointment (Minute 21 Feby last) of Porters, Police &c. for the Traffic Department, that some were already in the Company's employment as supernumeraries, and had been so for various periods of from 4 months to more than 12 months, and in one case more than two years, without being reported to the Board or brought before the Directors for approval. It was RESOLVED that in future all selections or engagements of the kind be reported, and the men brought before the Directors, prior to the men entering the service of the Company as supernumeraries or otherwise:

Bristol and Exeter Railway Company. The train of carriages is approaching Bristol; Clifton is in the distance. (Somerset Archaeological and Natural History Society)

717   The following men appeared before the Board and were appointed:-

Station	Name	Occupation
Bristol	Charles Mitchell	Porter
do	William Henry Staddon	do
do	Charles Mitchell	do
do	Thomas Francis Maunder	Number Taker
do	Charles Antill	Parcel Porter
do	George Libbey	Porter
do	James Eastmond	Policeman
Portishead	Alfred Nicholls	Porter
Weston	William Lovering	do
Highbridge	George Pile	do
Taunton	Frederic Levi Knight	do
Weston	Thomas James Goodland	do
Uphill	Albert Hayes	do
Taunton	William Henry Dobson	do

1st Dec 1875.

Station	Name	Occupation
Taunton	Alfred Hurd	Porter
do	Robert Harris	do
do	William Summer	do
do	Newman Bayley	Lampman
do	Eli Langdon	Porter
Burlescombe	Robert Morrish	do
Norton Fitzwarren	Thomas Seamen	Ticket Collector
Exeter	George Baker	Policeman
Barnstaple	Alfred Ackland	Porter

Bristol and Exeter Railway Company. Page showing lists of staff from the Minutes of the Board of Directors Meeting, 1 December 1875. (TNA, RAIL 75/47) and that Mr Dykes arrange accordingly so as to have a sufficiency of men brought forward from time to time for selection or provisional appointment subject to their afterwards passing the medical examination in due course and to subsequent confirmation of the appointment by the Board.

RAIL 75/47   Bristol and Exeter Railway Company
Board of Directors' Meetings

Wednesday 9 June 1875
404   Reported the following accident:
         The death of D. Ashton aged 70, killed by Up North Mail at Victory
         Crossing 14th May.
         W. Mills, ganger injured at Yatton 10th May, died subsequently.
         Charles Perkins crushed between buffers in Bristol Yard on 31 June.
         Verdict of accidental death in each case.

22 September 1875
570   Reported an application from P.C. Smith who was injured by falling in the Fire
         at Taunton on 10 March 1874 for a Wooden Arm. Granted!

RAIL 465/11   Manchester South Junction and Altrincham Railway Company
Board of Directors' Meetings

13 February 1903
With reference to the Salaried Staff over 60 years of age it was agreed that Mr Wardleworth, who has been 52 years in the service, be allowed to retire; the Company paying him £1 per week. The other 2 men over 60 years of age, Blease and Latham, were, upon the Secretary's recommendation, allowed to remain in the service.

RAIL 332/2   Kent and East Sussex Light Railway Company
Board of Directors' Meetings

7 May 1930
Apprenticeship Deed.   Mr Austin submitted an Apprenticeship Deed dated 28 March 1930 between the Guardians of the Poor of the Tenterden Union of the first part, John Hoad of High Street, Rolvenden, Kent of the second part and the Company of the third part, whereby the Company undertook to take John Hoad as a Locomotive fitter apprentice for five years at a weekly wage of 5s during the first year with yearly increases up to 15s per week in the fifth year. The Deed was executed by the Tenterden union and John Hoad, but not by the Company, although according to the Minutes this should have been done at the Board Meeting held on the 7th May 1930.
It was resolved that the seal of the Company be affixed to the Deed and this seal was affixed accordingly.

CHAPTER 5

COMMITTEE AND
SUB-COMMITTEE MEETINGS

Many railway companies had various committees to control specific administrative functions. Some of these were given the authority to recruit staff. The minutes of the meetings of these committees may therefore record staff appointments and other staff matters. The Great Western Railway Company had many such conmittees.

The following range of examples show various entries of staff.

RAIL 250/85   Great Western Railway Company
London Committee of Management

20 August 1838   Sub-Committee on Appointments
Thomas McClure a policeman in the Paddington District has resigned in consequence of being appointed the master of an Union Workhouse.

RAIL 250/108 Great Western Railway Company
Meeting of Sub-committee on the Progress of Works and other committees

Appointments Sub-committee
4 August 1840
The several hereinafter mentioned applicants for employment as conductors, guards, policemen and porters were individually called in, and their respective Testimonials referred to.
Approved as conductors at £2–2–0 per week
        Thomas J. Gawler
Approved as Sub-inspector of Police at 25/- per week
        Richard Burton

Approved as Guards at 25/- per week
        Simeon Cosgreave
        John Morgan Williams
        Henry Painter
        Edward Willey
        Thomas Harrill

Approved as Policemen at 19/- per week
> Thomas Morgan
> Thomas Cook
> Charles Lawrence
> Wm Buckingham, subject to further Inquiry
> William Chapman

Approved as Porters at 19/- per week
> William Chadwick
> Benjamin Boucher

Approved for Employment in Goods Yard [wages not given]
> Francis Norrish

Approved for Employment in Store Depot [wages not given]
> Horatio Dunn

Approved for future employment
> James Brow

RAIL 250/119 Great Western Railway Company
Minutes of the General Committee

22 June 1843
James Taylor and Daniel Derrick porters at the Bath Station were reported by Mr Starr, the former on account of disorderly conduct in the Tap Room of the Half Moon Inn, and the latter with having being intoxicated on the night of Sunday last the 17th Inst.

The offence of Derrick was further proved by evidence of Pudnor a porter.

It was ordered that James Taylor be fined in the sum of 10/- and Daniel Derrick be dismissed from the Company's Service.

RAIL 615/9 Shrewsbury and Birmingham Railway Company
Traffic Committee Minute Book

25 April 1849
Appointment of Servants
The Testimonials of the various applicants for situations were examined and the following appointments made:

Guards	William Ballinger, Thomas Hughes, Charles Heath, James Large and Henry Hemming
Breaksman [sic]	John Waller
Policeman	Alexander Corbett
Porters	Japhet Morris, James Moore, and Robert Grainger.

15 June 1848 [an error for 1849]
Company's Servants
The Secretary reported that Japhet Morris (appointed as porter at Oakengates) had accepted another appointment and that James Moore, also appointed a porter had since become unwell and unable to undertake the duties, and that in consequence Richard Hughes (late porter at the Jermingham Arms) had been appointed porter at Oakengates.

33

Officers
Salaries to,

Officers &
Servants
appointment of

Salaries to Officers –
Ordered
That the Salaries to Station Masters be as follows

Whampton (Temporary)	£100 —	per Annum
Shiffnal with House & Coals	80 — " " — " —
Albrighton Do Do	60 " " " —
Codsall Do Do	60 " " " —

Appointment of Officers & Servants

The candidates in attendance having been called in and examined the following appointments were subsequently made:

Station Masters

Wolverhampton Philip Jones it being understood that the appointment was temporary only, and that he should eventually receive an appointment in the Goods Department —

Codsall — John Dawson
Albrighton — James Davies
Shiffnal — Henry Wheeler

Goods Clerks

Shiffnal John Partridge at a Salary of 25/ per week.
Wellington James Hiles 15/ per week
Oaken Gates Alfred Atkins 15/ — " — " —

Porter & Housekeeper

Wolverhampton Mr & Mrs Shepherd at a Salary of £1. per week

Breaksmen

George Harvey.

Shrewsbury and Birmingham Railway Company. Page from the Minutes of the Traffic Committee, 12 September 1849. (TNA, RAIL 615/9)

Mr Parsons having reported that it was necessary to appoint an additional Policeman in order to prevent parties trespassing upon the Line between Oakengates and Wellington the several applications were examined and Thomas Tongue, having been sent for and his testimonials being satisfactory, was appointed.

RAIL 75/59   Bristol and Exeter Railway Company
Minutes of the Finance, Plant and Appointment Committee

Wednesday 28 November 1849, 12.35 o'clock
– – – – – reported that Mr Cooper at the Weston-Super-Mare Station had sent in his resignation.
Resolved.   That it be recommended to the Board to accept the resignation of Mr Cooper and to appoint Mr Robinson at £50 in his stead.

Wednesday 16 January 1850, 11 o'clock
Mr Alfred Larkman attended as a candidate for an appointment in the Accountant's Office connected with the proposed new system of booking Through Traffic. Age 28. Has been employed by London and So. Western Comp^y.
Recommended from Mr Storin at £80 y^r. 1 month trial. £150 Security.

Mr Harry Smith also attended as a candidate for a minor appointment in the same department. Age 23. Received by [blank] at £50 a year. 1 month trial. £150 Security.

Wednesday 23 January 1850, 12.35 o'clock
– – – – – reported a deception practiced by Ed Tollevey for the purpose of concealing his age to the Great Western Company, this Company and the Provident Society, by the last of which he had been expelled.
Resolved.   That Edward Tollevey be suspended and brought before the Board on Wednesday next.
Also reported that Mr I.S. Crawford clerk at the Tiverton Station had been guilty of charging 20/- too much for a Lady's fare from Tiverton to Paddington, and had omitted to return the excess to her, and that having obtained leave of absence to visit his mother in London, he had taken with him £5 of this Company's money.
Resolved.   That Mr Harriott be directed to take measures for prosecuting I.S. Crawford in case the Board shall so determine on Wednesday next.
In order to fill up the Vacancies occasioned by the dismissal of I.S. Crawford it was
Resolved.   That it be recommended to the Board to remove Henry Clark from Taunton to Tiverton at £80 a year, and to give an increase of 4/- per week to Charles Hinckley at Taunton for taking the Night Duty.

1 Suit of Clothes for Sub Inspector of police
consisting of 1 Great Coat   at 32/6
            1 dress d°   „ 34/-
            1 pair Trowsers „ 28/-

6 Suits for passenger Guards
each consisting of 1 Great Coat   „ 32/6
            1 Dress d°   „ 33/9
            1 Waistcoat   „ 6/-
            1 Pair Trowsers   „ 13/10
            1 Leather Belt
                & pouch   }   „ 31/6

4 Suits for Goods – Guards
each consisting of 1 Great Coat   „ 39/6
            1 Cloth round Jacket „ 17/6
            1 Pr. blue trowsers „ 12/6
            1 Waistcoat   „ 8/6

40 Suits for Porters
each consisting of
            1 Green Cord Jacket „ 10/3
            1 pr. d° trowsers   7/6
            1 badge for sleeve   9

10 Suits for Foremen Porters
each consisting of
            1 Green cloth jacket „ 17/6
            1 Pair cord trowsers „ 7/6

From
Gilpin & C°
Northumberland St.
Strand,
London.

Bristol and Exeter Railway Company. Page from the Minutes of the Finance Committee, giving descriptions of uniforms, 14 February 1849. (TNA, RAIL 75/58)

RAIL 250/167   Great Western Railway Company
Engineering Committee

15 December 1886
It was agreed to recommend increases of salary as follows:

			Present Salary £	Proposed Increase £
Mr James Hart, clerk	Engineer's Office,	Hereford	150	20
Mr W.J. Johnson	Chief Clerk's Office	"	130	10
Mr A.E. Johnson	Surveyor's Office	"	90	10
Mr R. Davies	Clerk	"	60	20
Mr A.W. Witterton	Clerk	"	55	15
Mr A.G. Smith	Clerk	Sudbrook	100	15

The transfer of Mr F.J. Dawe, a clerk in the Divisional Engineer's Office, Paddington, whose services are no longer required there, to a vacancy in the Accountant's Office was authorised. Mr Dawe's salary is £50 per annum.

RAIL 250/298   Great Western Railway Company
Refreshment Room Committee

21 April 1888
The Committee considered a recommendation of Mr Peach that the salary of Mr Hughes should be increased to £110 a year.

RAIL 250/148 Great Western Railway Company
Clerks Appointment Committee

16.5.88

Memo
The Clerks engaged on night duty at Paddington work regularly every night and are allowed £10 per annum each in addition to their salaries.
The hours are as under:–
Down Invoicing 7 p.m. to 11.30 p.m. and on Abstract Work 10 a.m. to 1 p.m.
Down Invoicing 7 p.m. to about 3 a.m.
Up Invoicing 12 midnight to about 8 a.m. the time of departure depending upon the nature of the work.
A Clerk doing Down Invoicing would leave work at, say 3 a.m. on Sunday and would be free from that time until 7 p.m. on the Monday.

Paddington Station
18 May 1887

Present

Minimum number of marks 40; maximum 54

1.	Hale, Arthur William	(Lad Clerk, Clause 14 circular 556)		19	Approved
2.	Poole, Edward George	"	"	18	Approved
3.	Horton, Charles	"	"	19	Approved
4.	Beak, Charles James	"	"	19	Approved
5.	Flint, James Fergusson	"	"	19	Approved

6.	Tanswell, Thomas	"	"	19	Approved
7.	Partridge, Charles Henry	"	"	19	Approved
8.	Robins, Arthur Henry	"	"	19	Approved
9.	Leavans, William	"	"	19	Approved
10.	Mills, Anther [sic] Blakeman	"	"	19	Approved
11.	O'Brien, Munro Tom	"	"	18	Approved
12.	Smith, Robert Russell	"	"	19	Approved
13.	Gale, Frank Arnold	"	"	19	Approved
14.	Brinton, Joseph Caleb	"	"	19	Approved
15.	Price, Thomas Murray	"	"	19	Approved
16.	Heywood, Joseph William	"	"	19	Approved
17.	Barrett, Walter Frank	"	"	19	Approved
18.	Nichols, John	"	"	19	Approved
19.	Garard, William	"	"	19	Approved
20.	Davis, William Edgar	"	"	19	Approved
21.	Layton, Edward Charles	"	"	20	Approved
22.	Robertson, Albert Augustus	"	"	19	Approved
23.	Taylor, Thomas	"	"	19	Approved
24.	Smith, William George	"	"	21	Approved
25.	Dyer, Archie Frederick	"	"	19	Approved
26.	Pepple, Albert Edward	"	"	18	Approved
27.	Artlett, Frederick George	"	"	18	Approved
28.	Bagley, George Charles	"	"	19	Approved
29.	Venn, James	"	"	18	Approved
30.	Raby, Arthur	"	"	19	Approved
31.	Denner, Henry John	"	"	19	To come again

*   F.G. Artlett appears in the following photograph

Great Western Railway Company, Paddington, Cricket Team, c. 1904. Back row, left to right:
B. Eydmann (umpire), P.R. Lindsay, G. Johnson, H.W. Ashurst, F.G. Artlett,
R.S. Wood. Front row: H.J. Humphrey, B. Gibbs, F.K. Honeyball, A.P. Bolland, F.B. Farr,
G.L. Bushell. (TNA, RAIL 253/459)

RAIL 250/268   Great Western Railway Company
Locomotive, Carriage and Stores Committee

17 December 1890

Mr Dean called attention to recent instances in which accidents on the Line had been prevented by the judicious and prompt action of Enginemen and Firemen in the Service and he submitted a memorandum giving particulars of the cases referred to. The Committee desired that the commendation of the Directors be conveyed to the several men as undermentioned and they recommended that gratuities, as specified, be given in certain of the cases, viz:

Wm Scott	Engineman, Salisbury	
Herbert Thos, Fox	Fireman, Salisbury	
Henry Hibberd	Engineman, Plymouth	
Walter E. Coldwell	Fireman, Paddington	20/-
Wm Viner	Engineman, Paddington	20/-
Chas. H. A'Court	Engineman, Paddington	20/-
John Neate	Engineman, Newport	40/-
Wm Bailey	Engineman, Trowbridge	40/-
Wm Henry Silcocks	Fireman, Trowbridge	20/-
Edward Morgan Williams	Engineman, New Milford	20/-
Chas. Nowlan	Engineman, Plymouth	20/-

RAIL 250/344   Great Western Railway Company
Traffic Committee

12 April 1905

That the following payments under the provisions of the Workmen's Compensation Act 1897 have been made:–

£297–12–11	to the widow of T. Evans, Inspector, fatally injured at Newport on the 12th of January last.
£292–10–4	to the widow of T. Nethercott, ganger, fatally injured at West London on the 21st of February last.
£236–19–1	to the widow of Wm Ellway, goods guard, fatally injured at Pontypool on the 31st of December last.
£221–4–1	to the widow of J. Williams, ganger, fatally injured at Risca on the 14th ultimo.

RAIL 250/304   Great Western Railway Company
Refreshment Room Committee

5 January 1922

A report by the General Manager

He states that in consequence of the unsatisfactory conduct of Stock Takers E.W. Griffiths and P.G. James, Paddington, it had been decided to reduce their positions, as from the 5th proximo as follows:

  E.W. Griffiths from class 3, £270 per annum to class 4, £240 per annum
  P.G. James from class 3, £250 per annum to class 5, £210 per annum

TOTTENHAM AND HAMPSTEAD JUNCTION RAILWAY.

OFFICERS' COMMITTEE.

28, Great George Street, Westminster,

April 29th and May 12th, 1885.

Mr. Noble (in the Chair) ... ...
 ,, Hodges ... ...
 ,, Harrison ... ... } *Midland Company.*
 ,, Langley ... ...
 ,, Needham ... ...

Mr. Birt ... ...
 ,, Robertson ... ...
 ,, Fearn ... ... } *Great Eastern Company.*
 ,, Wilson ... ...

1. It having been agreed by the Boards of the Midland and Great Eastern Companies that on and from *August* ~~July~~ 1st, 1885, the staff of the Tottenham and Hampstead Junction Railway shall be a joint staff, and that the line shall be managed and worked by a Joint Committee, it was agreed to recommend :—

2. That the working of the line be placed under the management of the General Managers of the two Management Companies.

3. That the following be considered the joint staff of the line :— Staff.

South Tottenham	Mapp, R. W.	Station-master	£85 per annum.
	Garrett, C.	Office youth	12s. ,, week.
	Warne, C.	Station porter	21s. ,, ,,
	Langridge, R. W.	Assistant porter	12s. ,, ,,
	Redfern, J. W.	Shunter	19s. and 2s. allowance per week.
	Fabian, C.	Signalman	25s. per week.
	Williams, G.	,,	25s. ,, ,,
St. Ann's Road	Heyward, R.	Station-master	£63 14s. 0d. per annum.
	Briant, C. H.	Office youth	6s. per week.
	Johnson, J.	Station porter	20s. ,, ,,
	Edwards, W.	Assistant porter	10s. ,, ,,
	Barnes, W.	Porter signalman	19s. ,, ,,
	Joyner, F.	Signalman	24s. ,, ,,
Haringay Park	Mansell, E.	Station-master	£62 8s. 0d. per annum.
	Dasley, A.	Station porter	21s. per week.
	Jones, T. E.	,,	19s. ,, ,,
	Downey, A.	Assistant porter	8s. ,, ,,
	Watts, A.	Signalman	24s. ,, ,,
	Foster, G.	,,	24s. ,, ,,
Crouch Hill	Britland, R.	Station-master	£90 ,, annum.
	Chapman, F.	Office youth	10s. ,, week.
	Barrs, J. W.	Station porter	21s. ,, ,,
	Stinchcombe, W.	,,	19s. ,, ,,
	Joyce, J.	Signalman	24s. ,, ,,
	Davison, A.	,,	24s. ,, ,,
Hornsey Road	Wallace, J.	Station-master	£67 12s. 0d. per annum.
	Males, F. E.	Assistant porter	10s. per week.
	Keys, T.	Signal porter	21s. ,, ,,
	White, A.	,, ,,	19s. ,, ,,

Tottenham and Hampstead Junction Railway Company. Page from the Minutes of the Officers' Committee, 29 April and 12 May 1885. (TNA, RAIL 697/12)

Great Western Railway Company, Ilminster station staff, 1902. The four men are, left to right: Mr Morrish, relief porter who became District Inspector at Penzance; Mr Churchill, signalman, who on retirement was station master at Dunball; Mr Johnson, porter; A.L. Saunders, lad clerk, who was station master at Dulverton when he retired. (TNA, RAIL 1014/36)

RAIL 250/134   Great Western Railway Company
Committee as to Allowances on Retirement

23 November 1939

It was agreed to grant the following gratuities to the undermentioned members of the staff who are retiring from the service through ill health:

Traffic Department			Gratuity
D.L. Jones	Porter	Saltash	£20
Engineering Department			
B .W. Ralph	Labourer	Bath	£10
Chief Mechanical Engineer's Department			
J. Evans	Boiler Scruffer	Caerphilly	£10

Resolved that William Waite be appointed Office Porter at a salary of eighteen shillings per week, and that Wiliiam Farmer be appointed a general porter at sixteen shillings per week. Resolved that the day of opening the Joint Station for public traffic be fixed for the 1 June and that the officers and servants of the Committee be required to enter upon their situations on the 29th instant.

Note: Further meetings name other staff appointed.

The following is of particular interest:

15 June 1855
Clothing of Station Servants
Ordered that it is desirable that the livery of servants of the Committee be distinctive from that adopted by either of the two Companies using the Station. That the colour of the Committee's livery be a dark reddish brown, with letters in white H.J'. S. that Mr Nash be instructed to ascertain the price paid for liveries by the Great Western Company and by the Shrewsbury and Hereford Company, and that he obtain tenders and patterns of cloth from such of the tailors of Hereford as may be willing to tender for the supply of this clothing.

Note: At the meeting of 17 September 1855 other items of clothing (boots, greatcoats, hats and caps) were discussed as to colours and patterns.

2 October 1855
John Evans (discharged, wounded from the army in the Crimea) was appointed Weighing Machine Clerk in the Coal Yard, at a salary of 16/- per week, and it was ordered that he be provided with the necessary books, tickets, &c.

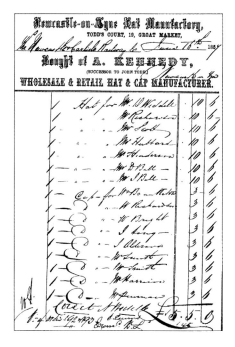

A bill from A. Kennedy of the Groat Market, Newcastle-upon-Tyne, listing hats and caps supplied to the Newcastle and Carlisle Railway Company. Note that the employees for whom the items had been ordered are named. (TNA, RAIL 509/133)

RAIL 744/4   Whitehaven Junction and Whitehaven and Furness Junction Railways Joint Committee
Minutes of Meetings

29 January 1858
Read petition from Ralph Turner for a subscription towards the expense of a Cork Leg he having lost his leg by being run over by an Engine while on duty at Preston Street Station in January 1856.

Ordered: That a Gratuity of £10 be awarded to Ralph Turner towards the expense of a Cork Leg

RAIL 686/1   Tebay Joint Station Committee
Minntes of Meetings

1 September 1862
Large cottages. Resolved they be let to the following viz. L. Longbottom, J. Holland, W. Middlehurst, Thos. Heald and Mrs Latimer and the Small Cottages to R. Smith, J. Yates, Nathan Clark, John Robinson, W. Sanderson, Thos. Ellison, Thomas Atkinson, Richard Radcliffe, John O'Neil, John Stamper, Thos Orchard and Jas. Stamper.

6 October 1862
Read letter from Mr Longbottom, Locomotive Manager also from Mr Scott, Station Master, representing the rents of the new Cottages at Tebay which are set at 3/6 per week as to [*sic*] high

Lancashire and Yorkshire Railway Company, Luddendenfoot station staff (undated).
(TNA, RAIL 1015/2)

and praying the Committee to take the same into consideration. Resolved that for the first year an abatement of 6d per week be made on the small class of Cottage.

Staff Changes at Tebay
Resolved that J. Atherton, pointsman be transferred to Mr Bores Department in place of Nelson J. Stamper to take the place of J. Atherton, pointsman at 18/- per week and that Wm Atkinson be appointed to be porter in place of Stamper at 16/- per week.

RAIL 404/177   London and North Western and Great Western Joint Committee Staff Register [indexed by station]

Shrewsbury Station

B. Evans	Yard Pointsman
Date of Entry Into Service	August 1863
Age	34
Wage	£1 per week
Increased Wage	
Oct. 1880	22/-
Nov. 1881	23/-
Feb. 1890	24/-
Feb. 1891	25/-
Porter	April 1876
Deceased	July 1891

RAIL 617/12 Shrewsbury and Hereford Joint Committee Minutes of Meetings

20 December 1864
A statement of Passes issued since the last meeting was submitted and also the following Staff changes which were sanctioned.

Dorrington	Wright from Church Stretton to be porter at 12/- pr week
Leebotwood	Heath from Ludlow to be signalman at 20/- pr week Painter, porter removed to Moreton J. Hodgkiss from Moreton to be signalman at 18/- pr week
Church Stretton	G. Shanks from Salop to be porter at 15/- pr week vice Wright removed to Dorrington
Marsh Brook	Thos. Clutton from Salop to be signalman at 18/- per week J. Pugh, porter to be increased from 14/- to 16/- pr week
Graven Arms	J. Hill removed to Onibury to be porter at 16/- per week R. Pritchard from Onibury to be signalman at 18/- pr week vice Hill
Onibury	T. Horton, Stationmaster to be Stationmaster at Tenbury at £90 pr annum vice Shiel dismissed at last meeting
Ludlow	W. Wright from Wooferton to be pointsman at 18/- pr week vice Heath removed to Leebotwood Pearce supernumerary at 15/- pr week
Wooferton	C. Hill from Permanent Way to be pointsman at 16/- pr week vice Wright removed to Ludlow

Tenbury	F. Coarse, yard foreman resigned
	E. May pointsman suspended for being drunk
	If it is decided to do away with the Block at Leebotwood Heath to fill May's place
Leominster	R. Pritchard, horsekeeper deceased. J. Edwards from Salop to be horsekeeper at 18/- pr week vice Pritchard
	J. Nash, booking clerk removed to Salop
Dinmore	Edwards's salary increased to £80
Moreton	W. Painter from Leebotwood to be porter at 14/- pr week vice Hodgkiss
Hereford	H. Jones, parcel porter to be increased from 8/- to 10/- pr week
	G. Jones, porter left the service
	D. Owens to be porter at 16/- pr week vice Jones

Pritchard pointsman at Craven Arms to be warehouseman at Tenbury. Man to be appointed to Craven Arms and an agent for Onibury.

RAIL 706/1   Vale of Towy Railway Joint Committee
Minutes of Meetings

April 1868	Statement of the men employed on the line was produced and approved; and ordered to be entered on the Minutes as follows, viz:		
	Traffic Department		
	Charles Berry, station master,	Llandovery	30/-
	Thos. R. Berry, telegraph clerk	"	10/-
	Rees Morgan, porter	"	15/-
	John Jones, porter	"	15/-
	William Thomas, porter	"	12/-
	John Morgan, station master	Llanwrda	20/-
	John Jones, porter	Llandovery	14/-
	Morgan Price, telegraph clerk	"	5/-
	William Evans, station master	Llangadock	17/-
	John Morris, porter	"	14/-
	E. Williams, telegraph clerk	"	5/-
	William Lover, station master	Glanrhyd	13/-
	John Thomas, station master	Talley Road	12/-
	William Harverson, telegraph inspector	Prop[n]	10/-
	Engineering Department		
	John Davies, ganger	Llandovery	16/-
	Thomas Rees, platelayer	"	14/-
	Ll. Jones, platelayer	"	14/-
	T. Thomas, platelayer	"	14/-
	Israel Griffiths, ganger	Llangadock	16/-
	John Davies, platelayer	"	14/-
	D. Jones, platelayer	"	14/-
	S. Evans, platelayer	"	14/-
	Timothy Thomas, fencer		14/-
	F.W. Tristram, inspector	Permanent Way, Prop[n]	12/-
			£16–14

Great Northern Railway Company, Doncaster station staff, *c.* 1905. The men's grades are given, although unfortunately only a few names. Back row, left to right: porter, lampmen. Second row: porter; porter, guard, porter (Barton), porter, lampmen, excess luggage porter (Burbidge).
Third row: no grade given, porter, porter, porter, ticket collector, ticket collector, signal lampman, porter, no grade given. Front row: passenger shunter (standing), horse shunter, station lampman (train lights), goods inspector (Hodges), station master (Bolt), chief inspector (Brummitt), station lampman (Cooper), porter, signal lampman (Crawley, standing). (TNA, RAIL 1014/33)

RAIL 736/6 West Riding and Grimsby Railway
Wakefield Station Minute Book

3 September 1868
The uniform of the Station Master to be a dark green Frock Coat with black buttons and with 'Station Master' in gold letters on the collar of the coat; dark green waistcoat, and black trousers both plain. Cap of dark green with gold letters 'W.J.S.'* on front and thin gold beading on bottom of cap.

Porters Uniform to be green cord with brass buttons, 'W.J.S.' to be on cap, collar of jacket and on buttons.

The Foreman Porter's cap to have a red band with 'Foreman Porter' in black letters. Cloth Jacket with 'W.J.S.' on collar.
Clothing to be provided with the stores.

* Wakefield Joint Station

RAIL 241/1 Great Western and Midland Railways Joint Committee
Minutes of Committee of Consultation

3 April 1873
Staff Employed at the Worcester Joint Station

Name	Occupation	Salary or Wages
F.W. Beauchamp	Station Master	£250 per annum
E. Bird	Parcels Clerk	£75 per annum
H.R. Jowling	" "	£60 per annum
G.A. Hobro	" "	£20 per annum
W. Remington	Inspector	34/- per week
A. Lipscomb	" "	34/- per week
F. Bundy	Foreman Porter	25/- per week
D. Davies	" "	25/- per week
W. Drew	Luggage Porter	21/- per week
H. Spiers	Ticket Examiner	18/- per week
W. Rostron	" "	20/- per week
H. Merrifield	Parcels Porter	21/- per week
E. Paine	" "	21/- per week
W. Goodman	" "	21/- per week
R. Hodgson	Shunter	21/- per week
S. Worman	"	21/- per week
W. Edkins	Cloak Room Porter	19/- per week
T. Finch	Horse Driver	17/- per week
R. Freeman	Lamp Porter	14/- per week
I. Wheeler	Cab Inspector	3/- per week
F. Richings	Porter	16/- per week
G. Lester	Porter	17/- per week
T. Tuffley	Porter	17/- per week
W. Huckfield	"	16/- per week
I. Neathway	"	17/- per week
W. Grubb	"	16/- per week
W. Parry	"	17/- per week
W. Lovell	"	17/- per week
G. Fowler	"	16/- per week
T. Workman	"	16/- per week
A. Page	"	16/- per week
C. Newman	Pointsman	20/- per week
C. Cole	"	22/- per week
Mrs Dale	Ladies Attendant	10/- per week
Mrs Spencer	Office Cleaner	10/- per week

In addition to the above mentioned Staff there are, one Relief Pointsman, eight Pointsmen and one Gatekeeper entered on the Joint Pay Bill, but as the question as to whether the Signalmen at the posts adjacent to the Joint Station shall be or shall not be looked upon as Joint Servants, is an outstanding one. The Midland Company have neither considered them as members of the Joint Staff nor filled up any vacancies which have, from time to time occurred.

The List to be without prejudice to either Company.

RAIL 309/1 Huddersfield Joint Station Committee
Minutes of Meetings

10 August 1874
Staff Changes and Advances of Salary
Reported as follows, viz:
London and North Western Railway and Lancashire and Yorkshire Joint Railways
Staff Changes Huddersfield Joint Station submitted 10 Aug. 1874 and submitted for approval.

Name	Present Duties and Station in the case of Guards or Breaksmen [sic] points of duty	Proposed Duties and Station in the case of Guards or Breaksmen points of duty	Present Salary or Wages	Proposed increase	Proposed Salary or Wages	Reason for Recommendation
Senior, James	Cloak Room Clerk	Cloak Room Clerk	20/-		20/-	To L. & NW Co.
Arksey, Thomas	New Appt.					vice Senior
Hill, Richard	Parcel deliverer		21/-			Dismissed for misconduct
Netherwood, W.H.	Porter	Parcel deliverer	17/6	3/6	21/-	vice Hill
Finney, William	Parcel deliverer		21/-			Dismissed for misconduct
Milnes, George	Porter	Parcel deliverer	17/6	3/6	21/-	vice Finney at 21/-
Stanley, B.	Night Watchman		20/-			Resigned
Turner, John	Signalman Middle Box		22/-			To L. & NW Co.
Pogson, Isaac	Porter	Signalman Middle Box	17/6	4/6	22/-	vice Turner at 22/-
Lees, William	New Appt.	Porter			17/6	vice Pogson at 17/6
Kendal, W.	Porter		17/6			Dismissed for insubordination
Benbow	New Appt.	Porter			17/6	vice Kendal at 17/6
Shaw, Joseph	Parcel Boy		10/-			Resigned
Tinsley, Alfred	New Appt.	Parcel Boy			10/-	vice Shaw at 10/-
Moore, Mary J.		Attendant Ladies Waiting Room			12/6	Additional. Joint Minute 415 of 13/4/74
Taylor, Mrs		Attendant Ladies Waiting Room			12/6	Additional. Joint Minute 415 of 13/4/74
Curthays	Signalman Bottom Box	24/-			Resigned	
Richardsons	Porter	Signalman Bottom Box	17/6	6/6	24/-	vice Curthays at 24/-
Gardner, Robt.	New Appt.	Porter			17/6	vice Richardson at 17/6
Pearson, T.	Signalman Middle Box		24/-			Resigned
Wilson, James	Porter	Signalman Middle Box	17/6		24/-	vice Pearson
Walker, James	New Appt.	Porter			17/6	vice Wilson at 17/6
Shaw, George	Signalman Bottom Box		24/-			Dismissed for refusing to remove to an inferior post
Wood, William	Do L. & NW Co'y*	Signalman Bottom Box	22/-	2/-	24/-	vice Shaw at 24/-
Glendinning, L.	New Appt.	Slip Boy			9/-	Additional. Joint Minute 416 of 13/4/74
Stevenson, W.	Porter		17/6			To L. & NW Co.
Hey, J.W.	New Appt.	Porter			17/6	vice Stevenson at 17/6
etc.						

* London and North Western Railway Company

	ORDER NO.	DATE 10th May 1875.					268

Huddersfield Joint Station
Staff changes recommended by Mr Phillipps for
the four Months ending 30th April 1875, and
submitted for approval. —

Name	Present duties and station in the case of Guards or Breakmen Points of duty	Proposed duties and stations in the case of Guards or Breakmen points of duty	Present Salary or Wages	Proposed increase	Proposed Salary or Wage	Reason for Recommendation	Remarks
Hirst William	Inspector		30/-	—	—	Resigned	
Carr J. E.	Do	same	27/6	2/6	30/-	vice Hirst at 30/-	
Woodhead L	Foreman	Inspector	23/-	4/6	27/6	" Carr at 27/6	
Richardson S.	Signalman	Foreman	24/-	—	23/-	" Woodhead at 23/-	at own desire
Barrand Geo.	Ground Do	Signalman	21/-	3/-	24/-	" Richardson	
Nelson C.	Goods Dept	Ground Pointsman	21/-	—	21/-	" Barrand	
Carr J. E.	Inspector		30/-	—	—	To Ltn & Coy	
Woodhead L	Do	same	27/6	2/6	30/-	Vice Carr	
Sutcliffe G.	Signalman	Inspector	25/-	2/6	27/6	" Woodhead	
Crowther S.	Do Ltn & Cy	Signalman	24/-	1/-	25/-	" Sutcliffe at 25/-	
Turner John	Signalman	Inspector in Goods yard.	25/-	5/-	30/-	additional	
Samuels A.	Do Ltn & Cy	Signalman	22/-	3/-	25/-	Vice Turner at 25/-	
Marsden S.	Signalman	Booking Office	25/-	—	21/-	additional	
Benbow W.	Porter	Do Do Breakman	17/6	3/6	21/-	Do	
Dye James	Lty Cy	Porter	—	—	17/6	Vice Benbow at 17/6	
Wood William	Signalman		24/-	—	—	To Ltn & Coy.	
Firth Harry	Ltn & Coy	Signalman	—	—	24/-	Vice Wood at 24/-	
Jones A. L	Porter		17/6	—	—	To Ltn & Cy.	
Tinker J. W.	Ltn & Cy	Porter.	17/6	—	17/6	Vice Jones at 17/6	
Holding H.	Porter.		17/6	—	—	To Ltn & Cy.	

Huddersfield joint Station Committee. Staff changes recommended by Mr Phillipps 10 May 1875. (TNA, RAIL 309/1)

111

RAIL 499/1   Monmouthshire Railways and Canal and Great Western Railway
Companies Consultation Committee
Minutes of Meetings

24 July 1878
It was agreed to allow porter Maynes half pay amounting to £2–4–1 for the time he was incapacitated from following his work.

RAIL 626/44   Somerset and Dorset Joint Line Committee
Staff Registers [arranged by station]

Evercreech New
W.J. Hayward porter 22 Mar. 1879 aged 22 wage 15/-

17/3/80   wage   16/-

Appointed B'man at Bath   18 July 1890
Repremanded for negligence and causing delay of goods traffic   30/8/81

Bath
W.J. Hayward breaksman [*sic*] (from Evercreech New)
17 Mar. 1879 aged 22

18/7/90   wage   19/-
18/7/91   20/-
18/7/92   21/-

Reprimanded for being late to duty and causing delay to Down Mail   3/12/99

Reprimanded for letting Goods Train run down at Radstock before receiving a proper signal   11/3/92

Goods Guard from 3 1/12/00

RAIL 521/15   North and South Western Junction Joint Committee
Minutes of Meetings

18 February 1885
Staff changes as under were approved

T.E. Bates	Train Register Boy	Acton Wells	8/-	Resigned
D.T. Wright	" " "	New Appointment	8/-	see Bates
A. Binnington	" " "	Acton	8/-	Resigned
H. Woodward	" " "	New Appointment	8/-	see Binnington
H. Grant	Signalman	Old Oak	23/-	Transferred to N.L. Line
A. Mundy	Collector	Acton	14/- to 15/-	

NORTH AND SOUTH WESTERN JUNCTION RAILWAY

JOINT COMMITTEE.

I, _William Thomas South_

being this _____ day of _____ 18____

engaged as _Booking Clerk_

in the service of the North and South Western Junction Railway Joint Committee, do hereby bind myself to observe and obey the Rules and Regulations of the Joint Committee, a copy of which I have received and which I have read (or heard read), and understand, and all other Rules, Regulations, and Instructions which may from time to time be issued for the better government of the North and South Western Junction Railway, so long as I continue in the service of the Joint Committee.

It is understood that one of the terms on which I am engaged is, that either party may determine the engagement, on any day in the year, by giving to the other one calendar month's notice in writing. If the Joint Committee determine the engagement, I am to be paid a proportionate part of my salary down to the time of the expiry of such notice. And a notice in writing, signed by the Secretary of the Joint Committee, is to be considered as sufficient on their part.

Dated this _23rd_ day of _September_ 18 _96_

William Thomas South

The foregoing Memorandum of Agreement, as to terms of engagement, dated this _Twenty third_ day of _September_ 189 _6_ was signed by

(write name at full length) _William Thomas South_

of the _Traffic_ Department, _Kew Bridge_ Station, in my presence.

Name _Alexander Joseph Palmer_

Occupation and Address } _Station Master_ _Kew Bridge_

North and South Western Junction Railway Joint Committee. The appointment of William Thomas South as a booking clerk, 23 September 1896. (TNA, RAIL 521/19)

RAIL521/15   North and South Western Junction Joint Committee
Minutes of Meetings

17 June 1885
Staff changes as under were approved

A. Stone	Junior Collector	South Acton	12/6 per week to 15/- as per scale from 26–4–85
E. Gibson	Porter	South Acton	18/- dismissed
W. Steel	Junior Collector to be	Kew Bridge Porter at South Acton	15/- to 17/6
W. Mills	Signalman to be Collector	Acton Wells Junction at Kew as from 20–4–85	24/- to 26/-
H. Grant	Signalman	N.L. Line to Acton Wells	24/- Junction
R. Perks	Relief Signalman	Transferred to N.L. Line	26/-
G.I. Inglis	Signalman	Hammersmith to be Relief	24/- to 26/- Signalman
R. Lilley	Signalman	Old Oak Junction to	24/- Hammersmith Junction
R. Crowe	Signalman	N.L. Line to Old Oak Junction	24/-

RAIL 462/2   Manchester, Sheffield and Lincolnshire and Midland Joint Lines Committee
Minutes of Meetings

3 May 1892
The appointment of four additional signalmen and the re-arrangement of the hours of duty recommended in minute No. 562 of the officers' meeting and involving an increased annual expenditure of £258–12–0 was approved.

6 April 1897
It was reported that Mr W.H. Hodges had retired from the position of Accountant to the Midland Co. and it was resolved that Mr J.J. Doughty be and he is hereby appointed Joint Auditor of the Committee in place of Mr Hodges resigned.

3 October 1899
On the recommendation of the General Manager it was agreed that the salary of Mr Hawkins, Station Master at Marple, be increased from £130 to £140 per annum, the same to date from the 1st instant.

RAIL 736/26   West Riding Railway Joint Committee
Accountant's Records
Abstract of wages [half year ending 30 June 1894]

Carcroft
example

Name   Askew W.
Grade   Clerk in Charge
Jan. 13   £2–10–0
Jan. 27   £2–10–0

Midland Railway Company, Barnsley Court House Joint station staff, 1899. Back row, left to right: George Hill (out porter), Frank Robinson (porter), John Bailey (porter), Harry Douglas (signalman), unknown. Second row: Jack Mallinder (parcel clerk), Harry Legge (signalman), Mr Bickerton (shunter, Midland), Mr Terry (porter, Midland), unknown (porter), Mr Gawkrodger (signalman, Midland), W. Bradshaw (porter), -?- (relief clerk, Midland). Third row: Percy Carter (foreman, Great Central), F.W. Freeman (chief booking clerk), J. Lane (relief clerk, Midland), J. Spencer (station master), G.W. Brinsley (booking clerk), C.J. Cooper (foreman, Midland), C. Eastwood (parcel clerk). Front row: Jack Maxwell (booking clerk), Arthur Douglas (lavatory attendant), Charlie Cragoe (parcel clerk), Mr Payne (guard, Midland). (TNA, RAIL 491/835)

Feb. 10	£2–10–0
Feb. 24	£2–10–0
Mar. 10	£2–10–0
Mar. 24	£2–10–0
Apr. 7	£2–10–0
Apr. 21	£2–10–0
May 5	£2–10–0
May 19	£2–10–0
June 2	£2–10–0
June 16	£2–10–0
June 30	£2–10–0
	£32–10–0

RAIL 465/11   Manchester South Junction and Altrincham Railway Company Joint Committee

Extract from the Minutes of the Meeting of the M.S.J. and A. Board held on 2 Dec. 1904.

Staff changes and advances on the M.S.J. & A. Rly approved by Minute No. 31 of the Joint Officers' Conference held at Euston on 17 Nov. 1904 were adopted as follows (Minute 8091):

Name	Grade	Station	Salary or Wage present	proposed	Date of Change 1904	Increase per Annum £ s d	Decrease per Annum £ s d	Remarks
Royle, A.	Shunter & Goods Guard	Oxford Rd.	25s/-		27 Aug.		65 0 0	Post dispensed with (experimentally)
Ure, A.	Lavatory Attendant	"	20/-		4 Sept.		52 0 0	"
Holcroft, T.	Lampman		21/-		4 "		54 12 0	"
Hannett, C.H.	Relief Signalman		30/-		27 Aug.		78 0 0	"
Neill, W.	Signalman	Charles St	23/-		4 Sept.		59 16 0	Left Service
Holt, E.	"		23/-	23/-	4 "			From Knott Mill vice Neill
Smith, W.J.	Signal lighter	Oxford Rd	23/-	23/-	2 "			Post vice Holt dispensed with
Webster, A.	Porter	Knott Mill	18/-		18 "		46 16 0	Post from Permanent Way Dept for convenience
Smith, Mrs	Charwoman	Old Strafford	8/-		24 "		20 16 0	Post dispensed with (experimentally)
Carney, P.	Porter	Sale	19/-		27 Aug.		49 8 0	"
Wall, Mrs	Charwoman		10/-		24 Sept.		26 0 0	"
Broady, L.H.	Signalman	Brooklands No 1	23/-		15 "		59 16 0	"
Brown, J.A.	"		23/-		20 "		59 16 0	"
Royle, Mrs	Charwoman	"	6/-		24 "		15 12 0	"
Greaves, J.	Porter	"	18/-		18 "		46 16 0	"
Wareham, Mrs	Charwoman	Timperley	6/-		24 "		15 12 0	"
Yates, G.	Porter	Altrincham	18/-		28 Aug.		46 16 0	"
Massey, D.	"	"	18/-		4 Sept.			Left Service
Leigh, A.	"	"	23/-	19/-	4 "	2 12 5	59 16 0	Reduced from Porter Guard to Porter vice Massey. Post vice Leigh dispensed with
Whittle, J.T.	Signal lighter	"	23/-	23/-	2 "			Post from Permanent Way Dept for convenience
Kyte, Mrs	Charwoman	London Rd.	5/-		24 "		13 0 0	Post dispensed with (experimentally)
Royle, E.	Signalman	Charles St.	23/-	23/-	22 "		59 16 0	Left Service
Drinkwater, G.	"	"	23/-	23/-	22 "			From Knott Mill vice Royal. Post vice Drinkwater dispensed with

etc.

LMA: Acc. 12971W&B/1/10   Whitechapel and Bow Railway Company Joint Committee
Minute Book No. 1

10 February 1903
Accidents   That the following accidents have occurred, viz:
                 Staff
Frederick Vickers, a ganger in the Permanent Way Staff, while attending to the points at Mile End Station on 10 January crushed the top of his left hand forefinger owing to the signalman at the same moment pulling the points over. He was attended at London Hospital and has not yet resumed duty, but is receiving half pay.

Porter Allen, while closing carriage doors at 1:26 p.m. up Ealing train at Stepney Green on 26 January twisted his wrist in turning the door handle. He was attended to at Charing Cross Hospital and resumed duty on 29 January.

RAIL 686/4   Tebay Joint Station Committee
Minutes of Meetings

6 October 1908
It was reported that in consequence of the delicate health of Mrs Scott, wife of the Tebay Station Master, and her Doctor having certified that it was necessary for her to have a change to the South, an exchange of posts between Mr Scott and Mr W. A. Mellor, the Station Master at Bicester has been carried out as from June 1st. The salary of Mr Mellor is £130, as against Mr Scott at £140 per annum.

LMA: Acc. 1297/MGCJ/1/1   Metropolitan and Great Central Joint Committee
Minute Book No. 1

13 March 1913
Joint Staff 60 years of age and over.
Reports were submitted from the Engineers upon men over 60 years of age, and the proposal to retire only plate-layer F. Smith, Aylesbury, and H. Brandon, Waddesdon Manor, at the present time, was agreed to, a retirement grant of three months wages (about £13) being voted to Brandon, and 5s pr week to Smith, during the Directors' pleasure, from January 1st, 1913 until he reaches 70 years of age, to be apportioned as under.
         Metropolitan Company   12 yrs 7 months
         Joint Committee   6 yrs 9 months

RAIL 356/10   Leeds New Station Joint Committee
Minutes of Meetings

12 October 1914
Married men leaving wife or wife and children.
The Army allowance to be supplemented by the Railway Company by 7/- per week for the wife and 1/- per week for each child under 16 years of age (maximum 10). This allowance may, however, be increased so that the minimum total allowance will not be less than 4/5ths of the

Midland Railway Company. Members of the Estate Agents Office who served in the First World War. (TNA, RAIL 491/1065)

man's standard railway wage. If on the other hand the supplemental allowance would bring his aggregate allowance from Army and Railway sources to more than the man's standard wage, then the supplemental allowance would be reduced so that the aggregate allowance would not exceed the amount of the man's standard wage.

Unmarried men or widowers without children leaving parents or other relatives dependent upon them.
An allowance to be paid equal to the sum normally paid by the man to the dependents provided the sum does not in any case exceed 4/5ths of the man's standard wage. If the man lived with the dependents and paid them, say 18/- per week, an amount of 7/- per week would be deducted in the calculations on account of food supplied, and the nett allowance to the dependents would be considered as being 11/- per week in such a case.

N.E.R.* Battalion of the Northumberland Fusiliers

Name	Grade
W.G. Batterby	Parcels Clerk
A. Fawcett	Platform Porter
T.J. Harker	Parcels Porter
L.A. Wright	Ticket Collector
J. Haullah	Platform Porter
H. Ibbotson	"
W. Eastwood	"
J. Swidenbank	"

*   North Eastern Railway

Leeds Joint station staff (undated). (NRM, 233/87)

Name	Grade	
H. Hardwick	Summer Porter	
F. Coote	"	
W. W. Fletcher	Parcels Porter	
H. Ellis	Luggage Room Porter	

Other Regiments

Name	Grade	
H. Hesslewood	Parcels Clerk	Territorial
T. Chapman	"	Lord Kitchener's Army
E. Pearson	"	"
T.W. Saunders	Clerk S.M.O.	Territorial
H. Hodgson	Parcels Porter	Lord Kitchener's Army
E. Stimpson	Ticket Collector	"
C. Boulton	Platform Porter	"
A. Owen	Ticket Collector	"
H. Darley	Lad Luggage Room Porter	"
J. Massey	Summer Porter	"

The positions for these men are being kept open for their return; temporary appointments have been, or are being made.

Badge Porters

Assisted on Station platform as shown below and in consequence were not able to use their carts

Date	Name	Number of days assisting on platforms	Amount deducted from cart rent s d
October	J.F. Brown	18	3 0
	W. Grimes	12	2 0
	T. Hardcastle	3	6
Easter	J.F. Brown	4	8
	H. Butterfield	6	1 0
	E. Durham	2	4
	J. Grimes	4	8
W.E. April 22	H. Butterfield	2	4
Whitsuntide	J.F. Brown	5	10
	J.T. Brown	5	10
	H. Butterfield	5	10
	J. Grimes	4	8
	E. Durham	2	4
	T. Hardcastle	5	10
August Bank Holiday	J.F. Brown	6	1 0
	J.T. Brown	2	4
	E. Durham	2	4
	J. Grimes	17	2 10
	T. Hardcastle	2	4
	Away ill and in consequence did not pay cart rent		
October 1913 and Aug[t] & Septr 1914	H. Butterfield	6	1 0

RAIL 110/160   Cheshire Lines Committee
Staff Irregularities

G. Bardsley
Grade	Shunter
Station Employed at	Heaton Mersey
Date	11 Feb. 1916
Nature of Irregularity	M.R. Wagons 40602 and 50784 off road and slightly damaged owing to failure to see No. 8 siding fouled.

A.V. Blyde
Grade	Shunter
Station Employed at	Brunswick
Date	19–3–26
Nature of Irregularity	Carelessness during shunting resulting in damage to stock. Suspended 2 days. Decision repealed as Blyde appealed and came before manager.

RAIL 110/20   Cheshire Lines Committee
Minutes of Meetings

3 July 1917
No. 10999
On the recommendation of the sub-committee a retiring allowance of £30 per annum was granted to Chief Delivery Clerk J.H. Cooke, Wellington Road Goods Station, Stockport.

7 May 1918
No. 11115
The manager reported that under the authority contained in Minute No. 10383, a gratuity of £19–19–0 had been made to J. Wallis, Foreman Shunter, Halewood, who had retired at the age of 71 after 41 years service.

RAIL 224/16   Great Central and Midland Railways Joint Committee
Minutes of Meetings

21 October 1931
Settlement of Compensation Claims for Personal injury.

Goods Porter G.C.S. Gaukrose, Widness.
Injured on 8th June 1931. Left instep bruised owing to a wagon door dropping on to it. Absent from the 9th to 15th June, and paid compensation for three days at the rate of 23s–11d per week. Total 12s–0d

Goods Porter L.D. Booth, Bredbury.
Injured on 27th July 1931. In the course of sheeting a railway wagon Booth stepped on a nail which was protruding from a piece of packing lying on the bottom of the wagon with the result the nail penetrated through his boot sole and pierced his foot. The man was off duty from 28th July to 1st August and was paid compensation at the rate of 23s–11d per week to a total of 8s.

CHAPTER 7

MISCELLANEOUS RECORDS OF STAFF AND OTHERS

In addition to the records already described in this book staff have been found recorded by name in all manner of miscellaneous records, the following being a list of examples of those given in this chapter:

Fines to staff
Miscellaneous staff details
Receipts for allowances
Notices and Instructions
Superannuation records
National Insurance records
Establishment records
Applications and Examinations
Time Books
Rent Rolls
Petitions
Reports on Staff Matters
Workmens' Compensation records
Railway Benevolent Institution gratuities and annuities
Retired Railway Officers' Society
Criminal records

RAIL 384/291 London and Birmingham Railway Company
Company Establishment; London Office

The following are the persons at present employed in the Office arranged in the order of seniority.

Clerks

Mr	Allen	14 Jan. 1831	Minute of Committee	£50 per ann.
	Pierson	21 Apr. 1832	Provisional	£2 weekly
	Saville	12 Sept. "	"	£1 "
	Brooke	5 Oct. "	"	£3 "
	Aitcheson	15 Jan. 1834	Minute of Committee	£150 per ann.
	Hemberrow	25 Apr. "	" Provisional	£120 "

Messengers

John Brown	21 Apr. 1832		£1.1 weekly
W. Self	18 Sept. 1832		£1 "

Their attendance and duties are as follows:

Mr Allen	Copies the Minutes fair in the Minute Books and makes the copies for Birmingham and Liverpool.
	Copies from the Secretary's rough statements the Weekly Call returns; Statements of Cash and Exchequer Bills; and detached Statement of Payments and Balance Sheet of the London Committee.
	Makes the Copies for Birmingham & Liverpool.
	Enters Letters in the Letter Book and makes fair copies from the rough drafts of the Secretary for him to sign.
Mr Pierson	Copies the Reports of the Engineers and Solicitors into the Report Books, and the letters referring thereto.
	Makes Copies of them when required for Birmingham and Liverpool.
	Copies the Contracts with Land Owners into the Land Contract Book.
	Copies the letters from the Secretary of the Birmingham Committee and from Public Bodies into the letter books.
	Prepares draft abstracts of Minutes, Reports and Letters from the Books in which they are entered for the Secretary to revise previously to their being entered fair.
	Fills up checks [*sic*] on the Bankers.
Mr Brooke	Enters in the Numerical sealed Register of the 25,000 Shares of the Company, the references to the entries of the names of new Proprietors.
	Makes the entries in the Rough Transfer Book 2, and fair Transfer Book 3.
	Makes out the Transfer Certificates for the Secretary to sign and keeps the Counterparts.
	Makes out the half yearly Registers 4, 5 and 6, and enters in 4 and 5 the particulars of all sums received for Calls, and of all changes made in the Proprietorship of shares in the course of each half year.
	Makes the entries in the Balance Book of Calls from the Numerical Call Book.
	Makes a copy of the Register No. 4 for the Non-resident Directors.
	Makes out an Alphabetical List of Proprietors at the date of the General half yearly meeting for the Birmingham Office.
	Assisted by Mr Saville, makes up and addresses the circulars to Proprietors for Calls and the Reports of General Meetings.

Mr Saville	Enters the particulars of sums received for calls into the Day Books from the returns of the respective Bankers.
	Makes copies of the weekly returns of calls furnished by the Liverpool and London Bankers to be sent to the Birmingham Office.
	Enters in the Call Book 7, the sums received on each share from the Register 4.
	Writes the endorsement of Transfers for the Secretary to sign on the Sealed Certificates.
	Makes rough Copies of letters which the Secretary writes after the regular Office hours.
	Reads off with Mr Brooke all entries which are made in the Register and checks them with him.
	Assists Mr Brooke in the issue of Circulars.
Mr Pierson	reads off with Mr Allen the documents which he copies.
Mr Aitcheson	keeps the Books under Head 4, and superintends the expenditure for works and has charge of all Plans.
Mr Hemberrow	makes out Plans for the Land Agents and Solicitors.

I have confined myself in the foregoing detail to the habitual duties of the Clerks, but I should add that it not infrequently occurs when copies of documents are suddenly called for that I am obliged to avail myself of their services without reference to the ordinary arrangement. On the proposed limited establishment this deviation from the general division of duties must still occasionally occur.

R. Creed

RAIL 667/443   Stockton and Darlington Railway Company
Shildon Works, Notices to Staff

Christmas Holidays

These works will be closed from Saturday night the 23rd of Dec. 1843 until Tuesday morning the 2nd of Jan. 1844.

Shildon Works 21/12/43

To leave at the end of this month:	Robert Pearson
To leave at the end of next month:	James Oliver

Shildon Works 4 Mo 26th/44

Men to leave at the end of this month:	Cornelius Toward
	Joseph Mitchell
	William Winthorpe
	Ralph Smurthwaite
	Thomas Lamb
	John Waite

8 Mo. 1 1844

To leave at the end of this month:	93 Thomas Gardiner
	149 Thomas Longstaff
	202 William Carling

Shildon Works 11th Mo. 1st 1844

Rules and Regulations,

TO BE-OBSERVED BY

THE WORKMEN,

IN THE EMPLOY OF THE

STOCKTON AND DARLINGTON RAILWAY COMPANY,

AT

NEW SHILDON.

I.   The Meal Times allowed, are from 8 to half-past 8 o'Clock in the Morning, for Breakfast; and from 12 to 1, for Dinner, at all times of the year.

II.   Overtime to be reckoned at the rate of 8 hours for a Day; but no Overtime to be entered till a whole Day of regular time has been worked.

III.   Every Workman to put on his Time-board with his Time, the name of the article or articles he has been working at during the Day, and what Engine or other Machinery they are for.

IV.   Every Workman who is provided with a Drawer, for his Tools, with Lock and Key, the Drawer and his Key to be numbered, and all his Tools to be marked with the same Number, and the Letters S D R W C; the Key to be left in the Office every night when the man has left work.

V.   Any Workman who is longer than a quarter of an hour after the Bell is rung, will lose a quarter Day.

VI.   Any Workman who does not call for his Time-board in the Morning, and return it to the Office in the Evening, or when done work, to be fined SIXPENCE.

VII.   Any Workman leaving his work without giving notice to the Clerk or to the Foreman, to be fined ONE SHILLING.

VIII.   Any Workman swearing, or using abusive language to a Shopmate, to be fined ONE SHILLING.

IX.   Should any one or more send for Beer, Ale, or Spirits, into the Works, (without leave) to be fined ONE SHILLING.

X.   Any Workman introducing a Stranger, or any person into the Works, (without leave) to be fined ONE SHILLING.

XI.   Any Workman giving in more time than he has wrought, to have double the time taken off that he has overcharged.

XII.   The Company's Time Piece at the Shops, to be the guide for the Workmen's time.

XIII.   Any Workman taking Tools from a Lathe or other piece of Machinery, to be fined SIXPENCE.

XIV.   Any Workman not returning Taps or Dies, or any general Tool, to the person who has the charge of them, to be fined SIXPENCE.

XV.   Should any Workman leave his Work for the purpose of Drinking, in working hours, he will be considered as having forfeited his situation.

August 17th, 1833.

Coates and Farmer, Printers, Darlington.

Stockton and Darlington Railway Company. Rules and Regulations for the workmen at New Shildon, 17 August 1833. (TNA, RAIL 667/633)

RAIL 772/60 York, Newcastle and Berwick Railway Company
Inspector's Time Book

9 Oct. 1847

Gatemen	Occupation	Time Week	Rate Week	£ s d
John Davidge	Belford Gate	2	14	1–8–0
Edward Pringle	Elwick Gate	"	"	"
William Middlmis	"	"	"	"
John Patterson	Lomoor Gate	"	"	"
William Fleming	"	"	"	"
Andrew Cockburn	Beal Gate	"	"	"
Bartholomew Watson	Windmill Hill Gate	"	"	"
Elijah Pearson	" "	"	"	"
William Cranson	Scramerston Gate	"	10	1–0–0
Charles Whillis	Spittell Gate	2	14	1–8–0
				13–12–0
Inspector				
William Teasdale		2	27	2–14–0

RAIL 532/26 North Staffordshire Railway Company
Reports to the Directors

Stoke
February 28, 1848

The opening of the Line

It is proposed to run 3 Passenger Trains and one Goods Train daily, each way for the first month. I have consulted the Engineers on this matter and they consider this as much as they shall he able to allow us to do at the commencement as they will require as much time as possible, between trains, for the repairs of the line.

All the necessary preliminaries for the working and settlement of the through Traffic to London, Birmingham, Liverpool, Manchester, &c, have been arranged with the Railway Clearing House Authorities.

I have received a communication from Captain Huish, asking this Company to join the London and North Western Company in erecting a small Goods Depot at Norton Bridge.

After carefully considering this proposition I would strongly recommend the Directors to agree to it as we shall find it necessary for supplying Eccleshall, and the district west of the Grand Junction line with Goods from the Potteries.

I am, Gentlemen
Your obedient Servant
S.P. Bidder

List of Staff required for Norton Bridge Branch

Names	Vocation	Weekly Pay £ s d	Annual Wages £ s d
Stoke Station			
Charles H. Barlee	Booking Clerk		100 – "
James Wilson	Parcel Clerk	18	46 – 16
William Woolgar	Station Inspector		70 "
George Wood	Assistant Clerk	12	31 – 4

Names	Vocation	Weekly Pay £ s d	Annual Wages £ s d
John Shufflebotham	Chief Guard	1 – 8	72 – 16
William Bell	Chief Guard	1 – 8	72 – 16
Edward Wright	Second Guard	1 – 4	62 – 8
James West	Second Guard	1 – 4	62 – 8
Thos. McNeil	Head Porter	1 "	52 "
Thomas Moss	Office Porter	18	46 – 16
Thomas Myers	Porter	16	41 – 12
Joseph Tittensor	Porter	16	41 – 12
William Johnson	Porter	16	41 – 12
Thomas Peake	Porter	16	41 – 12
Wm Edwards	Lampman	1 – 4	62 – 8
George Evans*	Pointman	1 – 1	54 – 12
Jonathan Tisley	Policeman	1 "	52 "
Trentham Station			
James Macbeth	Station Clerk	1 – 1	54 – 12
George Edge	Porter	16	41 – 12
Stone Station			
Andrew Anderson	Station Clerk		70 "
Edward Bean	Station Inspector	1 – 5	65 "
James Wardle	Porter	16	41 – 12
George Bates	Porter	16	41 – 12
Norton Bridge Station			
George Evans	Pointman	1 – 1	54 – 12
Gatemen at Level Crossing			
William Shropshire		12	31 – 4
William Dicks		12	31 – 4
Locomotive Department			
Robert Angus	Foreman		150 "
W. Worthington	Engine Driver	2 – 2	109 – 4
G. Quick	"	2 – 2	109 – 4
Alex^r Ballantine	"	2 – 2	109 – 4
Thos. Morgan	"	2 – 2	109 – 4
Thos. Jackson	Fireman	1 – 2	57 – 4
Jos. Fell	"	1 – 2	57 – 4
James Rigby	"	1 – 2	57 – 4
John Monk	"	1 – 2	57 – 4
George Gill	Smith	1 – 12	83 – 4
James Finnie	Fitter	1 – 12	83 – 4
[blank] Sandham	Striker	16	41 – 12
Carriage Department			
William Scales	Foreman		150 "
General Office			
James Hardman	Chief Clerk		130 "
George Green	Junr Clerk	5 "	13
[blank]	Boy		
Manager's Office			
Charles Cooper	[blank]		200
			2900 12

* This name has been crossed through and there follows: 'at Norton Bridge'

Schedule of Prices for clothing the Company's Servants from Messrs Hebbert & Co. of Pall Mall

Inspector	{	Dress Coat with Silver embroided Collar	61/-
		Trowsers	22/10
		Great Coat	68/-
Upper Guards	{	Frock Coat with Silver embroided Collar	61/-
		Trowsers	22/10
		Great Coat – strapped	82/7
Under Guards	{	Frock Coat with Worsted embroided Collar	48/9
		Trowsers	22/10
		Great Coats	82/7
Police	{	Dress Coat with embroided Collar	25/8
		Great Coat with embr^d Collar	31/6
		Capes	5/10
Porters	{	Jackets with embroided Collars	13/4
		Waistcoat	10/7
		Trowsers	7/-
		Wellington Boots	10/6
		Angle Boots	6/9

RAIL 414/527   London, Brighton and South Coast Railway Company
Traffic Manager's Notices to Station Staff

Traffic Manager's Office
Brighton
December 14th 1855

Sir,

I beg to advise you of the following circumstances, for the general information, and as a CAUTION to all persons employed in this department viz:

London Station
A. Wyatt, porter fined 1/- for coming late on duty and 2/- for being absent without leave.
S. Heughes and T. Freeman, porters, fined 2/- each for throwing a dustpan about the platform and destroying it.
J. Ridjer, carman, fined 2/6 for neglecting to collect some fish as directed by his superior officer.

West Croydon
W. Smith, porter, fined 2/6 for coming on duty late. Repeated offence.

H. Heath [Haywards Heath]
J. Muzzell, porter, fined 2/6 for neglecting to count sacks of wheat on receipt.

Brighton
John Head, goods guard, fined 5/- for causing damage to points by carelessly turning trucks on the wrong line.
W. Dunk, goods guard, fined 2/6 for carelessly causing a wagon to be thrown off the road, by giving the wrong signal.

Brighton station (undated). (TNA, RAIL 414/554)

Kingston Wharf
J. Holden Jun[r], porter, fined 1/- for carelessly losing a pass entrusted to his care.
J. Cook, clerk, fined 2/6 for neglecting to forward in due course, a letter containing Paybills.

Geo. Hawkins
Jno. F. Farmer

RAIL 667/798   North Eastern Railway Company
Petition from Platelayers for an Increase in Wages, 1868

To the Chairman & Directors of the North Eastern Railway Company (Darlington Section)
Gentlemen,
    We the undersigned platelayers (of the 1st Division) do hereby solicit you for an advance in wages of 2/- per week. The great prosperity there is in trade at present we think we are entitled to more than what we are receiving at present taking into consideration the amount of money that other working men are receiving round about this district. Will you please let it have your earliest attention.

James Sweeting	Robert Harrison	John Topam
W[m] Rymer	F Wilkinson	Thomas Johnson
John Smith	Matthew Herring	C. Ridgeway
William Robinson	Myers Graham	Edward Campbell
John Turner	George Carlton	Tom Overfield
T. Wilkinson	John Clarke	Thomas Stainsby

Cont.

Geo. Winter	William Newton	Thomas Gains
John Brown	James Mac	Wm Modd
James Tindale	Wm Grieveson	Wm Gales
John Skinner	Thomas Jones	E. Bowsfield
Mark Dawson	Robert Gales	John Bateman
John Wilkinson	John Hardy	F. Hanson
William Elcoat [?]	Wm Mason	Thomas Hall
Joseph Jennings	Robert Johnson	John Savage
John Swainson	John Seaton	Charles Gibson
H. Gildart	Wm Hardman	John Burnell
John Cartwright	George Stobart	James Fowler

RAIL 667/228   Stockton and Darlington Railway Company Superannuation Society Minute Book

Wednesday 17 Dec. 1873
It is reported that John Domville late Station Master at Appleby, who is now 63 years of age, has become infirm and incapable of attending to his duties and it is agreed that he shall receive Superannuation allowance in accordance with Rules.

RAIL 253/445   Great Western Railway Company Staff Duty Book, Stanton Station

Stanton Station
April 28, 84

William Taylor
Gateman Cricklade Crossing
To take charge of Cricklade Crossing and Gates.
The gates must be kept locked across the Turnpike Road by day when not required to be used. You must signal all trains during duty hours. You must not allow any vehicle or animal to cross the line at any time when a train is due. Rules 188 to 199 inclusive in Book of Rules and Regulations must be strictly observed. To signal all trains by flag by day and hand lamp at night. Gates must be closed across the line at night and locked until half an hour before the first train is due. Any special trains must be attended to as per notice. All the Rules in Book of Rules and Regulations and Gatemans duties and to all special instructions for working of the line.

On duty 7.15 a.m.
Off duty 8.40 p.m. if last train has past. Gate lamps must be kept as it is getting dark and you must keep a good look out for all approaching trains.

RAIL 527/1903   North Eastern Railway Company Application for Re-engagement

West Hartlepool
March 28th 1882

Mr E. Fletcher Esqr
Gateshead

My Dear Sir,
   It is with Regret that i now have to ask your sympathy on my behalf i hope and trust you will take into consideration the time i have been in the Service of the N.E. Ry. Co. and the Good

Continued. on p. 133

List of Cases assessed to Superannuation Fund on Salaries
where a deduction is made on account of expenses.

Station.	Name.		Grade.	Salary.	Deduc-tion.	Assess-ment.
				£.	£.	£.
	Sharpe,	C.	Sick Fund Inspector	130	10	120
ng's X. D.M.O.	Newell,	A.	Relief Clerk	145	60	85
	Knight,	G.S.	do.	145	※ 54	91
	Carroll,	A.C.	do.	145	※ 54	91
King's X. D.S.O.	Cullen,	R.H.	do.	170	60	110
	McElroy,	H.	do.	160	60	100
	Bingham,	R.O.	do.	160	※ 40	120
Hitchin Sack	Wigfall,	C.	Sack Auditor	65/-	15/-	50/-
Peterboro' D.M.O.	Porter,	R.	Relief Clerk	145	60	85
Grantham D.S.O.	Weston,	W.R.	do.	160	※ 56	104
Nottingham D.S.O.	Claydon,	H.	do.	170	60	110 / 85
	Peacock,	T.	do.	160	60	100
	Lee,	R.	do.	145	60	85
Nottingham D.M.O.	Simpson,	P.H.	do.	145	60	85
Retford Sack	Ainger,	J.	Sack Auditor	65/-	15/-	50/-
Wakefield	Ward,	H.	do.	65/-	15/-	50/-
Leeds D.S.O.	Hollin,	J.W.	Relief Clerk	160	※ 44	116
	Hurst,	J.G.	do.	145	※ 40	105
Leeds D.M.O.	Smithies,	H.	do.	145	60	85
	Harrabin,	G.E.	do.	145	60	85
Lynn Sack	Key,	F.E.	Sack Auditor	60/-	15/-	45/-
Boston D.S.O.	Halliday,	J.A.	Relief Clerk	160	60	100
	Rayner,	R.A.	do.	145	60	85
Boston D.M.O.	Cooke,	C.J.	do.	150	60	90

In these cases the full deduction is not in operation owing to default that if it were, the member's assessment would have been reduced, on promotion —

Great Northern Railway Company. Sack auditors and relief clerks' Superannuation Fund, 20 December 1906. (TNA, RAIL 783/331)

R251/6(1) 7 June

To the Committee of the London and Birmingham Railway Company.

The Humble Petition of John Brand lately a Porter of the London & Birmingham Railway Company at the Birmingham Station.—

Sheweth.

That having been in the Company's Employ at the Birmingham Station for 8 months as Porter and never having given any Cause for a Report or Complaint to be made against me for neglect of duty towards my Superiors in any Shape whatever during the time I was so employed until Monday Evening 13th May last, when unfortunately for me a Gentleman by the Liverpool Train put into my hands a Sixpence for putting his Luggage on a Car and before I could return him the Sixpence or explain to him that I was not allowed to accept of money, Mr. Reid my Inspector came and demanded what the Gentleman had put into my hand. I immediately held out my hand and showed him and wished to return the money to the Gentleman upon which Mr. Reid directed me to turn the Carriages off the Line and said he would Report me for taking it, which he accordingly did and the next Morning I was suspended, and on the Thursday following I went as usual to receive my Wages, when to my surprise I was

London and Birmingham Railway Company. Petition of John Brand, porter, who was dismissed for accepting a gratuity. (TNA, RAIL 1008/99)

ordered to bring in my Clothes and was told I was discharged, when other Porters before had only been fined for the like offence – and this being the only Charge against me during the above period I was in your Employ and having born a most excellent character at Birmingham I trust you will take my Case duly into consideration and take me into your Service again –

And your Petitioner will ever pray &c

John Brand

65 Middlesex Street
Somers Town

Carackter i have allways boarn i commencd under the N.E. Ry when i was nineteen years of age as a Spare fireman on December 28th 1870 was promoted to a Regular Fireman on May 2 1871 was Passed for a Driver on October 31st 1874 and have allways tried to do my best to further the interests of my Employers to the Best of my abilities but i Regret that unfortunetely on Feb 23 i absented my self from my duty for a short time giving those that was spitefull and ildesposed towards me the opertunity to Report me for which i am very Sorry that i ever gave them the opertunity i am Reported for Neglecting my Duty to agatate the men those Acusations i deny i have alway[s] Refrained from saying any thing when on duty for fear any ildisposed Person should Report me when my Fellow Workmen took up the Hours Movement i was chosen by a very large majority to be their Local Secretary and have only followed up the instructions that i have Received from my Fellow Workmen When i was off Duty But since i Received my Notice to leave the Co Service i have Severed my Connections with the Ry Servants Nine Hours Movement it was my intention if this had not occured to seek a situation under the Great Indian and Penninsular Railway Co in East India but with this Disgrace upon my Carackter i cannot Seek Employment to go into a Foreign Land if you will please to Reinstate me in my Former Position i will allways try to do my Duty towards my Employers to the Best of my abilities to Redeam the good Carackter i have now Lost Trusting i may be Reinstated in my Former Position i Remain your obediant Servant

Robert Royal
Engine Driver
32 James St
West Hartlepool

Mr E. Fletcher Esq
Gateshead

RAILWAY BENEVOLENT INSTITUTION FORMED MAY 1858

In 1880 the Special Benevolent Fund was raised to relieve cases of distress among officers and servants whether members of the Institution or not, and widows and orphans of those killed in the performance of their duties.

In 1875 an orphanage for the children of railway servants was opened at Derby, and in 1947 a home in Dorking, Surrey, was opened for aged railwaymen and their wives, and widows. The annual reports are available from 1881 to 1959 in RAIL 1166; details of annuities awarded to servants and widows of servants, dating from 1888, are found in piece numbers 81 to 86.

RAIL 1166/81   Railway Benevolent Institution
Annuity to Officers' Widows, Servants, and Servants' Widows [indexed]

May 1888
John Pinkerton
Application on behalf of John Pinkerton, aged 56, seventeen years service of Glasgow and South Western Railway as Foreman Boilermaker who joined the Institution February 1885, when over 45 years of age and is permanently incapacitated from following employment. Has £200, and receives 10s–6d per week from Glasgow and South Western Friendly Society.

Resolved – That a gratuity of £10 be granted to Mr Pinkerton.

May 1888
Mr James Edward Mumford
Application of Mr James Edward Mumford of Truro, aged 56 years, Porter and Station Master, Cornwall, Midland, and Midland and Great Western (Ireland) Railways, who joined the Institution in May 1861 and retired in December 1887, owing to failing eyesight and general debility. Applicant has one son aged 26 years and a cripple and asks a gratuity of £60 in lieu of becoming a candidate for an annuity as he wishes to open a small shop, and has only his savings amounting to £70.

Resolved – That a gratuity of £60 in full discharge of all claims be allowed to Mr Mumford.

Mar 1892
Mrs Kate Kiernan
Application of Mrs Kate Kiernan, aged 43 years, widow of lampman Peter Kiernan (sixteen years service) London and North Eastern Railway, Euston who joined the Institution in February 1887, and died in February 1892 leaving her with six children aged 15, 12, 10, 8, 5, and 2 years and only £10 from Provident Fund.

Resolved – That £5 be granted for the assistance of Mrs Kieman that she be admitted an application for an annuity.

Apr 1892
Mrs Mary Ann Whiting
Application of Mrs Mary Ann Whiting, aged 60 years, widow of Mr J.H.J. Whiting, for thirty one years Porter, Guard and Signalman South Eastern Railway, Deptford, who joined the Institution in February 1882 and died in February 1892, leaving her destitute.

Resolved – That £5 gratuity be paid to Mrs Whiting, and that she be admitted a candidate for an annuity.

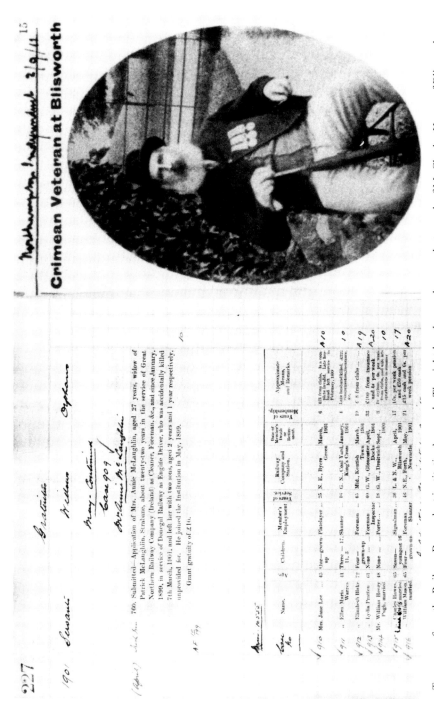

Two pages from the Railway Benevolent institution's records. The right-hand page shows a photograph of Mr Charles Hawes of Blisworth, at one time a signalman with the London and North Western railway Company. He was a Crimean War veteran. (TNA, RAIL 116/84)

May 1892

Mr Thomas Harrison

Application of Mr Thomas Harrison, aged 54 years, married with four children aged 22, 19, 16, and 13 years, for nineteen years Carriage Cleaner, Midland Railway, Leicester, who joined the Institution in May 1882, and who left the service in March suffering from pulmonary disease. Has no means of support, but his wife earns 12s per week as Bible-woman.

Resolved – That £10 be allowed for the assistance of Mr T. Harrison, and that his name be added to the list of applicants for annuities.

June 1889

George Henry Hawkins   Born 24/12/79

Aged 9 years, (both parents dead), late Father 20 years clerk

R.C.H.*

To be sent to the Derby Orphanage

June 1890

Cuthbert William Davison   Born Aug 17th 1882

Aged 7 years, son of Mrs Jane Davison (a Jubilee annuitant) and Mr John Davison, who was for sixteen years Chief Foreman, North Eastern Railway, Forth Goods Station, and who joined the Institution in August 1878, and was crushed between wagons and killed in December 1886.

Not admitted; mother remarried now Mrs Richardson.

RAIL 134/40   Cornwall Railway Company
Staff Details

Great Western Railway

Accountant's Office
Paddington, W.
27 May 1889

Mr Dear Sir,

You will remember that some time ago Mr W.R. Marshall was transferred to the Accountant's Office at Plymouth on account of his health; his salary is £65 per annum and it is possible that the Cornish Bank may take him on as a clerk, but if not he would be available as an assistant to Mr Fowler who I understand you promised should have one.

Mr Marshall is a very good clerk and we should be glad to take him back here but if he returned to London it would only be to die. Plymouth suits him very well as his health there is good.

Yours truly,
S. Matthews

To J.D. Higgins, Esq.

*   Railway Clearing House

RAIL 1014/4/21 Taff Vale Railway Company

Letter regarding diarrheoa [*sic*] medicine

> Taff Vale Railway Co.
> General Manager's Office
> Cardiff
> July 19th 1892

Dear Sir,

It has been the practice, I believe, for this Company to supply a medicine or Diarrhoea mixture to the men engaged in the various departments, but, as I find that this is not so in the case of the G.W.R. Co., nor the Rhymney and Barry Companies, I do not see why we should continue to supply such a medicine in future.

> Kindly note,
> Yours truly,
> A. Beasley

J.W. Brewer Esq.
Engineer

RAIL 1166/81   Railway Benevolent Institution

Case 628   June 1894

Mrs Mary Jane Farnham aged 38 years, widow of Mr Henry Farnham, twenty-three years in the service of the Great Eastern Railway as Porter and Station Master at Takeley, who joined the Institution (by collector's book) in May 1883, and died in September 1893, leaving only £138. She has five children aged 10, 8, 6 and 3 years, and 5 months.

Letter from   Railway Benevolent Institution
                   133 Seymour Street,
                   Euston Square
                   London
                   Feb. 1896

Dear Madam,

I beg to enclose you a cheque for £2–10–0, the amount of your quarterly allowance from this Institution. You must please sign the receipt at the foot of the cheque before presenting it for payment, and no other acknowledgement will be necessary. Any change in your address should be at once made known to us.

> Your faithful servant,
> W.F. Mills
> Secretary

Mrs M.J. Farnham

On the reverse side of this letter is written in a neat hand:

> Dear Sir,
> I return this cheque as I do not require any more assistance from this Institution.

A note has been appended:

> 'This was probably written just before Mrs Farnham murdered her children and committed suicide'.

The following newspaper cutting has been inserted in this file:

Daily Telegraph 20 February 1896

A terrible tragedy is reported from Wimblington a village near March. Since Michaelmas a widow named Mary Jane Farnham has, with four of her children, occupied a four-roomed cottage near the village. As nothing had been heard of them since Saturday night the police entered the residence. In one room upstairs they found two children, aged four and eleven respectively, lying dead with their throats cut, and in another bedroom the bodies of a girl aged three years, and a boy aged eight. Mrs Farnham was lying with her head on the babies body. She also was dead and a white-handled knife was still deeply embedded in the right side of the throat. There appears no doubt that Mrs Farnham murdered her children and afterwards committed suicide. Mrs Farnham appears to have led a very retired life, and is said to have been devoted to her children. She was possessed of means, her husband formerly station master at Takely [*sic*] on the Dunmow branch of the Great Eastern Railway, having left her provided for on his death about two years ago. She was deeply attached to him and had never recovered from the shock of the bereavement. A later telegram says that the crime was apparently premeditated. The police, on searching the house found £3–10–0 in a sealed envelope which bore the inscription 'Mr Fisher's rent'. It has also been ascertained that on Saturday night the eldest daughter went to the baker's shop to pay for two loaves of bread although it had previously been Mrs Farnham's invariable practice to pay on Wednesdays when the cart came round.

RAIL 491/986   Midland Railway Company
Fine Book, Wages Staff

Commercial Manager's Office Derby
William Hawkins, carter

24 Aug. 1898	Delivered case to Jackson, Wilford Street although plainly addressed 'Jackson Gunmaker'.
	His manner to me was anything but satisfactory, his argument practically being he had no right to be spoken to seeing he had given his explanation in writing and expressed his regret.
21 Jan. 1899	Had sheet to deliver case 213 to Benny Clark Ho [House] but wrongly delivered case 210 which belonged to Palmer and Mycroft.
	Resigned

A. Hardy, porter

3 Jan. 1900	This man attempted to move heavy barrel of oil from dray to platform by himself, weight 3.3.26 [*sic*] Dec. 30th 99, when half way off dray it slipped out of his hands fell to the ground one lag broken, not much contents lost.
	Resigned

RAIL 684/123   Taff Vale Railway Company
Workmen's Compensation: Minutes of Officers' Meetings

Workmen's Compensation Act. 1897.

Meeting of Officers. May 14th 1906.

PRESENT:

Mr Beasley.

Mr Harland.   Mr Cameron. (for Mr Riches)

Mr Tilley.   Mr W.J. Edwards. (for Mr Sibbering)

Mr S. Thomas.

Dr Joscelyne also attended.

TRAFFIC DEPARTMENT

T. Jones.	4742.	Mr Harland reported that this man has not failed since he resumed work on March 14th and continues, although not quite recovered, to follow his work with regularity.
J.J. Williams.	5186.	It was reported that the Barry Company have paid the compensation, amount to £7/3/9, due to this man, but that he has since been dismissed the service, having been convicted of a theft of coal at the Abercynon Police Court on April 25th.
R. Keene.	5202.	This man has been put on as Ticket Collector at Llandaff at his former wages (21/- a week), and will remain in that position until he is able to resume his old position, of groundman.
E.J. Luen.	5426.	Dr Joscelyne reported that he has seen the House Surgeon of the Cardiff Infirmary who states that Luen is still an inmate and is not likely to be able to leave for some time. His salary has been paid to the 24th April but it was ordered that no further payment is to be made without the authority of the Directors, and Mr Harland was accordingly instructed to prepare a recommendation for submission to the Traffic Committee on the 22nd instant.
H.D. Davies.	5263.	Paid £1/8/-.
T. Miles.	5266.	It was reported that this man has not yet resumed duty. The question of settling his claim for compensation by a lump sum payment, was considered by the Traffic Committee on April 3rd, when it was decided (see Minute No. 956) that the payment of compensation (19/3 a week) be continued, say until the Accident Fund pay ceases in February next, when it is anticipated that the man will be more ready to agree to a final settlement than he is at present.
T. Randell.	5269.	Resumed March 26th. Paid £2/8/-.
D. Hamblyn.	5287.	It was reported that the claim of the widow has been settled by payment of £267/18/10 which includes the cost of clothing and boots as directed by Traffic Minute 1502 of April 3rd.
G.W. Cairns.	5310.	Resumed April 30th. Paid £4/9/4.
W. Squire.	5322.	" " 2nd. Paid £2/15/5
T. Abbott.	5331.	It was reported that the application for compensation put forward by the father-in-law in this case, was submitted to the Directors on April 24th when it was ordered that all liability be declined, and that Mr Harland has written to the applicant accordingly.

April 8th 1918.

Received of The Taff Vale Railway Co.

—————— *Pounds,*

Three Shillings and four Pence,

for *Allowance for W E April 7/1918.*

R Barnett

NOTE.—Any person signing this Receipt on behalf of the party to whom the order is payable, must write his own name in full.

£ — 3:4.

This Receipt must be addressed to "THE SECRETARY, TAFF VALE RAILWAY COMPANY, CARDIFF."

April 8th 1918.

Received of The Taff Vale Railway Co.

—————— *Pounds,*

Two Shillings and six Pence,

for *Allowance for W E Apl 7/1918.*

NOTE.—Any person signing this Receipt on behalf of the party to whom the order is payable, must write his own name in full.

Received with thanks Ellen Davies

£ — 2:6:

This Receipt must be addressed to "THE SECRETARY, TAFF VALE RAILWAY COMPANY, CARDIFF."

Receipts for Taff Vale Railway Company allowances, 8 April 1918. (TNA, RAIL 684/79)

LOCOMOTIVE DEPARTMENT

J. Thomas	4421.	Mr Cameron reported that this man is still following his work satisfactorily, and the question of pensioning him was further deferred.
J. Lane.	4759.	It was reported that Mr Riches has seen this man as to a settlement of his claim by a lump sum payment but that he prefers to have work found for him rather than accept a lump sum in settlement. As, however, it was laid down at the Officers' Meeting on March 25th 1905 (see Minute No. 49) that on account of the additional risk not only to themselves but to other men involved in their re-employment, it is not desirable to retain in the service men who are maimed, it was considered that this man who has lost an arm, should not be reinstated. He is being paid 18/- a week by the Accident Fund and has also received a disablement allowance of £20 from the Amalgamated Society of Railway Servants, so that in addition to the half pay (16/10) which he is receiving under the Act he is in receipt of considerably more than he was earning while at work.
T.T. Fry.	4886.	A letter of 11th instant from Mr Riches was read stating that Fry adheres to his demand for £700 in settlement of his claim, and Mr Cameron was instructed to again reply that such a demand cannot be entertained and that the payment of the compensation, 12/3 a week, must therefore continue.
H. Beasant.	4901.	This man was reported to be following his work satisfactorily, and the question of pensioning him was accordingly further postponed.
R. Stradling.	5135.	A letter from Mr Riches dated 11th instant was read stating that this man does not desire any payment beyond the weekly compensation (amounting to £14/17/5) which he was paid for the 13 weeks he was away, up to the date of his pension (March 12th).
E. Humphreys.	5149.	It was reported that the joint [report] of Messrs Riches and Sibbering on the question of portions of a day being taken into account in calculating the time from which compensation should be paid, was not ready. It was pointed out that as under the Compensation Bill of this Session, as altered in Committee, compensation for accidents will be payable after three, instead of 14 days after the accident occurs, the precise time from which compensation is payable will require very careful consideration, as claims will probably be much more numerous than they are at present. It was therefore ordered that the joint report in question be made forthwith.
		Mr Harland stated that the commencement of incapacity in his Department is calculated on the same basis as that of Mr Sibbering's men, viz., from the morning of the day following the accident.
W.H. Boothby.	5181.	It was reported that the letter to the Board of Trade referred to at the last Meeting was sent on March 27th and that nothing has been heard from the Department since that date.
		It was suggested that, with a view to determining how far the use of brake sticks can be abolished, arrangements be made to test their

		efficacy, and Mr Harland was instructed to arrange for such tests to be made and report the result to the General Manager.
R. Davey	5199.	Resumed April 30th. Paid £9/7/11 The man has now applied for a pension which application will be submitted to the Directors in due course.
A. Gronow.	5258.	Resumed April 2nd. Paid £1/13/10.
R. Collard.	5303.	" March 26th. " £1/18/7.
S.J. Hughes.	5313.	" " " " 19/4.
C. Wakeley.	5325.	" " " " £1/2/-
M. Thompson.	5326.	Still away. To be paid.

RAIL 756/10   Wirral Railway Company

National Insurance Act, 1911 (Health Section)
Insurance Stamps/Cash Account

List of Employees for whom exemption was not claimed.

Mrs Little, Hoylake, Lady Attendant
Miss S. Cornish TMO* typist

List of Employees who have completed 3 years service.

W. Foster, Station Docks, Pass^r Guard
Entered Company's service May 1885

RAIL 684/78   Taff Vale Railway Company
Receipts for Allowances

8 Nov. 1916
Received of The Taff Vale Railway Co. Two pounds, thee shillings and six pence ½d for wages and war bonus due for two weeks ended October 22nd 1916 to A.H. Vowles.

[signed] Amelia Vowles

£2–3–6 ½

---

*   Traffic Manager's Office

RAIL 463/164   Rent Roll of the Manchester, Sheffield, and Lincolnshire Railway Rent Roll of Property [indexed]

No. of Property	Situation of Property	Description	Name of Tenant	Annual Rent	Dates When Payable	Remarks
14752	Audenshaw Junction	Land inside the fence	Alfred Earl (goods foreman)	5 – 0	June 24	In advance from 24/6/07
14813	Ashton	Privilege of drain water	Frank Marland	2 6	Sept. 29	In advance from 7/8/07
12973	Dukinfield, between Peak Forest Canal & Station St.	115 sq.yds. land From folios 396 G.C. Roll* Feb/08	J.G. Wagstaffe Ltd	2 15 4	Mar. 25 June 24 Sept. 29 Dec. 25	From 29/0/03
15197	Audenshaw	Land	W. Pattinson & Sons Ltd	1 – 0 – 0	Mar. 25 June 24 Sept. 29 Dec. 25	From 11/8/08
15628	Stalybridge Water Road	Land Stalybridge Joint Station Committee	John Young	0 – 5 – 0	Mar. 25	In advance from Jan. 1/09
3242	Audenshaw	Cottage	Joseph Turner	6 –10 – 0	2/6 weekly	From 24/7/09
	3, Tunnel Houses		Henry Wild	6 –10 – 0		
15989	Dukinfield, Clarendon Street	Privilege as to two windows	Samˡ Taylor	0 – 2 – 6		In advance from 25/12/09
16049	Ashton-u-Lyne	Privilege of erecting a wooden shop partly on land	Twiner Bros	0 – 5 – 0	June 24	In advance from 24/6/10
16067	Audenshaw Guide Lane	Privilege of erecting urinal on Co's land	Ashton-u-Lyne Corporⁿ	1 – 0 – 0		In advance from 25/12/09
16081	South Audenshaw, Hanover St.	Privilege of fixing drain pipes to bridge over Co's railway	Austin Hopkinson	1 – 0 – 0	July 1	In advance from 1 July 10
16082	Audenshaw	Privilege of laying pipe conveying roof water down embankment & fixing sump on Co's property	Austin Hopkinson	0 – 1 – 0	July 1	In advance from 1 July 10
16093	Dukinfield, King Street	Privilege of urinal on land	Dukinfield Corporation	0 – 2 – 6	Dec. 25	In advance from 25/12/06
16298	Ashton Moss	Land adjoining Cricket ground	The Ashton-under-Lyne Cricket Club	2 –10 – 0	June 24	From 24/6/11
16628	Dukinfield, Dewsnap Sidings	Land for storage of two boilers, now three	Mr Marler	5 – 4 – 0	2/- weekly	From 2/7/12
			Thos. do	7 –16 – 0	3/- weekly	From 30/11/12
			" "	5 – 4 – 0		
16723	Ashton-u-Lyne, Southampton St.	Privilege of electric cable across bridge	Ashton-under-Lyne Corporation	0 –10 – 0	2/- weekly	From 25/12/12
16819 etc.	Dunkinfield Dewsnap Sidings	Land for tool box	Edward Eastwood	1 – 1 – 0	Dec. 25	In advance from 25/12/12

*   Great Central Railway

143

RETIRED RAILWAY OFFICERS' SOCIETY

The Retired Railway Officers' Society was founded in the year 1902, through the initiative of Mr E.B. Ivatts, one time of the Midland Great Western Railway of Ireland. He acted as Honorary Secretary to the Society from its foundation to the day of his death on 4 May 1911.

The preliminary meeting at which its formation was discussed was held at the Railway Clearing House on 12 November 1901. Mr Ivatts, acting as Chairman, was able to announce that he had obtained promises of support from twenty-four retired officers, and recommendations for proceeding with the formation of the Society were unanimously adopted. The Society's first formal meeting was convened at the Railway Clearing House on 1 July 1902. At that meeting Mr Josiah Medcalf, late of the Great Northern Railway, was voted chairman. The following were elected to form the first Committee of Management:

Messrs G.P. Neele, London and North Western Railway
R. Johnson, Great Northern Railway
J. O'Connell, Bombay, Baroda and Central India Railway
J. Stephens, Great Western Railway

The election of Mr Josiah Medcalf to the Chair continued annually until the year 1911 when he expressed his desire to resign in order that other members might in turn occupy the Chair at the monthly meetings. Mr T.I. Allen, late of the Great Western Railway, was unanimously elected to succeed him.

Railway Clearing House, the Long Room, 1864. (TNA, RAIL 1085/79/12

James Watson Emmett, superintendent of Wagon Department, London and North Western Railway Company. This page is taken from an 'Official Album' of the Retired Railway Officers' Society. (TNA, RAIL 1156/13)

The first monthly social meeting was held on 25 September 1902, and these meetings took place regularly from that date.

The annual meeting was first held on 3 February 1903, and repeated each year. An annual summer excursion was also held for the entertainment of members' wives, families and friends.

In January 1910 Mr G.P. Neele, late of the London and North Western Railway, was elected President.

In February 1911, owing to the illness of Mr Ivatts, Mr W. Dawson, late of the Great Western Railway, was appointed Honorary Joint Secretary. On Mr Ivatts' death Mr Dawson was appointed Honorary Secretary.

The provision of a series of official albums was begun, in which portraits of each member with a short statement of his railway career were kept. These are now in RAIL 1156 pieces 12 to 26 covering the dates 1902 to 1963. Minutes of the meetings of the Society are in RAIL 1156/1 to 4, dated 1902 to 1944.

CRIMINAL RECORDS

Offences against railway companies (theft and fraud) are often found among Quarter Sessions records. The proceedings of such cases usually record the statements made by railway police and other railway employees who were called as witnesses.

The following are two examples from Somerset Quarter Sessions.

SOM RO   QS/1855/Midsummer
Somerset Quarter Session Rolls

Midsummer, 3 July 1855
Robert Warner charged with stealing wood from the Bristol and Exeter Railway Company.
The examination of William Blackmore of the City of Bristol, Superintendent of the Railway Police; William Green of the City of Exeter, Inspector of Railway Police; and John Nichols of Bridgwater in the said County, Inspector of Permanent Way to the Bristol and Exeter Railway Company.
Taken upon oath this fourth day of May in the year of our Lord one thousand eight hundred and fifty five at Bridgwater in the said County, before the undersigned John Lovell Sealy, Esquire, one of Her Majesty's Justices of the Peace in and for the said County, in the presence and hearing of Robert Warner who is brought before me charged with having within six calender months now last past at North Petherton in the said County, feloniously stolen, taken, and carried away a certain quantity of wood being portions of new and old fence rails and of a four inch drain pipe from the Bristol and Exeter Railway then and there situate, of the goods and chattels of the Bristol and Exeter Railway Company contrary to the Statute in that case made and provided.

This Deponent William Blackmore on his Oath saith: I am Superintendent of Police of the Bristol and Exeter Railway Company. That Railway runs through the parish of North Petherton and other parishes in this County. The prisoner was employed as a workman upon the said Railway to the twenty sixth of April last. There has been a field of fence railing taken down by Company's orders in the parish of North Petherton recently. Some portions within the last month. On the twenty sixth of last month I obtained a search warrant to search the prisoner's house. I first of all went on the Railway and prisoner came to me from his work. I told the prisoner I should go and search his premises for some fence railing. I had first told him I had been informed that he had a crib in his orchard made of the Company's fence. He said he had no crib there. On telling him I should go to see he said 'Very well I could'. I and William Green and John Venn and the Prisoner went to the prisoner's orchard but saw no crib there. I then told the prisoner for the first time I had a search warrant and should go and search his premises. I then went to the prisoner's house and sheds. The first shed I looked at I saw the rafters were evidently portion of the Company's fence. I told prisoner so; he said it was not. I then went to a small house or cellar, in which I found the greatest portion of the wood now produced all but two polished pieces which were found in the dwelling house. When I found it I said 'I suppose there is no question about this Warner, coming from the Company's premises; you can't deny this'. 'No', he said, 'it's no use denying that, I bought that from the line'.

I afterwards searched two or three other small sheds. After searching I told the prisoner that he should himself tie up all he had taken from the Line. He then tied up the bundle now produced.

Mr Reed.   Prisoner was permanently employed on the line, the Gang of which he formed would work under a Ganger and would work under him, but chiefly under Inspector Nichols. The Gauger is John Venn, but is not here today. The fence taken down was about quarter of a mile from Warner's house. Some of it might be rotten, some sound. The value of the wood produced is a shilling. Warner did not say Venn had given the men this timber, but Venn said he had given them leave to take away the rotten timber but certainly not the new. We did not compel

London, Brighton and South Coast Railway Company. A cautionary notice, February 1876. (TNA, RAIL 414/532

LONDON BRIGHTON AND SOUTH COAST RAILWAY.

CAUTION.

JOHN WEBB,

Engine Cleaner, New Cross, was charged at the Greenwich Police Court, on the 2nd Feb., before the presiding Magistrate, for negligently opening the regulator of an engine in steam at New Cross, on the 18th December last, whereby persons being upon the Company's Works might have been injured or their lives endangered, and he was Fined 10s. and Costs, or Seven Days' Imprisonment.

BY ORDER,

J. P. KNIGHT,

LONDON BRIDGE TERMINUS,

February, 1876.

General Manager.

PRINTED BY LETTS, SON & CO. LIMITED. LONDON.

prisoner to go to his house. The cellar was connected with the dwelling house at the end of it. The door was locked. There was more old timber there. Venn did not say that he had given the men leave to take away the rotten fire wood until upwards of an hour after we had searched Warner's house. Venn is still in the employ of the Company. He was suspended and fined. I have not seen him until yesterday. I had no conversation with him yesterday about the wood. He spoke of it yesterday before the Board. Prisoner was present Venn then said in prisoner's presence that he had given leave for the men to take away the rotten pieces but he certainly never gave them leave to take off the new for he should have objected to it. He did not state that he had given the men liberty to take the wood. The new wood in the bundle is worth about six pence. The Warrant was granted the twenty sixth of April. The prisoner was apprehended on it yesterday the third day of May. I waited for orders from the Board.

This Deponent William Green on his oath saith: 'I am Inspector of Police of the Bristol and Exeter Railway Company. On the twenty sixth of April last I accompanied the last witness in the search of prisoner's premises. I found the greatest portion of the wood now produced in the cellar: the remainder consisting of two pieces I found in the dwelling house. The prisoner stated in answer to an observation from Mr Blackmore he said he had bought the wood now produced from the Railway. Mr Blackmore asked him more particularly the pieces of wood which are blackened and the prisoner said they were part of a four inch trunk which had been damaged. Mr Blackmore ordered him to tie up all the wood he had brought from the Railway. Any in the heap which he had not brought from the Railway he was to throw back; the prisoner then tied up all the wood now produced and took it to the Railway.

Mr Reed.   I was present when Venn was spoken to on the subject Warner being present. Venn said he had given the men leave to carry away the old stuff. He might have said the damaged stuff I dont remember which but they were to carry away nothing useful or new. He was then over by the Railway. He said this more than once. It was said on Warners taking back the wood to the Railway. I never recollect Warner saying the ganger had given him leave. I wont swear he did not say so but to the best of my belief he did not. I ride over the Railway nearly every day by the Train. Not on foot. We searched another man's house and found some old fencing but none new, very little old, it was in a similar outhouse to Warners.

This Deponent John Nicholis on his oath saith:
    I am an Inspector of the permanent way of the Bristol and Exeter Railway and live at Bridgwater. There has been some railing removed by my orders in the parish of North Petherton; the prisoner has been employed in that removal, and is called a packer. The packers take their orders from the Gangers and the Gangers take their orders from me. About three months ago the prisoner was at work on the Railway and I said to him "Mind I don't catch you steal or take anything from the Railway or any one else." I have on other occasions in the prisoner's presence told the men that nothing is to be stolen or taken from the Line by the Company's men, no materials whatever. Two of the blackened pieces now produced to the best of my belief are portions of a four inch trunk of the Company. Judging from the general appearance the rest appears to be portions of a fence railing. To the best of my belief it is part of the fence taken down in the field in North Petherton part of which was taken down last week. It has all been taken down within the last two months. The trunks were issued about Christmas last, the men had not a privilege to take rotten or decayed wood off the Line. The rotten wood is used to light the Engine fires. The Gangers have no authority to give it to the men, nor have I any authority to do so.

By Mr Reed.   The men do not look upon taking the rotten wood as a privilege. My beat is from Weston to Durston, twenty miles and a quarter. Venn had a mile and a half and ten chains. I used to go there twice or three times a week. Venn's duty would be to obey my orders and the packers would obey Venn. I saw Venn yesterday, Warner was present. I fetched them from the station. Venn said he had given the men liberty to take home the old rotten fencing to burn. Warner said he had liberty to take it and he took it home to burn it.

The fence was taken down because it was no longer required. Some of the rails were down. I did not tell the men that if the Ganger gave them liberty they were not to take it. I have never been a Ganger of Packers. The Gangers on my district are under my control and they get their orders from me. If the Engineer came along he would give them orders.

Re-examined.

The wood produced, except the five pieces, is not sound wood. It is the duty of the Gangers and Packers to stack away the fence which was useful and that which is old would be taken to the Station.

The above Depositions of William Blackmore
William Green and John Nicholls were taken
and sworn at Bridgwater the day and year
first aforesaid.

Robert Warner stands charged before the undersigned one of Her Majesty's Justices of the Peace, in and for the County aforesaid, this fourth day of May in the year of our Lord one thousand eight hundred and fifty five for that he the said Robert Warner within six calendar months now last past at North Petherton in the said County of Somerset, did feloniously steal take and carry away certain wood the property of the Bristol and Exeter Railway Company.

AND the said charge being read to the said Robert Warner and the witnesses for the prosecution, William Blackmore, William Green and John Nicholls being severally examined in his presence, the said Robert Warner is now addressed by me as follows: "Having heard the evidence, do you wish to say anything in answer to the charge? You are not obliged to say anything, unless you desire to do so; but whatever you say, will be taken down in writing, and may be given in evidence against you upon your trial," whereupon the said Robert Warner saith as follows. "I have nothing to say".

Robert Warner was acquitted.

SOM RO QS/1869/Epiphany
Somerset Quarter Sessions Rolls

Epiphany, 5 January 1869
Edward Reding stands charged before the undersigned one of Her Majesty's Justices of the Peace in and for the County aforesaid, this 31st day of October in the year of our Lord one Thousand Eight Hundred and Sixty Eight for that he the said Edward Reding on the 10th day of October in the year of our Lord One Thousand Eight Hundred and Sixty Eight at the parish of Edington in the said County of Somerset, certain money to wit two pounds thirteen shillings and eleven pence of the money of the Somerset and Dorset Railway Company feloniously did steal, take and carry away against the peace of our Lady the Queen, Her Crown and Dignity.

AND the said charge having been read to the said Edward Reding and the witnesses for the

NORTH EASTERN RAILWAY.

It having come to the knowledge of the Directors that a person employed by the Company has been guilty of Poaching, Notice is hereby Given, that any Servant of the Company who may be convicted of Poaching, will be immediately dismissed.

(BY ORDER)   **W. O'BRIEN,**

York, 16th July, 1855.   *SECRETARY.*

GODDARD AND LANCASTER, STEAM PRINTERS, YORK AND HULL.

North Eastern Railway Company. A warning notice, 16 July 1855. (TNA, RAIL 1157/1)

Prosecution having been severally examined in his presence, the said Edward Reding is now addressed by me as follows: "Having heard the evidence do you wish to say anything in answer to the charge? Yon are not obliged to say any thing, unless you desire to do so, but whatever you say will be taken down in writing, and may be given in evidence against you upon your trial; and you are also clearly to understand that you have nothing to hope from any promise of favour, and nothing to fear from any threat which may have been holden out to you to induce you to make any admission or confession of your guilt; but whatever you shall now say, may be given in evidence against you upon your trial, notwithstanding such promise or threat;" whereupon the said Edward Reding saith as follows: "Not at present".

Taken before me

J.L. Sealy

The mark of

X

Edward Reding

An identical charge was read to Anthony Watts who stated: "I reserve my defence".

The Examinations of William Sandy of the parish of Edington in the County of Somerset, Station Master, Alfred Colson of Glastonbury in the said County Railway Clerk, Robert Lee of Burnham in the said County, Inspector of Railway Permanent Way, Job Hewlett of the parish of Edington in the said County, Labourer and Sargent Taylor of Chilton Polden in the said County, Police Constable, taken on Oath this Thirty first day of October in the year of our Lord One Thousand Eight Hundred and Sixty Eight at Bridgwater, in the County aforesaid, before the undersigned one of Her Majesty's Justices of the Peace for the said County, in the presence and hearing of Edward Reding and Anthony Watts who are charged this day before me for that they the said Edward Reding and Anthony Watts on the tenth day of October One Thousand Eight Hundred and Sixty Eight at the parish of Edington in the said County feloniously did steal take and carry away certain money to wit two pounds thirteen shillings and eleven pence of the money of the Somerset and Dorset Railway Company contrary to the form of the statute in that case made and provided, and against the peace of our Lady the Queen, her Crown and Dignity.

This Deponent William Sandy on his oath saith as follows: I am Station Master at the Edington

Station on the Somerset and Dorset Railway. I know the prisoners; they are employed as packers by the Somerset and Dorset Railway Company and work upon that portion of the Railway where my station is situated. On the 10th of October instant I received a package from Mr Robert Lee, Inspector of Permanent Way and a few minutes after I received the package I handed to several of the packers employed upon the Railway a small packet (or envelope) each containing their fortnights pay. I opened each envelope before handing it to the men and counted the money out to them. After I had paid these persons they signed the pay sheet and went away. The prisoners were not amongst those men I then paid. About half past 5 or a quarter to 6 o'clock the two prisoners came to my station to be paid their fortnights wages. I paid them their money out of the packet I had received from Mr Lee and after I had paid them there remained three men's wages in the packet. After paying them I asked them to sign the pay sheet and whilst they were doing so I had to go outside the Station to signal a train. When I went out of the station I left a bag with three men's money upon a form in the station. Before I went out of the station and after paying the two prisoners a man named Hewlett came to the door of the station and asked what time it was as he had often done before. I told him what time it was and he then remained standing upon the platform. Whilst Hewlett was standing upon the platform I went to signal the train. To do this I had to go to the platform a few yards from the office door, and hold out my hand. Whilst I was upon the platform I saw the two prisoners leave the office and go away. I said nothing to them. After the train had passed I put the signals right and Hewlett went with me to the gates and then went on his way home. The whole of the time I was upon the platform Hewlett had been standing by my side. I then returned to the office and found that the bag that I had left on the platform containing the 3 men's money was gone. There was no one in the office when I returned. No one could have entered the office during the time I was away from it. There is only one entrance to the office and that is facing the platform.

Cross-examined by Mr Reed the prisoner's Attorney.

Anthony Watts has worked 6 or 7 months upon the line I should say and the other prisoner for a less period. I did not open the three envelopes I left in the bag so I cannot say what they contained except from the pay sheet. The platform at Edington is 60 or 70 feet long I should say. The public highway is at one end of the platform. I had lights in the office that evening. The signal I gave that night was by holding up my hand whilst the train was a quarter of a mile off. To give that signal my side would be towards the station. After the train passed I went to the end of the platform to turn off the signal and to open the gates across the road. There is only one signal at the station. Four or 5 minutes before the train arrived I received a telegram that the train was coming and left the office to open the gates across the line and to turn round the signal light but at that time the prisoners had not arrived. As I was opening the gates they came up and I told them to go into the office and I would pay them their wages. I followed them in and paid them their wages. Hewlett walked with me from the platform to the gates and the office was then left without any one in it. I could not leave the station to go after the men that night. My last train was at 9 30 p.m. and I then left for the night. I did not go to the houses of either of the prisoners that night. I know that they live at Burtle about ½ a mile from Edington Station. I did not that night take any steps to ascertain where they lived. I saw at my station that night two men called Norris and Parsons. They came for their wages. I told them that I had not got the pay sheet. I said 'The pay sheet has not come'. I did not tell them that their money had not arrived. Their names were not upon the regular pay sheet as they were extra men. I afterwards paid the two men Norris and Parsons from my cash box. I did not pay the two prisoners money out of money I took from my pocket: I told of my loss to Parsons and Norris that night, and I told Mr Lee (the Inspector) of it the next day. I went to Burnham to tell him and I told him whom I suspected viz the two prisoners. I did not go to the prisoners' houses on the next day in consequence of orders. The prisoners came to their work on the following Monday morning. Reding was an extra man and he did not sign his sheet when I paid him on Saturday evening but he signed it on the following Monday and he then said to me 'Did I have your money'. He did not say to me that some money had been lost the previous Saturday and that they were charged with taking it. I said 'One or other of you had it'. At breakfast time Watts said to me 'It's a pretty (something) your saying I had the money'. I said 'I'll have nothing more to say until I see Mr Lee'. That was all I said. They did not say why do you blame us? On the Saturday following the prisoners came to my Station and met Mr Lee, they were working close to the Station. I was not present at the interview. The prisoners were working for the company on the day they were apprehended (yesterday the 30th Oct.).

Re-examined.   The names upon the 3 packets lost from Edington Station were Bishop, Norris and Parsons, and those three I did not pay.

[signed] W. Sandy

This Deponent Alfred Colson on his oath saith as follows: I live at Glastonbury and I am a Clerk in the permanent way department of the Somerset and Dorset Railway Company. On the 10th October I made up the wages for the men employed upon the Edington length of the Somerset and Dorset Railway. I put each man's money in a small envelope with the man's name and the amount of the money it contained upon it. I placed the envelopes containing the money in a bag and made it up into a parcel which I handed to Inspector Lee. In that packet were envelopes containing the wages of Charles Bishop (14s/-) H. Parsons (£1–3–1) and Norris (16s/10).

Cross-examined by Mr Reed.

I cannot tell how many parcels I made up that day, it may be 20; nor can I say the amount I sent away; I should say about £200. I made up all the parcels myself. I have referred to the pay sheet and I find that those men I have mentioned have not been paid. I checked the parcels with the pay sheet as I put them into the bag; the pay sheet has been returned to me.

[signed]   Alfred Colson

This Deponent Robert Lee on his oath saith as follows:

I am Inspector of Permanent Way upon the Somerset and Dorset Railway and I live at Burnham. On the 10th October I received a packet from the last witness at Glastonbury. I took the packet from Glastonbury to Edington and delivered it to Mr Lander the Stationmaster there. The packet was tied up and I did not open it.

Cross-examined by Mr Reed.

On 17th instant I was at Edington, the prisoners have been working on for the Company from the 10th to the 30th instant with the exception of lost time on their part. On 17th I sent for them at Edington from their work and they came. Mr Wood enquired of them in my presence what time they received their wages on the 10th and who paid them and they answered his questions. Mr Wood is the Inspector of Railway Police upon the Somerset and Dorset Railway. I saw them again on the 23rd, they were then coming to work. I said 'I want to speak to you'. I did not say 'Are you going to allow back the money' but I said 'Are you going to pay back the money'. Reding said 'I shall not give back any money, I never took any', and Watts said 'Neither shall I'. I believe I said 'Then you must stand the consequence' and they replied 'Then we must do that' or words to that effect. If they had paid back the money there would have been an end to this.

Re-examined at request of prosecutor.

I had no authority to say but I thought in my own mind that nothing more would be said about it.

[signed]   Robert Lee

No. 15.

London Brighton & South Coast Railway Company.

CAUTION.

LIST OF CONVICTIONS

For Offences against the Company's Acts and Bye-Laws.

NAME.	ADDRESS.	DESCRIPTION	NATURE OF OFFENCE	WHEN AND WHERE CASE HEARD.	RESULT OF CONVICTION.
T. W. MELLOR,	84, King William Street, E.C.	Civil Engineer.	Travelling without having paid his fare, and with intent to avoid payment thereof, 27th November, 1876.	11th January, 1877. Southwark Police Court.	Fined FORTY SHILLINGS and Two Shillings Costs, or a Month's Imprisonment.
JOSEPH LEACH,	9, Little East Street, Brighton.	...	Attempting to join a Train in motion, 26th December, 1876.	8th January, 1877. Steyning Police Court.	Fined Two Shillings and Sixpence and Nineteen and Sixpence Costs.
CHARLES McLEOD,	Egremont Villa, Knight's Hill, Lower Norwood, S.E.	...	Having paid his fare for a certain distance, knowingly and wilfully proceeding beyond such distance without previously paying the additional fare for the additional distance, and with intent to avoid payment thereof, December 10th, 1876.	9th January, 1877. Lambeth Police Court.	Fined FORTY SHILLINGS and Forty-two Shillings Costs.
JAMES FYFFE,	53, Mack's Road, Bermondsey, S.E.	Waterman.	Wilfully obstructing and impeding an officer of the Company in the execution of his duty, and assaulting a servant of the Company at the same time.	11th January, 1877. Thames Police Court.	Fined TWENTY SHILLINGS and Two Shillings Costs, or Fourteen Days Imprisonment for each offence.
T. W. MELLOR,	84, King William Street, E.C.	Civil Engineer.	Travelling without having paid his fare, and with intent to avoid payment thereof, 24th October, and 17th November, 1876.	13th January, 1877. Croydon Police Court.	Fined FORTY SHILLINGS and Nineteen Shillings and Sixpence Costs in each case.
SAMUEL JENNER,	5, Wallington Green, Wallington.	Grocer's Assistant.	Using a ticket on a day on which such ticket was not available, 21st December, 1876.	13th January, 1877. Croydon Police Court.	Fined TEN SHILLINGS and Costs.
WILLIAM MAYLIN,	Monument Yard, E.C.	...	Travelling without special permission in a superior class carriage to that for which he had taken a ticket, 14th December, 1876.	13th January, 1877. Croydon Police Court.	Fined FORTY SHILLINGS and Costs.
WILLIAM PARKER, CHARLES WHITTLE, GEORGE GYLES,	...	...	Assaulting a servant of the Company, 4th December, 1876.	15th January, 1877. Brighton Police Court.	Two MONTHS Hard Labour each.
JOHN CALDON,	...	Soldier.	Drunk and refusing to quit the Company's premises, 23rd January, 1877.	24th January, 1877. Shoreham Police Court.	Fined Two Shillings and Sixpence and Nine Shillings and Sixpence Costs.
PATRICK HAYES,	4, Star Court, Mint Street, Borough, S.E.	...	Being found on the Company's premises, supposed for an unlawful purpose, and making use of obscene language, 27th January, 1877.	29th January, 1877. Southwark Police Court.	Fined THIRTY SHILLINGS or One Month's Imprisonment.
GEORGE HUNT,	9, Clarina Road, Penge, S.E.	...	Travelling without having previously paid his fare, and with intent to avoid payment thereof, 25th January, 1877.	7th February, 1877. Lambeth Police Court.	Fined THIRTY SHILLINGS, and Ten Shillings Costs, or Three Weeks Imprisonment.
EDWARD BIRCH,	1, Farquhar Road, Upper Norwood, S.E.	...	Having paid his fare for a certain distance, knowingly and wilfully proceeding beyond such distance, without previously paying the additional fare for the additional distance, and with intent to avoid payment thereof, 10th January, 1877.	8th February, 1877. Brighton Police Court.	Fined FORTY SHILLINGS and Fourteen Shillings and Sixpence Costs.
WILLIAM FREEMAN,	3, Albert Terrace, Lower Road, Deptford.	...	Travelling without having previously paid his fare, and with intent to avoid payment thereof, 8th February, 1877.	21st February, 1877. Greenwich Police Court.	Fined TEN SHILLINGS and Two Shillings Costs
HENRY BARBER,	9, Stansfield Road, Brixton.	...	Travelling without the special permission of some duly authorized servant of the Company, in a carriage or by a train of a superior class to that for which he had taken a ticket, 15th & 19th February, 1877.	8th March, 1877. Southwark Police Court.	Fined FORTY SHILLINGS and Two Shillings Costs, in each case.
SYDNEY HOUGH,	Laurel Bank, Oakfield Road, Penge.	...	Assaulting one of the Company's servants, 20th February, 1877.	13th March, 1877. Lambeth Police Court.	Fined TWENTY SHILLINGS and Twelve Shillings Costs.
WILLIAM ABBELBY,	3, Riley Street, Abbey Street, Bermondsey.	Hawker.	Being in a state of intoxication using obscene and abusive language, and otherwise wilfully interfering with the comfort of other passengers, 27th February, 1877.	16th March, 1877. Southwark Police Court	Fined FORTY SHILLINGS and Twelve Shillings Costs

London Bridge Terminus.

[PRINTED BY LETTS, SON & CO LIMITED, LONDON]

London, Brighton and South Coast Railway Company. List of convictions, *c.* 1877. (TNA, RAIL 414/532)

This Deponent Job Hewlettt on his oath saith as follows:
I live at Edington, I work at Farmer Church's. On the 10th October (Saturday, 3 weeks ago tonight) I was on my way from work and at 10 minutes to 6 o'clock I went to the office door at Edington Station. I went to see what time it was. I saw the two prisoners sitting down upon a form in the office. I saw the Stationmaster also in the office; he had some paper in his hand. I then turned round and saw the train coming down the line. I stood upon the platform and watched the train. Whilst I was standing upon the platform I saw the prisoners walking along the platform towards the gates; the Station Master was then holding up his hand for the train to go by. After the train had passed the Station Master went to shut the gates and I went with him. I went through the little gate and then home. I did not go further into the office than the door.
Cross-examined by Mr Reed.
The prisoners would have to go the way they went to get off the platform on their way home and in doing so they passed me and the Station Master Sandy. It is 30 yards or more I should say from the Booking Office to the gates. It was getting dark. I wished Sandy good night at the gate. I saw no one at the office.

The mark of   X   Job Hewlett

This Deponent Sargent Taylor on his oath saith as follows:
Yesterday I arrested the 2 prisoners under a warrant for stealing £2–13–11 the money of the Somerset and Dorset Railway Co. They told me that they went together to the Station for their money and that Sandy was at the gates right for the train to pass; that they all went together into the Station and they pointed out to me where they had sat in the office and where they had received their money. They said that Mr Sandy took the money out of his pocket loose, and he had not enough by 6d and he went back to a little desk (pointing to one on the other side of the office) and took a sixpence from there. They said Mr Sandy left the office whilst they were there. Mr Sandy was present whilst the prisoners were making this statement and he denied it stating that he took the bag out of his pocket in which those men's money was, and that of three others. That he placed the bag upon the end of the stool he pointed out to me in the presence of the prisoners and that the bag was taken from there. He also pointed to the desk and showed me where he left the prisoner Watts signing the pay sheet and the other prisoner standing by his side when he went out to signal the train. And he said that the prisoners left whilst he was out signalling the train, and he then went to the gates to put them right for passengers to pass and to put the danger signal on, and when he returned to the office he found that both the bag and money was gone.
Cross-examined by Mr Reed.
I apprehended them without notice and from first to last they have denied all knowledge of the robbery. I have searched the prisoners but have found nothing upon them that has been identified. There is a desk in the office where they said Sandy went to take the sixpence.

[*signed*]   *Sargent Taylor*

The foregoing Examinations of William Sandy, Alfred Colson, Robert Lee, Job Hewlett and Sargent Taylor were severally taken and sworn before me one of Her Majesty's Justices of the peace in and for the County of Somerset this 31st day of October 1868 at Bridgwater in the said County.

[*signed*] J.L. Sealy

The Bill of Indictment was found 'ignoramus' and the prisoners were discharged.

CHAPTER 8

TRADES UNION APPEALS AND DISPUTES FROM MANAGEMENT AND CORRESPONDENCE FILES

The National Archives document record class RAIL 1172 is entitled 'Management and Correspondence Files'. Much of this collection in fact contains the minutes and reports from the Industrial Court which sat in judgement over disputes between railway companies and trades unions. These usually relate to wages and working conditions. Many of the disputes refer to general matters of principle while others relate specifically to named employees. Such disputes record in some detail the nature of the work carried out by individuals. These records date from 1920.

All disputes giving the names of employees have been included in the staff records of the related railways in their appropriate appendices. Those of a general nature have been omitted.

Most of these reports include, verbatim, the questions and answers put before the Court, each case covering several dozens of pages. Abstracts from a selection of cases are given in this chapter.

RAIL 1172/266   London, Midland and Scottish Railway Company
A. Goodlad and J.H. Davies

1.   The National Union of Railwaymen requested the Court's ruling upon the grading of A. Goodlad and J.H. Davies, electricians in the employ of the London, Midland and Scottish Railway at Redbank, Manchester.

   The Court heard representatives of the parties in London on 11th February, 1925.

2.   In the application of Decision No. 728, the men in question have been graded by the Company as Electricians, Grade II. The Union's claim is that they should be Grade I.

3. According to the evidence before the Court, the men examine the electric lighting in the railway coaches, inserting new electric bulbs as may be necessary; they test the strength of the batteries, filling them with water as required; and clean, oil and grease the dynamos. They carry out minor repairs only and in general replace defective parts from stores. Any substantial repairs are done by electricians at the Company's Newton Heath Carriage Works.

4. J.H. Davies entered the Company's service at the age of 26 years as a temporary washer and in due course worked up to his present post. A. Goodlad entered the Company's service as a 'brasser' and while in the Company's employment has been engaged in a number of occupations. He attended at the Manchester School of Technology and has passed an examination. The Court note that the Company hold examinations from time to time with a view to affording men opportunities for promotion. Goodlad worked for three months in the Newton Heath Shops.

5. The rate of wages of both men prior to Decision No. 728 was 39/- per week, plus war wage. Under the decision, they receive 42/- plus war wage.

6. The class of work which the men perform appears to be of a restricted character, and on the evidence the Court are of opinion that the men have not at the present time acquired that skill in the various branches of an electrician's trade as would entitle them to be placed in Grade I, and the Court decide accordingly.

WILLIAM W. MACKENZIE
J. McKIE BRYCE
P. S. BUTTON.

W.H. Reynolds,
  Secretary
    5, Old Palace Yard,
      London, S.W.I.

19th February, 1925.

RAIL 1172/286   Southern Railway Company
A.R. Tarr

MR REYNOLDS: The following is the letter from the National Union of Railwaymen raising this question: 'Dear Sir, A.R. Tarr: Assistant Fitter: Signal & Telegraph Department: Norwood Junction: Southern Railway. This case was discussed at a meeting between the Company's representatives and ours in December last, but they refused to alter his grading from that of an Assistant on the ground that he is only an assistant in the trade. My Committee have carefully considered his claim and in view of this they request the Court to fix a date for a hearing on the matter. I shall be glad if you will arrange for this and favour me with the date and time. Yours faithfully, C.T. Cramp'.

MR CARTER: A.R. Tarr is engaged in the Signal and Telegraph Department at Norwood Junction on the Southern Railway. His present grade is that of assistant fitter, and his rate is 38s.; the grade claimed is fitter Grade II and the rate claimed is 46s. Tarr started with the Company as messenger boy at 15 years of age. Prior to the Award he was in receipt of 26s.

base rate. His present work is repairing and finishing the following instruments for signal work in connection with the main line and single line requirements: Tyers instruments and parts; compound ringing keys, Sines' ringing keys, inside and not, Tyers ringing keys, inside and out, telephones, bells, etc. (telephones have to be taken to pieces to be cleaned and repairs [*sic*] afterwards Tarr has to re-assemble them); making new train staffs for use in instruments. He is capable of and does work in a turning lathe and has to set up his own jobs and finish them. All the work coming into the shop is distributed amongst the men, irrespective of grading, and a large amount of the work now done by Tarr is also performed by Grade I and Grade II fitters. That is our case at present.

In the view of the Court, the man concerned is in process of improving his status, but the facts and circumstances as proved in evidence are not such as to warrant a raising of his status at the present time, in the absence of a vacancy. The Court, therefore, decide not to disturb the existing position.

22 May 1925

RAIL 1172/313 Southern Railway Company
C. Bradford

MR THOMPSON: This case arises out of a letter from the National Union of Railwaymen dated June 26, 1925, which is as follows: 'Dear Sir, C. Bradford, Labourer, Exmouth Junction. I have had this case in correspondence with the Management of the Southern for the purpose of having Bradford re-graded as a Grade I labourer, but they will not agree, and in consequence my Committee request that the case be heard by the Industrial Court, as they are of the opinion he is entitled to Grade I rate. Yours faithfully, C.T.W Cramp'.

Mr W. Clements of Whitstable, Southern
Railway Company. (TNA, RAIL 1017/2)

MR BROWNING: The claim is on behalf of C. Bradford, who is engaged on the Southern Railway in the Engineer's Department at Exmouth Junction. He commenced with the Company as a labourer, and his rate at the commencement was £1 per week. He commenced with the Company on June 20, 1914. His rate prior to the Award was £1 and bonus, and his rate under the Award is 27s. plus 17s.6d. What he is claiming is that he should be a Grade I labourer. 'Bradford is graded as a Grade II Labourer, and is continually working with a first class craftsman. He has to do all the scaffolding and mixing of material for use on all buildings which he and the mason are called upon to repair. On one occasion Bradford was sent to Heldon Signal Box to put new slates on the roof by himself. During the last three months this man has been engaged erecting scaffolding for renovating the front of the Engineer's offices which consist of cement blocks. In addition, Bradford has had to assist the mason to fix the concrete panelling showing the name of the offices, and also draining work. At Sidmouth he has assisted the mason to build a new cattle dock wall, and at Newton Poppleford he has assisted in the rebuilding of a new wing wall to the bridge. The Court in Award 1083 states that men digging holes, loading or unloading, and such like operations, should be Grade II. This man is a builder's labourer, and as such has to be experienced in the mixing of mortar; erecting scaffolding and generally assisting masons or bricklayers in their work.'

In the opinion of the Court, the work performed by Bradford is something more than ordinary labouring work. They therefore decide that the appropriate rate payable to him is that operating to the Grade I labourers. This decision is to operate from the beginning of the first full pay following the date hereof.

23 July 1925

RAIL 1172/328   Southern Railway Company
D. Broomfield

MR THOMPSON: This letter from the National Union of Railwaymen, dated October 28, 1925, raising this case is as follows:— 'Dear Sir; D. Broomfield, Bricklayer, Twickenham. This man is graded as a Grade II bricklayer and claims that he is entitled to Grade I on the ground that prior to the Award he received the same rate as the other bricklayers and that this was a recognition of his capabilities as a Grade I man. I have been in communication with the Southern Railway Company with the object of him being re-graded to Grade I, but they decline to accede to my request. My Committee feel that a hearing is necessary by the Court, and in view of this I shall be glad if you will fix a date for same, and advise me in due course. Yours faithfully, C.T. Cramp'

MR CARTER: This man, D. Broomfield, has not served an apprenticeship, but has had 10 years' experience in the outside trade prior to entering the Company's service in 1907. In addition to this he pursued a course of technical training at a school for three years. When he commenced with the Company he received 5s.9d. per day, which was the same rate as paid to other bricklayers. Under the Award, Broomfield has been given the Grade II rate although he claims that he is doing the same work as other men who are Grade I, that is to say bricklaying, pointing, plastering, stone dressing, cutting away brickwork and stone work, also rendering brickwork and floors. During the last few months he has performed jobs at the following places: General repairs to brickwork, Wellington Road Bridge; new lamp room and oil stores at Surbiton; and reconstruction of No. 13 Bridge, Epsom. 5s.6d. per day was the highest rate paid to bricklayers at the Twickenham building depot.

Broomfield entered the Company's service as a bricklayer in 1907 at a rate of 5s.9d. per day. He has been employed as a bricklayer since 1897.

The man concerned appears to be fully skilled, and is engaged from time to time on work of a fully skilled bricklayer, and is therefore entitled to the Grade I rate, and should be paid accordingly as from the first full pay following the date of this decision.

9 December 1925

RAIL 1172/340 Southern Railway Company
S.F. Lane

MR REYNOLDS: The letter from the Union which raises this case is as follows: 'Dear Sir, S.F. Lane – Grade II. Machinist Grinder. Eastleigh Loco. Works. This case has been discussed between the Company's representatives and those of this Union but it has not been possible to arrive at an agreement. My committee have gone into the man's claim for regrading and they are of the opinion that he is entitled to that of a Grade I Machinist. I shall be glad if you will fix a date for a hearing, to decide the case. Yours faithfully, C.T. Cramp.'

MR CARTER: I think on the first page of the statement which I have handed in you will find all the particulars about this man Lane.

'This man is graded as a Grade II Machinist and claims that in view of the nature of the machine and the work he is called upon to do he is entitled to Grade I rate. Lane is working a 22" Churchill Centre Lathe, which is 10 feet long between centres. He has to perform all classes of work such as Piston Rods and Valve Spindles, and has had 20 years of Grinding and Lapping experience. When this machine was first put down at Eastleigh a representative of the firm attended as a demonstrator for 8 days whilst he was learning. The machine in question is a very sensitive one and works up to a quarter of thousand part of an inch by automatic adjustment and turns out the work in 50 per cent of the time previously taken. The following work was performed on this machine by Lane during four weeks in March and April of this year; which but for this machine would have had to be done by Turners.' And then there follow particulars of the work, which I need not read. That gives you the class of work that he did.

The Court are not satisfied on the evidence that the man's qualifications have been shown to be such as to bring him within Grade I, and they decide accordingly.

23 December 1925

RAIL 1172/349 London, Midland and Scottish Railway Company
A.E Smith

MR REYNOLDS: The parties before the Court are the National Union of Railwaymen and the London, Midland & Scottish Railway. The Union's letter raising the question is as follows: '26th March, 1926. Dear Sir; A.F. Smith – Carpenter, Derby. I have been in communication with the London, Midland & Scottish Company with a view to Smith being raised from Grade II to Grade I, but the Company cannot see their way to agree to this man receiving the Grade I rate. I am instructed by my Committee to ask you to fix a date for the hearing of this case. Yours faithfully, C.T. Cramp'

MR CARTER: This is the case of A.E Smith, of the London, Midland & Scottish Railway. He entered the Company's service in October 1918, and he commenced with the Company as a joiner. He had served an apprenticeship, and he has his indentures. He received the same rate as other men employed at his depot for the same trade, and his rate before the Award was 46s. plus 16s.6d. bonus. Under the Award he is getting 42s. plus 16s.6d. He is claiming to be graded as a Grade I carpenter.

This man was employed by the late Midland Section in 1917 as a carpenter and joiner, and passed the trade test at Leicester. When the local agreement at Derby was agreed to in 1919, the rate for skilled men was 43s. per week and 2s. per week service money. Smith, however, was overlooked, and after local effort he was given the same rate as other skilled men, namely, 46s. Since the operation of the 728 Award he has been graded as a Grade II man with a 42s. rate, and in consequence of this, local efforts were made to get him regraded, but without effect. The Company claim that he has been graded as a coach repairer. The work performed by Smith is mainly on vehicles that do not require to be sent in to the shop, but are repaired on the platform sidings.

The Court suggest that in the event of a vacancy arising for a Grade I Carpenter or Joiner the question of the employment of the workman concerned in the present reference should be considered by the company.

18 June 1926

RAIL 1172/358 Great Western Railway Company
A.R. Whatley and J. Evans

MR REYNOLDS: The parties before the Court are the National Union of Railwaymen and the Great Western Railway. The Union's letter raising this question is as follows: 'Dear Sir, A.R. Whatley and J. Evans. Claim for Danger Allowance – Masons working on Locks, Port Talbot, G.W.R. These men have been working on a staging 7 feet long and three feet six inches wide, erected one foot above the water level, and four feet below the dock quay. They were engaged refixing coping stones, pointing and bricklaying on the dock walls. Application has been made both locally and through the General Manager for payment of a danger allowance, but agreement cannot be reached. In view of this my Committee are of opinion that the question should be settled by the Industrial Court. In these circumstances, I shall be glad if you will favour me with a date for the hearing. Yours faithfully, C.T. Cramp'.

THE PRESIDENT: Will you present the case to us, Mr Carter?

MR CARTER: This is the case of A.R. Whatley and J. Evans, who are masons working on locks at Port Talbot Docks, and it is a claim for danger allowance. During the weeks ending February 6th and 13th these men were engaged refining coping stones, pointing and bricklaying on the dock walls at Port Talbot. The work was carried out on a staging 7 feet long and 3 feet 6 inches wide, which was erected 4 feet below the dock quay and 1 foot above the water level. The depth of the water was 30 feet, and the only means of protection afforded the men was lifebelts.

Application was made to the local engineer for a danger allowance, but he refused, and a subsequent effort was made with the General Manager, and the latter refused on the ground that there was no particular danger. It is, however, interesting to note that although the management state there was no particular danger, they supplied the men with lifebelts.

Repairs carried out by masons are generally those on bridges and viaducts. Where a river or deep ravine is directly below the bridge or viaduct and the men work on staging, they are generally paid a danger allowance; for instance, the case of the masons at Muirhouse, in which Award No. 1210 granted the men concerned 1d. per hour whilst so engaged. There is also the case of the carpenters at Deptford Wharf who were working on a swinging scaffold; they were granted 1s. per week by the Industrial Court. Additional to the above, it is not the general practice in the trade for masons to carry out repairs to dock walls on a staging over water without the position being recognised by the payment of an additional allowance.

That is our case for the present.

After careful consideration of the evidence and arguments submitted by the parties, the Court have come to their conclusion and so decide that in the circumstances referred to, the case is not one in which, having regard to the provisions of Condition 11 of Schedule F to Decision No. 728, an extra payment should be made.

GREAT WESTERN RAILWAY.

TERMS OF SETTLEMENT AS BETWEEN THE RAILWAY COMPANIES ON THE ONE HAND AND THE NATIONAL UNION OF RAILWAYMEN, ASSOCIATED SOCIETY OF LOCOMOTIVE ENGINEERS & FIREMEN, AND THE RAILWAY CLERKS' ASSOCIATION ON THE OTHER.

1. Those employees of the Railway Companies who have gone out on strike to be taken back to work as soon as traffic offers and work can be found for them. The principle to be followed in reinstating to be seniority in each grade at each station, depot or office.

2. The Trade Unions admit that in calling a strike they committed a wrongful act against the Companies and agree that the Companies do not by reinstatement surrender their legal rights to claim damages arising out of the strike from strikers and others responsible.

3. The Unions undertake:—
   (a) not again to instruct their members to strike without previous negotiations with the Companies.
   (b) to give no support of any kind to their members who take any unauthorised action.
   (c) not to encourage Supervisory employees in the Special Class to take part in any strike.

4. The Companies intimated that arising out of the strike it may be necessary to remove certain persons to other positions, but no such person's salary or wages will be reduced. Each Company will notify the Unions within one week the names of men whom they propose to transfer and will afford each man an opportunity of having an advocate to present his case to the General Manager.

5. The settlement shall not extend to persons who have been guilty of violence or intimidation.

On behalf of the General Managers' Conference:—	On behalf of the Railway Trade Unions:—	
Felix J. C. Pole.	J. H. Thomas,	National Union of Railwaymen.
H. G. Burgess.	C. T. Cramp,	
H. A. Walker.	J. Bromley,	Associated Society of Locomotive Engineers and Firemen.
R. L. Wedgwood.		
R. H. Selbie.	A. G. Walkden,	Railway Clerks' Association.

Dated this Fourteenth Day of May, Nineteen Hundred and Twenty-six.

Great Western Railway Company. Terms of settlement between the railway companies and the National Union of Railwaymen, the Associated Society of Locomotive Engineers & Firemen, and the Railway Clerks Association, 14 May 1926. (TNA, RAIL 786/6)

22 December 1926

RAIL 1172/383   Southern Railway Company
E. Allen

E. Allen, Engineering Department, Twickenham [as a result of war injuries is unable to do his former work]

Mr Harris for the National Union of Railwaymen

The place at which Allen [26 years service with the company] is employed is a depot for the Engineering Department, and is one of the centres from which is carried out the repair and maintenance of the company's property such as stations, buildings, offices, etc. There are about 100 men attached to the depot, and whilst a considerable number of them would be working in the depot during the day, others would be working away on the various jobs; but in a large number of cases those latter men would visit for various purposes such as booking on and off duty, and getting materials.

Allen's work consists of sweeping up and burning sawdust from the carpenter's shop, clearing out sawdust from the sawmill, checking scaffolding, barrows and wagon sheets in and out of the depot, loading and unloading material, and sweeping and clearing up the yard. In addition to these duties he has to clean out the earth latrines, of which there are three cubicles, and a trough containing sawdust in which the men urinate.

Allen has to take away the excrement from the earth latrines in an open iron wheel barrow and bury it in a spare piece of land. The water from the trough filters through the sawdust into a sump hole. Allen has to bale this out and dispose of it in the same piece of land, which is approximately 125 yards away. He also removes the saturated sawdust from the trough and fills it with clean sawdust. The saturated sawdust being buried with the other excrement…

I think it will be generally agreed that a man doing work of this nature even for a period of only two hours a day, is working in a very putrid atmosphere; and not only is he working in a

Southern Railway Company c.1930. Mr Charles Anderson (left) and his father. The man furthest from the camera is unknown. (TNA, RAIL 1017/2)

very putrid atmosphere, but the very nature of his work suggests to one's mind that his clothes are saturated not only with the stench, but possibly with the substance of the matter he is dealing with; and therefore we have no hesitation in putting forward the claim for an additional payment...

I am given to understand that even in the Army men doing this particular work are doled out an extra ration of rum.

… it is never too late to mend a wrong and get what we can for a man. I am reminded of the story of the three Scotchmen [sic] who came to London for a holiday, if I may venture to tell it. Each of them had an eight day railway ticket, and on the afternoon of the evening upon which they were due to return one of them died. The other men inquired of the Railway Company what the charge would be to take the corpse back to Aberdeen. The Railway Company said it would be the usual charge of 1s 6d a mile. The men could not see their way clear to pay that so they got a taxi, took the deceased man to Kings Cross and propped him up in the corner of the compartment. As the train was on the move a gentleman got in and said, 'Excuse me, I am a doctor, is that man a friend of yours?' and they said 'Yes'. 'Well,' said the doctor 'He looks very ill'. 'Yes' they said 'We know that'. Then approaching Grantham he said again 'Excuse me Gentlemen, I'm afraid your friend has expired'. 'Yes' they said, 'We know that, but his ticket has not.' Just as those men wanted to get full value for what had been paid to the Railway Company, so we are asking the Court this morning to take into consideration the claim that we have made…

'The Court have given careful consideration to the facts and arguments submitted to them and are of opinion that the work in question is not of such a nature as to warrant the payment of a special allowance.'

Sir Harold Morris
President
28 October 1929

RAIL 1172/413 London, Midland and Scottish Railway Company
A. Bird, C. Watts and A. Howlett

MR REYNOLDS: The parties before the Court are the National Union of Railwaymen and the London, Midland & Scottish Railway. The difference between the parties arises on an application for extra payment of ½d. per hour whilst working on electrified lines with current on – Grade 2 Carpenters A. Bird and C. Watts and Grade 2 Labourer A. Howlett, Hartland Road Bridge, from September 1st to 6th and 9th to 12th, 1930. The Union ask that the Industrial Court should determine whether the correct payment has been made under Clause 11 of Schedule F to Award No. 728.

MR HUMPHREYS: The application, Sir; is for extra payment of ½d per hour while working on electrified lines. It is made by Grade 2 Carpenters A. Bird and C. Watts and Grade 2 Labourer A. Howlett, Hartland Road Bridge, London, Midland & Scottish Railway.

We want to ask the Industrial Court to give a decision, as a point of interpretation, whether Grade 2 Carpenters A. Bird and C. Watts, and Grade 2 Labourer A. Howlett should be paid an additional ½d per hour for the whole of the period they were employed in connection with the renewing of certain timbers in between electrified lines, with the current on, from the 1st to 6th and 9th to 12th September; 1930.

The men are employed by the London, Midland & Scottish Railway Company. Carpenter A. Bird entered the service of the late Midland Railway Company on the 11th May, 1884, was promoted to Carpenter, and subsequently made a Chargeman in October, 1900. His wages are 48s. plus war wage 16s.6d. Carpenter C. Watts entered the service of the late Midland Railway

Company on the 5th March, 1900, as a Labourer, and was appointed Carpenter in 1908. His wages are 46s. plus war wage 16s.6d. Labourer A. Howlett entered the service of the Company on the 6th October, 1922, as a Grade 2 Labourer. His wages are 33s. plus war wage 16s.6d. The three men are stationed at Kentish Town Depot.

The men were employed on the fixing of timbers at Hartland Road Bridge. The running rails on the bridge are fixed on 10 inch square longitudinal timbers, interspaced by lengths of 5 inch timber fixed in horizontal position. There are also lengths of 5 inch timber between the bridge and the outside of the longitudinal timbers; in addition there are pieces of 5 inch timber which have to support the 5 inch timber between the bridge and the rail, these being placed in a vertical position against the side of the bridge.

The longitudinal timbers were placed in position under the running rails on Sunday, when the electrical power was 'off', but the other timbers were fixed during the ordinary working week, that is, Monday to Saturday, with the current 'on'. The wood was placed between the two positive rails in the 6 foot way, and the men had to get each piece of wood from this place as they required it for placing in its final position. This work involved the frequent crossing and re-crossing of the positive rails.

The Company have paid the men an additional ½d per hour in respect of 50 per cent of the time they were employed on the bridge. It is claimed, however, that payment should be made for the whole period, 70¾ hours.

The permanent way over the bridge is kept free from slag ballast by means of timbers which run the whole width of the bridge, that is to say, the lengths of timber run crosswise to the running rails to prevent ballast from encroaching on the bridge itself.

The rough sketches submitted may assist the members of the Court to an understanding of the actual conditions which exist at the site where the work was performed. Exhibit 'A' gives an end view, and Exhibit 'B' a side view of the place.

The portion of the work in respect of which payment has been made is for that marked 'A', that is, where the timber is nearest to the positive rail. The Company have refused to pay for the time occupied in renewing timbers which are 6 ft. 4 ins, from the positive rail. In support of their decision the Company have made reference to the Court's Award No. 1455. It is the view of the Union that the case dealt with in this Award is not analogous to the one now under consideration. The painters concerned in the case covered by the Award were working in an area where the protection boards were 1 inch higher than the live rail. In the claim now before the Court the men were working in an area where protection boards are not fixed. It will be appreciated, therefore, that the work was of an exceptionally dangerous character, and as such the claim under the provisions of Award No. 728, Schedule F, Clause 11, for payment for the whole period is justified by the facts.

I may add, Sir, that all the material was not only deposited but cut between the two positive rails of the up and down road and had to be carried across on to the bridge, the reason being that there was no room on the left hand side of Exhibit 'A'. There was no room there at all to deposit the timber or to work the material. I am informed also that ½d an hour extra has been paid to men doing such work. Therefore the Union considers that the facts of the case justify their claim. We have here the chargeman, A. Bird, as a witness to the facts.

The Court have given careful consideration to the contentions of the parties in regard to the present claim and are of opinion that the claim of the union has not been established. They award accordingly.

21 April 1932

RAIL 1172/419   London, Midland and Scottish Railway Company
A. Warren, R. White and F. West

MR HUMPHREYS: This is an application for Dangerous Work Allowance for Labourers

A. Warren, R. White and F. West of the Civil Engineer's Department, Willesden, London, Midland & Scottish Railway. The application before the Court is to ask the Court to determine by way of interpretation the claim of Grade II Labourers A. Warren, R. White and F. West, employed by the London, Midland & Scottish Railway Company in the Engineer's Department at Willesden, for extra payment in accordance with the provisions of Clause 11, Schedule F, of Industrial Court Award No. 728, when employed in connection with excavation work at Kensal Green Station during the period 6th June to 25th July, 1933. The history of the claim is as follows. Labourers A. Warren, R. White and F. West were employed from the 6th June to the 25th July, 1933, on the excavation of soil from the back of the retaining wall at Kensal Green Station. In their view, the work was of a dangerous character, and they submitted an application for payment of a Danger Allowance. The claim was refused by the local Management, and subsequently the application was referred to the Civil Engineer's Departmental Line Committee for consideration. The case was discussed at the meeting of the Committee held on the 27th September, 1933, when the representatives of the Company indicated that the claim could not be granted. The matter was referred to the Union, and representations were made to the Company's Headquarters with a view to securing the granting of the men's request. The Company, however, declined to make an allowance on the ground that the work was not of an exceptionally dangerous character.

The Union contends that, having regard to the depth at which the men were required to work and the danger which existed while they were working in the trench, the work was of an exceptionally dangerous character. The retaining wall in question is approximately 6 feet

Amalgamated Society of Railway Servants, Reading Branch, *c.* 1910. (TNA, RAIL 1057/3395)

wide at the top, battering out to 11 feet at the bottom. It supports a bank of earth, on the top of which are about thirty houses. The backs of the houses are about 37 feet from the inner edge of the retaining wall, and the distance between the fence at the bottom of the yards of the houses and the wall is about 7 feet. The excavations were necessary because the retaining wall had become badly cracked, and were made to allow of the wall being drilled to place eight tie rods and plates to hold it to the new concrete with which the trench was filled up. A crane was used for the removal of the earth and lowering of the concrete to fill up the trench. The material for the concrete was hoisted to the top of the bank at a point about 100 yards from the excavations, mixed up and transported to the site by means of a light railway. A rough sketch, showing the method adopted in timbering the trench, is submitted for the information of the Court. It will be seen that the shoring timbers were let into the wall at one end, and it is the considered opinion of the men that the danger of these timbers becoming loose existed by reason of the wall being 'on the move'. That is, it was creeping. They state that, after the struts of timber had been fixed, the wall moved half an inch, and there was always the possibility of a further move taking place. The necessity for strongly timbering the sides of the trench is also evidence of the danger which existed. Further, the weight of the houses and the bank of earth pressing against the shoring timbers, together with vibration arising from the passage of trains, added to the danger, and there was need for a constant watch to be kept on the condition of the retaining wall and the sides of the trench whilst the work was in progress.

The approximate measurements of the trench were 25 feet long; 4 feet, 6 inches wide; and the total depth reached was between 32 and 33 feet.

In addition to the strain imposed upon the men by these circumstances, the depth at which they had to work was exceptional, and this fact added to the dangerous nature of the job. Had a fall of earth taken place, or a piece of timber become dislodged, the possibility of injury to the men was greater than it would have been in a hole less deep. The Union, therefore, suggests that the circumstances outlined are indicative of the fact that the job was exceptionally dangerous, and ask the Court to decide that the claim for payment of Danger Allowance has been substantiated.

MR LAZENBY: The claim preferred in this case by the National Union of Railwaymen, as Mr Humphreys has stated, is on behalf of the three labourers named who are employed in the Civil Engineer's Department of the London, Midland & Scottish Railway. It is a claim for extra payment under the provisions of Clause 11, Schedule F, to Award No. 728, and relates to work performed whilst doing excavating at Kensal Green Station during the period from the 6th June to the 25th July, 1933. As was stated by Mr Humphreys, the claim is made on the ground that the work performed was of a dangerous nature.

As Mr Humphreys has also told you, the application was considered at a meeting of the Departmental Line Committee on the 27th September last, and I will read to you the minute, from which it will be seen that the claim then made was for five men; but two of them are not now in the Company's service.

The Court have given careful consideration to the evidence submitted and while they are not satisfied that in general the work was of an exceptionally dangerous character they are of opinion that having regard to the nature of the work, the conditions under which it was carried out, and the classification of the labourers employed, some allowance should be made to the men concerned. They suggest that the allowance should be 5s per man and that the Company should deal with the matter on this basis.

12 July 1934

RAIL 1172/436 Great Western Railway Company
F.C. Mundy

The facts of this case as agreed between the Company and the National Union of Railwaymen are as under:

F.C. Mundy entered the Company's service on June 10th, 1919, as a Labourer at the Civil Engineering Dept. Depot at West Ealing, and is still attached to that depot.

Under the provisions of Industrial Court Decision No. 728 he was graded as Labourer Grade 1 and paid at the rate of 32/6d. plus 16/6d. per week war wage from 1st October, 1922, and 34/- plus 16/6d. per week war wage as from 1st November, 1922.

On 9th June, 1930, he was transferred to a post as Fitter's Mate, his rate of pay being increased to 35/- per week plus 16/6d. war wage.

In November, 1933, Mundy met with an accident on duty which incapacitated him from employment as Fitter's Mate and since his return to duty on 8th January, 1934, he has been employed as a Labourer Grade 1 upon various light duties.

In his capacity either as a Labourer or Fitter's Mate attached to the West Ealing Depot he is liable, in common with the majority of the staff at that depot, to work at any point within the area of maintenance of the West Ealing Inspector of Mechanics.

Two regular Chainmen are attached to the West Ealing Depot and these are augmented as may be found necessary from time to time by obtaining volunteers from the labouring grades.

It has been the practice to pay such men up to the appropriate rate of chainmen and to apply to them the conditions applicable to the grade of Chainman during the time they are so employed.

The Inspector of Mechanics at the West Ealing Depot ordinarily provides from his staff Chainmen necessary to work with the technical staff of:

(a) The Chief Engineer (who covers the whole of the Great Western system) and
(b) the Paddington Divisional Engineer (who covers the London Division).

During 1935 Mundy was given the opportunity of employment as a temporary Chainman on various occasions and was employed as Chainman for 49 days between April and October 1935. On 14 of these days he was employed at Twyford which is in the London Engineering Division, but not within the area of the West Ealing Inspector, and it is in respect of these 14 days that the claim is made.

The Court have given careful consideration to the evidence submitted and the contentions of the parties and find that the man concerned is employed from time to time as a Chainman on the staff of the London Divisional Engineer. They also find that when so employed he is paid the rate for a chainman and that on material dates he was so employed and paid. The man's home station or district whilst so employed is the district under the control of the London Divisional Engineer within which Twyford is situated. The claim falls to be dealt with accordingly and the Court so award.

18 January 1938

CHAPTER 9

RAILWAY MAGAZINES AND NEWSPAPERS

Many of the larger railway companies produced their own magazines and included regular features on staff matters. Obituaries and marriages are recorded for all grades of staff and often include photographic portraits. Examples of some such entries are given in this chapter. Local newspapers too, should not be overlooked. A listing of railway magazines is given in the Bibliography.

RAILWAY MAGAZINES

The Railway Times Vol. XIV, No. 41, 11 October 1851

CARELESSNESS OF GUARDS AND DRIVERS

The following accidents, which have occurred during the week, form a sad exemplification of a great laxity of discipline among the working men of the railway system. The fear of punishment, as well as that of self-preservation, would indeed seem to have lost their influence where they are most required:

YORK AND NORTH MIDLAND.– An inquest was held at Burton Salmon on Saturday on view of the body of Thomas Gowland, guard, aged 24, who was killed on Friday near the Burton Salmon station. It appeared from the evidence that the deceased was the guard of a coke train which was on its way from York, when it was overtaken by a short goods train from Milford junction. The driver and guard of the latter train were aware of its proximity to deceased's train, and both trains were nearly at a standstill, when the goods train went slowly up to the other, with the intention of assisting to give it a start from the station. The coke train being, however, the more heavily laden of the two, and all the buffers being closed up, the engine of the goods train ran into the last carriage of the coke train, and caused it to bounce up, forcing it into the guard's van. Deceased fell out of the van with his face downwards across the rails. He was conveyed to the station, and medical assistance was procured, but he died about two hours after the accident, one of his arms and his body having been dreadfully crushed. The jury returned a verdict of 'accidentally killed.' At the same time they considered that there had been some negligence on the part of the driver of the engine of the second train in not sounding his whistle on approaching the coke train, and they trusted that the melancholy result of this accident would prove a caution to railway officials generally for the future.

EAST INDIA DOCK JUNCTION.—On Wednesday evening an accident took place on the railway, whereby an engine-driver, named William Baker, aged 32 years, received such fearful injuries that he expired shortly afterwards. The train which contained a number of passengers left the Camden Town station for the purpose of proceeding to the Blackwall terminus, Fenchurch Street, City. The night was dark, and when the train approached the Kingsland platform the stoker suddenly missed the engine-driver. The former shut off the steam, and the train was stopped when the officials and others after searching for the deceased found him on the roof of one of the carriages next to the tender. Mr Welsh, jun., surgeon, was promptly in attendance and rendered every assistance to the injured man, who died in great agony in a few minutes after the arrival of the medical gentleman. The general opinion is that the deceased must have gone along the roof of the carriage to close one of the doors which had been left open, and thereby met his death by being knocked down by the archway or tunnel passing under the Kingsland-road.

Great Western Railway Magazine and Temperance Union Record Vol. II, No. 20, June 1890

MR JAMES BRADLEY

In the biographical sketches which we gave of Mr Hugh Owen, and Mr Robert Roscoe, we introduced two personages of a thoroughly representative character, who, in their respective sections of the Service, linked the Great Western of the present with the Great Western of the long

Mr James Bradley.

G.W.R. Men who have Lost their Lives in the War.

Staff details from *Great Western Railway Magazine*, Vol. 27, No. 1, January 1915.

1.—E. W. TURNER, an army reservist, who was 27 years of age, had been in the G.W.R. service three months when called to the Colours, having been employed as a labourer in the Locomotive department at Old Oak Common. He died on October 26th from wounds received at a place unknown.

2.—A. J. BAILEY, a labourer in the Locomotive department at Old Oak Common, was an army reservist, and at the outbreak of war joined his old regiment, the 2nd Battalion Highland Light Infantry. He was 30 years old, and had been in the G.W.R. service eight years. He died in an ambulance hospital on September 23rd from wounds received at a place unknown.

3.—GEORGE STEVENS, who was 22 years of age, had been a porter in the Traffic department at Landore since January 1914.

4.—LAURENCE S. JOHNSON, for two years a packer in the Engineering department at Ruislip, volunteered for the Army immediately after the war broke out. He died of fever while serving with the Colours on October 21st. His age was 21.

5.—JOHN G. ILSLEY was an army reservist, 28 years of age. He entered the G.W.R. service as a labourer in the Signal Works at Reading in June, 1907, and was appointed as a riveter in November the following year.

6.—JAMES CARD, who was 29 years of age, was a packer in the Engineering department at Lawrence Hill. He joined the G.W.R. service in June, 1905. Being an army reservist, he was called to the Colours on the outbreak of the war.

7.—J. MONK, whose age was 22, was a temporary packer in the Engineering department at Stroud. He had been in the G.W.R. service since May 5th, 1913.

8.—G. H. PROWSE, a porter in the Goods department at Oxford, was a private in the Oxford and Bucks Light Infantry. He joined the G.W.R. service in 1908. His age was 30. He died of wounds in Boulogne hospital.

9.—WILLIAM RANKIN, who was attached to the Royal Field Artillery, had been a housekeeper in the Goods department at Hockley since October, 1913. He was killed in action on September 9th. His age was 27.

10.—E. THOMPSON was a fitter's labourer in the Locomotive department at Old Oak Common. He was an army reservist, and had been employed by the G.W.R. Co. one year when called to the Colours. His age was 29. He was a corporal in the 2nd Battalion Yorkshire Regiment, and was killed in action on October 22nd at a place unknown.

11.—G. F. LEE, carriage cleaner at Old Oak Common, was a naval reservist, and on the outbreak of war was given the position of 1st class stoker on board H.M.S. *Aboukir*, which was sunk in the North Sea on September 22nd, when he lost his life. He was 33 years old, and had been employed by the G.W.R. Co. a little over a year.

12.—HENRY F. MILTON, who was 26 years of age, had been in the G.W.R. Co.'s service a little over a year, first as a porter in the Traffic department at Newport High Street, and later as a signal porter at Pyle.

past, and following in the same groove we now bring to the front one of the oldest representatives of another section, Mr James Bradley, the Down Shed Superintendent, Paddington Goods Department.

Mr Bradley, who is a native of Four Oaks, near Sutton Coldfield, was born in 1815, and 29 years later he joined the porterage staff in Paddington Goods. The Goods yard and offices then occupied sites close to Bishop's Road Bridge, now covered by the Passenger station and the General offices, some of the arches of the bridge being utilized for the receipt of goods to be sent forward. The aspect of the surroundings was at that time of an almost rural character, the Goods yard was fringed with a large green field, extending in the direction of Praed Street, and on a portion of which the Great Western Hotel has since been built. The entrance to the yard was by a long avenue, a pretty lodge gate standing near the Royal Mint Tavern. Extending from the Mint to Bishop's Road, and bordering the canal, was a bank planted with flowers and evergreens, now no longer 'a bank whereon the wild thyme grows,' but a dreary looking receptacle for the contents of coal trucks. When Mr Bradley entered on his duties there were two Down and two Up trains forming the Company's whole goods train service, with 25 trucks to a train as a maximum. The whole of the Company's stock of Goods waggons was 319, and the Staff of Paddington Goods numbered 70. The development of the traffic in less than half-a-century may be gauged by the fact that the Goods waggon stock of the Line has increased from 319 to nearly 37,000, and that the staff under the present Paddington Goods Superintendent is 1,400.

The business life of Mr Bradley has been that of a quiet, plodding, hardworking servant, unvaried by any thrilling incident or sensational event, but it is needless to add he has witnessed many great changes in the railway world about him. In the commencement of his career, he saw the third class passenger 'stowed' in an open truck, travelling only though the hours of darkness or the grey morning by a goods train, and arriving at his destination after hours of tedious pace, covered not unfrequently with snow. The beginning of this month he sees the same class of passenger enjoying in an express train, which for speed beats the record, an expedition, coupled with even the luxuries of railway travelling. He has seen the green fields about Paddington one by one disappear, and although he has shifted his quarters westward to a more commodious goods station, he has lately witnessed that station, even with its many modern extensions and appliances, at times scarcely adequate to meet the exigencies of a still increasing traffic.

Mr Bradley's record of service may be briefly described. He has served under 10 Superintendents. His promotion to Foreman dates to 1845. His promotion to the position he now holds to 1865. He is a remarkable instance of both mental and physical vigour. Day by day, and in all weathers, he is still to be found at his post, directing the work with his old clearness and application, and when the day arrives that will sever his long connection with the Company, he willl bear away with him from the many with whom he has been associated that esteem and respect engendered by a thorough straightforwardness of character, and a warm heart.

Great Eastern Railway Magazine Vol. 2, No. 23, November 1912

Obituaries

MR THOMAS WILDERSPIN, ex foreman-platelayer, died on August 2nd.

The Way and Works staff at Hunstanton sent a wreath in token of sympathy and respect and the coffin was borne by four platelayers. An account of Mr Wilderspin's retirement, together with a photograph, appeared in our March number this year.

*　*　*

Top left: Mr Hatcher; top right: Miss Garrard. Bottom left: Mr G. Fairchild; bottom right: Mr Clibbens. (From *Great Eastern Railway Magazine*, Vol. 2, No. 23, November 1912.)

As the result of an accident, just before taking duty on September 30th, Mr William Hatcher, who had been cloak-room attendant at Liverpool St. since 1881, died on October 2nd. He entered the service at Bishopsgate in March, 1874, as ticket collector, and came to Liverpool Street in the same capacity the following month. The funeral took place at Woodgrange Park cemetery.

* * *

MISS MAUD GARRARD of the G.E.R. Steam Laundry Colchester, died on 14th Sept. from pleurisy after undergoing two operations. She had been employed at the laundry for about three years, and was much respected by her fellow workers, about seventy of whom attended the funeral which took place at St Michael's Church, Mile End, Colchester.

* * *

MR G. FAIRCHILD, who retired from the service in 1911, has recently died. Joining in 1866 as porter at Enfield, he was subsequently promoted to foreman-porter at the same station, and in 1907 was transferred to Bush Hill Park as ticket collector, where he remained until his retirement.

* * *

The death took place recently after an operation at the London Hospital, of Mr John Clibbens, Superior Foreman at Spitalfields. Mr Clibbens, who was held in very great esteem by all who knew him, was in the Company's service for 39 years, having started in the Spitalfields Granary in October, 1873, where he rose to the post of superior foreman, which he held for 29 years.

Retirements

MR J.H. PAIN, main-line passenger guard, has recently retired, at the age of sixty-three years. Entering the service as lad porter at Ipswich in 1867, he was transferred to the London district in 1872 as foreman-porter at Bruce Grove. He subsequently acted in a similar capacity at Noel Park and at Palace Gates, and in 1879 was appointed second guard at Wood Street, receiving promotion in 1883 to head passenger guard at the same station. In December, 1893, Mr Pain was appointed

Top: Mr J.H. Pain; middle: Mr G. Wilcox; bottom: Mr J. Gotts. (From *Great Eastern Railway Magazine*, Vol. 2, No. 23, November 1912.)

main-line passenger guard at Cambridge, where he remained until March last, when, owing to failing health, he retired on the pension supplemental fund after forty-five years' service.

* * *

MR GEORGE WILCOX, of the Way and Works Signal Fitters' Department, Stratford, recently retired from the service to go into business at Westcliff-on-Sea. He was presented with a well-filled smokers' cabinet by his fellow workmen.

* * *

MR JAMES BRADLY, Cashier at Bishopsgate Goods Station, retired at the end of September after a railway life of fifty years, thirty-four of which were spent with the Great Eastern Company.

Commencing his career with the South-Eastern Railway he entered the service of the Great Eastern Company in May, 1879, at Old Brick Lane Station Accounts Office; after serving some years at Bishopsgate was appointed canvasser; and in 1901 was made cashier.

On September 30th his colleagues and friends at Bishopsgate presented him with a kit bag and a purse of money as a token of their respect. Mr Clemson who presided spoke of the personal esteem in which Mr Bradly was held.

* * *

MR JOHN GOTTS, of the Way and Works Signal Fitters' Department, Stratford, retired on the 20th September, after thirty-seven years' service, and was presented by his fellow workmen with a walking-stick and his portrait painted in oils.

Marriages

CAMBRIDGE. – On September 25th at St. Barnabas Church, Miss Winifred Hutcherson – youngest daughter of Mr A.C. Hutcherson, District Goods Manager, Cambridge – was married to Mr T.A.W. Robinson. The service was conducted by the Vicar, the Rev. W. Norman.

Top: Mr B.G. Hooks; bottom: Mr and Mrs Botwright. (From *Great Eastern Railway Magazine*, Vol. 2, No. 23, November 1912.)

Numerous presents were received, among which was a cruet-stand presented by the District Goods Manager's staff.

* * *

WOODFORD. – On September 2nd Mr B.G. Hooks, booking clerk, was the recipient of a handsome tea service, which was subscribed for by the staff and friends on the occasion of his recent marriage.

The presentation was made by Mr Cadman (stationmaster) who voiced the feelings of the subscribers in wishing Mr Hooks long life and happiness.

* * *

BISHOPSGATE (LOW LEVEL). – On 7th October the staff presented Mr Botwright (ticket-collector) with a wedding gift which took the form of a marble clock. The presentation was made by Mr Gotts (stationmaster).

Mr Botwright was also the recipient of a pair of vases from the staff at Stratford Market, where he had been stationed for some months, till August last.

New Appointments

PARKESTON QUAY. – Mr C. Lazell, a clerk in the Continental Department, has lately resigned to take up a position in Australia.
He entered the service in June, 1907, and the best wishes of his colleagues are extended to him in his future career.

* * *

STRATFORD. – Mr S.J. Chignell, who entered the service as a fitter's apprentice in the Way and Works Department on 9th April, 1908, left on the 30th August to join the Metropolitan Police Force.

* * *

ANGEL ROAD. – Mr Reeve, stationmaster, who has recently been promoted to the charge of Lower Edmonton, was, on 17th August, the recipient of a sum of money from the tradesmen and travelling public using Angel Road station, and also a kit bag from past and present members of the staff.

374   GREAT EASTERN RAILWAY MAGAZINE.

Liverpool Street.—The Nineteenth Annual Outing of the Audit Department, which took place on September 21st, proved exceptionally enjoyable, Sir Walter Gilbey kindly granting permission for a visit to his property at Elsenham.

In the paddocks here are to be found some of the finest hackneys in the Country; these were paraded, and the party were charmed with the grace of the beautiful animals.

Next the aviaries, which contain many rare birds from all quarters of the globe, were inspected.

The treasures inside the Hall embracing the celebrated collection of sporting and other pictures, famous cups, and numerous art objects were also seen.

Photo by]   AUDIT OFFICE OUTING.   [F. Mayes, Audit Office.

We reproduce a photo of the party with the Hall in the background. The two central figures, sitting, are (left) Mr. D. P. Hine, son-in-law of Sir Walter, who kindly conducted the party and (right) Mr. H. Starling, head of the famous stud.

Later in the afternoon the journey was continued to Saffron Walden, (an old rendezvous) where a substantial meal was followed by music presided over by Mr. W. Brazier Martin. The general arrangements were made by Mr. F. McClean.

* * *

Mr. Philip H. Morgan, A.M.I.E.E., who for the past two and a half years has been engaged as a charge engineer in the lighting and power department, sailed for Montreal at the beginning of October to take up a position on one of the Canadian railways. Before leaving he was presented with a cheque subscribed by the Electrical Engineer and members of the staff. Prior to his engagement with the Company Mr. Morgan was for three years employed by the Great Western Railway at their Fishguard lighting and power station.

* * *

Mr. C. P. DAVIS who was an assistant attached to the signal section of the Engineer's Department, left the service on the 13th September and sailed for South Africa. His many friends wish him success in his new sphere.

MR. C. P. DAVIS.

Two members of the staff of the Goods Manager's Mineral Office have recently been married, the first wedding being that of Mr. Alfred Humphreys to Miss Florence Ward on the 7th September, and the second that of Mr. H. G. Dresch to Miss Katherine Cole on the 21st of the same month.

Each gentleman was the recipient of a present from his colleagues, that to Mr. Humphrey taking the form of a massive floor lamp and shade, and that to Mr. Dresch of a mahogany coal cabinet.

MR. A. HUMPHREYS.

MR. AND MRS. H. G. DRESCH.

* * *

Chingford.—Mr. A. V. Goodwin, booking clerk recently transferred to London Fields, was on September 25th presented with a kit-bag, oak tea-tray and pair of vases, by Mr. H. Markley (Station Master) on behalf of the staff at Chingford.

Staff details from *Great Eastern Railway Magazine*, Vol. 2, No. 23, November 1912.

Top left: Mr Lazell; top right: Mr S.G. Chignell. Bottom left: Mr Reeve; bottom right: Mr J. Faulkner. (From *Great Eastern Railway Magazine*, Vol. 2, No. 23, November 1912.)

Mr Doggett (shunter) made the presentation on behalf of the staff, and wished Mr Reeve success in his new appointment.

* * *

BRIMSDOWN. – An interesting ceremony took place at Brimsdown recently, the occasion being a presentation to Mr G.M. Green, who was stationmaster at Brimsdown for upwards of three years, till June last, when he was promoted to the charge of Ponder's End. The gift took the form of a gold watch, bearing the inscription 'Presented to Mr G.M. Green by his friends at Brimsdown, September, 1912.' The presentation was made by Mr W.A. Humfrey (Works Manager of the Brimsdown Lead Company) on behalf of the subscribers, supported by Mr Thomas Hills.

Presentations

ST MARGARET'S. – Our readers will be interested to know that H.M. The King has conferred upon Mr David Wheal, gate-porter, the Edward Medal for bravery. It will be remembered that Mr Wheal was the means of saving the life of an old lady at St Margaret's on 15th May, an account of which occurrence, together with Mr Wheal's portrait, appeared in our July number. Mr Wheal has also been the recipient of a silver watch, suitably inscribed, from the Carnegie Hero Fund.

* * *

STRATFORD MARKET. – Mr J. Sames, of the Printing Department, is leaving with his family for Australia, and on October 4th the compositors and members of the stereo section presented him with a silver watch, suitably inscribed, as a mark of their esteem.

Mr F. Pomphrey presided, and Mr H. Nichols, in making the presentation, wished Mr Sames every success in his new life.

* * *

TOTTENHAM. – On September 18th, Mr J. Faulkner, ticket-collector, on leaving the service for New Zealand, was presented with a handsome dressing-case and fountain pen from the staff; also a leather writing-folio from passengers.

Mr Chapman (foreman-porter), who made the presentation in the absence of the stationmaster, spoke of the esteem in which Mr Faulkner was held and wished him every success in his new life.

Mr Faulkner started as goods porter at Saffron Walden in January, 1899; was transferred to Stratford Market two months later; and in the following year was promoted to ticket-taker at Stepney. He subsequently served at Leman Street, but was soon transferred to Tottenham where he remained for nearly eleven years.

North Eastern & Scottish Magazine Vol. 14, No. 165, September 1924

Retirements

NORTH BRITISH RAILWAY INSURANCE SOCIETY
(Retirements)

Name	Grade	Station	Date of Retirement	Year of Service
Hunter, Robt.	Station Master	Drumchapel	18.7.24	33
Black, James	Porter	Lasswade	30.6.24	50
Hopper, Francis	Pass Guard	Stirling	19.7.24	38
Crawford, Thos.	Controller	Coatbridge	2.8.24	36
Stewart, Robert	Inspector	P.M.O*, Waverley	11.8.24	36
Adam, William	Inspector	Boness	14.7.24	46
Church, John	Stn. Foreman	Queen Street	7.8.24	46
Stewart, Robert	Station Master	Berwick	28.7.24	49

NORTH BRITISH RAILWAY SUPERANNUATION FUND
(Retirements)

Name	Grade and Dept	Date of Retirement
Andrew Cumming	Loco. Shed Foreman, Fort William	14.6.1924
Robert Stewart	Agent, Berwick	25.7.1924
Wm. Malcolm	Agent, Dumbarton	26.7.1924
Thomas Crawford	Controller, Coatbridge	1.8.1924
David P. Duguid	Goods Clerk, High Street	4.8.1924
George Tennant	Agent, East Linton	5.8.1924
Robert Stewart	Inspector, Passenger Manager's Office	9.8.1924

Obituaries

MR THOMAS MATSON, ganger, Croft Spa, met his death under tragic circumstances on July 8. He was out on his length and was killed by a passing train. Mr Matson, who was 68 years of age, had spent 38 years at Croft Spa. He commenced service with the Company in 1876 in the gang at Northallerton and spent practically the whole of his time on the Darlington – Northallerton length. MR JAMES K. MITCHELL, M.B.E., late Goods Agent, Waterloo, who died recently at the comparatively early age of 54, entered the service of the old G.N. of S. Company as a clerk at

---

*   Passenger Manager's Office

Auchnagatt in 1883, and after serving in that capacity at a number of stations was appointed Relief Agent in 1894. He was appointed Stationmaster at Cruden Bay in 1897 and in 1902 was transferred to Ellon, and to Peterhead in 1903. In 1911 he was appointed Inspector of Agencies and in 1913 became Goods Agent at Waterloo. During the war a large amount of extra work fell upon Mr Mitchell in connection with traffic for the Naval Base at Aberdeen, and in recognition of his services he was awarded the honour of M.B .E.

NEWSPAPERS

West Somerset Free Press September 1883

SHOCKING FATALITY TO A STATION-MASTER AT BLUE ANCHOR

Mr Henry Crang, aged sixty-eight, who had been station-master at Blue Anchor, on the Minehead branch railway, for the past seven years, met with his death in a shocking manner at that station on Friday last. It appears that just before the arrival of the mid-day up train from Minehead, Mr Crang, as usual, closed the gates at the level crossing below the station, and saw the line clear. He then stopped and looked over the gate on the Blue Anchor side, against which some of the railway men had been at work. He next went towards the line, and as the train approached stooped down over the metals, as though to pick up something, apparently not noticing or hearing the train, owing to his being rather deaf. He was seen by the fireman in this position, but too late to avert the disaster. The unfortunate man was struck by the axle box of one of the front wheels of the engine, and was hurled a distance of five feet into a hole by the side of the railway where the men had been at work. He was picked up and carried into the station, and died shortly afterwards from the injuries he had received. Mr Crang had been thirty-eight years in the employ of first the Bristol and Exeter and then the Great Western Railway Company, and was afflicted with slight lameness as well as deafness.

An inquest on the body was held on Saturday afternoon, at Mrs Henson's, the Cleeve Bay hotel, before W.W. Munckton, Esq., coroner for West Somerset. Mr Manning was appointed foreman of the jury. Mr Wm. Green, superintendent of police on the Great Western Railway, watched the proceedings on behalf of the company, and Mr Gibson, traffic manager, of Taunton, was also present. The following evidence was taken:

Peter Broomfield, fireman on the Great Western Railway, deposed:—The deceased was the station-master at Blue Anchor. On Friday last I left Minehead in the 11.45 a.m up-train, of which I was stoker. The train was about four minutes late. Joseph Jones was the engine driver. Just as we were approaching Blue Anchor station I saw deceased standing clear of the line at the crossing on the station side. When we got within a few yards of the crossing I saw him stoop down and put out his right hand towards the rail, apparently to pick something off the line, and immediately the leading axle box struck him. I turned round to my mate and told him of it, and he at once stopped the train. My mate went back to deceased. We were going slowly at the time, being on the point of stopping. Several men were standing on the same side of the line by the gate, which was shut. One of them stood inside the gate, a few yards off from deceased.

Robert Prior said: I am a labourer in the employ of the Great Western Railway Company. I was standing three yards from the gate on the Blue Anchor side, in the road, when the 11.45 train came in. I saw the deceased standing at the gate, as mentioned by last witness. He turned round from the gate towards the line, but I went on with my work, and did not notice him until a few seconds afterwards, when he was in a stooping position in a hole close to where I was working, about five feet from the rails. I did not see him thrown there. The gates had been closed three or four minutes, and the line was clear for the train. The train was coming in at the usual pace.

A juror (Mr Harrison) thought Mr Crang should have been on the platform at the time.

Mr Green said the deceased was quite at liberty to be where he was, but there was no necessity for it.

In reply to another juror, the coroner said it appeared that nothing had been found to account for deceased stooping over the line.

Mr Neate (a juror) remarked that deceased was deaf.

The coroner said that was so.

Mr Harrison thought if the gate had been put back earlier deceased would have been upon the platform at the time.

The witness Broomfield, recalled, said when he saw deceased he was quite clear of the line, and there was no necessity to whistle. After that there was no time to pull up more quickly than they did.

The coroner said it was evident that whatever deceased did he did of his own accord. No one touched him.

In answer to a juror, it was stated that deceased, who was lame, got so through slipping on the ice, and that the occurrence had nothing to do with his official duties.

Dr Thomas Clark, of Dunster, stated that he saw the body soon after two o'clock on Friday afternoon, at the station. There were marks of violence. There was a severe contusion on the right side of the head, the right leg was broken, and there were bruises about the body. The injuries were such as doubtless would have been caused in the way mentioned by the previous witnesses, whilst deceased was in a stooping position. In answer to the coroner, who asked the witness if he could offer any suggestion as to why deceased was stooping over the line, Dr Clark said he might mention, though he did not wish it to he taken as his evidence, that a lady told him that she had several times seen deceased stooping in the road as if he were picking up something. It seemed to be a habit he had got.

The coroner: There is nothing tangible about it at all. This is merely secondary evidence. We do not doubt that the death was the result of an accident, but should like to know what deceased was about.

Inspector Needs stated that at the crossing there is a check rail for the purpose of allowing vehicles to go over the running rail easier. His idea was that a stone might have been kicked by a horse between the metal and the check rail, which it would be necessary to take out, and that deceased was in the act of picking it up when knocked down by the train.

The coroner, having asked the jury if they required any further evidence, and received an answer in the negative, proceeded to sum up. He said deceased was well known to all of them, and was highly respected. He was rather deaf and lame. It appeared that he was stooping down over the line, just as the train came in, that he was struck by the engine, and received such injuries as to cause his death. The facts were quite clear, and there was no doubt as to the cause of death. They could not tell what deceased was doing at the time, but he thought the suggestion of the inspector the most probable one. Deceased was deaf, and could not have heard the approach of the train.

The jury at once returned a verdict of 'Accidental death'.

RAIL 1150/1   Great Northern Railway
Yorkshire Post 8 February 1896

DEATH OF MR FRANCIS COCKSHOTT

A large circle of the railway travelling public will learn with regret of the death of Mr Francis P. Cockshott, the ex-superintendent of the Great Northern Railway Company, and one of the pioneers of our modern railway organisation. Although Mr Cockshott was 70 years of age, and retired from the active duties of railway life with the close of last year, his death was sudden and entirely unexpected. The deceased gentleman had appeared in almost robust health since leaving King's Cross, and in company with two of his daughters spent Thursday evening at the house of a friend. He reached his home at Tufnell Park at about midnight, when he appeared in the best of health and spirits. After removing his coat and hat in the hall he went into the breakfast room, and a few minutes later, while talking with some of his family, suddenly became unwell. Medical aid was immediately summoned, but within about quarter of an hour of his arrival home Mr Cockshott was dead, and the doctor attributed his decease to an attack of syncope. Mr Cockshott's active railway career extended to the long period of 55 years, and may, indeed, be said to be an epitome of English railway history. As a schoolboy he often rode on the foot-plate of 'No. 1' of the Stockton and Darlington. He was on board the first ship that ever entered Middlesbrough Docks. While yet in his teens he became private secretary to Mr Edward Pease, M.P., treasurer of the Stockton and Darlington and Great North of England Railways, and in that capacity often attended meetings between Mr Pease and George Stephenson. Those were days when the English railway seemed a puny infant, and Edward Pease smiled incredulously at the prediction concerning the future of the locomotive; but the old Quaker was captured by the adroit Stephenson, who said, 'I think, sir, I have some knowledge of craniology, and from what I see of your head I feel sure that if you fairly buckle to this railway you are the man to successfully carry it through.' Mr Pease did buckle to, and did carry it through, and on this railway Mr Cockshott began his training. It was reckoned a big thing then that 'in some parts the speed was frequently 12 miles an hour.' Last August, in the railway race to the North, under Mr Cockshott's superintendence the Great Northern train ran from King's Cross to Grantham, 105 miles in 106½ minutes. If he recalled the conversations he overheard in his boyish days on the Stockton and Darlington Railway, he must have marvelled at the strides which railways had made in his own experience. From Darlington Mr Cockshott went, after a short training in the engineering shops of the Stockton Railway at Shildon, to Scotland as goods manager for [sic] and later on became superintendent of the Edinburgh and Northern, afterwards known as the Edinburgh, Perth, and Dundee, whose trains from Leith were hauled up by a stationary engine through the Scotland Street tunnel – now abandoned to mushroom growing – into the then new Waverley Station in Edinburgh. Leaving this company, whose financial position made it questionable whether the officers' salaries were certain to be paid, in 1851, he went to the South Devon, where the atmospheric system had only recently been abandoned. In 1858 he took charge of the Cornwall Railway also, and it was here he was associated with the famous Brunel, who designed the great bridge with its 19 spans across the Tamar at Saltash, and also the celebrated Cornish viaducts. It fell to Mr Cockshott to conduct Brunel, lying on his back on a carriage truck, to see for the first and last time his great Saltash Bridge completed. There, too, the intervention of a director, who urged him not to work himself to death, dragged him from the foot-plate of an engine which half-an-hour later ran off the line on a viaduct near St Germans and buried itself and its crew in the mud of the Tamar. In 1865 Mr Cockshott went to King's Cross as superintendent of the Great Northern Railway Company, long known as one of the most progressive as well as one of the largest of English companies, and in his 30 years' work there he worthily upheld its high traditions. When he entered the service of the Great Northern Company he found the best trains – reserved, of course, for first and second-class passengers – taking 10½, 11½, and 16 hours to Edinburgh, Glasgow, and Aberdeen respectively. Before his resignation he saw third-class trains run in 7½, 8, and 10½ hours respectively. But it was not only in the 'race to the North' that Mr Cockshott kept abreast with the times. He inaugurated a system of fast expresses between Manchester and King's Cross, which up to a short time ago were the fastest ordinary daily trains in the world, and in the organisation of the traffic to and from Doncaster at race meetings he achieved some notable reforms. Alluding to this point, in his book on 'Our Railways,' Mr John Pendleton says:

> There is always an enormous crowd at the St Leger; and Mr Francis Cockshott, the superintendent of the Great Northern, has sent me a special traffic sheet showing how they get the mass of people on their way home again. The winner's shout of delight and the loser's curse of despair are scarcely expressed before the exodus begins. On the St Leger Day in 1892 40 trains left the up platform at Doncaster during the afternoon and night. These were chiefly fast ordinary or special express trains, and included the private special excursion train engaged by the Duke of Portland to convey his house party down to Worksop, for Welbeck. No fewer than 43 ordinary and special expresses quitted the down platform. Then the excursion trains were many... no fewer than 173 trains altogether, many inconveniently and humorously crowded with human life, some of the compartments revealing such an amazing variety of struggling people and crushed hats that quietly disposed passengers preferred to seek refuge in the guard's van.

The Great Northern, under Mr Cockshott's superintendence, also largely developed the traffic for milk between the provinces and London, and their competition for the coal traffic of the Midlands is familiar to all. Mr Cockshott brought to bear upon his office work a ripe experience and an ability to grasp intricate detail which was conspicuous to all who were brought in contact with him, and he was courteous and considerate in his personal dealings both with the company's customers and their servants. When he retired it was with the general good wishes of a large circle of friends, who hoped that he might have long enjoyed his well-earned rest, and his sudden death will be the subject of widespread regret.

RAIL 102/9   **A letter from Charles Dickens**

Victoria Hotel
Thursday Twenty Second July 1847

Sir,

I had the honor of calling on you at your office this morning and sent a card to you by one of the gentlemen there. But you were missing engaged and could not be found. Hence I trouble you with this note.

What I desired to say is, that a large party of gentlemen connected with literature and art purpose going to Manchester on a public occasion by the ten o'clock train on Sunday morning next. As they are under my guidance I shall be much obliged if you will direct four compartments of first class carriages to be marked 'Engaged' in my name. (There will be four and twenty persons in the party), and that if I could, consistent with the official regulations, pay the fares before hand, it would be an additional convenience, perhaps.

> I am Sir,
> Your faithful Servant
> Charles Dickens

R Creed Esquire.

24 fares 1st Class by Day Mail one way to Manchester – £51

NOTES ON APPENDICES

Appendix 1 is an alphabetical list of all steam railway companies which have been found to run in England and Wales up to Nationalization in 1947. Additionally, it includes those horse-drawn 'tramways' which were eventually converted to steam or acted as 'feeders' to other steam railways. It also includes those Scottish railways which crossed into England. It does not include the many railways which were incorporated but never built.

Appendix 2 lists the railways which ran in each historic county in England and Wales, arranged chronologically by date of opening. These are in groups, separated at the time of each population census thus enabling a researcher to quickly identify the railways for which a family member, if mentioned in a census as a railway worker, may have worked.

Appendix 3 lists all the known staff registers for each railway company and includes other records where named staff have been found. Section 3.2 gives the railway companies taken over by the GWR at the 1923 Grouping. Sections 3.3, 3.4 and 3.5 list the railway companies which were united to form the LMS, the LNER and the SR respectively. In the latter four sections all known staff records are also given with their appropriate references.

Appendix 4 lists alphabetically all Railway Joint Committees which have been found to have surviving records (159 in total). The constituent companies which formed each Joint Committee are given. Minutes of meetings are listed and in the small number of instances where they exist, related staff registers are also given.

Appendix 5 lists staff records for the Railway Clearing House.

Appendix 6 lists the trades and occupations of employees of railway companies.

Appendix 7 is a selective list of the most important events in railway history.

APPENDIX 1

ALPHABETICAL LIST OF RAILWAY COMPANIES IN ENGLAND AND WALES UP TO NATIONALIZATION IN 1947

Each railway has been given a sequential number which appears in column 1. The name of the railway with any subsequent change of name is given in column 2. Column 3 lists the date of incorporation of the company. In many cases a company was formed by the amalgamation of two or more existing companies. In such cases the word 'amalg.' is given in brackets below the date of incorporation. 'Private' indicates that the railway was built privately and was not incorporated by an Act of Parliament. The relevant document record class at The National Archives is given in column 4. Where there is no dedicated class for a particular company, the record class in which records have been found is entered in brackets. In some instances records exist only in other repositories. In such cases, the abbreviation for the repository is entered in brackets. (A List of Abbreviations is given on p. xii.) Column 5 gives the overall dates covered by the records and column 6 indicates whether or not staff records exist. (Details of these records are given in Appendix 3 with the exception of staff records for joint railways. Surviving staff records for joint railways are given in Appendix 4.) The destiny of the company, whether an amalgamation with, or absorption by another company, or its closure, is given in column 7. This makes it possible to follow through the 'descent' of a company, enabling the researcher to identify and explore the records of the successors. (It has been discovered that some 'parent' companies have records of the staff of the companies they had taken over.)

Note: The spelling of place-names is as given in the original act of incorporation for the railway companies concerned e.g. Dolgelly, Festiniog, Llanelly, etc.

List No.	Name of Company	Date of Incorporation	TNA Record Class	Records		Change of Ownership or Control
				Dates covered	Staff	
1	Abbey Dolgarrog Light Railway Co.	1908	Nil		None	(Built during 1st World War)
2	Abbotsbury Railway Co.	6 Aug 1877	RAIL 1	1877–1896	None	Taken over by the GWR 7 August 1896
3	Abercarn Railway. See Hall's Tramroad, List No. 366					

List No.	Name of Company	Date of Incorporation	TNA Record Class	Records Dates covered	Staff	Change of Ownership or Control
4	Aberdare Railway Co.	31 Jul 1845	RAIL 2	1845–1902	None	Leased to the Taff Vale Railway Co. 1 January 1849 and vested in that company 31 July 1902
5	Aberdare Valley Railway Co.	2 Jul 1855	RAIL 3	1856–1864	None	Leased to the Vale of Neath Railway Co. 1 January 1857. Purchased by that company 21 July 1859
6	Aberford Railway Co.	Private	Nil		None	Abandoned in 1924
7	Aberystwyth and Welsh Coast Railway Co.	22 Jul 1861	RAIL 4	1862–1866	None	Amalgamated with the Cambrian Railways Co. 5 August 1865
8	Abingdon Railway Co.	15 Jun 1855	RAIL 5 (RAIL 1057)	1855–1904	None	Amalgamated with the GWR 1 July 1904
9	Alcester Railway Co.	6 Aug 1872	RAIL 6	1872–1879	None	Worked by the GWR from opening. Vested in the GWR and the Stratford-upon-Avon Railway Co. jointly 22 July 1878
10	Alexandra (Newport and South Wales) Docks and Railway Co.	6 Jul 1865	RAIL 7 (RAIL 1057)	1865–1922	Yes	Became part of the GWR in 1923
11	Alford and Sutton Tramway Co.	12 Aug 1880	Nil		None	Closed in 1889
12	Alton, Alresford and Winchester Railway Co. Re-named the Mid-Hants (Alton Lines) Railway Co. 1 January 1865	28 Jun 1861	Nil		None	Leased to the London and South Western Railway Co. 26 August 1880. Purchased by that company June 1884

List No.	Name of Company	Date of Incorporation	TNA Record Class	Records Dates covered	Staff	Change of Ownership or Control
13	Ambergate, Nottingham and Boston and Eastern Junction Railway Co. Re-named the Nottingham and Grantham Railway and Canal Co. 15 May 1860	16 Jul 1846 (amalg.)	RAIL 8 RAIL 545	1845–1923	None	Leased to the Great Northern Railway Co. 1 August 1861. Became part of the LNER in 1923
14	Amesbury and Military Camp Light Railway	24 Sep 1898	Nil		None	Owned and worked by the London and South Western Railway Co.
15	Andover and Redbridge Railway Co.	12 Jul 1858	RAIL 9 (RAIL 1057)	1857–1865	None	Amalgamated with the London and South Western Railway Co. 29 June 1863
16	Anglesey Central Railway Co.	13 Jul 1863	Nil		None	Purchased by the London and North Western Railway Co. 1 July 1876
17	Ashby and Nuneaton Joint Railway Co.	17 Jun 1867	RAIL 11 (App 4)	1867–1889	Yes App 4	Worked jointly by the London and North Western Railway Co. and the Midland Railway Co.
18	Ashover Light Railway Co.	4 Dec 1919	Nil		None	Remained independent until its closure in 1950
19	Ashton, Stalybridge and Liverpool Junction Railway Co.	19 Jul 1844	Nil		None	Vested in the Manchester and Leeds Railway Co. 9 July 1847
20	Avon and Gloucestershire Railway Co.	19 Jun 1828	RAIL 12	1828–1867	None	Purchased by the GWR 9 July 1852

List No.	Name of Company	Date of Incorporation	TNA Record Class	Records Dates covered	Records Staff	Change of Ownership or Control
21	Avonmouth Light Railway Co.	12 Dec 1893 (amalg.)	Nil		None	Purchased jointly by the GWR and the LMS in 1926
22	Axholme Joint Railway Co. (see List No. 325 and List No. 421)	31 Jul 1902	(RAIL 1057)		None	Vested jointly in the LNER and the LMS in 1923
23	Axminster and Lyme Regis Light Railway Co.	15 Jun 1899	RAIL 14	1900–1907	None	Purchased by the London and South Western Railway Co. 1 January 1907
24	Aylesbury and Buckingham Railway Co.	6 Aug 1860	(RAIL 1057)		None	Taken over by the Metropolitan Railway Co. 1 July 1891
25	Aylesbury and Rickmansworth Railway Co.	18 Jul 1881	Nil		None	Part of the Metropolitan Railway Co. Closed in 1967
26	Aylesbury Railway Co.	19 May 1836	RAIL 15	1835–1841	None	Vested in the London and Birmingham Railway Co. 16 July 1846
27	Bailey's Tramroad	Private (c. 1822)	Nil		None	Purchased by the Merthyr, Tredegar and Abergavenny Railway Co. 1 February 1859
28	Baker Street and Waterloo Railway Co.	28 Mar 1893	(RAIL 1057)		None	Taken over by the London Electric Railway Co. 1 July 1910
29	Bala and Dolgelly Railway Co.	30 Jun 1862	RAIL 16	1862–1877	None	Amalgamated with the GWR 23 July 1877
30	Bala and Festiniog Railway Co.	28 Jul 1873	RAIL 17	1873–1919	None	Amalgamated with GWR 1 July 1910

List No.	Name of Company	Date of Incorporation	TNA Record Class	Records		Change of Ownership or Control
				Dates covered	Staff	
31	Banbury and Cheltenham Direct Railway Co.	21 Jul 1873	RAIL 18	1874–1900	None	Vested in the GWR 1 July 1897
32	Bangor and Caernarvon Railway Co.	20 May 1851	RAIL 19	1851–1860	None	Vested in the Chester and Holyhead Railway Co. 10 July 1854
33	Banstead and Epsom Downs Railway Co.	17 Jul 1862	RAIL 20	1862–1864	None	Amalgamated with the London Brighton and South Coast Railway Co. in 1864
34	Barnoldswick Railway Co.	12 Aug 1867	RAIL 21	1867–1900	None	Vested in the Midland Railway Co. 1 July 1899
35	Barnsley Coal Railway Co.	22 Jul 1861	RAIL 22	1861–1863	None	Purchased by the South Yorkshire Railway and River Dun Navigation Co. 13 July 1863
36	Barnstaple and Ilfracombe Railway Co.	4 Jul 1870	Nil		None	Amalgamated with the London and South Western Railway Co. 16 July 1874
37	Barrington Light Railway Co.	15 Jul 1920	Nil		None	Became part of the LNER in 1923
38	Barry Dock and Railway Co. Re-named the Barry Railway Co. 5 August 1891	14 Aug 1884	RAIL 23 (RAIL 1057)	1884–1923	Yes	Amalgamated with the GWR 1 January 1922
39	Barry Railway Co. See Barry Dock and Railway Co., List No. 38					

List No.	Name of Company	Date of Incorporation	TNA Record Class	Records Dates covered	Staff	Change of Ownership or Control
40	Barton and Immingham Light Railway Co.	19 Jul 1907	RAIL 24	1909–1912	None	Purchased by the Humber Commercial Railway and Dock Co. 7 August 1912
41	Basingstoke and Alton Light Railway Co.	9 Dec 1897	Nil		None	Closed in 1916 and re-opened by the Southern Railway in 1924. Finally closed in 1937.
42	Basingstoke and Salisbury Railway Co.	13 Aug 1846	Nil		None	Taken over by the London and South Western Railway Co. 26 June 1849
43	Bedale and Leyburn Railway Co.	4 Aug 1853	RAIL 26	1852–1859	None	Vested in the North Eastern Railway Co. 8 August 1859
44	Bedford and Cambridge Railway Co. Originally promoted as the Bedford Potton and Cambridge Railway	6 Aug 1860	RAIL 27	1858–1864	None	Vested in the London and North Western Railway Co. 5 July 1865
45	Bedford and London and Birmingham Railway Co. Also known as the Bedford Railway	30 Jun 1845	Nil			Worked by the London and North Western Railway Co. and taken over by that company in 1885
46	Bedford and Northampton Railway Co.	5 Jul 1865	RAIL 28	1865–1886	None	Amalgamated with the Midland Railway Co. 31 December 1885
47	Bedford Railway. See Bedford and London and Birmingham Railway Co., List No. 45					
48	Belvoir Castle Railway	Private (1815)	Nil		None	Closed in 1918

List No.	Name of Company	Date of Incorporation	TNA Record Class	Records Dates covered	Staff	Change of Ownership or Control
49	Bentley and Bordon Light Railway Co.	6 Oct 1902	Nil		None	Built and run by the London and South Western Railway Co. Closed 4 April 1966
50	Bere Alston and Calstock Railway Co.	12 Jul 1900	Nil		None	Run by the Plymouth, Devonport and South Western Junction Railway Co. Became part of the SR in 1923
51	Berkshire and Hampshire Extension Railway Co.	13 Aug 1859	RAIL 29	1859–1887	None	Vested in the GWR 19 August 1882
52	Berkshire and Hampshire Railway Co.	30 Jun 1845	RAIL 30	1845–1851	None	Amalgamated with the GWR 14 May 1846
53	Bexley Heath Railway Co.	20 Aug 1883	RAIL 32	1882–1901	None	Worked by the South Eastern Railway Co. from 17 July 1890 and transferred to that company 10 July 1900
54	Bideford Extension Railway Co.	4 Aug 1853	RAIL 33	1852	None	Amalgamated with the London and South Western Railway Co. 1 January 1865
55	Bideford, Westward Ho! and Appledore Railway Co.	21 May 1896	Nil		None	Closed in 1917
56	Birkenhead, Lancashire and Cheshire Junction Railway Co. Re-named the Birkenhead Railway Co. 1 August 1859	26 Jun 1846	RAIL 35 (RAIL 1057)	1846–1925	Yes	Vested in the London and North Western Railway Co. and the GWR jointly 11 July 1861

List No.	Name of Company	Date of Incorporation	TNA Record Class	Records		Change of Ownership or Control
				Dates covered	Staff	
57	Birkenhead Railway Co. See Birkenhead, Lancashire and Cheshire Junction Railway Co., List No. 56					
58	Birmingham and Derby Junction Railway Co.	19 May 1836	RAIL 36	1836–1846	None	Amalgamated with the North Midland Railway Co. and the Midland Counties Railway Co. to form the Midland Railway Co. 10 May 1844
59	Birmingham and Gloucester Railway Co.	22 Apr 1836	RAIL 37	1835–1846	Yes	Taken over by the Midland Railway Co. 3 August 1846
60	Birmingham and Henley-in-Arden Railway Co. See Henley-in-Arden and Great Western Junction Railway Co., List No. 385					
61	Birmingham and Oxford Junction Railway Co.	3 Aug 1846	RAIL 39	1845–1855	Yes	Vested in the GWR 31 August 1848
62	Birmingham and Sutton Coldfield Extension Railway Co.	21 Jul 1863	RAIL 40	1863–1869	None	Apparently abandoned about 1869. Note: The London and North Western Railway Co. built a railway over most of the same route
63	Birmingham, Bristol and Thames Junction Railway Co. Re-named the West London Railway Co. 23 July 1840	21 Jun 1836	RAIL 733	1836–1907	None	Vested jointly in the GWR and the London and North Western Railway Co. 21 July 1854. Passed to the British Transport Commission in 1948

List No.	Name of Company	Date of Incorporation	TNA Record Class	Records		Change of Ownership or Control
				Dates covered	Staff	
64	Birmingham, North Warwickshire and Stratford-upon-Avon Railway Co.	25 Aug 1894	RAIL 42 (RAIL 1057)	1894–1900	None	Transferred to the GWR 30 July 1900
65	Birmingham West Suburban Railway Co.	31 Jul 1871	RAIL 43	1869–1875	None	Vested in the Midland Railway Co. 1 July 1875
66	Birmingham, Wolverhampton and Dudley Railway Co.	3 Aug 1846	RAIL 44	1845–1856	None	Vested in the GWR 31 August 1848
67	Birmingham, Wolverhampton and Stour Valley Railway Co.	3 Aug 1846	RAIL 45	1846–1867	None	Vested in the London and North Western Railway Co. 15 July 1867
68	Bishop Auckland and Weardale Railway Co.	15 Jul 1837	RAIL 46	1836–1848	None	Amalgamated with the Wear Valley Railway Co. 1847
69	Bishops Castle Railway Co.	28 Jun 1861	(RAIL 1057)		Yes	Remained independent until its closure in 1935
70	Bishops Stortford, Dunmow and Braintree Railway Co.	22 Jul 1861	RAIL 48	1862–1866	None	Vested in the Great Eastern Railway Co. 29 June 1865
71	Bishops Waltham Railway Co.	17 Jul 1862	RAIL 49	1861–1881	None	Worked by the London and South Western Railway Co. and taken over by that company 22 June 1863
72	Bisley Tramway	1890	Nil		None	Last operated 19 July 1952
73	Blackburn and Preston Railway Co.	6 Jun 1844	RAIL 50	1844–1846	None	Became part of the East Lancashire Railway Co. 3 August 1846
74	Blackburn, Burnley, Accrington and Colne	30 Jun 1845	RAIL 51	1844–1845	None	Became part of the East Lancashire *Cont.*

List No.	Name of Company	Date of Incorporation	TNA Record Class	Records		Change of Ownership or Control
				Dates covered	Staff	
	Extension Railway Co.					Railway Co. 3 August 1846
75	Blackburn, Clitheroe and North Western Junction Railway Co.	27 Jul 1846	Nil		None	Amalgamated with the Blackburn, Darwen and Bolton Railway Co. in 1847 to form the Bolton, Blackburn, Clitheroe and West Yorkshire Railway Co.
76	Blackburn, Darwen and Bolton Railway Co.	30 Jun 1845	Nil		None	Amalgamated with the Blackburn, Clitheroe and North Western Junction Railway Co. in 1847 to form the Bolton, Blackburn, Clitheroe and West Yorkshire Railway Co.
77	Blackburn Railway Co. See Bolton, Blackburn, Clitheroe and West Yorkshire Railway Co., List No. 90					
78	Blackpool and Fleetwood Tramway Co.	20 Jul 1896	Nil		None	Taken over by the Blackpool Corporation in 1919. Linked with the Lancashire and Yorkshire Railway Co. and the London and North Western Railway Co.
79	Blackpool and Lytham Railway Co.	17 May 1861	RAIL 53	1860–1871	None	Amalgamated with the Preston and Wyre Railway Harbour and Dock Co. 1 July 1871

List No.	Name of Company	Date of Incorporation	TNA Record Class	Records		Change of Ownership or Control
				Dates covered	Staff	
80	Blackwell Railway	Private	Nil		None	Purchased by the Midland Railway Co. 28 June 1877
81	Blaenavon Tramroad. Re-incorporated 31 July 1845 as the Monmouthshire Railway and Canal Co.	3 Jun 1792	RAIL 500	1794–1880	Yes	Amalgamated with the GWR 1 August 1880
82	Blandford Camp Railway	1918	Nil		None	Closed 1921
83	Blaydon, Gateshead and Hebburn Railway Co.	22 May 1834	RAIL 55	1834–1839	None	Vested in the Newcastle upon Tyne and Carlisle Railway Co. in 1835
84	Bluebell and Primrose Railway. An extension of the South Eastern Railway. See List No. 797					
85	Blyth and Tyne Railway Co.	30 Jun 1852	RAIL 56	1855–1915	Yes	Vested in the North Eastern Railway Co. 7 August 1874
86	Bodmin and Wadebridge Railway Co.	23 May 1832	RAIL 57	1832–1886	Yes	Shares taken over by the London and South Western Railway Co. in 1847. Formally amalgamated with the London and South Western Railway Co. 1 July 1886
87	Bognor Railway Co.	11 Jul 1861	RAIL 58	1861–1871	None	Amalgamated with the London, Brighton and South Coast Railway in 1871

List No.	Name of Company	Date of Incorporation	TNA Record Class	Records Dates covered	Records Staff	Change of Ownership or Control
88	Bolton and Leigh Railway Co.	31 Mar 1825	(RAIL 1057)		Yes	Consolidated with the Liverpool and Manchester Railway Co., and the Kenyon and Leigh Junction Railway Co. into the Grand Junction Railway Co. 8 August 1845
89	Bolton and Preston Railway Co.	15 Jul 1837	RAIL 59	1837–1844	None	Vested in the North Union Railway Co. 10 May 1844
90	Bolton, Blackburn, Clitheroe and West Yorkshire Railway Co. Re-named the Blackburn Railway Co. 24 July 1851	9 Jul 1847 (amalg.)	RAIL 52	1844–1862	None	Vested in the Lancashire and Yorkshire Railway Co. 12 July 1858
91	Border Counties Railway Co.	31 Jul 1854	Nil		None	Taken over by the North British Railway Co. 13 August 1860
92	Border Union (North British) Railway Co.	21 Jul 1859	Nil		None	Owned by the North British Railway Co.
93	Boston, Sleaford and Midland Counties Railway Co.	20 Aug 1853	(RAIL 1057)		None	Worked by the Great Northern Railway Co. Taken over by that company 25 July 1864
94	Bourne and Essendine Railway Co.	12 Aug 1857	Nil		None	Worked by the Great Northern Railway Co. Taken over by that company 25 July 1864
95	Bourton-on-the-Water Railway Co.	14 Jun 1860	RAIL 60	1860–1874	None	Amalgamated with the GWR 1 February 1874
96	Bowes Railway. See Pontop and Jarrow Wagonway, List No. 684					

List No.	Name of Company	Date of Incorporation	TNA Record Class	Records Dates covered	Staff	Change of Ownership or Control
97	Brackenhill Light Railway Co.	19 Mar 1901	RAIL 61	1901–1923	None	Worked by the North Eastern Railway Co. Became part of the LNER 1 January 1923
98	Bradford and Thornton Railways Co.	24 Jul 1871	RAIL 62	1871–1872	None	Amalgamated with the Great Northern Railway Co. 18 July 1872
99	Bradford, Eccleshill and Idle Railway Co.	26 Jun 1866	RAIL 63	1869	None	Vested in the Great Northern Railway Co. 24 July 1871
100	Bradford, Wakefield and Leeds Railway Co. Re-named the West Yorkshire Railway Co. 21 July 1863	10 Jul 1854	RAIL 739	1853–1865	None	Amalgamated with the Great Northern Railway Co. 5 July 1865
101	Brading Harbour Improvement and Railway Co. Re-named the Brading Harbour and Railway Co. 14 August 1896	7 Aug 1874	(RAIL 1057)		None	Worked by the Isle of Wight (Eastern Section) Railway Co. Later re-named the Isle of Wight Railway Co. Purchased by that company 2 August 1898
102	Brampton Railway	Private (c. 1799)	Nil		None	Leased to the North Eastern Railway Co. 29 October 1912
103	Brandling Junction Railway Co.	7 Sep 1835	RAIL 64	1833–1875	Yes	Purchased by George Hudson 13 August 1844 and transferred to the Newcastle and Darlington Junction Railway Co. 16 August 1844

List No.	Name of Company	Date of Incorporation	TNA Record Class	Records Dates covered	Records Staff	Change of Ownership or Control
104	Breakwater Railway [Portland, Dorset]	1874	Nil		None	Worked by the GWR and the London and South Western Railway Co. From 1923 worked by the SR
105	Brecon and Merthyr Tydfil Junction Railway Co.	1 Aug 1859	RAIL 65 (RAIL 1057)	1859–1922	Yes	Taken over by the GWR 1 July 1922
106	Bricklayers Arms Extension Railway		RAIL 66	1843–1845	None	Taken over by the South Eastern Railway Co. 12 November 1845
107	Bridestowe Railway. See Rattlebrook Peat Railway, List No. 708					
108	Bridgewater Railway Co.	18 Aug 1882	RAIL 68	1882–1922	None	Purchased by the London and South Western Railway Co. 31 December 1922
109	Bridport Railway Co.	5 May 1855	RAIL 69	1854–1901	None	Taken over by the GWR 1 July 1901
110	Brighton and Chichester Railway Co.	4 Jul 1844	RAIL 70	1844–1849	None	Purchased by the London and Brighton Railway Co. *c.* 1845
111	Brighton and Dyke Railway Co.	2 Aug 1877	Nil		None	Worked by the London, Brighton and South Coast Railway Co. Became part of the SR in 1923. Closed in 1939
112	Brighton, Lewes and Hastings Railway Co.	29 Jul 1844	RAIL 72	1844–1847	None	Purchased on day of incorporation by the London, Brighton and South Coast Railway Co.

List No.	Name of Company	Date of Incorporation	TNA Record Class	Records Dates covered	Staff	Change of Ownership or Control
113	Brighton, Uckfield and Tunbridge Wells Railway Co.	22 Jul 1861	RAIL 73	1861–1864	None	Taken over by the London, Brighton and South Coast Railway Co. 29 July 1864
114	Bristol and Exeter Railway Co.	19 May 1836	RAIL 75	1835–1878	Yes	Taken over by the GWR 1 August 1876
115	Bristol and Gloucester Railway Co. See Bristol and Gloucestershire Railway Co., List No. 116					
116	Bristol and Gloucestershire Railway Co. Re-named the Bristol and Gloucester Railway Co. 1 July 1839	19 Jun 1828	RAIL 76	1839–1846	None	Taken over by the Midland Railway Co. 7 May 1845
117	Bristol and North Somerset Railway Co.	21 Jul 1861	RAIL 77	1863–1884	None	Taken over by the GWR 1 July 1884
118	Bristol and Portishead Pier and Railway Co.	29 Jun 1863	(RAIL 1057)		None	Worked by the GWR from 1876. Purchased by the GWR 14 August 1884
119	Bristol and South Wales Union Railway Co.	27 Jul 1857	RAIL 78	1854–1870	None	Taken over by the GWR 1 August 1868
120	Bristol Harbour Railway Co.	28 Jun 1866	RAIL 79	1867–1879	None	Taken over by the GWR 1 August 1876
121	Bristol Port Railway and Pier Co. Included the Clifton Extension Railway	17 Jun 1862	RAIL 81	1862–1894	None	Vested in the GWR and Midland Railway Co. jointly 25 July 1890

List No.	Name of Company	Date of Incorporation	TNA Record Class	Records Dates covered	Staff	Change of Ownership or Control
122	Briton Ferry Floating Dock and Railway Co.	3 Jul 1851	RAIL 82	1850–1873	None	Originally worked by the Vale of Neath Railway Co. and transferred to the GWR 21 July 1873
123	Bromley Direct Railway Co.	16 Jul 1874	RAIL 83	1877–1879	None	Vested in the South Eastern Railway Co. 21 July 1879
124	Brompton and Piccadilly Circus Railway Co. Re-named the Great Northern, Piccadilly and Brompton Railway Co. 18 November 1902 (before opening). Re-named the London Electric Railway Co. 26 July 1910	6 Aug 1897	(RAIL 1057) and (LMA)	1897–1933	Yes	Taken over by the London Passenger Transport Board 1 July 1933
125	Brynmawr and Western Valleys Railway Co.	13 Jul 1899	(RAIL 1057)		None	Vested jointly in the London and North Western Railway Co. and the GWR 31 July 1902 (before opening)
126	Buckfastleigh, Totnes and South Devon Railway Co.	25 Jul 1864	RAIL 84	1864–1897	None	Vested in the GWR 1 July 1897
127	Buckingham and Brackley Junction Railway Co.	27 Jul 1846	RAIL 85	1846–1847	None	Amalgamated with the Oxford and Bletchley Junction Railway Co. 22 July 1847, to form the Buckinghamshire Railway Co. (before opening)
128	Buckinghamshire Railway Co.	22 Jul 1847 (amalg.)	RAIL 86 (RAIL 1057)	1845–1878	None	Vested in the London and North Western Railway Co. 21 July 1879

List No.	Name of Company	Date of Incorporation	TNA Record Class	Records Dates covered	Staff	Change of Ownership or Control
129	Buckley Railway Co.	14 Jun 1860	RAIL 87	1859–1905	None	Leased to the Wrexham Mold and Connah's Quay Railway Co. from 30 June 1873. Transferred to the Great Central Railway 22 July 1904
130	Budleigh Salterton Railway Co.	20 Jul 1894	RAIL 88	1895–1912	None	Worked by the London and South Western Railway Co. from 1 June 1903. Transferred to that company 1 January 1912
131	Bullo Pill Tramway Co. Re-incorporated as the Forest of Dean Railway Co. 5 May 1826. See also List No. 308	10 Jun 1809	RAIL 210	1826–1852	None	Purchased by the South Wales Railway Co. 2 July 1847
132	Burry Port and Gwendraeth Valley Railway Co.	5 Jul 1865	RAIL 89 (RAIL 1057)	1888–1922	None	Became part of the GWR 1 July 1922
133	Burton and Ashby Light Railway Co.	5 Nov 1902	(RAIL 491)	1906–1920	Yes	Built and worked by the Midland Railway Co. Closed in 1927
134	Bury and Tottington District Railway Co.	2 Aug 1877	RAIL 90	1878–1892	None	Vested in the Lancashire and Yorkshire Railway Co. 1 March 1889
135	Bury St Edmunds and Thetford Railway Co.	5 Jul 1865	Nil		None	Purchased by the Great Eastern Railway Co. 22 July 1878
136	Bute Docks Co. Re-named the Cardiff Railway Co. 6 August 1897	25 Jun 1886	RAIL 97 (RAIL 1057)	1867–1923	Yes	Became part of the GWR in 1923

List No.	Name of Company	Date of Incorporation	TNA Record Class	Records Dates covered	Staff	Change of Ownership or Control
137	Caldon Low Tramway Co.	13 May 1776	Nil		None	Purchased by the North Staffordshire Railway Co. in 1847
138	Caledonian Railway Co.	31 Jul 1845	(Scot RO)	1845–1923	Yes	Became part of the LMS in 1923
139	Callington and Calstock Railway Co. Re-named the East Cornwall Mineral Railway Co. 25 May 1871 (before opening)	9 Aug 1869	Nil		None	Purchased by the Plymouth, Devonport and South Western Junction Railway Co. 1 June 1891. Became part of the Bere Alston and Calstock Railway Co.
140	Calne Railway Co.	15 May 1860	RAIL 91	1859–1892	None	Taken over by the GWR 1 July 1892
141	Cambrian Railways Co.	25 Jul 1864 (amalg.)	RAIL 92 (RAIL 1057)	1864–1922	Yes	Became part of the GWR in 1923
142	Cannock Chase and Wolverhampton Railway Co.	Initially private then incorporated 29 Jul 1864	Nil		None	Part of this became a section of what is now the Chacewater Light Railway
143	Cannock Chase Railway Co.	15 May 1860	Nil		None	Taken over by the London and North Western Railway Co. 28 July 1863
144	Cannock Mineral Railway Co. Previously called the Derbyshire, Staffordshire and Worcestershire Junction Railway Co. See also List No. 224	14 Aug 1855	RAIL 94	1856–1869	None	Controlled by the London and North Western Railway Co. from opening in November 1859. Vested in that company 12 July 1869

List No.	Name of Company	Date of Incorporation	TNA Record Class	Records		Change of Ownership or Control
				Dates covered	Staff	
145	Canterbury and Whitstable Railway Co.	10 Jun 1825	(RAIL 1057)		None	Worked by the South Eastern Railway Co. from 29 September 1844. Taken over by that company 4 August 1853
146	Cardiff and Ogmore Valley Railway Co.	21 Jul 1873	RAIL 95 (RAIL 1057)	1873–1876	None	Amalgamated with the Llynvi and Ogmore Railway Co. 24 July 1876
147	Cardiff, Penarth and Barry Junction Railway Co.	6 Aug 1885	RAIL 96	1885–1889	None	Amalgamated with the Taff Vale Railway Co. 1 July 1889
148	Cardiff Railway Co. See Bute Docks Co., List No. 136					
149	Carlisle and Silloth Bay Railway and Dock Co.	16 Jul 1855	Nil		None	Leased by the North British Railway Co. from 3 June 1862. Taken over by that company 1 August 1880
150	Carmarthen and Cardigan Railway Co.	7 Aug 1854	RAIL 99	1853–1924	Yes	Amalgamated with the GWR 1 July 1881
151	Carmarthenshire Railway or Tramroad Co.	3 Jun 1802	RAIL 100	1873–1881	None	Purchased by the Llanelly and Mynydd Mawr Railway Co. 19 July 1875
152	Carnarvon and Llanberis Railway Co.	14 Jul 1864	RAIL 101	1864–1873	None	The London and North Western Railway Co. became part owners 29 May 1868. Vested in that company 4 July 1870

List No.	Name of Company	Date of Incorporation	TNA Record Class	Records Dates covered	Staff	Change of Ownership or Control
153	Carnarvonshire Railway Co.	29 Jul 1862	RAIL 102	1862–1868	None	Vested in the London and North Western Railway Co. 4 July 1870
154	Caterham Railway Co.	16 Jun 1854	Nil		None	Purchased by the South Eastern Railway Co. 7 July 1859
155	Cawood, Wistow and Selby Light Railway Co.	2 Jul 1896	RAIL 103	1897–1900	None	Purchased by the North Eastern Railway Co. 1 July 1900
156	Cefn and Pyle Railway	Private (c. 1797)	Nil		None	Purchased by the Port Talbot Railway Co. 27 July 1896
157	Central Cornwall Railway Co. See Launceston, Bodmin and Wadebridge Junction Railway Co., List No. 454					
158	Central London Railway Co.	5 Aug 1891	(LMA)	1891–1933	Yes	Vested in the London Passenger Transport Board 1 July 1933
159	Central Wales and Carmarthen Junction Railway Co. See Swansea and Carmarthen Railway Co., List No. 841					
160	Central Wales Extension Railway Co.	3 Jul 1860	(RAIL 1057)		None	Taken over by the London and North Western Railway Co. 25 June 1868
161	Central Wales Railway Co.	13 Aug 1859	(RAIL 1057)		None	Taken over by the London and North Western Railway Co. 25 June 1868

List No.	Name of Company	Date of Incorporation	TNA Record Class	Records Dates covered	Staff	Change of Ownership or Control
162	Chard Railway Co.	25 May 1860	RAIL 106	1859–1863	None	Taken over by the London and South Western Railway Co. 22 June 1863, 6 weeks after opening
163	Chard, Ilminster and Taunton Railway Co.	6 Aug 1861	Nil		None	Powers transferred to the Bristol and Exeter Railway Co. 8 June 1863 (before opening)
164	Charing Cross, Euston and Hampstead Railway Co.	24 Aug 1893	LMA	1893–1910	None	Leased by the Underground Electric Railways Company of London. Taken over by the London Electric Railway Co. 1 July 1910
165	Charing Cross Railway Co.	8 Aug 1859	RAIL 107	1859–1870	None	Taken over by the South Eastern Railway Co. 1 August 1864
166	Charlesworth's Railway Co. See Lake Lock Railroad, List No. 443					
167	Charnwood Forest Railway Co.	16 Jul 1874	RAIL 108 (RAIL 1057)	1874–1923	None	Worked partly by the London and North Western Railway Co. from 12 May 1881. Vested in the LMS in 1923
168	Chattenden and Upnor Railway	c. 1870	Nil		None	Taken over by the Admiralty in 1906 and closed in 1961
169	Chattenden Naval Tramway	24 Jul 1901	Nil		None	Worked by the Kingsnorth Light Railway Co. from 24 July 1926. Transferred to that company 25 July 1929

List No.	Name of Company	Date of Incorporation	TNA Record Class	Records		Change of Ownership or Control
				Dates covered	Staff	
170	Cheadle Railway Co. See Cheadle Railway, Mineral and Land Co., List No. 171					
171	Cheadle Railway, Mineral and Land Co. Re-named the Cheadle Railway Co. 7 August 1896	7 Aug 1888	Nil		None	Taken over by the North Staffordshire Railway Co. 1 January 1908
172	Cheddar Valley and Yatton Railway Co.	14 Jul 1864	(RAIL 75)	1866–1872	None	Powers transferred to the Bristol and Exeter Railway Co. 19 June 1865
173	Cheltenham and Great Western Union Railway Co.	21 Jun 1836	RAIL 109	1835–1846	None	Taken over by the GWR 10 May 1844
174	Cheshire Midland Railway Co.	14 Jun 1860	RAIL 111	1859–1868	None	Vested in the Cheshire Lines Committee 5 July 1865
175	Chester and Birkenhead Railway Co.	12 Jul 1837	RAIL 112	1836–1858	None	Vested in the Birkenhead, Lancashire and Cheshire Junction Railway Co. 22 July 1847
176	Chester and Crewe Railway Co.	30 Jun 1837	RAIL 776	*c.* 1838	None	Incorporated into the Grand Junction Railway Co. 1 July 1840
177	Chester and Holyhead Railway Co.	4 Jul 1844	RAIL 113 (RAIL 1057)	1843–1860	Yes	Worked by the London and North Western Railway Co. from 1 July 1856. Vested in that company with effect from 1 January 1859. (Continued in its own name until 21 July 1879)

List No.	Name of Company	Date of Incorporation	TNA Record Class	Records Dates covered	Staff	Change of Ownership or Control
178	Chester and West Cheshire Junction Railway Co.	5 Jul 1865	Nil		None	Powers transferred to the Cheshire Lines Committee 10 August 1866
179	Chichester and Midhurst Railway Co.	23 Jun 1864	RAIL 115	1864–1871	None	Line abandoned 31 July 1868. Revived by the London, Brighton and South Coast Railway Co. 13 July 1876
180	Chipping Norton Railway Co.	31 Jul 1854	Nil		None	Powers were obtained for this line by the Oxford, Worcester and Wolverhampton Railway Co. The company amalgamated with the GWR and the West Midland Railway Co. (who were successors of the Oxford, Worcester and Wolverhampton Railway Co.) in 1863
181	Chipstead Valley Railway Co.	27 Jul 1893	RAIL 116	1893–1899	None	Vested in the South Eastern Railway Co. 13 July 1899
182	Churnet Valley Railway Co.	26 Jun 1846	Nil		None	Formed as part of the North Staffordshire Railway Co.
183	City and South London Railway Co. See City of London and Southwark Subway Co., List No. 184					

List No.	Name of Company	Date of Incorporation	TNA Record Class	Records Dates covered	Staff	Change of Ownership or Control
184	City of London and Southwark Subway Co. Re-named the City and South London Railway Co. 25 July 1890	28 Jul 1884	(RAIL 1057) and (LMA)	1884–1933	None	Vested in the London Passenger Transport Board 1 July 1933
185	Clacton-on-Sea Railway Co.	2 Aug 1877	Nil		None	Worked by the Great Eastern Railway Co. Purchased by that company 1 July 1883
186	Clarence Railway Co.	23 May 1828	RAIL 117	1828–1854	None	Leased to the Stockton and Hartlepool Railway Co. 1 September 1844. Purchased by the West Hartlepool Harbour and Railway Co. 30 June 1852
187	Cleator and Workington Junction Railway Co.	27 Jun 1876	RAIL 119	1876–1923	Yes	Worked by the Furness Railway Co. from 28 June 1877. Became part of the LMS in 1923
188	Cleobury Mortimer and Ditton Priors Light Railway Co.	23 Mar 1901	RAIL 120 (RAIL 1057)	1901–1922	Yes	Became part of the GWR 1 January 1922
189	Cleveland Railway Co.	23 Jul 1858	RAIL 121	1847–1867	None	Amalgamated with the North Eastern Railway Co. 5 June 1865
190	Clifton Extension Railway. See Bristol Port Railway and Pier Co., List No. 121					
191	Cockermouth and Workington Railway Co.	21 Jul 1845	RAIL 122	1844–1866	None	Vested in the London and North Western Railway Co. 16 July 1866

List No.	Name of Company	Date of Incorporation	TNA Record Class	Records		Change of Ownership or Control
				Dates covered	Staff	
208	Cowbridge Railway Co.	29 Jul 1862	RAIL 141 (RAIL 1057)	1863–1889	Yes	Leased to the Taff Vale Railway Co. from 1 January 1876 and taken over by that company 26 August 1889
209	Cowes and Newport Railway Co.	8 Aug 1859	RAIL 142	1859–1887	None	Amalgamated with the Ryde and Newport Railway Co. and the Isle of Wight (Newport Junction)Railway Co. 31 July 1887 to form the Isle of Wight Central Railway Co.
210	Cranbrook and Paddock Wood Railway Co.	2 Aug 1887	RAIL 143	1890–1901	None	Worked by the South Eastern Railway Co. from opening. Absorbed by that company 10 July 1900
211	Croesor and Portmadoc Railway Co. Re-named the Portmadoc, Croesor and Beddgelert Tram Railway Co. 21 July 1879	5 Jul 1865	Nil		None	Purchased by the Portmadoc, Beddgelert and Snowdon Railway Co. 17 August 1901
212	Cromford and High Peak Railway Co.	2 May 1825	RAIL 144	1824–1887	None	Leased to the London and North Western Railway Co. from 30 June 1862. Taken over by that company 19 July 1887
213	Crowhurst, Sidley and Bexhill Railway Co.	15 Jul 1897	RAIL 145	1897–1907	None	Worked by the South Eastern and Chatham Railway Company's Managing Committee. Taken over by the South Western and Chatham Railway Co. 1 January 1907

List No.	Name of Company	Date of Incorporation	TNA Record Class	Records Dates covered	Staff	Change of Ownership or Control
214	Croydon and Epsom Railway Co.	29 Jul 1844	Nil		None	Purchased by the London and Croydon Railway Co. (before opening)
215	Croydon, Merstham and Godstone Iron Railway Co.	17 May 1803	Nil		None	Purchased by the London and Brighton Railway Co. 15 July 1837
216	Crystal Palace and South London Junction Railway Co.	17 Jul 1862	RAIL 146	1862–1876	None	Vested in the London, Chatham and Dover Railway Co. 19 July 1875
217	Culm Valley Light Railway Co.	15 May 1873	RAIL 147	1872–1902	None	Purchased by the GWR April 1880
218	Dare Valley Railway Co.	21 Jul 1863	RAIL 148	1863–1889	None	Leased to the Taff Vale Railway Co. from 1 January 1871. Taken over by that company 1 July 1889
219	Darlington and Barnard Castle Railway Co.	4 Jul 1854	RAIL 149	1842–1859	None	Amalgamated with the Stockton and Darlington Railway Co. 23 July 1858
220	Dartmouth and Torbay Railway Co.	27 Jul 1857	Nil		None	Worked by the South Devon Railway Co. Taken over by that company in 1866
221	Dearne Valley Railway Co.	6 Aug 1897	RAIL 150	1897–1922	None	Became part of the LMS in 1923
222	Dearness Valley Railway Co.	30 Jul 1855	RAIL 151	1855–1857	None	Purchased by the North Eastern Railway Co. 13 July 1857

List No.	Name of Company	Date of Incorporation	TNA Record Class	Records		Change of Ownership or Control
				Dates covered	Staff	
223	Denbigh, Ruthin and Corwen Railway Co.	23 Jul 1860	RAIL 152	1860–1879	None	Worked by the London and North Western Railway Co. from 1 July 1878. Vested in that company 1 July 1879
224	Derbyshire, Staffordshire and Worcestershire Junction Railway Co. Re-named the Cannock Mineral Railway Co. 14 August 1855 (before opening)	2 Jul 1847	RAIL 153	1852–1856	None	See Cannock Mineral Railway Co., List No. 144
225	Derwent Valley Light Railway Co.	19 Dec 1905	Nil		None	Remained independent until its closure in 1980
226	Devon and Cornwall Railway Co. See Okehampton Railway Co., List No. 651					
227	Devon and Somerset Railway Co.	29 Jul 1864	RAIL 155	1864–1901	None	Worked by the Bristol and Exeter Railway Co. Taken over by the GWR 26 July 1901
228	Devon Great Consols Tramway	Private (1859)	Nil		None	Closed in 1899
229	Didcot, Newbury and Southampton Junction Railway Co. Re-named the Didcot, Newbury and Southampton Railway Co. 16 July 1883	5 Aug 1873	RAIL 156 (RAIL 1057)	1876–1923	None	Became part of the GWR in 1923

List No.	Name of Company	Date of Incorporation	TNA Record Class	Records		Change of Ownership or Control
				Dates covered	Staff	
230	Dore and Chinley Railway Co.	28 Jul 1884	Nil		None	Vested in the Midland Railway Co. 24 July 1888 (before opening)
231	Dorset Central Railway Co.	29 Jul 1856	RAIL 159	1856–1872	None	Amalgamated with the Somerset Central Railway Co. to form the Somerset and Dorset Railway Co. 7 August 1862
232	Dover and Deal Joint Railway Co.	30 Jun 1874	Nil		None	Vested jointly in the South Eastern Railway Co. and the London, Chatham and Dover Railway Co. in 1899
233	Dowlais Railway Co.	28 Jul 1849	(RAIL 1057)		None	Owned by the Dowlais Iron Co. Closed in 1930
234	Downham and Stoke Ferry Railway Co.	24 Jul 1879	RAIL 160	1879–1897	None	Worked by the Great Eastern Railway Co. Purchased by the Great Eastern Railway Co. 1 July 1897
235	Dudley and Oldbury Junction Railway Co. Re-named the Oldbury Railway Co. 11 August 1881	21 Jul 1873	RAIL 550	1883–1894	None	Worked by the GWR from opening and taken over by that company 1 July 1894
236	Duffryn, Llynvi and Porthcawl Railway Co.	10 Jun 1825	RAIL 161	1825–1848	None	Purchased by the Llynvi Valley Railway Co. 22 July 1847
237	Dulas Valley Mineral Railway Co. Re-named the Neath and Brecon Railway Co. 13 July 1863	29 Jul 1862	RAIL 505 (RAIL 1057)	1862–1922	Yes	Became part of the GWR 24 July 1922

List No.	Name of Company	Date of Incorporation	TNA Record Class	Records		Change of Ownership or Control
				Dates covered	Staff	
238	Dunstable Railway Co.	30 Jun 1845	RAIL 163	1845–1846	None	Vested in the London and Birmingham Railway Co. from its incorporation
239	Durham and Sunderland Railway Co.	13 Aug 1834	RAIL 164	1834–1846	None	Purchased by the Newcastle and Darlington Junction Railway Co. 1 January 1847
240	Durham Junction Railway Co.	16 Jun 1834	RAIL 165	1834–1845	None	Purchased by the Newcastle and Darlington Junction Railway Co. 23 May 1844
241	Dursley and Midland Junction Railway Co.	25 May 1855	RAIL 166	1855–1861	None	Purchased by the Midland Railway Co. 28 June 1861
242	Ealing and South Harrow Railway Co.	25 Aug 1894	Nil		None	Vested in the Metropolitan District Railway Co. 1 July 1900
243	Easingwold Light Railway Co. See Easingwold Railway Co., List No. 244					
244	Easingwold Railway Co. Re-named the Easingwold Light Railway Co. in 1928	23 Aug 1887	RAIL 167	1891–1958	Yes	Remained independent until its closure 27 December 1957
245	East and West India Docks and Birmingham Junction Railway Co. Re-named the North London Railway Co. 1 January 1853	26 Aug 1846	RAIL 529	1845–1922	Yes	Leased by the London and North Western Railway Co. Became part of the LMS in 1923

List No.	Name of Company	Date of Incorporation	TNA Record Class	Records		Change of Ownership or Control
				Dates covered	Staff	
246	East and West Junction Railway Co.	23 Jun 1864	(RAIL 674) (RAIL 1057)	1873–1908	Yes	Amalgamated with the Stratford-upon-Avon, Towcester and Midland Junction Railway Co. and the Evesham, Redditch and Stratford-upon-Avon Railway Co. 1 January 1909 to form the Stratford-upon-Avon and Midland Junction Railway Co.
247	East and West Yorkshire Junction Railway Co.	16 Jul 1846	RAIL 169	1845–1852	None	Amalgamated with the York and North Midland Railway Co. 1 July 1851
248	East and West Yorkshire Union Railways Co.	2 Aug 1883	RAIL 170	1882–1923	Yes	Taken over by the LMS in 1923
249	East Anglian Railway Co.	22 Jul 1847 (amalg.)	RAIL 171	1851–1862	None	Amalgamated with the East Suffolk Railway Co., the Eastern Counties Railway Co., the Norfolk Railway Co. and the Eastern Union Railway Co. 7 August 1862 to form the Great Eastern Railway Co.
250	East Cornwall Mineral Railway Co. See Callington and Calstock Railway Co., List No. 139					
251	East Gloucestershire Railway Co.	29 Jul 1864	RAIL 173	1864–1890	None	Taken over by the GWR 1 July 1890

List No.	Name of Company	Date of Incorporation	TNA Record Class	Records		Change of Ownership or Control
				Dates covered	Staff	
252	East Grinstead, Groombridge and Tunbridge Wells Railway Co.	7 Aug 1862	RAIL 174	1862–1864	None	Purchased by the London, Brighton and South Coast Railway Co. 29 July 1864
253	East Grinstead Railway Co.	8 Jul 1853	(RAIL 1057)		None	Worked by the London, Brighton and South Coast Railway Co. from 28 June 1858
254	East Kent Light Railway Co.	19 Jun 1911	RAIL 175	1911–1949	None	Taken over by the British Transport Commission in 1948
255	East Kent Railway Co. Re-named the London, Chatham and Dover Railway Co. 1 August 1859	4 Aug 1853	RAIL 415	1853–1922	Yes	With the South Eastern Railway Co. ran jointly from 1 August 1899 under the name The South Eastern and Chatham Railway Companies' Managing Committee. Became part of the SR in 1923
256	East Lancashire Railway Co. See Manchester, Bury and Rossendale Railway Co., List No. 539					
257	East Lincolnshire Railway Co.	26 Jun 1846	RAIL 177	1845–1923	Yes	Leased to the Great Northern Railway Co. from 1 October 1848. Became part of the LNER 1 January 1923
258	East London Railway Co.	26 May 1865	RAIL 178	1865–1925	None	Vested in the Southern Railway Co. 1 January 1925

List No.	Name of Company	Date of Incorporation	TNA Record Class	Records Dates covered	Staff	Change of Ownership or Control
259	East Norfolk Railway Co.	23 Jun 1864	RAIL 180	1869–1881	None	Worked by the Great Eastern Railway Co. and vested in that company 3 June 1881
260	East Somerset Railway Co.	5 Jun 1856	RAIL 181	1855–1874	None	Taken over by the GWR 30 June 1874
261	East Suffolk Railway Co. See Halesworth, Beccles and Haddiscoe Railway Co., List No. 363					
262	East Usk Railway Co.	6 Aug 1885	RAIL 183	1886–1892	None	Vested in the GWR 28 June 1892
263	Eastern and Midlands Railway Co.	18 Aug 1882 (amalg.) with effect from 1 Jul 1883	RAIL 184	1882–1893	None	Incorporated into the Midland and Great Northern Joint Railway 1 July 1893
264	Eastern Counties and Thames Junction Railway Co.	4 Jul 1844	Nil		None	Purchased by the Eastern Counties Railway Co. 9 July 1847
265	Eastern Counties Railway Co. Initially called the Grand Eastern Counties Railway Co.	4 Jul 1836	RAIL 186	1835–1862	Yes	Amalgamated with the Norfolk Railway Co., the Eastern Union Railway Co., the East Anglian Railway Co. and the East Suffolk Railway Co. 7 August 1862 to form the Great Eastern Railway Co.
266	Eastern Union and Hadleigh Junction Railway Co.	18 Jun 1847	Nil		None	Purchased by the Eastern Union Railway Co. 2 January 1847

List No.	Name of Company	Date of Incorporation	TNA Record Class	Records		Change of Ownership or Control
				Dates covered	Staff	
267	Eastern Union Railway Co.	19 Jul 1844	RAIL 187	1844–1866	None	Amalgamated with the East Anglian Railway Co., the Eastern Counties Railway Co., the Norfolk Railway Co. and the East Suffolk Railway Co. 7 August 1862 to form the Great Eastern Railway Co.
268	Easton and Church Hope Railway Co.	25 Jul 1867	RAIL 188	1867–1945	None	Passed to the British Transport Commission 1 January 1948
269	Easton Neston Mineral and Towcester, Roade and Olney Junction Railway Co. Re-named the Stratford-upon-Avon, Towcester and Midland Junction Railway Co. 10 August 1882	15 Aug 1879	Nil		None	Amalgamated with the East and West Junction Railway Co. and the Evesham, Redditch and Stratford-upon-Avon Railway Co. 1 January 1909 to form the Stratford-upon-Avon and Midland Junction Railway Co.
270	Eden Valley Railway Co.	21 May 1858	RAIL 189	1854–1867	Yes	Amalgamated with the Stockton and Darlington Railway Co. 30 June 1862
271	Edenham and Little Bytham Railway Co.	Private (1856)	Nil		None	Closed 17 October 1871
272	Edge Hill Railway Co.	28 Jan 1919	Nil		None	Abandoned in 1925
273	Edgware and Hampstead Railway Co.	18 Nov 1902	(LMA)	1902–1912	None	Powers transferred to the London Electric Co. 7 August 1912 (before opening)

List No.	Name of Company	Date of Incorporation	TNA Record Class	Records Dates covered	Records Staff	Change of Ownership or Control
274	Edgware, Highgate and London Railway Co.	3 Jun 1862	RAIL 190	1862–1866	None	Transferred to the Great Northern Railway 15 July 1867
275	Elan Valley Railway Co.	27 Jun 1892	(RAIL 1057)		None	Closed in 1917
276	Elham Valley Railway Co.	18 Jul 1881	RAIL 191	1884–1891	None	Transferred to the South Eastern Railway Co. 28 July 1884
277	Elsenham and Thaxted Light Railway Co.	1906	Nil		None	Worked by the Great Eastern Railway Co. Became part of the LNER in 1923
278	Ely and Clydach Valleys Railway Co.	5 Aug 1873	RAIL 192	1875–1880	None	Vested in the GWR 6 August 1880
279	Ely and Huntingdon Railway Co.	30 Jun 1845	Nil		None	Amalgamated with the Lynn and Ely Railway Co. and the Lynn and Dereham Railway Co. 22 July 1847 to form the East Anglian Railway Co.
280	Ely and Newmarket Railway Co.	11 Aug 1875	RAIL 193	1876–1898	None	Leased to the Great Eastern Railway Co. from 1 January 1888. Vested in that company 1 July 1898
281	Ely and St Ives Railway Co. See Ely, Haddenham and Sutton Railway Co., List No. 282					

List No.	Name of Company	Date of Incorporation	TNA Record Class	Records		Change of Ownership or Control
				Dates covered	Staff	
282	Ely, Haddenham and Sutton Railway Co. Re-named the Ely and St Ives Railway Co. 10 May 1878	23 Jun 1864	RAIL 194	1864–1899	None	Leased to the Great Eastern Railway Co. from 21 July 1879. Vested in that company 1 July 1898
283	Ely Tidal Harbour and Railway Co. Re-incorporated as the Penarth Harbour Dock and Railway Co. 27 July 1857	21 Jul 1856	RAIL 561 (RAIL 1057)	1855–1922	None	Leased to the Taff Vale Railway Co. 22 June 1863. Became part of the GWR 1 January 1922
284	Ely Valley Extension Railway Co.	28 Jul 1863	Nil		None	Worked by the GWR. Amalgamated with the Ogmore Valley Railways Co. 5 July 1865
285	Ely Valley Railway Co.	13 Jul 1857	RAIL 195 (RAIL 1057)	1857–1903	None	Leased to the GWR from 1 January 1861. Taken over by that company 1 July 1903
286	Epping Railway Co.	13 Aug 1859	RAIL 196	1860–1863	None	Transferred to the Eastern Counties Railway Co. 29 July 1862
287	Epsom and Leatherhead Railway Co.	14 Jul 1856	RAIL 197	1856–1922	None	Transferred to the London and South Western Railway Co. 23 July 1860
288	Epsom Downs Extension Railway Co.	27 Jun 1892	RAIL 198	1892–1899	None	Vested in the South Eastern Railway Co. 13 July 1899
289	Evesham and Redditch Railway Co.	13 Jul 1863	RAIL 199 (RAIL 1057)	1863–1882	None	Vested in the Midland Railway Co. 1 July 1882

220

List No.	Name of Company	Date of Incorporation	TNA Record Class	Records Dates covered	Staff	Change of Ownership or Control
290	Evesham, Redditch and Stratford-upon-Avon Junction Railway Co.	5 Aug 1873	RAIL 777	1878	None	Worked from the opening by the East and West Junction Railway Co. Became part of the Stratford-upon-Avon and Midland Junction Railway Co. 1 January 1909
291	Exe Valley Railway Co.	30 Jun 1874	RAIL 200	1874–1875	None	Transferred to the Bristol and Exeter Railway Co. 19 July 1875
292	Exeter and Crediton Railway Co.	1 Jul 1845	RAIL 201	1844–1879	None	Leased to the London and South Western Railway Co. from 1 January 1862. Purchased by that company 13 July 1876
293	Exeter and Exmouth Railway Co. (A company of the same name was incorporated in 1846 but abandoned)	2 Jul 1855	Nil		None	Leased to the London and South Western Railway Co. from 6 August 1860. Taken over by that company 1 January 1866
294	Exeter Railway Co. See Exeter, Teign Valley and Chagford Railway Co., List No. 295					
295	Exeter, Teign Valley and Chagford Railway Co. Re-named the Exeter Railway Co. 12 August 1898	20 Aug 1883	RAIL 203 (RAIL 1057)	1881–1923	Yes	Became part of the GWR in 1923
296	Fairbourne Railway	Private (c. 1890)	Nil		None	Independent and still in use

List No.	Name of Company	Date of Incorporation	TNA Record Class	Records		Change of Ownership or Control
				Dates covered	Staff	
*	Fareham and Netley Railway Co.	See List No. 989				
297	Faringdon Railway Co.	13 Aug 1860	RAIL 204 (RAIL 1057)	1860–1886	None	Vested in the GWR 1 July 1886
298	Felixstowe Railway and Dock Co. See Felixstowe Railway and Pier Co., List No. 299					
299	Felixstowe Railway and Pier Co. Re-named the Felixstowe Railway and Dock Co. 21 July 1879	19 Jul 1875	(RAIL 1057)		Yes	Worked by the Great Eastern Railway Co. from 1 Sept 1879. Purchased by that company 5 July 1887
300	Festiniog and Blaenau Railway Co.	15 Aug 1862	RAIL 205	1876–1883	Yes	Vested in the GWR and Bala and Festiniog Railway Co. jointly 6 August 1880
301	Festiniog Railway Co.	23 May 1832	(RAIL 1057)		Yes	Closed in 1946. Re-opened as a tourist railway in 1954 and still in use
302	Firbeck Light Railway Co.	22 Feb 1916	Nil		None	Built by the South Yorkshire Joint Line Committee
303	Fishguard and Rosslare Railways and Harbours Co. See Fishguard Bay Railway and Pier Co., List No. 304					
304	Fishguard Bay Railway and Pier Co. Re-named the Fishguard and Rosslare Railways and Harbours Co. 31 July 1894	29 Jun 1893	RAIL 206	1898–1947	None	Remains independent

List No.	Name of Company	Date of Incorporation	TNA Record Class	Records Dates covered	Staff	Change of Ownership or Control
305	Fleetwood, Preston and West Riding Junction Railway Co.	27 Jul 1846	RAIL 207	1846–1868	None	Vested in the London and North Western Railway Co. and the Lancashire and Yorkshire Railway Co. jointly 17 June 1867
306	Forcett Railway Co.	2 Jun 1865	RAIL 208	1865–1922	Yes	Worked by the North Eastern Railway Co. Became part of the LNER in 1923
307	Forest of Dean Central Railway Co.	11 Jul 1856	RAIL 209 (RAIL 1057)	1856–1879	None	Worked by the GWR and became part of that company in 1923
308	Forest of Dean Railway Co. See Bullo Pill Tramway Co. List No. 131	5 May 1826				
309	Fovant Military Railway	1916	Nil		None	Closed 15 February 1924
310	Freshwater, Yarmouth and Newport Railway Co.	7 Jul 1873	RAIL 211	1886–1923	Yes	Abandoned 23 July 1877. A further company was incorporated under this name 26 August 1880. Became part of the SR in 1923
311	Frosterley and Stanhope Railway Co.	26 Jun 1861	RAIL 212	1860–1865	None	Amalgamated with the Stockton and Darlington Railway Co. 30 June 1862
312	Furness and Midland Joint Railway Co.	22 Jun 1863	RAIL 213 (App 4)	1863–1897	None	Became part of the LMS in 1923
313	Furness Railway Co.	23 May 1844	RAIL 214	1844–1928	Yes	Became part of the LMS in 1923

List No.	Name of Company	Date of Incorporation	TNA Record Class	Records Dates covered	Staff	Change of Ownership or Control
314	Furzebrook Tramway. Also called Pike's Tramway	Private (c. 1840)	Nil		None	Used locomotive traction from 1866. Closed in 1956
315	Garstang and Knott End Railway Co.	30 Jun 1864	RAIL 215	1864–1899	None	Purchased by the Knott End Railway Co. 1 July 1908
316	Garston and Liverpool Railway Co.	17 May 1861	RAIL 216	1861–1867	None	Joint ownership with the Midland Railway Co. 5 July 1865. Not included in the 1923 Grouping but managed jointly by the LNER and the LMS. Line passed to the British Transport Commission in 1947
317	Glasgow and South Western Railway Co.	28 Oct 1850 (amalg.)	(Scot RO)	1846–1923	Yes	Became part of the LMS in 1923
318	Glasgow, Dumfries and Carlisle Railway Co.	13 Aug 1846	(Scot RO)		None	Amalgamated with the Glasgow, Paisley, Kilmarnock and Ayr Railway Co. 28 October 1850 to form the Glasgow and South Western Railway Co.
319	Gloucester and Cheltenham Railway Co. Also known as the Gloucester and Cheltenham Tramroad	28 Apr 1809	(RAIL 1057)		None	Purchased jointly by the Birmingham and Gloucester Railway Co. and the Cheltenham and Great Western Union Railway Co. in 1837. Line abandoned in 1859

List No.	Name of Company	Date of Incorporation	TNA Record Class	Records		Change of Ownership or Control
				Dates covered	Staff	
320	Gloucester and Cheltenham Tramroad. See Gloucester and Cheltenham Railway Co., List No. 319					
321	Gloucester and Forest of Dean Railway Co.	27 Jul 1846	RAIL 217	1844–1874	None	Leased to the GWR from 3 July 1871. Amalgamated with that company 30 June 1874
322	Glyn Valley Tramway Co.	10 Aug 1870	Nil		None	Amalgamated with the Cheshire Lines Committee 15 August 1867
323	Goathorn Pier Mineral Tramway	Private	Nil		None	Closed 1936
324	Golden Valley Railway Co.	13 Jul 1876	RAIL 218 (RAIL 1057)	1876–1899	None	Vested in the GWR 1 August 1899
325	Goole and Marshland Light Railway Co.	17 Aug 1898	RAIL 219	1898–1902	None	Purchased by the North Eastern Railway Co., and the Lancashire and Yorkshire Railway Co. jointly 2 October 1901. Amalgamated with the Isle of Axholme Light Railway Co. 1 October 1902 to form the Axholme Joint Railway Co.
326	Gorseddau Junction and Portmadoc Railway Co.	25 Jul 1872	(RAIL 1057)		None	Closed in 1892
327	Gorseddau Tramway (originally 3 ft horse-drawn)	Private (c. 1856)	Nil		None	Taken over by the Gorseddau Junction and Portmadoc Railway Co. 25 July 1872

List No.	Name of Company	Date of Incorporation	TNA Record Class	Records		Change of Ownership or Control
				Dates covered	Staff	
328	Gowdall and Braithwell Railway Co.	16 Aug 1909	Nil		None	Owned jointly by the Hull and Barnsley Railway Co. and the Great Central Railway Co. Remained independent until its closure in 1970
329	Grand Eastern Counties Railway Co. See Eastern Counties Railway Co., List No. 265					
330	Grand Junction Railway Co.	6 May 1833	RAIL 220	1833–1856	Yes	Amalgamated with the London and Birmingham Railway Co., and the Manchester and Birmingham Railway Co. to form the London and North Western Railway Co. 16 July 1846
331	Gravesend and Rochester Railway Co. Also known as the North Kent Line	31 Jul 1845	Nil		None	Purchased by the South Eastern Railway Co. 3 August 1846
332	Gravesend Railway Co.	18 Jul 1881	RAIL 221	1881–1900	None	Vested in the London, Chatham and Dover Railway Co. 29 June 1883
333	Great Central and Midland Joint Railway Co.	31 Jul 1902	RAIL 224 (App 4)	1901–1947	None	
334	Great Central, Hull and Barnsley and Midland Joint Railway Co.	20 Jul 1906	RAIL 225 (App 4)	1906–1938	None	

List No.	Name of Company	Date of Incorporation	TNA Record Class	Records Dates covered	Staff	Change of Ownership or Control
335	Great Central Railway Co. See Manchester, Sheffield and Lincolnshire Railway Co., List No. 541					
336	Great Eastern Railway Co.	7 Aug 1862 (amalg.)	RAIL 227	1855–1922	Yes	Became part of the LNER in 1923
337	Great Grimsby and Sheffield Junction Railway Co.	30 Jun 1845	RAIL 228	1844–1850	None	Amalgamated with the Sheffield, Ashton-under-Lyne and Manchester Railway Co., the Sheffield and Lincolnshire Junction Railway Co., the Sheffield and Lincolnshire Extension Railway Co. and the Grimsby Dock Co. 1 January 1847 to form the Manchester, Sheffield and Lincolnshire Railway Co.
338	Great Marlow Railway Co.	13 Jul 1868	RAIL 230	1867–1897	None	Taken over by the GWR 1 July 1897
339	Great North of England, Clarence and Hartlepool Junction Railway Co.	3 Jul 1837	RAIL 231	1837–1923	None	Leased to the Hartlepool Dock and Railway Co. in 1845. Leased to the York, Newcastle and Berwick Railway Co. in 1848. Became part of the LNER in 1923
340	Great North of England Railway Co.	4 Jul 1836	RAIL 232	1835–1858	Yes	Purchased by the Newcastle and Darlington Junction Railway Co. 27 July 1846

List No.	Name of Company	Date of Incorporation	TNA Record Class	Records		Change of Ownership or Control
				Dates covered	Staff	
341	Great Northern and City Railway Co.	28 Jun 1892	(RAIL 1057) and (LMA)	1892–1913	None	Taken over by the Metropolitan Railway Co. 1 July 1913
342	Great Northern and Great Eastern Joint Railway Co.	3 Jul 1879	RAIL 233 (App 4)		None	
343	Great Northern and Lancashire and Yorkshire Joint Railway Co.	1 Aug 1870	Nil		None	
344	Great Northern and London and North Western Joint Railway Co.	30 Jul 1874	RAIL 234 (App 4)		None	
345	Great Northern and Manchester, Sheffield and Lincolnshire Joint Railway Co.	23 Jul 1858	RAIL 235 (App 4)		Yes App 4	
346	Great Northern, Piccadilly and Brompton Railway Co. See Brompton and Piccadilly Circus Railway Co., List No. 124					
347	Great Northern Railway Co.	26 Jun 1846	RAIL 236	1844–1926	Yes	Became part of the LNER in 1923
348	Great Western and Brentford Railway Co.	14 Aug 1855	RAIL 237	1854–1874	None	Leased to the GWR in 1859. Vested in that company 1 July 1871
349	Great Western and Great Central Joint Railway Co.	1 Aug 1899	RAIL 239 (App 4)		None	
350	Great Western and Rhymney Joint Railway Co.	15 Jul 1867	RAIL 244 (App 4)		None	

List No.	Name of Company	Date of Incorporation	TNA Record Class	Records Dates covered	Staff	Change of Ownership or Control
351	Great Western and Uxbridge Railway Co.	16 Jul 1846	RAIL 247	1852–1855	None	Vested in the GWR 22 July 1847
352	Great Western Railway Co. See App 3.2	31 Aug 1835	RAIL 250 to RAIL 282	1833–1947	Yes	Retained its name under the Absorption Scheme of 1922 and other companies became vested in this company
353	Great Yarmouth and Stalham Light Railway Co. Re-named the Yarmouth and North Norfolk Light Railway Co. 27 May 1878. Re-incorporated 11 August 1881 as the Yarmouth and North Norfolk Railway Co.	26 Jul 1876	Nil		None	Amalgamated with the Lynn and Fakenham Railway Co. and the Yarmouth Union Railway Co. 1 July 1883 to form the Eastern and Midlands Railway Co.
354	Grimsby District Light Railway Co.	15 Jan 1906	Nil		None	Built by the Great Central Railway Co.
355	Grosmont Railway Co.	12 May 1812	(RAIL 1057)		None	Purchased by the Newport, Abergavenny and Hereford Railway Co. in 1846
356	Guildford Junction Railway Co.	10 May 1844	Nil		None	Owned by the London and South Western Railway Co.
357	Guiseley, Yeadon and Headingley Railway Co. See Guiseley, Yeadon and Rawdon Railway Co., List No. 358					
358	Guiseley, Yeadon and Rawdon Railway Co. Re-named Guiseley, Yeadon and Headingley Railway Co. 5 August 1891	16 Jul 1885	Nil		None	Purchased by the Midland Railway Co. 1 June 1893 (before opening)

List No.	Name of Company	Date of Incorporation	TNA Record Class	Records		Change of Ownership or Control
				Dates covered	Staff	
359	Gwendraeth Valleys Railway Co.	30 Jul 1866	RAIL 285 (RAIL 1057)	1885–1922	None	Became part of the GWR in 1923
360	Hafan and Talybont Tramway. See Plynlimon and Hafan Tramway, List No. 682					
361	Halesowen and Bromsgrove Branch Railway Co. Re-named Halesowen Railway Co. 13 July 1876	5 Jul 1865	RAIL 286	1865–1910	None	Vested in the GWR and Midland Railway Co. jointly 20 July 1906
362	Halesowen Railway Co. See Halesowen and Bromsgrove Branch Railway Co., List No. 361					
363	Halesworth, Beccles and Haddiscoe Railway Co. Re-named the East Suffolk Railway Co. 3 July 1854	5 Jun 1851	RAIL 182	1853–1857	None	Amalgamated with the East Anglian Railway Co., the Eastern Counties Railway Co., the Norfolk Railway Co. and the Eastern Union Railway Co. 7 August 1862 to form the Great Eastern Railway Co.
364	Halifax High Level and North and South Junction Railway Co.	7 Aug 1884	Nil		None	Vested jointly in the Great Northern Railway Co. and the Lancashire and Yorkshire Railway Co. 1 October 1894
365	Halifax, Thornton and Keighley Railway Co.	5 Aug 1873	Nil		None	Worked by the Great Northern Railway Co.

List No.	Name of Company	Date of Incorporation	TNA Record Class	Records Dates covered	Records Staff	Change of Ownership or Control
366	Hall's Tramroad. Later called the Abercarn Railway	Private (1810)	(RAIL 1057)		None	Leased by the GWR in 1877. Continued in use until 1979
367	Hammersmith and City Railway Co.	22 Jul 1861	(LMA)	1861–1867	None	Worked by the GWR. Vested jointly in the GWR and the Metropolitan Railway Co. 15 July 1867
368	Hammersmith Extension Railway Co.	7 Jul 1873	Nil		None	Absorbed by the Metropolitan District Railway Co. on opening 9 September 1874
369	Hampstead Junction Railway Co.	20 Aug 1853	RAIL 291	1852–1866	Yes	Vested in the London and North Western Railway Co. 15 July 1867
370	Harborne Railway Co.	28 Jun 1866	RAIL 292	1876–1923	None	Became part of the LMS in 1923
371	Harecastle and Sandbach Railway Co.	26 Jun 1846	Nil		None	Part of the North Staffordshire Railway Co.
372	Harrington and Lowca Light Railway	Private (c. 1858)	Nil		None	Remained independent until its closure in 1973
373	Harrow and Rickmansworth Railway Co.	6 Aug 1880	Nil		None	Built and run by the Metropolitan Railway Co.
374	Harrow and Stanmore Railway Co.	25 Jun 1886	RAIL 293	1888–1890	None	Vested in the London and North Western Railway Co. 1 July 1899
375	Harrow and Uxbridge Railway Co.	6 Aug 1897	(LMA)	1898–1905	None	Worked by the Metropolitan Railway Co. Taken over by that company 25 February 1904

List No.	Name of Company	Date of Incorporation	TNA Record Class	Records		Change of Ownership or Control
				Dates covered	Staff	
376	Hartlepool Dock and Railway Co.	1 Jun 1832	RAIL 294	1831–1872	Yes	Leased to the York, Newcastle and Berwick Railway Co. from 1 July 1848. Vested in the North Eastern Railway Co. 13 July 1857
377	Hatfield and St Albans Railway Co.	30 Jun 1862	RAIL 295	1862–1884	None	Vested in the Great Northern Railway Co. 1 November 1883
378	Hay Railway Co.	25 May 1811	(RAIL 1057)		None	Parts were purchased by the Hereford, Hay and Brecon Railway Co., the Mid-Wales Railway Co. and the Brecon and Merthyr Tydfil Junction Railway Co. 6 August 1860
379	Hayle Railway Co.	27 Jun 1834	(RAIL 1057)		None	Taken over by the West Cornwall Railway Co. 3 December 1846
380	Hayling Railway Co.	23 Jul 1860	RAIL 298	1863–1923	None	Leased to the London, Brighton and South Coast Railway Co. from 30 June 1874. Transferred to the London, Brighton and South Coast Railway Co. 31 December 1922
381	Heads of the Valleys Line. See Merthyr, Tredegar and Abergavenny Railway Co., List No. 560					

List No.	Name of Company	Date of Incorporation	TNA Record Class	Records		Change of Ownership or Control
				Dates covered	Staff	
382	Helston Railway Co.	9 Jul 1880	RAIL 299 (RAIL 1057)	1879–1898	None	Vested in the GWR 1 July 1898
383	Hemel Hempstead Railway Co.	13 Jul 1863	Nil		None	Worked by the Midland Railway Co. Absorbed by that company 25 June 1886
384	Hendre Ddu Tramway	Private	Nil		None	Linked with the Mawddwy Railway Co. Closed c. 1940
385	Henley-in-Arden and Great Western Junction Railway Co. Re-named the Birmingham and Henley-in-Arden Railway Co. 7 August 1888	5 Aug 1873	RAIL 38 (RAIL 1057)	1893–1900	None	Taken over by the GWR 1 July 1900
386	Hereford, Hay and Brecon Railway Co.	8 Aug 1859	RAIL 300 (RAIL 1057)	1858–1885	None	Amalgamated with the Brecon and Merthyr Tydfil Junction Railway Co. 5 July 1865. This amalgamation was annulled in 1868 and the company re-instated. Vested in the Midland Railway Co. in 1876
387	Hereford Railway Co.	26 May 1826	(RAIL 1057)		None	Purchased by the Newport, Abergavenny and Hereford Railway Co. in 1846
388	Hereford, Ross and Gloucester Railway Co.	5 Jun 1851	RAIL 302 (RAIL 1057)	1850–1866	None	Taken over by the GWR 29 July 1862

List No.	Name of Company	Date of Incorporation	TNA Record Class	Records Dates covered	Staff	Change of Ownership or Control
389	Herne Bay and Faversham Railway Co. Re-named the Margate Railway Co. 13 August 1859. Re-named the Kent Coast Railway 6 August 1861	17 Aug 1857	RAIL 333	1857–1874	None	Leased to the London, Chatham and Dover Railway Co. Amalgamated with that company 1 July 1871
390	Hertford and Welwyn Junction Railway Co.	3 Jul 1854	Nil		None	Worked jointly by the Great Northern Railway Co. and the Eastern Counties Railway Co. Amalgamated with the Luton, Dunstable and Welwyn Junction Railway Co. 28 June 1858 to form the Hertford, Luton and Dunstable Railway Co.
391	Hertford, Luton and Dunstable Railway Co.	28 Jun 1858 (amalg.)	Nil		None	Worked by the Great Northern Railway Co. and the Eastern Counties Railway Co. until 1860. Absorbed by the Great Northern Railway Co. 12 June 1861
392	Hetton Colliery Railway	Private (1822)	Nil		None	Remained independent until its closure in 1959
393	Hexham and Allendale Railway Co.	19 Jun 1865	RAIL 303	1864–1883	None	Vested in the North Eastern Railway Co. 13 July 1876
394	Holywell Railway Co.	29 Jul 1864	RAIL 304	1892–1895	None	Purchased by the London and North Western Railway Co. 4 March 1897

List No.	Name of Company	Date of Incorporation	TNA Record Class	Records		Change of Ownership or Control
				Dates covered	Staff	
395	Horncastle and Kirkstead Junction Railway Co. Re-named the Horncastle Railway Co. in 1861	10 Jul 1854	RAIL 305	1853–1923	None	Worked by the Great Northern Railway Co. Became part of the LNER in 1923
396	Horncastle Railway Co. See Horncastle and Kirkstead Junction Railway Co., List No. 395					
397	Horsham and Guildford Direct Railway Co.	6 Aug 1860	RAIL 306	1860–1864	None	Purchased by the London, Brighton and South Coast Railway Co. 29 July 1864
398	Horsham, Dorking and Leatherhead Railway Co.	17 Jul 1862	RAIL 307	1862–1870	None	Taken over by the London, Brighton and South Coast Railway Co. 1 May 1867
399	Hounslow and Metropolitan Railway Co.	26 Aug 1880	(RAIL 1057) and (LMA)	1880–1903	None	Worked by the District Railway Co. Vested in that company 21 July 1903
400	Hoylake and Birkenhead Rail and Tramway Co. See Hoylake and Birkenhead Tramway Co., List No. 401					
401	Hoylake and Birkenhead Tramway Co. Re-incorporated as the Hoylake and Birkenhead Rail and Tramway Co. 18 July 1872. Re-named the Seacombe, Hoylake and Deeside Railway Co. 18 July 1881	1862	RAIL 599	1874–1891	None	Became part of the Wirral Railway Co. 1 July 1891

List No.	Name of Company	Date of Incorporation	TNA Record Class	Records		Change of Ownership or Control
				Dates covered	Staff	
402	Hoylake Railway Co.	28 Jul 1863	(RAIL 1057)		None	Purchased by the Hoylake and Birkenhead Tramway Co. 18 July 1872
403	Huddersfield and Manchester Railway and Canal Co.	21 Jul 1845	RAIL 308	1845–1851	None	Vested in the London and North Western Railway Co. 9 July 1847
404	Huddersfield and Sheffield Junction Railway Co.	30 Jun 1845	Nil		None	Taken over by the Manchester and Leeds Railway Co. 27 July 1846.
405	Hull and Barnsley and Great Central Joint Railway Co.	26 Jul 1910	RAIL 310 (App 4)		None	
406	Hull and Barnsley Railway Co. See Hull, Barnsley and West Riding Junction Railway and Dock Co., List No. 411					
407	Hull and Holderness Railway Co.	8 Jul 1853	RAIL 313	1852–1862	Yes	Worked by the North Eastern Railway Co. from 1 January 1860. Vested in that company 7 July 1862
408	Hull and Hornsea Railway Co.	30 Jun 1862	RAIL 314	1861–1866	None	Vested in the North Eastern Railway Co. 16 July 1866
409	Hull and Selby Railway Co.	1 Jun 18362	RAIL 315	1834–1872	Yes	Leased to the York and North Midland Railway Co. from 1 July 1845. Purchased by the North Eastern Railway Co. 1 March 1872

List No.	Name of Company	Date of Incorporation	TNA Record Class	Records		Change of Ownership or Control
				Dates covered	Staff	
410	Hull and South Yorkshire Extension Railway Co.	6 Aug 1897	Nil		None	Amalgamated with the Hull and Barnsley Railway Co. 25 July 1898
411	Hull, Barnsley and West Riding Junction Railway and Dock Co. Re-named the Hull and Barnsley Railway Co. 30 June 1905	26 Aug 1880	RAIL 312	1880–1946	Yes	Taken over by the North Eastern Railway Co. 1 April 1922
412	Humber Commercial Railway and Dock Co.	22 Jul 1904	RAIL 317	1900–1923	None	Leased to the Great Central Railway Co. 15 June 1904. Taken over by the LNER 1 January 1923
413	Hundred of Hoo Railway Co.	21 Jul 1879	RAIL 320	1879–1882	None	Vested in the South Eastern Railway Co. 11 August 1881
414	Hundred of Manhood and Selsey Railway Co. Re-named the West Sussex Railway Co. January 1924	29 Apr 1896	Nil		None	Closed in 1935
415	Hunslet Railway Co.	27 Jul 1893	Nil		None	Amalgamated with the Great Northern Railway Co. 3 July 1894 (before opening)
416	Hunstanton and West Norfolk Railway Co.	8 Jun 1874 (amalg.)	RAIL 321	1874–1892	None	Vested in the Great Eastern Railway Co. 1 July 1890
417	Hylton, Southwick and Monkwearmouth Railway Co.	25 May 1871	RAIL 322	1870–1884	None	Vested in the North Eastern Railway Co. 29 June 1883
418	Hythe and Sandgate Railway Co.	25 Jan 1870	RAIL 323	1870 only	None	Leased to the South Eastern Railway Co. 24 March 1870 in perpetuity

List No.	Name of Company	Date of Incorporation	TNA Record Class	Records		Change of Ownership or Control
				Dates covered	Staff	
419	Idle and Shipley Railway Co.	12 Aug 1867	RAIL 324	1870–1871	None	Vested in the Great Northern Railway Co. 24 July 1871
420	Ipswich and Bury St Edmunds Railway Co.	21 Jul 1845	RAIL 326	1845–1849	None	Amalgamated with the Eastern Union Railway Co. 9 July 1847
421	Isle of Axholme Light Railway Co.	11 Mar 1899	Nil		None	Amalgamated with the Goole and Marshland Light Railway Co. 1 October 1902 to form the Axholme Joint Railway Co.
422	Isle of Wight Central Railway Co.	31 Jul 1887 (amalg.)	RAIL 328	1860–1924	Yes	Taken over by the London and South Western Railway Co. 31 December 1922
423	Isle of Wight (Newport Junction) Railway Co.	31 Jul 1868	RAIL 329	1868–1887	None	Amalgamated with the Cowes and Newport Railway Co., and the Ryde and Newport Railway Co. to form the Isle of Wight Central Railway Co. 31 July 1887
424	Isle of Wight Railway Co.	23 Jul 1860	RAIL 330	1859–1922	Yes	Taken over by the London and South Western Railway Co. 31 December 1922
425	Keighley and Worth Valley Railway Co.	30 Jun 1862	RAIL 331	1861–1886	None	Vested in the Midland Railway Co. 1 July 1881
426	Kelvedon, Tiptree and Tollesbury Pier Light Railway Co.	29 Jan 1901	(RAIL 1057)		None	Worked by the Great Eastern Railway Co. Became part of the LNER in 1923

List No.	Name of Company	Date of Incorporation	TNA Record Class	Records Dates covered	Records Staff	Change of Ownership or Control
427	Kendal and Windermere Railway Co.	30 Jun 1845	Nil		None	Leased to the Lancaster and Carlisle Railway Co. 1 May 1858. Vested in the London and North Western Railway Co. 21 July 1879
428	Kent and East Sussex Light Railway Co. See Rother Valley Light Railway Co., List No. 723					
429	Kent Coast Railway Co. See Herne Bay and Faversham Railway Co., List No. 389					
430	Kenyon and Leigh Junction Railway Co.	14 May 1829	Nil		None	Consolidated with the Bolton and Leigh Railway Co., the Liverpool and Manchester Railway Co. into the Grand Junction Railway Co. 8 August 1845.
431	Kettering and Thrapstone Railway Co. Re-incorporated as the Kettering, Thrapstone and Huntingdon Railway Co. 28 July 1863	29 Jul 1862	Nil		None	Worked by the Midland Railway Co. Vested in the Midland Railway Co. 6 August 1897
432	Kettering, Thrapstone and Huntingdon Railway Co. See Kettering and Thrapstone Railway Co., List No. 431					
433	Kidwelly and Burry Port Railway Co.	5 Jul 1865	Nil		None	Amalgamated with the Burry Port and Gwendraeth Valley Railway Co. 30 April 1866

List No.	Name of Company	Date of Incorporation	TNA Record Class	Records Dates covered	Staff	Change of Ownership or Control
434	Kiltonthorpe Railway	Private	Nil		None	Purchased by the North Eastern Railway Co. 16 July 1874
435	Kings Lynn Docks and Railway Co.	19 Jun 1865	RAIL 334	1846–1956	None	Vested in the British Transport Commission in 1947
436	Kingsbridge and Salcombe Railway Co.	24 Jul 1882	RAIL 335	1883–1888	None	Vested in the GWR 13 August 1888
437	Kingsbury and Harrow Railway Co.	16 Jul 1874	Nil		None	Worked by the Metropolitan Railway Co.
438	Kingsnorth Light Railway	c. 1915	Nil		None	An extension of the Chattenden Naval Tramway
439	Kington and Eardisley Railway Co.	30 Jun 1862	RAIL 336	1862–1898	None	Vested in the GWR 1 July 1897
440	Kington Tramway	23 May 1818	(RAIL 1057)		None	Purchased by the Kington and Eardisley Railway Co. in 1862
441	Knighton Railway Co.	21 May 1858	(RAIL 1057)		None	Merged with the Central Wales Railway Co. 22 June 1863
442	Knott End Railway Co.	12 Aug 1898	RAIL 337	1921–1923	Yes	Became part of the LMS in 1923
443	Lake Lock Railroad Included an extension known as Charlesworth's Railway which opened in 1805	Private (1793)	Nil		None	Abandoned by 1840
444	Lambourn Valley Railway Co.	2 Aug 1883	RAIL 338 (RAIL 1057)	1883–1905	None	Vested in the GWR 1 July 1905
445	Lambton Wagonway	Private (c. 1770)	Nil		None	Worked by the North Eastern Railway Co. from 1864

List No.	Name of Company	Date of Incorporation	TNA Record Class	Records Dates covered	Records Staff	Change of Ownership or Control
446	Lampeter, Aberayron and New Quay Light Railway Co.	9 Oct 1906	RAIL 339 (RAIL 1057)	1908–1922	None	Taken over by the GWR 1 July 1922
447	Lancashire and Yorkshire and Lancashire Union Railways Joint Railway Co.	26 May 1865	RAIL 342 (App 4)	1865–1889	None	
448	Lancashire and Yorkshire Railway Co. Previously called the Manchester and Leeds Railway Co. See also List No. 533	9 Jul 1847 (amalg.)	RAIL 343 (RAIL 1057)	1835–1924	Yes	Amalgamated with the London and North Western Railway Co. 1 January 1922
449	Lancashire, Derbyshire and East Coast Railway Co.	5 Aug 1891	RAIL 344	1890–1907	Yes	Purchased by the Great Central Railway Co. 1 January 1907
450	Lancashire Union Railways Co.	25 Jul 1864	RAIL 345	1864–1883	None	Vested in the London and North Western Railway Co. 1 July 1883
451	Lancaster and Carlisle Railway Co.	6 Jun 1844	RAIL 346	1843–1879	None	Vested in the London and North Western Railway Co. 21 July 1879
452	Lancaster and Preston Junction Railway Co.	5 May 1837	RAIL 347	1836–1859	None	Taken over by the Lancaster and Carlisle Railway Co. 10 September 1859
453	Launceston and South Devon Railway Co.	30 Jun 1862	RAIL 348	1862–1874	None	Taken over by the South Devon Railway Co. 24 June 1869
454	Launceston, Bodmin and Wadebridge Junction Railway Co. Re-named the Central Cornwall Railway Co. 6 July 1865. Powers lapsed and it was re-incorporated as the North Cornwall Railway Co. 18 August 1882	29 Jul 1864	RAIL 522 (RAIL 1057)	1883–1923	None	Worked by the London and South Western Railway Co. Became part of the SR in 1923

List No.	Name of Company	Date of Incorporation	TNA Record Class	Records		Change of Ownership or Control
				Dates covered	Staff	
455	Lee Moor Tramway Co.	24 Jul 1854	Nil		None	Built by the Devon and Tavistock Railway Co. Later owned by Lord Morley. Closed in 1960
456	Lee-on-the-Solent Railway Co.	1890	RAIL 349	1890–1923	None	Became part of the SR in 1923
457	Leeds and Bradford Extension Railway Co.	4 Jul 1844	RAIL 350	1843–1859	None	Incorporated in the Midland Railway Co. 24 July 1851
458	Leeds and Selby Railway Co.	29 May 1830	RAIL 351	1829–1859	None	Purchased by the York and North Midland Railway Co. May 1844
459	Leeds and Thirsk Railway Co. Re-named the Leeds Northern Railway Co. 3 July 1851	21 Jul 1845	RAIL 357	1844–1858	Yes	Amalgamated with the York and North Midland Railway Co. and the York, Newcastle and Berwick Railway Co. 31 July 1854 to form the North-eastern Railway Co.
460	Leeds, Bradford and Halifax Junction Railway Co.	30 Jun 1852	RAIL 352	1851–1865	None	Amalgamated with the Great Northern Railway Co. 5 September 1865
461	Leeds, Castleford and Pontyfract Junction Railway Co.	21 Jul 1873	RAIL 353	1873–1880	None	Vested in the North Eastern Railway Co. 13 July 1876
462	Leeds, Dewsbury and Manchester Railway Co.	30 Jun 1845	RAIL 355	1845–1848	None	Vested in the London and North Western Railway Co. 4 July 1847
463	Leeds Northern Railway Co. See Leeds and Thirsk Railway Co., List No. 459					

List No.	Name of Company	Date of Incorporation	TNA Record Class	Records		Change of Ownership or Control
				Dates covered	Staff	
464	Leek and Manifold Valley Light Railway Co.	6 Mar 1899	RAIL 358	1898–1923	None	Worked and maintained by the North Staffordshire Railway Co. Became part of the LMS in 1923
465	Leicester and Swannington Railway Co.	29 May 1830	RAIL 359	1829–1854	None	Purchased by the Midland Railway Co. 27 July 1846
466	Leominster and Bromyard Railway Co.	13 Jul 1874	RAIL 362	1874–1888	None	Vested in the GWR 13 August 1888
467	Leominster and Kington Railway Co.	10 Jul 1854	RAIL 363	1853–1898	None	Leased to the GWR from 1 July 1862 and taken over by that company 2 August 1898
468	Lewes and East Grinstead Railway Co.	10 Aug 1877	RAIL 364	1876–1884	None	Amalgamated with the London, Brighton and South Coast Railway Co. 17 June 1878
469	Lewes and Uckfield Railway Co.	27 Jul 1857	RAIL 365	1857–1861	None	Purchased by the London, Brighton and South Coast Railway Co. 31 May 1860
470	Liskeard and Caradon Railway Co.	27 Jun 1843	RAIL 366 (RAIL 1057)	1854–1909	None	Vested in the GWR 1 July 1909
471	Liskeard and Looe Railway Co. See Liskeard and Looe Union Canal Co., List No. 472					
472	Liskeard and Looe Union Canal Co. Re-named the Liskeard and Looe Railway Co. 6 July 1895	27 Jun 1825	RAIL 367 (RAIL 1057)	1825–1922	None	Became part of the GWR in 1923

List No.	Name of Company	Date of Incorporation	TNA Record Class	Records		Change of Ownership or Control
				Dates covered	Staff	
473	Liverpool and Bury Railway Co.	31 Jul 1845	RAIL 368	1844–1846	None	Vested in the Manchester and Leeds Railway Co. 27 July 1846
474	Liverpool and Manchester Railway Co.	5 May 1826	RAIL 371	1836–1845	Yes	Consolidated with the Kenyon and Leigh Junction Railway Co. and the Bolton and Leigh Railway Co. into the Grand Junction Railway Co. 8 August 1845
475	Liverpool, Crosby and Southport Railway Co.	2 Jul 1847	RAIL 372	1845–1855	None	Purchased by the Lancashire and Yorkshire Railway Co. 1 January 1855
476	Liverpool, Ormskirk and Preston Railway Co.	18 Aug 1846	RAIL 373	1844–1846	None	Purchased by the East Lancashire Railway Co. 3 August 1846
477	Liverpool Overhead Railway Co.	24 Jul 1888	RAIL 778	undated	None	An electric railway. Remained independent until its closure in 1956
478	Liverpool, St Helens and South Lancashire Railway Co. See St Helens and Wigan Junction Railway Co., List No. 735					
479	Liverpool, Southport and Preston Junction Railway Co.	7 Aug 1884	RAIL 375	1884–1897	None	Vested in the Lancashire and Yorkshire Railway Co. 1 July 1897
480	Llanelly and Mynydd Mawr Railway Co.	19 Jul 1875	RAIL 376 (RAIL 1057)	1875–1922	None	Became part of the GWR in 1923
481	Llanelly Railway. See Llanelly Railway and Dock Co., List No. 482					

List No.	Name of Company	Date of Incorporation	TNA Record Class	Records Dates covered	Staff	Change of Ownership or Control
482	Llanelly Railway and Dock Co. Also known locally as the Llanelly Railway. Part of this railway was re-incorporated as the Swansea and Carmarthen Railway Co. See List No. 841	21 Aug 1835	RAIL 377	1835–1889	Yes	Worked by the GWR from 1 July 1873. Taken over by that company 24 June 1889
483	Llangollen and Corwen Railway Co.	6 Aug 1860	RAIL 378	1859–1896	None	Taken over by the GWR 1 July 1896
484	Llanidloes and Newtown Railway Co.	4 Aug 1853	RAIL 379	1852–1865	None	Amalgamated with the Oswestry and Newtown Railway Co., the Oswestry, Ellesmere and Whitchurch Railway Co. and the Newtown and Machynlleth Railway Co. 25 July 1864 to form the Cambrian Railways Co.
485	Llantrissant and Taff Vale Junction Railway Co.	7 Jun 1861	RAIL 380	1861–1889	None	Leased to the Taff Vale Railway Co. from 1 July 1875. Amalgamated with that company 1 July 1889
486	Llanvihangel Railway Co.	25 May 1811	Nil		None	Purchased by the Newport, Abergavenny and Hereford Railway Co. 3 August 1846
487	Llynvi and Ogmore Railway Co.	28 Jun 1866 (amalg.)	RAIL 382	1866–1883	None	Absorbed by the GWR 1 July 1883
488	Llynvi Valley Railway Co.	7 Aug 1846	RAIL 383	1845–1882	None	Amalgamated with the Ogmore Valley Railways Co. to form the Llynvi and Ogmore Railway Co. 28 June 1866

List No.	Name of Company	Date of Incorporation	TNA Record Class	Records		Change of Ownership or Control
				Dates covered	Staff	
489	London and Birmingham Railway Co.	6 May 1833	RAIL 384	1830–1850	Yes	Amalgamated with the Grand Junction Railway Co. and the Manchester and Birmingham Railway Co. 16 July 1846 to form the London and North Western Railway Co.
490	London and Blackwall Railway Co. See Commercial Railway Co., List No. 198					
491	London and Brighton Railway Co.	15 Jul 1837	RAIL 386	1835–1851	None	Amalgamated with the London and Croydon Railway Co. to form the London, Brighton and South Coast Railway Co. 27 July 1846
492	London and Croydon Railway Co.	12 Jun 1835	RAIL 388	1834–1846	None	Amalgamated with the London and Brighton Railway Co. to form the London, Brighton and South Coast Railway Co. 27 July 1846
493	London and Greenwich Railway Co.	17 May 1833	RAIL 389	1831–1923	None	Leased to the South Eastern Railway Co. from January 1845. Became part of the SR in 1923
494	London and North Eastern Railway. See App 3.4	Railway Act 19 Aug 1921	RAIL 390 to RAIL 401	1923–1948	Yes	
495	London and North Western and Furness Joint Railway Co.	17 Jun 1878	RAIL 403 (App 4)		Yes	

List No.	Name of Company	Date of Incorporation	TNA Record Class	Records Dates covered	Records Staff	Change of Ownership or Control
496	London and North Western Railway Co.	16 Jul 1846 (amalg.)	RAIL 410 (RAIL 625) (RAIL 1057)	1846–1933	Yes	Became part of the LMS in 1923
497	London and South Western Railway Co. See also London and Southampton Railway Co., List No. 498	4 Jun 1839 (Re-named)	RAIL 411 (RAIL 1057)	1841–1923	Yes	Became part of the SR in 1923
498	London and Southampton Railway Co. Re-named the London and South Western Railway Co. 4 June 1839. See also List No. 497	25 Jul 1834	RAIL412	1834–1845	None	
499	London, Brighton and South Coast Railway Co.	27 Jul 1846 (amalg.)	RAIL 414	1846–1945	Yes	Became part of the SR in 1923
500	London, Chatham and Dover Railway Co. See East Kent Railway Co., List No. 255					
501	London, Deptford and Dover Railway Co. Re-named the South Eastern Railway Co. c. 1844	21 Jun 1836	RAIL 635 (RAIL 1057)	1836–1922	Yes	Became part of the SR in 1923
502	London Electric Railway Co. See Brompton and Piccadilly Circus Railway Co., List No. 124					
503	London, Midland and Scottish Railway. See App 3.3	Railway Act 19 Aug 1921	RAIL 418 to RAIL 432 and (Scot RO)	1923–1947	Yes	
504	London Necropolis and National Mausoleum Co. Re-named the London Necropolis Co. in 1927.	30 Jun 1852	Nil		None	Run by the LSWR until 1923. Run by the SR from 1923.

List No.	Name of Company	Date of Incorporation	TNA Record Class	Records		Change of Ownership or Control
				Dates covered	Staff	
505	London, Tilbury and Southend Railway Co.	17 Jun 1852	RAIL 437	1852–1928	Yes	Leased to Peto, Brassey and Petts in 1854 for 21 years. Run by the North London Railway Co. from 18 May 1869. Vested in the Midland Railway Co. 1 January 1912
506	Longmoor Military Railway. See Woolmer Instructional Military Railway, List No. 968					
507	Longton, Adderley Green and Bucknall Railway Co.	16 Jul 1866	Nil		None	Worked by the North Staffordshire Railway Co. Purchased by that company in 1895
508	Lostwithiel and Fowey Railway Co.	30 Jun 1862	RAIL 1176	1863–1894	None	Closed 31 December 1879. Purchased by the Cornwall Mineral Railway 27 June 1892 and re-opened September 1895
509	Louth and East Coast Railway Co.	18 Jul 1872	RAIL 439	1871–1908	None	Purchased by the Great Northern Railway Co. 14 October 1908
510	Louth and Lincoln Railway Co.	6 Aug 1866	RAIL 440	1865–1883	None	Vested in the Great Northern Railway Co. 30 June 1883
511	Lowestoft and Beccles Railway Co.	23 Jun 1856	Nil		None	Became part of the East Suffolk Railway Co. 23 July 1858
512	Lowestoft Junction Railway Co.	6 Aug 1897	Nil		None	Operated by the LNER from 1 October 1936

List No.	Name of Company	Date of Incorporation	TNA Record Class	Records Dates covered	Staff	Change of Ownership or Control
513	Lowestoft Railway and Harbour Co.	30 Jun 1845	RAIL 441	1845–1864	None	Leased to the Norfolk Railway Co. 3 July 1846. Passed to the Eastern Counties Railway Co. in 1848
514	Ludlow and Clee Hill Railway Co.	22 Jul 1861	RAIL 442	1860–1892	None	From 1 January 1877 worked by the Great Western Railway Co. and the London and North Western Railway Co. and vested jointly in these companies 1 January 1893
515	Luton, Dunstable and Welwyn Junction Railway Co.	16 Jul 1855	Nil		None	Amalgamated with the Hertford and Welwyn Junction Railway Co. 28 June 1858 to form the Hertford, Luton and Dunstable Railway Co.
516	Lydd Railway Co.	8 Apr 1881	RAIL 443	1882–1895	None	Vested in South Eastern Railway Co. 20 June 1895
517	Lydney and Lidbrook Railway Co. Re-named the Severn and Wye Railway and Canal Co. 21 June 1810	10 June 1809	RAIL 604	1809–1879	None	Amalgamated with the Severn Bridge Railway Co. to form the Severn and Wye and Severn Bridge Railway Co. 21 July 1879
518	Lymington Railway Co.	7 Jul 1856	Nil		None	Transferred to the London and South Western Railway Co. 31 October 1878

List No.	Name of Company	Date of Incorporation	TNA Record Class	Records		Change of Ownership or Control
				Dates covered	Staff	
519	Lynn and Dereham Railway Co.	21 Jul 1845	Nil		None	Amalgamated with the Lynn and Ely Railway Co. and the Ely and Huntingdon Railway Co. 22 July 1847 to form the East Anglian Railway Co.
520	Lynn and Ely Railway Co.	30 Jun 1845	Nil		None	Amalgamated with the Lynn and Dereham Railway Co. and the Ely and Huntingdon Railway Co. 22 July 1847 to form the East Anglian Railway Co.
521	Lynn and Fakenham Railway Co.	13 Jul 1876	Nil		None	Amalgamated with the Yarmouth and North Norfolk Railway Co. and the Yarmouth Union Railway Co. 1 July 1883 to form the Eastern and Midlands Railway Co.
522	Lynn and Hunstanton Railway Co.	1 Aug 1861	RAIL 444	1862–1874	None	Amalgamated with the West Norfolk Junction Railway Co. to form the Hunstanton and West Norfolk Railway Co. 8 June 1874
523	Lynn and Sutton Bridge Railway Co.	6 Aug 1861	RAIL 445	1861–1866	None	Amalgamated with the Spalding and Bourn Railway Co. to form the Midland and Eastern Railway Co. 23 July 1866

List No.	Name of Company	Date of Incorporation	TNA Record Class	Records Dates covered	Records Staff	Change of Ownership or Control
524	Lynton and Barnstaple Railway Co.	27 Jun 1895	RAIL 446 (RAIL 1057)	1895–1923	Yes	Became part of the SR in 1923
525	Macclesfield, Bollington and Marple Railway Co.	14 Jul 1864	RAIL 448	1864–1938	None	Vested in the North Staffordshire and Great Central Railways Committee 25 May 1871; the name was then changed to the Macclesfield Committee
526	Maenclochog Railway	Private (1874)	Nil		None	Leased to the Rosebush and Fishguard Railway Co. 11 August 1878
527	Maidstone and Ashford Railway Co.	12 Aug 1880	RAIL 450	1880–1884	None	Vested in the London, Chatham and Dover Railway Co. 27 June 1883
528	Maldon, Witham and Braintree Railway Co.	18 Jun 1846	RAIL 451	1845–1850	None	Purchased by the Eastern Counties Railway Co. in 1846
529	Malmesbury Railway Co.	25 Jul 1872	RAIL 452	1872–1883	None	Vested in the GWR 1 July 1880
530	Malton and Driffield Junction Railway Co.	26 Jun 1846	RAIL 453	1845–1863	None	Amalgamated with the North-eastern Railway Co. 28 October 1854
531	Mamhead Military Railway	c. 1914	Nil		None	Closed 1918
532	Manchester and Birmingham Railway Co.	30 Jun 1837	RAIL 454	1837–1854	None	Amalgamated with the London and Birmingham Railway Co. and the Grand Junction Railway Co. 16 July 1846 to form the London and North Western Railway Co.

251

List No.	Name of Company	Date of Incorporation	TNA Record Class	Records Dates covered	Staff	Change of Ownership or Control
533	Manchester and Leeds Railway Co. Re-named the Lancashire and Yorkshire Railway Co. 9 July 1847. See also List No. 448	4 Jul 1836	RAIL 1175	1837–1850	None	Took over the Huddersfield and Sheffield Junction Railway Co., the Liverpool and Bury Railway Co. 27 July 1846 and the Ashton, Stalybridge and Liverpool Junction Railway Co., the Wakefield, Pontefract and Goole Railway Co., the West Riding Union Railway Co. and the Manchester, Bolton and Bury Canal Navigation and Railway Co. on 9 July 1847 to become the Lancashire and Yorkshire Railway Co.
534	Manchester and Lincoln Union Railway Co.	7 Aug 1846	Nil		None	Taken over by the Manchester, Sheffield and Lincolnshire Railway Co. 9 July 1847 (before opening)
535	Manchester and Milford Railway Co.	23 Jul 1860	RAIL 456 (RAIL 1057)	1860–1911	Yes	Leased to the GWR from 1 July 1906. Vested in that company 1 July 1911
536	Manchester and Southport Railway Co.	22 Jul 1847	RAIL 457	1846–1855	None	Vested jointly in the East Lancashire Railway Co. and the Lancashire and Yorkshire Railway Co. 3 July 1854

List No.	Name of Company	Date of Incorporation	TNA Record Class	Records Dates covered	Staff	Change of Ownership or Control
537	Manchester and Stockport Railway Co.	24 Jun 1869	Nil		None	Taken over jointly by the Manchester, Sheffield and Lincolnshire Railway Co. and the Midland Railway Co. 24 June 1869 (before opening)
538	Manchester, Bolton and Bury Canal Navigation and Railway Co.	13 May 1791	RAIL 458	1790–1851	Yes	Amalgamated with the Manchester and Leeds Railway Co. 18 August 1846. This company on 9 July 1847 was re-named the Lancashire and Yorkshire Railway Co.
539	Manchester, Bury and Rossendale Railway Co. Re-named the East Lancashire Railway Co. 21 July 1845	4 Jul 1844	RAIL 176	1843–1859	None	Absorbed by the Lancashire and Yorkshire Railway Co. 13 May 1859
540	Manchester, Buxton, Matlock and Midland Junction Railway Co.	16 Jul 1846	RAIL 459	1844–1871	None	The line was worked by the Midland Railway Co. Leased to the London and North Western Railway Co. and the Midland Railway Co. jointly from 1 July 1852. Vested in the Midland Railway Co. 1 July 1871
541	Manchester, Sheffield and Lincolnshire Railway Co. Re-named the Great Central Railway Co. 1 August 1897	1 Jan 1847 (amalg.)	RAIL 463 RAIL 226 (RAIL 1057)	1847–1958	Yes	Became part of the LNER in 1923

List No.	Name of Company	Date of Incorporation	TNA Record Class	Records Dates covered	Staff	Change of Ownership or Control
542	Manchester Ship Canal Company (Railways)	6 Aug 1885	Nil		None	Remained independent until Nationalization in 1947
543	Manchester South District Railway Co.	5 Aug 1873	Nil		None	Powers transferred to the Manchester and Stockport Railway Co. in 1876. Vested in the Sheffield and Midland Committee 11 August 1876
544	Manchester South Junction and Altrincham Railway Co.	21 Jul 1845 (amalg.)	RAIL 465	1842–1938	Yes	This company was formed by uniting the Manchester and Birmingham Railway Co. with the Sheffield, Ashton-under-Lyne and Manchester Railway Co. 16 July 1846. The Manchester and Birmingham Railway Co. was amalgamated with the Grand Junction Railway Co. and the London and Birmingham Railway Co. to form the London and North Western Railway Co. At the same time the Sheffield, Ashton-under-Lyne and Manchester Railway Co. became part of the Manchester, Sheffield and Lincolnshire Railway Co.

List No.	Name of Company	Date of Incorporation	TNA Record Class	Records Dates covered	Staff	Change of Ownership or Control
545	Mansfield and Pinxton Railway Co.	16 Jun 1817	RAIL 467	1817–1847	None	Purchased by the Midland Railway Co. 8 July 1847
546	Mansfield Railway Co.	26 Jul 1910	RAIL 468	1910–1923	None	Became part of the LNER in 1923
547	Margate Railway Co. See Herne Bay and Faversham Railway Co., List No. 389					
548	Marland Light Railway	Private (1880)	Nil		None	Became part of the North Devon and Cornwall Junction Light Railway Co.
549	Marlborough and Grafton Railway Co.	7 Aug 1896	RAIL 469 (RAIL 1057)	1895–1900	None	Vested in the Midland and South Western Junction Railway Co. 1 August 1899
550	Marlborough Railway Co.	22 Jul 1861	RAIL 470	1861–1896	None	Taken over by the GWR 1 July 1896
551	Marple, New Mills and Hayfield Junction Railway Co.	15 May 1860	RAIL 471	1859–1865	None	Vested in the Manchester, Sheffield and Lincolnshire Railway Co. 5 July 1865 and jointly with the Midland Railway Co. 24 June 1869
552	Maryport and Carlisle Railway Co.	12 Jul 1837	RAIL 472	1835–1923	Yes	Became part of the LMS in 1923
553	Mawddwy Railway Co.	5 Jul 1865	RAIL 473 (RAIL 1057)	1865–1922	None	Became part of the GWR in 1923
554	Mellis and Eye Railway Co.	5 Jul 1865	Nil			Worked by the Great Eastern Railway Co. Purchased by that company 1 July 1898

List No.	Name of Company	Date of Incorporation	TNA Record Class	Records Dates covered	Records Staff	Change of Ownership or Control
555	Merchants Railway. See Portland Railway Co., List No. 691					
556	Merrybent and Darlington Railway Co.	11 Jun 1866	RAIL 474	1865–1878	None	Company wound up 17 June 1878. The undertaking was purchased by the North Eastern Railway Co. in 1890
557	Mersey Docks and Harbour Board. [Railways at the docks of Birkenhead and Liverpool]	12 Jul 1858	(RAIL 1057)		None	Closed c1973
558	Mersey Pneumatic Railway Co. Re-named the Mersey Railway Co. 31 July 1868	28 Jun 1866	RAIL 475	1866–1948	Yes	Passed to the British Transport Commission in 1947
559	Mersey Railway Co. See Mersey Pneumatic Railway Co., List No. 558					
560	Merthyr, Tredegar and Abergavenny Railway Co. Also known as the Heads of the Valleys Line	1 Aug 1859	RAIL 476	1858–1866	None	Leased to the London and North Western Railway Co. from 7 August 1862. Transferred to that company 30 July 1866
561	Metropolitan and Metropolitan District Joint Railway Co.	11 Aug 1879	Nil		None	
562	Metropolitan and St Johns Wood Railway Co.	29 Jul 1864	(LMA)	1864–1883	None	Worked by the Metropolitan Railway Co. Absorbed by that company 3 July 1882

List No.	Name of Company	Date of Incorporation	TNA Record Class	Records Dates covered	Staff	Change of Ownership or Control
563	Metropolitan District Railway Co.	29 Jul 1864 (amalg.)	(RAIL 1057) and (LMA)	1864–1926	None	Passed to the London Passenger Transport Board 1 July 1933
564	Metropolitan Inner Circle Completion Railway Co.	7 Aug 1874	Nil		None	Taken over jointly by the Metropolitan Railway Co. and the Metropolitan District Railway Co. 11 August 1879 (before opening)
565	Metropolitan Railway Co. See North Metropolitan Railway Co., List No. 629					
566	Mid-Hants (Alton Lines) Railway Co. See Alton, Alresford and Winchester Railway Co., List No. 12					
567	Mid-Kent and North Kent Railway Co.	23 Jul 1855	Nil		None	Amalgamated with the South Eastern Railway Co. 29 July 1864
568	Mid-Kent (Bromley to St Mary Cray) Railway Co.	21 Jul 1856	RAIL 478	1856–1923	None	Leased to the London, Chatham and Dover Railway Co. from 1 September 1863. Became part of the SR in 1923
569	Mid-Suffolk Railway Co.	Light Railways Act 1896	RAIL 479	1900–1924	Yes	Became part of the LNER in 1923
570	Mid-Sussex and Midhurst Junction Railway Co.	13 Aug 1859	RAIL 480	1859–1874	None	Purchased by the London, Brighton and South Coast Railway Co. June 1874

List No.	Name of Company	Date of Incorporation	TNA Record Class	Records		Change of Ownership or Control
				Dates covered	Staff	
571	Mid-Sussex Railway Co.	10 Aug 1857	RAIL 481	1857–1860	None	Purchased by the London, Brighton and South Coast Railway Co. 31 May 1860
572	Mid-Wales Railway Co.	1 Aug 1859	RAIL 482 (RAIL 1057)	1859–1902	Yes	Worked by the Cambrian Railways Co. from 2 April 1888. Vested in that company 1 July 1904
573	Middlesbrough and Guisborough Railway Co.	17 Jun 1852	RAIL 483	1851–1859	Yes	Vested in the Stockton and Darlington Railway Co. 23 July 1858
574	Middlesbrough and Redcar Railway Co.	21 Jul 1845	RAIL 484	1844–1878	Yes	Leased to the Stockton and Darlington Railway Co. from 1 October 1847. Vested in that company 23 July 1858
575	Middleton Railway Co.	9 Jun 1758	Nil		None	Remained independent until its closure in 1958. Re-opened in 1960 as a preservation society
576	Midland and Eastern Railway Co.	23 Jul 1866 (amalg.)	RAIL 485	1866–1883	None	Incorporated into the Eastern and Midlands Railway Co. 1 July 1883
577	Midland and Great Eastern Joint Railway Co. See Tottenham and Hampstead Junction Railway Co., List No. 873					

List No.	Name of Company	Date of Incorporation	TNA Record Class	Records Dates covered	Staff	Change of Ownership or Control
578	Midland and Great Northern Joint Railway Co.	1 Jul 1893	RAIL 487 (App 4)	1866–1936	Yes App 4	Became part of the LNER and the LMS in 1923
579	Midland and North Eastern Joint Railway Co.	16 Jul 1874	RAIL 488 (App 4)	1874–1923	None	
580	Midland and South Western Junction Railway Co.*	14 Jul 1864	Nil		None	Taken over by the Midland Railway Co. 30 July 1874
581	Midland and South Western Junction Railway Co.	23 Jun 1884 (amalg.)	RAIL 489 (RAIL 1057)	1884–1923	Yes	Became part of the GWR in 1923
582	Midland Counties Railway Co.	21 Jun 1836	RAIL 490 RAIL 491	1834–1846	None	Amalgamated with the Birmingham and Derby Junction Railway Co. and the North Midland Railway Co. to form the Midland Railway Co. 10 May 1844
583	Midland Counties and South Wales Railway Co. See Northampton and Banbury Junction Railway Co., List No. 640					
584	Midland Railway Co.	10 May 1844 (amalg.)	RAIL 491 (RAIL 1057)	1844–1923	Yes	Became part of the LMS in 1923
585	Milford Haven Docks and Railway Co.	23 Jul 1861	Nil		None	Still runs as an independent company
586	Milford Railway Co.	5 Jun 1856	RAIL 492	1856–1896	None	Taken over by the GWR 1 July 1896

* There were two companies with the same name.

List No.	Name of Company	Date of Incorporation	TNA Record Class	Records		Change of Ownership or Control
				Dates covered	Staff	
587	Millwall Extension Railway Co.	19 Jun 1865	Nil		None	Owned by the Port of London Authority. Closed in 1966
588	Minehead Railway Co.	5 Jul 1865	RAIL 493	1865–1897	None	Company dissolved in 1870. Re-incorporated 29 June 1871 by the West Somerset Railway Co. Leased to the Bristol and Exeter Railway Co. from opening. The company was absorbed by the GWR 6 August 1897
589	Mitcheldean Road and Forest of Dean Junction Railway Co.	13 Jul 1871	RAIL 494	1871–1880	None	Taken over by the GWR 6 August 1880
590	Mold and Denbigh Junction Railway Co.	6 Aug 1861	RAIL 495	1861–1923	None	Worked by the London and North Western Railway Co. from 12 November 1868. Became part of the LMS in 1923
591	Mold Railway Co.	9 Jul 1847	RAIL 496	1847–1853	None	Purchased by the Chester and Holyhead Railway Co. 30 March 1849
592	Monmouth Railway Co.	24 May 1810	RAIL 498	1808–1876	None	Part of the line purchased by the Coleford, Monmouth, Usk and Pontypool Railway Co. in 1853. Remainder purchased by the Coleford Railway Co. in 1876

List No.	Name of Company	Date of Incorporation	TNA Record Class	Records		Change of Ownership or Control
				Dates covered	Staff	
593	Monmouthshire Railway and Canal Co. See Blaenavon Tramroad, List No. 81					
594	Morecambe Harbour and Railway Co.	16 Jul 1846	Nil		None	Leased by the Midland Railway Co. 1 January 1859. Purchased by that company 1 June 1871
595	Moretonhampstead and South Devon Railway Co.	7 Jul 1862	RAIL 501	1858–1872	None	Worked by the South Devon Railway Co. and absorbed by that company 1 July 1872
596	Much Wenlock and Severn Junction Railway Co.	21 Jul 1859	RAIL 502	1859–1897	None	Vested in the GWR 1 July 1896
597	Muswell Hill and Palace Railway Co. See Muswell Hill Railway Co., List No. 598					
598	Muswell Hill Railway Co. Re-named the Muswell Hill and Palace Railway Co. 25 September 1886	30 Jul 1866	RAIL 503	1866–1911	None	Worked by the Great Northern Railway Co. Line ceased operation in August 1882. Re-opened on 8 April 1898 and worked by the Great Northern Railway Co. Purchased by that company 18 August 1911
599	Nantlle Railway Co.	20 May 1825	Nil		None	Vested in the Caernarvonshire Railway Co. 25 July 1867

List No.	Name of Company	Date of Incorporation	TNA Record Class	Records		Change of Ownership or Control
				Dates covered	Staff	
600	Nantwich and Market Drayton Railway Co.	7 Jun 1861	RAIL 504	1860–1897	None	Taken over by the GWR 1 July 1897
601	Narberth Road and Maenclochog Railway Co.	24 Jun 1872	(RAIL 1057)		None	Taken over by the North Pembroke and Fishguard Railway Co. and extended to Fishguard in 1893
602	Neath and Brecon Railway Co. See Dulas Valley Mineral Railway Co., List No. 237					
603	Nerquis Railway	Private (c. 1846)	Nil		None	Purchased by the London and North Western Railway Co. in 1868
604	Newark and Leicester Railway Co.	6 Aug 1872	Nil		None	Became part of the LMS and part of the LNER in 1923
605	Newbottle Wagonway	Private (c. 1770)	Nil		None	Purchased by the Lambton Wagonway in 1822
606	Newcastle and Berwick Railway Co.	31 Jul 1845	RAIL 506	1845–1847	None	Amalgamated with the York and Newcastle Railway Co. to form the York, Newcastle and Berwick Railway Co. 9 August 1847
607	Newcastle and Carlisle Railway Co.	22 May 1829 for use of horse power only. 17 Jun 1835 for use of locomotives	RAIL 509	1825–1887	Yes	Worked by the York, Newcastle and Berwick Railway Co. from 1 July 1848 to 31 December 1849. Worked by the company from 1 January 1850. Amalgamated with the North Eastern Railway Co. 17 July 1862

List No.	Name of Company	Date of Incorporation	TNA Record Class	Records Dates covered	Records Staff	Change of Ownership or Control
608	Newcastle and Darlington Junction Railway Co. Re-named the York and Newcastle Railway Co. 3 August 1846	18 Jun 1842	RAIL 772	1847–1848	Yes	Amalgamated with the Newcastle and Berwick Railway Co. 9 July 1847 to become the York, Newcastle and Berwick Railway Co.
609	Newcastle and North Shields Railway Co.	21 Jun 1836	RAIL 507	1835–1861	None	Vested in the Newcastle and Berwick Railway Co. 31 July 1845
610	Newent Railway Co.	5 Aug 1873	RAIL 510	1873–1892	None	Taken over by the GWR 1 July 1892
611	Newmarket and Chesterford Railway Co. Re-named the Newmarket Railway Co. 8 June 1847	16 Jul 1846	RAIL 512	1852–1853	None	Worked by the Eastern Counties Railway Co. from 1 Oct 1848
612	Newmarket Railway Co. See Newmarket and Chesterford Railway Co., List No. 611					
613	Newport, Abergavenny and Hereford Railway Co.	3 Aug 1846	RAIL 513	1845–1860	None	Amalgamated with the Worcester and Hereford Railway Co. and the Oxford, Worcester and Wolverhampton Railway Co. 14 June 1860 to form the West Midland Railway Co.
614	Newport, Godshill and St. Lawrence Railway Co. See Shanklin and Chale Railway Co., List No. 757					

List No.	Name of Company	Date of Incorporation	TNA Record Class	Records Dates covered	Staff	Change of Ownership or Control
615	Newquay and Cornwall Junction Railway Co.	4 Jul 1864	RAIL 516	1863–1884	None	Transferred to the Cornwall Minerals Railway Co. 21 July 1873
616	Newtown and Machynlleth Railway Co.	27 Jul 1857	RAIL 517	1856–1864	None	Amalgamated with the Oswestry, Ellesmere and Whitchurch Railway Co., the Oswestry and Newtown Railway Co., and the Llanidloes and Newtown Railway Co. to form the Cambrian Railways Co. 25 July 1864
617	Nidd Valley Light Railway Co.	30 Mar 1901	Nil		None	Closed in 1936
618	Norfolk and Suffolk Joint Railway Co.	25 Jul 1898	RAIL 518 (App 4)	1897–1938	None	Worked by the Midland and Great Northern Joint Railway Co. Remained independent until Nationalization in 1947
619	Norfolk Railway Co.	30 Jun 1845 (amalg.)	RAIL 519	1845–1865	None	Amalgamated with the East Anglian Railway Co., the Eastern Counties Railway Co., the Eastern Union Railway Co. and the East Suffolk Railway Co. 7 August 1862 to form the Great Eastern Railway Co.

List No.	Name of Company	Date of Incorporation	TNA Record Class	Records		Change of Ownership or Control
				Dates covered	Staff	
620	North and South Western Junction Railway Co.	24 Jul 1851	RAIL 521	1851–1923	Yes	Leased to the London and North Western Railway Co. and the Midland and North London Railway Co. jointly 1 January 1871. Became part of the LMS in 1923
621	North British Railway Co.	4 Jul 1844	(RAIL 1057) and (Scot RO)	1850–1946	Yes	Became part of the LNER in 1923
622	North Cornwall Railway Co. See Launceston, Bodmin and Wadebridge Junction Railway Co., List No. 454					
623	North Devon and Cornwall Junction Light Railway Co.	28 Aug 1914	RAIL 523	1914–1947	None	Was not part of the 1923 Grouping. Passed to the British Transport Commission in 1948
624	North Devon Railway and Dock Co. See Taw Vale Railway and Dock Co., List No. 857					
625	North-eastern Railway Co. Later recorded as the North Eastern Railway Co.	31 Jul 1854 (amalg.)	RAIL 527 (RAIL 1057)	1854–1923	Yes	Became part of the LNER in 1923
626	North Kent Line. See Gravesend and Rochester Railway Co., List No. 331					
627	North Lindsey Light Railway Co.	29 Jan 1900	RAIL 528	1905–1923	None	Became part of the LNER in 1923

List No.	Name of Company	Date of Incorporation	TNA Record Class	Records		Change of Ownership or Control
				Dates covered	Staff	
640	Northampton and Banbury Junction Railway Co. Re-named the Midland Counties and South Wales Railway Co. in 1866 but reverted to its original name 14 July1870	28 Jul 1863	RAIL 538	1861–1911	None	Purchased by the Stratford-upon-Avon and Midland Junction Railway Co. 1 July 1910
641	Northern and Eastern Railway Co.	4 Jul 1836	RAIL 541	1835–1909	None	Leased to the Great Eastern Railway Co. Vested in that company 1 July 1902
642	Northumberland Central Railway Co.	28 Jul 1863	Nil		None	Taken over by the North British Railway Co. 18 July 1872
643	Norwich and Brandon Railway Co.	10 May 1844	Nil		None	Amalgamated with the Yarmouth and Norwich Railway Co. 30 June 1845 to become the Norfolk Railway Co.
644	Norwich and Spalding Railway Co.	4 Aug 1853	RAIL 544	1856–1877	None	Leased to the Midland and Eastern Railway Co. 23 July 1866. Vested in that company 12 July 1877
645	Nottingham and Grantham Railway and Canal Co. See Ambergate, Nottingham and Boston and Eastern Junction Railway Co., List No. 13					

List No.	Name of Company	Date of Incorporation	TNA Record Class	Records Dates covered	Staff	Change of Ownership or Control
646	Nottingham, Erewash Valley and Ambergate Railway Co.	4 Aug 1845	Nil		None	Amalgamated with the Nottingham and Boston Railway Co. and the Nottingham, Vale of Belvoir and Grantham Railway Co. 16 July 1846 to form the Ambergate, Nottingham and Boston and Eastern Junction Railway Co.
647	Nottingham Suburban Railway Co.	25 Jun 1886	RAIL 547	1886–1923	None	Worked by the Great Northern Railway Co. Became part of the LNER in 1923
648	Nottingham, Vale of Belvoir and Grantham Railway	Never incorporated	RAIL 548	1845	None	Amalgamated with the Nottingham, Erewash Valley and Ambergate Railway Co., and the Nottingham and Boston Railway Co. 16 July 1846 to form the Ambergate, Nottingham and Boston and Eastern Junction Railway Co.
649	Nuneaton and Hinckley Railway Co. Re-named the South Leicestershire Railway Co. 14 June 1860	18 Aug 1850	RAIL 636	1861–1863	None	Vested in the London and North Western Railway Co. 15 July 1867
650	Ogmore Valley Railways Co.	13 Jul 1863	RAIL 549	1863–1866	None	Amalgamated with the Llynvi Valley Railway Co. to form the Llynvi and Ogmore Railway Co. 28 June 1866

List No.	Name of Company	Date of Incorporation	TNA Record Class	Records		Change of Ownership or Control
				Dates covered	Staff	
651	Okehampton Railway Co. Re-named the Devon and Cornwall Railway Co. 26 July 1870	17 Jul 1862	RAIL 154	1865–1875	None	Purchased by the London and South Western Railway Co. 1 January 1872
652	Oldbury Railway Co. See Dudley and Oldbury Junction Railway Co., List No. 235					
653	Oldham, Ashton-under-Lyne and Guide Bridge Junction Railway Co.	10 Aug 1857	RAIL 551	1857–1947	None	30 June 1862 leased to the London and North Western Railway Co. (subsequently the LMS) and the Manchester, Sheffield and Lincolnshire Railway Co. (later the Great Central Railway Co. and subsequently the LNER). Passed to the British Transport Commission in 1948
654	Oswestry and Newtown Railway Co.	26 Jun 1855	RAIL 552	1855–1864	None	Amalgamated with the Oswestry, Ellesmere and Whitchurch Railway Co., the Llanidloes and Newtown Railway Co. and the Newtown and Machynlleth Railway Co. 25 July 1864 to form the Cambrian Railways Co.

List No.	Name of Company	Date of Incorporation	TNA Record Class	Records Dates covered	Staff	Change of Ownership or Control
655	Oswestry, Ellesmere and Whitchurch Railway Co.	1 Aug 1861	RAIL 553	1860–1864	None	Amalgamated with the Oswestry and Newtown Railway Co., the Llanidloes and Newtown Railway Co. and the Newtown and Machynlleth Railway Co. 25 July 1864 to form the Cambrian Railways Co.
656	Otley and Ilkley Joint Railway Co.	11 Jul 1861	RAIL 554 (App 4)	1861–1923	Yes App 4	Built and managed jointly by the Midland Railway Co. and the North Eastern Railway Co. The line was run jointly by the LNER and the LMS from 1 January 1923
657	Oxford and Aylesbury Tramroad Co. Ran only as the Wotton Tramway. See List No. 972	7 Aug 1888	Nil		None	Leased to the Metropolitan Railway Co. 1 December 1899. Run by the Metropolitan and Great Central Joint Committee from 2 April 1906. Closed in 1935
658	Oxford and Bletchley Junction Railway Co.	26 Jun 1846	RAIL 555	1840–1847	None	Amalgamated with the Buckingham and Brackley Junction Railway Co. (before opening) to form the Buckinghamshire Railway Co. 22 July 1847

List No.	Name of Company	Date of Incorporation	TNA Record Class	Records Dates covered	Staff	Change of Ownership or Control
659	Oxford and Rugby Railway Co.	4 Aug 1845	RAIL 556	1840–1850	None	Became part of the Birmingham and Oxford Junction Railway Co. (before opening). Taken over by the GWR 14 May 1846
660	Oxford Railway Co.	11 Apr 1843	RAIL 557	1843	None	Taken over by the GWR 10 May 1844 (before opening)
661	Oxford, Worcester and Wolverhampton Railway Co.	4 Aug 1845	RAIL 558 RAIL 784	1844–1863	Yes	Amalgamated with the Newport, Abergavenny and Hereford Railway Co. and the Worcester and Hereford Railway Co. 14 June 1860 to form the West Midland Railway Co.
662	Oxted and Groombridge Railway Co.	11 Aug 1881	Nil		None	Taken over by the London, Brighton and South Coast Railway Co. 3 July 1884
663	Oystermouth Railway Co. Reconstituted as the Swansea and Mumbles Railway Co. 26 July 1893	29 Jun 1804	(RAIL 1057)		None	Worked by the Swansea Improvements and Tramway Co. from 1884. Became part of the GWR in 1923
664	Padarn Railway	Private (c. 1842)	Nil		None	Remained independent until its closure in 1961
665	Palleg Tramroad	Private (c. 1806)	Nil		None	Purchased by the Swansea Vale Railway Co. 7 June 1861

List No.	Name of Company	Date of Incorporation	TNA Record Class	Records Dates covered	Records Staff	Change of Ownership or Control
666	Park Prewett Hospital Railway (Near Basingstoke)	Private (1912)	Nil		None	Worked by the London and South Western Railway Co. Became part of the SR in 1923. Closed in 1954
667	Peak Forest Tramway Co.	28 Mar 1794	Nil		None	Taken over by the Sheffield, Ashton-under-Lyme and Manchester Railway Co. 27 July 1846
668	Pembroke and Tenby Railway Co.	21 Jul 1859	RAIL 559	1859–1898	None	Leased to the GWR from 1 July 1896 and amalgamated with that company 1 July 1897
669	Penarth Extension Railway Co.	11 Aug 1876	RAIL 560	1876–1922	None	Worked by the Taff Vale Railway Co. and became part of the GWR in 1923
670	Penarth Harbour Dock and Railway Co. See Ely Tidal Harbour and Railway Co., List No. 283					
671	Penllwyn Tramroad	Private (c. 1824)	Nil		None	Part purchased by the London and North Western Railway Co. in 1876. The rest abandoned
672	Penrhyn Railway	Private (1801)	Nil		None	Remained independent until its closure in 1962
673	Pensnett Railway. Also known as the Shut End Railway	Private (1829)	Nil		None	
674	Pentewan Railway	Private (c. 1828)	Nil		None	Closed in 1918

| List No. | Name of Company | Date of Incorporation | TNA Record Class | Records | | Change of Ownership or Control |
				Dates covered	Staff	
675	Penydarren Tramway	1796	Nil		None	Closed *c.* 1884
676	Peterborough, Wisbeach and Sutton Bridge Railway Co.	28 Jul 1863	RAIL 564	1863–1874	None	Taken over by the Eastern and Midland Railway Co. 1 July 1883
677	Petersfield Railway Co.	23 Jul 1860	RAIL 565	1863–1883	None	Purchased by the London and South Western Railway Co. 22 June 1863
678	Pike's Tramway. See Furzebrook Tramway, List No. 314					
679	Plymouth and Dartmoor Railway Co.	2 Jul 1819	RAIL 566 (RAIL 1057)	1819–1923	None	Became part of the SR in 1923
680	Plymouth, Devonport and Exeter Railway. See South Devon Railway Co., List No 795					
681	Plymouth, Devonport and South Western Junction Railway Co.	25 Aug 1883	RAIL 567	1883–1923	None	Became part of the SR in 1923
682	Plynlimon and Hafan Tramway. Also known as the Hafan and Talybont Tramway	Private (*c.* 1892)	(RAIL 1057)		None	Closed 12 August 1898
683	Pontcysyllte Tramway. See Ruabon Brook Railway, List No. 727					
684	Pontop and Jarrow Wagonway. Re-named the Bowes Railway	Private (*c.* 1729)	(TWAS)		Yes	Closed in 1887
685	Pontop and South Shields Railway Co.	23 May 1842	RAIL 569	1833–1861	None	Purchased by the Newcastle and Darlington Junction Railway Co. 3 August 1846 which then changed its name to the York and Newcastle Railway Co.

List No.	Name of Company	Date of Incorporation	TNA Record Class	Records Dates covered	Staff	Change of Ownership or Control
686	Pontypool, Caerleon and Newport Railway Co.	5 Jul 1865	RAIL 570	1870–1877	None	Vested in the GWR 13 July 1876
687	Pontypridd, Caerphilly and Newport Railway Co.	8 Aug 1878	RAIL 571 (RAIL 1057)	1878–1897	None	Vested in the Alexandra (Newport and South Wales) Docks and Railway Co. 31 December 1897
688	Poole and Bournemouth Railway Co.	26 May 1865	RAIL 572	1865–1882	None	Purchased by the London and South Western Railway Co. 1 January 1882
689	Port Carlisle Dock and Railway Co.	4 Aug 1853	Nil		None	Leased by the North British Railway Co. from 1 August 1862. Absorbed by that company 1 August 1880
690	Port Talbot Railway and Docks Co.	31 Jul 1894	RAIL 573 RAIL 574 (RAIL 1057)	1836–1922	Yes	Became part of the GWR 1 January 1922
691	Portland Railway Co. Also known as the Merchants Railway	10 Jun 1825	(RAIL 1057)		None	Closed in 1939
692	Portmadoc, Beddgelert and South Snowdon Railway Co.	17 Aug 1901	Nil		None	Purchased by the Welsh Highland Railway Co. 1 January 1922
693	Portmadoc, Croesor and Beddgelert Tram Railway Co. See Croesor and Portmadoc Railway Co., List No. 211					

List No.	Name of Company	Date of Incorporation	TNA Record Class	Records Dates covered	Staff	Change of Ownership or Control
694	Portsmouth Railway Co.	8 Jul 1853	RAIL 575	1852–1861	None	Leased to the London and South Western Railway Co. 21 July 1859. Company dissolved 21 August 1861
695	Potteries, Biddulph and Congleton Railway Co.	24 Jul 1854	Nil		None	Became part of the North Staffordshire Railway Co.
696	Potteries Junction Railway Co.	15 May 1863	RAIL 1180	1863	None	Became part of the North Staffordshire Railway Co. and never ran as a separate company
697	Potteries Railway Co.	26 Jun 1846	Nil		None	Became part of the North Staffordshire Railway Co. on the day of incorporation
698	Potteries, Shrewsbury and North Wales Railway Co.	16 Jul 1866 (amalg.)	(RAIL 1057)		None	Part closed 18 July 1881. Remainder worked by the Cambrian Railways Co.
699	Preston and Longridge Railway Co.	14 Jul 1836	RAIL 576	1866–1889	None	Purchased by the Fleetwood, Preston and West Riding Junction Railway Co. 31 August 1856
700	Preston and Wigan Railway Co.	22 Apr 1831	RAIL 534	1831–1833	None	Amalgamated with the Wigan Branch Railway Co. 22 May 1834 to form the North Union Railway Co.
701	Preston and Wyre Dock Co.	5 May 1837	RAIL 577	1836–1847	None	These two companies were combined to form the Preston and Wyre Railway Harbour and Dock Co. 1 July 1839
702	Preston and Wyre Railway and Harbour Co.	3 Jul 1835	Nil		None	

List No.	Name of Company	Date of Incorporation	TNA Record Class	Records Dates covered	Records Staff	Change of Ownership or Control
703	Preston and Wyre Railway Harbour and Dock Co.	1 Jul 1839 (amalg.)	RAIL 577	1836–1847	None	Vested in the London and North Western Railway Co. and the Lancashire and Yorkshire Railway Co. jointly 28 July 1849
704	Princetown Railway Co.	13 Aug 1878	RAIL 578	1879–1922	None	Became part of the GWR 1 January 1922
705	Radstock Tramway	c. 1815	Nil		None	Purchased by the Somerset and Dorset Railway Co. 21 August 1871
706	Ramsey and Somersham Railway Co.	2 June 1875	Nil		None	Became part of the Great Northern and Great Eastern Joint Railway Co. 1 January 1897
707	Ramsey Railway Co.	22 Jul 1861	Nil		None	Worked by the Great Northern Railway Co. Purchased by the Great Eastern Railway Co. 19 July 1875
708	Rattlebrook Peat Railway. Also known as the Bridestowe Railway	Private (1879)	Nil		None	Closed c. 1910
709	Ravenglass and Eskdale Railway Co.	26 May 1873	Nil		None	Became a tourist railway in 1960
710	Reading, Guildford and Reigate Railway Co.	16 Jul 1846	RAIL 579	1845–1852	None	Leased to the South Eastern Railway Co. from 15 March 1850. Purchased by that company 11 June 1852

List No.	Name of Company	Date of Incorporation	TNA Record Class	Records		Change of Ownership or Control
				Dates covered	Staff	
711	Redditch Railway Co.	23 Jul 1858	RAIL 580	1858–1875	None	Purchased by the Midland Railway Co. 4 October 1865
712	Redlake Tramway	1911	Nil		None	Closed in 1932
713	Redruth and Chasewater Railway Co.	17 Jun 1824	Nil		None	Closed in 1915
714	Rhondda and Swansea Bay Railway Co.	10 Aug 1882	RAIL 581 (RAIL 1057)	1880–1922	Yes	Worked by the GWR from 1 January 1906. Became a subsidiary of the GWR 1 January 1922
715	Rhondda Valley and Hirwain Junction Railway Co.	12 Aug 1867	RAIL 582	1879–1889	None	Amalgamated with the Taff Vale Railway Co. 1 July 1889
716	Rhymney Railway Co.	24 Jul 1854	RAIL 583 (RAIL 1057)	1853–1922	Yes	Taken over by the GWR 1 January 1922
717	Richmond Railway Co.	24 Jul 1845	RAIL 584	1845–1847	None	Purchased by the London and South Western Railway Co. 1 January 1847
718	Ringwood, Christchurch and Bournemouth Railway Co.	8 Aug 1859	RAIL 585	1859–1874	None	Transferred to the London and South Western Railway Co. 1 January 1874
719	Romney, Hythe and Dymchurch Railway	Private (c. 1920)	Nil		None	Continues as an independent concern
720	Rosebush and Fishguard Railway Co. Re-named the North Pembrokeshire and Fishguard Railway Co. 7 August 1884	8 Aug 1878	RAIL 531	1878–1899	None	Vested in the GWR 12 February 1898

List No.	Name of Company	Date of Incorporation	TNA Record Class	Records Dates covered	Records Staff	Change of Ownership or Control
721	Ross and Ledbury Railway Co.	28 Jul 1873	RAIL 586	1874–1892	None	Taken over by the GWR 1 July 1892
722	Ross and Monmouth Railway Co.	5 Jul 1865	RAIL 587 (RAIL 1057)	1865–1922	None	Became part of the GWR 1 July 1922
723	Rother Valley Light Railway Co. Re-named the Kent and East Sussex Light Railway Co. 1 June 1904	2 Jul 1896	RAIL 332	1897–1948	None	Passed to the British Transport Commission in 1947
724	Rotherham, Maltby and Laughton Railway Co.	4 Aug 1905	(RAIL 1057)		None	Transferred to the Great Central Railway Co. 20 July 1906
725	Rowrah and Kelton Fell (Mineral) Railway Co.	16 Jul 1874	Nil		None	Closed in 1926
726	Royston and Hitchin Railway Co.	16 Jul 1846	RAIL 588	1845–1897	None	Leased to the Great Northern Railway Co. 1 August 1850. Leased to the Great Eastern Railway Co. 23 June 1864 to 1 April 1866. Vested in the Great Northern Railway Co. 1 July 1897
727	Ruabon Brook Railway. Also known as the Pontcysyllte Tramway	Private (c1800)	Nil		None	Leased to the London and North Western Railway Co. 2 July 1847
728	Rugby and Leamington Railway Co. Provisionally known as the Rugby, Leamington and Warwick Railway Co.	13 Aug 1846	RAIL 589	1845–1846	None	Purchased by the London and North Western Railway Co. 17 November 1846

List No.	Name of Company	Date of Incorporation	TNA Record Class	Records		Change of Ownership or Control
				Dates covered	Staff	
729	Rugby, Leamington and Warwick Railway Co. See Rugby and Leamington Railway Co., List No. 728					
730	Rumney Railway Co.	20 May 1825	RAIL 590	1852–1863	None	Vested in the Brecon and Merthyr Tydfil Junction Railway Co. 28 July 1863
731	Ryde and Newport Railway Co.	25 Jul 1872	RAIL 591	1872–1887	None	Amalgamated with the Cowes and Newport Railway Co., and the Isle of Wight (Newport Junction) Railway Co. to form the Isle of Wight Central Railway Co. 1 July 1887
732	Ryde Pier and Tramway Co.	Originally incorporated in 1812 as horse-drawn. Steam authorized 23 July 1877	RAIL 592	1812–1923	None	Transferred to the SR 1 June 1924
733	Rye and Camber Railway	Private (1894)	Nil		None	Requisitioned by the Admiralty in 1914
734	St Helens and Runcorn Gap Railway Co.	29 May 1830	Nil		None	Amalgamated with the Sankey Brook Navigation Co. to become the St Helens Canal and Railway Co. 21 July 1845
735	St Helens and Wigan Junction Railway Co. Re-named the Liverpool, St Helens and South Lancashire Railway Co. 26 July 1889	22 Jul 1855	RAIL 374	1885–1905	None	Taken over by the Great Central Railway Co. 1 January 1906

List No.	Name of Company	Date of Incorporation	TNA Record Class	Records		Change of Ownership or Control
				Dates covered	Staff	
736	St Helens Canal and Railway Co.	21 Jul 1845 (amalg.)	RAIL 593	1830–1864	None	Taken over by the London and North Western Railway Co. 29 July 1864
737	Saffron Walden Railway Co.	22 Jul 1861	Nil		None	Purchased by the Great Eastern Railway Co. 1 January 1877
738	Salisbury and Dorset Junction Railway Co.	22 July 1861	RAIL 594	1862–1883	None	Worked by the London and South Western Railway Co.
739	Salisbury and Yeovil Railway Co.	7 Aug 1854	RAIL 595	1854–1878	None	Worked by the London and South Western Railway Co. and purchased by the L&SW, 4 July 1878
740	Salisbury Railway and Market House Co.	14 Jul 1856	Nil		None	Remained independent until its closure in 1964
741	Sand Hutton Light Railway	Private (1910)	Nil		None	Remained independent until its closure in 1932
742	Sandy and Potton Railway	Private (c. 1857)	Nil		None	Purchased by the Bedford and Cambridge Railway Co. 7 July 1862
743	Saundersfoot Railway and Harbour Co.	1 Jun 1829	Nil		None	Remained independent until its closure in 1939
744	Scarborough and Whitby Railway Co.	29 Jun 1871	RAIL 596	1871–1898	None	Vested in the North Eastern Railway Co. 1 July 1898
745	Scarborough, Bridlington and West Riding Junction Railways Co.	6 Aug 1885	RAIL 597	1885–1916	None	Purchased by the North Eastern Railway Co. 1 July 1914

List No.	Name of Company	Date of Incorporation	TNA Record Class	Records		Change of Ownership or Control
				Dates covered	Staff	
746	Scotswood, Newburn and Wylam Railway Co.	16 Jun 1871	RAIL 598	1872–1883	None	Vested in the North Eastern Railway Co. 29 June 1883
747	Seacombe, Hoylake and Deeside Railway Co. See Hoylake and Birkenhead Tramway Co., List No. 401					
748	Seaham and Sunderland Railway	Private (1853)	Nil		None	Became part of the North Eastern Railway Co.
749	Seaton and Beer Railway Co.	13 Jul 1863	RAIL 601	1863–1888	None	Transferred to the London and South Western Railway Co. 1 January 1888
750	Seghill Railway	Private (1840)	Nil		None	Worked by the Newcastle and North Shields Railway Co. from 25 June 1844. Became part of the Blyth and Tyne Railway Co. 30 June 1852
*	Settle and Carlisle Railway	See List No. 990				
751	Sevenoaks, Maidstone and Tunbridge Railway Co. See Sevenoaks Railway Co., List No. 752					
751	Sevenoaks Railway Co. Re-named the Sevenoaks, Maidstone and Tunbridge Railway Co. 17 July 1862	1 Aug 1859	RAIL 602	1858–1874	None	Vested in ther London, Chatham and Dover Railway Co. 21 July 1879
753	Severn and Wye and Severn Bridge Railway Co.	21 Jul 1879 (amalg.)	RAIL 603	1879–1895	None	Vested in the GWR and the Midland Railway Co. jointly 1 July 1894

List No.	Name of Company	Date of Incorporation	TNA Record Class	Records		Change of Ownership or Control
				Dates covered	Staff	
754	Severn and Wye Railway and Canal Co. See Lydney and Lidbrook Railway Co., List No. 517					
755	Severn Bridge Railway Co.	18 Jul 1872	RAIL 605	1871–1879	None	Amalgamated with the Severn and Wye Railway and Canal Co. to form the Severn and Wye and Severn Bridge Railway Co. 21 July 1879
756	Severn Valley Railway Co.	20 Aug 1853	RAIL 606	1852–1873	None	Leased to the West Midland Railway Co. 2 November 1860. Amalgamated with the GWR 1 August 1870
757	Shanklin and Chale Railway Co. Re-named the Newport, Godshill and St Lawrence Railway Co. 12 August 1889	14 Aug 1885	RAIL 514	1892–1913	None	Absorbed by the Isle of Wight Central Railway Co. 8 April 1913
758	Sheffield and Lincolnshire Extension Railway Co.	3 Aug 1846	Nil			Amalgamated with the Manchester, Sheffield and and Lincolnshire Railway Co. 1 January 1847
759	Sheffield and Lincolnshire Junction Railway Co.	3 Aug 1846	RAIL 607	1844–1849	None	On incorporation was amalgamated with the Sheffield, Ashton-under-Lyne and Manchester Railway Co., the Great Grimsby and Sheffield Junction Railway Co., the Sheffield and Lincolnshire

Cont.

283

List No.	Name of Company	Date of Incorporation	TNA Record Class	Records Dates covered	Staff	Change of Ownership or Control
						Extension Railway Co. and the Grimsby Dock Co. to form the Manchester, Sheffield and Lincolnshire Railway Co.
760	Sheffield and Midland Joint Railway Co.	24 Jun 1869	RAIL 224 (App 4)	1875–1909	None	
761	Sheffield and Rotherham Railway Co.	4 Jul 1836	RAIL 609	1841–1846	None	Worked by the Midland Railway Co. from 10 October 1844. Vested in that company 21 July 1845
762	Sheffield, Ashton-under-Lyne and Manchester Railway Co.	5 May 1837	RAIL 610	1836–1848	None	Amalgamated with the Great Grimsby and Sheffield Junction Railway Co., the Sheffield and Lincolnshire Junction Railway Co., the Sheffield and Lincolnshire Extension Railway Co. and the Grimsby Dock Co. 6 January 1847 to form the Manchester, Sheffield and Lincolnshire Railway Co.
763	Sheffield District Railway Co.	14 Aug 1896	RAIL 611	1896–1923	Yes	Became part of the LNER in 1923
764	Sheffield, Rotherham, Barnsley, Wakefield, Huddersfield and Goole Railway Co.	7 Aug 1846	RAIL 612	1847–1858	None	Leased partly to the Manchester and Leeds Railway Co. and partly to the South Yorkshire, Doncaster and Goole Railway Co. 5 October 1846 Vested in the Lancashire and Yorkshire Railway Co. 2 August 1858

List No.	Name of Company	Date of Incorporation	TNA Record Class	Records		Change of Ownership or Control
				Dates covered	Staff	
765	Sheppey Light Railway Co.	3 Apr 1899	Nil		None	Worked by the South Eastern and Chatham Railway Co. Purchased by the London, Chatham and Dover Railway Co. 31 October 1905
766	Shildon Tunnel Railway	Private (1842)	(RAIL 1057)		None	Purchased by the Wear Valley Railway Co. 22 July 1847
767	Shireoaks, Laughton and Maltby Railway Co.	9 Aug 1901	RAIL 613	1902–1904	None	Vested jointly in the Great Central Railway Co. and the Midland Railway Co. 31 July 1902
768	Shortlands and Nunhead Railway Co.	12 Aug 1889	RAIL 614	1889–1896	None	Worked by the London, Chatham and Dover Railway Co. from 1 July 1892. Vested in that company 1 September 1896
769	Shrewsbury and Birmingham Railway Co. Provisionally called the Shrewsbury and Wolverhampton Railway Co., and also the Shrewsbury, Wolverhampton, Dudley and Birmingham Railway Co.	3 Aug 1846	RAIL 615 (RAIL 1057)	1844–1854	None	Taken over by the GWR 1 September 1854
770	Shrewsbury and Chester Railway Co.	27 Jul 1846 (amalg.)	RAIL 616 (RAIL 1057)	1843–1855	None	Amalgamated with the GWR 1 September 1854

List No.	Name of Company	Date of Incorporation	TNA Record Class	Records Dates covered	Staff	Change of Ownership or Control
771	Shrewsbury and Hereford Railway Co.	3 Aug 1846	RAIL 617 (RAIL 1057)	1845–1881	Yes	Leased to the London and North Western Railway Co., the GWR and the West Midland Railway Co. 29 July 1862. The affairs of the Shrewsbury and Hereford Railway Co. were managed by the Shrewsbury and Hereford Joint Committee from August 1862 to September 1867. Vested in the GWR and the London and North Western Railway Co. jointly 4 July 1870
772	Shrewsbury and North Wales Railway Co. See the West Shropshire Mineral Railway Co., List No. 929					
773	Shrewsbury and Potteries Junction Railway Co.	5 Jul 1855	Nil		None	Amalgamated with the Shrewsbury and North Wales Railway Co. to form the Potteries, Shrewsbury and North Wales Railway Co. 16 July 1866
774	Shrewsbury and Stafford Railway Co.	3 Aug 1846	Nil		None	Amalgamated with the Newton and Crewe Railway Co. and the Chester and Wolverhampton Railway Co. 3 August 1846 before being built, to form the Shropshire Union Railways and Canal Co.

List No.	Name of Company	Date of Incorporation	TNA Record Class	Records Dates covered	Staff	Change of Ownership or Control
775	Shrewsbury and Welshpool Railway Co.	29 Jul 1856	Nil		None	Worked by the London and North Western Railway Co. Purchased jointly by the GWR and the London and North Western Railway Co. 5 July 1865
776	Shrewsbury and Wolverhampton Railway Co. See Shrewsbury and Birmingham Railway Co., List No. 769					
777	Shrewsbury, Oswestry and Chester Junction Railway Co.	30 Jun 1845	(RAIL 616)	1845–1846	None	Amalgamated with the North Wales Mineral Railway Co. 27 July 1846 to form the Shrewsbury and Chester Railway Co.
778	Shrewsbury, Wolverhampton, Dudley and Birmingham Railway Co. See Shrewsbury and Birmingham Railway Co., List No. 769					
779	Shropshire and Montgomeryshire Light Railway Co.	11 Feb 1909	RAIL 621	1909–1947	None	Passed to the British Transport Commission 1947
780	Shropshire Union Railways and Canal Co.	3 Aug 1846 (amalg.)	RAIL 623	1834–1948	Yes	Leased to the London and North Western Railway Co. 2 July 1847. Became part of the LMS in 1923
781	Shut End Railway See Pensnett Railway, List No. 673					

List No.	Name of Company	Date of Incorporation	TNA Record Class	Records		Change of Ownership or Control
				Dates covered	Staff	
782	Sidmouth Railway Co.	29 Jun 1871	Nil		None	Became part of the SR in 1923
783	Silkstone Railway	Private (1809)	Nil		None	Abandoned in 1860
784	Silverdale and Newcastle Railway Co.	Private. Became a public company 13 Aug 1859	Nil		None	Leased by the North Staffordshire Railway Co. 31 August 1860. Closed before the 1923 Grouping
785	Sirhowy Railway Co. See Sirhowy Tramroad, List No. 786					
786	Sirhowy Tramroad. Re-named the Sirhowy Railway Co. 25 May 1860	26 Jun 1802	RAIL 624	1860–1876	None	Vested in the London and North Western Railway Co. 13 July 1876
787	Sittingbourne and Sheerness Railway Co.	7 Jul 1856	Nil		None	Worked by the London, Chatham and Dover Railway Co. Transferred to that company 19 July 1865
788	Snailbeach District Railways Co.	5 Aug 1873	Nil		None	Remained independent until its closure in 1959
789	Sneyd's Railway Co.	28 Jun 1861	Nil		None	Leased by the North Staffordshire Railway Co. 29 July 1864
790	Snowdon Mountain Railway	Private (1893)	Nil		None	Still continues to run as an independent concern
791	Solway Junction Railway Co.	30 Jun 1864	Nil		None	Taken over by the Caledonian Railway Co. 6 July 1895

List No.	Name of Company	Date of Incorporation	TNA Record Class	Records Dates covered	Records Staff	Change of Ownership or Control
792	Somerset and Dorset Railway Co.	7 Aug 1862 (amalg.)	RAIL 626 RAIL 627 (See also App 4)	1862–1923	Yes	Vested jointly in the South Western Railway Co. and the Midland Railway Co. 1 November 1875
793	Somerset Central Railway Co.	17 Jun 1852	RAIL 628	1851–1862	None	Vested jointly in the South Western Railway Co. and the Midland Railway Co. 1 November 1875
794	South Devon and Tavistock Railway Co.	24 Jul 1854	RAIL 629	1852–1865	None	Amalgamated with the South Devon Railway Co. 1 July 1865
795	South Devon Railway Co. (originally called the Plymouth, Devonport and Exeter Railway)	4 Jul 1844	RAIL 631 (RAIL 1057)	1844–1878	Yes	Absorbed by the GWR 1 Feb 1876
796	South Durham and Lancashire Union Railway Co.	13 Jul 1857	RAIL 632	1856–1874	Yes	Amalgamated with the Stockton and Darlington Railway Co. 30 June 1862
797	South Eastern Railway Co. See London, Deptford and Dover Railway Co., List No. 501					
798	South Hampshire Railway and Pier Co.	25 Jun 1886	(RAIL 1057)		None	Line was completed by the Totton, Hythe and Fawley Light Railway Co. Became part of the SR in 1923
799	South Leeds Junction Railway Co.	24 Aug 1893	Nil		None	Worked by the East and West Yorkshire Union Railway Co. Absorbed by that company 2 July 1896

List No.	Name of Company	Date of Incorporation	TNA Record Class	Records Dates covered	Staff	Change of Ownership or Control
800	South Leicestershire Railway Co. See Nuneaton and Hinckley Railway Co., List No. 649					
801	South Shields Light Railway. See South Shields, Marsden and Whitburn Colliery Railway, List No. 802					
802	South Shields, Marsden and Whitburn Colliery Railway. Re-named the South Shields Light Railway in 1920	Private	Nil		None	Nationalized in 1947
803	South Staffordshire Junction Railway Co.	3 Aug 1846	RAIL 638	1845–1867	None	Before opening amalgamated with the Trent Valley, Midlands, and Grand Junction Railway Co. to form the South Staffordshire Railway Co. 6 October 1846
804	South Staffordshire Railway Co.	6 Oct 1846 (amalg.)	Nil		None	Leased to the London and North Western Railway Co. February 1861. Taken over by the London and North Western Railway Co. 15 June 1867
805	South Wales Mineral Railway Co.	10 Aug 1853	RAIL 639 (RAIL 1057)	1853–1922	None	Became part of the GWR in 1923
806	South Wales Railway Co.	4 Aug 1845	RAIL 640 (RAIL 1057)	1844–1863	Yes	Amalgamated with the GWR 1 August 1863

List No.	Name of Company	Date of Incorporation	TNA Record Class	Records Dates covered	Staff	Change of Ownership or Control
807	South Yorkshire, Doncaster and Goole Railway Co. Re-named the South Yorkshire Railway and River Dun Navigation Co. 19 April 1850	22 Jul 1847	Nil		None	Transferred to the Manchester, Sheffield and Lincolnshire Railway Co. 16 July 1874
808	South Yorkshire Joint Railway Co.	14 Aug 1903	RAIL 641 (App 4)	1903–1939	None	Worked by the Great Central Railway Co., the Great Northern Railway Co., the Lancashire and Yorkshire Railway Co., the Midland Railway Co. and the North Eastern Railway Co. Became part of the LMS and the LNER in 1923
809	South Yorkshire Junction Railway Co.	14 Aug 1890	RAIL 642	1891–1930	None	Became part of the LNER in 1923
810	South Yorkshire Railway and River Dun Navigation Co. See South Yorkshire, Doncaster and Goole Railway Co., List No. 807					
811	Southampton and Dorchester Railway Co.	21 Jul 1845	RAIL 644	1845–1848	None	Amalgamated with the London and South Western Railway Co. 22 Jul 1848
812	Southampton and Netley Railway Co.	1 Aug 1861	Nil		None	Amalgamated with the London and South Western Railway Co. 1 January 1864
813	Southern Railway. See App 3.5	Railway Act 22 Dec 1922	RAIL 645 to RAIL 654	1923–1947	Yes	

List No.	Name of Company	Date of Incorporation	TNA Record Class	Records		Change of Ownership or Control
				Dates covered	Staff	
814	Southport and Cheshire Lines Extension Railway Co.	11 Aug 1881	RAIL 656	1880–1948	None	Vested in the British Transport Commission 1 January 1948
815	Southsea Railway Co.	26 Aug 1880	Nil		None	Worked by the London and South Western Railway Co. Purchased jointly by the London and South Western Railway Co. and the London, Brighton and South Coast Railway Co. 18 November 1882. Closed 6 August 1914
*	Southwold Railway Co.	See List No. 991				
816	Spalding and Bourn Railway Co.	28 Jul 1862	RAIL 657	1862–1866	None	Amalgamated with the Lynn and Sutton Bridge Railway Co. 23 July 1866 (before opening) to form the Midland and Eastern Railway Co.
817	Spilsby and Firsby Railway Co.	7 Jul 1865	RAIL 658	1864–1890	None	Vested in the Great Northern Railway Co. 25 July 1890
818	Stafford and Uttoxeter Railway Co.	29 Jul 1862	Nil		None	Worked by the Great Northern Railway Co. Purchased by that company 1 August 1881
819	Staines and West Drayton Railway Co.	7 Jul 1873	RAIL 659	1881–1900	None	Taken over by the GWR 1 July 1900
820	Staines, Wokingham and Woking Railway Co.	8 Jul 1853	RAIL 660	1852–1879	None	Leased to the London and South Western Railway Co. 25 March 1858. Absorbed by that company 4 July 1878

List No.	Name of Company	Date of Incorporation	TNA Record Class	Records		Change of Ownership or Control
				Dates covered	Staff	
821	Stamford and Essendine Railway Co.	15 Aug 1853	RAIL 662	1853–1920	None	Worked by the Great Northern Railway Co. from 1 January 1894. Became part of the LNER in 1923
822	Stanhope and Tyne Railroad Co. See also List No. 907.	3 Feb 1834	RAIL 663	1835–1844	None	The company was dissolved on 5 February 1841. Part of the line was incorporated into the Pontop and South Shields Railway Co. 23 May 1842
823	Stockport and Woodley Junction Railway Co.	15 May 1860	RAIL 664	1860–1865	None	Vested in the Manchester, Sheffield and Lincolnshire Railway Co. and the Great Northern Railway Co. 5 July 1865
824	Stockport, Disley and Whaley Bridge Railway Co.	31 Jul 1854	RAIL 665	1853–1866	None	Transferred to the London and North Western Railway Co. 23 July 1866
825	Stockport, Timperley and Altrincham Junction Railway Co.	22 Jul 1861	RAIL 666	1861–1865	None	Transferred to the Manchester, Sheffield and Lincolnshire Railway Co. and the Great Northern Railway Co. 5 July 1865
826	Stocksbridge Railway Co.	30 Jun 1874	Nil		None	Remained independent until its closure in 1931
827	Stockton and Darlington Railway Co.	19 Apr 1821	RAIL 667 (RAIL 1057)	1818–1879	Yes	Taken over by the North Eastern Railway Co. 13 July 1863

List No.	Name of Company	Date of Incorporation	TNA Record Class	Records		Change of Ownership or Control
				Dates covered	Staff	
828	Stockton and Hartlepool Railway Co.	30 Jun 1842	RAIL 668	1839–1857	None	Amalgamated with the Hartlepool West Harbour and Dock Co. 30 June 1852 to form the West Hartlepool Harbour and Railway Co.
829	Stokes Bay Railway and Pier Co.	14 Aug 1855	RAIL 669	1855–1875	None	Leased to the London and South Western Railway Co. in 1872. Purchased by that company 17 June 1875
830	Stonebridge Railway Co.	19 May 1836	Nil		None	Closed in 1930
831	Stonehouse and Nailsworth Railway Co.	13 Jul 1863	Nil		None	Taken over by the Midland Railway Co. 1 July 1878
832	Storeton Tramway	Private (1837)	Nil		None	Abandoned *c.* 1905
833	Stourbridge Railway Co.	14 June 1860	RAIL 671	1860–1869	None	Vested in the Great Western Railway Co. 1 February 1870
834	Stratford and Moreton Railway Co.	28 May 1821	RAIL 673	1821–1869	None	Leased to the Oxford, Worcester and Wolverhampton Railway Co. 18 December 1845. Taken over by that company 1 January 1852
835	Stratford-upon-Avon and Midland Junction Railway Co.	1 Aug 1908	RAIL 674	1873–1923 (Early records relate to the East and West Junction Railway Co.)	Yes	Became part of the LMS in 1923
836	Stratford-upon-Avon Railway Co.	10 Aug 1858	RAIL 675	1856–1884	Yes	Taken over by the GWR 1 Jul 1883

List No.	Name of Company	Date of Incorporation	TNA Record Class	Records Dates covered	Records Staff	Change of Ownership or Control
837	Stratford-upon-Avon, Towcester and Midland Junction Railway Co. See Easton Neston Mineral and Towcester, Roade and Olney Junction Railway Co., List No. 269					
838	Surrey Iron Railway Co.	21 May 1801	Nil		None	Closed in 1846
839	Sutton and Willoughby Railway Co.	28 Jul 1884	RAIL 677	1884–1902	None	Worked by the Great Northern Railway Co. from its opening. Amalgamated with that company 22 July 1902
840	Sutton Veny Camp Railway	c. 1914	Nil		None	Taken over by the GWR in 1918 and closed in 1926
841	Swansea and Carmarthen Railway Co. Re-named the Central Wales and Carmarthen Junction Railway Co. 21 July 1873	16 Jun 1871	RAIL 104	1871–1891	None	Worked by the London and North Western Railway Co. Vested in that company 21 July 1873
842	Swansea and Mumbles Railway Co. See Oystermouth Railway Co., List No. 663					
843	Swansea and Neath Railway Co.	6 Aug 1861	RAIL 678	1861–1863	None	Purchased by the Vale of Neath Railway Co. 5 August 1863
844	Swansea Vale and Neath and Brecon Junction Railway Co.	29 Jul 1864	(RAIL 1057)		None	Running powers were granted to the Severn Valley Railway Co. (before opening)

List No.	Name of Company	Date of Incorporation	TNA Record Class	Records		Change of Ownership or Control
				Dates covered	Staff	
845	Swansea Vale Railway Co. See Swansea Valley Railway Co., List No 846					
846	Swansea Valley Railway Co. Re-incorporated as the Swansea Vale Railway Co. 15 June 1855	2 Jul 1847	RAIL 679 RAIL 680	1847–1853	None	Vested in the Midland Railway Co. 11 August 1876
847	Swindon and Cheltenham Extension Railway Co.	18 Jul 1881	RAIL 681 (RAIL 1057)	1881–1884	Yes	Amalgamated with the Swindon, Marlborough and Andover Railway Co. 23 June 1884 to form the Midland and South Western Junction Railway Co.
848	Swindon and Highworth Light Railway Co.	29 Jun 1875	RAIL 682	1873–1882	None	Purchased by the GWR 1 July 1882
849	Swindon, Marlborough and Andover Railway Co.	21 Jul 1873	RAIL 683 (RAIL 1057)	1872–1884	None	Amalgamated with the Swindon and Cheltenham Extension Railway Co. 23 June 1884 to form the Midland and South Western Junction Railway Co.
850	Swinton and Knottingley Joint Railway Co.	16 Jul 1874	Nil		None	Worked by the Midland Railway Co., the Great Northern Railway Co., the North Eastern Railway Co. and the Manchester, Sheffield and Lincolnshire Railway Co.

List No.	Name of Company	Date of Incorporation	TNA Record Class	Records		Change of Ownership or Control
				Dates covered	Staff	
851	Syston and Peterborough Railway Co.	30 Jun 1845	Nil		None	Sponsored and owned by the Midland Railway Co.
852	Taff Vale Railway Co.	21 Jun 1836	RAIL 684	1835–1922	Yes	Became part of the GWR in 1923
853	Talyllyn Railway Co.	5 Jul 1865	(RAIL 1057)		None	Still in use; now run by the Talyllyn Railway Preservation Society
854	Tamar, Kit Hill and Callington Railway Co.	29 Jul 1864	Nil		None	Taken over by the Callington and Calstock Railway Co. (before completion).
855	Tanat Valley Light Railway Co.	1899	RAIL 685 (RAIL 1057)	1899–1918	None	Absorbed by the Cambrian Railways Co. 12 March 1921
856	Tanfield Wagonway	Private (c. 1632)	Nil		None	Taken over by the Newcastle and Darlington Junction Railway Co. c. 1845
857	Taw Vale Railway and Dock Co. Re-named the North Devon Railway and Dock Co. 24 July 1851 (before opening)	11 Jun 1838	RAIL 524	1845–1847	None	Worked by the Bristol and Exeter Railway Co. Leased by the London and South Western Railway Co. from 1 January 1863. Taken over by the London and South Western Railway Co. 1 January 1865
858	Tees Valley Railway Co.	19 Jun 1865	RAIL 687	1864–1882	Yes	Vested in the North Eastern Railway Co. 19 June 1882

List No.	Name of Company	Date of Incorporation	TNA Record Class	Records Dates covered	Records Staff	Change of Ownership or Control
859	Teign Valley Railway Co.	13 Jul 1863	RAIL 688 (RAIL 1057)	1864–1918	None	Became part of the GWR in 1923
860	Tenbury and Bewdley Railway Co.	3 Jul 1860	RAIL 689 (RAIL 1057)	1859–1870	None	Vested in the GWR 12 July 1869
861	Tenbury Railway Co.	21 Jul 1859	RAIL 690 (RAIL 1057)	1858–1881	None	Worked by the Shrewsbury and Hereford Railway Co. Transferred to the GWR and the London and North Western Railway Co. jointly 1 January 1869
862	Tendring Hundred Railway Co.	13 Aug 1859	RAIL 691	1860–1884	None	Vested in the Great Eastern Railway Co. 29 June 1883
863	Tewkesbury and Malvern Railway Co.	25 May 1860	Nil		None	Worked by the Midland Railway Co. Purchased by that company 1 January 1877
864	Thames Haven Dock and Railway Co.	4 Jul 1836	Nil		None	Purchased by the London, Tilbury and Southend Railway Co. in 1854 (before opening)
865	Thames Valley Railway Co.	17 Jul 1862	RAIL 693	1861–1866	None	Amalgamated with the London and South Western Railway Co. 1 January 1867
866	Thetford and Watton Railway Co.	16 Jul 1866	RAIL 694	1865–1898	None	Leased to the Great Eastern Railway Co. from 1 March 1880. Vested in that company 1 July 1897
867	Tickhill Light Railway Co.	7 Aug 1901	Nil		None	Transferred to the Great Northern Railway Co. in 1907 (before opening)

List No.	Name of Company	Date of Incorporation	TNA Record Class	Records Dates covered	Records Staff	Change of Ownership or Control
868	Ticknall Tramway Co.	May 1794	Nil		None	Purchased by the Midland Railway Co. in 1846
869	Tiverton and North Devon Railway Co.	19 Jul 1875	RAIL 695	1865–1894	None	Amalgamated with the GWR 1 July 1894
870	Tooting, Merton and Wimbledon Railway Co.	29 Jul 1864	Nil		None	Taken over jointly by the London, Brighton and South Coast Railway Co. and the London and South Western Railway Co. 5 July 1865
871	Torbay and Brixham Railway Co.	25 Jul 1864	(RAIL 1057)		None	Leased to the South Devon Railway Co. Purchased by the GWR 19 May 1882
872	Tottenham and Forest Gate Railway Co.	4 Aug 1890	RAIL 696	1890–1923	None	Worked by the Midland Railway Co. from 1 January 1914. Became part of the LMS in 1923
873	Tottenham and Hampstead Junction Railway Co.	29 Jul 1862	RAIL 697	1863–1936	None	Worked jointly by the Great Eastern Railway Co. and the Midland Railway Co. from 1885. Vested in these companies jointly from 1 July 1902
874	Totton, Hythe and Fawley Light Railway Co.	10 Nov 1903	Nil		None	Taken over by the SR in 1923 (before opening)
875	Treferig Valley Railway Co.	21 Jul 1879	(RAIL 1057)		None	Leased to the Taff Vale Railway Co. 14 July 1884. Taken over by that company 26 August 1889

List No.	Name of Company	Date of Incorporation	TNA Record Class	Records		Change of Ownership or Control
				Dates covered	Staff	
876	Treffry Estates Tramway	Private (1842)	Nil		None	Together with the Newquay and Cornwall Junction Railway Co. it formed the Cornwall Minerals Railway Co. 21 July 1873
877	Trent, Ancholme and Grimsby Railway Co.	22 Jul 1861	RAIL 698	1861–1881	None	Vested in the Manchester, Sheffield and Lincolnshire Railway Co. 12 July 1882
878	Trent Valley, Midlands and Grand Junction Railway Co.	3 Aug 1846	Nil		None	Amalgamated with the South Staffordshire Junction Railway Co. 6 October 1846 (before opening) to form the South Staffordshire Railway Co.
879	Trent Valley Railway Co.	21 Jul 1845	RAIL 699	1844–1848	Yes	Purchased by the London and Birmingham Railway Co. 15 April 1846
880	Tunbridge Wells and Eastbourne Railway Co.	5 Aug 1873	Nil		None	Vested in the London, Brighton and South Coast Railway Co. 27 June 1876 (before opening)
881	Ulverstone and Lancaster Railway Co.	24 Jul 1851	RAIL 700	1851–1862	None	Purchased by the Furness Railway Co. 21 January 1862
882	Vale of Clwyd Railway Co.	23 Jun 1850	(RAIL 1057)		Yes	Worked by the London and North Western Railway Co. from 25 July 1867. Vested in the London and North Western Railway Co. 15 July 1867

List No.	Name of Company	Date of Incorporation	TNA Record Class	Records Dates covered	Staff	Change of Ownership or Control
883	Vale of Glamorgan Railway Co.	26 Aug 1889	RAIL 702 (RAIL 1057)	1889–1922	Yes	Worked by the Barry Railway Co. Became part of the GWR in 1923
884	Vale of Llangollen Railway Co.	1 Aug 1859	RAIL 703	1854–1896	None	Taken over by the GWR 1 July 1896
885	Vale of Neath Railway Co.	3 Aug 1846	RAIL 704 (RAIL 1057)	1845–1867	Yes	Amalgamated with the GWR 1 February 1865
886	Vale of Rheidol Light Railway Co.	6 Aug 1897	RAIL 705 (RAIL 1057)	1901–1913	None	Amalgamated with the Cambrian Railways Co. 1 July 1913
887	Vale of Towy Railway Co.	10 Jul 1854	(RAIL 1057)		None	Leased jointly to the Central Wales Extension Railway Co., the Central Wales Railway Co., and the Llanelly Railway and Dock Co. Vested jointly in the GWR and the London and North Western Railway Co. 28 July 1884
888	Van Railway Co.	3 Jun 1870	(RAIL 1057)		None	Taken over by the GWR in 1923. Closed 4 November 1940
889	Victoria Station and Pimlico Railway Co.	23 Jul 1858	RAIL 707	1858–1922	None	Became part of the SR in 1923
890	Volks Electric Railway	c. 1883	Nil		None	Purchased by the Brighton Corporation 1 April 1940
891	Wainfleet and Firsby Railway Co.	13 May 1869	(RAIL 1057)		None	Worked by the Great Northern Railway Co. Purchased by that company 1 January 1896

List No.	Name of Company	Date of Incorporation	TNA Record Class	Records		Change of Ownership or Control
				Dates covered	Staff	
892	Wakefield, Pontefract and Goole Railway Co.	31 Jul 1845	Nil		None	Became part of the Lancashire and Yorkshire Railway Co. 9 July 1847 (before opening)
893	Wallingford and Watlington Railway Co.	25 Jul 1864	RAIL 708 (RAIL 1057)	1863–1873	Yes	Vested in the GWR 18 July 1872
894	Wansbeck Railway Co.	8 Aug 1859	Nil		None	Taken over by the Great Northern Railway Co. 21 July 1863
895	Wantage Tramway Co.	7 Aug 1874	Nil		None	Closed in 1940
896	Ware, Hadham and Buntingford Railway Co.	12 Jul 1858	RAIL 709	1856–1870	None	Purchased by the Great Eastern Railway Co. 1 September 1868
897	Warrington and Altrincham Junction Railway Co. Re-named the Warrington and Stockport Railway Co. 4 August 1853	3 Jul 1851	RAIL 710	1853–1856	None	Leased to the London and North Western Railway Co. and the St Helens Canal and Railway Co. jointly 13 August 1859. Purchased by the London and North Western Railway Co. 15 July 1867
898	Warrington and Newton Railway Co.	14 May 1829	Nil		None	Purchased by the Grand Junction Railway Co. 31 December 1834
899	Warrington and Stockport Railway Co. See Warrington and Altrincham Junction Railway Co., List No. 897					

List No.	Name of Company	Date of Incorporation	TNA Record Class	Records		Change of Ownership or Control
				Dates covered	Staff	
900	Warwick and Leamington Union Railway Co.	18 Jun 1842	RAIL 711	1839–1845	None	Vested in the London and Birmingham Railway Co. 3 April 1843
901	Waterloo and City Railway Co.	27 Jul 1893	RAIL 713 (RAIL 1057)	1894–1907	None	Transferred to the London and South Western Railway Co. 1 January 1907
902	Watford and Rickmansworth Railway Co.	3 Jul 1860	(RAIL 1057)		None	Purchased by the London and North Western Railway Co. 27 June 1881
903	Watlington and Princes Risborough Railway Co.	26 Jul 1869	RAIL 785 (RAIL 1057)	1870–1883	None	Worked by the GWR from opening. Vested in that company 1 July 1883
904	Watton and Swaffham Railway Co.	12 Jul 1869	RAIL 714	1872–1898	Yes	Leased to the Great Eastern Railway Co. from 1 March 1880. Vested in that company 15 July 1897
905	Waveney Valley Railway Co.	3 Jul 1851	RAIL 715	1855–1857	None	Taken over by the Great Eastern Railway Co. 21 July 1863
906	Wear and Derwent Junction Railway. (Unofficial name given to the Weardale Extension Railway, see List No. 910)					
907	Wear and Derwent Railway. (Name given to the western part of the disused Stanhope and Tyne Railroad line on its revival.) See also List No. 822		Nil		None	Leased to the Stockton and Darlington Railway Co. from 1 January 1845. Purchased by the Wear Valley Railway Co. 22 July 1847

List No.	Name of Company	Date of Incorporation	TNA Record Class	Records		Change of Ownership or Control
				Dates covered	Staff	
908	Wear Valley Extension Railway Co.	20 Jun 1892	RAIL 717	1893–1894	None	Transferred to the North Eastern Railway Co. 31 July 1894
909	Wear Valley Railway Co.	31 Jul 1845	RAIL 718	1845–1858	Yes	Leased to the Stockton and Darlington Railway Co. 1 October 1847. Amalgamated with that company 23 July 1858
910	Weardale Extension Railway Co. Also known locally as the Wear and Derwent Junction Railway.	Private (1837)	RAIL 716			Purchased by the Wear Valley Railway Co. 22 July 1847
911	Wellington and Drayton Railway Co.	7 Aug 1862	RAIL 719	1863–1877	None	Amalgamated with the GWR 12 July 1869
912	Wellington and Severn Junction Railway Co.	28 Aug 1853	RAIL 720 (RAIL 1057)	1853–1890	None	Leased to the GWR and the West Midland Railway Co. 1 August 1861. Vested in the GWR 1 July 1892
913	Wells and Fakenham Railway Co.	24 Jul 1854	RAIL 721	1855–1859	None	Worked by the Norfolk Railway Co. Became part of the Great Eastern Railway Co. 1 September 1862
914	Welsh Highland Railway Co.	30 Mar 1922	(RAIL 1057)		None	Leased by the Festiniog Railway Co. 9 July 1934. Closed 1 June 1937
915	Welshpool and Llanfair Light Railway Co.	8 Sep 1899	RAIL 722 (RAIL 1057)	1897–1922	None	Worked by the Cambrian Railways Co. Became part of the GWR in 1923

List No.	Name of Company	Date of Incorporation	TNA Record Class	Records Dates covered	Staff	Change of Ownership or Control
916	Wenlock Railway Co.	22 Jul 1861	RAIL 723	1861–1897	None	Worked by the GWR and taken over by that company 1 July 1896
917	West Cheshire Railway Co. (From 1867 managed by the Cheshire Lines Committee. See App 4)	11 Jul 1861	RAIL 724	1861–1865	None	Worked by the Manchester, Sheffield and Lincolnshire Railway Co. Vested in the Manchester, Sheffield and Lincolnshire Railway Co. and the Great Northern Railway Co. jointly 5 July 1865
918	West Cornwall Railway Co.	3 Aug 1846	RAIL 725 (RAIL 1057)	1845–1876	Yes	Leased to the GWR, Bristol and Exeter Railway Co. and the South Devon Railway Co. 1 January 1865. Purchased jointly by the GWR and the South Devon Railway Co. 27 June 1876
919	West Durham Railway Co.	4 Jul 1839	RAIL 728	1837–1870	None	Vested in the North Eastern Railway Co. 1 September 1870
920	West End of London and Crystal Palace Railway Co.	4 Aug 1853	RAIL 729	1852–1860	None	Purchased by the London, Brighton and South Coast Railway Co. January 1864
921	West Hartlepool Harbour and Railway Co.	30 Jun 1852 (amalg.)	RAIL 730	1844–1873	None	Amalgamated with the North Eastern Railway Co. 30 June 1865

List No.	Name of Company	Date of Incorporation	TNA Record Class	Records		Change of Ownership or Control
				Dates covered	Staff	
922	West Lancashire Railway Co.	14 Aug 1871	RAIL 731	1873–1897	None	Vested in the Lancashire and Yorkshire Railway Co. 1 July 1897
923	West London Extension Railway Co.	13 Aug 1859	RAIL 732 (RAIL 623)	1859–1947	Yes	Passed to the British Transport Comm-ission in 1947
924	West London Railway Co. See Birmingham, Bristol and Thames Junction Railway Co., List No. 63					
925	West Midland Railway Co.	14 Jun 1860 (amalg.)	RAIL 734	1860–1863	None	Vested in the GWR 13 July 1863
926	West Norfolk Junction Railway Co.	23 Jun 1864	RAIL 735	1864–1874	None	Amalgamated with the Lynn and Hunstanton Railway Co. to form the Hunstanton and West Norfolk Railway Co. 8 June 1874
927	West Riding and Grimsby Joint Railway Co.	7 Aug 1862	RAIL 736 (App 4)	1862–1923	Yes App 4	Transferred jointly to the Great Northern Railway Co. and the Manchester, Sheffield and Lincolnshire Railway Co. 1 February 1866
928	West Riding Union Railway Co.	18 Aug 1846 (amalg.)	(RAIL 1057)		None	Vested in the Manchester and Leeds Railway Co. in 1846
929	West Shropshire Mineral Railway Co. Re-named the Shrewsbury and	29 Jul 1862	RAIL 622	1888–1946	None	Amalgamated with the Shrewsbury and Potteries Junction Railway

Cont.

List No.	Name of Company	Date of Incorporation	TNA Record Class	Records Dates covered	Records Staff	Change of Ownership or Control
	North Wales Railway Co. in 1864					Co. 16 July 1866 to form the Potteries, Shrewsbury and North Wales Railway Co.
930	West Somerset Mineral Railway Co.	16 Jul 1855	Nil		None	Leased to the Ebbw Vale Co. of South Wales 24 September 1865. Closed in 1910
931	West Somerset Railway Co.	17 Aug 1857	RAIL 737 (RAIL 1057)	1857–1922	None	Initially worked by the Bristol and Exeter Railway Co. Worked by the GWR from 8 June 1863. Became part of the GWR 1 January 1922
932	West Sussex Railway Co. See Hundred of Manhood and Selsey Railway Co., List No. 414					
933	West Wickham and Hayes Railway Co.	9 Jul 1880	RAIL 738	1880–1883	None	Transferred to the South Eastern Railway Co. 11 August 1881
934	West Yorkshire Railway Co. See Bradford, Wakefield and Leeds Railway Co., List No. 100					
935	Westerham Valley Railway Co.	24 Jul 1876	RAIL 740 (RAIL 1057)	1880–1881	None	Amalgamated with the South Eastern Railway Co. 11 August 1881
936	Weston-super-Mare, Clevedon and Portishead Railway Co.	6 Aug 1885	RAIL 781	1899–1927	None	Remained independent until its closure in 1940

List No.	Name of Company	Date of Incorporation	TNA Record Class	Records Dates covered	Staff	Change of Ownership or Control
937	Weymouth and Portland Railway Co.	30 Jun 1862	RAIL 741	1862–1947	None	Worked by the GWR and the London and South Western Railway Co. jointly. Passed to the British Transport Commission in 1947
938	Whitby and Pickering Railway Co.	6 May 1833	RAIL 742	1833–1923	None	Purchased by the York and North Midland Railway Co. 30 June 1845
939	Whitby, Redcar and Middlesbrough Union Railway Co.	16 Jul 1866	RAIL 743	1866–1889	None	Leased to the North Eastern Railway Co. 19 July 1875. Vested in that company 5 July 1889
940	Whitechapel and Bow Railway Co.	6 Aug 1897	Nil		None	Taken over by the Midland Railway Co. 1 January 1912 and remained independent until Nationalization in 1947
941	Whitehaven and Furness Junction Railway Co.	21 Jul 1845	RAIL 744	1845–1866	Yes	Taken over by the Furness Railway Co. 16 July 1866
942	Whitehaven, Cleator and Egremont Railway Co.	16 Jun 1854	RAIL 745	1853–1878	None	Vested in the London and North Western Railway Co. 1 July 1877
943	Whitehaven Junction Railway Co.	4 Jul 1844	RAIL 746	1845–1866	None	Vested in the London and North Western Railway Co. 16 July 1866
944	Whitland and Cardigan Railway Co. See Whitland and Taff Vale Railway Co., List No. 945					

List No.	Name of Company	Date of Incorporation	TNA Record Class	Records		Change of Ownership or Control
				Dates covered	Staff	
945	Whitland and Taff Vale Railway Co. Re-named the Whitland and Cardigan Railway Co. in 1877	12 Jul 1869	RAIL 747 (RAIL 1057)	1869–1899	Yes	Worked by the GWR. Vested in that company 1 July 1890
946	Whittingham Railway	Private (1888)	Nil		None	Owned by the Lancashire County Council. Closed in 1957
947	Widnes Railway Co.	7 Jul 1873	RAIL 748	1873–1874	None	Vested in the Manchester, Sheffield and Lincolnshire Railway Co. and the Midland Railway Co. jointly 29 June 1875
948	Wigan Branch Railway Co.	29 May 1830	RAIL 534	1830–1834	None	Amalgamated with the Preston and Wigan Railway Co. to form the North Union Railway Co. 22 May 1834
949	Wigan Junction Railway Co.	16 Jul 1874	RAIL 749	1874–1906	None	Vested in the Great Central Railway 1 January 1906
950	Wiltshire, Somerset and Weymouth Railway Co.	30 Jun 1845	RAIL 750 (RAIL 1057)	1844–1858	Yes	Vested in the GWR 3 July 1854
951	Wimbledon and Croydon Railway Co.	8 Jul 1853	RAIL 751	1852–1863	None	Leased to the London, Brighton and South Coast Railway Co. 21 July 1856. Purchased by that company 1 January 1866
952	Wimbledon and Dorking Railway Co.	27 Jul 1857	RAIL 752	1856–1865	None	Transferred to the London and South Western Railway Co. 3 June 1862

List No.	Name of Company	Date of Incorporation	TNA Record Class	Records Dates covered	Staff	Change of Ownership or Control
953	Wimbledon and Sutton Railway Co.	26 Jul 1910	RAIL 753	1910–1924	None	Taken over by the SR 1 January 1924
954	Windsor, Staines and South Western Railway Co.	25 Jun 1847	RAIL 755	1846–1850	None	Became part of the London and South Western Railway Co. in 1850
955	Wirral Railway Co.	13 Jun 1883	RAIL 756	1883–1926	Yes	Became part of the LMS in 1923
956	Wisbech, St Ives and Cambridge Junction Railway Co.	7 Aug 1846	Nil		None	Became part of the Great Northern and Great Eastern Junction Railway Co. in 1882
957	Wissington Tramway	Private (c. 1905)	Nil		None	Remained independent until its closure in 1957
958	Witney Railway Co.	1 Aug 1859	RAIL 757	1859–1891	None	Vested in the GWR 1 July 1890
959	Wivenhoe and Brightlingsea Railway Co.	11 Jul 1861	RAIL 758	1860–1895	None	Worked by the Great Eastern Railway Co. from opening. Purchased by that company 9 June 1893
960	Wolverhampton and Walsall Railway Co.	29 Jun 1865	(RAIL 1057)		None	Leased to the London and North Western Railway Co. 19 July 1875. Purchased by the Midland Railway Co. 11 August 1876
961	Wolverhampton, Walsall and Midland Junction Railway Co.	6 Aug 1872	Nil		None	Taken over by the Midland Railway Co. 30 July 1874
962	Wolverton and Stony Stratford and District Tramway Co. See Wolverton and Stony Stratford Tramway Co., List No. 964					

310

List No.	Name of Company	Date of Incorporation	TNA Record Class	Records Dates covered	Records Staff	Change of Ownership or Control
963	Wolverton and Stony Stratford District New Tramway Co. See Wolverton and Stony Stratford Tramway Co., List No. 964					
964	Wolverton and Stony Stratford Tramway Co. Re-incorporated as the Wolverton and Stony Stratford and District Tramway Co. 16 July 1883. Re-named the Wolverton, Stony Stratford and District Light Railway Co. 5 October 1886. Re-incorporated as the Wolverton and Stony Stratford District New Tramway Co. 15 September 1893	Nov 1882	Nil		None	Purchased by the London and North Western Railway Co. in 1920. The line was closed in 1926
965	Wolverton, Stony Stratford and District Light Railway Co. See Wolverton and Stony Stratford Tramway Co., List No. 964					
966	Woodside and South Croydon Railway Co.	6 Aug 1880	RAIL 760	1881–1923	None	Transferred jointly to the South Eastern Railway Co. and the London, Brighton and South Coast Railway Co. 10 August 1882
967	Woodstock Railway Co.	25 Sep 1886	RAIL 761	1888–1897	None	Vested in the GWR 6 August 1897

List No.	Name of Company	Date of Incorporation	TNA Record Class	Records		Change of Ownership or Control
				Dates covered	Staff	
968	Woolmer Instructional Military Railway. Re-named the Longmoor Military Railway in 1935	1902	Nil		None	Built by the Royal Engineers. Closed in 1969
969	Worcester and Hereford Railway Co.	15 Aug 1853	RAIL 762	1851–1860	None	Amalgamated with the Newport, Abergavenny and Hereford Railway Co. and the Oxford, Worcester and Wolverhampton Railway Co. 14 June 1860 to become the West Midland Railway Co.
970	Worcester, Bromyard and Leominster Railway Co.	11 Aug 1861	RAIL 763	1860–1889	None	Vested in the GWR 1 July 1888
971	Worsborough Railway	Private (*c.* 1820)	Nil		None	Purchased by the South Yorkshire Railway Co. *c.* 1851. Closed in 1918
972	Wotton Tramway. See also Oxford and Aylesbury Tramroad Co., List No 657	Private (1870)	Nil		None	Leased to the Oxford and Aylesbury Tramroad Co. 17 July 1888. Taken over by the Metropolitan and the Great Central Railway Joint Committee 2 April 1906
973	Wrexham and Ellesmere Railway Co.	31 Jul 1885	RAIL 765 (RAIL 1057)	1887–1922	Yes	Became part of the GWR in 1923
974	Wrexham and Minera Railway Co.	17 May 1861	(RAIL 1057)		None	Leased jointly to the GWR and the London and North Western Railway Co. and became the Wrexham and Minera Joint Railway Co. 11 June 1866

List No.	Name of Company	Date of Incorporation	TNA Record Class	Records Dates covered	Staff	Change of Ownership or Control
975	Wrexham and Minera Joint Railway Co.	11 Jun 1866	(RAIL 1057)		None	Worked by the London and North Western Railway Co. Remained independent until its closure in 1950
976	Wrexham, Mold and Connah's Quay Railway Co.	7 Aug 1862	RAIL 767	1861–1905	None	Vested in the Great Central Railway Co. 1 January 1905
977	Wrington Vale Light Railway Co.	18 Mar 1897	Nil		None	Worked by the GWR. Closed in 1931
978	Wycombe Railway Co.	27 Jul 1846	RAIL 768	1845–1867	Yes	Leased to the GWR from opening. Taken over by that company 1 February 1867
979	Wye Valley Railway Co.	10 Aug 1866	Nil		None	Vested in the GWR 4 August 1905
980	Yarmouth and Haddiscoe Railway Co.	7 Jul 1856	Nil		None	Amalgamated with the East Suffolk Railway Co. 23 July 1858
981	Yarmouth and North Norfolk Light Railway Co. See Great Yarmouth and Stalham Light Railway Co., List No. 353					
982	Yarmouth and North Norfolk Railway Co. See Great Yarmouth and Stalham Light Railway Co., List No. 353					
983	Yarmouth and Norwich Railway Co.	18 Jun 1842	(RAIL 1057)		None	Amalgamated with the Norwich and Brandon Railway Co. to form the Norfolk Railway Co. 30 June 1845

List No.	Name of Company	Date of Incorporation	TNA Record Class	Records		Change of Ownership or Control
				Dates covered	Staff	
984	Yarmouth Union Railway Co.	26 Aug 1880	Nil		None	Amalgamated with the Yarmouth and North Norfolk Railway Co. and the Lynn and Fakenham Railway Co. 1 July 883 to form the Eastern and Midlands Railway Co.
985	York and Newcastle Railway Co. See Newcastle and Darlington Junction Railway Co., List No. 608					
986	York and North Midland Railway Co.	21 Jun 1836	RAIL 770	1835–1875	Yes	Amalgamated with the Leeds Northern Railway Co. and the York, Newcastle and Berwick Railway Co. 31 July 1854 to form the Northeastern Railway Co.
987	York, Newcastle and Berwick Railway Co.	9Aug 1847 (amalg.)	RAIL 772	1842–1857	Yes	Amalgamated with the York and North Midland Railway Co. and the Leeds Northern Railway Co. 31 July 1854 to become the Northeastern Railway Co.
988	Yorkshire Dales Railway Co.	6Aug 1897	RA1L 774	1897–1923	None	Worked by the Midland Railway Co. from opening. Became part of the LMS in 1923

Addenda

989	Fareham and Netley Railway Co.	29 June 1865			None	
990	Settle and Carlisle Railway Co.					Part of the Midland Railway Co. See List No. 584
991	Southwold Railway Co.	24 Jul 1876			None	Closed 12 April 1929

APPENDIX 2

COUNTY LISTS OF RAILWAY COMPANIES IN ENGLAND AND WALES UP TO THE 1923 GROUPING

Column 1 gives the list number as given in Appendix 1. The name of the railway company, with any subsequent change of name, is given in column 2. Column 3 lists the earliest date the railway opened or ran in the particular county. When a company was formed by the amalgamation of two or more operating companies then the date of amalgamation is given as the opening date, the lines being already in use. In many instances dates of opening vary from one source to another. Some quote the unofficial or official opening, or the first goods traffic or passenger train. In every case the earliest recorded date has been given. Researchers should note, however, that all railways must have recruited some staff before the rail traffic was operating. Clerks and accountants were required to keep records, manual workers were used to build the railway and station staff would have undertaken a certain amount of instruction prior to taking up their formal duties.

Anglesey

Appendix 1 List No.	Name of Railway Company	Date of Initial Opening within this County
177	Chester and Holyhead Railway Co.	1 August 1848
496	London and North Western Railway Co.	1 January 1859
16	Anglesey Central Railway Co.	16 December 1864

Bedfordshire

Appendix 1 List No.	Name of Railway Company	Date of Initial Opening within this County
45	Bedford and London and Birmingham Railway Co. (Also known as the Bedford Railway)	17 November 1846
496	London and North Western Railway Co.	17 November 1846
238	Dunstable Railway Co.	1848
347	Great Northern Railway Co.	5 August 1850

Cont.

Appendix 1 List No.	Name of Railway Company	Date of Initial Opening within this County
584	Midland Railway Co.	15 April 1857
742	Sandy and Potton Railway	23 June 1857
515	Luton, Dunstable and Welwyn Junction Railway Co.	5 April 1858
391	Hertford, Luton and Dunstable Railway Co.	28 June 1858
44	Bedford and Cambridge Railway Co.	1 August 1862
46	Bedford and Northampton Railway Co.	10 June 1872

Berkshire

Appendix 1 List No.	Name of Railway Company	Date of Initial Opening within this County
352	Great Western Railway Co.	4 June 1838
52	Berkshire and Hampshire Railway Co.	21 December 1847
710	Reading, Guildford and Reigate Railway Co.	4 July 1849
954	Windsor, Staines and South Western Railway Co.	1 December 1849
797	South Eastern Railway Co.	11 June 1852
978	Wycombe Railway Co.	1 August 1854
8	Abingdon Railway Co.	2 June 1856
820	Staines, Wokingham and Woking Railway Co.	4 June 1856
51	Berkshire and Hampshire Extension Railway Co.	11 November 1862
297	Faringdon Railway Co.	1 June 1864
893	Wallingford and Watlington Railway Co.	2 July 1866
895	Wantage Tramway Co.	1 October 1875
229	Didcot, Newbury and Southampton Junction Railway Co.	13 April 1882
444	Lambourn Valley Railway Co.	2 April 1898

Breconshire otherwise Brecknockshire

Appendix 1 List No.	Name of Railway Company	Date of Initial Opening within this County
785	Sirhowy Railway Co.	1805
665	Palleg Tramroad	1807
486	Llanvihangel Railway Co.	1814
671	Penllwyn Tramroad	1824
885	Vale of Neath Railway Co.	24 September 1851
925	West Midland Railway Co.	14 June 1860

Appendix 1 List No.	Name of Railway Company	Date of Initial Opening within this County
560	Merthyr, Tredegar and Abergavenny Railway Co. (Also known as the Heads of the Valleys Line)	29 September 1862
105	Brecon and Merthyr Tydfil Junction Railway Co.	23 April 1863
572	Mid-Wales Railway Co.	23 August 1864
386	Hereford, Hay and Brecon Railway Co.	1 September 1864
602	Neath and Brecon Railway Co.	2 October 1864
352	Great Western Railway Co.	10 August 1866
160	Central Wales Extension Railway Co.	1 November 1866
496	London and North Western Railway Co.	15 July 1867
584	Midland Railway Co.	1876
275	Elan Valley Railway Co.	1894
141	Cambrian Railways Co.	24 June 1904
125	Brynmawr and Western Valleys Railway Co.	12 July 1905

Buckinghamshire

Appendix 1 List No.	Name of Railway Company	Date of Initial Opening within this County
489	London and Birmingham Railway Co.	9 April 1838
352	Re-named the London and South Western Railway Co. 4 June 1839	4 June 1838
26	Great Western Railway Co. Aylesbury Railway Co.	27 May 1839
496	London and North Western Railway Co.	16 July 1846
45	Bedford and London and Birmingham Railway Co. (Also known as the Bedford Railway)	17 November 1846
954	Windsor, Staines and South Western Railway Co.	22 August 1848
128	Buckinghamshire Railway Co.	30 March 1850
978	Wycombe Railway Co.	1 August 1854
24	Aylesbury and Buckingham Railway Co.	23 September 1868
657	Oxford and Aylesbury Tramroad Co.	1 April 1871
972	Wotton Tramway	1 April 1871
338	Great Marlow Railway Co.	27 June 1873
819	Staines and West Drayton Railway Co.	9 August 1884
965	Wolverton and Stony Stratford and District Light Railway Co.	27 May 1887
25	Aylesbury and Rickmansworth Railway Co.	8 July 1889
837	Stratford-upon-Avon, Towcester and Midland Junction Railway Co.	13 April 1891
335	Great Central Railway Co.	1 August 1897
835	Stratford-upon-Avon and Midland Junction Railway Co.	1 January 1909

Caernarvonshire

Appendix 1 List No.	Name of Railway Company	Date of Initial Opening within this County
672	Penrhyn Railway	July 1801
599	Nantlle Railway Co.	1828
301	Festiniog Railway Co.	20 April 1836
664	Padarn Railway	3 March 1843
177	Chester and Holyhead Railway Co.	1 May 1848
32	Bangor and Carnarvon Railway Co.	1 March 1852
327	Gorseddau Tramway	c. 1856
496	London and North Western Railway Co.	1 January 1859
200	Conway and Llanrwst Railway Co.	17 June 1863
211	Croesor and Portmadoc Railway Co. Re-named the Portmadoc, Croesor and Beddgelert Tram-Railway Co. 21 July 1879	1 August 1864
153	Carnarvonshire Railway Co.	2 September 1867
7	Aberystwyth and Welsh Coast Railway Co.	10 October 1867
152	Carnarvon and Llanberis Railway Co.	1 July 1869
326	Gorseddau Junction and Portmadoc Railway Co.	2 September 1875
636	North Wales Narrow Gauge Railway Co.	21 May 1877
790	Snowdon Mountain Railway	6 April 1896
692	Portmadoc, Beddgelert and South Snowdon Railway Co.	1904
1	Abbey Dolgarrog Light Railway Co.	c. 1914
914	Welsh Highland Railway Co.	1 June 1923

Cambridgeshire

Appendix 1 List No.	Name of Railway Company	Date of Initial Opening within this County
641	Northern and Eastern Railway Co.	30 July 1845
279	Ely and Huntingdon Railway Co.	27 October 1846
520	Lynn and Ely Railway Co.	29 October 1846
956	Wisbech, St Ives and Cambridge Junction Railway Co.	3 March 1847
249	East Anglian Railway Co.	22 July 1847
612	Newmarket Railway Co.	3 January 1848
347	Great Northern Railway Co.	3 August 1851
726	Royston and Hitchin Railway Co.	3 August 1851
44	Bedford and Cambridge Railway Co.	1 August 1862
336	Great Eastern Railway Co.	7 August 1862
496	London and North Western Railway Co.	5 July 1865

Appendix 1 List No.	Name of Railway Company	Date of Initial Opening within this County
432	Kettering, Thrapstone and Huntingdon Railway Co.	21 February 1866
282	Ely, Haddenham and Sutton Railway Co.	6 April 1866
	Re-named the Ely and St Ives Railway Co. 10 May 1878	
676	Peterborough, Wisbeach and Sutton Bridge Railway Co.	1 June 1866
280	Ely and Newmarket Railway Co.	1 September 1879
263	Eastern and Midlands Railway Co.	1 July 1883
37	Barrington Light Railway Co.	c. 1921

Cardiganshire

Appendix 1 List No.	Name of Railway Company	Date of Initial Opening within this County
7	Aberystwyth and Welsh Coast Railway Co.	1 July 1863
150	Carmarthen and Cardigan Railway Co.	3 June 1864
535	Manchester and Milford Railway Co.	1 January 1866
945	Whitland and Taff Vale Railway Co.	c. 1878
	Re-named the Whitland and Cardigan Railway Co.	
	2 August 1877 before opening in this county	
352	Great Western Railway Co.	1 July 1881
682	Plynlimon and Hafan Tramway. (Also known as the Hafan and Talybont Tramway)	28 March 1898
886	Vale of Rheidol Light Railway Co.	22 December 1902
446	Lampeter, Aberayron and New Quay Light Railway Co.	10 April 1911

Carmarthenshire

Appendix 1 List No.	Name of Railway Company	Date of Initial Opening within this County
151	Carmarthenshire Railway or Tramroad Co.	1804
482	Llanelly Railway and Dock Co. (Also known as the Llanelly Railway)	1 June 1839
806	South Wales Railway Co.	11 October 1852
887	Vale of Towy Railway Co.	1 April 1858
150	Carmarthen and Cardigan Railway Co.	3 September 1860
352	Great Western Railway Co.	1 August 1863
572	Mid-Wales Railway Co.	23 August 1864

Cont.

319

Appendix 1 List No.	Name of Railway Company	Date of Initial Opening within this County
841	Swansea and Carmarthen Railway Co. Re-named the Central Wales and Carmarthen Junction Railway Co. 21 July 1873	1 June 1865
433	Kidwelly and Burry Port Railway Co.	*c.* 1866
535	Manchester and Milford Railway Co.	1 January 1866
132	Burry Port and Gwendraeth Valley Railway Co.	30 April 1866
668	Pembroke and Tenby Railway Co.	4 September 1866
845	Swansea Vale Railway Co.	18 June 1868
160	Central Wales Extension Railway Co.	6 October 1868
496	London and North Western Railway Co.	6 October 1868
359	Gwendraeth Valleys Railway Co.	1871
945	Whitland and Taff Vale Railway Co. Re-named the Whitland and Cardigan Railway Co. in 1877	24 March 1873
584	Midland Railway Co.	11 August 1876
480	Llanelly and Mynydd Mawr Railway Co.	1 January 1883
141	Cambrian Railways Co.	24 June 1904

Cheshire

Appendix 1 List No.	Name of Railway Company	Date of Initial Opening within this County
330	Grand Junction Railway Co.	4 July 1837
832	Storeton Tramway	14 August 1838
532	Manchester and Birmingham Railway Co.	4 June 1840
175	Chester and Birkenhead Railway Co.	22 September 1840
176	Chester and Crewe Railway Co.	1 October 1840
533	Manchester and Leeds Railway Co. Re-named the Lancashire and Yorkshire Railway Co. 9 July 1847	5 October 1840
762	Sheffield, Ashton-under-Lyne and Manchester Railway Co.	8 August 1844
736	St Helens Canal and Railway Co.	21 July 1845
496	London and North Western Railway Co.	16 July 1846
19	Ashton, Stalybridge and Liverpool Junction Railway Co.	5 October 1846
177	Chester and Holyhead Railway Co.	4 November 1846
541	Manchester, Sheffield and Lincolnshire Railway Co. Re-named the Great Central Railway Co. 1 August 1897	1 January 1847
632	North Staffordshire Railway Co.	9 October 1848
697	Potteries Railway Co.	9 October 1848
770	Shrewsbury and Chester Railway Co.	16 October 1848
182	Churnet Valley Railway Co.	13 June 1849
544	Manchester South Junction and Altrincham Railway Co.	20 July 1849
403	Huddersfield and Manchester Railway and Canal Co.	1 August 1849
56	Birkenhead, Lancashire and Cheshire Junction Railway Co. Re-named the Birkenhead Railway Co. 1 August 1859	18 December 1850

Appendix 1 List No.	Name of Railway Company	Date of Initial Opening within this County
371	Harecastle and Sandbach Railway Co.	21 January 1852
899	Warrington and Stockport Railway Co.	1 November 1853
824	Stockport, Disley and Whaley Bridge Railway Co.	9 June 1857
695	Potteries, Biddulph and Congleton Railway Co.	3 August 1859
174	Cheshire Midland Railway Co.	12 May 1862
823	Stockport and Woodley Junction Railway Co.	12 January 1863
352	Great Western Railway Co.	1 July 1863
600	Nantwich and Market Drayton Railway Co.	19 October 1863
551	Marple, New Mills and Hayfield Junction Railway Co.	1 July 1865
402	Hoylake Railway Co.	2 July 1866
825	Stockport, Timperley and Altrincham Junction Railway Co.	1 December 1866
525	Macclesfield, Bollington and Marple Railway Co.	2 August 1869
917	West Cheshire Railway Co.	1 September 1870
400	Hoylake and Birkenhead Rail and Tramway Co. Re-named the Seacombe, Hoylake and Deeside Railway Co. 18 July 1881	1 August 1872
178	Chester and West Cheshire Junction Railway Co.	2 November 1874
537	Manchester and Stockport Railway Co.	15 February 1875
947	Widnes Railway Co.	3 April 1877
559	Mersey Railway Co.	20 January 1886
955	Wirral Railway Co.	2 January 1888

Cornwall

Appendix 1 List No.	Name of Railway Company	Date of Initial Opening within this County
713	Redruth and Chasewater Railway Co.	30 January 1826
674	Pentewan Railway	June 1829
86	Bodmin and Wadebridge Railway Co.	4 July 1834
379	Hayle Railway Co.	23 December 1837
876	Treffry Estates Tramway	1844
470	Liskeard and Caradon Railway Co.	28 November 1844
918	West Cornwall Railway Co.	11 March 1852
202	Cornwall Railway Co.	2 May 1859
472	Liskeard and Looe Union Canal Co. Re-named the Liskeard and Looe Railway Co. 6 July 1895	27 December 1869
453	Launceston and South Devon Railway Co.	1 June 1865
508	Lostwithiel and Fowey Railway Co.	1 June 1869
615	Newquay and Cornwall Junction Railway Co.	1 July 1869
250	East Cornwall Mineral Railway Co.	7 May 1872
201	Cornwall Minerals Railway Co.	1 June 1874
352	Great Western Railway Co.	27 June 1876

Cont.

Appendix 1 List No.	Name of Railway Company	Date of Initial Opening within this County
497	London and South Western Railway Co.	1 July 1886
622	North Cornwall Railway Co.	21 July 1886
382	Helston Railway Co.	9 May 1887
50	Bere Alston and Calstock Railway Co.	2 March 1908

Cumberland

Appendix 1 List No.	Name of Railway Company	Date of Initial Opening within this County
102	Brampton Railway	1799
607	Newcastle and Carlisle Railway Co.	19 July 1836
552	Maryport and Carlisle Railway Co.	15 July 1840
943	Whitehaven Junction Railway Co.	19 January 1846
451	Lancaster and Carlisle Railway Co.	17 December 1846
191	Cockermouth and Workington Railway Co.	28 April 1847
138	Caledonian Railway Co.	9 September 1847
941	Whitehaven and Furness Junction Railway Co.	21 July 1849
317	Glasgow and South Western Railway Co.	28 October 1850
318	Glasgow, Dumfries and Carlisle Railway Co.	28 October 1850
689	Port Carlisle Dock and Railway Co.	22 May 1854
942	Whitehaven, Cleator and Egremont Railway Co.	11 January 1856
149	Carlisle and Silloth Bay Railway and Dock Co.	28 August 1856
372	Harrington and Lowca Light Railway	1858
92	Border Union (North British) Railway Co.	12 October 1861
625	North Eastern Railway Co.	17 July 1862
192	Cockermouth, Keswick and Penrith Railway Co.	26 October 1864
791	Solway Junction Railway Co.	13 September 1869
709	Ravenglass and Eskdale Railway Co.	24 May 1875
584	Midland Railway Co.	August 1875
725	Rowrah and Kelton Fell (Mineral) Railway Co.	1 January 1877
187	Cleator and Workington Junction Railway Co.	4 August 1879
496	London and North Western Railway Co.	1 June 1880

Denbighshire

Appendix 1 List No.	Name of Railway Company	Date of Initial Opening within this County
727	Ruabon Brook Railway. (Also known as the Pontcysyllte Tramway)	*c.* 1800
584	Midland Railway Co.	10 May 1844
635	North Wales Mineral Railway Co.	4 November 1846
770	Shrewsbury and Chester Railway Co.	4 November 1846
177	Chester and Holyhead Railway Co.	1 May 1848

Appendix 1 List No.	Name of Railway Company	Date of Initial Opening within this County
591	Mold Railway Co.	14 September 1849
352	Great Western Railway Co.	1 September 1854
882	Vale of Clwyd Railway Co.	5 October 1858
496	London and North Western Railway Co.	1 January 1859
884	Vale of Llangollen Railway Co.	1 December 1861
223	Denbigh, Ruthin and Corwen Railway Co.	1 March 1862
974	Wrexham and Minera Railway Co.	22 May 1862
200	Conway and Llanrwst Railway Co.	17 June 1863
483	Llangollen and Corwen Railway Co.	1 May 1865
976	Wrexham, Mold and Connah's Quay Railway Co.	1 January 1866
590	Mold and Denbigh Junction Railway Co.	11 September 1869
975	Wrexham and Minera Joint Railway Co.	27 January 1872
322	Glyn Valley Tramway Co.	April 1873
973	Wrexham and Ellesmere Railway Co.	2 November 1895
855	Tanat Valley Light Railway Co.	4 January 1904
335	Great Central Railway Co.	1 January 1905
1	Abbey Dolgarrog Light Railway Co.	1917

Derbyshire

Appendix 1 List No.	Name of Railway Company	Date of Initial Opening within this County
667	Peak Forest Tramway Co.	31 August 1796
868	Ticknall Tramway Co.	1802
545	Mansfield and Pinxton Railway Co.	13 April 1819
212	Cromford and High Peak Railway Co.	29 May 1830
582	Midland Counties Railway Co.	4 June 1839
58	Birmingham and Derby Junction Railway Co.	5 August 1839
630	North Midland Railway Co.	11 May 1840
584	Midland Railway Co.	10 May 1844
762	Sheffield, Ashton-under-Lyne and Manchester Railway Co.	8 August 1844
541	Manchester, Sheffield and Lincolnshire Railway Co. Re-named the Great Central Railway Co. 1 August 1897	1 January 1847
540	Manchester, Buxton, Matlock and Midland Junction Railway Co.	4 June 1848
759	Sheffield and Lincolnshire Junction Railway Co.	12 February 1849
534	Manchester and Lincoln Union Railway Co.	17 July 1849
551	Marple, New Mills and Hayfield Junction Railway Co.	1 July 1865
80	Blackwell Railway	1871

Cont.

Appendix 1 List No.	Name of Railway Company	Date of Initial Opening within this County
347	Great Northern Railway Co.	23 August 1875
496	London and North Western Railway Co.	27 June 1892
230	Dore and Chinley Railway Co.	6 November 1893
449	Lancashire, Derbyshire and East Coast Railway Co.	15 December 1896
335	Great Central Railway Co.	1 August 1897
133	Burton and Ashby Light Railway Co.	13 June 1906
18	Ashover Light Railway Co.	6 April 1925

Devonshire

Appendix 1 List No.	Name of Railway Company	Date of Initial Opening within this County
679	Plymouth and Dartmoor Railway Co.	26 September 1823
114	Bristol and Exeter Railway Co.	1 May 1844
795	South Devon Railway Co.	30 May 1846
292	Exeter and Crediton Railway Co.	12 May 1851
624	North Devon Railway and Dock Co.	12 July 1854
54	Bideford Extension Railway Co.	2 November 1855
455	Lee Moor Tramway Co.	24 September 1858
202	Cornwall Railway Co.	2 May 1859
794	South Devon and Tavistock Railway Co.	22 June 1859
220	Dartmouth and Torbay Railway Co.	2 August 1859
228	Devon Great Consols Tramway	November 1859
497	London and South Western Railway Co.	18 July 1860
293	Exeter and Exmouth Railway Co.	1 May 1861
453	Launceston and South Devon Railway Co.	1 June 1865
651	Okehampton Railway Co. Re-named the Devon and Cornwall Railway Co. 26 July 1870	1 November 1865
595	Moretonhampstead and South Devon Railway Co.	4 July 1866
871	Torbay and Brixham Railway Co.	28 February 1868
749	Seaton and Beer Railway Co.	16 March 1868
126	Buckfastleigh, Totnes and South Devon Railway Co.	1 May 1872
227	Devon and Somerset Railway Co.	1 November 1873
782	Sidmouth Railway Co.	6 July 1874
36	Barnstaple and Ilfracombe Railway Co.	20 July 1874
217	Culm Valley Light Railway Co.	12 May 1876
352	Great Western Railway Co.	1 August 1876
708	Rattlebrook Peat Railway. (Also known as the Bridestowe Railway)	1879
548	Marland Light Railway	1880

Appendix 1 List No.	Name of Railway Company	Date of Initial Opening within this County
859	Teign Valley Railway Co.	9 October 1882
704	Princetown Railway Co.	11 August 1883
869	Tiverton and North Devon Railway Co.	1 August 1884
291	Exe Valley Railway Co.	1 May 1885
681	Plymouth, Devonport and South Western Junction Railway Co.	1 June 1890
436	Kingsbridge and Salcombe Railway Co.	19 December 1893
130	Budleigh Salterton Railway Co.	15 May 1897
524	Lynton and Barnstaple Railway Co.	11 May 1898
55	Bideford, Westward Ho! and Appledore Railway Co.	24 April 1901
294	Exeter Railway Co.	1 July 1903
23	Axminster and Lyme Regis Light Railway Co.	23 August 1903
50	Bere Alston and Calstock Railway Co.	2 March 1908
712	Redlake Tramway	11 September 1911
623	North Devon and Cornwall Junction Light Railway Co.	27 July 1925

Dorsetshire

Appendix 1 List No.	Name of Railway Company	Date of Initial Opening within this County
691	Portland Railway Co. (Also known as the Merchants Railway)	October 1836
314	Furzebrook Tramway. (Also called Pike's Tramway)	c. 1840
811	Southampton and Dorchester Railway Co.	1 June 1847
497	London and South Western Railway Co.	22 July 1848
352	Great Western Railway Co.	3 July 1854
109	Bridport Railway Co.	12 November 1857
739	Salisbury and Yeovil Railway Co.	1 May 1859
231	Dorset Central Railway Co.	1 November 1860
792	Somerset and Dorset Railway Co.	1 September 1862
937	Weymouth and Portland Railway Co.	9 October 1865
323	Goathorn Pier Mineral Tramway	c. 1866
738	Salisbury and Dorset Junction Railway Co.	20 December 1866
688	Poole and Bournemouth Railway Co.	2 December 1872
104	Breakwater Railway (Portland)	29 May 1874
2	Abbotsbury Railway Co.	9 November 1885
268	Easton and Church Hope Railway Co.	1 October 1900
23	Axminster and Lyme Regis Light Railway Co.	23 August 1903
82	Blandford Camp Railway	1918

325

Durham

Appendix 1 List No.	Name of Railway Company	Date of Initial Opening within this County
856	Tanfield Wagonway	*c.* 1632
445	Lambton Wagonway	*c.* 1770
605	Newbottle Wagonway	1813
392	Hetton Colliery Railway	18 November 1822
827	Stockton and Darlington Railway Co.	27 September 1825
186	Clarence Railway Co.	1836
822	Stanhope and Tyne Railroad Co. (The western part of this railroad was also known as the Wear and Derwent Railway)	15 May 1834
376	Hartlepool Dock and Railway Co.	1 January 1835
607	Newcastle and Carlisle Railway Co.	9 March 1835
239	Durham and Sunderland Railway Co.	5 July 1836
83	Blaydon, Gateshead and Hebburn Railway Co.	March 1837
240	Durham Junction Railway Co.	24 August 1838
103	Brandling Junction Railway Co.	15 January 1839
339	Great North of England, Clarence and Hartlepool Junction Railway Co.	18 March 1839
828	Stockton and Hartlepool Railway Co.	12 November 1839
919	West Durham Railway Co.	12 June 1840
340	Great North of England Railway Co.	1 January 1841
684	Pontop and Jarrow Wagonway. Re-named the Bowes Railway	1842
68	Bishop Auckland and Weardale Railway Co.	19 April 1842
766	Shildon Tunnel Railway	19 April 1842
608	Newcastle and Darlington Junction Railway Co. Re-named the York and Newcastle Railway Co. 3 August 1846	18 June 1844
685	Pontop and South Shields Railway Co.	19 August 1844
910	Weardale Extension Railway Co. (Known locally as the Wear and Derwent Junction Railway)	14 May 1845
909	Wear Valley Railway Co.	3 August 1847
987	York, Newcastle and Berwick Railway Co.	9 August 1847
921	West Hartlepool Harbour and Railway Co.	30 June 1852
748	Seaham and Sunderland Railway	17 January 1854
625	North Eastern Railway Co.	31 July 1854
219	Darlington and Barnard Castle Railway Co.	8 July 1856
222	Dearness Valley Railway Co.	1 January 1858
796	South Durham and Lancashire Union Railway Co.	4 July 1861
311	Frosterley and Stanhope Railway Co.	22 October 1862
858	Tees Valley Railway Co.	12 May 1868
802	South Shields, Marsden and Whitburn Colliery Railway Re-named the South Shields Light Railway in 1920	1870
556	Merrybent and Darlington Railway Co.	1 June 1870
417	Hylton, Southwick and Monkwearmouth Railway Co.	1 July 1876
908	Wear Valley Extension Railway Co.	21 October 1895

Essex

Appendix 1 List No.	Name of Railway Company	Date of Initial Opening within this County
265	Eastern Counties Railway Co.	18 June 1839
641	Northern and Eastern Railway Co.	9 August 1841
264	Eastern Counties and Thames Junction Railway Co.	19 April 1846
267	Eastern Union Railway Co.	1 June 1846
194	Colchester, Stour Valley, Sudbury and Halstead Railway Co.	1 April 1847
638	North Woolwich Railway Co.	14 June 1847
612	Newmarket Railway Co.	3 January 1848
528	Maldon, Witham and Braintree Railway Co.	15 August 1848
505	London, Tilbury and Southend Railway Co.	13 April 1854
864	Thames Haven Dock and Railway Co.	7 June 1855
197	Colne Valley and Halstead Railway Co.	16 April 1860
336	Great Eastern Railway Co.	7 August 1862
862	Tendring Hundred Railway Co.	6 May 1863
286	Epping Railway Co. (Opened after absorption by Eastern Counties Railway Co. in 1862)	24 April 1865
737	Saffron Walden Railway Co.	21 November 1865
959	Wivenhoe and Brightlingsea Railway Co.	18 April 1866
70	Bishops Stortford, Dunmow and Braintree Railway Co.	22 February 1869
185	Clacton-on-Sea Railway Co.	4 July 1882
203	Corringham Light Railway Co.	1 January 1901
426	Kelvedon, Tiptree and Tollesbury Pier Light Railway Co.	1 October 1904
584	Midland Railway Co.	1 January 1912
277	Elsenham and Thaxted Light Railway Co.	1 April 1913

Flintshire

Appendix 1 List No.	Name of Railway Company	Date of Initial Opening within this County
177	Chester and Holyhead Railway Co.	4 November 1846
770	Shrewsbury and Chester Railway Co.	4 November 1846
591	Mold Railway Co.	14 August 1849
496	London and North Western Railway Co.	1 January 1859
974	Wrexham and Minera Railway Co.	22 May 1862
129	Buckley Railway Co.	7 June 1862
141	Cambrian Railways Co.	25 July 1864
603	Nerquis Railway	before 1866
976	Wrexham, Mold and Connah's Quay Railway Co.	1 January 1866
394	Holywell Railway Co.	1867

Cont.

Appendix 1 List No.	Name of Railway Company	Date of Initial Opening within this County
590	Mold and Denbigh Junction Railway Co.	11 September 1869
352	Great Western Railway Co.	27 January 1872
541	Manchester, Sheffield and Lincolnshire Railway Co. Re-named the Great Central Railway Co. 1 August 1897	3 August 1889
973	Wrexham and Ellesmere Railway Co.	2 November 1895

Glamorganshire

Appendix 1 List No.	Name of Railway Company	Date of Initial Opening within this County
156	Cefn and Pyle Railway	1798
675	Penydarren Tramway	c. 1802
663	Oystermouth Railway Co.	April 1806
236	Duffryn, Llynvi and Porthcawl Railway Co.	1829
482	Llanelly Railway and Dock Co. (Also known as the Llanelly Railway)	1 June 1839
852	Taff Vale Railway Co.	9 October 1840
4	Aberdare Railway Co.	6 August 1846
806	South Wales Railway Co.	18 June 1850
233	Dowlais Railway Co.	21 August 1851
885	Vale of Neath Railway Co.	24 September 1851
122	Briton Ferry Floating Dock and Railway Co.	April 1852
846	Swansea Valley Railway Co.	December 1852
613	Newport, Abergavenny and Hereford Railway Co.	6 December 1853
5	Aberdare Valley Railway Co.	December 1855
716	Rhymney Railway Co.	25 February 1858
670	Penarth Harbour Dock and Railway Co.	July 1859
845	Swansea Vale Railway Co.	21 February 1860
925	West Midland Railway Co.	14 June 1860
285	Ely Valley Railway Co.	2 August 1860
488	Llynvi Valley Railway Co.	1 August 1861
805	South Wales Mineral Railway Co.	1 September 1861
284	Ely Valley Extension Railway Co.	8 January 1862
560	Merthyr, Tredegar and Abergavenny Railway Co. (Also known as the Heads of the Valleys Line)	29 September 1862
352	Great Western Railway Co.	15 July 1863
843	Swansea and Neath Railway Co.	15 July 1863
485	Llantrisant and Taff Vale Junction Railway Co.	1 December 1863
602	Neath and Brecon Railway Co.	2 October 1864
208	Cowbridge Railway Co.	February 1865
650	Ogmore Valley Railways Co.	1 August 1865
218	Dare Valley Railway Co.	1866

Appendix 1 List No.	Name of Railway Company	Date of Initial Opening within this County
841	Swansea and Carmarthen Railway Co. Re-named the Central Wales and Carmarthen Junction Railway Co. 21 July 1873	January 1866
487	Llynvi and Ogmore Railway Co.	28 June 1866
105	Brecon and Merthyr Tydfil Junction Railway Co.	1 August 1868
496	London and North Western Railway Co.	1 August 1868
844	Swansea Vale and Neath and Brecon Junction Railway Co.	26 July 1869
584	Midland Railway Co.	11 August 1876
146	Cardiff and Ogmore Valley Railway Co.	2 October 1876
715	Rhondda Valley and Hirwain Junction Railway Co.	1878
669	Penarth Extension Railway Co.	20 February 1878
278	Ely and Clydach Valleys Railway Co.	10 August 1878
875	Treferig Valley Railway Co.	April 1883
687	Pontypridd, Caerphilly and Newport Railway Co.	25 July 1884
714	Rhondda and Swansea Bay Railway Co.	26 February 1885
147	Cardiff, Penarth and Barry Junction Railway Co.	1 December 1887
39	Barry Railway Co.	20 December 1888
207	Cowbridge and Aberthaw Railway Co.	1 October 1892
690	Port Talbot Railway and Docks Co.	1 September 1897
883	Vale of Glamorgan Railway Co.	1 December 1897
148	Cardiff Railway Co.	15 May 1909

Gloucestershire

Appendix 1 List No.	Name of Railway Company	Date of Initial Opening within this County
319	Gloucester and Cheltenham Railway Co. (Also known as the Gloucester and Cheltenham Tramroad)	1810
131	Bullo Pill Tramway Co. Re-incorporated as the Forest of Dean Railway Co. 5 May 1826	c. 1810
754	Severn and Wye Railway and Canal Co.	1 August 1812
592	Monmouth Railway Co.	17 August 1812
834	Stratford and Moreton Railway Co.	5 September 1826
20	Avon and Gloucestershire Railway Co.	10 January 1831
116	Bristol and Gloucestershire Railway Co. Re-named the Bristol and Gloucester Railway Co. 1 July 1839	6 August 1835
59	Birmingham and Gloucester Railway Co.	24 June 1840
352	Great Western Railway Co.	31 August 1840
173	Cheltenham and Great Western Union Railway Co.	31 May 1841
584	Midland Railway Co.	3 August 1846
321	Gloucester and Forest of Dean Railway Co.	19 September 1851
806	South Wales Railway Co.	19 September 1851
388	Hereford, Ross and Gloucester Railway Co.	11 July 1853

Cont.

Appendix 1 List No.	Name of Railway Company	Date of Initial Opening within this County
241	Dursley and Midland Junction Railway Co.	25 August 1856
195	Coleford, Monmouth, Usk and Pontypool Railway Co.	12 October 1857
661	Oxford, Worcester and Wolverhampton Railway Co.	12 July 1859
925	West Midland Railway Co.	14 June 1860
958	Witney Railway Co.	14 November 1861
95	Bourton-on-the-Water Railway Co.	1 March 1862
119	Bristol and South Wales Union Railway Co.	8 September 1863
863	Tewksbury and Malvern Railway Co.	1 May 1864
121	Bristol Port Railway and Pier Co. (included the Clifton Extension Railway)	6 March 1865
831	Stonehouse and Nailsworth Railway Co.	1 February 1867
307	Forest of Dean Central Railway Co.	25 May 1868
120	Bristol Harbour Railway Co.	11 March 1872
251	East Gloucestershire Railway Co.	15 January 1873
753	Severn and Wye and Severn Bridge Railway Co.	21 July 1879
755	Severn Bridge Railway Co.	17 October 1879
31	Banbury and Cheltenham Direct Railway Co.	1 June 1881
196	Coleford Railway Co.	1 September 1883
847	Swindon and Cheltenham Extension Railway Co.	18 December 1883
581	Midland and South Western Junction Railway Co.	23 June 1884
610	Newent Railway Co.	27 July 1885
589	Mitcheldean Road and Forest of Dean Junction Railway Co.	4 November 1907
21	Avonmouth Light Railway Co.	c. 1918

Hampshire

Appendix 1 List No.	Name of Railway Company	Date of Initial Opening within this County
498	London and Southampton Railway Co. Re-named the London and South Western Railway Co. 4 June 1839	29 September 1838
352	Great Western Railway Co.	14 May 1846
811	Southampton and Dorchester Railway Co.	1 June 1847
52	Berkshire and Hampshire Railway Co.	1 November 1848
710	Reading, Guildford and Reigate Railway Co.	4 July 1849
797	Sooth Eastern Railway Co.	11 June 1852
42	Basingstoke and Salisbury Railway Co.	3 July 1854
518	Lymington Railway Co.	1 July 1858
694	Portsmouth Railway Co.	24 January 1859
739	Salisbury and Yeovil Railway Co.	1 June 1860
718	Ringwood, Christchurch and Bournemouth Railway Co.	13 November 1862
829	Stokes Bay Railway and Pier Co.	6 April 1863

Appendix 1 List No.	Name of Railway Company	Date of Initial Opening within this County
71	Bishops Waltham Railway Co.	1 June 1863
677	Petersfield Railway Co.	1 September 1864
380	Hayling Railway Co.	19 January 1865
812	Southampton and Netley Railway Co.	5 March 1865
15	Andover and Redbridge Railway Co.	6 March 1865
566	Mid-Hants (Alton Lines) Railway Co.	2 October 1865
738	Sailsbury and Dorset Junction Railway Co.	21 December 1866
688	Poole and Bournemouth Railway Co.	15 June 1874
584	Midland Railway Co.	30 July 1874
849	Swindon, Marlborough and Andover Railway Co.	1 May 1882
798	Sooth Hampshire Railway and Pier Co.	c. 1884
581	Midland and South Western Junction Railway Co.	23 June 1884
229	Didcot, Newbury and Southampton Railway Co.	1 May 1885
815	Southsea Railway Co.	1 July 1885
989	Fareham and Netley Railway Co.	2 Sept. 1889
456	Lee-on-the-Solent Railway Co.	12 May 1894
41	Basingstoke and Alton Light Railway Co.	1 June 1901
49	Beatley and Bordon Light Railway	11 December 1905
968	Woolmer Instructional Military Railway	1906
	Re-named the Longmoor Military Railway in 1935	
666	Park Prewett Hospital Railway [near Basingstoke]	1914
874	Totton, Hythe and Fawley Light Railway Co.	25 July 1925

Hampshire – Isle of Wight

Appendix 1 List No.	Name of Railway Company	Date of Initial Opening within this County
209	Cowes and Newport Railway Co.	16 June 1862
424	Isle of Wight Railway Co.	23 August 1864
732	Ryde Pier and Tramway Co.	29 August 1864
423	Isle of Wight (Newport Junction) Railway Co.	1 February 1875
731	Ryde and Newport Railway Co.	20 December 1875
497	London and South Western Railway Co.	5 April 1880
101	Brading Harbour Improvement and Railway Co.	27 May 1882
	Re-named the Brading Harbour and Railway Co. 14 August 1896	
422	Isle of Wight Central Railway Co.	1 July 1887
310	Freshwater, Yarmouth and Newport Railway Co.	10 September 1888
614	Newport, Godshill and St Lawrence Railway Co.	20 June 1897

Herefordshire

Appendix 1 List No.	Name of Railway Company	Date of Initial Opening within this County
378	Hay Railway Co.	7 May 1816
440	Kington Tramway	1 May 1820
387	Hereford Railway Co.	2 September 1829
771	Shrewsbury and Hereford Railway Co.	30 July 1852
613	Newport, Abergavenny and Hereford Railway Co.	16 January 1854
388	Hereford, Ross and Gloucester Railway Co.	2 June 1855
467	Leominster and Kington Railway Co.	2 August 1857
969	Worcester and Hereford Railway Co.	16 May 1860
925	West Midland Railway Co.	14 June 1860
352	Great Western Railway Co.	29 July 1862
386	Hereford, Hay and Brecon Railway Co.	24 October 1862
722	Ross and Monmouth Railway Co.	4 August 1873
584	Midland Railway Co.	1 July 1874
439	Kington and Eardisley Railway Co.	3 August 1874
970	Worcester, Bromyard and Leominster Railway Co.	22 October 1877
324	Golden Valley Railway Co.	1 September 1881
466	Leominster and Bromyard Railway Co.	1 March 1884
721	Ross and Ledbury Railway Co.	27 July 1885

Hertfordshire

Appendix 1 List No.	Name of Railway Company	Date of Initial Opening within this County
489	London and Birmingham Railway Co.	20 July 1837
641	Northern and Eastern Railway Co.	15 September 1840
496	London and North Western Railway Co.	16 July 1846
347	Great Northern Railway Co.	5 August 1850
726	Royston and Hitchin Railway Co.	21 October 1850
584	Midland Railway Co.	15 April 1857
390	Hertford and Welwyn Junction Railway Co.	1 March 1858
391	Hertford, Luton and Dunstable Railway Co.	28 June 1858
515	Luton, Dunstable and Welwyn Junction Railway Co.	1 September 1860
902	Watford and Rickmansworth Railway Co.	1 October 1862
896	Ware, Hadham and Buntingford Railway Co.	3 July 1863
336	Great Eastern Railway Co.	29 June 1865
377	Hatfield and St Albans Railway Co.	16 October 1865
70	Bishops Stortford, Dunmow and Braintree Railway Co.	22 February 1869
383	Hemel Hempstead Railway Co.	16 July 1877
335	Great Central Railway Co.	1 August 1897

Huntingdonshire

Appendix 1 List No.	Name of Railway Company	Date of Initial Opening within this County
249	East Anglian Railway Co.	22 July 1847
279	Ely and Huntingdon Railway Co.	17 August 1847
956	Wisbech, St Ives and Cambridge Junction Railway Co.	1 February 1848
347	Great Northern Railway Co.	5 August 1850
336	Great Eastern Railway Co.	7 August 1862
707	Ramsey Railway Co.	1 August 1863
432	Kettering, Thrapstone and Huntingdon Railway Co.	21 February 1866
282	Ely, Haddenham and Sutton Railway Co. Re-named the Ely and St Ives Railway Co. 10 May 1878	10 May 1878
706	Ramsey and Somersham Railway Co.	16 September 1889
584	Midland Railway Co.	6 August 1897

Isle of Wight – see end of Hampshire

Kent

Appendix 1 List No.	Name of Railway Company	Date of Initial Opening within this County
145	Canterbury and Whitstable Railway Co.	3 May 1830
493	London and Greenwich Railway Co.	12 February 1836
501	London, Deptford and Dover Railway Co. Re-named the South Eastern Railway Co. c. 1844	31 August 1842
331	Gravesend and Rochester Railway Co. (Also known as the North Kent Line)	10 February 1845
499	London, Brighton and South Coast Railway Co.	27 July 1846
492	London and Croydon Railway Co.	January 1847
567	Mid-Kent and North Kent Railway Co.	11 January 1857
920	West End of London and Crystal Palace Railway Co.	1 October 1857
255	East Kent Railway Co. Re-named the London, Chatham and Dover Railway Co. 1 August 1859	25 January 1858
568	Mid-Kent (Bromley to St Mary Cray) Railway Co.	5 July 1858
787	Sittingbourne and Sheerness Railway Co.	19 July 1860
547	Margate Railway Co. Re-named the Kent Coast Railway Co. 6 August 1861	1 August 1860
113	Brighton, Uckfield and Tunbridge Wells Railway Co.	1 October 1866
252	East Grinstead, Groombridge and Tunbridge Wells Railway Co.	1 October 1866
751	Sevenoaks, Maidstone and Tunbridge Railway Co.	1 June 1874
768	Shortlands and Nunhead Railway Co.	6 July 1874

Cont.

Appendix 1 List No.	Name of Railway Company	Date of Initial Opening within this County
418	Hythe and Sandgate Railway Co.	9 October 1874
168	Chattenden and Upnor Railway	*c.* 1875
123	Bromley Direct Railway Co.	1 January 1878
232	Dover and Deal Joint Railway Co.	15 June 1881
935	Westerham Valley Railway Co.	7 July 1881
516	Lydd Railway Co.	5 December 1881
413	Hundred of Hoo Railway Co.	1 April 1882
933	West Wickham and Hayes Railway Co.	29 May 1882
527	Maidstone and Ashford Railway Co.	1 July 1884
332	Gravesend Railway Co.	10 May 1886
276	Elham Valley Railway Co.	4 July 1887
662	Oxted and Groombridge Railway Co.	2 January 1888
210	Cranbrook and Paddock Wood Railway Co.	1 October 1892
53	Bexley Heath Railway Co.	1 May 1895
723	Rother Valley Light Railway Co. Re-named the Kent and East Sussex Light Railway Co. 1 June 1904	26 March 1900
765	Sheppey Light Railway Co.	1 August 1901
169	Chattenden Naval Tramway	*c.* 1902
438	Kingsnorth Light Railway	1915
254	East Kent Light Railway Co.	16 October 1916
719	Romney, Hythe and Dymchurch Railway	16 July 1927

Lancashire

Appendix 1 List No.	Name of Railway Company	Date of Initial Opening within this County
88	Bolton and Leigh Railway Co.	1 August 1828
474	Liverpool and Manchester Railway Co.	15 September 1830
430	Kenyon and Leigh Junction Railway Co.	3 January 1831
898	Warrington and Newton Railway Co.	25 July 1831
734	St Helens and Runcorn Gap Railway Co.	21 February 1833
330	Grand Junction Railway Co.	4 July 1837
538	Manchester, Bolton and Bury Canal Navigation and Railway Co.	29 May 1838
634	North Union Railway Co.	21 October 1838
533	Manchester and Leeds Railway Co. Re-named the Lancashire and Yorkshire Railway Co. 9 July 1847	4 July 1839
699	Preston and Longridge Railway Co.	1 May 1840
532	Manchester and Birmingham Railway Co.	4 June 1840
452	Lancaster and Preston Junction Railway Co.	5 June 1840
703	Preston and Wyre Railway, Harbour and Dock Co.	15 July 1840
89	Bolton and Preston Railway Co.	4 February 1841

Appendix 1 List No.	Name of Railway Company	Date of Initial Opening within this County
762	Sheffield, Ashton-under-Lyne and Manchester Railway Co.	8 August 1844
736	St Helens Canal and Railway Co.	21 July 1845
19	Ashton, Stalybridge and Liverpool Junction Railway Co.	13 April 1846
73	Blackburn and Preston Railway Co.	1 June 1846
313	Furness Railway Co.	3 June 1846
496	London and North Western Railway Co.	16 July 1846
451	Lancaster and Carlisle Railway Co.	22 September 1846
256	East Lancashire Railway Co.	28 September 1846
541	Manchester, Sheffield and Lincolnshire Railway Co. Re-named the Great Central Railway Co. 1 August 1897	1 January 1847
448	Lancashire and Yorkshire Railway Co.	9 July 1847
76	Blackburn, Darwen and Bolton Railway Co. Became part of the Bolton, Blackburn, Clitheroe and West Yorkshire Railway Co. 9 July 1847 before opening	3 August 1847
90	Bolton, Blackburn, Clitheroe and West Yorkshire Railway Co. Re-named the Blackburn Railway Co. 24 July 1851	3 August 1847
594	Morecombe Harbour and Railway Co.	12 June 1848
74	Blackburn, Burnley, Accrington and Colne Extension Railway Co.	19 June 1848
475	Liverpool, Crosby and Southport Railway Co.	24 July 1848
462	Leeds, Dewsbury and Manchester Railway Co.	31 July 1848
473	Liverpool and Bury Railway Co.	20 November 1848
476	Liverpool, Ormskirk and Preston Railway Co.	2 April 1849
544	Manchester South Junction and Altrincham Railway Co.	20 July 1849
637	North Western Railway Co.	17 November 1849
305	Fleetwood, Preston and West Riding Junction Railway Co.	14 January 1850
75	Blackburn, Clitheroe and North West Junction Railway Co. Became part of the Bolton, Blackburn, Clitheroe and West Yorkshire Railway Co. 9 July 1847 before opening	22 June 1850
56	Birkenhead, Lancashire and Cheshire Junction Railway Co. Re-named the Birkenhead Railway Co. 1 August 1859	18 December 1850
899	Warrington and Stockport Railway Co.	1 May 1854
536	Manchester and Southport Railway Co.	1 May 1855
881	Ulverstone and Lancaster Railway Co.	10 August 1857
199	Coniston Railway Co.	18 June 1859
653	Oldham, Ashton-under-Lyne and Guide Bridge Junction Railway Co.	31 July 1861
79	Blackpool and Lytham Railway Co.	6 April 1863
316	Garston and Liverpool Railway Co.	1 June 1864
450	Lancashire Union Railways Co.	1 November 1869
315	Garstang and Knott End Railway Co.	5 December 1870
584	Midland Railway Co.	1871
537	Manchester and Stockport Railway Co.	17 May 1875
947	Widnes Railway Co.	3 April 1877
922	West Lancashire Railway Co.	19 February 1878
949	Wigan Junction Railway Co.	16 October 1879
543	Manchester South District Railway Co.	1 January 1880

Cont.

Appendix 1 List No.	Name of Railway Company	Date of Initial Opening within this County
134	Bury and Tottington District Railway Co.	6 November 1882
814	Southport and Cheshire Lines Extension Railway Co.	1 September 1884
559	Mersey Railway Co.	20 January 1886
479	Liverpool, Southport and Preston Junction Railway Co.	1 September 1887
946	Whittingham Railway	June 1888
477	Liverpool Overhead Railway Co.	6 March 1893
542	Manchester Ship Canal Co. (Railways)	1 January 1894
478	Liverpool, St Helens and South Lancashire Railway Co.	1 July 1895
335	Great Central Railway Co.	1 August 1897
78	Blackpool and Fleetwood Tramway Co.	14 July 1898
557	Mersey Docks and Harbour Board	*c.* 1900
442	Knott End Railway Co.	30 July 1908

Leicestershire

Appendix 1 List No.	Name of Railway Company	Date of Initial Opening within this County
868	Ticknall Tramway Co.	1802
48	Belvoir Castle Railway	June 1815
465	Leicester and Swannington Railway Co.	17 July 1832
582	Midland Counties Railway Co.	5 May 1840
584	Midland Railway Co.	10 May 1844
851	Syston and Peterborough Railway Co.	1 September 1846
495	London and North Western Railway Co.	1 May 1850
800	South Leicestershire Railway Co.	1 January 1864
17	Ashby and Nuneaton Joint Railway Co.	1 September 1873
347	Great Northern Railway Co.	29 October 1875
604	Newark and Leicester Railway Co.	1 April 1878
167	Charnwood Forest Railway Co.	16 April 1883
335	Great Central Railway Co.	1 August 1897
133	Burton and Ashby Light Railway Co.	2 July 1906

Lincolnshire

Appendix 1 List No.	Name of Railway Company	Date of Initial Opening within this County
40	Barton and Immingham Light Railway Co.	1 December 1810
584	Midland Railway Co.	2 October 1846
851	Syston and Peterborough Railway Co.	2 October 1846

Appendix 1 List No.	Name of Railway Company	Date of Initial Opening within this County
257	East Lincolnshire Railway Co.	November 1847
337	Great Grimsby and Sheffield Junction Railway Co.	1 March 1848
541	Manchester, Sheffield and Lincolnshire Railway Co. Re-named the Great Central Railway Co. 1 August 1897	1 March 1848
347	Great Northern Railway Co.	17 October 1848
759	Sheffield and Lincolnshire Junction Railway Co.	17 July 1849
496	London and North Western Railway Co.	1 May 1850
13	Ambergate, Nottingham and Boston and Eastern Junction Railway Co. Re-named the Nottingham and Grantham Railway and Canal Co. 15 May 1860	15 July 1850
758	Sheffield and Lincolnshire Extension Railway Co.	7 August 1850
395	Horncastle and Kirkstead Junction Railway Co. Re-named the Horncastle Railway Co. in 1861	11 August 1855
93	Boston, Sleaford and Midland Counties Railway Co.	16 June 1856
271	Edenham and Little Bytham Railway Co.	1 November 1856
821	Stamford and Essendine Railway Co.	1 November 1856
644	Norwich and Spalding Railway Co.	9 August 1858
94	Bourne and Essendine Railway Co.	16 May 1860
877	Trent, Ancholme and Grimsby Railway Co.	1 May 1866
676	Peterborough, Wisbeach and Sutton Bridge Railway Co.	1 June 1866
576	Midland and Eastern Railway Co.	23 July 1866
816	Spalding and Bourn Railway Co. Amalgamated with the Lynn and Sutton Bridge Railway Co. to form the Midland and Eastern Railway Co. 23 July 1866 (before opening)	1 August 1866
817	Spilsby and Firsby Railway Co.	1 May 1868
891	Wainfleet and Firsby Railway Co.	24 October 1871
510	Louth and Lincoln Railway Co.	1 December 1876
509	Louth and East Coast Railway Co.	17 October 1877
342	Great Northern and Great Eastern Joint Railway Co.	6 March 1882
263	Eastern and Midlands Railway Co.	1 July 1883
11	Alford and Sutton Tramway Co.	2 April 1884
839	Sutton and Willoughby Railway Co.	23 September 1886
449	Lancashire, Derbyshire and East Coast Railway Co.	15 December 1896
22	Axholme Joint Railway Co.	10 August 1903
354	Grimsby District Light Railway Co.	May 1906
627	North Lindsey Light Railway Co.	3 September 1906
421	Isle of Axholme Light Railway Co.	5 January 1909
412	Humber Commercial Railway and Dock Co.	29 June 1910
867	Tickhill Light Railway Co.	26 August 1912

Merionethshire

Appendix 1 List No.	Name of Railway Company	Date of Initial Opening within this County
301	Festiniog Railway Co.	20 April 1836
204	Corris, Machynlleth and River Dovey Tramroad Co. Re-named the Corris Railway Co. 25 July 1864	30 April 1859
7	Aberystwyth and Welsh Coast Railway Co.	November 1863
223	Denbigh, Ruthin and Corwen Railway Co.	6 October 1864
553	Mawddwy Railway Co.	1865
483	Llangollen and Corwen Railway Co.	1 May 1865
206	Corwen and Bala Railway Co.	16 July 1866
853	Tal-y-llyn Railway Co.	1 October 1866
300	Festiniog and Blaenau Railway Co.	29 May 1868
29	Bala and Dolgelly Railway Co.	4 August 1868
352	Great Western Railway Co.	23 July 1877
496	London and North Western Railway Co.	22 July 1879
30	Bala and Festiniog Railway Co.	1 November 1882
296	Fairbourne Railway	1890

Middlesex (including London)

Appendix 1 List No.	Name of Railway Company	Date of Initial Opening within this County
489	London and Birmingham Railway Co.	20 July 1837
352	Great Western Railway Co.	4 June 1838
265	Eastern Counties Railway Co.	18 June 1839
641	Northern and Eastern Railway Co.	15 September 1840
490	London and Blackwall Railway Co.	January 1841
924	West London Railway Co.	27 May 1844
496	London and North Western Railway Co.	16 July 1846
954	Windsor, Staines and South Western Railway Co.	1 December 1849
497	London and South Western Railway Co.	1 February 1850
347	Great Northern Railway Co.	5 August 1850
245	East and West India Docks and Birmingham Junction Railway Co. Re-named the North London Railway Co. 1 January 1853	26 September 1850
620	North and South Western Junction Railway Co.	15 February 1853
820	Staines, Wokingham and Woking Railway Co.	4 June 1856
351	Great Western and Uxbridge Railway Co.	8 September 1856
584	Midland Railway Co.	1857
255	East Kent Railway Co. Re-named the London, Chatham and Dover Railway Co. 1 August 1859	25 February 1858
920	West End of London and Crystal Palace Railway Co.	27 March 1858

Appendix 1 List No.	Name of Railway Company	Date of Initial Opening within this County
348	Great Western and Brentford Railway Co.	15 July 1859
369	Hampstead Junction Railway Co.	2 January 1860
889	Victoria Station and Pimlico Railway Co.	1 October 1860
336	Great Eastern Railway Co.	7 August 1862
565	Metropolitan Railway Co.	10 January 1863
923	West London Extension Railway Co.	2 March 1863
165	Charing Cross Railway Co.	11 January 1864
797	South Eastern Railway Co.	11 January 1864
367	Hammersmith and City Railway Co.	13 June 1864
865	Thames Valley Railway Co.	1 November 1864
587	Millwall Extension Railway Co.	1867
274	Edgware, Highgate and London Railway Co.	22 August 1867
562	Metropolitan and St Johns Wood Railway Co.	13 April 1868
873	Tottenham and Hampstead Junction Railway Co.	21 July 1868
580	Midland and South Western Junction Railway Co.	1 October 1868
563	Metropolitan District Railway Co.	24 December 1868
258	East London Railway Co.	6 January 1869
598	Muswell Hill Railway Co. Re-named the Muswell Hill and Palace Railway Co. 25 September 1886	24 May 1873
368	Hammersmith Extension Railway Co.	9 September 1874
437	Kingsbury and Harrow Railway Co.	2 August 1880
399	Hounslow and Metropolitan Railway Co.	1 May 1883
819	Staines and West Drayton Railway Co.	9 August 1884
564	Metropolitan Inner Circle Completion Railway Co.	6 October 1884
373	Harrow and Rickmansworth Railway Co.	25 May 1885
183	City and South London Railway Co.	18 December 1890
374	Harrow and Stanmore Railway Co.	18 December 1890
872	Tottenham and Forest Gate Railway Co.	9 July 1894
335	Great Central Railway Co.	1 August 1897
901	Waterloo and City Railway Co.	11 July 1898
158	Central London Railway Co.	30 July 1900
940	Whitechapel and Bow Railway Co.	2 June 1902
242	Ealing and South Harrow Railway Co.	23 June 1903
341	Great Northern and City Railway Co.	14 February 1904
375	Harrow and Uxbridge Railway Co.	30 June 1904
28	Baker Street and Waterloo Railway Co.	10 March 1906
346	Great Northern, Piccadilly, and Brompton Railway Co. Re-named the London Electric Railway Co. 26 July 1910	15 December 1906
164	Charing Cross, Euston and Hampstead Railway Co.	22 June 1907
273	Edgware and Hampstead Railway Co.	19 November 1923

Monmouthshire

Appendix 1 List No.	Name of Railway Company	Date of Initial Opening within this County
81	Blaenavon Tramroad	*c.* 1795
	Re-incorporated 31 July 1845 as the Monmouthshire Railway and Canal Co.	
786	Sirhowy Tramroad	1805
	Re-named the Sirhowy Railway Co. 25 May 1860	
366	Hall's Tramroad (later called the Abercarn Railway)	*c.* 1811
592	Monmouth Railway Co.	17 August 1812
486	Llanvihangel Railway Co.	1814
730	Rumney Railway Co.	1816
355	Grosmont Railway Co.	*c.* 1818
27	Bailey's Tramroad	18 November 1822
671	Penllwyn Tramroad	1828
387	Hereford Railway Co.	21 September 1829
806	South Wales Railway Co.	15 June 1850
593	Monmouthshire Railway and Canal Co.	1 July 1852
613	Newport, Abergavenny and Hereford Railway Co.	2 January 1854
195	Coleford, Monmouth, Usk and Pontypool Railway Co.	2 June 1856
716	Rhymney Railway Co.	25 February 1858
925	West Midland Railway Co.	14 June 1860
560	Merthyr, Tredegar and Abergavenny Railway Co. (Also known as the Heads of the Valleys Line)	29 September 1862
119	Bristol and South Wales Union Railway Co.	8 September 1863
352	Great Western Railway Co.	28 December 1863
496	London and No.rth Western Railway Co.	15 July 1867
722	Ross and Monmouth Railway Co.	4 August 1873
686	Pontypool, Caerleon and Newport Railway Co.	17 September 1874
10	Alexandra (Newport and South Wales) Docks and Railway Co.	13 April 1875
979	Wye Valley Railway Co.	1 November 1876
687	Pontypridd, Caerphilly and Newport Railway Co.	25 July 1884
262	East Usk Railway Co.	4 April 1898
125	Brynmawr and Western Valleys Railway Co.	12 July 1905

Montgomeryshire

Appendix 1 List No.	Name of Railway Company	Date of Initial Opening within this County
204	Corris, Machynlleth and River Dovey Tramroad Co. Re-named the Corris Railway Co. 25 July 1864	30 April 1859
484	Llanidloes and Newtown Railway Co.	30 April 1859
654	Oswestry and Newtown Railway Co.	1 May 1860
775	Shrewsbury and Welshpool Railway Co.	27 January 1862
616	Newtown and Machynlleth Railway Co.	3 January 1863
7	Aberystwyth and Welsh Coast Railway Co.	1 July 1863
141	Cambrian Railways Co.	25 July 1864
572	Mid-Wales Railway Co.	23 August 1864
698	Potteries, Shrewsbury and North Wales Railway Co.	13 August 1866
384	Hendre Ddu Tramway	c. 1867
888	Van Railway Co.	14 August 1871
322	Glyn Valley Tramway Co.	April 1873
915	Welshpool and Llanfair Light Railway Co.	9 March 1903
855	Tanat Valley Light Railway Co.	4 January 1904
779	Shropshire and Montgomeryshire Light Railway Co.	13 April 1911

Norfolk

Appendix 1 List No.	Name of Railway Company	Date of Initial Opening within this County
983	Yarmouth and Norwich Railway Co.	1 May 1844
619	Norfolk Railway Co.	30 June 1845
643	Norwich and Brandon Railway Co.	30 July 1845
519	Lynn and Dereham Railway Co.	27 October 1846
520	Lynn and Ely Railway Co.	27 October 1846
513	Lowestoft Railway and Harbour Co.	3 May 1847
249	East Anglian Railway Co.	22 July 1847
261	East Suffolk Railway Co.	4 December 1854
905	Waveney Valley Railway Co.	1 December 1855
913	Wells and Fakenham Railway Co.	1 December 1857
980	Yarmouth and Haddiscoe Railway Co.	1 June 1859
336	Great Eastern Railway Co.	7 August 1862
522	Lynn and Hunstanton Railway Co.	3 October 1862
576	Midland and Eastern Railway Co.	23 July 1866
926	West Norfolk Junction Railway Co.	17 August 1866
523	Lynn and Sutton Bridge Railway Co.	18 July 1867
866	Thetford and Watton Railway Co.	26 January 1869
435	Kings Lynn Dock and Railway Co.	1870

Cont.

Norfolk (continued)

Appendix 1 List No.	Name of Railway Company	Date of Initial Opening within this County
416	Hunstanton and West Norfolk Railway Co.	1 July 1874
259	East Norfolk Railway Co.	20 October 1874
904	Watton and Swaffham Railway Co.	20 September 1875
135	Bury St Edmunds and Thetford Railway Co.	1 March 1876
353	Great Yarmouth and Stalham Light Railway Co. Re-named the Yarmouth and North Norfolk Light Railway Co. 27 May 1878. Re-incorporated 11 August 1881 as the Yarmouth and North Norfolk Railway Co.	7 August 1877
521	Lynn and Fakenham Railway Co.	16 August 1879
984	Yarmouth Union Railway Co.	15 May 1882
234	Downham and Stoke Ferry Railway Co.	1 August 1882
263	Eastern and Midlands Railway Co.	18 August 1882
578	Midland and Great Northern Joint Railway Co.	9 June 1893
618	Norfolk and Suffolk Joint Railway Co.	20 June 1898
512	Lowestoft Junction Railway Co.	13 July 1903
957	Wissington Tramway	c. 1905

Northamptonshire

Appendix 1 List No.	Name of Railway Company	Date of Initial Opening within this County
127	Buckingham and Brackley Junction Railway Co.	1850
347	Great Northern Railway Co.	5 August 1850
496	London and North Western Railway Co.	1 June 1850
584	Midland Railway Co.	15 April 1857
432	Kettering, Thrapstone and Huntingdon Railway Co.	21 February 1866
640	Northampton and Banbury Junction Railway Co. Re-named the Midland Counties and South Wales Railway Co. in 1866 but reverted to its original name on 14 July 1870	1 May 1866
821	Stamford and Essendine Railway Co.	9 August 1867
46	Bedford and Northampton Railway Co.	10 June 1872
246	East and West Junction Railway Co.	1 July 1873
837	Stratford-upon-Avon, Towcester and Midland Junction Railway Co.	13 April 1891
335	Great Central Railway Co.	1 August 1897
835	Stratford-upon-Avon and Midland Junction Railway Co.	1 January 1909

Northumberland

Appendix 1 List No.	Name of Railway Company	Date of Initial Opening within this County
607	Newcastle and Carlisle Railway Co.	9 March 1835
609	Newcastle and North Shields Railway Co.	19 June 1839
750	Seghill Railway	1 June 1840
608	Newcastle and Darlington Junction Railway Co.	18 June 1844
	Re-named the York and Newcastle Railway Co. 3 August 1846	
621	North British Railway Co.	18 June 1846
606	Newcastle and Berwick Railway Co.	1 March 1847
987	York, Newcastle and Berwick Railway Co.	9 August 1847
625	North Eastern Railway Co.	31 July 1854
91	Border Counties Railway Co.	5 April 1858
85	Blyth and Tyne Railway Co.	31 October 1860
894	Wansbeck Railway Co.	23 July 1862
393	Hexham and Allendale Railway Co.	19 August 1867
642	Northumberland Central Railway Co.	1 November 1870
746	Scotswood, Newburn and Wylam Railway Co.	12 July 1875
633	North Sunderland Railway Co.	1 August 1898

Nottinghamshire

Appendix 1 List No.	Name of Railway Company	Date of Initial Opening within this County
545	Mansfield and Pinxton Railway Co.	13 April 1819
582	Midland Counties Railway Co.	30 May 1839
584	Midland Railway Co.	10 May 1844
534	Manchester and Lincoln Union Railway Co.	17 July 1849
347	Great Northern Railway Co.	4 September 1849
541	Manchester, Sheffield and Lincolnshire Railway Co.	2 April 1850
	Re-named the Great Central Railway Co. 1 August 1897	
13	Ambergate, Nottingham and Boston and Eastern Junction Railway Co.	15 July 1850
	Re-named the Nottingham and Grantham Railway and Canal Co. 15 May 1860	
758	Sheffield and Lincolnshire Extension Railway Co.	7 August 1850
80	Blackwell Railway	1871
342	Great Northern and Great Eastern Joint Railway Co.	5 July 1879
647	Nottingham Suburban Railway Co.	2 December 1889
449	Lancashire, Derbyshire and East Coast Railway Co.	15 December 1896
546	Mansfield Railway Co.	13 June 1913

343

Oxfordshire

Appendix 1 List No.	Name of Railway Company	Date of Initial Opening within this County
352	Great Western Railway Co.	12 June 1844
660	Oxford Railway Co.	12 June 1844
128	Buckinghamshire Railway Co.	30 March 1850
658	Oxford and Bletchley Junction Railway Co. Amalgamated with the Buckingham and Brackley Junction Railway Co. 22 July 1847 to form the Buckinghamshire Railway Co. (before opening)	30 March 1850
61	Birmingham and Oxford Junction Railway Co.	2 September 1850
659	Oxford and Rugby Railway Co.	2 September 1850
661	Oxford, Worcester and Wolverhampton Railway Co.	4 June 1853
180	Chipping Norton Railway Co.	1 June 1855
8	Abingdon Railway Co.	2 June 1856
925	West Midland Railway Co.	14 June 1860
958	Witney Railway Co.	14 November 1861
978	Wycombe Railway Co.	1 August 1862
903	Watlington and Princes Risborough Railway Co.	15 August 1872
251	East Gloucestershire Railway Co.	15 January 1873
496	London and North Western Railway Co.	21 July 1879
31	Banbury and Cheltenham Direct Railway Co.	6 April 1887
967	Woodstock Railway Co.	19 May 1890
335	Great Central Railway Co.	1 June 1900

Pembrokeshire

Appendix 1 List No.	Name of Railway Company	Date of Initial Opening within this County
743	Saundersfoot Railway and Harbour Co.	1832
806	South Wales Railway Co.	2 January 1854
668	Pembroke and Tenby Railway Co.	30 July 1863
352	Great Western Railway Co.	1 August 1863
586	Milford Railway Co.	7 September 1863
945	Whitland and Taff Vale Railway Co. Re-named the Whitland and Cardigan Railway Co. in 1877	October 1874
601	Narberth Road and Maenclochog Railway Co.	19 September 1876
526	Maenclochog Railway	December 1876
585	Milford Haven Docks and Railway Co.	19 January 1882
303	Fishguard and Rosslare Railways and Harbours Co.	14 March 1895
631	North Pembrokeshire and Fishguard Railway Co.	14 March 1895

Radnorshire

Appendix 1 List No.	Name of Railway Company	Date of Initial Opening within this County
440	Kington Tramway	1 May 1820
441	Knighton Railway Co.	1 October 1860
572	Mid-Wales Railway Co.	23 August 1864
161	Central Wales Railway Co.	10 October 1865
160	Central Wales Extension Railway Co.	1 November 1866
496	London and North Western Railway Co.	25 June 1868
275	Elan Valley Railway Co.	1894

Rutland

Appendix 1 List No.	Name of Railway Company	Date of Initial Opening within this County
584	Midland Railway Co.	20 March 1848
851	Syston and Peterborough Railway Co.	20 March 1848
496	London and North Western Railway Co.	2 June 1851
821	Stamford and Essendine Railway Co.	1 November 1856
94	Bourne and Essendine Railway Co.	16 May 1860
347	Great Northern Railway Co.	25 July 1864

Shropshire

Appendix 1 List No.	Name of Railway Company	Date of Initial Opening within this County
770	Shrewsbury and Chester Railway Co.	14 October 1848
777	Shrewsbury, Oswestry and Chester Junction Railway Co.	23 December 1848
780	Shropshire Union Railways and Canal Co.	23 December 1848
769	Shrewsbury and Birmingham Railway Co.	1 June 1849
771	Shrewsbury and Hereford Railway Co.	30 July 1852
352	Great Western Railway Co.	1 September 1854
773	Shrewsbury and Potteries Junction Railway Co.	13 August 1856
912	Wellington and Severn Junction Railway Co.	1 May 1857
496	London and North Western Railway Co.	1 September 1858
654	Oswestry and Newtown Railway Co.	1 May 1860
441	Knighton Railway Co.	1 October 1860
775	Shrewsbury and Welshpool Railway Co.	14 February 1861
861	Tenbury Railway Co.	1 August 1861
596	Much Wenlock and Severn Junction Railway Co.	1 February 1862
756	Severn Valley Railway Co.	1 February 1862
655	Oswestry, Ellesmere and Whitchurch Railway Co.	20 April 1863

Cont.

345

Appendix 1 List No.	Name of Railway Company	Date of Initial Opening within this County
600	Nantwich and Market Drayton Railway Co.	20 October 1863
141	Cambrian Railways Co.	25 July 1864
514	Ludlow and Clee Hill Railway Co.	24 August 1864
916	Wenlock Railway Co.	1 November 1864
69	Bishops Castle Railway Co.	24 October 1865
698	Potteries, Shrewsbury and North Wales Railway Co.	13 August 1866
911	Wellington and Drayton Railway Co.	16 October 1867
788	Snailbeach District Railways Co.	1873
973	Wrexham and Ellesmere Railway Co.	2 November 1895
855	Tanat Valley Light Railway Co.	4 January 1904
188	Cleobury Mortimer and Ditton Priors Light Railway Co.	1 July 1908
779	Shropshire and Montgomeryshire Light Railway Co.	13 April 1911

Somersetshire

Appendix 1 List No.	Name of Railway Company	Date of Initial Opening within this County
705	Radstock Tramway	20 July 1815
352	Great Western Railway Co.	31 August 1840
114	Bristol and Exeter Railway Co.	14 June 1841
950	Wiltshire, Somerset and Weymouth Railway Co.	7 October 1850
793	Somerset Central Railway Co.	28 August 1854
260	East Somerset Railway Co.	9 November 1858
930	West Somerset Mineral Railway Co.	28 September 1859
739	Salisbury and Yeovil Railway Co.	1 June 1860
497	London and South Western Railway Co.	18 July 1860
931	West Somerset Railway Co.	31 March 1862
792	Somerset and Dorset Railway Co.	1 September 1862
162	Chard Railway Co.	8 May 1863
163	Chard, Ilminster and Taunton Railway Co.	11 September 1866
118	Bristol and Portishead Pier and Railway Co.	12 April 1867
172	Cheddar Valley and Yatton Railway Co.	3 August 1869
584	Midland Railway Co.	4 August 1869
227	Devon and Somerset Railway Co.	8 June 1871
117	Bristol and North Somerset Railway Co.	3 September 1873
588	Minehead Railway Co.	16 July 1874
108	Bridgewater Railway Co.	21 July 1890
936	Weston-super-Mare, Clevedon and Portishead Railway Co.	1 December 1897
977	Wrington Vale Light Railway Co.	4 December 1901

Staffordshire

Appendix 1 List No.	Name of Railway Company	Date of Initial Opening within this County
137	Caldon Low Tramway Co.	1777
673	Pensnett Railway. (Also known as the Shut End Railway)	1829
330	Grand Junction Railway Co.	4 July 1837
58	Birmingham and Derby Junction Railway Co.	5 August 1839
584	Midland Railway Co.	10 May 1844
496	London and North Western Railway Co.	16 July 1846
879	Trent Valley Railway Co.	15 September 1847
804	South Staffordshire Railway Co.	1 November 1847
697	Potteries Railway Co.	17 April 1848
632	North Staffordshire Railway Co.	May 1848
780	Shropshire Union Railways and Canal Co.	1 June 1849
182	Churnet Valley Railway Co.	13 June 1849
769	Shrewsbury and Birmingham Railway Co.	12 November 1849
784	Silverdale and Newcastle Railway Co.	1850
371	Harecastle and Sandbach Railway Co.	21 January 1852
67	Birmingham, Wolverhampton and Stour Valley Railway Co.	1 July 1852
661	Oxford, Worcester and Wolverhampton Railway Co.	1 December 1853
66	Birmingham, Wolverhampton and Dudley Railway Co.	14 November 1854
352	Great Western Railway Co.	14 November 1854
142	Cannock Chase and Wolverhampton Railway Co.	1 February 1858
695	Potteries, Biddulph and Congleton Railway Co.	3 August 1859
144	Cannock Mineral Railway Co.	November 1859
925	West Midland Railway Co.	14 June 1860
789	Sneyd's Railway Co.	January 1861
143	Cannock Chase Railway Co.	1867
833	Stourbridge Railway Co.	1 April 1867
818	Stafford and Uttoxeter Railway Co.	10 December 1867
960	Wolverhampton and Walsall Railway Co.	1 November 1872
370	Harborne Railway Co.	10 August 1874
507	Longton, Adderley Green and Bucknall Railway Co.	September 1875
961	Wolverhampton, Walsall and Midland Junction Railway Co.	19 May 1879
347	Great Northern Railway Co.	1 August 1881
171	Cheadle Railway, Mineral and Land Co. Re-named the Cheadle Railway Co. 7 August 1896	7 November 1892
578	Midland and Great Northern Joint Railway Co.	13 July 1903
464	Leek and Manifold Valley Light Railway Co.	27 June 1904
133	Burton and Ashby Light Railway Co.	13 June 1906

Suffolk

Appendix 1 List No.	Name of Railway Company	Date of Initial Opening within this County
643	Norwich and Brandon Railway Co.	30 July 1845
267	Eastern Union Railway Co.	1 June 1846
420	Ipswich and Bury St Edmunds Railway Co.	30 November 1846
513	Lowestoft Railway and Harbour Co.	3 May 1847
266	Eastern Union and Hadleigh Junction Railway Co.	20 August 1847
612	Newmarket Railway Co.	3 January 1848
194	Colchester, Stour Valley, Sudbury and Halstead Railway Co.	2 July 1849
261	East Suffolk Railway Co.	4 December 1854
511	Lowestoft and Beccles Railway Co.	1 June 1859
980	Yarmouth and Haddiscoe Railway Co.	1 June 1859
905	Waveney Valley Railway Co.	2 November 1860
336	Great Eastern Railway Co.	7 August 1862
554	Mellis and Eye Railway Co.	1 April 1867
135	Bury St Edmunds and Thetford Railway Co.	1 March 1876
299	Felixstowe Railway and Pier Co.	
	Re-named the Felixstowe Railway and Dock Co. 21 July 1879	1 May 1877
991	Southwold Railway Co.	24 Sept. 1879
578	Midland and Great Northern Joint Railway Co.	13 July 1903
618	Norfolk and Suffolk Joint Railway Co.	13 July 1903
569	Mid-Suffolk Railway Co.	20 September 1904
957	Wissington Tramway	c. 1905

Surrey

Appendix 1 List No.	Name of Railway Company	Date of Initial Opening within this County
838	Surrey Iron Railway Co.	26 July 1803
215	Croydon, Merstham and Godstone Iron Railway Co.	24 July 1805
493	London and Greenwich Railway Co.	14 December 1836
498	London and Southampton Railway Co.	21 May 1838
	Re-named the London and South Western Railway Co. 4 June 1839	
492	London and Croydon Railway Co.	1 June 1839
491	London and Brighton Railway Co.	12 July 1841
501	London, Deptford and Dover Railway Co.	31 August 1842
	Re-named the South Eastern Railway Co. c1844	
106	Bricklayers Arms Extension Railway	1 May 1844
356	Guildford Junction Railway Co.	1 May 1845
499	London, Brighton and South Coast Railway Co.	27 July 1846
717	Richmond Railway Co.	27 July 1846
214	Croydon and Epsom Railway Co.	10 May 1847
954	Windsor, Staines and South Western Railway Co.	22 August 1848
710	Reading, Guildford and Reigate Railway Co.	4 July 1849

Appendix 1 List No.	Name of Railway Company	Date of Initial Opening within this County
504	London Necropolis and National Mausoleum Co.	7 November 1854
951	Wimbledon and Croydon Railway Co.	22 October 1855
820	Staines, Wokingham and Woking Railway Co.	9 July 1856
154	Caterham Railway Co.	5 August 1856
920	West End of London and Crystal Palace Railway Co.	1 October 1857
694	Portsmouth Railway Co.	24 January 1859
287	Epsom and Leatherhead Railway Co.	1 February 1859
952	Wimbledon and Dorking Railway Co.	4 April 1859
165	Charing Cross Railway Co.	11 January 1864
568	Mid-Kent (Bromley to St Mary Cray) Railway Co.	4 April 1864
33	Banstead and Epsom Downs Railway Co.	22 May 1865
216	Crystal Palace and South London Junction Railway Co.	1 August 1865
397	Horsham and Guildford Direct Railway Co.	2 October 1865
398	Horsham, Dorking and Leatherhead Railway Co.	11 March 1867
870	Tooting, Merton and Wimbledon Railway Co.	1 October 1868
768	Shortlands and Nunhead Railway Co.	6 July 1874
966	Woodside and South Croydon Railway Co.	10 August 1885
662	Oxted and Groombridge Railway Co.	2 January 1888
72	Bisley Tramway	14 July 1890
183	City and South London Railway Co.	18 December 1890
288	Epsom Downs Extension Railway Co.	*c.* 1893
181	Chipstead Valley Railway Co.	1 September 1897
901	Waterloo and City Railway Co.	11 July 1898
28	Baker Street and Waterloo Railway Co.	10 March 1906
953	Wimbledon and Sutton Railway Co.	7 July 1929

Sussex

Appendix 1 List No.	Name of Railway Company	Date of Initial Opening within this County
491	London and Brighton Railway Co.	12 May 1840
110	Brighton and Chichester Railway Co.	24 November 1845
112	Brighton, Lewes and Hastings Railway Co.	8 June 1846
499	London, Brighton and South Coast Railway Co.	27 July 1846
797	South Eastern Railway Co.	13 February 1851
253	East Grinstead Railway Co.	9 July 1855
469	Lewes and Uckfield Railway Co.	11 October 1858
571	Mid-Sussex Railway Co.	10 October 1859
87	Bognor Railway Co.	1 June 1864
497	London and South Western Railway Co.	1 September 1864

Cont.

Appendix 1 List No.	Name of Railway Company	Date of Initial Opening within this County
677	Petersfield Railway Co.	1 September 1864
397	Horsham and Guildford Direct Railway Co.	2 October 1865
252	East Grinstead, Groombridge and Tunbridge Wells Railway Co.	1 October 1866
113	Brighton, Uckfield and Tunbridge Wells Railway Co.	1 October 1867
570	Mid-Sussex and Midhurst Junction Railway Co.	15 October 1866
398	Horsham, Dorking and Leatherhead Railway Co.	1 May 1867
880	Tunbridge Wells and Eastbourne Railway Co.	14 May 1879
179	Chichester and Midhurst Railway Co.	11 July 1881
468	Lewes and East Grinstead Railway Co.	1 August 1882
890	Volks Electric Railway	3 August 1883
111	Brighton and Dyke Railway Co.	1 September 1887
662	Oxted and Groombridge Railway Co.	1 October 1888
733	Rye and Camber Railway	13 July 1895
414	Hundred of Manhood and Selsey Railway Co. Re-named the West Sussex Railway Co. January 1924	27 August 1897
723	Rother Valley Light Railway Co. Re-named the Kent and East Sussex Light Railway Co. 1 June 1904	26 March 1900
213	Crowhurst, Sidley and Bexhill Railway Co.	1 June 1902

Warwickshire

Appendix 1 List No.	Name of Railway Company	Date of Initial Opening within this County
834	Stratford and Moreton Railway Co.	11 February 1836
330	Grand Junction Railway Co.	4 July 1837
489	London and Birmingham Railway Co.	9 April 1838
58	Birmingham and Derby Junction Railway Co.	5 August 1839
830	Stonebridge Railway Co.	12 August 1839
582	Midland Counties Railway Co.	30 June 1840
59	Birmingham and Gloucester Railway Co.	16 August 1841
584	Midland Railway Co.	10 May 1844
900	Warwick and Leamington Union Railway Co.	9 December 1844
496	London and North Western Railway Co.	16 July 1846
879	Trent Valley Railway Co.	15 September 1847
728	Rugby and Leamington Railway Co.	1 March 1851
67	Birmingham, Wolverhampton and Stour Valley Railway Co.	February 1852
61	Birmingham and Oxford Junction Railway Co.	1 October 1852
352	Great Western Railway Co.	1 October 1852
66	Birmingham, Wolverhampton and Dudley Railway Co.	14 November 1854
661	Oxford, Worcester and Wolverhampton Railway Co.	12 July 1859
925	West Midland Railway Co.	14 June 1860

Appendix 1 List No.	Name of Railway Company	Date of Initial Opening within this County
836	Stratford-upon-Avon Railway Co.	10 October 1860
800	South Leicestershire Railway Co.	1 January 1862
62	Birmingham and Sutton Coldfield Extension Railway Co.	2 June 1862
246	East and West Junction Railway Co.	1 July 1873
17	Ashby and Nuneaton Joint Railway Co.	1 September 1873
370	Harborne Railway Co.	10 August 1874
65	Birmingham West Suburban Railway Co.	3 April 1876
9	Alcester Railway Co.	4 September 1876
961	Wolverhampton, Walsall and Midland Junction Railway Co.	19 May 1879
290	Evesham, Redditch and Stratford-upon-Avon Junction Railway Co.	2 June 1879
60	Birmingham and Henley-in-Arden Railway Co.	6 June 1894
335	Great Central Railway Co.	1 August 1897
64	Birmingham, North Warwickshire and Stratford-upon-Avon Railway Co.	9 December 1907
835	Stratford-upon-Avon and Midland Junction Railway Co.	1 January 1909
272	Edge Hill Railway Co.	1920

Westmorland

Appendix 1 List No	Name of Railway Company	Date of Initial Opening within this County
427	Kendal and Windermere Railway Co.	22 September 1846
451	Lancaster and Carlisle Railway Co.	22 September 1846
796	South Durham and Lancashire Union Railway Co.	4 July 1861
270	Eden Valley Railway Co.	December 1861
625	North Eastern Railway Co.	13 July 1863
584	Midland Railway Co.	August 1875
496	London and North Western Railway Co.	26 June 1876

Wiltshire

Appendix 1 List No.	Name of Railway Company	Date of Initial Opening within this County
352	Great Western Railway Co.	17 December 1840
173	Cheltenham and Great Western Union Railway Co.	31 May 1841
497	London and South Western Railway Co.	27 January 1847
52	Berkshire and Hampshire Railway Co.	21 December 1847
950	Wiltshire, Somerset and Weymouth Railway Co.	5 September 1848

Cont.

Wiltshire (continued)

Appendix 1 List No.	Name of Railway Company	Date of Initial Opening within this County
42	Basingstoke and Salisbury Railway Co.	1 May 1857
740	Salisbury Railway and Market House Co.	May 1859
739	Salisbury and Yeovil Railway Co.	2 May 1859
51	Berkshire and Hampshire Extension Railway Co.	11 November 1862
140	Calne Railway Co.	3 November 1863
550	Marlborough Railway Co.	14 April 1864
738	Salisbury and Dorset Junction Railway Co.	20 December 1866
529	Malmesbury Railway Co.	17 December 1877
849	Swindon, Marlborough and Andover Railway Co.	1 May 1882
848	Swindon and Highworth Light Railway Co.	9 May 1883
847	Swindon and Cheltenham Extension Railway Co.	18 December 1883
581	Midland and South Western Junction Railway Co.	23 June 1884
549	Marlborough and Grafton Railway Co.	26 June 1898
14	Amesbury and Military Camp Light Railway	1 October 1901
193	Codford Camp Railway	c. 1914
840	Sutton Veny Camp Railway	c. 1914
309	Fovant Military Railway	1916

Worcestershire

Appendix 1 List No.	Name of Railway Company	Date of Initial Opening within this County
834	Stratford and Moreton Railway Co.	11 February 1836
59	Birmingham and Gloucester Railway Co.	24 June 1840
661	Oxford, Worcester and Wolverhampton Railway Co.	5 October 1850
66	Birmingham, Wolverhampton and Dudley Railway Co.	14 November 1854
711	Redditch Railway Co.	19 September 1859
969	Worcester and Hereford Railway Co.	c. 1860
925	West Midland Railway Co.	14 June 1860
861	Tenbury Railway Co.	1 August 1861
756	Severn Valley Railway Co.	1 February 1862
863	Tewkesbury and Malvern Railway Co.	1 July 1862
833	Stourbridge Railway Co.	1 April 1863
860	Tenbury and Bewdley Railway Co.	13 August 1864
584	Midland Railway Co.	1 October 1864
289	Evesham and Redditch Railway Co.	16 June 1866
352	Great Western Railway Co.	1 February 1870
361	Halesowen and Bromsgrove Branch Railway Co. Re-named the Halesowen Railway Co. 13 July 1876	1 March 1872

Appendix 1 List No.	Name of Railway Company	Date of Initial Opening within this County
970	Worcester, Bromyard and Leominster Railway Co.	2 May 1874
290	Evesham, Redditch and Stratford-upon-Avon Junction Railway Co.	2 June 1879
652	Oldbury Railway Co.	7 November 1884

Yorkshire

Appendix 1 List No.	Name of Railway Company	Date of Initial Opening within this County
443	Lake Lock Railroad	1793
783	Silkstone Railway	1809
575	Middleton Railway Co.	12 August 1812
971	Worsborough Railway	*c.* 1820
827	Stockton and Darlington Railway Co.	27 December 1830
458	Leeds and Selby Railway Co.	22 September 1834
938	Whitby and Pickering Railway Co.	8 June 1835
761	Sheffield and Rotherham Railway Co.	1 November 1838
986	York and North Midland Railway Co.	29 May 1839
630	North Midland Railway Co.	11 May 1840
409	Hull and Selby Railway Co.	1 July 1840
533	Manchester and Leeds Railway Co.	5 October 1840
340	Great North of England Railway Co.	1 January 1841
584	Midland Railway Co.	10 May 1844
6	Aberford Railway Co.	*c.* 1845
762	Sheffield, Ashton-under-Lyne and Manchester Railway Co.	14 July 1845
574	Middlesbrough and Redcar Railway Co.	4 June 1846
457	Leeds and Bradford Extension Railway Co.	1 July 1846
541	Manchester, Sheffield and Lincolnshire Railway Co. Re-named the Great Central Railway Co. 1 August 1897	1 January 1847
496	London and North Western Railway Co.	4 July 1847
448	Lancashire and Yorkshire Railway Co.	9 July 1847
403	Huddersfield and Manchester Railway and Canal Co.	2 August 1847
987	York, Newcastle and Berwick Railway Co.	9 August 1847
459	Leeds and Thirsk Railway Co. Re-named the Leeds Northern Railway Co. 3 July 1851	5 January 1848
892	Wakefield, Pontefract and Goole Railway Co.	1 April 1848
347	Great Northern Railway Co.	6 June 1848
462	Leeds, Dewsbury and Manchester Railway Co.	31 July 1848
247	East and West Yorkshire Junction Railway Co.	30 October 1848
759	Sheffield and Lincolnshire Junction Railway Co.	12 February 1849
637	North Western Railway Co.	31 July 1849
807	South Yorkshire, Doncaster and Goole Railway Co. Re-named the South Yorkshire Railway and River Dun Navigation Co. 19 April 1850	10 November 1849
305	Fleetwood, Preston and West Riding Junction Railway Co.	14 January 1850
928	West Riding Union Railway Co.	9 May 1850
404	Huddersfield and Sheffield Junction Railway Co.	1 July 1850

Cont.

Yorkshire (continued)

Appendix 1 List No.	Name of Railway Company	Date of Initial Opening within this County
337	Great Grimsby and Sheffield Junction Railway Co.	16 July 1850
530	Malton and Driffield Junction Railway Co.	19 May 1853
573	Middlesbrough and Guisbrough Railway Co.	11 November 1853
407	Hull and Holderness Railway Co.	26 June 1854
625	North Eastern Railway Co.	31 July 1854
460	Leeds, Bradford and Halifax Junction Railway Co.	1 August 1854
764	Sheffield, Rotherham, Barnsley, Wakefield, Huddersfield and Goole Railway Co.	4 September 1854
43	Bedale and Leyburn Railway Co.	24 November 1855
100	Bradford, Wakefield and Leeds Railway Co. Re-named the West Yorkshire Railway Co. 21 July 1863	3 October 1857
639	North Yorkshire and Cleveland Railway Co.	27 March 1861
796	South Durham and Lancashire Union Railway Co.	4 July 1861
189	Cleveland Railway Co.	23 November 1861
408	Hull and Hornsea Railway Co.	28 March 1864
656	Otley and Ilkley Joint Railway Co.	February 1865
927	West Riding and Grimsby Joint Railway Co.	1 February 1866
306	Forcett Railway Co.	October 1866
425	Keighley and Worth Valley Railway Co.	15 April 1867
35	Barnsley Coal Railway Co.	28 January 1870
34	Barnoldswick Railway Co.	8 February 1871
434	Kiltonthorpe Railway	11 June 1873
99	Bradford, Eccleshill and Idle Railway Co.	4 May 1874
419	Idle and Shipley Railway Co.	1 May 1874
826	Stocksbridge Railway Co.	14 April 1877
98	Bradford and Thornton Railways Co.	August 1877
461	Leeds, Castleford and Pontyfract Junction Railway Co.	12 August 1878
850	Swinton and Knottingley Joint Railway Co.	19 May 1879
342	Great Northern and Great Eastern Joint Railway	3 July 1879
365	Halifax, Thornton and Keighley Railway Co.	3 September 1882
939	Whitby, Redcar and Middlesbrough Union Railway Co.	5 December 1883
744	Scarborough and Whitby Railway Co.	16 July 1885
411	Hull, Barnsley and West Riding Junction Railway and Dock Co. Re-named the Hull and Barnsley Railway Co. 30 June 1905	20 July 1885
745	Scarborough, Bridlington and West Riding Junction Railways Co.	18 April 1890
364	Halifax High Level and North and South Junction Railway Co.	1 August 1890
248	East and West Yorkshire Union Railways Co.	19 May 1891
244	Easingwold Railway Co. Re-named the Easingwold Light Railway Co. in 1928	1 July 1891
357	Guiseley, Yeadon and Headingley Railway Co.	26 February 1894
809	South Yorkshire Junction Railway Co.	1 September 1894
799	South Leeds Junction Railway Co.	6 April 1895

Appendix 1 List No.	Name of Railway Company	Date of Initial Opening within this County
155	Cawood, Wistow and Selby Light Railway Co.	16 February 1898
415	Hunslet Railway Co.	3 July 1899
325	Goole and Marshland Light Railway Co.	8 January 1900
763	Sheffield District Railway Co.	28 May 1900
410	Hull and South Yorkshire Extension Railway Co.	31 March 1902
988	Yorkshire Dales Railway Co.	29 July 1902
22	Axholme Joint Railway Co.	10 August 1903
767	Shireoaks, Laughton and Maltby Railway Co.	2 October 1905
617	Nidd Valley Light Railway Co.	11 September 1907
808	South Yorkshire Joint Railway Co.	1 January 1909
421	Isle of Axholme Light Railway Co.	5 January 1909
221	Dearne Valley Railway Co.	17 May 1909
724	Rotherham, Maltby and Laughton Railway Co.	1 October 1909
741	Sand Hutton Light Railway	1910
867	Tickhill Light Railway Co.	26 August 1912
225	Derwent Valley Light Railway Co.	12 October 1912
97	Brackenhill Light Railway Co.	1 July 1914
328	Gowdall and Braithwell Railway Co.	1 May 1916
302	Firbeck Light Railway Co.	December 1924

APPENDIX 3

RAILWAY STAFF RECORDS

In the cases of records held by the The National Archives the relevant RAIL reference is given. Where records are held by another repository the abbreviation for that repository is given together with the relevant document references. A description of each type of record is given together with its overall covering dates. (Gaps in records are not recorded.) The number given in brackets after the name of the railway company refers to the List No. in Appendix 1.

3.1 Companies formed before 1923, excluding the Great Western Railway

Alexandra (Newport and South Wales) Docks and Railway Co. (No. 10)

TNA Reference			
Class	Piece No.	Dates	Description
RAIL 1057	1865	1916	Accident to R. Wilson
	2710	1914 to 1918	List of Railwaymen killed in First World War

Barry Dock and Railway Co. (No. 38). Re-named the Barry Railway Co. 5 August 1891

TNA Reference			
Class	Piece No.	Dates	Description
RAIL 23	46	1886 to 1922	Register of Clerical Staff
	47	1890 to 1923	Register of Stores Staff
	48	1888 to 1923	Register of Staff
			Locomotive Dept. Staff
	49	*c.* 1888 to 1922	Drivers
	50 & 51	*c.* 1889 to 1921	Firemen
	52	1913 to 1917	Accidents: Locomotive Dept.
	53	1907 to 1922	Accidents: Passengers and Staff

TNA Reference		Dates	Description
Class	Piece No.		
RAIL 23 (cont.)	54 to 60	1898 to 1922	Wages Staff
	64 & 65	1898 to 1922	Workmen's Compensations: payments by settlement or award
RAIL 1057	2245	1898 to 1903	Accidents to Staff (named)
	2710	1914 to 1918	List of Railwaymen killed in First World War
A. Miller		1888 to 1912	Traffic Staff Record Book*

* This document is held by Mr A. Miller, 2 Luddington Road, Great Gidding. Huntingdon, PE17 5PA, who is prepared to answer written enquiries.

Birkenhead, Lancashire and Cheshire Junction Railway Co. Re-named the Birkenhead Railway Co. 1 August 1859 (No. 56)

TNA Reference		Dates	Description
Class	Piece No.		
RAIL 35	24/2	1848	Report on Staff necessary (names not included)
	24/3	1850	Report from Engineer (W. Bragg) on Maintenance (includes Lists of Staff)
	24/5	1852	Report from engineer (George Douglas, includes Lists of Staff and Rates of Pay)
	33	1854	Apprenticeship Indenture of Thomas Tierney
	34	1854	Apprenticeship Indenture of Thomas Davies
	35	1858	Apprenticeship Indenture of Francis Dodd
	38	1848	List of Staff and amount paid per annum on Birkenhead, Lancashire and Cheshire Junction Railway Co.
	45	1852	Lists of Working Staff
	46	1856	Lists of Working Staff
	48	1858	Subscription List for the widow of Thomas Stratford, Gatekeeper at Birkenhead
	51	1875 to 1925	Volume containing details of Staff Payments (formerly kept at Monks Ferry)

Birmingham and Gloucester Railway Co. (No. 59)

TNA Reference		Dates	Description
Class	Piece No.		
RAIL 1020	4	1841	Diary of Herbert Spencer, Engineering Assistant

Birmingham and Oxford Junction Railway Co. (No. 61)

TNA Reference			
Class	Piece No.	Dates	Description
RAIL 39	15	1852 to 1853	Accountant's Vouchers (includes salary and wages receipts with signatures)

Bishops Castle Railway Co. (No. 69)

TNA Reference			
Class	Piece No.	Dates	Description
RAIL 1057	2710	1914 to 1918	List of Railwaymen killed in First World War

Blaenavon Tramroad (No. 81). Re-incorporated as the Monmouthshire Railway and Canal Co. 31 July 1845

TNA Reference			
Class	Piece No.	Dates	Description
RAIL 500	43	1801	Petition of George Harris for increase in wages
		1819	Petition of Henry Howel, lock-keeper, for a house
		1822	Petition of John Howells, lock-keeper, for a house
		1824	Petition from carpenters for a rise in wages
		1824	Petition from labourers protesting against their low wages (names not included)
		1824	Petition from carpenters asking that their reduced wage of 16 shillings per week should be increased by 2 shillings
		1824	Petition from carpenters for increase in wages (names not included)
		1827	Petition from Thomas Jones, blocklayer and keeper of the Blaenavon Rail Road, for building of a house
		1827	Petition from W. Williams, lock-keeper, for a house
		1827	Petition from James Parry, (fifteen years smith with the company) for a house
		1827	Petition from William Jones, Blocklayer, for a house
		1843	Petition from blocklayers protesting against proposed reduction in wages (names not included)
		1854	Petition from firemen for increase in wages (names not included)
		1863	Petition from guard G. Hadden in connection with accusations against his character
		1864	Petition from guards protesting that they had to work 14 to 16 hours each day without extra pay in contrast to drivers and firemen who were paid for all time worked. Draft reply
		1864	Petition from guards protesting against low wages and lack of prospects

TNA Reference			
Class	Piece No.	Dates	Description
RAIL 500 (cont.)	43	1864	Petitions from guards expressing disappointment at non-receipt of advance in wages, and tendering their notice to leave the service of the company
		1864	Protests from guards Giddings and Shoebridge against dismissal and applying for reinstatement; denying they were ringleaders in the petition of 7 June
		1871	Memorial from workmen for increase in wages and reduction of hours of duty
		1877	Memorial from old engine drivers protesting against high cost of joining GW Mutual Assurance Society
	65	1865	Applications for transfer clerk
	66	1866	Applications for accountant
	69	1870	Locomotive foremen and drivers; statements of income for tax purposes
	72	1870 to 1871	Requests for salary increases (individual letters)
	74	1872	G. Harrison's relinquishment of engineering duties
	80	1875	Appointment of engineer T.D. Roberts
RAIL 1057	2744	1851	Historical file (includes schedule of times of trains with their drivers

Blyth and Tyne Railway Co. (No. 85)

TNA Reference			
Class	Piece No.	Dates	Description
RAIL 56	6	1853 to 1856	Agenda Book of Directors' Meetings (includes names and addresses of staff)
	32	1874	Letter from A. Mather, driver, reporting disagreement with Robinson, coal guard

Bodmin and Wadebridge Railway Co. (No. 86)

TNA Reference			
Class	Piece No.	Dates	Description
RAIL 57	19	1863 to 1884	Wages Lists
RAIL 1017	1/134 to 1/150	1873 to 1881	Wages Lists: Blocklayers (on reverse side of various posters)
Brun/Cl Reference Box2		1866, 1867, 1871	Pay Sheets (includes names)
Corn RO Reference FS,3/1549		1876, 1877, 1881 1871, 1872	Pay Sheets (includes names)

Bolton and Leigh Railway Co. (No. 88)

TNA Reference Class	Piece No.	Dates	Description
RAIL 1057	3390	1857 to 1899	Method of accounting devised by John Diggle, clerk (includes biography)

Brandling Junction Railway Co. (No. 103)

TNA Reference Class	Piece No.	Dates	Description
RAIL 64	8	1839 to 1843	Lists of Staff with their duties and rates of pay
	10	Undated	Proposed Appointment of Superintendent (not named)

Brecon and Merthyr Tydfil Junction Railway Co. (No. 105)

TNA Reference Class	Piece No.	Dates	Description
RAIL 65	31	1880 to 1888	Permanent Way Staff
	32	1880 to 1888	Locomotive Staff
	33	1880 to 1888	Station Staff
	34 & 35	1912 to 1922	Accident Books
RAIL 1014	3/65	1880	Letter from guard John Powell complaining about stoppage of pay; absent with bowel complaint
RAIL 1057	32	1882	Accident: John Davies, driver
	35	1883	Accident: James Reed, ganger
	36	1883	Accident: James Johnson, labourer
	37	1883	Accident: George Lewis, goods guard
	39	1885	Accident: William Edwards, signalman
			Accident: William Coston, passenger
			Accident: S. Thomas, passenger
	40	1885	Accident: J. Powell, platelayer
	42	1886	Accident: William Adams, goods guard
	43	1887	Accident: David Griffiths, platelayer
	44	1882	Accident: Frederick Smith, wagon examiner
	45	1882	Accident: Steadman, guard
	47	1884	Accident: David Davies, passenger driver
	48	1885	Accident: William Colston, (died)
	49	1888	Accident: Robert Thorpe, goods guard
	50	1887	Accident: Mrs Edwards, passenger
	51	1891 to 1892	Accident: W.J. Grant, passenger
	2710	1914 to 1918	List of Railwaymen killed in First World War

Bristol and Exeter Railway Co. (No. 114)

TNA Reference Class	Piece No.	Dates	Description
RAIL 75	124	1864 to 1867	Accountant's Vouchers (includes paybills and names) List of Staff at Carriage Dept., Bridgwater, 1 August 1867 Accident to John Legg, fitter, 1867 Lists of Officers at Bristol Station, with salaries, 1864 to 1867
	272	8 March 1821	Will of Joseph Carde of Burnham, Somerset
Som RO Reference			
T/PH/br.C/1372	1862		Henry Britton, Locomotive Dept 6 years, Proficiency Certificate

Brompton and Piccadilly Circus Railway Co. (No. 124) – see London Electric Railway Co., (No. 502) in this Appendix

Burton and Ashby Light Railway Co. (No. 133)

TNA Reference Class	Piece No.	Dates	Description
RAIL 491	1038	1906 to 1920	Staff Register

Bute Docks Co. (No. 136) – see Cardiff Railway Co. (No. 148) in this Appendix

Caledonian Railway Co. (No. 138)

Scot RO Reference	Dates	Description
BR/CAL/4/1 & 2	1908 to 1911	Returns of Staff, Emoluments and Duties
48	1919 to 1921	Salaries and Wages Staff Agreements
49	1900 to 1923	Salaried Staff Retirements (Extracts of Minutes, etc.)
50	1911	Salaried Clerical Staff
56A & 56B	1900	Photographs of Officers
153 to 155	1907 to 1919	Registers of Accidents to Company's Servants, Compensation, etc.
163	1900	Photographs of Officers
BR/CAL/5/17	1846 to 1895	List of Locomotive Superintendents

Cont.

Caledonian Railway Co. (continued)

Scot RO Reference	Dates	Description
BR/CAL/74	1914	Memorial from Clerical Staff re salaries
5	1916	Memorial from Clerical Staff re increased cost of living
BR/CAL/15/9 to 11	1901 to 1907	Traffic Dept Staff, hours and wages
14	1904 to 1920	Staff Emoluments and Duties
15	1920 to 1923	Staff and Emoluments
16	1923	Casualties and Offences Letter Book
17	1892 to 1932	Individual Staff Histories
		Notes: 1. Records dated from 1923 relate to LMS
		2. There are also other records which relate specifically to Scottish regions

Cambrian Railways Co. (No. 141)

TNA Reference Class	Piece No.	Dates	Description
RAIL 92	136	1909	Group Photographs of Oswestry Works Staff (includes names)
	140	1892	Newspaper cuttings regarding the wrongful dismissal of John Hood, Station Master
	142	1898 to 1922	Staff Register: Locomotive Dept.
	143	1915 to 1944	Medical Examination Book, Traffic Dept.
	144	1904 to 1913	Register of Staff Promotions and Tranfers
	145	c. 1870 to 1922	Outdoor Staff: Goods Dept.
	146	c. 1870 to 1922	Uniformed Station Staff
	147 & 148	1898 to 1922	Registers of Accidents to Staff on Duty
RAIL 1057	1868	1911 to 1922	Staff Pensions (includes names)
	1995/1 to 1995/117	1913 to 1922	Accidents to Employees (Class List at PRO includes names of employees)
	2710	1914 to 1918	List of Railwaymen killed in First World War
Ches RO Reference			
NPR2/25 to 27		c. 1865 to 1945	Staff registers
			Note: Records in this class dating from 1923 relate to the GWR

Cardiff Railway Co. Previously the Bute Docks Co. (No. 136)

TNA Reference Class	Piece No.	Dates	Description
RAIL 97	32	1880 to 1922	Engineer's Dept.
	33	1871 to 1922	Clerical Staff
	34	1870 to 1922	Supervisory Staff
	35 & 36	1867 to 1922	General Staff
	37 to 43	1908 to 1923	Accidents
			Accident Claims
RAIL 1057	1266	1910 to 1911	Daniel Barry
	1268	1916	Arthur Bates
	1269	1916 to 1917	Sidney Barnett (fatal)
	1272	1892 to 1899	William Collins
	1279	1899	William Davies
	1285	1913	Eli England
	1286	1913	Morgan Eliott
	1288	1918	Charles Edwards
	1289	1916	J.R. Evans
	1290	1921 to 1922	Benjamin Evans
	1297	1909	Mrs Nellie Gill
	1298	1912 to 1913	David Gash
	1309	1909 to 1910	Henry Hobbs (fatal)
	1310	1896	Thomas Jenkins (fatal)
	1381/3	1913	Henry Roe, chief engineer's resignation
	2710	1914 to 1918	List of Railwaymen killed in First World War

Carmarthen and Cardigan Railway Co. (No. 150)

TNA Reference Class	Piece No.	Dates	Description
RAIL 99	57 to 60	1869 to 1875	Vouchers with Wage Lists (includes names)

Central London Railway Co. (No. 158)

LMA Reference	Dates	Description
Acc 1297/CLR4/1	1892 to 1903	Henry Tennant's papers (Henry Tennant was General Manager, later Director of the North Eastern Railway Co., and Chairman of the Central London Railway Co.)

Chester and Holyhead Railway Co. (No. 177)

TNA Reference		Dates	Description
Class	Piece No.		
RAIL 1057	2857	*c.* 1856	List of Staff

Cleator and Workington Junction Railway Co. (No. 187)

TNA Reference		Dates	Description
Class	Piece No.		
RAIL 119	13	1879 to 1923	Staff Register: Traffic Dept.
RAIL 1057	2710	1914 to 1918	List of Railwaymen killed in First World War

Cleobury Mortimer and Ditton Priors Light Railway Co. (No. 188)

TNA Reference		Dates	Description
Class	Piece No.		
RAIL 1057	410/2	1908 to 1919	Staff Matters, List of Staff, applications for wage increases, etc.

Cockermouth, Keswick and Penrith Railway Co. (No. 192)

TNA Reference		Dates	Description
Class	Piece No.		
RAIL 1057	2710	1914 to 1918	List of Railwaymen killed in First World War

Colne Valley and Halstead Railway Co. (No. 197)

TNA Reference		Dates	Description
Class	Piece No.		
RAIL 1057	2710	1914 to 1918	List of Railwaymen killed in First World War
	2747	1904 to 1924	Register of Accidents (includes names)

Cornwall Railway Co. (No. 202)

TNA Reference		Dates	Description
Class	Piece No.		
RAIL 134	40	1889	Amalgamation with the GWR giving lists of staff
	54	1860s	Form of Application for appointment as clerk or salaried officer
	55	1864	Security bond for employment of Thomas Stephens

TNA Reference Class	Piece No.	Dates	Description
RAIL 134 (cont.)	60	1859	Memorial on behalf of John Melhuish for situation as guard or clerk
	62	1871	Protest by Inhabitants of St. Austell regarding the dismissal of W. Tucker, railway policeman and attendant
	79	1854 to 1889	Miscellaneous papers (includes staff applications)
Brun/Cl Reference			
HE 3017.S68		1873, 1874	Establishment Reports (Lists of staff arranged by stations)
Wilts RO Reference			
(no ref)		1847 to 1889	Probate Register

Cowbridge Railway Co. (No. 208)

TNA Reference Class	Piece No.	Dates	Description
RAIL 1057	1834	1872	Historical file (f. 12. staff pay (gangers, cleaners, etc.))

Dulas Valley Mineral Railway Co. (No. 237) – see Neath and Brecon Railway Co. (No. 602) in this Appendix

Easingwold Railway Co. (No. 244)

TNA Reference Class	Piece No.	Dates	Description
RAIL 1057	2710	1914 to 1918	List of Railwaymen killed in First World War

East and West India Docks and Birmingham Junction Railway Co. (No. 245) – see North London Railway Co. (No. 628) in this Appendix

East and West Junction Railway Co. (No. 246)

TNA Reference Class	Piece No.	Dates	Description
RAIL 674	11	1873 to 1908	Staff Register Note: Entries from 1909, include staff for the Stratford-upon-Avon and Midland Junction Railway Co.

East and West Yorkshire Union Railways Co. (No. 248)

TNA Reference Class	Piece No.	Dates	Description
RAIL 1057	2710	1914 to 1918	List of Railwaymen killed in First World War

East Kent Railway Co. (No. 255) – see London, Chatham and Dover Railway Co. (No. 500) in this Appendix

East Lincolnshire Railway Co. (No. 257)

TNA Reference Class	Piece No.	Dates	Description
RAIL 177	21	1848 to 1850	Pay Lists for Permanent Way Staff at various stations, workmen engaged on construction of the line, railway police, etc.

Eastern Counties Railway Co. (No. 265)

TNA Reference Class	Piece No.	Dates	Description
RAIL 186	99	1844	Diary and Expenses Book of Mr James Beadel, surveyor
	100	1851 to 1901	History of George How and the number of accidents in which he was involved (with other documents)
	105	1851 to 1857	Occupations and Rates of Pay of Men employed at Stafford Works
	109 & 110	1856	Posters naming persons convicted of evasion of fares
RAIL 1016	1/64	1850	List of engine drivers and firemen who resigned their situations 12 August 1850
RAIL 1021	11/13	1850	ditto

Eden Valley Railway Co. (No. 270)

TNA Reference Class	Piece No.	Dates	Description
RAIL 189	12	1858	Paybill ledger (contractors only)

Exeter Railway Co. (No. 294)

TNA Reference		Dates	Description
Class	Piece No.		
RAIL 1057	178/3	1903	Station Masters' House Applications (G.A. Haywood, C. Kemp and J. Hill)

Felixstowe Railway and Dock Co. (No. 298)

TNA Reference		Dates	Description
Class	Piece No.		
RAIL 1057	2710	1914 to 1918	List of Railwaymen killed in First World War

Festiniog and Blaenau Railway Co. (No. 300)

TNA Reference		Dates	Description
Class	Piece No.		
RAIL 205	1	1876 to 1883	Accountant's Vouchers (includes wage lists with names of staff)

Festiniog Railway Co. (No. 301)

TNA Reference		Dates	Description
Class	Piece No.		
RAIL 1057	2846/10	*c.* 1930	Photograph of Woman Station master [Bessie Jones] at Tan-y-Bwlch

Forcett Railway Co. (No. 306)

TNA Reference		Dates	Description
Class	Piece No.		
RAIL 208	8 to 13	1877 to 1922	Paybill Abstracts (includes some names)

Freshwater, Yarmouth and Newport Railway Co. (No. 310)

TNA Reference		Dates	Description
Class	Piece No.		
RAIL 1057	2710	1914 to 1918	List of Railwaymen killed in First World War

Furness Railway Co. (No. 313)

TNA Reference Class	Piece No.	Dates	Description
RAIL 214	97 to 101	1867 to 1901	Staff Registers – Traffic Dept.
	102 & 103	1852 to 1902	Staff Registers
	106 to 110	1898 to 1923	Engineer's Record Books
RAIL 1057	2710	1914 to 1918	List of Railwaymen killed in First World War

Glasgow and South Western Railway Co. (No. 317)

Scot RO Reference	Dates	Description
GD422/1/89	1874 to 1922	Register of Uniformed Staff
BR/GSW/15/1	1912	Clerical Staff Salary Scales and Classification of Offices and Stations
		Note: There are other staff records which relate only to Scotland

Grand Junction Railway Co. (No. 330)

TNA Reference Class	Piece No.	Dates	Description
RAIL 1021	8/24	1810 to 1886	Notes re Nathaniel Worsdell Superintendent of Carriage Department

Great Central Railway Co. (No. 335) – see also Manchester, Sheffield and Lincolnshire Railway Co. (No. 541)

TNA Reference Class	Piece No.	Dates	Description
RAIL 226	178 & 179	1893 to 1915	Labourers' Houses, Loughborough, with plans (tenants not named)
	193 to 195	1857 to 1923	Staff Books, Secretary's Office
	196	1882 to 1920	Register of Officers
	197	c. 1915 to 1923	Staff Record Book, Sack Depot at Grimsby

TNA Reference			
Class	Piece No.	Dates	Description
RAIL 226	198	1899 to 1946	Staff History Book, Goods Dept., Leicester
(cont.)	199	1872 to 1949	Staff Register, Goods Dept., Leicester
			The following Staff Records are arranged by Employees' Staff Numbers and have name indices
	200 to 225	1899 to 1926	5743 to 11397 Index
	226	1 January 1910	Staff Register
	227	1919 to 1927	Staff Register, Audit Accountants'
			Registers of Staff at Joint Agencies
	228 229	1897 to 1906	207 to 456 Index
	230 231 232	1906 to 1922 1921 to 1925	457 to 850 Index
	233		Index
	234	1867 to 1920	Register of Officers, Assistant Officers and Chief Officers
	386	1898 to 1904	Workmen's and passengers' Compensation Claims (names not included)
	401	1899 to 1905	Competition for Railway Ambulance Shield (includes names of staff in winning teams)
	404	1900	Dismissal of Shop Foremen of Gorton (William Kilshaw and John Taylor)
	508	1906 to 1920	Clerical Staff aged 60 or over, for Retirement or Retention
RAIL 1174	213	1906 to 1920	Pension Fund Voucher Book (lists of contributors)
	276 to 280	1943 to 1971	Friendly Society Accident and Pension Fund; Probate Registers

Great Eastern Railway Co. (No. 336)

TNA Reference			
Class	Piece No.	Dates	Description
RAIL 227	342	1892 to 1894	Misdemeanours and Punishments. Bishopsgate Station
	363	1910	Retirement Presentation, John Wilson, Chief Engineer
	371	1888 to 1919	Staff Lists, Sack Dept.
	376	c. 1899 to 1910	Photographs, J. Gooday, General Manager, H.G. Drury, Superintendent of Line and J. Holden, Locomotive Superintendent

Cont.

Great Eastern Railway (continued)

Class	Piece No.	Dates	Description
RAIL 227 (cont.)	445	1914	Staff Details, Locomotive, Carriage and Wagon Dept.
	446	c. 1870 to 1922	Staff Record Book, Sack Superintendent's Dept.
	447	1860 to 1918	Staff Register, Clerical
	448	1870 to 1913	Staff Contract Register, Audit Dept.
	449	1870 to 1919	Staff Register of Officers' and Clerks' Salaries
			Histories of Salaried Staff (Arranged by Staff Number) Superintendent's Dept.
	450 to 455	1855 to 1923	1 to 3000
			Goods Dept.
	456 & 457	1868 to 1923	1 to 1000
			Passenger Dept.
	458	1875 to 1917	2001 to 2500
			Histories of Wages Staff (arranged by Staff Number) Traffic Dept.
	459 to 479	1859 to 1925	1 to 11000
			Goods Dept.
	480 to 486	1872 to 1930	1 to 3500
	487	1858 to 1903	Register of Goods Staff, Clerical and Wages, Bishopsgate
	509	1893	Photograph, Chairman, General Manager, Secretary and Delegates of Pension Fund
	510	1894	Photograph, Chairman, General Manager, Members of Management, Secretary and Delegates of Pension Fund
	511	c. 1913	Photographs, Liverpool Street Station Swimming Club
	514 to 520	1904 to 1921	Wages Staff, Historic Registers; drivers and firemen
	521		Index
	522 to 532	1876 to 1950	Awards and Cautions, Works and Locomotive Staff (alphabetical)
	533 & 534	1866 to 1936	Staff Register, Temple Mills Wagon Shop
	535	1853 to 1911	Staff Register, Locomotive and Wagon Shop No. 1
	540	1877 to 1930	Staff Register, Carriage Workshop
	541	1903 to 1922	Accident Book, all Grades

TNA Reference			
Class	Piece No.	Dates	Description
RAIL 227	542	1942 to 1946	Staff Alterations, all Depots
(cont.)	543	1875 to 1958	Staff Register, Stratford, Carriage and Wagon Engineers
	544	1879 to 1940	Staff Register, Stratford, Accountants, Chief Mechanical Engineers, Locomotive Running Superintendent, Chemist etc.
	545 & 546	1886 to 1954	Staff Register, Chief Mechanical Engineer's Dept.
RAIL 463	217 to 221	1847 to 1926	Staff Registers; Audit Dept. (These were once believed to be for Manchester, Sheffield and Lincolnshire Railway Co.)
RAIL 1016	1/42	1891	Certificate of membership of pension fund
RAIL 1021	8/24	1881	Note re Thomas William Worsdell, Works Manager, Crewe
RAIL 1057	2710	1914 to 1918	List of Railwaymen killed in First World War
Suf RO (no reference)		20th century	Various photographs of Staff
			Note: Records from 1923 relate to the LNER Records from 1948 relate to British Railways

Great North of England Railway Co. (No. 340)

TNA Reference			
Class	Piece No.	Dates	Description
RAIL 232	54 & 55	1840 to 1847	Paybill Books (includes Wages Lists with names)

Great Northern Railway Co. (No. 347)

TNA Reference			
Class	Piece No.	Dates	Description
RAIL 236	727	c. 1861 to 1924	Sack Dept. Staff Register (indexed)
	728	1910 to 1925	Staff Sickness Register (indexed)
	729	1862 to 1943	Locomotive Dept. Register of Salaried Staff (indexed)
	730	1862 to 1913	Register of Office Staff (indexed)
	731	1903 to 1916	Hours and Pay of Drivers and Firemen
	732	1915	Unfair Promotion at Bradford. C. Dalby, cleaner to fireman.

Cont.

Great Northern Railway Co. (continued)

TNA Reference			
Class	Piece No.	Dates	Description
RAIL 236 (cont.)	732		A. Panter, cleaner to fireman
			Staff Histories of Engine Drivers and Firemen (arranged by Staff Number)
	733	1848 to 1919	3 to 402 Leeds District
	734	1882 to 1919	403 to 592 Leeds District
	735	1894 to 1924	1 to 400 Leeds District
	736	1883 to 1924	401 to 697 Leeds District
	737	1894 to 1924	Index
	738 & 739	1848 to 1924	Seniority Books of Drivers and Firemen at Leeds, Ardsley, Bradford, Ingrow and Holmfield
	740	1879 to 1919	Register of Cleaners and Firemen recommended for promotion
	741	1889 to 1926	Register of New Entrants to the Locomotive Dept., Leeds District
			Superintendent's Office
	742 to 744	1865 to 1912	Registers of Clerks
	745	1886 to 1920	Register of Clerks' commencing dates. Includes Army Reserve List
RAIL 393	225 & 226	1897 to 1927	Station Master's Staff Books, Gainsborough. Refers to named staff, accidents, attendance, transfers, etc.
RAIL 783	331	1906 to 1908	Superannuation Fund (includes names)
	383	1911 to 1921	Female staff: Kings Cross, Farringdon Street, Peterborough, Nottingham Goods, Bradford Goods, Leeds Goods, Manchester D.M.O.
	384 to 387	1915 to 1920	War Bonus. Lists of staff
	394	1917 to 1918	Application for Doncaster District wage rates (includes names of some union representatives and some workmen)
	395	1916 to 1919	Farrier's and saddler's short working week. General correspondence (names not included)
	396	1919 to 1921	Holidays. General correspondence (name not included)
	397	1919	Holidays (includes some names)
	398	1920 to 1921	Public holidays. Staff arrangements (names not included)
	33/24	*c.* 1905	Photograph, Doncaster Staff
	33/25	*c.* 1909	Photograph, Doncaster Staff
RAIL 1016	1/38	*c.* 1895	Letter from Duchess of Rutland to Station Master at Bottesford re omission of gratuity
RAIL 1057	2710	1914 to 1918	List of Railwaymen killed in First World War
RAIL 1150	1	1841 to 1896	Francis Pickersgill Cockshott, Superintendent

| TNA Reference | | Dates | Description |
Class	Piece No.		
RAIL 1172	90	1920	Sack Dept., Boston. Shed Staff. A. A. Mitcham, Supt. Foreman H. White, porter; G. Lockwood, cutter; William Mitcham, labourer; H. Dickenson, labourer; N. Hooper, messenger
RAIL 1174	305 to 309	1937 to 1970	Sick and Funeral Allowance Fund and Register of Probates (includes date of marriage and name of spouse, dates of death and executors)
			Note: Records from 1923 relate to the LNER

Hampstead Junction Railway Co. (No. 369)

| TNA Reference | | Dates | Description |
Class	Piece No.		
RAIL 291	6	1857 to 1859	Check Time Book (names not included)
	7	1857 to 1860	Pay Book (contractors' employees)

Hartlepool Dock and Railway Co. (No. 376)

| TNA Reference | | Dates | Description |
Class	Piece No.		
RAIL 294	48 to 50	1832 to 1842	Wages lists

Hull and Holderness Railway Co. (No. 407)

| TNA Reference | | Dates | Description |
Class	Piece No.		
RAIL 313	22	1859 to 1860	Fortnightly Wages Lists (includes names)

Hull and Selby Railway Co. (No. 409)

| TNA Reference | | Dates | Description |
Class	Piece No.		
RAIL 315	30	1845 to 1875	Staff Register

Hull, Barnsley and West Riding Junction Railway and Dock Co. (No. 411) Re-named the Hull and Barnsley Railway Co. 30 June 1905

TNA Reference Class	Piece No.	Dates	Description
RAIL 312	77	1885 to 1922	Register of Traffic Dept.: Uniformed Staff
	78	1890 to 1925	Register of Permanent Staff, Goods and Docks Depts
	79	1913 to 1921	Files of Wages Statements (Summary accounts. Includes names of a few senior staff only)
	80	1900 to 1927	Register of Engine Drivers and Firemen with Rates of Pay
	81	1885 to 1927	Register of Engine Drivers and Firemen with Commendations and Punishments. Indexed
	130	1911	Appointment of Special Constables, Alexandra Dock (includes names)
	140 to 172	1875 to 1931	Diaries kept by Matthew Stirling, Locomotive Superintendent
RAIL 1057	2710	1914 to 1918	List of Railwaymen killed in First World War
			Note: Records from 1923 are for the LNER

Isle of Wight Central Railway Co. (No. 422)

TNA Reference Class	Piece No.	Dates	Description
RAIL 328	18	1860 to 1915	Staff Register
RAIL 1057	2710	1914 to 1918	List of Railwaymen killed in First World War

Isle of Wight Railway Co. (No. 424)

TNA Reference Class	Piece No.	Dates	Description
RAIL 328	16	1864 to 1915	Staff Register
	17	1884 to 1923	Staff Register
RAIL 1057	2710	1914 to 1918	List of Railwaymen killed in First World War

Knott End Railway Co. (No. 442)

TNA Reference Class	Piece No.	Dates	Description
RAIL 1057	2710	1914 to 1918	List of Railwaymen killed in First World War

Lancashire and Yorkshire Railway Co. (No. 448)

TNA Reference Class	Piece No.	Dates	Description
RAIL 343	722	1851	Officer's Notebook (includes List of Officers for 1850)
	725	1917	Photograph, Chief Mechanical Engineer's Dept., female workers
	755	1915	Roll of Honour of Men of Various Depts who joined the Forces 1914 to 1915
	827 & 828	1903 to 1912	Pay Lists, Accountant's Dept.
	829 & 830	1908 to 1921	Pay Lists, Officers' Salaries
	831 to 833	1913 to 1919	Pay Lists, Chief Cashier's Dept.
	834	1917 to 1921	Pay Lists, Chief Goods Manager's Personal Staff
	835 & 836	1903 to 1911	Pay Lists, Chief Traffic Manager's Officers
	837	1922 to 1924	Pay Lists, Divisional Accountant's Officers
	838	1903 to 1905	Pay Lists, Secretary's Officers
	839 & 840	1919 to 1922	Pay Lists, Superintendent of Line, Officers
	841	1922 to 1923	Pay Lists, General Superintendent's Officers
	842	1915 to 1921	Salary Advances of Officials and Supervisory Staff of Traffic Dept., etc.
	843	1887 to 1927	Register of Drivers and Firemen
	844	1863 to 1941	Register of Back-up Locomotive Dept.
	845	1853 to 1872	Hindley Station Staff Time Book
	901	1919	Carriage Cleaner, Alice Gould killed at Manchester. Enquiry into accident
			Note: Records in this Class for 1922 are for the London and North Western Railway Co. Records from 1923 are for the LMS
RAIL 623	67 68	1862 to 1897 Index	Staff Register (with Shropshire Union Railways and Canal Co.)
RAIL 1057	2710	1914 to 1918	List of Railwaymen killed in First World War
G Man RO Reference			
A18		*c.* 1880 to *c.* 1920	Horwich Works, Staff History Cards
A18/1/1/to 41		1898 to 1935	Horwich Works, Accident Registers
A18/1/4 1 to 7		1898 to 1935	Horwich Works, Accident Correspondence

Lancashire, Derbyshire and East Coast Railway Co. (No. 449)

TNA Reference			
Class	Piece No.	Dates	Description
RAIL 344	56	1904 to 1906	Appointment of Mr Harry Wilmott as General Manager and Chief Officer

Leeds and Thirsk Railway Co. (No. 459). Re-named the Leeds Northern Railway Co. 3 July 1851

TNA Reference			
Class	Piece No.	Dates	Description
RAIL 357	29	1847 to 1858	Wages Book for Bramhope Contract, Inspector's Dept. and Wellington Street, Goods Dept.
	33	1850 to 1853	List of Staff and Incomes
	35	1852	Memorandum Book of Henry Tennant, Traffic Superintendent. (This item is actually recorded for the Leeds and Thirsk Railway though it had already been re-named the Leeds Northern Railway by the time it was written)
	36	1845 to 1846	Time Book, Bramhope Contract (names with signatures)
	37	1846	Time Book, Pannal Contract (names with signatures)
	38	1846 to 1849	General Time Book (names with signatures)
	39 & 40	1847 to 1849	Time Books, Police (includes names)

Leeds Northern Railway Co. – see Leeds and Thirsk Railway Co. (No. 459) in this Appendix

Liverpool and Manchester Railway Co. (No. 474)

TNA Reference			
Class	Piece No.	Dates	Description
RAIL 371	23	1839 to 1845	Lists of Salaries with earlier Salary Receipts
RAIL 1021	8/24	1810 to 1886	Notes re Nathaniel Worsdell
		1818 to 1893	Thomas Worsdell
		1821 to 1912	George Worsdell
		1838 to 1916	Thomas William Worsdell
			All sons of T. C. Worsdell, Superintendent Carriage Builder

Llanelly Railway and Dock Co. (No. 482)

TNA Reference			
Class	Piece No.	Dates	Description
RAIL 377	30	1873	Staff Lists

London and Birmingham Railway Co. (No. 489)

TNA Reference Class	Piece No.	Dates	Description
RAIL 384	204 & 205	1835 to 1836	Men employed, London and Birmingham Divisions (names of contractors only)
	258	1833 to 1848	Establishment Papers (staff regulations)
	261	1835	Watford Tunnel Accident, names of men killed
	284	1833 to 1846	Salaries Register
	285 to 287	1838 to 1847	Registers of Permanent Officers and Servants
	288 & 289		Index to above Registers
	290	1840	Regulations approved by the Board for future Salaries and Promotions of Clerks in the several Depts
	291	1834	Company Establishment, London Office: Report (includes list of staff)
RAIL 1007	234	1838	Tombstone inscription of Thomas Port (son of John Port) of Burton-upon-Trent, who had both legs severed in train accident
RAIL 1008	99	1837 to 1884	John Brand, porter, Birmingham, dismissed for accepting gratuity

London and North Western Railway Co. (No. 496)

TNA Reference Class	Piece No.	Dates	Description
RAIL 410	1797 to 1799	1850 to 1901	Staff, Coaching, Traffic and Police Depts
	1800	1902 to 1910	Staff, Coaching Dept.
	1801	1902 to 1910	Staff of Traffic, Police and Telegraph Depts, (includes Staff of the Joint Company with the Ashby and Nuneaton Railway)
	1802	1875 to 1911	Staff, Coaching and Police Depts
	1803 & 1804	1894 to 1910	Staff, Coaching, Police and Traffic Depts
	1805 to 1808	1837 to 1893	Staff Registers
	1809 & 1810	1903 to 1923	Staff Records, Superintendent of Line, Euston and Crewe
	1811	1852 to 1923	Staff, Rolling Stock Section, Crewe

Cont.

London and North Western Railway Co. (continued)

TNA Reference Class	Piece No.	Dates	Description
RAIL 410 (cont.)	1812 & 1813	1861 to 1896	Staff, Superintendent's Dept.
	1814 & 1815	1861 to 1914	Staff Registers, Northampton: Coaching, Police and Traffic Depts
	1816 to 1822	1895 to 1924	Caution Books
	1823	1894 to 1899	Punishments Book
	1824 & 1825	1899 to 1922	Suspension Books
	1826 & 1827	1898 to 1911	Cautions and Suspension Books
	1828	1876 to 1923	Guards
	1829	1887 to 1923	Conditions of Service: Retiring Allowances, Scales of Pay and General Staff Matters
	1830	1877 to 1881	Staff, London Road, Manchester
	1831	1865 to 1920	Staff, Broad Street
	1832 & 1833	1872 to 1915	Police Dept.: Discipline Books
	1834	1854 to 1922	Staff, Bushbury Motive Power Depot
	1835	1897 to 1922	Staff Register, Birmingham New Street
	1836	1911 to 1922	Staff Punishment Book, Birmingham New Street
	1837	1845 to 1878	Salaried Officers, Goods Dept.
	1838 to 1843	1851 to 1918	Salaried Staff Registers, Goods Dept.
	1844 to 1847	1839 to 1917	Salaried Staff Registers, Coaching Dept.
	1848 to 1850	1840 to 1918	Salaried Staff Registers
	1851 to 1853		Indexes to Salaried Staff Registers
	1854	1838 to 1878	Permanent Salaried Officers
	1855 to 1860	1833 to 1878	Permanent Officers and Servants
	1861	1855 to 1917	Permanent Officers and Servants, including Staff on North London, and North and South Western Junction Railway Companies' Stations
	1862	1848 to 1862	Permanent Officers and Servants, including Staff transferred from Chester and Holyhead, and Lancaster and Carlisle Railways

TNA Reference			
Class	Piece No.	Dates	Description
RAIL 410 (cont.)	1863 to 1868		Indexes to Registers of Permanent Officers and Servants
	1869	1832 to 1856	Salaried Offcers, Southern Division
	1870	1838 to 1856	Salaried Officers, North Eastern Division
	1871	1831 to 1863	Salaried Officers
	1872	Index	
	1873	1868 to 1903	Staff Register
	1874	1864 to 1907	Staff Book
	1875	1914 to 1921	Salaries, Hotels and Refreshment Rooms (lists of grades at various stations, sometimes including names)
	1876 to 1884	1830 to 1927	Salaries Alteration Books
	1885	1915 to 1922	Wages Alteration Book
	1886	1921 to 1922	Staff in Hotels, Refreshment Rooms and Laundry; Alteration Books
	1887 & 1888		Indexes to Registers of Salaried Officers (Audit Dept.) Registers missing
	1889	1897 to 1922	Allowances and Gratuities to Salaried Staff £500 per annum and over
	1890 & 1891	1877 to 1921	Salaried Staff Record Cards
	1892	1882 to 1926	Wages Staff Record Cards
	1893	1900 to 1923	LNW Guarantee Fund: Papers and Forms
	1894	1918 to 1924	National Health Insurance Acts: Papers
	1895	1920 to 1921	National Unemployment Insurance: Papers
	1896	1919	Special Instructions for Bonus Payments to Staff during Railway Strike
	1897	1921	List of Staff with present and proposed positions on the Amalgamation of the LNW and the Lancashire and Yorkshire Railway from 1 January 1922
	1898	1918 to 1919	Classification of Male and Female Clerical Staff, Station Masters, Goods Agents, etc.
	1899	1915 to 1920	War Bonuses and War Wages
	1900 & 1901	1866 to 1878	Salary Payment Books, Northampton District
	1902 & 1903	1917 to 1920	Staff Engagement Agreements: Nos 14751 to 15292
	1904	c. 1862 to 1905	Staff, Camden Goods Station
	1905 to 1970 and 2213 to 2222	1854 to 1930	Staff Registers, Crewe Works

Cont.

London and North Western Railway Co. (continued)

TNA Reference Class	Piece No.	Dates	Description
RAIL 410	1971	1847 to 1927	Staff, Chester Locomotive Shed
(cont.)	1972	1865 to 1888	Register of Fines
	1973 to 1976	1869 to 1920	Supervisory and Clerical Staff, Liverpool Goods Depot
	1977	1879 to 1926	Supervisory and Clerical Staff at Liverpool Goods Depot formerly of Lancashire and Yorkshire Railway
	1978	1873 to 1926	Supervisory and Clerical Staff at Liverpool Goods Depot formerly of Midland Railway
	1979 & 1980	1869 to 1926	Clerical Staff at Liverpool Goods Depots 'Unappointed' (dismissed or resigned)
	1981	1872 to 1925	Clerical and Wages Staff, Brunswick Goods Station
	1982	1877 to 1929	Wages Staff, Alexandra Dock Goods Station
	1985	c. 1880 to 1912	Staff, Carriage and Goods Depts at Broad Street and Shoreditch
	1986	1869	Returns of Accident Pay
	2212	1853 to 1903	Staff, Longsight Shops
RAIL 623	67	1886 to 1897	Staff Register (in Shropshire Union Railways and Canal Co. Staff Register)
	68		Index
RAIL 1007	609	1857	Apprenticeship Indenture, T.A. Peterkin
RAIL 1057	2710	1914 to 1918	List of Railwaymen killed in First World War
RAIL 1015	2		Roll of Honour of men in First World War granted Distinguished Conduct Medal and mentioned in dispatches
Ches RO Reference			
NPR 1/14		1891 to 1910	Staff Rates of Pay, Running Dept.
NPR2/10 & NPR2/11		c. 1875 to 1913	Staff Registers
NPR2/12		1908	Goods Staff, Holyhead
Leic RO Reference			
Misc.122			Letters regarding the Appointment of A. J. Higginson as Assistant Porter at Stirchley
Staf RO Reference			
D1225		19th century	Stafford Station, Staff Register
Ang RO Reference			
WM 363		1898 to 1927	Holyhead Staff Register

London and South Western Railway Co. (No. 497)

TNA Reference Class	Piece No.	Dates	Description
RAIL 411	413	1910	Staff, Chief Mechanical Engineer's Dept.
	418	[c. 1930]	Staff, Equipment, Engines, etc., at Eastleigh (staff named)
	423	1860 to 1869	General Instructions to Staff at Liss Station
	424	1891 to 1906	General Instructions to Staff at Farnborough
	433	1896	Notice of Instructions to signalmen at Semley Station
	483	1887 to 1897	Staff Register, Devonport
	484	1889 to 1907	Staff Register, Godalming
	485	1865 to 1866	Staff Pay Book, Exeter Goods Dept.
	486 to 490	c. 1889 to 1944	Black Book – Cautions and Commendations to Enginemen
	491 to 497	1838 to 1921	Clerical Staff Character Books
	498	1865 to 1925	Staff Register, Agents (includes Station Masters)
	499 to 502	1841 to 1924	Salaried Staff Registers
	503	1913	Index to Staff Registers
	504 & 505	1873 to 1924	Clerical Staff Registers
	506	1915 to 1924	Clerical Staff Registers – Female
	507 to 516	1861 to 1927	Registers of Wages Staff
	517 to 519	1866 to 1924	Staff Registers – Goods Dept.
	520	1886 to 1920	Salaried Staff Register, Nine Elms
	521	1889 to 1896	Black Book – Fines to Drivers and Firemen
	522 & 523	1870 to 1924	Staff Registers: Locomotive Dept.
	524 to 526 and 528 to 530	1844 to 1894	Staff Registers: Various Locomotive and Carriage and Wagon Depots
	527		Index to part of above
	574	1865 to 1866	Expenses (f535) Income Tax; List of Clerks
	665	1842 to 1920	Staff Register, Nine Elms Locomotive Dept.
	666	1871 to 1929	Staff Register, Shed and Shop, Locomotive Dept.
	667	1903 to 1917	Register of Workmen, Locomotive Dept.

Cont.

London and South Western Railway Co. (continued)

TNA Reference Class	Piece No.	Dates	Description
RAIL 1017	1/34	1889	Petition to Board for better conditions. Senior clerks Nine Elms Station (93 names)
	1/156	1895	Group photograph of Station staff at Byfleet
RAIL 1057	2710	1914 to 1918	List of Railwaymen killed in First World War
Dev RO Reference			
328OB/A6		1899 to 1925	Time Book (includes names)
328OB/A2		1904 to 1908	Wages Book
328OB/A3		1924 to 1925	Wages Book

London, Brighton and South Coast Railway Co. (No. 499)

TNA Reference Class	Piece No.	Dates	Description
RAIL 414	234	1850	Increase of Salaries to Principal Officers
	527 to 532 and 551 to 553	1849 to 1920	Instruction to Staff
	554		Various Documents (includes Lists of Staff)
	565	1867	Strike: Printed Statements of Men
	569	1868	Returns of Staff – All Depts
	572 & 573	1870 to 1888	Salaries Payable to the Staff of the Locomotive and Carriage Depts
	574	1921 to 1928	Appropriation of Salaries, Wages, etc.
	600 to 611	1872 to 1934	Changes of Staff, with Rates of Pay, Locomotive and Carriage Depts
	625 & 626	1914 to 1940	Staff with Rates of Pay, Carriage Dept.
	627 & 628	1934 to 1943	Staff with Rates of Pay, Locomotive Dept. (Southern Railway, Central Section)
	630 to 632	1901 to 1921	Engine cleaners passed as firemen, and firemen passed as drivers
	636	1889 to 1924	Staff absent from duty, Locomotive Dept.
	644	1851 to 1923	Benevolent and Pension Funds. (Notices with names)
	648	1910	Album presented to Chief Traffic Inspector H. Etherington

TNA Reference			
Class	Piece No.	Dates	Description
RAIL 414	750	1899 to 1904	Workmen's Compensation Scheme – Annual Returns
(cont.)	751	1866 to 1876	List of Apprentices
	752	1882 to 1908	Staff in Locomotive Superintendent's Dept.
	753 & 754	1873 to 1874 and 1882	Applications for employment (Locomotive and Carriage Dept., Brighton Works)
	755	1875	Applications for Employment (Locomotive and Carriage Dept., Brighton Works)
	756 & 757	1892 to 1902	Names of Staff claiming benefit under Workmen's Compensation Scheme, Brighton Works, Book 1
	758	1909 to 1922	Memoranda of meetings held between the Locomotive Engineer and Delegates appointed by the Staff
	759	1862 to 1863	Names, offences, punishments etc. of various members of operating staff (black book)
	760 to 762	1858 to 1913	Registers of Appointments
	763 to 766	1871 to 1891	Registers of Staff in All Depts (with salary or wages)
	767	1856	Traffic Staff Histories based on questionnaire and relating to staff appointed 1836–1854
	768 & 769	1836 to 1902	Registers of Salaried Staff appointed
	770 to 784	1837 to 1921	Traffic Staff: Registers of Appointments (indexed)
	785	1852 to 1905	Portsmouth Joint Staff
	786	1854 to 1905	Staff Register, Willow Walk & Newhaven Harbour
	787 & 788	1854 to 1922	Staff Registers, Willow Walk & Newhaven Harbour and Portsmouth Joint Staff
	789	1855 to 1923	Register of Portsmouth Joint Staff appointed
	790	1873 to 1925	Register of Clerical Staff appointed 1873–1923
	791 & 792	1914 to 1920	Register of Staff of All Depts on active service during the First World War Index
	793	2 Dec 1885	Indenture of Apprenticeship for Percival Gordon Gay
	794	15 Nov 1875	Indenture of Apprenticeship for John Wm Geering
	863 to 872	1854 to 1936	Staff Histories, Locomotive Dept.
	873	1911	Workmen's Compensation Cases – indexed
RAIL 1057	2710	1914 to 1918	List of Railwaymen killed in First World War
			Note: Records from 1923 refer to the Southern Railway

London, Chatham and Dover Railway Co. (No. 500). Previously the East Kent Railway Co. (No. 255)

TNA Reference			
Class	Piece No.	Dates	Description
RAIL 415	104	c. 1859 to 1910	Staff, Secretary's Dept., Audit Office
	108	1880 to 1891	Register of Injuries to Workmen
	109 ⎫		Registers of Staff, Longhedge, Blackfriars, Victoria,
	& ⎬	1860 to 1918	Beckenham, Bickley, Sevenoaks, Farningham,
	110 ⎭		Canterbury, Herne Hill, Sheerness, Chatham,
			Faversham, Margate, Maidstone, Dover
	173	1898	Staff List, Locomotive, Carriage and Marine
			Depts

London Electric Railway Co. (No. 502)

TNA Reference			
Class	Piece No.	Dates	Description
RAIL 1057	2710	1914 to 1918	List of Railwaymen killed in First World War

London, Tilbury and Southend Railway Co. (No. 505)

TNA Reference			
Class	Piece No.	Dates	Description
RAIL 437	44 ⎫		
	to ⎬	1861 to 1923	Staff Registers
	55 ⎭		
	56 ⎫		
	& ⎬	1894 to 1912	Railway Clearing System Superannuation Fund
	57 ⎭		Association Ledgers (with name index)
	42	1912	Photographs: includes photos of Thomas Whitelegg
			and Robert Whitelegg, Locomotive Superintendents

Lynton and Barnstaple Railway Co. (No. 524)

TNA Reference			
Class	Piece No.	Dates	Description
RAIL 1172	51	1921 to 1924	Complaints by Staff (only a few staff named)

Manchester and Milford Railway Co. (No. 535)

TNA Reference			
Class	Piece No.	Dates	Description
RAIL 456	13	1873 & 1880	Lists of Staff
	15	1905 to 1911	Papers relating to Pensions and Gratuities to Staff after Amalgamation with the GWR
	27	1867	Memorial from Railway Servants regarding Working Hours (names not included)

Manchester, Bolton and Bury Canal Navigation and Railway Co. (No. 538)

TNA Reference			
Class	Piece No.	Dates	Description
RAIL 458	13	1833 to 1840	Journal of R. Cunliffe, Company Agent (some staff are named)

Manchester, Sheffield and Lincolnshire Railway Co. (No. 541) – see also Great Central Railway Co. (No. 335)

TNA Reference			
Class	Piece No.	Dates	Description
RAIL 226	178 & 179	1896	Labourers' houses, Loughborough with plans (tenants not named)
RAIL 463	164	1879 to 1914	Rent Roll (includes staff tenants. Indexed)
	174	1855 to 1857	Paybill Book, Hazlehead Bridge (names with signatures)
	176	1895 to 1957	Rent Roll Book (tenants named; some staff) (from 1897 Great Central Railway Co.; from 1923 LNER; from 1948 British Rail)
	177	1870 to 1894	Staff Register, Trafford Park Locomotive Depot
	188	1870 to 1967	Rent Roll for Market Rasen Station (tenants named; some staff) (from 1897 Great Central Railway Co.; from 1923 LNER; from 1948 British Rail)
	192	c. 1898 to 1943	Rent Roll (tenants named; some staff)
	210 & 211	1851 to 1898	Staff Registers: Audit Office
	212 & 213	1864 to 1913	Staff Registers: Goods Audit Office
	214 to 216	1864 to 1925	Staff Registers: Accountant's Depts: Manchester, Grimsby, Ardwick, Hull, Marylebone, Gorton Stores, Hexthorpe, Sheffield, etc.
	222 & 223	1863 to 1920	Registers of Officers

Cont.

Manchester, Sheffield and Lincolnshire Railway Co. (continued)

TNA Reference Class	Piece No.	Dates	Description
RAIL 463	224	1862 to 1912	Register of Principal Staff
(cont.)	225	1870 to 1925	Register of Staff: Accountant's Dept., General Office
	226	1870 to 1914	Staff Register arranged by Sections
	227	1852 to 1901	Staff Register: Joint Lines
	228		General Index to Staff Registers
	229 to 246	1845 to 1899	Staff Registers with Indexes Note: This series is continued in RAIL 226/200
	247	1881 to 1896	Register of Staff at Joint Agencies
	248	Index	Note: For later volumes see RAIL 226/228 to 233
	249	1869 to 1906	Staff Register kept at Sheffield (includes Diary of Events 1879 to 1892)
	305 to 312	c. 1856 to 1901	Staff Registers
	313 to 315	1862 to 1867	Accountant's Personal Staff
	316	1894 to 1903	Alphabetical List: Extension to London, Tenants' Compensation
	317 to 319	1890 to 1903	Alphabetical List: Extension to London, Payments exclusive of Tenants' Compensation
RAIL 1016	1/80	1865	Paybill, Brunswick Station (includes names and grades)

Manchester South Junction and Altrincham Railway Co. (No. 544)

TNA Reference Class	Piece No.	Dates	Description
RAIL 465	53	1904	Presentation to R. H. Brown on Retirement as Secretary and Manager
	55 & 56	1906 to 1908	Wages Bills for Staff at Sale and Ashton-on-Mersey
	57	1892 to 1893	Driver's Log (staff not named)

Maryport and Carlisle Railway Co. (No. 552)

TNA Reference Class	Piece No.	Dates	Description
RAIL 472	50	1891 to 1910	Wages Sheets
	51	1861 to 1912	Accidents and Offences of Drivers and Firemen
	53	1917	Photograph of Staff at Mealsgate Station
RAIL 1057	2710	1914 to 1918	List of Railwaymen killed in First World War

Cum RO Reference	Dates	Description
DX/485/1 to 3	1867 to 1910	Includes Memorandum regarding Employees' Fines
DX/1008/1	1880 & 1885	Testimonials; W. Bewley of Maryport

Mersey Railway Co. (No. 559). Previously the Mersey Pneumatic Railway Co. (No. 558)

TNA Reference			
Class	Piece No.	Dates	Description
RAIL 475	41	1885 to 1907	Staff Register, Birkenhead Central Station
RAIL 1057	2710	1914 to 1918	List of Railwaymen killed in First World War

Metropolitan Railway Co. (No. 565). Previously the North Metropolitan Railway Co. (No. 629)

TNA Reference			
Class	Piece No.	Dates	Description
RAIL 1057	2710	1914 to 1918	List of Railwaymen killed in First World War

Mid-Suffolk Railway Co. (No. 569)

TNA Reference			
Class	Piece No.	Dates	Description
RAIL 1057	2710	1914 to 1918	List of Railwaymen killed in First World War

Mid-Wales Railway Co. (No. 572)

TNA Reference			
Class	Piece No.	Dates	Description
RAIL 482	17	1862 to 1902	Probate Register (347 will abstracts with dates of death of testators)

Middlesbrough and Guisbrough Railway Co. (No. 573)

TNA Reference			
Class	Piece No.	Dates	Description
RAIL 483	26	1853	Memorial from the Inhabitants of Guisbrough recommending George Page as first Station Master at Guisbrough

Middlesbrough and Redcar Railway Co. (No. 574)

TNA Reference Class	Piece No.	Dates	Description
RAIL 484	23	1847	Memorial from Workmen for Compensation for the loss of their tools in a fire at Redcar Station
	28	1846 to 1847	Correspondence including Resignation of John Tweddell, Policeman
	33	1845 to 1857	Staff Employed
	40	1847	Platelayers' Monthly Time and Wages
	41	1845 to 1847	Police Monthly Paybills (includes names and signatures) and Accounts for Staves, Lanterns and Handcuffs
	46	1846	Workmen attending Opening Ceremony

Midland and South Western Junction Railway Co. (No. 581)

TNA Reference Class	Piece No.	Dates	Description
RAIL 489	21	1891 to 1921	Staff Register, Locomotive and Carriage Dept.
RAIL 1014	36/16	1901	Photograph, Ludgershall Staff
RAIL 1057	318	1885	Appointment of James Rew Shopland as Engineer
	319	1884 to 1888	Appointment and Termination of Service of B. L. Fearnley, General Manager
	351	1874 to 1887	Claim for Salary and Professional Fees by James R. Shopland, Engineer
	2171	1891 to 1892	Accident to Guard James Choules. Also names various staff with duties
	2710	1914 to 1918	List of Railwaymen killed in First World War

Midland Railway Co. (No. 584)

TNA Reference Class	Piece No.	Dates	Description
RAIL 491	835	1899	Photograph, Staff at Barnsley Court House Station
	966	1866 to 1901	Letters, including Appointment and Resignation of W. H. Hodges, Accountant
	969 & 970	c. 1870 to 1924	Staff Registers, Goods Manager's Office, St Pancras
	971 & 972	1903 to 1927	Staff Registers, Carting and Stable staff, St Pancras (indexed)
	973	1914 to 1925	Staff Registers, Carting Depots, London Area Depots
	974 & 975	c. 1880 to 1936	Staff Registers, Office and Station Staff, Somers-Town (indexed)
	976	c. 1880 to 1927	Staff Register, Whitecross Street, Victoria Docks, Poplar and Bow (indexed)

TNA Reference Class	Piece No.	Dates	Description
RAIL 491 (cont.)	977	*c.* 1900 to 1913	Staff Register, Carting Depots, London (indexed)
	978	*c.* 1911 to 1926	Staff Register, Commercial Offices, London Area (indexed)
	979	*c.* 1880 to 1913	Staff Register, Outlying Depots, London (indexed)
	980	*c.* 1900 to 1910	Staff Register, London District, Bedford District, Northampton, Southampton, Brighton, etc. (indexed)
	981	*c.* 1900 to 1913	Staff Register, Victoria Docks and Poplar (indexed)
	982	*c.* 1900 to 1913	Staff Register, Goods Manager's Office, Whitecross Street (indexed)
	983	*c.* 1900 to 1913	Staff Register, Goods Manager's Office, City Depot (indexed)
	984	*c.* 1900 to 1913	Staff Register, Goods Manager's Office, Bow (indexed)
	985	*c.* 1872 to *c.* 1920	Staff Register, Goods Manager's Office, Liverpool, Victoria Station
	986	1897 to 1916	Wages Staff Fine Book, District Commercial Manager's Office, Derby
	987	1886 to 1921	Clerical Staff Fine Book, District Commercial Manager's Office, Derby
	988 to 993	1873 to 1911	Staff Registers, Telegraph Dept.
	994	1899 to 1907	Staff Register, Superintendent's Dept.
	995 & 996	1901 to 1909	Staff Registers, District Superintendent's Personal Staff
	997	1897 to 1911	Staff Register, Birmingham New Street Joint Station
	998	1878 to 1911	Staff Register, Bristol Joint Station
	999	1876 to 1908	Staff Register, Burton
	1000	1880 to 1908	Staff Register, Cudworth, Sheepbridge, and Eckington, etc.
	1001	1876 to 1907	Staff Register, Derby
	1002	1876 to 1908	Staff Register, Gloucester, Bath and Bristol
	1003	1880 to 1908	Staff Register, Kettering, Northampton, and Luton
	1004	1876 to 1908	Staff Register, Leeds
	1005	1876 to 1908	Staff Register, Leicester
	1006	1876 to 1908	Staff Register, Masbrough, Staveley and Chesterfield
	1007	1876 to 1908	Staff Register, Nottingham and Beeston
	1008 & 1009	1876 to 1908	Staff Registers, St Pancras
	1010	1876 to 1908	Staff Register, Saltley and Birmingham
	1011	1876 to 1908	Staff Register, Sheffield
	1012	1876 to 1908	Staff Register, Skipton, Keighley, Shipley and Hellifield
	1013	1876 to 1908	Staff Register, Toton
	1014	1876 to 1908	Staff Register, Trent, Lincoln, Mansfield and Westhouses
	1015 to 1020	1871 to 1913	New Appointments

Cont.

Midland Railway Co. (continued)

TNA Reference Class	Piece No.	Dates	Description
RAIL 491 (cont.)	1021	1906 to 1930	Additional Appointments
	1022 & 1023	1880 to 1908	Staff Registers, Goods Guards
	1024 to 1027	1871 to 1908	Staff Registers, Coaching Dept.
	1028	1902 to 1908	Staff Register, Marshalling Staff
	1029 to 1031	1860 to 1921	Staff Register, Mineral Office
	1032 & 1033	1868 to 1902	Staff Register
	1034 to 1037	1870 to 1920	Joint Staff Lists (includes Dates of Opening of Joint Lines and Stations)
	1038	1906 to 1920	Staff Register, Burton and Ashby Light Railway
	1039	1859 to 1866	Staff List (indexed by Station)
	1040 & 1041	undated / undated	Pedigree Lists (alphabetical lists of Staff at Stations)
	1042 to 1057	1908 to 1915	Workmen's Compensation: Cases Settled
	1058 to 1062	1875 to 1921	Register of Accidents to Company's Servants and others not in Company's Service
	1063	1901 to 1922	Staff Register (with cautions and reprimands)
	1064	1890 to 1930	Alterations of Staff (name, trade, age)
	1065	1914 to 1918	Estate Agent's Office, Derby. Photographs of Staff who served with H.M. Forces during the First World War
	1066	c. 1912	Goods Stations: Numbers of Staff, Minimum Wages, Local Demands for Labour, etc.
	1067 to 1069	1864 to 1909	Staff Registers, Locomotive Dept., Foremen, Clerks, Timekeepers, Pupils, Draughtsmen, Photographers, Stewards, Cooks, Messengers, etc.
	1070 & 1071	1897 to 1922	Salary Books, Locomotive Dept.
	1072	c. 1890 to 1931	Staff Register, Bromsgrove Wagon Works
	1073 & 1074	c. 1833 to 1898	Staff Registers, Sheffield Station
	1075	c. 1901 to 1924	Staff Register, Sheffield Goods Station and Depots
	1076	1914	Staff on Salary List
	1077	1908	Annual Leave Entitlement for Henry Vardy
	1079	1919	Regulation and Rates of Pay for Privileged Apprentices at Locomotive Works

TNA Reference			
Class	Piece No.	Dates	Description
RAIL 491 (cont.)	1080	*c.* 1877 to 1916	Staff Book, Locomotive Dept., Manchester District
	1981	1874 to 1919	Staff Record of George Simmons
	1259	1921	Employees killed in action in First World War
RAIL 1015	2	1876, 1897 1909–1910	Gangers' Time Record Book. D. Carlton of Griseburn (Settle and Carlisle Railway) Gives names of gangers etc.
RAIL 1057	2710	1914 to 1918	List of Railwaymen killed in First World War
	2840	1898 to 1924	Westhouses Railway School, Staff Book
Brist Ref. Lib.			
(no ref)		1914 to 1919	Roll of Honour, Bristol Goods Station Staff, First World War
Beds RO			
X 770/6		1914 to 1918	List of Railwaymen killed, wounded, taken prisoner and decorated in First World War
Cum RO Reference			
DX/1122/1		1906	Appointment of Assistant Porter, Ormside
Leic RO Reference			
DE 2503/3		*c.* 1895 to 1912	Staff Register, Loughborough

Monmouthshire Railway and Canal Co. (No 593) – see Blaenavon Tramroad (No. 81) in this Appendix

Neath and Brecon Railway Co. (No. 602). Previously the Dulas Valley Mineral Railway Co. (No. 237)

TNA Reference			
Class	Piece No.	Dates	Description
RAIL 505	13	1903 to 1922	Staff Register, Traffic Staff
RAIL 1057	1498	1904 to 1910	(folio 4) Employees Sick and Benefit Society and petition re uniforms with signatures (guards and brakesmen)
	2340	1898 to 1899	Station Master at Cray acting as Postmaster (name not included)
	2420	1897 to 1915	Accidents to Staff
	2431	1872	Staff pay (includes names)
	2710	1914 to 1918	List of Railwaymen killed in First World War

Newcastle and Carlisle Railway Co. (No. 607)

TNA Reference			
Class	Piece No.	Dates	Description
RAIL 509	58	*c.* 1840	List of Salaries (names and grades)
	85	1852 to 1855	Officers' Book on Working Arrangements at Stations (names not included)
	96	1845 to 1848	Record Book of Wages Paid at Newcastle (names and grades)

Cont.

Newcastle and Carlisle Railway Co. (continued)

TNA Reference Class	Piece No.	Dates	Description
RAIL 509 (cont.)	128 & 129	1860 to 1862	Paybill Books, Alston Branch (includes names)
	133	1856 to 1862	Vouchers (includes receipts for hats, caps and uniforms for employees; some named)
RAIL 1157	1/29	1840	Epitaph to Oswald Gardner, Locomotive Engineman, killed at Stokesfield Station

Newcastle and Darlington Junction Railway Co. (No. 608) – see York and Newcastle Railway Co. (No. 985) in this Appendix

North and South Western Junction Railway Co. (No. 620)

TNA Reference Class	Piece No.	Dates	Description
RAIL 521	19	1883 to 1916	Staff Agreements (with name index)

North British Railway Co. (No. 621)

TNA Reference Class	Piece No.	Dates	Description
RAIL 1057	2710	1914 to 1918	List of Railwaymen killed in First World War
Scot RO Reference Class	Piece No.		
BR/NBR/4	1	1850	List of Salaried Officers
	2 to 11	1869 to 1915	Accident Books
	53 to 60 & 66 to 71 & 79 to 92	1851 to 1892	Pass Registers and Returns
	287	1856	Station Traffic and Staff Book
	309 & 310	1879 & 1898	Photographs of Principal Officers
	315		Album (includes group photographs of employees)

Scot RO Reference			
Class	Piece No.	Dates	Description
BR/NBR/7	1	1917	Memorial from Stationmasters
	2	1914	Memorial from Clerical Staff re salaries
	3	1916	Memorial from Clerical Staff re increased cost of living
BR/NBR/15/	1 to 4	1867 to 1920	Staff Books (Southern Section)
	5	1920 to 1927	Staff (Central and Southern Sections)
	17 to 19 & 52 & 53	1820 to 1936	Staff, Head and District Offices
	23	1920 to 1926	Staff Book (Stations A to L) [for Carlisle etc.]
	36	1916 to 1921	Staff Book (Southern District)
	45	1910 to 1936	Staff (Northern and Southern Districts)
	56	1928 to 1934	List of Office Cleaners (All Districts)
	58	1894 to 1920	Register of Servants fined or cautioned
	59	1926 to 1930	Record of Punishments Inflicted
	60	1930 to 1948	Discipline Book
	63 & 64	1919 to 1922	Staff Agreements and Circulars
	65 to 86	1870 to 1922	Weekly Staff Changes
	87	1920	Special Staff Lists
	88	1920 to 1948	Weekly Schedule of Staff Changes
	89 to 92	1908 to 1916	Miscellaneous Staff Statements
	93	1922 to 1946	Register of Discipline Cases
	94	1905 to 1928	Register of Servants who have obtained Certificates of Proficiency in Ambulance Work
	120	1879 to 1892	Staff (Western and Southern Sections)
	149 to 166	1849 to 1940	Staff Books (Southern Section)
	167 to 170	1865 to 1921	Staff Books (Borders and Carlisle)
BR/NBR/23/	138	1870 to 1871	Voucher Book (includes lists of staff)
			Note: 1. Records from 1923 relate to the LNER
			2. There are also other records which relate specifically to Scottish regions

North Eastern Railway Co. (No. 625)

TNA Reference			
Class	Piece No.	Dates	Description
RAIL 527	97 to 99	1880 to 1922	Salaries Committee (includes Lists of Staff)
	1655	1860	Petition from Employees of Gateshead Works (with signatures of four representing the other workers)
	1656	1865	Petition from 29 Engine Drivers at Gateshead against being fined for late arrival
	1657	1862	Petition from 600 Employees at Tyne Dock for assistance to build Mechanics Institute and a day school for their children
	1658	1864	Petition from Draymen at Leeds
	1683	1873	Petition from Workmen for cottages
	1699	1897	Petition from Engine Drivers at West Auckland against having to pay higher rents than other grades
	1701	1874	Petition from Staff in Locomotive Dept. at Carlisle for houses
	1702	1857	Petition from Goods Clerks at York, calling attention to unfit state of offices
	1705	1860	Petition from Workmen in Locomotive Dept. at York for privilege fares for their wives when travelling alone
	1706	1867	Petition from Enginemen regarding wages
	1707	1873	Petition from Porters, Signalmen, Platelayers etc., regarding wages, hours, Sunday working etc.
	1708	1873 to 1882	Various Memorials from Employees
	1730	1872 to 1881	Petition from Salaried Officers and Clerks asking directors for superannuation fund etc.
	1895	1855 to 1919	Appointments and Salaries for Clerical Staff and Draughtsmen in the NER Workshops
	1896	1854 to 1918	Appointments and Salaries for Locomotive Foremen and Inspectors in the NER Workshops
	1897	1843 to 1919	Appointments and Salaries of Carriage and Wagon Foremen in the NER Workshops
	1898	1866 to 1874	Salaries of Officers, Darlington Section
	1899	1866	Indiscipline: Discussions between Management and Enginemen
	1900	1873 to 1882	Traffic Officer's attitude towards Petitions for Increased Wages and Shorter Hours
	1901	1881	Railway Servants' Nine Hour Movement
	1902	1882	Cases of Dismissal for Petty Theft
	1903	1882	Validity of Verbal Dismissal of Engine Driver, Robert Royal
	1904	1881 to 1882	Injury to Engineman, F. Smith of Hull
	1905	1875	Application for Free Passes, with details of the Practices of other Railway Companies
	1906	1881 to 1882	Introduction of Piece Work at York Carriage Works: 130 men gave notice to leave

TNA Reference		Dates	Description
Class	Piece No.		
RAIL 527 (cont.)	1907	1882 to 1883	Enginemen's Request for Higher Pay, and Uniform Clothing
	1908	1894	Guards' Rest Hours
	1909	1859 to 1957	Staff Register, Spennymoor
	1910	1878	Staff at Bishop Auckland
	1911	1916	Traffic Staff, Hours and Wages
	1912 & 1913	1872 to 1955	Station Masters' Appointments
	1914	1918	Regulations affecting Wages Staff employed in Chief Mechanical Engineers's Dept.
	1915	1919	Meeting of Staff Clerks regarding retention of Female Clerks and Holiday Relief Arrangements, etc.
	1916	1911	Regulations affecting Engine Drivers, Firemen, etc. regarding hours, wages, and conditions of service
	1917	1902 to 1912	Statement of Clerical Staff with details of Salaries
	1918	1906	Proposed transfer of Rulleymen to the Operating Dept. Note: A Rulley is a four-wheeled dray
	1919	1907 to 1917	Correspondence concerning Railway Clerks Association
	1920	1911	Chemist at Gateshead, Salary and Duties
	1921	1912	Salary Survey of Senior Clerks. Average Rates of Pay of Clerical Grades and Station Masters with a Cost of Living Summary for 1896 to 1910 (names not included)
	1922	1912	Claim by a Clerk, J. Martin, involved in an accident whilst travelling on duty
	1923	1913	Regulations for Appointment and Promotion of Clerical Staff
	1924	1913	Shop Clerks' Wages and Duties
	1925	1913 to 1916	Memorials from Staff regarding Increases in Salaries
	1926	1916	Temporary Female Clerks and Staff from the Chief Mechanical Engineer's Department on HM Service (includes names)
	1927	1918	Restrictions on Issue of Passes, Special Facilities to Company's Employees for investments in National Bonds and Payment of Staff for Armistice Day (names not included)
	1928	1919 to 1923	Rates of Pay and Conditions of Service of Hydraulic Enginemen and Firemen and of Graving Dock Enginemen and Firemen (names not included)
	1929	1919 to 1924	Reports of Apprentices attending Day Classes (includes names)
	1930 to 1933	1920	Station Masters' Salaries, Rents, and Traffic Receipts (alphabetical order)
	1934 to 1936	Undated	Rates of Pay, Wagon Works, Carriage Works and Engineering Works (names not included)
	1937	1913 to 1916	Piece Work Profits, Darlington Locomotive Works (names not included)

Cont.

North Eastern Railway Co. (continued)

TNA Reference			
Class	Piece No.	Dates	Description
RAIL 527 (cont.)	1938	1908 to 1924	Pension Book (includes names with dates of death)
	1939 & 1940	1854	Paybills for Engine Drivers, Firemen, Fitters, Night Watchmen, Cleaners and Water Station Attendants, etc. (names with signatures) Note: These records are headed 'York, Newcastle and Berwick; York and North Midland; and Leeds Northern Railways'
	1941	1874 to 1881	Salaries Register, Supervisory Staff, North Road Works (includes names)
	1942	*c.* 1912	Organisation Charts, with names, grades and pay, Northern and Southern Divisions
	1943 to 1945	1840 to 1876	Wages Books, Apprentices, Shildon Works
	1946 & 1947	1872 to 1901	Staff Register, Shildon Works
	1948	1891 to 1906	Histories of Signalmen, Hull District
	1949	1895 to 1930	Fines imposed on Footplate and Electric Train Drivers for non-observance of Rules
	1950	1917 to 1930	Histories of Staff who served in the First World War
	1951 & 1952	1856 to 1954	Histories of Staff, Darlington District
	1953	1862 to 1922	Histories of Staff, Hull District
	1954	1918	Information respecting Conference Staff
	1955	1890 to 1913	Agreements with Men and Arbitrators' Awards
	1956	1862 to 1897	Applications for positions as Guards, Porters, etc., Darlington District
	1957	1912 to 1922	Fine Ticket Book, Shildon Works
	1958	1898	Salaries of Senior Staff, Darlington District Superintendent's Office
	1959	1908 to 1926	Register of Complaints made against Enginemen, Newcastle District
	1960	1914 to 1927	Record of Fines, Reprimands, etc., against Shed Staff, Northern Division
	1961	1904 to 1927	Record of Fines, Reprimands, etc., against Shed Staff, Central Division
	1962	1903 to 1927	Record of Fines, Reprimands, etc., against Shed Staff, Southern Division
	1963	1914 to 1919	Conditions of Service of Men in Chief Civil Engineer's Dept.
	1964	1887	Paybill, Widdrington (includes names)
	1965	1916	List of Candidates for Junior Male Clerks
	1984	1866 to 1948	Staff Details, Spennymoor and Byers Green
	2054	1899 to 1900	Deductions from Clerks etc., for Mutual Assurance Fund
	2252	1912	Officers at Stations
	2255	1914	Special Constables, Hull Joint Dock

TNA Reference			
Class	Piece No.	Dates	Description
RAIL 527 (cont.)	2258	Undated	Fire Brigade (names) at Newcastle and Gateshead
	2272 to 2276	1861 to 1931	Staff Registers
	2279		Index
	2277	Undated	Staff List, Hull and York
RAIL 667	1500	1867	Wages Paybills, Way and Works Dept., Darlington Section
RAIL 1021	8/24	1885 to 1893	Note re Thomas William Worsdell Locomotive, Carriage and Wagon Superintendent
	11/17	1825	Apprenticeship indenture of William Hedley to John Watson of Willington
	11/32	1867	Application for engine driver from William Simpson
	11/40	1872	Agreement between Shildon Works Co. and Anthony Douthwaite, Engine Driver
RAIL 1057	2710	1914 to 1918	List of Railwaymen killed in First World War
TWAS Reference			
DT/NER		1872 to 1959	Staff Register
			Note: Records from 1923 relate to the LNER

North London Railway Co. (No. 628). Previously the East and West India Docks and Birmingham Juntion Railway Co. (No. 245)

TNA Reference			
Class	Piece No.	Dates	Description
RAIL 529	130	1907	Staff Register, New Entrants
	131	1906	Staff Register, Coaching and Police Depts
	132 to 135	1854 to 1895	Staff Registers
	136	1912 to 1920	Engagement Agreements
	137 & 138	1882 to 1896	Clerks' Agreements

North Midland Railway Co. (No. 630)

TNA Reference			
Class	Piece No.	Dates	Description
RAIL 530	10	1840 to 1844	Sheffield Station Committee (includes details of staff appointments with names and pay)

North Staffordshire Railway Co. (No. 632)

TNA Reference Class	Piece No.	Dates	Description
RAIL 532	26	1847 to 1868	Reports to Directors (includes Lists of Staff and details of uniforms)
	58 & 59	1869 to 1917	Staff Registers, Traffic Dept.
	60 & 61	1870 to 1923	Staff Registers, Telegraph Dept.
	62 to 64	1873 to 1923	Staff Registers (by Staff Numbers)
	65		Index
	66	1878 to 1914	Staff Register, Traffic Staff
	67	1847 to 1922	Staff Register, Clerks, Station Masters, Traffic Staff, etc.
RAIL 1057	2710	1914 to 1918	List of Railwaymen killed in First World War
	3522	1854	Indenture of Apprenticeship of William Douglas Phillipps to John Scott
	3523	1912	Portrait, William Douglas Phillipps, General Manager

North Sunderland Railway Co. (No. 633)

TNA Reference Class	Piece No.	Dates	Description
RAIL 533	26	1931	Financial History of Company with Staff Details (Statistics, names not included)
	75	1893	Letter from A.W. Price, Chartered Accountant at Newcastle, applying for position of Auditor
	76	1931 to 1948	Staff Employed, with wages, conditions of service, grades, etc.

North Union Railway Co. (No. 634)

TNA Reference Class	Piece No.	Dates	Description
RAIL 534	29	1841 to 1862	Book of Orders to Staff signed by James Chapman, Secretary, Treasurer and General Superintendent (includes names of some staff)

Oxford, Worcester and Wolverhampton Railway Co. (No. 661)

TNA Reference		Dates	Description
Class	Piece No.		
RAIL 558	32	1856	Staff Reports (includes Lists of Staff with grades and pay)

Pontop and Jarrow Wagonway (No. 684). Re-named Bowes Railway

TWAS Reference	Dates	Description
1566/1	*c.* 1875 to 1951	Workmen's Engagement Book with Family Details

Port Talbot Railway and Docks Co. (No. 690)

TNA Reference		Dates	Description
Class	Piece No.		
RAIL 574	13	1883 to 1918	Register of Staff
RAIL 1057	1530	1903	(folio 21) Driver A. Pitt shooting game while driving
	1534	1898 to 1899	(folio 9) Old pilots employed by company (only a few named)
	1568/11	1898, 1906 to 1909	Applications to join Railway Clearing System Superannuation Fund, with list of members
	2484	1898 to 1912	Employees Sick and Benefit Society (names with grade)
	2504	1903 to 1911	Accidents: staff claims B to M
	2505	1905 to 1916	Accidents: staff claims N to W
	2608	1910 to 1914	Workmen's Compensation Insurance. General correspondence with a few names
	2643 to 2646	1897 to 1911	Accidents: staff claims
	2710	1914 to 1918	List of Railwaymen killed in First World War
Wilts RO Reference			
(no ref)		1916	Register of Compensation

Rhondda and Swansea Bay Railway Co. (No. 714)

TNA Reference		Dates	Description
Class	Piece No.		
RAIL 581	36	1882 to 1920	General Staff Book
	37	1882 to 1922	Staff Register
RAIL 1057	1560	1891 to 1895	(folio 1) Payment for medical attendance by employees (includes lists of members of sick fund and a petition with 80 signatures)

Cont.

TNA Reference Class	Piece No.	Dates	Description
RAIL 1057 (cont.)	1568	1896	Historical file (folio 19). Petition from guards and brakesmen with signatures (folio 20). Includes lists of enginemen
	2013	Various dates	Accidents to staff; B to K
	2014	Various dates	Accidents to staff; M to W
	2057	1896	Accident to ganger, Philip Powell
Wilts RO Reference			
(no ref)		1916 to 1917	Register of Compensation

Rhymney Railway Co. (No. 716)

TNA Reference Class	Piece No.	Dates	Description
RAIL 583	41 to 53	1860 to 1922	Wages Books
	54 to 59	1869 to 1922	Staff Registers
	60	1918 to 1921	Time Book, Locomotive, Carriage and Wagon Dept., Caerphilly
	61	1896 to 1922	Accidents and Superannuation Allowances
	62 to 65	1907 to 1922	Registers of Accidents
RAIL 1057	1594	1861	Medical attention to staff (petition with names)
	1642	1898 to 1922	Accidents to employees and compensation paid (names with grades)
	2710	1914 to 1918	List of Railwaymen killed in First World War

Sheffield District Railway Co. (No. 763)

TNA Reference Class	Piece No.	Dates	Description
RAIL 611	25	1904 to 1916	Appointment of Mr Harry Willmott as General Manager
	26	1897	Agreement with R.E. Cooper and J. Wilson for their employment as engineers for lines in Sheffield area

Shrewsbury and Hereford Railway Co. (No. 771)

TNA Reference Class	Piece No.	Dates	Description
RAIL 617	29	1848 to 1862	Memoranda including List of Staff

Shropshire Union Railways and Canal Co. (No. 780)

TNA Reference Class	Piece No.	Dates	Description
RAIL 623	66	1844 to 1879	Staff Book
	67	1862 to 1897	Staff Register (includes West London Extension
	&		Railway, and London and North Western and
	68	Index	Lancashire and Yorkshire Joint Stations)

Somerset and Dorset Railway Co. (No. 792) – see also Somerset and Dorset Joint Line Committee in Appendix 4

TNA Reference Class	Piece No.	Dates	Description
RAIL 627	6	1863 to 1877	Register of Stations and Staff

South Devon Railway Co. (No. 795)

TNA Reference Class	Piece No.	Dates	Description
RAIL 631	28	1858	Staff Establishment on Opening of the Cornwall Railway. Reports from Secretary and Traffic Superintendent (names not included)
	39	1875 to 1878	Sick Fund and Widows' and Orphans' Fund Reports and Papers
	62	1860	Time Book of William Pike, Policeman at Torre Station
	108	1856 to 1869	Half-yearly Accounts of Traffic (includes List of Directors, Officers, Engine Drivers, etc., under the heading of Income Tax)
RAIL 1014	3	1853	(folio 36) Paybills, Torquay (names with grades)
	16	1859	(folio 2) Paybills, Torquay (names with grades)
Brun/Cl Reference			
HE 3017.S68		1873, 1874	Establishment Reports (Lists of Staff arranged by stations)

South Durham and Lancashire Union Railway Co. (No. 796)

TNA Reference Class	Piece No.	Dates	Description
RAIL 632	42 to 44	1857 to 1863	Paybill Ledgers (Mostly contractors and tradesmen; a few staff)
	54	1858	Details of police duties, pay and uniform

Cont.

South Durham and Lancashire Union Railway Co. (continued)

TNA Reference			
Class	Piece No.	Dates	Description
RAIL 632	56	1861 to 1874	Accidents on the South Durham and Eden Valley Lines
(cont.)	61	1859 to 1864	Report on requirement for operating the Railway, List of Staff. Applications and cost of Joint Working of Tebay Station

South Eastern Railway Co. (No. 797) Previously the London, Deptford and Dover Railway Co. (No. 501)

TNA Reference			
Class	Piece No.	Dates	Description
RAIL 635	196	1851	Staff Book; giving particulars of Staff at Various Stations
	197	1889 to 1896	Paybill Register, Deptford High Street (includes names)
	201 to 204	1842 to 1898	Staff Books, Audit Office
	206	1860 to 1877	Staff Register, Wadhurst Station
	211	1858 to 1895	General Instructions to Staff at Bridge Station
	213	1855 to 1888	Letter Book of Engineer's Dept. concerning Staff and Stores
	217	1872	Table of working hours and wages for 28 grades of railway shopmen compared with those for 13 other railway companies
	302 to 304	1868 to 1920	Staff Register, Bricklayers Arms: Drivers, Firemen, Labourers, etc.
	305	c1869 to 1944	Punishments and Awards, Enginemen
	306	1847 to 1910	Staff Register, Goods Staff
	307 & 308	1845 to 1900	Register of Workmen, Locomotive Depots
	309	1845 to 1905	Register of Workmen, Carriage and Wagon Dept.
	399	1864 to 1919	Register of Enginemen; Marine Locomotive Dept.
RAIL 1057	2935	1880 to 1881	Staff Serving on Local and other Councils

South Wales Railway Co. (No. 806)

TNA Reference			
Class	Piece No.	Dates	Description
RAIL 640	30	1853 to 1861	Reports (includes Lists of Staff)
	45	1864	List of Staff of all Depts
	47	1852 to 1857	List of Fines levied on Enginemen; Punishments and Discharges
	55 & 56	1844 to 1860	Register of Clerks

Stockton and Darlington Railway Co. (No. 827)

TNA Reference			
Class	Piece No.	Dates	Description
RAIL 667	228	1860 to 1882	Superannuation Society Minute Book (gives names, indexed)
	261 & 262	1849 to 1862	Register of Probates
	344 to 346	1850 to 1853	Contract Agreements for the supply of Clothing for Guards, Policemen and Porters. Agreement for employment of William Bulmer, John Greenhill, Joseph Nevins and John Battyas Clerks
	400	1857 to 1858	Scrapbook regarding Edward Pease
	418	1830 to 1834	Report Book of Thomas Storey (Engineer and General Traffic Manager)
	419	1862 to 1876	Report Book of George Stephenson (Goods, Passenger and Traffic Manager)
	427	1831 to 1861	Notes of Incidents regarding the Stockton and Darlington Railway dictated to Mr H. Oxtoby by Mr G. Graham who drove Engine No. 1 *Locomotion* and whose father was the Traffic Manager of the Stockton and Darlington Railway
	432	1840 to 1845	Pay Book, Shildon Works (includes names)
	443	1840 to 1867	Notices issued by Management to Staff, Shildon Works
	452	1831	Safety Regulations: Cautions to Enginemen
	484	1840 to 1841	Fines Imposed for Indiscipline
	491	1847 to 1880	Notices to Staff and Printed Public Notices
	504	1847 to 1849	Fines for Negligence, Damage, Misconduct and Accidents
	506	1854	Sixty Letters for a Clerical Post at Darlington
	523	1849	Superannuation Scheme: Return of Employees and their Wives
	530	1854	Draft Proposal for an Employees' Accident and Sickness Fund
	551	1851 to 1859	Superannuation Proposals for Railwaymen
	555	1840 to 1855	Salary Register Shildon Works (includes names)
	594	1844 to 1846	Wages Lists: Signalmen of Shildon Tunnel
	600	Undated	Instruction to Signalmen and Platelayers regarding Accidents
	603	*c.* 1835	List of Officials and Passenger Guards with their Salaries
	609	1869	Obituary of Thomas McNay Secretary to the Company, 1849 to 1869
	616	1841 to 1844	Employees Duties and Wages, including proposals for wage reductions and dismissals
	625	1846 to 1860	Rules for Workmen
	633	1833 to 1865	Rules and Regulations for Workmen at New Shildon, 1833. Guidance of Police Officers, 1842. Working of Trains on Barnard Castle Line, 1856. Working of Line between Sunnyside and Carrhouse, 1865

Cont.

Stockton and Darlington Railway Co. (continued)

TNA Reference			
Class	Piece No.	Dates	Description
RAIL 667	654	1825	Names of first engines, builders and drivers
(cont.)	676	1865 to 1874	Three lists of locomotives at Darlington with a list of workmen employed at Shildon in 1865
	786	1844	Petition from Gatekeepers
	791	1864	Petition from Members of Traffic Dept.
	793	1865	Petition Regarding Wages
	795	1867	Petition from Engine Drivers and Firemen
	798	1868	Petition from Platelayers regarding Wages
	801	Undated	Petition from Employees of the Carriage Works, Darlington for the adoption of the nine hours system, and a general advance of wages and weekly payments
	803	Undated	Petition from inhabitants of Kirby Thore regarding Station Master (Mr Barley) not to be dismissed (61 signatures)
	820	1872	Petition from signalmen of Shildon Tunnel asking for an increase in wages because of their great responsibility, rise in the cost of living and lack of promotion
	822	1876	Petition from workmen at Tow Law asking for houses to be built
	826	1843	Petition from friends of Christopher Day, to learn why he has been discharged
	830	1832	Petition from workmen regarding the death of a colleague through drinking stolen spirits
	834	Undated	Petition from inhabitants of Middleton St George recommending that John West take charge of depots at Fighting Cocks
	835	Undated	Memorial from users of Yarm Station expressing their entire satisfaction concerning parcels dealt with by Thomas Temple and his wife
	846	1853	Petition from employees for wages to be paid fortnightly
	848	1855	Petition from Euston Station householders for supply of pure water as they have to rely on obtaining same from locomotives
	855	1818	Letter from Thomas Meynell, Company's first Chairman, urging Richard Miles to engage George Overton, rather than John Rennie to make a survey
	856	1818	Letter from Richard Miles to George Overton for the latter to survey Tram Road as an alternative to a canal
	857	1818	Letter from Jonathan Backhouse regarding meeting of Committee with George Overton
	948	1825	Fourteen letters of application for employment
	956	c. 1825	List of names of workmen and fines paid by them
	959	1826	Letters from employees: B. Tully, G. Jackson, Joseph Stephenson
	971	1826	Letters re applications for employment
	1024	1830	Applications for employment etc.
	1028	1831	Applications for employment etc.

TNA Reference			
Class	Piece No.	Dates	Description
RAIL 667	1044	1832	Applications for employment etc.
(cont.)	1060	1834	Applications for employment at Yarm etc.
	1070	1835	Applications for employment etc.
	1077	1836	Claims for loss and injury etc.
	1081	1836	Driver Holmes running over and killing five hounds
	1095	1837	Applications for employment etc.
	1104	1838	Letters from employees re staff matters
	1114	1839	Letters re staff matters, including guard Arnott
	1117	1839	Fines imposed on engine drivers etc.
	1125	1840	Applications for employment etc.
	1143	1854	Appointment of William English of Leeds as Superintendent of mineral traffic
	1159	1841 to 1859	Letters from John Harris, engineer
	1162	1856 to 1861	Ralph Ward Jackson, Chairman of West Hartlepool Harbour and Railway Co., on amalgamation policy
	1163	1853	Letter from Joseph Nevins of Stockton, one of the oldest railway servants, seeking employment for his son
	1209	1825 to 1845	Letters from Thomas Manton, Police Superintendent regarding accidents
	1220	1839 to 1845	Letters re staff in trouble including one from Smiles Richardson a well-known guard
	1244	1835 to 1849	Attack on guard Harland, policeman Scott and Joseph Nevins
	1246	1837 to 1849	Letters re personal accidents
	1248	1846 to 1849	Letters from Thomas Manton, Chief of Police re accidents. Includes George Watkinson sentenced to transportation for 14 years for breaking open a cabin and stealing a coat
	1262	1830 to 1864	Misc. correspondence including reference to interference by railway officials
	1265	1850 to 1856	Correspondence of police department re accidents naming those injured or killed
	1278	1846 to 1850	New Shildon Mechanics Institute membership record book
	1283	1835 to 1849	Applications for employment including letters from Joseph Nevins, Passenger Guard and later Station Master at Stockton
	1284	1835 to 1849	Letters requesting increase in wages
	1285	1838 to 1849	Letters from railway servants replying to allegations of misconduct
	1286	1837 to 1848	Railway servants' applications for leave
	1287	1840 to 1848	Various letters re clerical work with one from a schoolmaster of the railway school
	1288	1842	Monthly Paybill for clerks, guards, etc. (includes names)
	1289	1855	Alterations to wages of guards, porters, etc.
	1290	1856	Fines
	1291	1849	List of Gatekeepers
	1299	1829 to 1842	Tonnage – includes engine drivers' names

Cont.

Stockton and Darlington Railway Co. (continued)

TNA Reference Class	Piece No.	Dates	Description
RAIL 667 (cont.)	1301	1840 to 1841	Monthly Paybill abstracts, contractors and staff (includes names)
	1302	1840 to 1841	Monthly pay to employees at Middlesbrough (includes names)
	1303	1840 to 1847	Monthly pay at Shildon (incomplete)
	1304	1836 to 1839	Names and wages of guards, enginemen, etc. in Coach and Carrying Dept.
	1305	1846 to 1847	Names of drivers and earnings
	1307	1840 to 1847	Monthly pay of Company's Police Officers, gatekeepers and watchmen (incomplete)
	1308	1840 to 1847	Monthly pay in Carrying Dept.
	1309	1840 to 1847	Monthly accounts of wages, etc. in Coaching Dept. (includes names and grades)
	1311	1840 to 1847	Monthly pay at Brusselton Bank and Black Boy (includes names)
	1326	1841 to 1862	Accounts for Medical Services to workmen and others (railwaymen named)
	1335	1834 to 1835	Bills and Receipts for Poor Rates, contractors payments, salaries, etc.
	1370	1840 to 1841	Book of payments, including wages to staff (appears to name contractors only)
	1425	1849 to 1852	Paybill ledger (contractors only)
	1426	1840 to 1847	Monthly Paybills (contractors and staff)
	1427	1846 to 1849	
	1430 to 1433	1852 to 1864	Paybill Ledgers. Payments to contractors; and wages summaries (staff not named)
	1450 to 1455	1825 to 1843	Leaders Books (daily records of tonnages and destinations with payments to engine drivers who are named)
	1476 to 1488	1848 to 1863	Voucher Books, containing wages lists for guards, porters, mechanics, clerks, etc.
	1497	1844 to 1845	Fortnightly Wages for Stanhope Railway
	1498	1854	Wages List for Permanent Way carpenters and masons
	1499	1865	Wages List , police gatekeepers
	1500	1837 to 1847	Wages Lists, Way and Works Dept. (includes names)
	1502 to 1526	1822 to 1846	Paybills for construction workers (includes signatures)
	1527	1825 to 1826	Wages Lists, Locomotives and Traffic Dept.
	1529	1826 to 1827	Wages Lists, enginemen, etc. (includes signatures)
	1532	1822	Wages Lists for work at Brusselton and Etherley Quarries
	1567	1840 to 1841	Two Paybills for inspection, to George Graham and Thomas Sommerson
RAIL 1057	2885	1824 to 1825	Employees of original railway

Stratford-upon-Avon and Midland Junction Railway Co. (No. 835)

TNA Reference			
Class	Piece No.	Dates	Description
RAIL 674	11	1873 to 1923	Staff Register. (Entries before 1909 relate to the East and West Junction Railway Co.)
RAIL 1057	2710	1914 to 1918	List of Railwaymen killed in First World War

Stratford-upon-Avon Railway Co. (No. 836)

TNA Reference			
Class	Piece No.	Dates	Description
RAIL 675	20	1857 to 1869	Accountant's Vouchers; includes fortnightly paybills (includes names)
	22	1858 to 1860	Report by C. Sanderson, Engineer
	24	1858	Applications from Engineers for construction of the railway
	26	1860 to 1862	Copies of Letters and Reports from C. Sanderson, Engineer

Swindon and Cheltenham Extension Railway Co. (No. 847)

TNA Reference			
Class	Piece No.	Dates	Description
RAIL 1057	351	1874 to 1887	Claim by J.R. Shopland for Salary etc.

Taff Vale Railway Co. (No. 852)

TNA Reference			
Class	Piece No.	Dates	Description
RAIL 258	532	1922 to 1947	Accident Fund Papers
RAIL 684	55	1858	List of Policemen and other records including clothing Specifications
	62	1823	Plan of Intended Railway by George Overton, Engineer, and David Davies, Surveyor
	73 to 76	1893 to 1922	Applications for Pensions
	77	1892 to 1922	Register of Retiring Allowances
	78 to 82	1914 to 1920	Pension Allowances and Compensation Receipts (includes signatures)

Cont.

407

Taff Vale Railway Co. (continued)

TNA Reference Class	Piece No.	Dates	Description
RAIL 684 (cont.)	94 to 105	1840 to 1924	Staff Registers, Traffic Dept., Uniformed Staff
	106 to 113	1852 to 1920	Staff Registers, Locomotive Dept., Maintenance Staff
	114 & 115	1864 to 1922	Staff Registers, Goods Dept., Clerical and Wages Staff
	116 to 119	1864 to 1922	Registers of Accidents to Company's Servants
	120	1916 to 1921	Returns to Board of Trade regarding Accidents to Staff
	123 to 125	1905 to 1922	Workmen's Compensation, Minutes of Officers' Meetings
RAIL 1014	4/21	1892	Letter re cessation of issue of diarrhoea mixture to staff
	4/41	1842	Memorial from Michael Driscoll, a suspended servant in hope of re-instatement
RAIL 1057	1825	1905 to 1913	E.S. May. Claim for loss of both legs
	1857/2	1895 to 1917	Staff particulars and Register of Staff appointed 1840 to 1890
	1857/16	1903 to 1929	Employees' Accident Fund	general
	1857/16A	1903 to 1929	Employees' Hospital Fund correspondence,
	1857/16B	1903 to 1929	Employees' Benevolent Fund no names
	2697	1895 to 1896	Recruitment of fitters from North and Midland to replace men who had left owing to dispute. Issue of free travel vouchers (some names)
	2710	1914 to 1918	List of Railwaymen killed in First World War

Tees Valley Railway Co. (No. 858)

TNA Reference Class	Piece No.	Dates	Description
RAIL 687	11	1873 to 1881	Engineers' Reports to Directors
	16	1865 to 1870	Paybill Book (tradesmen, no staff)

Trent Valley Railway Co. (No. 879)

TNA Reference Class	Piece No.	Dates	Description
RAIL 699	5	1845 to 1846	Returns of men and horses employed (names of men not included)

Vale of Clwyd Railway Co. (No. 882)

TNA Reference Class	Piece No.	Dates	Description
RAIL 1057	3774	c. 1858	Includes testimonials in favour of John Lloyd's application as Station Master

Vale of Glamorgan Railway Co. (No. 883)

TNA Reference Class	Piece No.	Dates	Description
RAIL 1057	1014/5	1892	Appointment of James Bell of Cardiff as resident engineer
	1021	1894 to 1896	Entrants into Railway Clearing System Superannuation Fund Association
	2245 & 2248	1899 to 1900	Accidents to staff (includes names)

Vale of Neath Railway Co. (No. 885)

TNA Reference Class	Piece No.	Dates	Description
RAIL 704	17	1851 to 1904	Paybills, Merthyr Road, 1851 to 1853; Llwydcoed 1853 to 1904 (includes names)
RAIL 1057	2951	1859	Amalgamation with GWR, with lists of officers and clerks, with salaries

Wallingford and Watlington Railway Co. (No. 893)

TNA Reference Class	Piece No.	Dates	Description
RAIL 708	12	1865	Letter from Michael Lane (GWR Paddington Engineer) to James Grierson (GWR General Manager)

Watton and Swaffham Railway Co. (No. 904)

TNA Reference Class	Piece No.	Dates	Description
RAIL 714	7	1875	Paysheets (includes names)

Wear and Derwent Junction Railway Co. (No. 906)

TNA Reference		Dates	Description
Class	Piece No.		
RAIL 716	7	1846	Monthly Paybills (includes names)

Wear Valley Railway Co. (No. 909)

TNA Reference		Dates	Description
Class	Piece No.		
RAIL 667	1481	1849	Voucher Book; (f174) Labourers' Times (includes names)

West Cornwall Railway Co. (No. 918)

TNA Reference		Dates	Description
Class	Piece No.		
RAIL 725	6	1833 to 1851	Testimonials: Edward Austin, Clerk to the West Cornwall Railway Co.

West London Extension Railway Co. (No. 923)

TNA Reference		Dates	Description
Class	Piece No.		
RAIL 623	67	1886 to 1897	Staff Register (in Shropshire Union Railways and
	68	Index	Canal Co. Staff Register)
RAIL 732	41	1908 to 1913	Notices and Instructions to staff and train alterations (some staff named)

Whitehaven and Furness Junction Railway Co. (No. 941)

TNA Reference		Dates	Description
Class	Piece No.		
RAIL 744	9	1856	Staff Register (arranged by stations)

Whitland and Cardigan Railway Co. (No. 944)

TNA Reference Class	Piece No.	Dates	Description
RAIL 747	21	1883	Appointment of J.B. Walton, Engineer
	35*		
	to	1876 to 1886	Voucher Book, with Wages Lists (includes names)
	38	1877	
RAIL 981	521	1879	Working Timetable with Staff Regulations
			* pieces 35 and 37 also contain Wages Lists for Whitland and Taff Vale Railway Co.

Whitland and Taff Vale Railway Co. (No. 945)

TNA Reference Class	Piece No.	Dates	Description
RAIL 747	35 & 37	1876 to 1877	Voucher Book with wages lists; Locomotive, Permanent Way and Traffic Staff (includes names)

Wiltshire, Somerset and Weymouth Railway Co. (No. 950)

TNA Reference Class	Piece No.	Dates	Description
RAIL 750	14 to 16	1845 to 1858	Paybill Books (contain names of only some top salaried staff and some labourers)

Wirral Railway Co. (No. 955)

TNA Reference Class	Piece No.	Dates	Description
RAIL 756	10	1884 to 1926	Staff Register with Cash Accounts
	11	1892 to 1921	Staff Register, Birkenhead Park Station Committee
RAIL 1057	2710	1914 to 1918	List of Railwaymen killed in First World War

Wrexham and Ellesmere Railway Co. (No. 973)

TNA Reference Class	Piece No.	Dates	Description
RAIL 1057	632	1898 to 1901	Appointment of A.J. Collins as Engineer, and Retirement and Death of G. Owen

411

Wycombe Railway Co. (No. 978)

TNA Reference		Dates	Description
Class	Piece No.		
RAIL 768	14	1858 to 1861	Appointment of E.F. Murray as Engineer

York and Newcastle Railway Co. (No. 985). Previously the Newcastle and Darlington Junction Railway Co.

TNA Reference		Dates	Description
Class	Piece No.		
RAIL 772	121	1847 to 1848	Paybill Book, Richmond, Thirsk, Malton, Boroughbridge and Bedale

York and North Midland Railway Co. (No. 986)

TNA Reference		Dates	Description
Class	Piece No.		
RAIL 770	14	1850 to 1851	Reports by Thomas Cabry, Engineer
	15	1842	Reports by Robert Stephenson, Chief Engineer
	46	1852	Paybills, Hull Goods Dept. (includes names)
	52	1853	Wages Payments (summary lists, no names)
	66	1855	List of Station Masters, Goods Agents and Mineral Agents
	77	1848	Paybills, Coaching Dept. and Secretary's Office (includes names)
	78	1848	Paybills, Normanton (includes names)
	79	1848	Staff, Whitby to Pickering Branch
	80	1848	Staff, Beverley, Bridlington, Driffield, Hull and Selby
	81	1843 to 1850	Staff, York and Newcastle Central

York, Newcastle and Berwick Railway Co. (No. 987)

TNA Reference		Dates	Description
Class	Piece No.		
RAIL 667	1195	1843 to 1851	Correspondence re appointment of a signalman Elias Binns at Darlington
	1251	1846 to 1849	Letters from James Allport, General Manager
RAIL 772	60	1847	Inspector's Time Book
	61	1848	Pay Book, Engineering Dept. (includes names with signatures)
	62	1850	Paybill Book, Men's Time Repairing Engines (includes names with signatures)
	77	1848	Time Book, Engineering Dept., Carlisle (includes names)
	79	1845	Inspector's Time Book, Newcastle and Darlington (includes names)

TNA Reference Class	Piece No.	Dates	Description
RAIL 772 (cont.)	99	1845	Testimonial From James Allport, General Manager, Newcastle and Darlington Railway, to Henry Tennant, later General Manager and Director of the North Eastern Railway
	106	1845	Paybills, Engineering, Locomotive and Carriage Dept. of the Newcastle and Darlington Railway at Gateshead (includes names)
	121	1847 to 1848	Paybill Book: Richmond, Thirsk, Malton, Boroughbridge and Bedale (includes names)
	123	1845 to 1850	Paybill Book, Berwick District (includes names)
	124	1852 to 1857	Paybill Book, Bishop Auckland (includes names)
	125	1858 to 1860	Paybill Book, Bishop Auckland and Jarrow Dock (includes names)

3.2 The Great Western Railway (GWR)

The Great Western Railway Co. was incorporated 31 August 1835 initially to run from London to Bristol. Its headquarters were at Paddington. One hundred and fifty other railway companies were taken over by the GWR before the Grouping in 1923. This was the only company to survive the Grouping. At the Grouping it absorbed the following companies:

1   The Alexandra (Newport and South Wales) Docks and Railway Co.
2   The Barry Railway Co.
3   The Brecon and Merthyr Tydfil Junction Railway Co.
4   The Burry Port and Gwendraeth Valley Railway Co.
5   The Cambrian Railways Co.
6   The Cleobury Mortimer and Ditton Priors Light Railway Co.
7   The Didcot, Newbury and Southampton Railway Co.
8   The Exeter Railway Co.
9   The Forest of Dean Central Railway Co.
10 The Gwendraeth Valleys Railway Co.
11 The Lampeter, Aberayron and New Quay Light Railway Co.
12 The Liskeard and Looe Railway Co.
13 The Llanelly and Mynydd Mawr Railway Co.
14 The Mawddwy Railway Co.
15 The Midland and South Western Junction Railway Co.
16 The Neath and Brecon Railway Co.
17 The Penarth Extension Railway Co.
18 The Penarth Harbour, Dock and Railway Co.
19 The Port Talbot Railway and Docks Co.
20 The Princetown Railway Co.
21 The Rhondda and Swansea Bay Railway Co.
22 The Rhynmey Railway Co.
23 The Ross and Monmouth Railway Co.
24 The South Wales Mineral Railway Co.
25 The Taff Vale Railway Co.

26 The Teign Valley Railway Co.
27 The Vale of Glamorgan Railway Co.
28 The Van Railway Co.
29 The Welshpool and Llanfair Light Railway Co.
30 The West Somerset Railway Co.
31 The Wrexham and Ellesmere Railway Co.

Staff Records

TNA Reference			
Class	Piece No.	Dates	Description
RAIL 250	128 to 134	1893 to 1947	Allowances on retirement
RAIL 252	13	1864	Apprenticeship indenture, John Maslin to Joseph Armstrong, fitter, Swindon
	179	29 Sept 1873	Articles of Apprenticeship of Thomas Walklate to Locomotive and Carriage Depts
RAIL 253	83	1856 to 1877	Paybills, Chirk Station (staff named)
	174 & 175	1868 to 1870	Paybill Book, General Manager's Office (staff named)
	266	1916 to 1918	Complaints
	321	1904 to 1910	Staff Applications in Locomotive, Carriage and Stores Dept. Swindon (indexed)
	322	1932 to 1934	Staff in Chief Mechanical Engineer's Dept. Applications and Accidents (indexed)
	445	1884	Duty Book, Stanton Station (staff named)
	459	c. 1904	Photograph: GWR cricket team
	508	1906	Illuminated volume with names of subscribers to testimonial to William Catton, Station Master at St Columb Road
	511 & 512	1891 to 1928	Instructions to Staff, Reading Station (some staff named)
	516	1915 to 1918	Letters from Paddington Audit Office Staff in HM Forces (includes photographs)
RAIL 258	264	1910	G.K. Mills, Secretary, retirement
	265	1910	A.E. Bolter, Secretary, appointment
	266	1926 to 1947	F.R.E. Davis, Secretary, appointment
	340	1945	Chief Engineer: appointment of mining assistant
	468		Retirement of Staff: customary practice of Port Talbot Railway and Dock Co.
	469		Retirement of Staff: Rhondda and Swansea Bay Railway Co.
	470		Retirement of Staff: Rhymney Railway
	471		Retirement of Staff: Swansea Harbour Trustees
	472		Retirement of Staff: Taff Vale Railway

TNA Reference Class	Piece No.	Dates	Description
RAIL 258 (cont.)	473		Retirement of Staff: Burry Port and Gwendraeth Valley Railway
	474		Retirement of Staff: Cambrian Railways
	475		Retirement of Staff: Cardiff Railway
	476		Retirement of Staff: Corris Railway
	477		Retirement of Staff: Alexandra, Newport and S. Wales Docks and Railway Co.
	478		Retirement of Staff: Barry Railway
	479		Retirement of Staff: Brecon and Merthyr Railway
	480		Retirement of Staff: Llanelly and Mynydd Mawr Railway
	481		Retirement of Staff: Midland and South Western Railway
	482		Retirement of Staff: Neath and Brecon Railway
	483		Retirement of Staff: Great Western Railway
	484	1900 to 1946	Retired officers GWR
	485	1925	GWR Swindon Retired Workman's Association
	486	1924 to 1945	United Kingdom Railway Officers' and Servants' Association
	487	1937 to 1947	'Old Contemptibles' and 1914/15 Star GWR Association
	538	c. 1903 to 1947	Appointments of secretaries to various pension and provident societies
	550	1940 to 1941	Appointment of Mr James Milne as a director
	412	1875 to 1912	Policy on retirement of staff, with list
	413	1886 to 1927	Stores dept., appointments etc.
	419	1940 to 1947	Salaried staff retirements
RAIL 264	1 to 9	1835 to 1910	Register of Clerks, entry into service
	10 to 16	1900 to 1946	Memorandum books relating to locomotive staff matters including medical examinations, mileage worked by enginemen, allowances, leave, etc.
	17		Index

Registers of Drivers and Firemen (arranged by staff number)

TNA Reference Class	Piece No.	Dates	Description
RAIL 264 (cont.)	18 to 130	1841 to 1941	110 volumes. Note: 3 volumes missing from this series
	131	Index from 1 March 1906	
	132	Index from 17 February 1920	
	133	Index	

Cont.

415

Staff Record Books: Employees at Stations and Depots

TNA Reference Class	Piece No.	Dates	Description
RAIL 264 (cont.)	135 to 147	1840 to 1914	Old Oak Common Division 9 volumes. Note: 4 volumes missing from this series
	148 to 161	1863 to 1920	Swindon Division
	162 to 173	1846 to 1920	Bristol Division 10 volumes. Note: 2 volumes missing from this series
	174 to 187	1846 to 1920	Newton Abbot Division
	188 to 202	1840 to 1920	Newport Division
	203 to 218	1851 to 1920	Neath Division 15 volumes. Note: 1 volume missing from this series
	219 to 234	1856 to 1920	Wolverhampton Division 14 volumes. Note: 2 volumes missing from this series
	235 to 240	1859 to 1921	Worcester Division

Locomotive, Carriage and Wagon Depts

TNA Reference Class	Piece No.	Dates	Description
RAIL 264 (cont.)	241 & 242	1881 to 1938	Station registers of staff: Swindon
	243	1882 to 1938	Station register of staff: all divisions

TNA Reference			
Class	Piece No.	Dates	Description
RAIL 264	244		Index to pieces 241 to 243
(cont.)	245	1880 to 1941	Numerical register of salaried staff: Nos 1118 to 2355 (continues from Piece No. 254)
	246	1838 to 1902	Numerical register of weekly paid staff: Nos 1 to 603
	247	1913 to 1925	Station register of salaried staff: foremen, inspectors and draughtsmen
	248 & 249	1888 to 1913	Station registers of staff
	250	1890 to 1901	Numerical register of weekly paid staff: shop clerks, time and store keepers, etc. Nos 1 to 692
	251 to 253	1892 to 1925	Station register of weekly paid staff: shop clerks, time and store keepers, etc.
	254	1840 to 1944	Numerical register of staff: officers, draughtsmen and clerks Nos 1 to 1117; and junior clerks Nos 1 to 569
	255	1910 to 1923	Alphabetical register of office boys and messengers (continues from piece No. 268)
	256 & 257	1852 to 1946	Numerical register of weekly paid staff: clerks and messengers 1 to 2706
	258	1846 to 1944	Numerical register of weekly paid staff: foremen, inspectors, etc.
	259 & 260	1919 to 1938	Station register of salaried staff: officers, technical, male and female clerks
	261 & 262	1910 to 1940	Numerical register of female clerks: 1 to 1060
	263	1914 to 1935	Numerical register of engine cleaners: 1 to 2988
	264 to 266	1910 to 1927	Alphabetical register of characters
	267	1946 to 1947	Chronological register of enquiries as to character received from prospective employers of employees of the company, with index to names of employees
	268	1887 to 1910	Alphabetical register of office boys and messengers
	269 & 270	1850 to 1887	Station register of officers, draughtsmen, inspectors, foremen, etc.
	271	1872 to 1913	Locomotive Accounts Dept., staff register
	272 & 273	1858 to 1899	Staff registers of clerks
	274	1932 to 1934	Register of new workshop staff
	275	1848 to 1902	Alphabetical register of clerks, draughtsmen, superintendents, etc.
	276 & 277	1845 to 1902	Alphabetical registers of men

Cont.

TNA Reference		Dates	Description
Class	Piece No.		
RAIL 264	278	1859 to 1908	Staff register of clerks
(cont.)	279 to 286	1864 to 1947	Registers of apprentices
	287 to 291	1879 to 1934	Pupils' time books
	292	1903 to 1912	Attendance register of apprentices at Swindon and North Wilts Technical School
	293 to 295	1912 to 1935	Attendance registers of apprentices at Swindon and North Wilts Technical School with examination results
	296 to 299	1869 to 1881	Monthly paybill books (includes names)
	300	1892 to 1923	Register of men, late Barry Railway
	301	1873 to 1923	Register of men, late Brecon and Merthyr Railway, Neath and Brecon Railway and Alexandra Docks Railway
	302	1884 to 1923	Register of men, late Cardiff Bute Docks Railway, Cardiff Gas Works and Mynydd Mawr Railway
	303	1874 to 1923	Register of men, Oswestry
	304	1889 to 1923	Register of men, late Rhymney Railway
	305 & 306	1886 to 1923	Register of men, late Taff Vale Railway
	307	1874 to 1925	Registers of officers, salaried and supervisory staff taken over from amalgamated railways
	308	1883 to 1927	Register of salaried staff taken over from amalgamated Railways and Docks and Electrical Dept.
	309	c. 1923	Service particulars of drivers, firemen and cleaners taken over from amalgamated railways
	310	1867 to 1923	Register of enginemen employed on amalgamated lines
	311	1922	Charts and lists of supervisory and clerical staff taken over from the Barry Railway
	312	1922	Charts and lists of supervisory and clerical staff taken over from the Cambrian Railways
	313	1922	Charts and lists of supervisory and clerical staff taken over from the Alexandra (Newport and South Wales) Docks and Railway
	314	1932 to 1937	Charts of supervisory and clerical staff at the Dock Mechanical Engineers' Offices
	315 & 316	1925 to 1929	Charts of supervisory and technical staff
	317 & 318	1925 to 1929	Charts of clerical staff

TNA Reference			
Class	Piece No.	Dates	Description
RAIL 264 (cont.)	319	*c.* 1923	Service particulars of drivers, firemen and cleaners from absorbed railways
	320	1900 to 1907	Record book of examination candidates for appointment as shunting firemen
	321	1914 to 1921	Staff register of clerks, draughtsmen, etc.
	322	1867 to 1869	Record book of monthly paybills
	323 to 327	1883 to 1911	Advances and vacancies book – clerks
	328 to 331	1923 to 1941	Vacancies book – technical, supervisory and clerical staff
	332	1914 to 1919	Pension fund book, members' deductions
	333 & 334	1903 to 1914	Registers of staff, Electrical Engineer's Dept.
	335 & 336	1918 and 1928	Census of staff – numbers in various grades (names not included) engineering, passenger, goods and signal depts
	337	1922	List of officers and staff occupying first and special class positions employed by the constituent companies in the Western Group
	338	1922	List of staff alterations – salaried and supervisory staff
	339	1925	Tables of authorized staff establishment
	240	1922	Authorized traffic staff establishment at stations and offices
	341 to 353	1842 to 1915	Registers of uniformed staff. First Series; 12 volumes (1 volume missing)
	458		Index
	354 to 366	1870 to 1915	Register of uniformed staff. Second Series; 13 volumes
	459		Index
	367		missing
	368 to 379	1878 to 1915	Register of uniformed staff. Third series; 12 volumes (1 volume missing)
	460		Index
	380 & 381	1918 to 1938	Registers of uniformed staff – new men appointed
	382	1905 to 1913	Register of weekly staff: London District
	384 & 385	1870 to 1877	Register of lad clerks
			Index
	386 & 387	1872 to 1890	Register of lad clerks

419

TNA Reference		Dates	Description
Class	Piece No.		
RAIL 264	388		Index
(cont.)	390 to 392	1897 to 1911	Register of lad clerks
	393		Index
	394	1835 to 1863	Register of clerks
	395		Index
	396 & 397	1836 to 1867	Registers of clerks
	398		Index
	399	1838 to 1876	Register of clerks
	400		Index
	401	1835 to 1860	Register of clerks
	402		Index
	403 to 405	1838 to 1855	Register of clerks
	406	1899 to 1909	Register of clerks permanently appointed
	407	1912 to 1916	Register of clerks' promotions
	408	1911 to 1919	Register of new clerks
	409	1843 to 1899	Register of clerks: Accountant's Dept.
	410	1859 to 1940	Register of clerks: Accountant's Dept.
	411	1894 to 1908	Register of staff changes and promotions at Aylesbury Joint Station. (Great Western and Metropolitan Railways)
	412 & 413	1939 to 1962	Registers of staff, Oswestry Works
	414	1839 to 1877	Register of inspectors, booking constables and booking porters
			Registers of weekly staff passengers and goods
	415	1896 to 1906	London Division
	416	1898 to 1913	Birmingham Division
	417	1898 to 1909	Chester Division
	418	1898 to 1907	Hereford Division
	419	1898 to 1907	Worcester Division
	420	1898 to 1914	Cardiff Division
	421	1898 to 1905	Bristol Division
	422	1898 to 1907	Exeter Division
	423	1898 to 1915	Bristol, Exeter and Plymouth Divisions
	424	1910 to 1915	Chester Division
	425	1905 to 1912	Cardiff Division
	426	1907 to 1915	Pontypool Road Division
	427	1910 to 1915	Birmingham Division
	428	1902	Staff in office and works of Signal Depts, Reading
	429	1876 to 1877	Paybill book, Reading Station (includes names)
	430 to 439	1861 to 1936	Registers of traffic staff at stations in Wales

TNA Reference			
Class	Piece No.	Dates	Description
RAIL 264 (cont.)	440	1900 to 1958	Register of Locomotive Dept., clerks and foremen in Wales
	441	1841 to 1904	Register of audit clerks – indexed
	442	1880 to 1962	Register of audit clerks (includes clerks from amalgamated lines) – indexed
	443	1880 to 1962	Register of chief accountant's clerks, audit section
	444	*c.* 1851 to 1901	Register of staff, Stationery and Ticket Depts
	445 to 447	1911 to 1914	General Manager's Office: registers of accidents and incidents
	448	1916 to 1918	Inquiries and reports into accidents to staff
	449	1850 to 1924	Wolverhampton area, permanent way dept.: register of inspectors, sub-inspectors and foremen entering service between 1850 and 1909
	450	1860 to 1926	Wolverhampton Engineering Offices: register of staff commencing employment 1860 to 1926
	451 & 452	1891 to 1952	Registers of pensions allowed to permanent way workmen (includes medical examinations)
	453	1920 to 1921	Bristol Division: reports on station staff (number of staff at each station and duties)
	457	*c.* 1870 to 1922	Unidentified staff register (interleaved are some staff history sheets for Cardiff)
	461	1913 to 1919	Summary of wages paid to various grades
	462	1943	Rates of pay for salaried and conciliation staff
	463	Undated	Index to register of salaried staff (register missing)
	464	1930 to 1937	Pooling of staff
	465	Undated	Statement of salaried clerical positions, Traffic Dept.
	466	Undated	Statement of salaried clerical positions, Goods Dept.
	467	Undated	Statement of salaried clerical positions, station masters, goods agents and yard masters
	468	Undated	Statement of salaried clerical positions, Secretary's, Accountant's, Locomotive, Engineering, Stores, Signal, Surveyor's, Electrical, Stationery and Marine Depts, Plymouth Docks, special police and widows and orphans fund
	469	1923 to 1935	Staff discharges through trade depression and promised reinstatement, applications for transfer and redundant staff
	470	1854 to 1916	Station staff register. Staff entering service 1854–1900 – indexed
RAIL 267	152	31 Jan 1866	Defalcation at Bath
	163	1875	Report on the duties of the staff in the Deeds Dept. (names of staff not included)
	173	1888	Telegraph staff. Report by Mr Spagnoletti (staff named)
RAIL270	1 to 30	1920 to 1929	Registers of accidents and related records
RAIL 276	22	1870 to 1899	Mechanics Institute, Swindon (various reports with names of candidates and exam results)

Cont.

TNA Reference Class	Piece No.	Dates	Description
RAIL 343	725	1917	Photograph: chief mechanical engineer's dept.; female staff
RAIL 786	9	1926	Deed room staff (includes payments to some named individuals during general strike)
RAIL 1005	316	1838 to 1953	List of superintendents
RAIL 1014	3/32 to 3/35	1820 to 1837	Applications for appointment from Cornelius Evans, John Hyde, Joseph Bavis, John Wilson Bart, William Bullock, William Windus. Specimen of handwriting; John Harris
	6/39	1863 to 1866	Lists of staff employed in Secretary's Office
	6/40	1840	Request for employment from Francis Nixon
	8/3	1842 to 1890	Papers: James Hurst, GWR's first engine driver
	16/20	1840	John Starling, workman; life and funeral
	33/22	1904	Photograph: Westbourne Park, uniformed staff
	33/23	c. 1912	Photograph: Paddington Cartage staff
	36/16	1901	Photograph: Ludgersall staff (missing at time of going to press)
	36/17	1902	Photograph: Ilminster staff
	37/7/2	1900	Photograph: GWR Infantry Company 2nd South Middlesex Volunteers
	38/32	Undated	Photograph: Swindon's first band
	48/31	Undated	Photograph: Swindon's Firemen's Group
RAIL 1057	2710	1914 to 1918	List of Railwaymen killed in First World War
	2933	1896 to 1903	List of staff, signalling, Telegraph and Electrical Depts
	2935	1880 to 1901	Servants (named) serving on local and other councils
	2971	1881	Rent of GWR houses (staff are named)
RAIL 1115	25	1914 to 1939	Staff Friendly Society (includes lists of widows and orphans, 1925 to 1939)

Management and Correspondence Files

TNA Reference Class	Piece No.	Dates	Description
RAIL 1172	358	1926	A.R. Whatley, J. Evans, masons, Port Talbot
	361	1940 to 1949	F. Gibbons, N.A. Pickering, H.W.T. Streetly, W.T. King, F. Payne, A.J. Powell, A. Barnes, W. Sweeper, E.T. Lucas, W.H.A.M. Sharp, R.C. Pithouse, setters-up, Swindon
	379	1927 to 1928	– Allen, holder-up, Birkenhead
	433	1937 to 1938	A.R. Pugh, painter, Shrewsbury
	436	1937 to 1938	F.C. Mundy, labourer, West Ealing
	207	1924	W.J. Nicholls, painter, Truro; – Jenkins, painter, Carmarthen
	265	1924 to 1925	A. Evans, carpenter; – Jones, blacksmith, Carmarthen

Ches RO Reference		
NPR2/22 & 23	*c.* 1900 to 1958	Staff registers (from 1948 British Railways)
Dev RO Reference		
588M/F5 3644Z/ZI	1874 c1917	Certificate of service, George Stuart, policeman Retirement: W.P. Parkhouse, inspector, Exeter
Wilts RO Reference		
(no ref)	1907 to 1918	Register of compensation

3.3 The London, Midland and Scottish Railway (LMS)

The London, Midland and Scottish Railway was formed by the 1923 Grouping from the amalgamation of the following companies:

1   The Arbroath and Forfar Railway Co.
2   The Brechin and Edzell District Railway Co.
3   The Caledonian Railway Co.
4   The Callander and Oban Railway Co.
5   The Cathcart District Railway Co.
6   The Charnwood Forest Railway Co.
7   The Cleator and Workington Junction Railway Co.
8   The Cockermouth, Keswick and Penrith Railway Co.
9   The Deane Valley Railway Co.
10 The Donoch Light Railway Co.
11 The Dundee and Newtyle Railway Co.
12 The Furness Railway Co.
13 The Glasgow and South Western Railway Co.
14 The Harborne Railway Co.
15 The Highland Railway Co.
16 The Killin Railway Co.
17 The Knot End Railway Co.
18 The Lanarkshire and Ayrshire Railway Co.
19 The Leek and Manifold Light Railway Co.
20 The London and North Western Railway Co.
21 The Maryport and Carlisle Railway Co.
22 The Midland Railway Co.
23 The Mold and Denbigh Junction Railway Co.
24 The North London Railway Co.
25 The North and South Western Junction Railway Co.
26 The North Staffordshire Railway Co.
27 The Shropshire Union Railways and Canal Co.
28 The Stratford-upon-Avon and Midland Junction Railway Co.
29 The Wick and Lybster Light Railway Co.
30 The Wirral Railway Co.
31 The Yorkshire Dales Railway Co.

Staff Records

TNA Reference			
Class	Piece No.	Dates	Description
RAIL 426	1 to 7	1938 to 1946	Registers of scale advances
	8	1923 to 1933	Register of staff (salary over £400 pa)
	9	1933 to 1939	Register of staff (salary over £500 pa)
	10	1922 to 1923	Summaries of staff (salaries over £500 pa)
	11 & 12	1926	Grants to loyal staff in railway strike
	13	1938	Proposed payments to clerical staff during strike in London
	14	1923 to 1937	History sheets of retired clerical staff
	15	1932 to 1936	Register of workshop staff, Crewe

Management and Correspondence Files

TNA Reference			
Class	Piece No.	Dates	Description
RAIL 1172	176	1923	J. Critchley, labourer, Horwich
	182	1923 to 1924	W. Jones, W. Owen, H. Owen, masons, H. Barker, carpenter, H. Williams, joiner, Bangor
	228	1924	F. Caffrey, W. Heath, J. Binns, blacksmiths, H. Keefe, plumber, Walsall
	231	1924	W. Rumney, mortar grinder, Lancaster
	233	1924	H.P. Dimmock, E.T. Gamble, W. Levick, bricklayers, Bletchley
	235	1924	G.W. Elliott, H. Minton, C. Palmer, carpenters, T. Watts, painter, Birmingham
	239	1924	W. Saunders, dipper, bronzer and plater, Crewe
	247	1924	J. Billington, C. Clarke, labourers, Wolverton
	248	1924	S. Gammon, bricklayer, Northampton
	249	1924	I. Harries, painter, Builth Road
	250	1924	J. Betton, carriage cleaner, Lancaster
	252	1924 to 1925	F. Dunn, wagon repairer, Birmingham
	266	1924 to 1925	A. Goodland, J.H. Davis, electricians, Manchester
	267	1925	W. Crowson, carpenter, Camden
	296	1925	E. Cope, P. Austin, A. Page, A.E. Wallis, S. Dawney, D. Baker, platers' helpers, Derby
	297	1925	– Adamson, – Pemberton, – Horley, – Pettifer, – Garner, – Elks, – Layon, – Wosley, – Grant, machinists, Derby
	299	1925	A. Hancock, wagon examiner, Newton Heath
	304	1925	H. Lythgoe, painter, Wolverhampton
	309	1925	W.J. Barnfield, machinist, St Rollox; R. Skilling, blacksmith, Polmadie; T.S. Nichols, labourer, West Ham

TNA Reference Class	Piece No.	Dates	Description
RAIL 1172 (cont.)	319	1925	T.S. Nichols, West Ham
	341	1920	Includes two lists (total 72 names) of artisans in Engineering Dept., Birmingham
	349	1929	A.F. Smith, carpenter, Derby
	374	1927	J. Henneby, W. Terry, labourers, Newton Heath
	377	1924 to 1927	– Perkins, – Cave, – Brown, – Dyde, – Routledge, – Whiting, – Stone, bricklayers, J. Dennehy, W. Terry, labourers, St Pancras and Belsize Tunnels
	408	1932	P. Smith, sawyer, Bolton
	413	1932	A. Bird and C. Watts, carpenters, A. Howlett, labourer, Hartland Road
	415	1933	E. Martin, E. Butcher, G. Hibbs, J. Morgan, A. Stevens, T. Hardiman, G. Hunt, painters, Kentish Town ·
	419	1934	A. Warren, R. White, F. West, labourers, Willesden
	421	1936	J. Clews, E. Crawford, E. Taylor, joiners, J. Russel, scaffolder, S. Chapman, plumber, J. Green, labourer, Crewe
	422	1936	H. Hewitt, J.W. Shaw, out-station repairers, Salford
	435	1937	– Carlon, labourer, Earlestown
	437	1937	H.A. Stiff, painter, Kentish Town
	456	1938	W. Hardern, J.W. Whitney, pulverizing plant assistants, Crewe
	467	1940	H. Roberts, machinist, Crewe

3.4 The London and North Eastern Railway (LNER)

The London and North Eastern Railway was formed by the 1923 Grouping from the amalgamation of the following companies:

1 The Brackenhill Light Railway Co.
2 The Colne Valley Halstead Railway Co.
3 The East Lincolnshire Railway Co.
4 The East and West Yorkshire Union Railways Co.
5 The Edinburgh and Bathgate Railway Co.
6 The Elsenham and Thaxted Light Railway Co.
7 The Forcett Railway Co.
8 The Forth and Clyde Junction Railway Co.
9 The Gifford and Garvald Light Railway Co.
10 The Great Central Railway Co.
11 The Great Eastern Railway Co.
12 The Great North of England, Clarence and Hartlepool Junction Railway Co.
13 The Great North of Scotland Railway Co.
14 The Great Northern Railway Co.
15 The Horncastle Railway Co.
16 The Humber Commercial Railway and Dock Co.
17 The Kelvedon, Tiptree and Tollesbury Pier Light Railway Co.
18 The Kilsyth and Bonnybridge Railway Co.

19 The Lauder Light Railway Co.
20 The London and Blackwall Railway Co.
21 The Mansfield Railway Co.
22 The Mid-Suffolk Light Railway Co.
23 The Newburgh and North Fife Railway Co.
24 The North British Railway Co.
25 The North Eastern Railway Co.
26 The North Lindsey Light Railway Co.
27 The Nottingham and Grantham Railway and Canal Co.
28 The Nottingham Suburban Railway Co.
29 The South Yorkshire Junction Railway Co.
30 The Stamford and Essendine Railway Co.
31 The West Riding and Grimsby Joint Railway Co.

Staff Records

TNA Reference Class	Piece No.	Dates	Description
RAIL 390	46 & 47	1923 to 1947	Salaries Committee
	133	1923 to 1947	Salaries Committee
	275	1923 to 1924	Loans to company's staff to buy houses
	351	1923 to 1947	Superannuation arrangements
	374	1923	Donations and allowances to retiring staff
	375	1923	Appointment of station masters
	380	1923	Payment of wages. Liverpool to Wrexham journey
	732	1929 to 1940	Great Northern Railway Superannuation Fund
	749	1929	Southern Area Local Board. Appointment of station masters
	794	1930 to 1936	Railwaymen's wages
	809	1930	Appointment of station masters
	810	1930 to 1931	Southern Area Local Board. Donations and retiring allowances
	812	1930	Appointment of chief chemist
	829	1931 to 1932	Admission of new entrants to benefit funds and savings banks
	846	1931	Southern Area Local Board. Appointment of station masters
	859	1931	Deductions from salaries of officers and special staff
	862	1931 to 1933	Educational schemes for clerical staff
	873	1932 to 1936	Artisans' dwellings at Whitechapel, Nottingham, Leicester, Loughborough, Manchester, Stratford and Hackney
	882	1932	Admission of new entrants to benefit funds and savings banks
	888	1932	Donations granted to retired staff
	897	1932	Appointment of station masters
	912	1933 to 1934	Admission of new entrants to benefit funds and savings banks

TNA Reference			
Class	Piece No.	Dates	Description
RAIL 390	928	1933 ⎫	
(cont.)	938	1934 ⎬	Appointment of station masters
	992	1935 ⎭	
	1019	1935 ⎫	
	1037	1935 ⎬	Admission of new entrants to benefit funds and
	1053	1936 ⎭	savings banks
	1059	1936	Appointment of station masters
	1076	1936	
	1081	1937	
	1095	1937	
	1126	1938	
	1131	1938	Admission of new entrants to benefit funds and
	1170	1939	savings banks
	1186	1939	
	1189	1940 to 1942	
	1209	1942	
	1210	1943	
	1107	1937	
	1177	1938 to 1939	
	1188	1940	
	1190	1940	Appointment of station masters
	1201	1941	
	1206	1941	
	1112	1937	Donations and allowances to retiring staff
	1208	1941 to 1944	Awards to railwaymen for gallantry
	1214	1942	
	1220	1943	
	1226	1943	
	1236	1944	
	1237	1944	
	1238	1944	
	1243	1945	
	1245	1945	
	1247	1945	Appointment of station masters
	1262	1946	
	1264	1946	
	1280	1946	
	1281	1947	
	1282	1947	
	1289	1947	
	1294	1947	
	1217	1943	
	1234	1944	
	1242	1945	
	1248	1945	Admission of new entrants to benefit funds and
	1258	1946	savings banks
	1259	1946	
	1297	1947	
	1300	1946	(includes list of members)
	1577	1923 to 1947	Appointment of station masters

Cont.

TNA Referece		Dates	Description
Class	Piece No.		
Rail 390	1580	1923 to 1939	North Eastern Railway cottage homes and benefit fund
(cont.)	1584	1923 to 1947	Police Annual Reports, general correspondence; (only a few names)
	1634	1926 to 1935	North Eastern Railway Superannuation Fund. Admission at over 40 years of age
	1825	1939	Appointment of station master at York
	1918	1925 to 1928	North Eastern Area staff clerks' meeting
RAIL 393	93		Circulars and instructions 'Guard Book'
	94	1927	Includes report on the visit of the King and Queen to Stratford Works 6 July 1927. Mentions foremen H. Knott, W.J. Wisbey and A. Farrow. Also men with over 50 years' service: G. Crabb, engine turner; W. Covell, engine turner; F. Gower, coachmaker; J. Mahon, smith; A. Splatt, engine turner; W.J. Osborn, engine fitter.
	106 to 110	1921 to 1947	Guard books
	170	1925	Medical examinations
	244	1927 to 1945	Log books, Widdrington Station
	246	1937 to 1947	Guard book of circulars
	310 to 315	1937 to 1962	Staff (D to Z)
RAIL 397	1 & 2	1939	Returns of staff at stations
	3	c. 1923 to 1942	Salaries and wages book; Sack Dept., Lincoln and East India Dock
	4	1924 and 1926	Strike of locomotive men
	5	1926	Analysis of examining and greasing posts in Carriage and Wagon Dept. (names are not included)
	6	1929	Officers' salary list: Locomotive Dept.
	7	1939	Chief Civil Engineer's Dept.; investigation into clerical costs (names not included)
	8	1923 to1929	Drivers, foremen and motormen's time book, Heaton steam shed and South Gosforth electric shed
	11	c. 1920 to 1938	Staff register: Bow and Old Ford Station
	12	1923 to 1948	Passed firemen. Record of awards and cautions. London and East Anglia Depots
RAIL 397	13	1914 to 1963	Staff histories: Stratford Works

Scot RO Reference	Date	Description
BR/LNE/14/92	1930	Station clerical staff booklet; Passenger Manager's Dept.
BR/LNE/15/4	1930 to 1943	Offence book
BR/LNE/15/9 to 22	1923 to 1936	Weekly staff changes
BR/LNE/15/23 to 37	1941 to 1946	Census of staff
BR/LNE/15/38 to 40	1925	Staff books (includes southern section)
BR/LNE/15/41	1935 to 1944	Staff applications
BR/LNE/15/42	1933 to 1935	Application for probationary clerks
BR/LNE/15/43	1937 to 1947	Junior clerks' examination; list of candidates
BR/LNE/15/46	1925 to 1947	Servants who have obtained certificate of proficiency in ambulance work

SoG	Dates	Description
Special Collections LNER (2846 cards of 2402 employees)	1923 to 1960s*	Staff Cards of Railway Employees in York area (alphabetical) *includes employees of British Rail after Nationalisation

Management and Correspondence Files

TNA Reference Class	Piece No.	Dates	Description
RAIL 1172	216	1924	F. Lewis, bricklayer, Ipswich
	229	1924	F.G. Stewart, bricklayer, Wickford
	232	1924	J. Adams, painter; V.A. Allen, crane fitter, Ipswich
	253	1924 to 1925	M. Mallows, bricklayer, Parkeston Quay, Felixstowe and Harwich
	270	1925	A.E. Cocks, labourer, Stratford
	281	1925	W.H. Ward, driller, Darlington
	285	1925	G.W. Brown, H.A. Brown, D.H. Davies, electricians, Shildon
	288	1925	57 men (listed) in signal dept. with their respective depots (Great Eastern Section)
	291	1925	S.G. Pring, fitter, Stratford
	293	1925	E. Way, wood machinist, S.G. Spring, fitter, Stratford; G.W. Brown, H.A. Brown, D.H. Davies, electricians, Shildon
	314	1925 to 1926	T.G. Hewitt, R. Etherington, G. Holdsworth, J.H. Crowther, T. Clulow, T. Horley, E.J. Hickman, M. Swainston, J.G. Kennedy, J.F. Harrison, W. Hadrick, J. Gibson, J.R. Hardy, T.E. Simpson, machinists, Darlington
	317	1925	J. Bolam, Heaton
	320	1925	W. Marley, F. Langhorn, A.W. Scott, wood machinists, Darlington
	324	1925	W. Chalmers, boilermaker, Thornton
	339	1925	C. Glass, machinist, Darlington
	354	1926	J.E.F. Mayes, W. Adamson, A. Parker, T. Ward, J.F. Tong, G. Harland, P.M. Rogers, J.H. Burton, P.J. Weaving, T. Sullivan, G.W. Adamson, J.T. Walmsley, G. Walker, labourers, Hull
	369	1927	F. Weston, fitter, Stanningley
	373	1927	– Timms, – Stimson, – Lister, – Hall, – Knight, – Fixter, C. Beetles, S. Norwell, F. Brooksbank, J.W. Ward, W. Dunkley, J. Netley, jointmakers, Peterborough. H. Parker, machinist, New England
	409	1932	W.J. Martin, J.V. Jordan, A.J. Halls, W.A. Ramsden, crane drivers, Stratford
	418	1934	A. Gell, plumber, Derby
	439	1937 to 1939	S. Draper, slater, A. Phillips, labourer, Stratford
	450	1938	C.A. Deaville, fitter, Kings Cross
	462	1938 to 1940	G. Fieldsend, J. Spenceley, fitters, Hull
	463	1938 to 1940	A. Care, machinist, Hull Docks

Cont.

LNER (continued)

TNA Referece		Dates	Description
Class	Piece No.		
RAIL 1172	464	1939	S. Penadrich, machinist, Gateshead
RAIL 1174	238		
	to	1946 to 1964	Superannuation Fund, Register of Probates and
	240		Letters of Administration

3.5 The Southern Railway (SR)

The Southern Railway was formed by the 1923 Grouping from the amalgamation of the following companies:

1   The Bridgewater Railway Co.
2   The Brighton and Dyke Railway Co.
3   The Freshwater, Yarmouth and Newport Railway Co.
4   The Hayling Railway Co.
5   The Isle of Wight Central Railway Co.
6   The Isle of Wight Railway Co.
7   The Lee-on-the-Solent Light Railway Co.
8   The London, Brighton and South Coast Railway Co.
9   The London, Chatham and Dover Railway Co.
10   The London and Greenwich Railway Co.
11   The London and South Western Railway Co.
12   The Lynton and Barnstaple Railway Co.
13   The Mid-Kent (Bromley to St Mary Cray) Railway Co.
14   The North Cornwall Railway Co.
15   The Plymouth and Dartmoor Railway Co.
16   The Sidmouth Railway Co.
17   The South Eastern Railway Co.
18   The Totton, Hythe and Fawley Light Railway Co.
19   The Victoria Station and Pimlico Railway Co.

Staff Records

TNA Reference		Dates	Description
Class	Piece No.		
RAIL 648	131	1926	Staff census (names not included)
RAIL 649	59	1930 to 1942	Register of repairs to locomotives and men (named) who undertook the work
RAIL 651	1		
	&	c. 1923 to 1944	Black books of cautions and commendations to enginemen
	2		
	3	1939 to 1945	Decisions regarding staff during the Second World War

TNA Reference Class	Piece No.	Dates	Description
RAIL 651 (cont.)	4	1927 to 1957	Accident compensation cases at Brighton Works
	5	1925 to 1947	Piecework earnings at Brighton Works. Smiths' shop
	6	1927 to 1941	Piecework percentages at Brighton Works. Locomotive shops
	7	1923 to 1927	Staff history, register of station masters entering service 1873 to 1915
	8	1933 to 1937	Monthly salary lists, Southampton Marine, Jersey, Guernsey and St Malo
	9	1924 to 1927	Correspondence regarding proposed amalgamation of docks and marine labour
	10	c. 1923 to 1929	Staff register, Marine Dept., Dover
RAIL 1017	2/25		Photograph of Inspector J. Banes, Bricklayers Arms Cabin
	2/26		Photograph of station masters at Chartham, Hawkhurst and Whitstable
	2/27	c. 1933	Photograph of W. Clements, Whitstable

Management and Correspondence Files

TNA Reference Class	Piece No.	Dates	Description
RAIL 1172	210	1924	R.H. Norton, blacksmith, Wimbledon
	213	1924	– Dixon, painter, Dover
	243	1924	G. West, carpenter, Folkestone
	246	1924	– Baker, – Wetherby, – Stanmer, signal fitters, New Cross
	258	1924 to 1925	– Anderson, – Lower, – Stace, painters, Newhaven
	259	1925	– Lester, painter, Dover
	260	1925	A.L. James, coachmaker, New Cross Gate
	271	1925	R.A. Harris, bridge examiner, Deptford
	272	1925	F.R. Scholey, painter, Angerstein Works
	273	1925	W. Clayson, plumber, Battersea
	275	1925	A. Skinner, blacksmith, New Cross
	279	1925	G. Collins, bricklayer, Ashford
	280	1925	W.F. Hills, bricklayer, Ashford
	282	1925	R.W. Emmett, signal fitter, Wimbledon
	283	1925	F. Mitchell, fitter, Exeter
	284	1925	S. Taylor, carpenter, Faversham
	286	1925	A.R. Tarr, fitter, Norwood Junction
	287	1925	W. Beck, W. Goss, painters, East Croydon
	289	1925	– Bignall, fitter, Durnsford Road Power House
	290	1925	J. Graves, carpenter, Ashford
	292	1925	J. Coomber, bricklayer, Wimbledon; – Bignall, fitter, Durnsford Road Power House
	294	1925	W.H. Kite, painter, Tunbridge Wells
	295	1925	– Knight, tinsmith, Brighton
	298	1925	H. Larkin, carpenter, Ashford
	300	1925	E.J. Gear, brake fitter, Eastleigh

Cont.

TNA Reference			
Class	Piece No.	Dates	Description
RAIL 1172 (cont.)	301	1925	T.G. Maile, J.H. Gunning, W.J. Flynn, A.H. Reeves, J.H. Lord, wagon repairers, New Cross
	302	1925	J. Head, carpenter, Eastleigh
	303	1925	A. Kinge, A. Attwood, W. Martin, F.A. Williams, R. Knight, painters, Angerstein Works
	305	1925	G. Hutchings, W. Sims, painters, Glastonbury
	306	1925	C. Bradford, Exmouth Junction
	308	1925	H. Smith, machinist, Chatham
	312	1925 to 1947	T. Sayer, W. Halke, H. Fleet, J. Halke, F. Harris, W. Smith, G. Sayer, J. King, B. King, W. Jones, E. Moreton, boilersmiths, Newhaven; J. Casey, B. Ford, holders-up, Newhaven
	313	1925	C. Bradford, labourer, Exmouth Junction
	314	1925 to 1926	
	323	1925	– Filce, – Wells, carpenters, Croydon
	325	1925	H. Tunton, plumber, Glastonbury
	327	1925	B.J. Booker, plumber, Ashford
	328	1925	D. Broomfield, bricklayer, Twickenham
	331	1925	E. Wadham, painter, Exmouth Junction
	334	1925	– Laker, – Page, – Norman, – Carwardine, – Upton, – Edwards, labourers, West Grinstead
	336	1925	A. Parsons, storeman, Tonbridge
	337	1925	P. Millar, machinist, Eastleigh
	340	1925	S.F. Lane, grinder, Eastleigh
	343	1925 to 1948	– Wiggins, – Aldridge, – Spreadbury, – Allen, watchmen, Twickenham
	344	1925 to 1926	E.A.C. Woodward, E.A. Dober, W.W. Thorne, E. Williams, C.H. Miles, A. Swift, F.J. Mitchell, machinists, Eastleigh
	346	1926	S. Sansom, T. Regan, P.S. Worsfold, S. Farnes, W.J. Mansbridge, labourers, Brighton
	350	1926	A.G. Longhurst, S.R. King, fitters, Selhurst
	351	1926	E.C. Watts, painter, Dover marine dept.
	352	1926	W.G. Ash, W.G. Clements, labourers, Exmouth
	353	1926	– Tilson, – Green, – Smith, R.T. Maskell, F.W. Harlock H.J. Maskell, S.F. West, painters, Eastleigh
	366	1925 to 1927	H.T. Taylor, wood machinist, Bricklayers Arms
	367	1927	C. Weeks, G. Payne, painters, New Cross
	370	1927	– Matthews, painter, Angerstein Works
	371	1927	W.V. Martin, A. Kinge, painters, Angerstein Works
	372	1927	D. Franks, fitter, London Bridge
	375	1925 to 1927	A. Welfare, plumber, Brighton
	376	1927	W.V. Martin, painter, London Bridge
	378	1927 to 1928	F. Hocking, S. Sergeant, F. Mantell, lifters; S. Ackland, C. Wood, J. Wright, S. Turk, E. Martin, S. Stagg, E. Turner, R. Chess, J. Hubert, R. Dalley, L.G. May, A.E. Barter, labourers' Slades Green
	383	1928 to 1929	– Allen, labourer, Twickenham ('as a result of war injuries unable to do his former work')

TNA Reference			
Class	Piece No.	Dates	Description
RAIL 1172	392	1933	A.A. Mitchard, mason, Radstock
(cont.)	405	1931	H.H. Knight, asphalter, Nine Elms
	424	1936	J.A. Warwick, fitter, Wimbledon and Richmond
	431	1937	A. Bellerby, bodymaker, Selhurst
	432	1937	T. Kane, painter, Waterloo
	434	1937	H. Glen, fitter, New Cross Gate
	449	1937	C.H. West, W.H. Perkins, F. Brook, wagon makers, Exmouth Junction
	461	1938	A. Marson, fitter, Tonbridge
			Note: Records dating from 1948 relate to British Railways Southern Region

APPENDIX 4

JOINT COMMITTEES – MINUTES AND STAFF RECORDS

Where records are held by The National Archives the relevant RAIL reference is given. Where records are held by another repository the abbreviation for that repository is given together with the relevant document references.

Ashby and Nuneaton Lines Joint Committee

| Constituent companies: | 1. London and North Western Railway Co. |
| | 2. Midland Railway Co. |

The functions of this committee were transferred to the London and North Western and Midlands Joint Committee in 1923.

TNA Reference Class	Piece No.	Dates	Description
RAIL 11	1 to 8	1867 to 1889	Minutes
RAIL 410	1801	1902 to 1910	Staff, Traffic, Police and Telegraph Depts

Axholme Joint Railway Committee

| Constituent companies: | 1. North Eastern Railway Co. |
| | 2. Lancashire and Yorkshire Railway Co. |

TNA Reference Class	Piece No.	Dates	Description
RAIL 13	1 to 3	1902 to 1946	Minutes

Bedford and Cambridge Railway Co. and London and North Western Railway Co. Joint Committee

Constituent companies:		1. Bedford and Cambridge Railway Co. 2. London and North Western Railway Co.	
TNA Reference			
Class	Piece No.	Dates	Description
RAIL 27	5	1860 to 1863	Minutes

Birkenhead Joint Committee

Constituent companies:		1. Birkenhead Railway Co. 2. London and North Western Railway Co. 3. Great Western Railway Co. (from 1860)	
TNA Reference			
Class	Piece No.	Dates	Description
RAIL 35	14 to 23	1852 to 1867	Minutes

Birkenhead Park Station Committee – see Mersey and Wirral Railways Joint Committee

Birmingham West Suburban Railway and Midland Railway Joint Committee

Constituent companies:		1. Birmingham West Suburban Railway Co. 2. Midland Railway Co.	
TNA Reference			
Class	Piece No.	Dates	Description
RAIL 43	4	1874 to 1875	Minutes

Bishop Auckland Station Joint Committee

Constituent companies:		1. North Eastern Railway Co. 2. Stockton and Darlington Railway Co.	
TNA Reference			
Class	Piece No.	Dates	Description
RAIL 47	1	1858 to 1862	Minutes

435

Blackburn Railway and Lancashire and Yorkshire Railway Joint Traffic Committee

| Constituent companies: | 1. Blackburn Railway Co. |
| | 2. Lancashire and Yorkshire Railway Co. |

TNA Reference			
Class	Piece No.	Dates	Description
RAIL 52	3	1850 to 1858	Minutes

Blackburn Railway Joint Committee

Constituent companies:	1. Blackburn Railway Co.
	2. Lancashire and Yorkshire Railway Co.
	3. East Lancashire Railway Co.

TNA Reference			
Class	Piece No.	Dates	Description
RAIL 52	4 & 5	1858 to 1862	Minutes

Brighton and Croydon Railways Committee of Amalgamation

| Constituent companies: | 1. London and Brighton Railway Co. |
| | 2. London and Croydon Railway Co. |

TNA Reference			
Class	Piece No.	Dates	Description
RAIL 71	1	1845 to 1846	Minutes

Brighton and South Eastern (Croydon and Oxted) Joint Committee

| Constituent companies: | 1. London, Brighton and South Coast Railway Co. |
| | 2. South Eastern Railway Co. |

TNA Reference			
Class	Piece No.	Dates	Description
RAIL 414	202 to 209	1884 to 1922	Minutes

Brighton, Croydon and Dover Joint Station Committee (London Bridge Station)

Constituent companies:	1. London and Croydon Railway Co.
	2. London and Brighton Railway Co.
	3. South Eastern Railway Co.

TNA Reference			
Class	Piece No.	Dates	Description
RAIL 386	28 to 35	1840 to 1851	Minutes

Bristol Harbour Railway Joint Committee

Constituent companies:	1. Great Western Railway Co.
	2. Bristol and Exeter Railway Co.
	3. Bristol Corporation

TNA Reference			
Class	Piece No.	Dates	Description
RAIL 79	1 to 3	1867 to 1879	Minutes

Bristol Joint Station Committee

Constituent companies:	1. Great Western Railway Co.
	2. Midland Railway Co.
	3. Bristol and Exeter Railway Co.

The functions of this committee were transferred to the Great Western and Midland Railway Companies Joint Committee in 1894 which became the Great Western and London, Midland and Scottish Railways Joint Committee in 1923.

TNA Reference			
Class	Piece No.	Dates	Description
RAIL 80	1 to 6	1863 to 1894	Minutes
Brun/Cl Reference			
Cup 5; Box 3/7		1878 to 1880, 1883, 1888, 1892	Extracts of Minutes
Cup 5; Box 3/10		1878 to 1880	Police and Staff Reports

437

Bristol Port Railway and Pier Co. Joint Committee

Constituent companies:	1. Great Western Railway Co. 2. Midland Railway Co. 3. Bristol Port Railway and Pier Co.	22 Nov 1870 to 17 April 1871
	1. Great Western Railway Co. 2. Midland Railway Co. 3. Clifton Extension Railway	from 20 June 1871

TNA Reference Class	Piece No.	Dates	Description
RAIL 81	1 & 2 5 to 8	1870 to 1880	Minutes

Carlisle Citadel Station Committee

Two committees were formed to manage this station:

1. Carlisle Goods Traffic Committee
2. Carlisle Citadel Station Committee

Constituent companies:
1. London and North Western Railway Co.
2. Caledonian Railway Co.

Both committees passed to the London, Midland and Scottish Railway in 1923.

TNA Reference Class	Piece No.	Dates	Description
RAIL 98	1 to 5	1844 to 1922	Minutes

Cheshire Lines Committee

The Cheshire Lines Committee was set up in 1865 to manage the West Cheshire Railway Co.

Constituent companies:
1. Manchester, Sheffield and Lincolnshire Railway Co.
2. Great Northern Railway Co.
3. West Cheshire Railway Co.
4. Midland Railway Co.

In 1923 this committee passed to the London and North Eastern Railway and London, Midland and Scottish Railway, and in 1948 to the British Transport Commission.

TNA Reference Class	Piece No.	Dates	Description
RAIL 110	1 to 121	1863 to 1947	Minutes
	160	1915 to 1926	Staff Irregularities (staff are named)
	353	1882	
	354	1889	Rents, Occupiers of Railway Properties
	355	1892	
RAIL 783	333	1913 to 1916	Accidents, St James Station, Liverpool
	369	1914 to 1919	Salaries and Wages (includes list of accountant's staff, February 1914, and staff alterations)
	370	1916	Proposed Staff Advances (includes list of clerks, agents and station masters)
	371	1916	Proposed Staff Advances
	372	1917 to 1918	Salary Increases, with lists of staff
	374	1918 to 1920	Railway Clearing House System Superannuation Fund (staff are named)

Chester Joint Station Committee

Constituent companies:	1. London and North Western Railway Co.
	2. Chester and Holyhead Railway Co.
	3. Shrewsbury and Chester Railway Co.
	4. Chester and Birkenhead Railway Co.
	5. Birkenhead, Lancashire and Cheshire Junction Railway Co.

TNA Reference Class	Piece No.	Dates	Description
RAIL 114	1 to 9	1846 to 1867	Minutes
			Staff Records
	11	1849	Report from Braithwaite Poole and R.L. Jones (Manager) upon Merchandise and Mineral Traffic at Chester, giving details of staff
	12	1849	John Stewart's Report on Rating Valuation of Station
	13	1850	Manager's Report on Principles of Work for Each Company
	14	1852	Alfred King's report on position of lamps in Passenger Station
	15	1855	Manager's Report on Accommodation for Goods Business
	16	1855 to 1863	Manager's reports on Expenditure on Chester Joint Station, 1855 to 1857, and 1859, with balance sheets and expenditure statements 1851 to 1863
	17	1861	Manager's Report with statistics of Chester General Station for 1860 to 1861

City Lines and Extension Joint Committee – see Metropolitan and District Railway Joint Committee

Cleator and Furness Railway Committee

Constituent companies:	1. Furness Railway Co. 2. Whitehaven, Cleator and Egremont Railway Co.		
TNA Reference Class Piece No.	Dates	Description	
RAIL 118 1	1866 to 1870	Minutes	

Cleator and Workington Junction and Furness Railways Joint Committee

Constituent companies:	1. Cleator and Workington Junction Railway Co. 2. Furness Railway Co.		
TNA Reference Class Piece No.	Dates	Description	
RAIL 119 6 to 8	1878 to 1911	Minutes	

Clifton Extension Railway Joint Committee

Constituent companies:	1. Great Western Railway Co. 2. Midland Railway Co.		
TNA Reference Class Piece No.	Dates	Description	
RAIL 81 9	1881 to 1894	Minutes	
Brist RO Reference			
Acc. 12167/28 to 30	1870 to 1882	Minutes	

Cockermouth Joint Station Committee

Constituent companies:	1. Cockermouth and Workington Railway Co. 2. Cockermouth, Keswick and Penrith Railway Co. 3. London and North Western Railway Co.
The Cockermouth and Workington Railway Co. was vested in the London and North Western Railway Co. 16 July 1866	

TNA Reference Class	Piece No.	Dates	Description
RAIL 122	6 & 7	1864 to 1896	Minutes
RAIL 123	11 to 13	1863 to 1896	Minutes

Cornwall and West Cornwall Joint Railway

Constituent companies:	1. Cornwall Railway Co. 2. West Cornwall Railway Co.	
Brun/Cl Reference	Dates	Description
4338	1875 to 1877	Truro Joint Station Line Clear Book (has signalmen's initials only)

Cornwall Minerals and Great Western Railway Companies Joint Committee

Constituent companies:	1. Cornwall Minerals Railway Co. 2. Great Western Railway Co.	
TNA Reference Class	Piece No.	Dates	Description
RAIL 132	1	1881 to 1888	Minutes

Cornwall Railway Joint Committee

Constituent companies:	1. Cornwall Railway Co. 2. Great Western Railway Co. 3. Bristol and Exeter Railway Co. 4. South Devon Railway Co.	
TNA Reference Class	Piece No.	Dates	Description
RAIL 134	5 to 14	1858 to 1889	Minutes
Brun/C1 Reference			
3344 3345		1862 to 1888	Minutes

East and West Junction, Stratford-upon-Avon, Towcester and Midland Junction Railway Companies Joint Committee

| Constituent companies: | 1. East and West Junction Railway Co. |
| | 2. Stratford-upon-Avon, Towcester and Midland Junction Railway Co. |

TNA Reference Class	Piece No.	Dates	Description
RAIL 168	1	1903 to 1909	Minutes

East and West Yorkshire Junction Railway and Leeds and Thirsk Railway Joint Committee

| Constituent companies: | 1. East and West Yorkshire Junction Railway Co. |
| | 2. Leeds and Thirsk Railway Co. |

TNA Reference Class	Piece No.	Dates	Description
RAIL 169	3	1849 to 1852	Minutes

East Lancashire and Lancashire and Yorkshire Railways United Board Committee

| Constituent companies: | 1. East Lancashire Railway Co. |
| | 2. Lancashire and Yorkshire Railway Co. |

TNA Reference Class	Piece No.	Dates	Description
RAIL 176	46 to 49	1857 to 1858	Minutes

East Lancashire Railway and Blackburn and Preston Railway Joint Committee

| Constituent companies: | 1. East Lancashire Railway Co. |
| | 2. Blackburn and Preston Railway Co. |

TNA Reference Class	Piece No.	Dates	Description
RAIL 176	50	1845 to 1847	Minutes

East Lancashire Railway Co. Joint Stations Committee

| Constituent companies: | 1. Lancashire and Yorkshire Railway Co. |
| | 2. East Lancashire Railway Co. |

TNA Reference Class	Piece No.	Dates	Description
RAIL 176	37 to 43	1852 to 1859	Minutes

East London Railway Joint Committee

Constituent companies:	1. London, Brighton and South Coast Railway Co.
	2. South Eastern Railway Co.
	3. London, Chatham and Dover Railway Co.
	4. Metropolitan Railway Co.
	5. Metropolitan District Railway Co.
	6. East London Railway Co.

The East London Railway Co. granted leases to the London, Brighton and South Coast Railway Co., the South Eastern Railway Co., the London, Chatham and Dover Railway Co., the Metropolitan Railway Co. and the Metropolitan District Railway Co. Two representatives from these companies together with two from the East London Railway Co. formed a joint committee which managed and controlled the East London Railway Co. The East London Railway Co. was transferred to the Southern Railway Co. by the Southern Railway Act of 1925 but the line was leased to the Metropolitan Railway Co., the Metropolitan District Railway Co. and the London and North Eastern Railway. The joint committee passed to the British Transport Commission in 1948.

TNA Reference Class	Piece No.	Dates	Description
RAIL 179	1 to 33	1884 to 1933	Minutes (with indexes)
	37	1884	Return of Traffic Staff
RAIL 1057	2710	1914 to 1918	List of Railwaymen killed in First World War

Eastern Counties and East Suffolk Railways Joint Committee

Constituent companies:	1. Eastern Counties Railway Co.
	2. East Suffolk Railway Co.

TNA Reference Class	Piece No.	Dates	Description
RAIL 185	1	1859 to 1862	Minutes

Eastern Counties, Norfolk and Eastern Union Joint Committee

Constituent companies:	1. Eastern Counties Railway Co.
	2. Norfolk Railway Co.
	3. Eastern Union Railway Co.

Cont.

TNA Reference Class	Piece No.	Dates	Description
RAIL 186	66	1854 to 1862	Minutes

Eastern Union Railway Joint Committee

Constituent companies:	1. Eastern Union Railway Co. 2. Ipswich and Bury St Edmunds Railway Co.		
TNA Reference Class	**Piece No.**	**Dates**	**Description**
RAIL 187	19	1847	Minutes

Furness and Midland Railways Joint Committee

Constituent companies:	1. Furness Railway Co. 2. Midland Railway Co.		
TNA Reference Class	**Piece No.**	**Dates**	**Description**
RAIL 213	1 & 2	1863 to 1882	Minutes

Garston and Liverpool Railway Committee

Constituent companies:	1. Manchester, Sheffield and Lincolnshire Railway Co. 2. Great Northern Railway Co.		
TNA Reference Class	**Piece No.**	**Dates**	**Description**
RAIL 216	1 to 4	1861 to 1866	Minutes

Great Central and London and North Western Railways Joint Committee

Constituent companies:	1. Great Central Railway Co. 2. London and North Western Railway Co.		
TNA Reference Class	**Piece No.**	**Dates**	**Description**
RAIL 222	1 to 3	1905 to 1931	Minutes

Great Central and Metropolitan Railways Joint Committee

| Constituent companies: | 1. Great Central Railway Co. |
| | 2. Metropolitan Railway Co. |

TNA Reference Class Piece No.	Dates	Description
RAIL 223 1	1899 only	Minutes
LMA Reference		
Acc.1297/MGCJ1/1 to 5	1906 to 1922	Minutes

Great Central and Midland Railways Joint Committee

Constituent companies:	1. Great Central Railway Co.
	2. Midland Railway Co.
	1. London and North Eastern Railway Co. ⎤ from 1923
	2. London, Midland and Scottish Railway Co. ⎦

TNA Reference Class Piece No.	Dates	Description
RAIL 224 9 to 12 & 16 & 20	1904 to 1929	Minutes

Great Central, Hull and Barnsley, and Midland Railways Joint Committee

Constituent companies:	1. Great Central Railway Co.
	2. Hull and Barnsley Railway Co.
	3. Midland Railway Co.

TNA Reference Class Piece No.	Dates	Description
RAIL 225 1 to 4	1906 to 1929	Minutes

Great Grimsby and Sheffield Junction Railway, and Sheffield and Lincolnshire Railway Joint Committee

| Constituent companies: | 1. Great Grimsby and Sheffield Junction Railway Co. |
| | 2. Sheffield and Lincolnshire Railway Co. |

TNA Reference Class Piece No.	Dates	Description
RAIL 229 1	1846	Minutes

Great Northern and Great Eastern Railways Joint Committee

Constituent companies:	1. Great Northern Railway Co. 2. Great Eastern Railway Co.		
TNA Reference Class Piece No.		Dates	Description
RAIL 233 1 to 15		1879 to 1922	Minutes
RAIL 393 225 & 226		1897 to 1927	Station master's Staff Book, Gainsborough (memoranda re staff attendance, transfers, etc.)

Great Northern and London and North Western Railways Joint Committee

Constituent companies:	1. Great Northern Railway Co. 2. London and North Western Railway Co.		
TNA Reference Class Piece No.		Dates	Description
RAIL 234 1 to 5		1874 to 1929	Minutes

Great Northern and Manchester, Sheffield and Lincolnshire Railways Joint Committee

Constituent companies:	1. Great Northern Railway Co. 2. Manchester, Sheffield and Lincolnshire Railway Co.		
TNA Reference Class Piece No.		Dates	Description
RAIL 235 1 to 7		1849 to 1872	Minutes (with index)
RAIL 783 279		1912	Retirement of goods guard, John Bingham

Great Western and Bristol and Exeter Railways Joint Committee

Constituent companies:	1. Great Western Railway Co. 2. Bristol and Exeter Railway Co.		
TNA Reference Class Piece No.		Dates	Description
RAIL 238 1		1875	Minutes

Great Western and Great Central Railways Joint Committee

Constituent companies:	1. Great Western Railway Co. 2. Great Central Railway Co.		
TNA Reference Class Piece No.	Dates	Description	

RAIL 239   1
          to
          4
	1899 to 1946	Minutes	

Great Western and London and South Western Railways Joint Committee

Constituent companies:	1. Great Western Railway Co. 2. London and South Western Railway Co. 1. Great Western Railway Co. 2. Southern Railway Co. } from 1923		
TNA Reference Class Piece No.	Dates	Description	

RAIL 240   1
          to
          10
	1877 to 1938	Minutes	

Great Western and Midland Railway Companies Joint Committee

Constituent companies:	1. Great Western Railway Co. 2. Midland Railway Co.		
TNA Reference Class Piece No.	Dates	Description	

RAIL 241   1
          to
          23
	1869 to 1923	Minutes	

28	1865 to 1915	Staff Register	

Great Western and Port Talbot Railway and Docks Companies Consultation Committee

Constituent companies:	1. Great Western Railway Co. 2. Port Talbot Railway and Docks Co.		
TNA Reference Class Piece No.	Dates	Description	

RAIL 242   1
          &
          2
	1908 to 1919	Minutes	

Great Western and Rhondda and Swansea Bay Railway Companies Consultation Committee

Constituent companies:	1. Great Western Railway Co. 2. Rhondda and Swansea Bay Railway Co.		
TNA Reference Class Piece No.		Dates	Description
RAIL 243 1 & 2		1903 to 1916	Minutes

Great Western and Rhymney Railway Companies Joint Committee

Constituent companies:	1. Great Western Railway Co. 2. Rhymney Railway Co.		
TNA Reference Class Piece No.		Dates	Description
RAIL 244 1 to 4		1869 to 1922	Minutes (Bargoed Railways Joint Committee)

Great Western and Southern Railways Joint Committee

Constituent companies:	1. Great Western Railway Co. 2. Southern Railway Co.		
TNA Reference Class Piece No.		Dates	Description
RAIL 245 1 & 2		1925 to 1938	Minutes

Great Western and Stratford-upon-Avon Railway Companies Joint Committee of Management

Constituent companies:	1. Great Western Railway Co. 2. Stratford-upon-Avon Railway Co.		
TNA Reference Class Piece No.		Dates	Description
RAIL 246 1		1860 to 1877	Minutes

Great Western and Vale of Neath Railways Joint Committee

Constituent companies:	1. Great Western Railway Co. 2. Vale of Neath Railway Co.		
TNA Reference Class Piece No.	Dates	Description	
RAIL 704 16	1866 to 1867	Minutes	

Great Western and West Midland Railway Companies Joint Committee

Constituent companies:	1. Great Western Railway Co. 2. West Midland Railway Co.		
TNA Reference Class Piece No.	Dates	Description	
RAIL 248 –		No Minutes (other records 1862 to 1863)	

Great Western and Whitland and Cardigan Railways Joint Committee

Constituent companies:	1. Great Western Railway Co. 2. Whitland and Cardigan Railway Co.		
TNA Reference Class Piece No.	Dates	Description	
RAIL 747 3 to 5	1883 to 1887	Minutes	

Great Western, Bristol and Exeter, and South Devon Railways Joint Committee

Constituent companies:	1. Great Western Railway Co. 2. Bristol and Exeter Railway Co. 3. South Devon Railway Co.		
TNA Reference Class Piece No.	Dates	Description	
RAIL 249 1 to 4	1870 to 1876	Minutes	

449

Great Western, Shrewsbury and Chester and Shrewsbury and Birmingham Railway Companies Joint Traffic Committee

Constituent companies:	1. Great Western Railway Co.
	2. Shrewsbury and Chester Railway Co.
	3. Shrewsbury and Birmingham Railway Co.

TNA Reference Class	Piece No.	Dates	Description
RAIL 283	1 & 2	1851 to 1855	Minutes

Great Western, West Midland and South Wales Railway Companies Joint Committee

Constituent companies:	1. Great Western Railway Co.
	2. West Midland Railway Co.
	3. South Wales Railway Co.

TNA Reference Class	Piece No.	Dates	Description
RAIL 284	1	1861 to 1863	Minutes

Halesowen Railway Joint Committee

| Constituent companies: | 1. Great Western Railway Co. |
| | 2. Midland Railway Co. |

This committee was formed 9 January 1884 and continued its meetings until 2 May 1894 after which its functions passed to the Great Western and Midlands Railways Joint Committee. This latter committee on 1 January 1923 became the London, Midland and Scottish and Great Western Railways Joint Committee. It ceased on Nationalization 1 January 1948.

TNA Reference Class	Piece No.	Dates	Description
RAIL 287	1 to 3	1884 to 1894	Minutes (with index)

Halifax and Ovenden Joint Committee

| Constituent companies: | 1. Great Northern Railway Co. |
| | 2. Lancashire and Yorkshire Railway Co. |

The Halifax and Ovenden Junction Railway Co. was incorporated 30 June 1864 and subscribed to by the Great Northern Railway Co. and the Lancashire and Yorkshire Railway Co. By an Act of 1 August 1870 the company was vested in the Great Northern Railway Co. and the Lancashire and Yorkshire Railway Co. jointly with a joint committee of four members from each company.

TNA Reference Class	Piece No.	Dates	Description
RAIL 288	1 & 2	1884 to 1929	Minutes

Halifax High Level Railway Joint Committee

Constituent companies:	1. Lancashire and Yorkshire Railway Co. 2. Great Northern Railway Co.		
TNA Reference Class	**Piece No.**	**Dates**	**Description**
RAIL 290	1	1889 to 1929	Minutes

Hammersmith and City Railway Joint Committee

Constituent companies:	1. Metropolitan Railway Co. 2. Great Western Railway Co.	
LMA Reference	**Dates**	**Description**
Acc.1297/HCJ1/1 to 11	1865 to 1948	Minutes
Acc.1297/HCJ4/1	1865 to 1922	Register of Staff

Hereford Joint Station Construction and Traffic Committees

Constituent companies:	1. Great Western Railway Co. 2. Shrewsbury and Hereford Railway Co.		
Management of the Joint Station passed to the Shrewsbury and Hereford Joint Committee which was taken over by the London and North Western and Great Western Railways Joint Committee 4 October 1867.			
TNA Reference Class	**Piece No.**	**Dates**	**Description**
RAIL 301	1 to 7	1854 to 1863	Minutes

Huddersfield Joint Station Committee

Constituent companies:	1. Lancashire and Yorkshire Railway Co.	
	2. London and North Western Railway Co.	
TNA Reference		
Class Piece No.	Dates	Description
RAIL 309 1	1865 to 1879	Minutes

Hull and Barnsley, and Great Central Railways Joint Committee

Constituent companies:	1. Hull and Barnsley Railway Co.	
	2. Great Central Railway Co.	
TNA Reference		
Class Piece No.	Dates	Description
RAIL 310 1 to 3	1909 to 1922	Minutes (with index)

Hull Joint Dock Committee

Constituent companies:	1. North Eastern Railway Co.	
	2. Hull and Barnsley Railway Co.	
TNA Reference		
Class Piece No.	Dates	Description
RAIL 527 114	1913 to 1922	Minutes

Kingston and London Railway Joint Committee

Constituent companies:	1. London and South Western Railway Co.	
	2. Metropolitan and District Railway Co.	
LMA Reference	Dates	Description
Acc.1297/KL1/1	1881 to 1891	Minutes

Lancashire and Yorkshire, and Great Eastern Railways Joint Committee

Constituent companies:	1. Lancashire and Yorkshire Railway Co.	
	2. Great Eastern Railway Co.	
TNA Reference		
Class Piece No.	Dates	Description
RAIL 340 1	1864 to 1865	Minutes

Lancashire and Yorkshire, and Great Northern Joint Stations Committee

Constituent companies:	1. Lancashire and Yorkshire Railway Co.
	2. Great Northern Railway Co.
	1. London, Midland and Scottish Railway Co. ⎫
	2. London and North Eastern Railway Co. ⎬ from 1923

TNA Reference Class Piece No.	Dates	Description

RAIL 341   1 ⎫
              to ⎬
              6 ⎭
	1884 to 1929	Minutes

7	*undated*	Photograph of staff at Knottingley Station (before 1907)

Lancashire and Yorkshire, and Lancashire Union Joint Committee

Constituent companies:	1. Lancashire & Yorkshire Railway Co. ⎫ 1865 to 1872
	2. Lancashire Union Railway Co. ⎬
	1. London & North Western Railway Co. ⎫ 1872 to 1889
	2. Lancashire & Yorkshire Railway Co. ⎬

TNA Reference Class Piece No.	Dates	Description

RAIL 342   1 ⎫
              & ⎬
              2 ⎭
	1865 to 1889	Minutes

Lancashire and Yorkshire Railway and London and North Western Officers' Meeting

Constituent companies:	1. Lancashire and Yorkshire Railway Co.
	2. London and North Western Railway Co.

Meetings to discuss Traffic and Accountants' Depts at Manchester, Mosley Street, Smith-field Market, Bolton, Bradford, Leeds and Belfast. (Some staff are named for each of these places.)

TNA Reference Class Piece No.	Dates	Description
RAIL 343 540	1905	Minutes: Joint Office Accommodation

453

Leeds New Joint Station Committee

Constituent companies:	1. London and North Western Railway Co. 2. North Eastern Railway Co. 3. Lancashire and Yorkshire Railway Co.	1866 to 1937
	1. London and North Eastern Railway Co. 2. London, Midland and Scottish Railway Co.	from 1923

TNA Reference Class Piece No.	Dates	Description
RAIL 356 1 to 20	1866 to 1937	Minutes

Liverpool, Crosby and Southport and East Lancashire Railways Joint Committee

Constituent companies:	1. Liverpool, Crosby and Southport Railway Co. 2. East Lancashire Railway Co.

TNA Reference Class Piece No.	Dates	Description
RAIL 372 8 & 9	1848 to 1854	Minutes

Liverpool Joint Entrance Committee

Constituent companies:	1. East Lancashire Railway Co. 2. Lancashire and Yorkshire Railway Co.

TNA Reference Class Piece No.	Dates	Description
RAIL 176 51 & 52	1849 to 1853	Minutes

Llynvi and Ogmore, and Great Western Railways Joint Committee

Constituent companies:	1. Llynvi and Ogmore Railway Co. 2. Great Western Railway Co.

TNA Reference Class Piece No.	Dates	Description
RAIL 381 1 to 6	1873 to 1883	Minutes

London and North Western, and Brecon and Merthyr Railways Joint Committee

| Constituent companies: | 1. London and North Western Railway Co. |
| | 2. Brecon and Merthyr Tydfil Junction Railway Co. |

In 1923 this committee became the London, Midland and Scottish, and Great Western Railways Joint Committee (London and North Western and Brecon and Merthyr Section)

TNA Reference Class	Piece No.	Dates	Description
RAIL 402	1 to 3	1879 to 1925	Minutes

London and North Western, and Furness Railways Joint Committee

| Constituent companies: | 1. London and North Western Railway Co. |
| | 2. Furness Railway Co. |

TNA Reference Class	Piece No.	Dates	Description
RAIL 403	1 to 4	1877 to 1908	Minutes
	7	1899 to 1906	Lists of staff with rates of pay
RAIL 1057	2710	1914 to 1918	List of Railwaymen killed in First World War

London and North Western and Great Western Joint Committee

Constituent companies:	1. London and North Western Railway Co.
	2. Great Western Railway Co.
	3. West Midland Railway Co. (to 9 July 1863)

This joint committee was originally set up as the London and North Western, Great Western and West Midland Joint Committee 17 March 1863. The joint committee became the London Midland and Scottish, and Great Western Joint Committee in 1923 and ceased on Nationalization in 1947.

TNA Reference Class	Piece No.	Dates	Description
RAIL 404	1 to 50 & 78 to 101	1863 to 1947	Minutes
	177 to 180	1871 to 1897	Registers of Staff on Joint Lines

Cont.

455

Ches RO Reference	Dates	Description
NPR 2/1 to NPR 2/8	*c.* 1869 to 1922	Staff Registers
NPR 2/9	*undated*	Index to unidentified register

London and North Western, and Lancashire and Yorkshire Railways Joint Committee

Constituent companies:	1. London and North Western Railway Co. 2. Lancashire and Yorkshire Railway Co.

TNA Reference Class Piece No.	Dates	Description
RAIL 405 1 to 10	1857 to 1921	Minutes: Joint Committee
11 to 17	1863 to 1889	Minutes: Joint Traffic Committee
18 to 21	1881 to 1914	Minutes: Officers of Joint Committee
22 & 37	1889 to 1921	Minutes: Amalgamated Joint Committee
Brun/Cl Reference		
4339	1901 to 1905	Minutes: Joint Committee

London and North Western, and Midland Railways Joint Committee

Constituent companies:	1. London and North Western Railway Co. 2. Midland Railway Co.

TNA Reference Class Piece No.	Dates	Description
RAIL 406 1 to 7	1849 to 1922	Minutes (Joint Committee and other Committees, includes Birmingham New Street)
16	1861 to 1911	Staff Register of Coaching and Police Depts at New Street and Derby Stations

London and North Western, and Rhymney Railway Companies Joint Line Committee

Constituent companies:	1. London and North Western Railway Co. 2. Rhymney Railway Co.

TNA Reference Class Piece No.	Dates	Description
RAIL 407 3	1868 to 1878	Minutes

London and North Western and Shropshire Union Railways and Canal Co. Joint Committee

Constituent companies:	1. London and North Western Railway Co. 2. Shropshire Union Railways and Canal Co.		
TNA Reference Class Piece No.	Dates	Description	
RAIL 623 36	1847 to 1870	Minutes	

London and North Western, Manchester, Sheffield and Lincolnshire, and Great Northern Railway Companies Joint Committee

Constituent companies:	1. London and North Western Railway Co. 2. Manchester, Sheffield and Lincolnshire Railway Co. 3. Great Northern Railway Co.		
TNA Reference Class Piece No.	Dates	Description	
RAIL 408 1 to 4	1858 to 1861	Minutes	

London and North Western, Midland and North London Railways Joint Committee

Constituent companies:	1. London and North Western Railway Co. 2. Midland Railway Co. 3. North London Railway Co.		
TNA Reference Class Piece No.	Dates	Description	
RAIL 521 9 to 17	1871 to 1922	Minutes	

London and North Western, Midland, Manchester, Sheffield and Lincolnshire Railway Companies Joint Committee

Constituent companies:	1. London and North Western Railway Co. 2. Midland Railway Co. 3. Manchester, Sheffield and Lincolnshire Railway Co.		
TNA Reference Class Piece No.	Dates	Description	
RAIL 409 1	1854 to 1855	Minutes	

London and York Railway and Direct Northern Railway Joint Board

Constituent companies:	1. London and York Railway Co.
	2. Direct Northern Railway Co.

Note: Neither of these railways was built

TNA Reference Class	Piece No.	Dates	Description
RAIL 236	6	1846	Minutes

London, Brighton and South Coast Railway and London and South Western Railway Joint Committee

Constituent companies:	1. London, Brighton and South Coast Railway Co.
	2. London and South Western Railway Co.

TNA Reference Class	Piece No.	Dates	Description
RAIL 414	196 to 201	1864 to 1915	Minutes

London, Midland and Scottish, and Great Western Railways Joint Committee

Constituent companies:	1. London, Midland and Scottish Railway Co.
	2. Great Western Railway Co.

TNA Reference Class	Piece No.	Dates	Description
RAIL 416	1 & 2 & 11 & 12	1926 to 1947	Minutes
	20 & 21	1923 to 1925	Minutes, London and North Western, and Rhymney Section Joint Committee

London, Midland and Scottish, and London and North Eastern Joint Committee

Constituent companies:	1. London, Midland and Scottish Railway Co.
	2. London and North Eastern Railway Co.

TNA Reference		Dates	Description
Class	Piece No.		
RAIL 417	1 to 11	1930 to 1947	Minutes (various committees)
	16	1891 to 1938	Staff Register, Traffic and Parcels Depts, Leeds New Station
Scot RO Reference			
BR/LMLN/1/12 to 14		1930 to 1947	Group Committee Minutes

London, Tilbury and Southend, and East and West India Dock Companies Joint Committee

Constituent companies:	1. London, Tilbury and Southend Railway Co.
	2. East and West India Dock Co.

TNA Reference		Dates	Description
Class	Piece No.		
RAIL 437	22	1885 to 1887	Minutes

London, Tilbury and Southend, and Metropolitan District Railways, Whitechapel and Bow Railway Joint Committee

Constituent companies:	1. London, Tilbury and Southend Railway Co.
	2. Metropolitan District Railways Co.
	3. Whitechapel and Bow Railway Co.

From 1912 this became the Midland and Metropolitan District Railways, Whitechapel and Bow Railway Joint Committee. From 1934 this committee became the London Passenger Transport Board and London, Midland and Scottish Railway, Whitechapel and Bow Joint Committee.

LMA Reference	Dates	Description
Acc.1297/W&B1/6A & 6B & Acc.1297/W&Bl/10 to 12	1902 to 1948	Minutes

London, Tilbury and Southend Extension Railway Joint Committee

Constituent companies:	1. London, Tilbury and Southend Railway Co.
	2. London and Blackwall Railway Co.

TNA Reference		Dates	Description
Class	Piece No.		
RAIL 437	23	1852 to 1862	Minutes

Macclesfield Joint Station Committee

Constituent companies:	1. London and North Western Railway Co. 2. North Staffordshire Railway Co.		
TNA Reference Class Piece No.	Dates	Description
RAIL 449 1 & 2	1847 to 1851	Minutes

Manchester and Leeds and Lancashire and Yorkshire Railway Companies Joint Committees

Constituent companies:	1. Manchester and Leeds Railway Co. 2. Lancashire and Yorkshire Railway Co.		
TNA Reference Class Piece No.	Dates	Description
RAIL 343 478	1846 to 1847	Finance Committee
484	1835 to 1855	Various Minutes
491 to 506	1846 to 1856	Traffic Committee
519	1846 to 1848	Locomotive and Carriage Committee

Manchester and Leeds, Grand Junction and North Union Railways Joint Committee

Constituent companies:	1. Manchester and Leeds Railway Co. 2. Grand Junction Railway Co. 3. North Union Railway Co.		
TNA Reference Class Piece No.	Dates	Description
RAIL 534 8 to 26	1840 to 1889	Minutes

Manchester and Milford, and Pembroke and Tenby Railway Companies Joint Committee

Constituent companies:	1. Manchester and Milford Railway Co. 2. Pembroke and Tenby Railway Co.		
TNA Reference Class Piece No.	Dates	Description
RAIL 455 1	1879 to 1881	Minutes

Manchester Joint Station Committee (London Road)

Constituent companies:	1. London and North Western Railway Co. 2. Manchester, Sheffield and Lincolnshire Railway Co.		
TNA Reference Class	Piece No.	Dates	Description
RAIL 435	1 to 6	1842 to 1904	Minutes
RAIL 463	71	1858 to 1859	Minutes

Manchester, Sheffield and Lincolnshire, and Great Northern Railway Companies Joint Line Committee

Constituent companies:	1. Manchester, Sheffield and Lincolnshire Railway Co. 2. Great Northern Railway Co.		
TNA Reference Class	Piece No.	Dates	Description
RAIL 461			No Minutes (plans only, 1894)

Manchester, Sheffield and Lincolnshire, and Midland Joint Lines Committee

Constituent companies:	1. Manchester, Sheffield and Lincolnshire Railway Co. 2. Midland Railway Co.		
TNA Reference Class	Piece No.	Dates	Description
RAIL 462	1 to 3	1869 to 1901	Minutes

Manchester South Junction and Altrincham, and Warrington and Stockport Joint Committee

Constituent companies:	1. London and North Western Railway Co. 2. Manchester, Sheffield and Lincolnshire Railway Co. 3. Warrington and Stockport Railway Co.		
TNA Reference Class	Piece No.	Dates	Description
RAIL 464	1	1856 to 1857	Minutes

461

Mersey and Wirral Railways Joint Committee

Re-named Birkenhead Park Station Committee 5 June 1902

Constituent companies:	1. Mersey Railway Co. 2. Wirral Railway Co.		
TNA Reference Class Piece No.	Dates	Description	
RAIL 475 22	1887 to 1924	Minutes	

Methley Joint Railway Committee

Constituent companies:	1. Great Northern Railway Co. 2. Lancashire and Yorkshire Railway Co. 3. North Eastern Railway Co.		
TNA Reference Class Piece No.	Dates	Description	
RAIL 477 1 & 2	1864 to 1929	Minutes	
4	1870 to 1910	Minutes etc.	

Metropolitan and District Railway Joint Committee

Re-named City Lines and Extension Joint Committee November 1893

Constituent companies:	1. Metropolitan District Railway Co. 2. Metropolitan Railway Co.	
LMA Reference	Dates	Description
Acc.1297/M&DJ1/1 to 66	1868 to 1903	Minutes

Midland and Glasgow, and South Western Joint Committee

| Constituent companies: | 1. Midland Railway Co. |
| | 2. Glasgow and South Western Railway Co. |

| TNA Reference | | | |
Class	Piece No.	Dates	Description
RAIL 486	1 to 3	1873 to 1921	Minutes

Midland and Great Northern Railways Joint Committee

| Constituent companies: | 1. Midland Railway Co. |
| | 2. Great Northern Railway Co. |

| TNA Reference | | | |
Class	Piece No.	Dates	Description
RAIL 487	1 to 10	1866 to 1929	Minutes
	78	1917 to 1921	Time Book, Melton Constable: Cleaners, Locomotive Dept.
	79 & 80	1917 to 1938	Time Books, Melton Constable: Drivers and Firemen, Locomotive Dept.
	115	1879 to 1893	Register of Staff, Eastern Section
RAIL 783	332	1914 to 1915	Superannuation Fund

Midland, and London, Tilbury and Southend, and Tottenham and Forest Gate Railways Joint Committee

Constituent companies:	1. Midland Railway Co.
	2. London, Tilbury and Southend Railway Co.
	3. Tottenham and Forest Gate Railway Co.

| TNA Reference | | | |
Class	Piece No.	Dates	Description
RAIL 696	6 & 7	1894 to 1914	Minutes

Midland and North Eastern Railway Companies Committee (Swinton and Knottingley Railway)

Constituent companies:	1. Midland Railway Co.	
	2. North Eastern Railway Co.	
TNA Reference		
Class Piece No.	Dates	Description
RAIL 488 1 to 11	1874 to 1923	Minutes

Monmouthshire Railway and Canal, and Great Western Railway Companies Consultation Committee

Constituent companies:	1. Monmouthshire Railway and Canal Co.	
	2. Great Western Railway Co.	
TNA Reference		
Class Piece No.	Dates	Description
RAIL 499 1 to 3	1875 to 1880	Minutes (with index)

Newport Street Joint Committee

Constituent companies:	1. Great Western Railway Co.	
	2. Corporation of Newport	
TNA Reference		
Class Piece No.	Dates	Description
RAIL 515 1	1873 to 1876	Minutes

Newport Joint Station Committee [Isle of Wight]

Constituent companies:	1. Ryde and Newport Railway Co.	
	2. Cowes and Newport Railway Co.	
	3. Isle of Wight (Newport Junction) Railway Co.	
TNA Reference		
Class Piece No.	Dates	Description
RAIL 591 5	1879	Minutes

Norfolk and Suffolk Joint Railways Committee

Constituent companies:	1. Great Eastern Railway Co.
	2. Midland Railway Co.
	3. Great Northern Railway Co.

The Great Eastern Railway Co. and the Great Northern Railway Co. were each vested in the London and North Eastern Railway Co. from 1 January 1923. The Midland Railway Co. was vested in the London, Midland and Scottish Railway Co. 1 January 1923. From the dates of the surviving records it is clear that this committee continued to function under its original name after the 1923 Grouping. This committee was vested in the British Transport Commission 1 January 1948.

TNA Reference Class	Piece No.	Dates	Description
RAIL 518	1 to 7 & 10	1898 to 1929	Minutes etc.

Norfolk Joint Committee

Constituent companies:	1. Norfolk Railway Co.
	2. Eastern Counties Railway Co.

TNA Reference Class	Piece No.	Dates	Description
RAIL 186	65	1848 to 1853	Minutes

Normanton Joint Station Committee

Constituent companies:	1. North Eastern Railway Co.	
	2. Lancashire and Yorkshire Railway Co.	
	1. Lancashire and Yorkshire Railway Co.	
	2. Midland Railway Co.	from 20 October 1859
	3. York and North Midland Railway Co.	

TNA Reference Class	Piece No.	Dates	Description
RAIL 520	1 to 11	1850 to 1929	Minutes

465

North Eastern Railway and Hull and Barnsley and West Riding Junction Railway and Dock Company Joint Committee

Constituent companies:	1. North Eastern Railway Co.	
	2. Hull and Barnsley and West Riding Junction Railway and Dock Co.	

TNA Reference Class / Piece No.	Dates	Description
RAIL 525 1 & 2	1898 to 1919	Minutes

North Eastern and Hull and Barnsley Railways Joint Committee

Constituent companies:	1. North Eastern Railway Co.	
	2. Hull and Barnsley Railway Co.	

TNA Reference Class / Piece No.	Dates	Description
RAIL 527 416 & 417	1898 to 1922	Minutes

North Eastern and Newcastle and Carlisle Railways Joint Committee

Constituent companies:	1. North Eastern Railway Co.	
	2. Newcastle and Carlisle Railway Co.	

TNA Reference Class / Piece No.	Dates	Description
RAIL 527 244	1859 to 1862	Minutes

North Eastern Railway and Lancashire and Yorkshire Railway Joint Committee

Constituent companies:	1. North Eastern Railway Co.	
	2. Lancashire and Yorkshire Railway Co.	

TNA Reference Class / Piece No.	Dates	Description
RAIL 526 1	1906	Minutes

Nottingham Joint Station Committee

Constituent companies:	1. Great Central Railway Co. 2. Great Northern Railway Co.		
TNA Reference Class Piece No.		Dates	Description
RAIL 546 1 to 5		1897 to 1923	Minutes
RAIL 783 278		1911	Inspectors – Pensions

Otley and Ilkley Joint Line Committee

Constituent companies:	1. Midland Railway Co. 2. North Eastern Railway Co.		
This committee was formed to manage the Otley and Ilkley Extension Railway built jointly by the Midland Railway Co. and the North Eastern Railway Co.			
TNA Reference Class Piece No.		Dates	Description
RAIL 554 1 to 13		1861 to 1923	Minutes
24 & 25		1865 to 1901	Staff Lists

Penrith Joint Station Committee

Constituent companies:	1. London and North Western Railway Co. 2. Stockton and Darlington Railway Co. 3. Cockermouth, Keswick and Penrith Railway Co. 4. North Eastern Railway Co. from 19 April 1866		
TNA Reference Class Piece No.		Dates	Description
RAIL 563 1		1863 to 1874	Minutes

Plymouth Joint Station Committee

Constituent companies:	1. South Devon Railway Co.	
	2. Cornwall Railway Co.	

TNA Reference Class Piece No.	Dates	Description
RAIL 568 1 to 4	1859 to 1888	Minutes

Preston and Longridge Railway Joint Committee

The Preston and Longridge Railway Co. was incorporated 14 July 1836 and opened 1 May 1840. The company was sold to the Fleetwood, Preston and West Riding Junction Railway Co. by an agreement dated 14 March 1856 to take effect from 31 August 1856. The Fleetwood, Preston and West Riding Junction Railway Co. was vested jointly in the London and North Western Railway Co., and the Lancashire and Yorkshire Railway Co. 17 June 1867. From this time the Preston and Longridge Line was managed by the Preston and Longridge Railway Joint Committee with representatives from:

      1. The London and North Western Railway Co.
      2. The Lancashire and Yorkshire Railway Co.

From 1 January 1889 the responsibilities of this joint committee were taken over by the London and North Western, and Lancashire and Yorkshire Railways Joint Committee.

TNA Reference Class Piece No.	Dates	Description
RAIL 576 1 to 3	1866 to 1889	Minutes

Ryde and Newport, and Cowes and Newport Railway Companies Joint Committee

Constituent companies:	1. Ryde and Newport Railway Co.	
	2. Cowes and Newport Railway Co.	

TNA Reference Class Piece No.	Dates	Description
RAIL 591 4	1875 to 1887	Minutes

Sheffield and Lincolnshire Junction Railway, and Manchester and Lincoln Union Railway and Canal Joint Committee

| Constituent companies: | 1. Sheffield and Lincolnshire Junction Railway Co. |
| | 2. Manchester and Lincoln Union Railway and Canal Co. |

TNA Reference Class	Piece No.	Dates	Description
RAIL 608	1	1846	Minutes

Sheffield and Midland Railway Companies Joint Committee

| Constituent companies: | 1. Great Central Railway Co. |
| | 2. Midland Railway Co. |

TNA Reference Class	Piece No.	Dates	Description
RAIL 224	1 to 9	1875 to 1909	Minutes

Shrewsbury and Hereford Joint Committee

Constituent companies:	1. London and North Western Railway Co.
	2. Great Western Railway Co.
	3. West Midland Railway Co.

The Shrewsbury and Hereford Railway Co. was incorporated 3 August 1846. From 1 July 1862 the company was leased to the London and North Western Railway Co., the Great Western Railway Co. and the West Midland Railway Co. The West Midland Railway Co. was amalgamated with the Great Western Railway Co. 1 August 1863 and the affairs of the Shrewsbury and Hereford Railway Co. were thenceforth managed by the Shrewsbury and Hereford Joint Committee. This committee was taken over by the London and North Western and Great Western Railways Joint Committee 4 October 1867.

TNA Reference Class	Piece No.	Dates	Description
RAIL 617	12 to 14 & 16 to 18	1862 to 1867	Minutes
	29	1848 to 1862	Memoranda (includes Lists of Staff)

Shrewsbury and Wellington Joint Line Committee

Constituent companies:	1. Shrewsbury and Birmingham Railway Co. 2. Shropshire Union Railway Co.		
TNA Reference Class Piece No.		Dates	Description
RAIL 618 1 to 8		1846 to 1867	Minutes

Shrewsbury Joint Station Committee

Constituent companies:	1. Shrewsbury and Birmingham Railway Co. 2. Shropshire Union Railway Co. 3. Shrewsbury and Hereford Railway Co. 4. Shrewsbury and Chester Railway Co.		
This committee was formed 16 April 1847 and continued to function until it was taken over by the London and North Western and Great Western Railways Joint Committee 4 October 1867.			
TNA Reference Class Piece No.		Dates	Description
RAIL 619 1 to 7		1847 to 1867	Minutes

Sittingbourne and Sheerness, and London, Chatham and Dover Railways Joint Traffic Committee

Constituent companies:	1. Sittingbourne and Sheerness Railway Co. 2. London, Chatham and Dover Railway Co.		
TNA Reference Class Piece No.		Dates	Description
RAIL 625 1		1860 to 1865	Minutes

Somerset and Dorset Joint Line Committee

The Somerset and Dorset Railway Co. was formed by the amalgamation of the Somerset Central Railway Co. and the Dorset Central Railway Co. 7 August 1862. The Somerset and Dorset Railway Co. was leased to the London and South Western Railway Co. and the Midland Railway Co. jointly 1 November 1875. From this date the Somerset and Dorset Railway Co. was managed by the Somerset and Dorset Joint Line Committee with representatives from:
 	
    1. London and South Western Railway Co.
    2. Midland Railway Co.

The Somerset and Dorset Railway Co. was transferred to the Southern Railway Co. and the London, Midland and Scottish Railway Co. jointly 1 January 1923 and the Somerset and Dorset Lines continued to be managed by the joint committee. The joint committee passed to the British Transport Commission in 1948.

TNA Reference Class	Piece No.	Dates	Description
RAIL 626	1 to 15	1875 to 1923	Minutes
	39	1924 to 1930	Register of Clothing of Joint Railway Staff
	44 to 47	1877 to 1928	Staff Books
	48 to 53	1920 to 1927	Lists of Staff at Stations
RAIL 972	1	1875 to 1876	Working Timetables (printed on covers are lists of punishments imposed on staff)

South Devon, Cornwall and West Cornwall Railways Joint Committee

Constituent companies:	1. South Devon Railway Co. 2. Cornwall Railway Co. 3. West Cornwall Railway Co.

TNA Reference Class	Piece No.	Dates	Description
RAIL 630	1	1874 to 1875	Store Committee Meetings (nothing else in this class)

South Eastern and Brighton Joint Committee

Constituent companies:	1. South Eastern Railway Co. 2. London, Brighton and South Coast Railway Co.

TNA Reference Class	Piece No.	Dates	Description
RAIL 635	80 to 84	1855 to 1898	Minutes

South Eastern and Chatham Railway Companies' Managing Committee

Constituent companies:	1. South Eastern Railway Co. 2. London, Chatham and Dover Railway Co.

Cont.

This committee was set up to manage the above companies jointly from 1 August 1899. By the Railways (Southern Group) Amalgamation Scheme of 22 December 1922 this managing committee became part of the Southern Railway Co.

See also the South Eastern and London, Chatham and Dover (Dover and Deal) Railways Joint Committee and South Eastern and London, Chatham and Dover Railways Joint Committee.

TNA Reference Class	Piece No.	Dates	Description
RAIL 633	1 to 55	1899 to 1923	Minutes
	343 to 345	1901 to 1944	Register of Punishments and Awards to Enginemen
	346	1853 to 1922	Staff Book, Management and Clerical Staff
	347 to 357	From 1899	Staff Books, Coaching Dept.
	358 to 361	From 1899	Staff Books, Goods Dept.
	362	1862 to 1922	Staff Book, Continental and Marine Dept.
	363	1900 to 1911	Register of Staff
	364 & 365	1905 to 1908	Staff Reports and Orders
	366	1918 to 1923	Register of Staff Appointments, Advances, Transfers and Resignations
	367	1874 to 1911	Register of Superannuation Fund Entrants
	368 & 369	1860 to 1913	Registers of Workmen at Various Depots
	370 & 371	1865 to 1924	Register of Workmen, Locomotive Dept.
	372 & 373	1853 to 1924	Registers of Workmen, Carriage and Wagon Dept.
	374	1914 to 1919	Register of Staff Employed in Works
	375 & 376	c. 1858 to 1924	Staff Books, Audit Accountant's Office
	377	1850 to 1922	Register of Clerks, Accountant's Offices, Ashford
	378	1904	Numbers of Various Tradesmen employed at Ashford
	379	c. 1882 to 1922	Register of Staff, Marine Dept.
	440	1920	Rules and Regulations for Officers and Men
	441	1912	Minor Accident Reports
	442 & 443	1898 to 1923	Allowances and Pensions to all Classes of Staff (Indexed)
RAIL 1025	80	1920 to 1922	List of Head Office and Workshop Supervisory Staff, Ashford
RAIL 1057	2710	1914 to 1918	List of Railwaymen killed in First World War

South Eastern and London, Chatham and Dover (Dover and Deal) Railways Joint Committee

Constituent companies:		1. South Eastern Railway Co. 2. London, Chatham and Dover Railway Co.	
TNA Reference Class	Piece No.	Dates	Description
RAIL 635	85 to 89	1874 to 1922	Minutes

South Eastern and London, Chatham and Dover Railways Joint Committee

Constituent companies:		1. South Eastern Railway Co. 2. London, Chatham and Dover Railway Co.	
TNA Reference Class	Piece No.	Dates	Description
RAIL 635	90 to 97	1863 to 1898	Minutes

South Wales Railway Joint Traffic Committee

Constituent companies:		1. South Wales Railway Co. 2. Great Western Railway Co.	
TNA Reference Class	Piece No.	Dates	Description
RAIL 640	18 to 22	1852 to 1863	Minutes etc.

South Western and Brighton Joint Committee (Epsom and Leatherhead Railway)

Constituent companies:		1. London and South Western Railway Co. 2. London, Brighton and South Coast Railway Co.	
TNA Reference Class	Piece No.	Dates	Description
RAIL 197	2 & 3	1883 to 1922	Minutes

South Yorkshire Joint Line Committee

Incorporated under the South Yorkshire Joint Railway Act 14 August 1903, this joint committee was formed to manage the building and running of 20 miles of line from Dinnington to Kirk Sandall which opened 1 January 1909.

Constituent companies:
1. North Eastern Railway Co.
2. Lancashire and Yorkshire Railway Co.
3. Great Northern Railway Co.
4. Midland Railway Co.
5. Great Central Railway Co.

From the 1923 Grouping the South Yorkshire Joint Line Committee continued to function with the London and North Eastern Railway and the London, Midland and Scottish Railway as its constituent members until it was vested in the British Transport Commission in 1948.

| TNA Reference | | | |
Class	Piece No.	Dates	Description
RAIL 641	1 to 12	1903 to 1939	Minutes of Various Committees

Stalybridge Joint Station Committee

Constituent companies:
1. London and North Western Railway Co.
2. Manchester, Sheffield and Lincolnshire Railway Co.

| TNA Reference | | | |
Class	Piece No.	Dates	Description
RAIL 661	1 to 3	1879 to 1904	Minutes

Stokes Bay Railway and Pier Co., and Isle of Wight Ferry Co. Joint Meetings

Constituent companies:
1. Stokes Bay Railway and Pier Co.
2. Isle of Wight Ferry Co.

| TNA Reference | | | |
Class	Piece No.	Dates	Description
RAIL 669	3	1855 to 1864	Minutes (included with Minutes of Board Meetings of the Stokes Bay Railway and Pier Co.)

Taff Vale Railway and Penarth Harbour, Dock and Railway Joint Committee

Constituent companies:
1. Taff Vale Railway Co.
2. Penarth Harbour, Dock and Railway Co.

TNA Reference Class	Piece No.	Dates	Description
RAIL 562	1	1862 to 1865	Minutes

Tebay Joint Station Committee

Constituent companies:	1. London and North Western Railway Co. 2. South Durham and Lancashire Union Railway 3. Stockton and Darlington Railway Co. 4. North Eastern Railway Co. when it took over the Stockton and Darlington Railway Co. 13 July 1863

TNA Reference Class	Piece No.	Dates	Description
RAIL 686	1 to 6	1860 to 1909	Minutes

Tooting, Merton and Wimbledon, Epsom and Leatherhead, Portsmouth Railway Joint Committees and Portsmouth, Southsea and Ryde Joint Railways Steam Packets Committee

Constituent companies:	1. London and South Western Railway Co. 2. London, Brighton and South Coast Railway Co.

TNA Reference Class	Piece No.	Dates	Description
RAIL 414	199	1876 to 1888	Minutes

Tooting, Merton and Wimbledon Joint Committee

Constituent companies:	1. London and South Western Railway Co. 2. London, Brighton and South Coast Railway Co.

TNA Reference Class	Piece No.	Dates	Description
RAIL 414	197 & 198	1882 to 1922	Minutes

Tottenham and Hampstead Junction Railway Joint Committee

From July 1885 the Tottenham and Hampstead Junction Railway was run by a joint committee:
Constituent companies: 1. Great Eastern Railway Co.   2. Midland Railway Co.

Cont.

TNA Reference Class	Piece No.	Dates	Description
From 1923 the constituent companies became the London, Midland and Scottish Railway and the London and North Eastern Railway.

TNA Reference Class	Piece No.	Dates	Description
RAIL 697	6 to 8 & 11	1885 to 1922	Minutes
	9 & 12	1885 to 1922	Joint Officers' Conference; Minutes (includes Lists of Joint Staff)

United Board of the Birmingham and Oxford Junction Railway Co. and the Birmingham, Wolverhampton and Dudley Railway Co.

Constituent companies:	1. Birmingham and Oxford Junction Railway Co.
	2. Birmingham, Wolverhampton and Dudley Railway Co.

TNA Reference Class	Piece No.	Dates	Description
RAIL 39	3	1846 to 1851	Minutes

Vale of Towy Railway Joint Committee

Constituent companies:	1. London and North Western Railway Co.
	2. Llanelly Railway and Dock Co.

The Vale of Towy Railway Co. was incorporated 10 August 1854 and leased from 1 April 1868 to the Knighton Railway Co., the Central Wales Railway Co., the Central Wales Extension Railway Co., and the Llanelly Railway and Dock Co. The Vale of Towy Railway Co. was vested in the London and North Western Railway Co. 1 July 1884 but the Llanelly Railway and Dock Co. retained the power to lease the Vale of Towy Railway. On amalgamation of the Llanelly company with the Great Western Railway Co. 1 July 1889 the Vale of Towy Railway Joint Committee was merged with the London and North Western and Great Western Railways Joint Committee. At the 1923 Grouping this committee became the London, Midland and Scottish and Great Western Railways Joint Committee and ceased on Nationalization in 1948.

TNA Reference Class	Piece No.	Dates	Description
RAIL 706	1 to 5	1868 to 1889	Minutes

476

Wakefield (Westgate) Station Joint Committee

Constituent companies:	1. West Riding and Grimsby Railway Co.
	2. Manchester, Sheffield and Lincolnshire Railway Co.
	3. South Yorkshire Railway and River Dun Navigation Co.
	4. Midland Railway Co.

TNA Reference Class	Piece No.	Dates	Description
RAIL 736	6 & 7	1864 to 1869	Minutes

West Cornwall Railway Joint Committee

Constituent companies:	1. West Cornwall Railway Co.
	2. Bristol and Exeter Railway Co.
	3. South Devon Railway Co.

TNA Reference Class	Piece No.	Dates	Description
RAIL 726	1 to 3	1865 to 1879	Minutes

West Riding and Grimsby Railway Co. Joint Committee

Constituent companies:	1. West Riding and Grimsby Joint Railway Co.
	2. Great Northern Railway Co.
	3. Manchester, Sheffield and Lincolnshire Railway Co.

The West Riding and Grimsby Railway Co. was taken over jointly by the Great Northern Railway Co. and the Manchester, Sheffield and Lincolnshire Railway Co. 1 February 1866. From this date the line was managed by the joint committee.

TNA Reference Class	Piece No.	Dates	Description
RAIL 736	1	1862 to 1870	Board Minutes (includes the Minutes of the Joint Committee 1867 to 1870)
	26	1894 to 1897	Abstracts of Wages (includes names)

477

West Riding Railway Joint Committee

Constituent companies:	1. Great Northern Railway Co. 2. Manchester, Sheffield and Lincolnshire Railway Co.

The West Riding and Grimsby Railway Co. was incorporated 7 August 1862. The company was vested jointly in the Great Northern Railway Co., and the Manchester, Sheffield and Lincolnshire Railway Co. 28 June 1867. From this date the line was managed by the West Riding Railway Joint Committee.

TNA Reference Class	Piece No.	Dates	Description
RAIL 736	1	1867 to 1870	Joint Committee Minutes (with Board of Directors' Minutes of West Riding and Grimsby Railway Co.)
	4 & 5	1885 to 1923	Minutes

Whitehaven Junction and Whitehaven and Furness Junction Railways Joint Committee

Constituent companies:	1. Whitehaven Junction Railway Co. 2. Whitehaven and Furness Junction Railway Co.

TNA Reference Class	Piece No.	Dates	Description
RAIL 744	4	1854 to 1866	Minutes

Wolverhampton Joint Committees

Joint Station Committee, Through Traffic Committee, Executive Committee, Management and Use Committee, High Level Station Committee and Low Level Station Committee. These committees were formed at various times by representatives from the following companies:

1. Shrewsbury and Birmingham Railway Co.
2. Birmingham, Wolverhampton and Stour Valley Railway Co.
3. Oxford, Worcester and Wolverhampton Railway Co.
4. West Midland Railway Co.
5. London and North Western Railway Co.
6. Great Western Railway Co.

TNA Reference Class	Piece No.	Dates	Description
RAIL 759	1 to 11	1848 to 1863	Minutes of Various Committee Meetings

Woodside and South Croydon Railway Joint Committee

Constituent companies:	1. London, Brighton and South Coast Railway Co. 2. South Eastern Railway Co.	June 1884 to December 1908
	1. London, Brighton and South Coast Railway Co. 2. South Eastern and Chatham Railway Companies Joint Management Committee	February 1909 to December 1922

The Woodside and South Croydon Railway Co. was incorporated 6 August 1880. This company was vested in the London, Brighton and South Coast Railway Co. and the South Eastern Railway Co. jointly 10 August 1882. From this date the management of the Woodside and South Croydon Line was undertaken by the Woodside and South Croydon Railway Joint Committee. The joint committee continued to function until the Grouping of 1923 when the line became part of the Southern Railway.

TNA Reference		Dates	Description
Class	Piece No.		
RAIL 760	3 to 11	1884 to 1922	Minutes of Various Joint Committee Meetings

Worcester and Hereford Railway Joint Committee

Constituent companies:	1. Worcester and Hereford Railway Co. 2. Newport, Abergavenny and Hereford Railway Co. 3. Midland Railway Co. 4. Oxford, Worcester and Wolverhampton Railway Co.

TNA Reference		Dates	Description
Class	Piece No.		
RAIL 762	6	1859	Minutes

Wrexham and Minera Railway Joint Committee

Constituent companies:	1. Great Western Railway Co. 2. London and North Western Railway Co.

The Wrexham and Minera Railway Co. was incorporated 17 May 1861. Part of the line was vested in the Wrexham and Minera Railway Joint Committee on 11 June 1866 and the remaining part of the line was vested in the Great Western Railway Co. The joint committee was abolished 1 September 1871 and the management of the Wrexham and Minera Railway was taken over by the London and North Western and Great Western Railways Joint Committee.

TNA Reference		Dates	Description
Class	Piece No.		
RAIL 766	1	1866 to 1871	Minutes

York Joint Station Committee

| Constituent companies: | 1. York and North Midland Railway Co. |
| | 2. York, Newcastle and Berwick Railway Co. |

| TNA Reference | | | |
Class	Piece No.	Dates	Description
RAIL 771	1 & 2	1851 to 1853	Minutes

York, Newcastle and Berwick, and Great North of England Railways Joint Committee

| Constituent companies: | 1. York, Newcastle and Berwick Railway Co. |
| | 2. Great North of England Railway Co. |

| TNA Reference | | | |
Class	Piece No.	Dates	Description
RAIL 772	18	1848	Minutes

York, Newcastle and Berwick; York and North Midland; and Leeds Northern Railways Joint Committee

Constituent companies:	1. York, Newcastle and Berwick Railway Co.
	2. York and North Midland Railway Co.
	3. Leeds Northern Railway Co.

| TNA Reference | | | |
Class	Piece No.	Dates	Description
RAIL 527	1939 & 1940	1854	Paybills for engine drivers, firemen, fitters, nightwatchmen, cleaners, water station attendants, etc. (Note: these records are listed as North Eastern Railway Co.)
RAIL 773	1 & 2	1853 to 1865	Minutes

APPENDIX 5

THE RAILWAY CLEARING HOUSE

As more and more railways were built it became possible to travel long distances by transferring from one railway to another at appropriate junctions. It was then possible to book a through fare from the beginning to the end of a journey regardless of how many railways the journey encompassed. The proportion of the fare paid to each of these railways was allotted in proportion to the mileage travelled. Such calculations were carried out by the Railway Clearing House which was founded in 1842 at Euston. It also employed many hundreds of 'number takers', working at all the major railway junctions throughout the country. The number takers recorded the number, name and owner with the destination of every railway company's wagon, carriage and van when they passed from one company's line to another.

The Railway Clearing House was also responsible for the standardization of signalling and telegraphic codes, and organized a lost property office. It has been described as the nerve centre of the railways. At one time it employed over 2,500 clerks.

The following lists the surviving staff records:

Staff Records

TNA Reference			
Class	Piece No.	Dates	Description
RAIL 1057	2710	1914 to 1918	List of Railwaymen killed in First World War
RAIL 1085	14	1888 to 1915	Weekly Wages Staff Register
	70	1872	Memorial from Clerks for Revision of Salaries
	71	1842 to 1849	Staff Salary Register
	79		Photographs of Chairman and Officers
	128	1873 to 1921	Clerical Staff, Salaries, Sonditions of Service, etc.
RAIL 1086	2	1895 to 1905	Superannuation Fund Papers
RAIL 1096	1	1862 to 1901	Numbers of Staff only (names not included)
	2	1939 to 1941	General File of Staff (includes names)
	3	1940 to 1948	Staff Salaries (includes names)
RAIL 1172	1701 to 1705	1931 to 1960	Clerical Staff. Claims for increases in pay etc. (includes names)
	1708	1945 to 1948	Salaried Staff (includes some names)

APPENDIX 6

STAFF TRADES AND OCCUPATIONS

Goods Staff

Bookers, brakesmen, callers off, capstan men, checkers, clerks, crane attendants, deliverers, gasmen, goods agents, hookers on, invoice clerks, labellers, loaders, messengers, number takers, porters, receivers, scalesmen, searchers, sheeters, shippers, shunt-horse drivers, shunters, slate counters, slip boys, timber loaders, timber measurers, van washers, wagon berthers, warehousemen, weighers, winchmen, yardsmen, yard inspectors, yard loaders.

Cartage Staff

Book carriers, busmen, bus drivers, bus conductors, carmen, cart drivers, carters, chain boys, draymen, grooms, housekeepers, quarrymen, parcel van drivers, stablemen/ostlers, van setters, van men, wagoners.

Maintenance Staff

Carriage cleaners, fitters, gangers, lengthmen, platelayers.

Operating Staff

Dining car attendants, drivers, firemen, goods guards, hotel staff, kitchen staff, locomotive cleaners, passenger guards, post firemen, railway police, ships' crews (ferry), shunters, signalmen, sleeping car attendants.

Station Staff

Booking office clerks, cleaners, clerks, foreman porters, inspectors, lavatory attendants, messengers, parcel porters, platform inspectors, porters, railway police, refreshment room staff, station masters, telegraph operators, ticket collectors, typists.

Engineering Staff

Adzers, asphalters, blacksmiths, boat builders, boatmen, boilermakers, borers, brass finishers, bricklayers, canalmen, carpenters, carters, chainmen, checkers, concrete makers, contracting staff, controllers, crane testers, cranemen, creosoters, drainmen, drivers, electricians, engine drivers, erectors, fencers, firemen, flagmen, flagmen (steam rollers), gangers, gas linemen, gatemen, glaziers, handymen, inspectors, labourers, lavatory attendants and cleaners, lime washers, lock-keepers, locksmiths, machine operators, machinists, masons, meter readers, nurserymen, office cleaners, office women, packers, painters passengers, paviors pitchers, plankeepers, plasterers, plumbers, riveters, road roller drivers sawyers, scaffolders, screw cutters, shunters and tallymen, sleeper chairers, stone weighers, storekeepers, storemen, strikers, timbermen, timekeepers, toolboys, toolmen, wages clerks, watchmen.

Office Staff

Accountants, auditors, cleaners, clerks, managers, messengers, telegraph operators, telephonists, typists, wages clerks.

APPENDIX 7

MAJOR EVENTS IN BRITISH RAILWAY HISTORY

1801	Incorporation of public horse-tram road companies
1812	The first regular use of locomotives; Middleton Colliery, near Leeds
1821	The Stockton and Darlington Railway authorized
1826	The Liverpool and Manchester Railway authorized
1829	The Rainhill Trials won by Stephenson's *Rocket*
1842	The Railway Clearing House established
1844	The Railways Act; Gladstone empowers public purchase of railways
1844	The Railways Board established
1850	Locomotives change from using coke to coal
1864	The Railway Construction Facilities Act
1864	The Railway and Canal Act
1892	Conversion by the Great Western Railway from broad gauge to narrow gauge
1914–18	Railways taken over by the State during the First World War
1919	The National Rail Strike
1920	White Paper on proposals for the future organization of transport
1921	The Railways Act; four companies formed (LMS, LNER, SR, GWR)
1923	The Grouping of the four companies
1933	The Road and Rail Traffic Act
1939–45	Railways taken over by the State during the Second World War
1947	The Transport Act; Nationalization of the railways and the British Transport Commission formed

BIBLIOGRAPHY

Place of publication is given only if outside London.

RAILWAY HISTORY

Allen, C. *The London and North Eastern Railway*, Ian Allan, Addlestone, 1966
——, *The Great Eastern Railway*, Ian Allan, Addlestone 1968
——, *The North Eastern Railway*, Ian Allan, Addlestone 1964
Athill, R. *The Somerset and Dorset Railway*, David & Charles, Newton Abbot, 1967
Awdry, C. *Encyclopaedia of British Railway Companies*, Patrick Stephens Ltd, Yeovil, 1990
Bagwell, P. *The Railway Clearing House in the British Economy*, George Allen and Unwin, 1968
Baker, C. *The Metropolitan Railway*, Oakwood Press, 1951
Barnett, A.L. *Railways of the South Yorkshire Coalfield*, Railway Correspondence and Travel Society [RCTS] 1984
Barrie, D.S. *The Taff Vale Railway*, Oakwood Press, 1939
——, *The Barry Railway*, Oakwood Press, 1962
Barrie, D.S. and Clinker, C.R. *The Somerset and Dorset Railway*, Oakwood Press, 1948
Barton, D.B. *The Redruth and Chacewater Railway*, Bradford Barton, 1966
Baughan, P. *The Chester and Holyhead Railway*, David & Charles, Newton Abbot, 1972
Borley, H.V. *Chronology of London Railways*, The Railway and Canal Historical Society, 1982
Boyd, J.I.C. *Narrow Gauge Railways in South Caernarvonshire*, Oakwood Press, 1972
——, *Narrow Gauge Railways in Mid-Wales*, Oakwood Press, 1952
——, *Narrow Gauge Railways to Portmadoc*, Oakwood Press, 1949
——, *The Festiniog Railway*, Oakwood Press, 1956
Bradley, D.L. *A Locomotive History of Railways on the Isle of Wight*, RCTS, 1982
Bradshaw, *Bradshaw's Railway Guides*, W.J. Adams, Bradshaw and Blacklock, 1852 to 1923
——, *Bradshaw's Railway Almanacks*, 1848 and 1849
Brown, G.A., Prideaux, J.D.C. and Radcliffe, HG. *The Lynton and Barnstaple Railway*, David & Charles, Newton Abbot, 1964
Carlson, R.E. *The Liverpool and Manchester Railway Project, 1821 to 1831*, David & Charles, Newton Abbot, 1969
Carter, B. *An Historical Geography of the Railways of the British Isles*, Cassell, 1959

——, *The Railway Encyclopaedia*, Harold Starke, Publishers Ltd, Eye, 1963

Casserley, H.C. *Britain's Joint Lines*, Ian Allan, Addlestone, 1968

Catchpole, L.T. *The Lynton and Barnstaple Railway*, Oakwood Press, 1936

Christiansen, R. *Forgotten Railways: North and Mid-Wales*, David & Charles, Newton Abbot, 1976

——, *Forgotten Railways: Severn Valley and Welsh Borders*, David & Charles, Newton Abbot, 1988

——, *Forgotten Railways: West Midlands*, David & Charles, Newton Abbot, 1985

Christiansen, R. and Miller, R.W. *The North Staffordshire Railway*, David & Charles, Newton Abbot, 1985

——, *The Cambrian Railways*, 2 volumes, David & Charles, Newton Abbot, 1968 and 1971

Clark, R.H. *The Midland and Great Northern Joint Railway*, Goose & Son, 1967

Clew, K. *The Somerset Coal Canal and Railways*, David & Charles, Newton Abbot, 1970

Clinker, C.R. *A Chronology of Opening and Closing Dates of Lines and Stations 1900 to 1960*, David and Charles, Newton Abbot, 1961

——, *The Birmingham and Derby Junction Railway*, Avon Anglia, 1982

Conolly, W.P. *British Railways Pre-Grouping Atlas and Gazetteer*, Ian Allan, Addlestone, date?

Course, E.A. *Railways of Southern England*, Batsford, 1973

——, *The Bexley Heath Railway*, Woolwich and District Antiquarian Society, 1954

Crombleholme, Stuckey, Whetmath and Gibson. *Callington Railways*, Forge Books, 1985

Davies, R. and Grant, M.D. *Forgotten Railways: Chilterns and Cotswolds*, David & Charles, Newton Abbot, 1984

Dendy Marshall, C.E. *History of the Southern Railway*, Ian Allan, Addlestone, 1963

Derby Railway History Research Group. *The Midland Counties Railway and Canal Historical Society*, 1989

Donaghy, T.J. *Liverpool and Manchester Railway Operations*, David & Charles, Newton Abbot, 1972

Dow, G. *Great Central*, 3 volumes, Ian Allan, Addlestone, 1959 to 1965

——, *The First Railway in Norfolk*, LNER, 1944

Edwards, Cliff. *Railway Records*, Public Record Office, 2001

Elliott, B.J. *The South Yorkshire Joint Railway*, Oakwood Press, 1971

Franks, D.L. *The Stamford and Essendine Railway*, Turntable Enterprises, 1971

Gough, J. *The Northampton and Harborough Line*, The Railway and Canal Historical Society, 1984

——, *The Midland Railway – A Chronology*, J.V. Gough, 1986

Gould, D. *The London and Birmingham Railway*, David & Charles, Newton Abbot, 1987

Gray, A. *The London, Chatham and Dover Railway*, Meresborough Books, 1984

Greville, M.D. *Chronology of the Railways of Lancashire and Cheshire*, RCHS, 1981

Grinling, C.H. *History of the Great Northern Railway*, Methuen, 1898

Hamilton Ellis, C. *The London, Brighton and South Coast Railway*, Ian Allan, Addlestone, 1960

——, *British Railway History 1830 to 1876*, George Allen and Unwin, 1956

——, *British Railway History 1877 to 1947*, George Allen and Unwin, 1959

——, *The Midland Railway*, Ian Allan, Addlestone, 1953

Hartley, K.E. *The Cawood, Wistow and Seiby Light Railway*, Turntable Enterprises, 1973

Highet, C. *The Glasgow and South Western Railway*, Oakwood Press, 1965

HMSO. *Index to Local and Personal Acts*, HMSO, 1949

Hoole, K. *Forgotten Railways: North East England*, David & Charles, Newton Abbot, 1984

——, *Stockton and Darlington Railway*, Dalesman Publishing Co. Ltd, Skipton, 1974

——, *The Hull and Barnsley Railway*, David & Charles, Newton Abbot, 1972

Howard, Anderson P. *Forgotten Railways: The East Midlands*, David & Charles, Newton Abbot, 1985

Isherwood, J. *Slough Estates Railway*, Wild Swan Publications, 1989

Jackson, A.A. *London's Metropolitan Railway*, David & Charles, Newton Abbot, 1986

James, L. A *Chronology of the Construction of Britain's Railways 1778 to 1855*, Ian Allan, Addlestone, 1983

James, L. *A Chronology of the Construction of Britain's Railways 1856 to 1922*, Manuscript at Brunel University

Joby, R.S. *Forgotten Railways: East Anglia*, David & Charles, Newton Abbot, 1977

Jowett, A. *Jowett's Railway Atlas*, Guild Publishing, 1989

Joy, D. *Cumbrian Coast Railways*, Dalesman Publishing Co. Ltd, Skipton, 1968

——, *Whitby and Pickering Railway*, Dalesman Publishing Co. Ltd, Skipton, 1969

Klapper, C. *London's Lost Railways*, Routledge & Kegan Paul, 1976

Lewin, H.G. *The Railway Mania and Its Aftermath*, David & Charles, Newton Abbot, 1968

Lewis, M.J.T. *Early Wooden Railways*, Routledge & Kegan Paul, 1970

——, *The Pentewan Railway*, Bradford Barton, 1980

Long, P.J. and Awdry, Revd W. *The Birmingham and Gloucester Railway*, Alan Sutton, Gloucester, 1987

MacDermot, E.T. *History of the Great Western Railway*, 2 volumes, GWR, 1927, 1931

Maggs, C.G. *The Midland and South Western Junction Railway*, David & Charles, Newton Abbot, 1967

Maggs, C.G. and Paye, P. *The Sidmnouth, Seaton and Lymne Regis Branches*, Oakwood Press, 1977

'Manifold'. *The North Staffordshire Railway*, Henstock, 1952

Marshall, J. *Forgotten Railways: North West England*, David & Charles, Newton Abbot, 1981

Moffat, H. *East Anglia's First Railway*, Terence Dalton, Sudbury, 1987

Mowat, C.L. *The Golden Valley Railway*, Cardiff University of Wales Press, 1964

Nabarro, Sir G. *Severn Valley Steam*, Routledge & Kegan Paul, 1971

Nock, O.S. *The South Eastern and Chatham Railway*, Ian Allan, Addlestone, 1961

——, *The Great Western in the Nineteenth Century*, Ian Allan, Addlestone, 1962

——, *The Great Western in the Twentieth Century*, Ian Allan, Addlestone, 1964

——, *The London and South Western Railway*, Ian Allan, Addlestone, 1965

——, *The Lancashire and Yorkshire Railway*, 1969

Nokes, G.A. *A History of the Great Western Railway*, Digby, Long, 1895

Norris, J. *The Stratford and Moreton Tramway*, RCHS, 1987

Ottley, G. *Bibliography of British Railway History*, George Allen and Unwin, 1965 and HMSO 1983 and supplement 1988.

Paar, H.W. *Severn and Wye Railway*, David & Charles, Newton Abbot, 1963

Page, J.H.R. *Forgotten Railways: South Wales*, David & Charles, Newton Abbot, 1979

Pope, How and Karau, *The Severn and Wye Railway*, Wild Swan Publications, 1983

Popplewell, L. *A Gazetteer of the Railway Contractors and Engineers of Central England*, Melledgen Press, 1986

——, *A Gazetteer of the Railway Contractors and Engineers of Wales and the Borders 1830 to 1914*, Melledgen Press, 1984

Potts, C.R. *The Newton Abbot to Kingswear Railway 1844–1988*, Oakwood Press, 1989

Richards, T. *Was Your Father a Railwayman?*, 2nd edn, Federation of Family History Societies, 1989

Roberts, B. *Railways and Mineral Tramways of Rossendale*, Oakwood Press, 1974

Ruddock and Pearson, R.E. *The Railway History of Lincoln*, Ruddock and Partners, 1974

Simmons, J. *The Railways in Town and Country 1830 to 1914*, David & Charles, Newton Abbot, 1986

Simpson, B. *The Aylesbury Railway*, Oxford Publishing Co., Oxford, 1989

Smith, P. *Forest of Denim Railways*, Oxford Publishing Co., Oxford, 1983

Stone, R.A. *The Meon Valley Railway*, Kingfisher Railway Productions, 1983

Stuckey, D. *The Bideford, Westward Ho! and Appledore Railway*, Forge Books, 1983

Taylor, R.S. and Tonks, E.S. *The Southwold Railway*, Ian Allan, Addlestone, 1979

Thomas, D.L. A*shby and Nuneaton Joint Railway*, Turntable Publications, 1975

Thomas, R.I *The Liverpool amid Manchester Railway*, Batsford, 1980

——, *London's First Railway: The London amid Greenwich*, Batsford, 1972

Thomas, D. St.J. *A Regional History of the Railways of Great Britain Volume 1: The West Country*, David & Charles, Newton Abbot, 1988

Tomlinson, W.W. *The North Eastern Railway*, David & Charles, Newton Abbot, 1987

Welch, H.D. *The London, Tilbury and Southend Railway*, Oakwood Press, 1951

Whetmath, C.F.D. *The Bodmin and Wadebridge Railway*, Town and Country Press, 1972

Whetmath and Stuckey, *The North Devon and Cornwall Junction Light Railway*, Forge Books, 1980

White, H.P. *Forgotten Railways: South East England,* David & Charles, Newton Abbot, 1986

Whittle, G. *The Railways of Consett and North West Durham*, David & Charles, Newton Abbot, 1971

Williams, F.S. *The Midland Railway: Its Rise and Progress*, David & Charles, Newton Abbot, 1976

Williams, R.A. *The London and South Western Railway*, David & Charles, Newton Abbot, 1968

Wilson, J.M. *The Imperial Gazetteer of England and Wales*, A. Fullerton & Co., 1870

Woodfin, R.J. *The Cornwall Railway, Bradford and Barton*, 1972

Wrottesley, A.J. *The Great Northern Railway*, 3 volumes, Batsford, 1981

——, *The Midland and Great Northern Joint Railway*, David & Charles, Newton Abbot, 1970

RAILWAY MAGAZINES AND JOURNALS

Furness Railway Magazine, 1921 to 1923

Great Central Railway Journal, 1905 to 1918

Great Eastern Railway Magazine, 1911 to 1926

Great Western Railway Magazine, 1888 to 1947

Herapath 's Railway and Commercial Journal, 1840 to 1865

The Jigger, 1921 to 1938. A magazine for members of the Railway Clearing House.

Journal of the Institute of Locomotive Engineers, 1911 to 1971

Locomotive Engineer's and Fireman's Journal, 1887 to 1903. This became the *Locomotive Journal*, 1904 to 1909.

Locomotive Magazine, 1897 to 1914. Before 1897 this was *Moore's Monthly Magazine*.

The Locomotive Railway, Carriage and Wagon Review, 1915 to 1959. Before 1915 this was *The Locomotive Magazine*.

London, Midland and Scottish Railway Magazine, 1923 to 1947

The London and North Eastern Railway Magazine, 1927 to 1947. Before 1927 this was the *North Eastern and Scottish Magazine*.

The London and North Western Railway Gazette, 1912 to 1923

Moore's Monthly Magazine, 1896. In 1897 this became *The Locomotive Magazine*.

The North Eastern Railway Magazine, 1911 to 1924. From June 1924 this became *The North Eastern and Scottish Magazine*.

The North Eastern and Scottish Magazine, 1924 to 1926. Before July 1924 this was *The North Eastern Railway Magazine*.

Over The Points, 1929 to 1940. A quarterly review of matters concerning the Southern Railway.

The Railway Chronical, 1844 to 1849.

The Railway Clerk, 1911 to 1913.

The Railway Engineer, 1880 to 1935.

The Railway Fly Sheet, 1887 to 1882.

The Railway Gazette, 1907 to 1970.

The Railway Gazette and Mining Chronicle, 1851 only.

Railway Intelligence, 1857 to 1877.

The Railway Magazine, 1897 to present.

The Railway Magazine and Steam Navigation Journal, (Herapath's Journal) 1835 to 1839.

Railway News, 1864 to 1918.

The Railway Official Gazette, 1883 to 1893.

The Railway Record, 1844 to 1901.

The Railway Signal or Light Along The Line, 1895 to 1896.

The Railway Times, 1839 to 1914.

The Railway Year Book, 1898 to 1932.

Railways, 1939 to 1952. After 1952 this became the *Railway World*.

The South Western Gazette, 1881 to 1883.

The South Western Railway Magazine, 1919 to 1922.

The Southern Railway Magazine, 1923 to 1947.

Transport and Railroad Gazette, 1904 to 1906.

Transport and Travel Monthly, 1920 to 1922.

Universal Directory of Railway Officials, 1895 to 1932.

Universal Directory of Railway Officials and Railway Year Book, 1932 to present.

INDEX OF PERSONS

Where no first name or initial is given, the index follows the text in the use or omission of 'Mr'. Persons with surname only are listed first, then those with title only (Mr/Mrs/Miss), then those with first name or initial. Where names are identical, they are distinguished by place or company. Numbers in italics refer to illustration captions.

INDEX OF RAILWAY
COMPANIES, STATIONS AND
INSTITUTIONS

507